TRAFALGAR

By the same author

EMILE ZOLA: A BIOGRAPHY

LYAUTEY IN MOROCCO: PROTECTORATE ADMINISTRATION 1912–1925

TRAFALGAR

COUNTDOWN TO BATTLE
1803–1805

ALAN SCHOM

ATHENEUM
New York   1990

Maxwell Macmillan International
New York   Oxford   Singapore   Sydney

To Sarah and Emma

Atheneum
Macmillan Publishing Company
866 Third Avenue, New York, NY 10022

Collier Macmillan Canada, Inc.
1200 Eglinton Avenue East, Suite 200
Don Mills, Ontario M3C 3N1

Library of Congress Cataloging-in-Publication Data

Schom, Alan.
    Trafalgar : countdown to battle, 1803–1805 / Alan Schom.—1st American ed.
        p.   cm.
    Includes bibliographical references (p.   ) and index.
    ISBN 0-689-12055-9
    1. Trafalgar (Cape), Battle of, 1805.   2. Napoleonic Wars, 1800–1814.   I. Title.
    DA88.5 1805.S36   1990   90-776   CIP
    940.2′7—dc20

Macmillan books are available at special discounts for bulk purchases
for sales promotions, premiums, fund-raising, or educational use.
For details, contact:

Special Sales Director
Macmillan Publishing Company
866 Third Avenue
New York, NY 10022

Maps by Peter McClure
Line drawings by Ken Smith

First American Edition 1990

10   9   8   7   6   5   4   3   2   1

PRINTED IN THE UNITED STATES OF AMERICA

CONTENTS

ACKNOWLEDGEMENTS   vi

LIST OF ILLUSTRATIONS   vii

MAP OF EUROPE IN 1803   x

PREFACE   1

1: 'THE FATE OF THE UNIVERSE'   5

2: 'OUR KING! OUR COUNTRY! AND OUR GOD!'   42

3: BUILDING AN ARMADA   63

4: INVASION PREPARATIONS   97

5: 'THE SAFETY OF THE COUNTRY WILL NEVER BE AT HAZARD'   128

6: THE POLITICS OF WAR   148

7: STEPPING UP OPERATIONS   160

8: 'AS MANY TRICKS AS A MONKEY'   182

9: PHANTOM FLEETS   219

10: THE LAST HOMECOMING   243

11: CADIZ   275

12: 'A PELL-MELL BATTLE'   307

13: A STATE FUNERAL   357

APPENDIX 1: Chronology of Events   371

APPENDIX 2: Biographical Sketches   378

APPENDIX 3: Fleets   390

NOTES AND SOURCES   394

INDEX   405

ACKNOWLEDGEMENTS

I should like to take this opportunity to express my gratitude to the following individuals and institutions for their assistance during the preparation of this book: The National Maritime Museum, Greenwich; Colin S. White, Head Curator of the Royal Naval Museum, Portsmouth; Evan Davies and Richard Kennell of the Britannia Royal Naval College, Dartmouth; the Public Record Office; the Bodleian Library, Oxford University; Grace Dempsey of the British Library; the Bibliothèque Nationale and Archives Nationales, Paris; Mme Huyghues des Etages, Conservateur of the Musée de la Marine, Paris; Mme Astorkia of the Service Historique de la Marine, Toulon; and Rear-Admiral Chatelle, Conservateur of the Service Historique de la Marine, Vincennes. And lastly I should like to thank the Royal Navy for the special tour they arranged for me aboard the *Victory*.

ILLUSTRATIONS

1. William Pitt the Younger (detail, by J. Hoppner, *National Portrait Gallery, London*)
2. Colonel Commandant of the Cinque Ports (detail, by Stadler after Hubert, *National Army Museum, London*)
3. The Admiralty (detail, by J. C. Stadler after J. Gendall, *National Maritime Museum, Greenwich*)
4. Interior of the Admiralty (detail, by Hill after Rowlandson and Pugin, *National Maritime Museum*)
5. Henry Dundas, Viscount Melville (detail, by T. Lawrence, *National Portrait Gallery*)
6. Blackwall yard (detail, by F. Holman, *National Maritime Museum*)
7. Sheerness dockyard and fortifications (by P. C. Canot after T. Milton and J. Cleveley, *National Maritime Museum*)
8. Chatham dockyard (by P. C. Canot after R. Paton and J. Mortimer, *National Maritime Museum*)
9. The Earl of St Vincent (by C. Turner after Carbonnier, *National Maritime Museum*)
10. Henry Addington, Viscount Sidmouth (detail, by G. Richmond, *National Portrait Gallery*)
11. Frederick, Duke of York (detail, by C. Turner after W. M. Beechey, *National Army Museum, London*)
12. George III reviewing troops (by J. Collyer after E. Dayes, *National Army Museum, London*)
13. General Orders to Volunteer Units (*National Army Museum, London*)
14. Martello Towers ring Great Britain (detail, after C. Stanfield, *National Maritime Museum*)
15. Walmer Castle (detail, *National Maritime Museum*)
16. 'In case of actual Invasion' (*National Army Museum, London*)
17. Beach defences along the Sussex coast (detail, *National Maritime Museum*)

18. Napoleon Bonaparte (by J. L. David, *National Gallery of Art, Washington D.C./Bridgeman Art Library*)
19. Napoleon witnesses the launch of a ship (detail, by Van Brée, *Musée de Versailles*)
20. Pierre Forfait (by Van Brée, *Musée de la Marine, Paris*)
21. Napoleon's plan of Boulogne (*Musée de la Marine*)

22. Marshal Soult (by Cassaert, after Mlle de Noireterre, *Musée de la Marine*)
23. Napoleon at Boulogne (detail, by Mollé, *Musée de la Marine*)
24. Admiral Decrès (attrib. to A. Ansiaux, *Musée de Versailles*)
25. Marshal Berthier (by Delpech, *Musée de la Marine*)
26. The National Flotilla poised at Boulogne (detail, by Baugeaun, *Musée de la Marine*)
27. Admiral de Bruix (by Lemoine after Maurin, *Musée de la Marine*)
28. Admiral Lacrosse (by C. J. Fuhr, *Musée de la Marine*)
29. Britain's Watch-dogs (detail, by W. B. Wollen, *National Army Museum, London*)
30. General Beurnonville (by Delpech, *Musée de la Marine*)
31. Admiral Verhuell (by Maurin, *Musée de la Marine*)
32. Marshal Davout (by Mauduison, *Musée de la Marine*)
33. Marshal Ney (*Musée de la Marine*)
34. Admiral Ganteaume (by Maurin, *Musée de la Marine*)
35. Brest (detail, by Morel Fatio, *Musée de la Marine*)
36. Invasion plans (Collection de Vinck, *Bibliothèque Nationale, Paris*)
37. Fulton's submarine, *Nautilus* (*Archives Nationales, Paris*)

38. Admiral Cornwallis (by C. Warren after T. Uwins, *reproduced by courtesy of the Trustees of the British Museum, London*)
39. Admiral Cotton (detail, by H. Meyer after J. Ramsay, *National Maritime Museum*)
40. Admiral Lord Nelson (detail, by L. F. Abbott, *National Maritime Museum*)
41. Admiral Collingwood (detail, after H. Howard, *Royal Naval Museum*)
42. Captain Hardy (detail, by R. Evans, *Royal Naval Museum, Portsmouth*)
43. The *Victory* at Portsmouth (by O. W. Brierly, *National Maritime Museum*)
44. Admiral Calder (detail, by L. F. Abbott, *National Maritime Museum*)
45. Captain Blackwood (detail, by J. Hopper RA, *National Maritime Museum*)
46. Admiral Villeneuve (*Musée de la Marine*)
47. The *Bucentaure* (detail, *Musée de la Marine*)
48. Admiral Gravina (*Musée de la Marine*)
49. Admiral Magon (by Lemoine, *Musée de la Marine*)
50. Captain Lucas (*Musée de la Marine*)
51. The battle of Trafalgar (detail, *Musée de la Marine*)
52. *Victory*'s log (*Crown copyright material in the Public Record Office, London, is reproduced by permission of the Controller of Her Majesty's Stationery Office, document reference ADM 51/4514*)
53. Nelson's funeral procession on the Thames (detail, by J. T. Smith, *Royal Naval Museum*)

54. Nelson's cortège reaches St Paul's (by M. Merigot after C. A. Pugin,
   Royal Naval Museum)

(Copyright holders and artists, where known, given in brackets)

MAPS

Europe in 1803   x
Boulogne   114–15
The Lesser Antilles   221

LINE DRAWINGS

Vessels of the National Flotilla   76
Commencement of Hostilities at Trafalgar   322
Victory engaging *Bucentaure*   326
Redoutable engaging *Victory*   328
Leviathan engaging *San Agustín*   336
Royal Sovereign engaging *Santa Ana*   339
Belleisle under attack from all sides   341
Tonnant engaging *Algésiras*   343
Bellerophon engaging *Aigle, Monarca* and *Montañes* 345
The Battle at 3.10 pm   347

Europe in 1803.

Preface

THE BATTLE OF Trafalgar, fought on 21st October 1805, was the high point and, in a sense, the culmination of an intense twenty-nine-month campaign (begun effectively in June 1803) waged by the Royal Navy to prevent a French invasion of Great Britain. Yet this obvious, well documented historical reality has either been ignored or misinterpreted by most British naval historians, including William James (the author of the distinguished five-volume *Naval History of Great Britain, 1793-1820*) to a certain degree, and Sir Julian Corbett (a former lecturer in history at the Royal Naval War College, and author of several works including *The Campaign of Trafalgar, England in the Mediterranean*, and *England in the Seven Years' War*) in particular. Indeed, the latter makes the extraordinary claim that the campaign only began on 11th January 1805 when Rear-Admiral E. T. de Burgues Missiessy's small squadron escaped from Rochefort, destined for the West Indies, a squadron whose actions in fact were of no serious or direct consequence to the happenings at Trafalgar! Only one Englishman and one Frenchman recognised that the long campaign leading up to and resulting in the events of 21st October 1805 had begun back in 1803.

Historian John Leyland acknowledged this when analysing and editing the Royal Navy's correspondence and signals found in his valuable work, *Dispatches and Letters Relating to the Blockade of Brest, 1803-1805*, which begins with the resumption of the blockade by Admiral Cornwallis and concludes in the late summer of 1805 as the ships from Ushant are sent to southern Spain. Trafalgar was no isolated battle, but rather an integral aspect and natural consequence of the Brest campaign. Colonel Edouard Desbrière linked inextricably the French invasion preparations, the British blockade and the subsequent battle of 21st October in his rigorous five-volume series on the subject, *Projets et Tentatives de Débarquement aux Iles Britanniques, 1803-1805*, and in *Trafalgar: La Campagne Maritime de 1805*. The Royal Navy documents in the Public Record Office, and the superb collection of thousands of French army and naval documents in the Archives Nationales, attest to and confirm this irrefutably. I hope that my own book will now demonstrate clearly that the naval battle fought off Cape Trafalgar in the autumn of 1805 was indeed part of the campaign involving the blockade and the invasion preparations (whose flotilla the Combined Franco-Spanish Fleet had been specially created and directed by Napoleon himself to escort and protect).

It was Vice-Admiral Lord Nelson who ultimately devised the strategy and personally directed operations that day off Trafalgar which resulted in the 'annihilation' of the Combined Fleet, thereby establishing British naval supremacy and preventing the French and Spanish from carrying out any further immediate major operations in the Channel or against British warships and merchantmen elsewhere in European waters, while at the same time breaking the spirit of those two navies for decades to come. But Nelson's own effective role along Europe's Atlantic coast began and ended there. He had nothing else to do with the 'blockade of Brest', as it is often called, when over thirty ships were deployed to form a battle line along French and Spanish shores between 1803 and 1805, which was responsible for, and largely successful in, keeping French men-of-war from leaving port and thus from joining and spearheading the invasion flotilla of 2,343 ships assembled between Boulogne and Dunkirk in order to transport three crack French army corps – a force totalling 167,500 men and later known collectively as the *Grande Armée* – to the shores of Kent and the Thames Estuary.

The man responsible for commanding and maintaining the Channel Fleet throughout this entire arduous two-and-a-half-year period and, in the final analysis, the one responsible both for successfully preventing the French invasion of Britain and deciding on the necessity of creating and dispatching to Spanish waters the nucleus of the fleet that Nelson was to command at Trafalgar – Admiral Sir William Cornwallis – was, however, never thanked by a grateful nation for his singular services. Although he, more than any other individual serving naval officer, directly saved his country, his name was then forgotten immediately and, indeed, has been overshadowed ever since by the charismatic Nelson. The failure to honour or even remember the distinctive role played by Admiral Cornwallis is one of the greatest disservices to, and distortions and omissions of, modern British history.[1]

Corbett's celebrated *Campaign of Trafalgar* neglected to acknowledge the significance of Cornwallis' contribution made during this period, but John Leyland rightly praised the otherwise forgotten Admiral for his 'courage, endurance, resource, and generally for . . . [his] great strategic and tactical ability'. He was, said Nelson, 'a gallant, good officer'. His 'extraordinary vigilance', claimed Leyland, nearly a century after the events of this crucial period, 'deserves . . . even a higher place among our great seamen than has hitherto been assigned to him . . . Cornwallis' great blockade', he concluded, 'was a masterpiece of administrative and seaman-like handling of a great naval force in operations of supreme importance to the country.'[2]

Unlike Nelson, Cornwallis was not known to the man in the street and was never stopped and cheered by patriotic Londoners, nor was he a boastful man. Indeed, he was the antithesis of Nelson, a quiet, retiring gentleman who assiduously avoided public acclaim as much as Nelson relished it. Unlike Nelson, too, he was neither a self-publicist nor even an adequate chronicler and left much less material for historians to study than did almost any other admiral of the time. Rarely present in the heat of action and often only in the background of this narrative, Cornwallis nonetheless remains a hero, if an unobtrusive one, whose steady guiding hand skilfully directed Channel operations during a most perilous period. As for Nelson, his victory at Trafalgar stands out today, as it did then, as one of the most enterprising achievements of any admiral at a single battle in the history of the Royal Navy. History, though, has room for two heroes.

The threat of invasion was no mere political ploy or scare-tactic manipulated by Napoleon and Pitt. Britain was under genuine threat and roused both by fear and patriotic fervour, while Napoleon undertook such preparations as to have bewildered even William Pitt had he but been aware of their full extent.

This then is the story of the French and their preparations, and of the men sent to sea over a period of nearly two-and-a-half years to prevent Napoleon from launching his forces against the British Isles.

1

'The Fate of the Universe'

England and France have long held the earth's destiny in their hands, and that of European civilisation in particular. What harm we have done to each other! How much good we can do instead!

I have shown France what she is capable of achieving; now let her do it.

Napoleon

THE CONCORDAT OF 1801, re-establishing normal relations between France and the Vatican, had prepared the way and now Napoleon Bonaparte had as good as demanded – albeit phrased in uncustomarily diplomatic language (prepared by the unseen hand of Talleyrand) – that the sixty-two-year-old Gregorio Luigi Barnaba Chiaramonti, in his capacity as Pope Pius VII, officiate at the French Imperial Coronation in Paris on 2nd December of that year, anno Domini 1804. It was bitterly ironic, however, as his predecessor, Pius VI, had condemned the French Revolution's Civil Constitution of the Clergy, which had removed French priests from Vatican authority, only to see the Papal States invaded by French forces, and himself arrested by General Berthier and removed to southern France where he was held prisoner until the time of his death in 1799.

In mid-November 1804, Pope Pius VII, a slender, quiet aristocrat, reached the nearly 13,000-foot Mont Cenis pass at the crest of the Alps, separating Turin in Italy from Grenoble in France. Standing behind him, his Vatican staff shivered in the unaccustomed cold, despite layers of clothing and heavy capes, while General Menou, the administrator of the newly acquired French territory of Piedmont, saw to quarters for the Pope's military escort. Napoleon (as he had been styling himself since the Senate had proclaimed him Emperor in May) had taken the trouble to send up army engineers to level the pass, have the road filled in with fresh rock and gravel after the damage suffered from the previous spring's snows and new stone barriers erected to make the carriage journey a little safer, although the narrow, twisting road already lay hidden beneath ice and an early snowfall. Napoleon did not want anything to happen to the Pope while he was on French soil and under French protection – the death of a second Pope would have been too embarrassing. In another week no carriage would find this desolate road passable, hence time was of the essence, for Napoleon could not afford to postpone the coronation yet again.

What were the thoughts of the seemingly resigned Pope Pius VII as he looked over the barren wasteland of ice, snow and rock? And, reluctantly facing westward again, toward the gloomy mountains through which the carriages must shortly wend their way, leading to the warmer plains of France . . . what then? The fate of his predecessor certainly was an unpleasant reality that could not escape his mind and this Napoleon, with his troops in northern Italy, was not an easy man to deal with.

The successor to the brave but unfortunate Pope Pius VI had been summoned to Paris – the situation was quite medieval in its implications and fraught with complexities. If the Holy Father did not attend to this 'Imperial summons', much would be at risk, namely the Concordat, which brought the recalcitrant and lawless French under the sway of the Vatican once again and allowed French churches to reopen (though the French retained the right to name their own bishops) for the first time since the beginning of the Revolution. How many prayers had he said for the return of a land that had for centuries prided itself on being the pillar of the Church, from whence the great Crusades had been launched creating the Kingdom of Jerusalem? With a violent military man such as Bonaparte – it was said he even beat his servants with his riding crop – the physical fate of Rome and the Vatican would be at stake again. The regaining of millions of French Catholic souls, cut off from the Church for so long, was a major achievement for Pius VII, not to be lost now just because he felt himself in danger or because his pride had been hurt. Pius VII, the scion of an ancient and noble family, had to consider a higher, long-term view of the consequences of this event. Europe was in transition, new powers and alliances were constantly forming. Thanks to Napoleon, Habsburg might was a thing of the past, despite the glitter and splendour of the Viennese court. Meanwhile, in France, the Bourbon supremacy, which had been replaced by a new Revolutionary heritage, was now being replaced in turn by an even mightier new Bonaparte dynasty that, alas, this Pope would now have to sanction and sanctify in Notre-Dame Cathedral within a fortnight's time. But what was the lifetime of one man in the history of a country? After all, Napoleon would not live for ever. Popes had suffered greater indignities in the past for the greater good of the Church and Christendom. Clearly the mountain had to be traversed.

*

France, which the Pope was about to enter, was, like all of Europe, already greatly altered since the coming to power of Napoleon, a land which had proved to be remarkably malleable, both politically and socially. The law courts, churches, schools and commercial world of the *ancien régime* had all disappeared or changed considerably in the waves of disruption and destruction following the fall of the Bastille in 1789. Monarchy and the traditions of centuries had been swept aside by a variety of Revolutionary governments that had not only replaced previous political and social customs, but utterly eradicated them in the process. Each of the preceding ones had been 'wrong', each of their successors had been unalterably 'right' and yet each had then been replaced in turn.

Fear and brutality had been the two catalytic forces required to bring about this malleability – lawlessness enabling strangers and private individuals (usually without any political authority) to rampage, cast suspicion, accuse, pillage, rape, terrorise and destroy. People were seized in their homes or in the streets, often never to be seen again, their property and houses plundered while the nominal public authorities frequently did virtually nothing to restrain, prevent, hinder, discourage or condemn such anarchy; the Revolution's children had run amok. Jean-Baptiste Carrier had ordered the drowning of hundreds of citizens at Nantes, Robespierre had blessed national terror everywhere and Joseph Fouché had given it a new dimension with the murder of 1,900 people at Lyons, many of them priests, wealthy bourgeois and aristocrats. Fouché in particular was typical of the amoral individuals put in charge of government plans to reform society in their own image. Finally, the corrupt Directory had been overthrown by the Consulate, Napoleon Bonaparte assuming by force of arms the position of leadership, *primus inter pares*, in the newly emerging triumvirate.

The dapper general then began transforming French society into yet another image, creating the values and institutions required to ensure the fulfilment of *his* plans, not so much for a renewed and better France, but rather for an immense, new, efficiently operated Bonaparte fiefdom, encompassing first the whole of France, then much of Europe. In his own way, however, at least at times, he was methodical in the execution of this new blueprint, creating for the present, but also for the long-term future. To this end he set up the *lycée* system of education (replacing the Central Schools of the Directory), which gave him access to the training and indoctrination of the educated élite of the land, allowing him to control the minds and values of pupils who would one day hold positions of leadership throughout the country. Now they marched briskly to class in smart military uniform to the roll of drums while their teachers instilled in them the concepts of loyalty to the State, that is, until 1804 when the 'Imperial Catechism' substituted a loyalty oath to Napoleon *first* and the State *second*. If Napoleon's revival of the Académie française was not seen as a threatening gesture, it was, in fact, representative of the sweeping detailed interest he was taking in the total reorganisation of the country – not simply the government, but the nation's very foundations, reflecting the complete control he wished to extend to all facets of life. No politician in Great Britain, whether Henry Addington or William Pitt, grasped the full significance of all this.

Finances, too, were revamped with the creation of the Banque de France in 1800, bringing badly needed new faith in the country's future from businessmen and property-owners, not to mention the establishment of a more efficient new system of centralised tax collection. Public works, including highways, bridges and canals, were initiated on a large scale, greatly reducing the number of unemployed – always popular with a political leader's public – while increasing the efficiency of transportation for commerce (and the military). New technical schools, prizes for inventions and industrial exhibitions brought a fresh appreciation for the accomplishments of science, though Napoleon's re-establishment of slavery (ended earlier by the Revolutionary government) was hardly a step forward.

When Napoleon added his various new law codes on legal procedure, commerce and criminal proceedings and, in particular, the Civil, or, 'Napoleonic' Code of 1804 (espousing civil equality, religious toleration and the protection of private property), it was a further indication of the seriousness of the French dictator's designs for the French Republic and of how efficiently he was planning to control every aspect of the country permanently.

Despite plots and opposition, which the British both prayed and often paid for, including attempts at *coups d'état* and assassinating Bonaparte himself, signs of his tightening grip on French affairs were to be seen almost monthly. It was hardly surprising that one of the first things he did upon seizing control of the government in 1799 was reduce the number of political newspapers in the country from seventy to thirteen and, ultimately, to three! No democrat he . . . He could not tolerate criticism from within the society he led. Madame de Staël's caustic remarks about the First Consul turned Emperor, made during her weekly salons, ultimately led to her banishment from Paris on Bonaparte's personal orders. Equally, when Benjamin Constant led twenty other political colleagues to address the Tribunate, questioning the quality of Justice in France, they were purged expeditiously. After all it was difficult for the new Emperor to restore France to the full stature of her former greatness while having to tolerate the myopic criticisms of chattering women and interfering politicians.

First and foremost, Bonaparte was a soldier. Bent on aggrandisement and blatant geographical expansion, the international complications wrought by his meteoric rise caused nothing but consternation and misery for the member states of the Second Coalition and the peoples of central and western Europe.

The Coalition itself was not as monolithic as it appears, consisting rather of a series of partnerships drafted in treaty form between May 1789 and June 1800 that led to Russia, Austria, Naples, the Ottoman Empire and Great Britain being bound together, albeit fairly loosely, to oppose further French territorial advances.[1] Not only was the Anglo-Austrian link weak to begin with – Austria only accepting a nine-month agreement from June 1800 to February 1801 – but Prussia had refused to partake altogether.

French aggression and the occupation of Rome had activated the Second Coalition as the French armies challenged not only Naples' position but that of Austria and Russia as well, as fighting spread in Italy again and in the Rhineland. Although the Allies got the French out of Italy (for the moment), not so in Holland and Switzerland. There French forces had been in occupation even before Napoleon's *coup d'état* of November 1799, the earlier Treaty of Campo Formio of 1798 having acknowledged the extension of the French frontier to the Rhine and the addition of the Austrian Netherlands, Savoy and the Ionian Islands, not to mention control of the United Provinces and part of Italy.

By the summer of 1800 First Consul Bonaparte was on the march again, seizing northern Italy. However, despite the capture of Valletta, the capital of Malta, by Britain in September 1800, Tsar Paul was determined to opt out of the fighting and, on 16th December 1800, signed a convention with Sweden and Denmark forming the Armed Neutrality of the North, at once destroying the shaky Coalition. Britain immediately denounced this neutrality pact and then smashed it, thanks to Nelson's great naval victory at the Battle of Copenhagen on 2nd April 1801, while the French Army in Egypt capitulated that September. Napoleon was now preparing for a temporary retrenchment, having signed a Franco-American Convention in Paris early in September 1800 (to maintain not only peace, but free trade between the two nations, which naturally distressed the British government) and a similar Franco-Portuguese pact in June 1801. These were then followed by a treaty with Russia on 8th October 1801, confirming French interests in Germany and reaffirming friendly ties between France and Russia.

More importantly, the Treaty of Lunéville, concluded between France and Austria on 9th February 1801, stipulated the independence of the Helvetic (Swiss), Batavian (Dutch), Cisalpine and Ligurian Republics (France agreeing to evacuate all four republics), while confirming the cession of the former Austrian Netherlands (Belgium) to France. In this treaty Austria also agreed to a French restructuring of the Habsburg lands in Germany and the Rhineland. This was further defined by the Austro-French-Russian Treaty of Paris on 27th December 1802 and ratified in the form of an Imperial Recess on 27th April 1803, thereby anticipating the death knell of the Holy Roman Empire. Its dissolution was all but a reality, reducing the fifty-one free Imperial cities to a mere six (Hamburg, Lübeck, Bremen, Frankfurt-am-Main, Augsburg and Nürnberg) while suppressing an additional 112 German states. Another major consequence of this agreement was the replacement of Catholic influence in the former Austrian Rhineland states with that of the Protestants who now held the new majority in the electoral college and Diet. In addition the Vatican now lost 2,500,000 subjects and some 21,000,000 florins in annual revenue, not to mention eighteen universities and dozens of monasteries. Thus at this time Austria ceded the entire left bank of the Rhine to Prussia, Baden, Bavaria and Württemberg, which emerged with correspondingly extended frontiers, while France, of course, seized control of northern and central Italy, the Cisalpine Republic extending its frontier to the Adige. The Austrians no doubt recalled Napoleon's words of 17th October 1798 at the signing of the treaty of Campo Formio (another treaty disadvantageous to their country): 'The [Holy Roman] Empire,' General Bonaparte had said, 'is an old woman-servant, accustomed to being raped by everybody.' So thorough was the violation of the Empire on this occasion and the subsequent reshaping of the Germanic world that it clearly prepared the way for the new French version of the 1,000-year-old Empire that was to replace it in 1806 as the Confederation of the Rhine.

With the Treaty of Lunéville now out of the way, and peace of sorts re-established on the Continent, it only remained for Britain and France to negotiate an agreement to render peace general and complete. In

December 1801 Lord Hawkesbury, the British Foreign Secretary, dispatched a special diplomatic envoy, Charles, Marquis Cornwallis, to Amiens with plenipotentiary powers, to meet with his French negotiating counterpart, Napoleon's brother, Joseph Bonaparte. If at first he appeared an unlikely Foreign Office representative (for this was the same General Lord Cornwallis who had surrendered the British army to the Americans at Yorktown in 1781) he was a most able diplomat and statesman, having already served successfully as Lord-Lieutenant of Ireland and as Governor-General of India. If Cornwallis' son, Viscount Brome, who had accompanied him to France at this time, found most of the influential Frenchmen he now met distinctly unpleasant ('with the dress of mountebanks and manners of assassins'), not so Lord Cornwallis who met almost daily with Joseph Bonaparte at the Hôtel de Ville in Amiens. The First Consul's elder brother, Cornwallis noted in a private letter to Lord Hawkesbury in mid December 1801, was 'a very sensible, modest, gentleman-like man, totally free from diplomatic chicanery, and fair and open in all his dealings'. Despite their rapport, however, it was not the envoys of either country who dictated what was to be negotiated, but rather the Prime Minister, Henry Addington, in London and General Bonaparte in Paris. Thus, regardless of his skill and perspicacity, Lord Cornwallis found himself in a most humiliating situation, ordered as he was by his Government to give in to the French no matter what the cost, relinquishing nearly everything Britain had gained during the long years of war between the two countries.

Addington had replaced Pitt at Downing Street in February 1801 with the promise of peace, fully supported, it would seem, by the merchant class, clamouring for reduced taxes and a resumption of full-scale commercial activities. However, if it was peace at any price that the Prime Minister was willing to accept, that is precisely what he got in the articles of agreement that were finally exchanged at Amiens on 24th March 1802. Britain returned most of the French and Dutch possessions which she had earlier seized, including the Cape of Good Hope, the French Antilles, Elba and Minorca, retaining only the small sugar-producing island of Trinidad and Ceylon, and, further, promised to evacuate Malta within three months, returning that island to the Order of St John of Jerusalem, while France in turn evacuated the Kingdom of Naples and had already been expelled from Egypt by the British.

'The ambitious man could ask no more of his country', a delighted Talleyrand commented on the results of Amiens. The French were stupefied by their own success, gaining so much for so little. 'The epoch of the peace of Amiens must be considered as the most glorious in the history of France, not excepting the splendid period of Louis XIV's victories', Napoleon's one-time secretary, Bourrienne, later enthusiastically declared with a little exaggeration. If the Treaty of Amiens was hardly an inspiring document for Great Britain, she had been exhausted by the many years of war, first with the American colonies and then with the French. Also, enormous subsidies had been sent to the Continent to maintain allies who, for all that, had met with defeat, followed by their abandonment of Pitt's Second Coalition. This left Britain crippled with debt and isolated diplomatically. Addington, therefore, felt he had no choice in the matter. Nevertheless, few in London were sanguine about long-term prospects, least of all Lord Hawkesbury who, when he nominated Marquis Cornwallis for the task at Amiens, had privately warned him about Napoleon, declaring him to be 'a person who is likely to take every unfair advantage in concluding business with others and should therefore be treated with more than usual caution and circumspection', while both were aware of the unscrupulous foreign policy being pursued by the First Consul's Foreign Minister, Talleyrand, and 'the spirits of chicanery and intrigue' that he 'so eminently possesses'. By 1802 no one in Europe, it seemed, had any illusions about the French Government under the leadership of Napoleon Bonaparte.

If peace had given Britain a much-needed respite, it had also worked to Bonaparte's advantage. Everywhere a feeling of militarism was in the air. Talleyrand, at Napoleon's behest, was naming French army officers to represent the French Republic's embassies (General Brune at Constantinople, General Gouvion St Cyr at Madrid, Colonel Sebastiani in Egypt and General Beurnonville at Berlin); uniformed *lycée* students marched briskly to class and French armies were sent to new camps at home and abroad. Despite the restrictive clauses of the Treaties of Campo Formio and Lunéville, French garrisons not only remained illegally in the newly declared Batavian Republic, but were strengthened during this period of European peace. Also, another French army reoccupied Switzerland in 1803 as Talleyrand drew up the 'Act of Mediation' at the Tuileries on 19th February 1803, providing a federal constitution for the nineteen 'sovereign Swiss states', requiring a perpetual defensive alliance with France and an annual contribution of 16,000 Swiss troops to French legions. Meanwhile, to the south, Bonaparte openly annexed Piedmont, meeting British criticism of this act with feigned surprise – referring to his seizure of Piedmont and Switzerland as 'mere bagatelles'. He had already outraged the British earlier by his assumption of the presidency of the Cisalpine, or Italian, Republic in Milan in December 1801. This, among other such hostile acts, ultimately led an exasperated Ambassador, Lord Whitworth (named to this post in Paris following the conclusion of the Treaty of Amiens), to describe Bonaparte to the Foreign Secretary as 'a scourge to himself and the nation, which for his punishment he has subdued to his will'. When, in turn, Britain refused to evacuate Malta after all, an astonished Bonaparte chided her: 'It is necessary to respect treaties; woe to those who do not do so. They shall be responsible to all Europe for the consequences'. This Napoleon said to Whitworth in the Tuileries before 200 guests in March 1803, regardless of his own recent shocking international expropriations and frequent contraventions of treaties and promises. 'The English want war', the indignant Bonaparte thundered, 'but if they are the first to draw the sword, I shall be the last to lay it down . . . from now on they [the peace treaties] will be covered with black crêpe.' Whitworth left, red-faced and shaking, afterwards relating to London: 'It seemed to me that I was listening to a captain of dragoons rather than to the head of one of the most powerful states of Europe.' A few weeks later Napoleon introduced the high-tariff law against imported British manufactured items and followed this with his declaration of war against Britain on 18th May 1803, using as a pretext the failure to evacuate Malta, while he nevertheless adamantly refused to withdraw troops from occupied Holland, Switzerland, Piedmont and the Italian Republic.[2] 'Buonaparte', *The Times* warned, 'is not yet gorged with his plunder'.

Such was the France Pius VII saw before him and the complex international situation he faced. Once he had entered France, however, more mundane matters quickly shifted such larger questions aside. The niceties of protocol, especially where a strong ego was concerned, were not only absorbing and perplexing but quite embarrassing. Napoleon, however, was merely amused by such problems, though within his new court the ancient etiquette of the Bourbons had already been reintroduced, both at St Cloud and at the Tuileries, so vigorously as to satisfy a punctilious Spanish grandee, or, indeed, Charles V himself.

The French Emperor first met the Pope a few days later when he arrived at Fontainebleau. Pius VII was to rest there for a day before proceeding the last few miles to Paris for the ceremony. They approached each other at the same time on the flat Nemours road in the hushed solitude of the immense forest surrounding the Château while Napoleon was out with friends on a hunting party. Pius VII, exhausted by

the long journey from the Alps via Grenoble and Lyons, descended from
his dust-laden carriage and walked slowly towards the Emperor, who had
by now dismounted from his small grey horse. Upon being invited by the
Pope to continue the remaining mile or so of the journey with him in his
carriage, Napoleon accepted and, as Napoleon's faithful valet, Constant,
put it: 'I don't know whether or not the Emperor took certain precautions,
carefully planning to avoid any compromise of his dignity, but what I do
indeed know is that no one could have gone to greater pains to make the
venerable old gentleman more comfortable upon his arrival.'

Now, on the crisp frosty morning of 2nd December, under a high
pearl-covered sky, the problems of protocol seemed to fall into place.
The Pope in his immaculate white chasuble preceded Napoleon to the Ile
de la Cité and the 600-year-old Notre-Dame Cathedral at nine o'clock in
a closed state carriage bearing the papal tiara and insignia, drawn by eight
dappled grey horses, preceded in turn by the Pope's principal chamberlain carrying a silver cross astride a somewhat reluctant donkey, which
raised a laugh from an otherwise sombre crowd. Even in the Tuileries
Palace overlooking the Seine and the still very medieval Paris of the Left
Bank, protocol had been neatly skirted and eased by the wishes of the
Pope himself, who chose to decline invitations to many of the ceremonies
and dinners. He was given a large suite of rooms in the Pavillon de Flore
where he was no doubt surprised to find the furniture carefully arranged
(on his host's orders) so as to duplicate exactly the layout of the papal
apartments he had left behind in the Vatican. 'The dinners served him
[the Pope] were not merely munificent but indeed sumptuous', said
Constant, Chambertin being added at the Pope's request and the vintage
wine removed, but the Pope otherwise scarcely touching his food.

The political problems and events of the day now seemed quite remote as
the procession left the Tuileries and crossed the Seine via the Pont du
Carrousel. Even the kidnapping of the Duke d'Enghien on German
territory earlier that year – an act initiated by Talleyrand, put into effect in
such devilish haste on Napoleon's personal orders and followed by the
expeditious murder of that unfortunate captive of Vincennes – now
seemed far from everyone's mind. There were, however, reminders and
the solemn looks of more than one German envoy were a bit disconcerting. Then there was the matter of the Tsar's missing ambassador, he
having been recalled by an irate Russian Emperor who had ordered his
court to officially mourn d'Enghien's death, meanwhile issuing secret

orders to his high military command to prepare for hostilities, something even Napoleon had not foreseen.

Another more recent French kidnapping scandal still very much alive in people's minds also took place on German soil. Sir George Rumbold, the British diplomatic envoy to Cuxhaven (at the mouth of the Elbe on the North Sea), was arrested on the orders of Fouché, the Police Minister, in October 1804 in an attempt to link the Court of St James officially with a plot to overthrow Bonaparte, but nothing of an incriminating nature could be found in the diplomat's papers. While King Frederick William III of Prussia was angered by this act, yet another flagrant intervention on sovereign German soil, his Foreign Minister, Karl von Hardenberg, was far more furious, this being the fourth such kidnapping of a British subject by French agents! Pitt's Government had lodged complaints and London newspapers maintained a running commentary on developments for the next few weeks. For his part, von Hardenberg wanted the Prussian King to mobilise the army along with the military support of Tsar Alexander (who had succeeded his murdered father, Paul, in 1801), and jointly order the release of Rumbold and the French evacuation of adjacent Hanover (still legally the property of the Elector of Hanover, George III). Instead, Frederick William artfully dodged both of these formal commitments (except the mutual defence alliance with Russia signed back on 24th May 1804) and international pressure from Britain and France, preferring instead to work with France to gain Hanover for himself, peacefully. Earlier negotiations to this end had failed, however, and were broken off with France in April 1804 when as the price for this evacuation Napoleon asked him to become a fully fledged French ally against the Austrians (in Italy) and Russia (in their Ottoman interests). Frederick William nonetheless put what diplomatic pressure he could on Napoleon (who did not want a hostile army facing his troops at this particular moment, joined no doubt by powerful contingents from a still irate Tsar Alexander) and Sir George Rumbold was released prior to the coronation ceremony.

Thus Napoleon and his ministers – 'the Atheist Emperor, and his gang of infidel advisers', as one English reporter irreverently referred to them – had gone on with the preparations for the ceremony as if quite unaware of their own recent acts and of subsequent world opinion.

Now, despite the plenitude of soldiers in a variety of regimental uniforms and colours, including the brilliant Imperial Guard and the thousands of troops lining the streets of the procession route, war seemed the furthest thing from people's minds, though, as already noted,

Napoleon had declared war over seventeen months earlier following the collapse of the short-lived Amiens accord.

And yet, if it was bad news one was in search of at the end of 1804, a most inauspicious year, there was no shortage of it, although the significance of a minor item from Madrid probably went unnoticed by most: 'It is asserted that Admiral Gravina will be recalled from Paris, to have the command of a fleet and in the interval to direct the preparations for war.' Of a little more immediate concern to British observers was a bulletin noting the Swedish King's progress as he reviewed his troops in Stralsund, Pomerania, while German princes were strengthening their military and city fortifications. And this, followed by a reliable Swedish source, warned 'that a body of 50,000 Frenchmen were now marching into Holland, in order to take possession of Hamburgh, and attack Stralsund', even as Napoleon entered his gilded coach for the procession to Notre-Dame cathedral.

From another sphere of operations, London was informed that, 'Russia continues her preparations for attack or defence. All the efficient force in the Provinces of Courland, Livonia, and Esthonia, is under orders to march at a moment's notice. It is expected that an army of eighty to one hundred thousand men will be collected on the frontiers of Russian Poland within a few weeks.' Of equal importance to British investors were the reports reaching Lloyd's Coffee House in London of the effects of war and Napoleon's embryonic Continental System, created to oust British manufactured goods and products from Europe. Thus John Bull was disturbed to hear that General Marmont himself was in Holland at that very moment ensuring that 'rigorous measures' were being taken to halt further British exports. London noted that '. . . strong remonstrances have been sent to Paris to have the difficulties on our [Dutch] commerce removed.' Meanwhile, owing to shipping losses at French hands, the Royal Navy was requested to increase convoy escorts, from the West Indies to the Indian Ocean, thereby stretching British naval capability to its very limits.

Troubled by the news of the Prusso-Russian defence pact of May 1804, the French Emperor's scarcely veiled subsequent threat to the Tsar that summer had only added to the already tense international scene: 'The Emperor of the French wishes for Peace on the Continent,' Talleyrand had informed St Petersburg. 'He has made all possible advances to re-establish it with Russia; he has spared nothing to maintain it, but with the assistance of God, and the might of his own arms, he is not in a situation to fear anyone', to which the presence of his troops reaching from the Apennines to the North Sea already attested. The threat was real enough. In the south of Italy 'the Usurper . . . has assumed a position sufficiently formidable to out-threaten the [Austrian] threateners', one English correspondent noted, while along the banks of the Rhine he had 'mustered a force capable of making headway against the fiercest storm' he might encounter by 'any combination of opposing forces'.

The French Emperor had indeed been making plans ever since the conclusion of the Treaty of Lunéville in February 1801, ably abetted in drafting his grandiose European designs by Talleyrand, around whom a mystique had already evolved and without whose aid many of these important events doubtless would not have occurred. It seemed to one and all, whether French or English, that Charles Maurice de Talleyrand-Périgord must have been born an arrogant rake and cynic, for no one could remember his having been otherwise. Anything was to be expected from the former Bishop of Autun (a title he had borne before being excommunicated by Pope Pius VII). This man who did little to conceal his numerous affairs was also a formidable statesman, capable of having written a political manual with new chapters for Machiavelli himself, who during his long career had served as foreign minister under the government of revolutionary France (though himself once on that dreaded list of *émigrés* and an exile in England and America) and under Napoleon (as both consul and emperor), and would later serve under Louis XVIII, finally being recalled to service in his eighties, as ambassador to London. This renegade of the Church had consecrated new bishops during the Revolution, while proposing the measure that was to be adopted for confiscating the landed property of the Church throughout the country, and later had masterminded the kidnapping and assassination of the Duke d'Enghien, not to mention helping in the execution of two successful *coups d'état*, that of Napoleon in November 1799 and of Louis-Philippe in July 1830.

The bribes he demanded from those soliciting his good offices were legendary, but for all his sophisticated rapacity, Talleyrand could also represent the titled *ancien régime* and the legitimacy it reflected, a commodity which Napoleon greatly valued. What is more, Talleyrand was not a mere symbol or title of a bygone era. He was a brilliant politician who devised ingenious ways of coping with tangled international problems, frequently in a legally satisfactory fashion, though certainly not shirking from the necessity of employing less palatable forms when the moment required (as in the case of the Duke d'Enghien). In the final analysis the ends always justified the means, and no one could ever accuse him of cant! He could also give Napoleon very good advice, though it was sometimes declined, as when Talleyrand strongly opposed the resumption of hostilities with Great Britain in May 1803, as well as the ill-fated invasion of Russia later in 1812. Whether he agreed with Talleyrand or not, Napoleon needed him badly at this time, when extensive Imperial designs were being prepared for all of Europe.

All these events formed the complex background, then, to the coronation ceremony.

Twenty-four state carriages thus slowly made their way to Notre-Dame. Spectators could occasionally catch glimpses of some of the major personalities of the day, including Cardinals Caprara and Fesch, Prince Joseph and his wife Princess Julia (soon to become King and Queen of Naples) and Prince Louis and Princess Hortense (shortly to assume the throne of Holland), Napoleon's sisters, Pauline and Elisa and, indeed, all his family, except the troublesome Lucien who had been banished to Italy with his unacceptable wife. The high Imperial officers in the procession included Napoleon's first Grand Chamberlain (Foreign Minister Talleyrand), the Grand Marshal of the Palace, the Grand Master of the Ceremonies, the Elector Arch-Chancellor of the Empire, important senators, the Ministers of War, Religion, Police, the Interior, Finances, the Public Treasury and the Secretary of State, as well as the High Court Judge, the head of the Military Board and nine Counsellors of State (all nine newly created Marshals of France: Augereau, Bessières, Davout, Lannes, Lefebvre, Masséna, Moncey, Ney and Soult) – not to mention a still numerous Diplomatic Corps, uniformed, beplumed, beribboned and girded with ceremonial swords.

Naturally, though, it was Napoleon, accompanied by Josephine, whom everyone awaited with such eagerness. Nor were the jostling crowds to be disappointed as the gilded imperial carriage drawn by eight light bay elaborately caparisoned horses finally emerged from the Carrousel and the last imposing arch of the Tuileries, crossing the Seine; even in this somewhat dull wintry light its splendour astonished the sightseers. Unlike any of the other vehicles either in that procession or, indeed, any other ever seen in the French capital, Napoleon's had, instead of wooden panels on the sides and doors, glass, over which was encrusted in gold the Imperial crown, supported by four golden eagles in flight. Even a Parisian crowd, inured to French pageantry, was dazzled by this novelty.

As if that were not enough, the Emperor was preceded by two enormous columns of infantry in colourful uniforms, marching on either side of 10,000 cavalry, their shining helmets and polished scabbards glittering and turned out on the finest mounts. They were accompanied by military bands playing martial and ceremonial music, often outdone by the unceasing pealing of hundreds of church bells from every quarter of the city, which in turn were sporadically drowned out by bursts of cannon fire from atop Montmartre and the Champ de Mars. Fouché reckoned that the crowd of spectators numbered about half a million. The streets had been cleaned beforehand and fresh sand spread everywhere within sight of the ceremonial route. Hanging from houses and apartments were flags and tapestries while shops along the Quai des Orfèvres were festooned with flowers.

As the column of magnificent carriages approached the Archbishop's Palace and the cathedral, the most splendid sacred music could be heard through the open doors of Notre-Dame – compositions of Messieurs Pasïello, Rose and Lesueur, the Imperial Chapel Masters, accompanied by two large orchestras and four choirs, totalling some three hundred musicians. The orchestras were themselves accompanied by the court's celebrated singer, M. Laïs, and principal violinists, Kreutzer and Baillot. Not to be outshone, the innumerable military bands outside continued to blare forth their marches, including one especially commissioned by Napoleon for the newly formed invasion forces, the 'Armée de Boulogne' (his own secret message to those gathered today). 'As for me,' noted Constant, 'this music left me pale and trembling.'

Most of the officials had assumed their seats in the twelfth-century Gothic cathedral at least two hours before the arrival of the Imperial couple. Descending from their carriage in the courtyard of the Archbishop's Palace, Napoleon and Josephine now donned the final outer ceremonial robes – long crimson and ermine mantles, lined in white satin and embroidered with the Bonaparte bee-design in gold. In Napoleon's case this was placed over a shorter cloak, also embroidered with bees, covering in part a shorter court jacket with facings of white velvet and embroidered from top to bottom in dazzling gold. Beneath this lay a much lighter crimson jacket, also lined in white satin, linked across the chest with a chain of diamonds, and under this a fine linen shirt with cuffs of delicate lace, a lace neckpiece and a white muslin cravate. His white velvet knee breeches were embroidered in gold while diamond-studded ceremonial garters secured white silk stockings, also embroidered with golden thread, including crests of the Imperial crown. As the outer ceremonial mantle of ermine and satin itself weighed some eighty-five pounds, although supported by four high officers, Napoleon still looked quite crushed by the weight and bulk of these clothes over the next few hours.

Just outside the building, the black toque with the two long, elegant, white heron plumes was replaced by a Roman laurel leaf diadem in gold and silver. The other ceremonial ornaments included the Hand of Justice, a simple golden crown and a golden ceremonial sword encrusted with silver and gems, all created by the celebrated jeweller Biennais. Finally, he carried the famous Sceptre of Office, designed by Odiot, with a base of solid silver, a golden serpent entwined about the handle surmounted by a sphere upon which a miniature golden Charlemagne sat enthroned (this last detail suggested solemnly by Talleyrand who liked the world to see the results of his little pranks).

Claire Comtesse de Rémusat, Josephine's Lady-in-waiting, described the Empress as 'especially resplendent in diamonds, her hair up high in a thousand curls in imitation of the court syle of Louis XIV', which made her look much younger than her forty-one years, the glitter momentarily distracting one's view from her mouthful of decaying teeth and a complexion prematurely wrinkled by some twenty-five years of uninhibited drinking. She wore a long, white satin gown and an even longer mantle of the same material, both with intricate gold and silver embroidery – 'She carried it all off with her unusual, inimitable natural grace.' It was her jewellery, however, that really attracted everyone's attention, particularly the intricate golden crown, which so fascinated Napoleon that he insisted she wear it at the State dinner following the ceremonies. In this the superb craftsman Margueritte surely surpassed himself in delicacy of design. It comprised eight intricate golden branches, decorated with diamonds, gradually meeting as one piece beneath a golden sphere upon which a golden cross was fixed. Its band bearing eight large emeralds harmonised with a string of sparkling amethysts lower over the forehead. The small diadem, however, was not to be overlooked as a piece of art, composed as it was of four simple sets of the finest pearls, interlaced with leaves of perfectly assorted diamonds and, at the front, even larger ones. Setting off her elegant gown, beneath a charming décolletage, was a golden belt encrusted with thirty-nine rubies. She was followed by her sisters-in-law, all wearing a surfeit of gems, indeed, such a quantity as to evoke a condescending smile from the Emperor, though he was genuinely proud of his Josephine, the only woman with whom he had ever been madly in love. The procession was led by the herald at arms, the pages, the assistant masters of ceremonies, the deputy masters of ceremonies, the Grand Master of Ceremonies, Marshal Serrurier, carrying the Empress' coronation ring on a cushion, Marshal Moncey with the basket for the ceremonial mantle and Marshal Murat with the Empress's crown, each person ten paces apart.

Josephine, who preceded Napoleon, was supported by her First Groom of the Bedchamber and her First Chamberlain, followed by the Lady of Honour and the Lady of the Bedchamber, then Marshal Kellerman carrying Charlemagne's crown, Marshal Perignon with Charlemagne's sceptre, Marshal Lefebvre, the sword, Marshal Berna-dotte (the future King of Sweden) carrying Napoleon's diamond collar, he in turn followed by Colonel-General Eugène Beauharnais (Josephine's son) with the Emperor's ring, Marshal Berthier, the Imperial Orbe, and the Grand Chamberlain (Talleyrand) with the basket in which Napoleon's mantle was to be placed.

Napoleon himself then approached, the princes and dignitaries carrying the train of his mantle, followed by the Chief Groom, the General of the Imperial Guard and the Grand Marshal, all walking in single file, followed by the ministers and the highest military officers of the realm walking four abreast. Upon reaching the porch of the cathedral the Cardinal Archbishop of Paris presented the Empress, and then Napoleon, with holy water as their Majesties advanced under a canopy borne by four canons as far as the sanctuary where Napoleon and Josephine then sat on their thrones.

Pope Pius VII now descended from his throne, approaching the altar where he began the *Veni Creator*. Following this hymn and the prayers, the Emperor was presented with the Hand of Justice and the golden Sceptre, while the Grand Chancellor removed the laurel crown and the Grand Chamberlain his collar of diamonds, then the immense ermine mantle, as Napoleon drew his sword, handing it to the Constable. At the same time, Josephine's mantle and crown were also being removed. Meanwhile the Grand Dignitaries filed in succession to the altar where they placed the various ceremonial ornaments.

The Sovereign Pontiff approached Napoleon as the Grand Almoner (his uncle, Cardinal Fesch) presented the *Book of the Gospels* to his Majesty, asking Napoleon in Latin if he would swear to the creed. The Emperor, placing both hands on the Gospels, replied '*Profiteor*' (I profess). Upon the completion of the remaining prayers by the senior clergy, the Grand Almoner of France, the senior French cardinals and bishops approached the Imperial couple with a profound reverence, conducting them to the foot of the altar to receive the holy unction. The Pope then began the mass as he consecrated the crowns, sword, mantles and rings. The Emperor received the ring, sword, mantle, Hand of Justice, sceptre and crown. It was at this moment that Napoleon so startled the Pope, the cardinals, indeed, everyone, by suddenly crowning first himself then Josephine who, on her knees before him, received the resplendent crown from his hands with tears of happiness and emotion. Pope Pius VII regained control of himself, after this humiliating rebuff from Napoleon – he having come all the way from Rome for the sole purpose of crowning the Emperor – and, standing before the seated Emperor and Empress, he recited a prayer, kissed Napoleon on the cheek and, turning to the vast audience, proclaimed in a loud voice: '*Vivat Imperator in aeternum!*' (may the Emperor live forever). The assistants responded: '*Vivent l'Empereur et l'Impératrice*'.

Next came one of the most dramatic parts of the ceremony, when following the mass, the Grand Almoner once again presented the *Book of the Gospels* to the Emperor, and the President of the Senate, accompanied by the Presidents of the Legislative Body and the Tribunate, offered Napoleon the *Constitutional Oath*, which Napoleon recited from memory, as the Chief Herald at Arms proclaimed in a resounding voice:

> The most glorious and most august Emperor of the French is crowned and enthroned.
> Long live the Emperor! [This was repeated by the assistant heralds.]
> Long live the Emperor! [Again repeated by the heralds.]

Everyone was jolted as a reverberating discharge of artillery announced to Paris and the world the coronation and enthronement of the Imperial couple. The Pope then recited the *Te Deum*, as the parchment bearing the Imperial oath was presented to Napoleon for his signature.

After nearly four gruelling hours, an exhausted but exhilarated Emperor and Empress of France descended from their thrones. As the Imperial couple emerged from the archway of the Archbishop's Palace in their glass carriage, hundreds of cannons thundered and bells resounded from every church steeple in Paris – and, indeed, across the whole of France. Mighty cannons continued to reverberate throughout the city on the hour, every hour, from six o'clock that evening until midnight. From Toulon to Bordeaux to Brest and Boulogne, ceremonial artillery fire signalled the birth of an Empire, their sound echoing across the Channel to Kent . . . a sound to which the British, and indeed all Europe, were soon to become accustomed for the next eleven years.

GEORGE III, A consistent foe of Revolutionary France and of Napoleon Bonaparte in particular – 'the Corsican usurper', as he called him – was a man little understood by the people he ruled. He was, in many respects, an anachronism and a puzzle. Having ascended to the throne at the age of twenty-two, in 1760, he had already been ruling for over forty years when Bonaparte achieved national prominence.

Young George grew up during the reign of his uncle, George II, whose court was still more German than English, indeed where English was all but a foreign language. His father, Frederick, having died when he was only twelve, had only occasionally shown a fatherly concern for his son, a concern that George III was later to take a little more seriously regarding his own sons.

As he became older, the Prince showed a real sense of duty to the nation and interest in his responsibilities, though even early after his coronation he displayed a tendency to revert to a monarchical authority and prerogative that had been gradually transferred to Parliament and Government ministers. He made it perfectly clear that he did not wish to be considered a mere figurehead monarch, and the French witticism, '*Le roi règne et ne gouverne pas*', was anathema to him.

A tall, heavy, awkward, ugly man – like his forebears and many children – he assumed the British throne a virgin King, which astonished and amused the members of an eighteenth-century court where mistresses for princes, married or not, were considered the norm. He was surprisingly puritanical; although he later ate a great deal, he always drank sparingly, which also amused the court.

Insisting he would marry only an English lady, he fell in love with a foreigner – Mary Charlotte, the daughter of the Duchess of Mecklenburg-Strelitz, and she with him. Although never considered a beauty, she was to be the only woman in his life and bore him fifteen children. Horace Walpole commented drily on 'her want of personal charms', while her Chamberlain, Colonel Disbrowe, was once overheard sighing, 'Yes, I do think the bloom of her ugliness is going off.' The young king was very protective of her and they shared a mutual interest in music, imbibing the delights of flute and violin.

Early in his reign George III purchased for £28,000 the residence that is so often associated with the Royal family, Buckingham House (also known thereafter as the Queen's House), with its large grounds, vast number of elms, gardens and fields where cattle grazed amid Queen Charlotte's own special pets, including her two elephants – all in the heart of London. It was literally a country house then and was only razed to the ground and totally rebuilt in 1825, becoming the Buckingham Palace we know today.

The political world of eighteenth-century England was indeed small, but nevertheless it is interesting that both William Pitt's father and namesake, as well as Charles James Fox's, held responsible governmental posts during the reign of George II.

The haughtiness and sheer arrogance of the Pitts was notorious and the King was often at a loss as to how to deal with the younger William Pitt. Nor, decades later, could King George dismiss from his mind the snub he and his family had received on the Lord Mayor's Day, 9th November 1761, when the senior William Pitt was wildly acclaimed by all those present, while the twenty-three-year-old George was virtually ignored.

As for Fox's father, he was a man the King entrusted with the position of Secretary of State, but his son's gambling debts (amounting to nearly five times the cost of Buckingham House) brought him down, nearly destroying him in the process. Although the young King could get on with the elder Fox, whose politics were reasonably close to his own, not so later those of the son, Charles James Fox. The younger Fox was outspoken about his pro-Jacobin sympathies and admiration for Bonaparte – who was to irritate the King as few men could.

George III's 'insanity' has been the butt of many jokes and even more conjecture, but there was nothing humorous about the medical afflictions that first came seriously to the notice of his physicians in 1762. That the medical profession was stymied – though hardly about to admit it – during the King's lifetime, was not to be wondered at, as the real problem was only correctly diagnosed over 200 years later in the late 1960s. The symptoms first began showing themselves when the King was under extreme emotional or political pressure and were so multifarious as to amaze and bewilder. They included colic, constipation, nausea, acute chest or stomach pains and cramps, lesions of the skin, delirium, profuse sweating and fever, accompanied by a rapid pulse, incoherence of speech, laryngitis, extreme insomnia, polyneuritis, attended by swelling and pain in the joints of arms and legs, a deterioration of the senses, in particular, an inability to taste, and diminished sight, and at such times he could not bear to have anything touch his body. All this was accompanied by gross irritability, mental aberration and delusions, and on occasion, he could be found wandering round Kew or Windsor in his nightshirt babbling incoherently. These bouts were to occur periodically over the years, notably in 1788 and 1789, 1801 and 1804, after which he declined rapidly. That the problem might prove hereditary never seemed to occur to anyone, for the Royal couple continued begetting offspring with alarming regularity. It was many decades later that the first sign of this disease, porphyria, which is caused by a metabolic imbalance, was noted, albeit in milder form, in George, the Prince of Wales. Surely one of the strangest episodes involving this affliction came when, during the annual vacation at Weymouth, the King was found entering a church . . . on horseback!

Although the King was often in conflict with his ministers and Parliament over Royal authority and prerogative, his greatest problems arose from his inability to cope with his children and much of the blame for this must be put on Queen Charlotte – a cold, insensitive, indomitable and egotistical woman who had little interest in cuddling babies. That most of the King's Royal offspring were alienated from either or both of their parents over the years was especially sad for George as he, at least, was deeply concerned about their welfare. Their incredible adventures, however, must have aggravated his mental problems. While the daughters avoided their mother completely during the last years, the most obvious problems were with the numerous sons, two in particular.

George, the Prince of Wales, was a notorious reprobate even before reaching his majority, and the decades following only saw the list of his follies – whoring, gambling, drinking and eating – increased. By 1790 he was over sixteen stone, which led the witty Charles Lamb to describe him as the 'Prince of Whales'. By 1795 the Prince's debts had reached such an astronomical figure that the King himself was left speechless, some £600,000 (or one twenty-fifth of the country's entire annual budget)! And yet the Prince of Wales still begged for positions of responsibility at court and, in particular, the command of an army. 'I ask to be allowed to display the best energies of my character; to shed the last drop of my blood in support of your Majesty's person, crown and dignity,' to which his long-suffering father replied: 'Though I applaud your zeal and spirit . . . yet, considering the repeated declarations I have made of my determination [against this], on your former applications to the same purpose, I had flattered myself to have heard no further on the subject.'

Although the other sons were more often than not exiled to distant lands – Hanover, Switzerland, Gibraltar, the Indies or Canada – where they would be less bothersome to the King, one of them, Frederick, Duke of York, ultimately ended up in his good graces. While young, Frederick was as wild as the Prince of Wales, but unlike his eldest brother, Frederick matured and became 'a reformed character' by 1793-94, so much so as to be given command of armies against French forces in Holland, though that appears to have required abilities he did not possess, resulting in his recall at the request of Prime Minister Pitt. But with the renewed threat from France, in 1803, it was the young Duke of York who was to assume the post of Commander-in-Chief of forces on British soil, while the Prince of Wales had to settle with the command of a mere regiment, and the rank of colonel.

Despite the endless personal problems within the royal family, there were times when the King was relatively worry-free and that was during the annual summer sojourn at Weymouth on the Dorset coast, where he was literally in his glory, riding, sailing, rowing, reviewing troops, attending plays nightly and bathing: as Fanny Burney recorded, 'the King bathes and with great success: a machine follows the Royal one into the sea, filled with fiddlers who play "God save the King" as His Majesty takes his plunge.'

However, a few weeks at the seaside would pass all too quickly amid growing political anxieties, declining health, the endless demands from his sons for fresh honours and from his daughters for husbands, not to mention a sexual boycott imposed by his wife (in defiance of Cabinet orders!), and a new military threat from the French – such was the state of the Royal family when Bonaparte declared the Treaty of Amiens null and void.

William Pitt the younger was a bit of a curiosity and an unknown quantity not only to the King, but to the public at large, for no man could have been more private in character, a trait that emerged early in youth. Fragile as a child and frequently ill, his parents, the Baroness Chatham (née Hester Grenville) and his father William Pitt (the Earl of Chatham), were frequently called to the ailing boy's bedside, where he was treated by the family physician, Anthony Addington, father of one of the young Pitt's childhood friends (future Prime Minister and political foe), Henry Addington. Dr Addington believed that William had inherited his father's tendency to gout, which he treated with soot bark and blistering, feeling that a 'cordial confection' would 'root out . . . something morbid that had long lurk'd in the boy's body'. It would seem that Dr Addington's son would inherit the same inability to diagnose and cope with the ills of his country decades later.

Born on 28th May 1759, ten years before his arch-foe Napoleon Bonaparte, William grew up on a sheltered and quiet estate in Kent and later at Burton-Pynsent, in Somerset. It was no doubt from his father that the boy acquired many of his traits, though not the former's obsession with landscape gardening, which sometimes found him in dress coat, tie and wig inspecting flowerbeds in the middle of the night by torchlight. The Earl was most punctilious about manners, however, and was always both aloof and 'extremely dignified'. He frequently took on political causes in opposition to the young King George, including the hostilities in the American colonies for, as he put it, 'You may ravage, you cannot conquer'. He was also keen on improving the Government of Ireland, a cause that his son was also to take up. Pitt the elder, however, was rarely a popular man in any circle, Walpole describing his speeches as being delivered with 'coolness, dignity, and art'. The discourses and manners of his son were often to be likened to those of his father, as was his view on the defence of the country: 'The first great and acknowledged object of national defence in this country', proclaimed Pitt the elder, 'is to maintain such a superior naval force at home that even the united fleets of France and Spain may never be masters of the Channel'. The younger Pitt was to echo these same sentiments thirty-four years later against the same two foes – *plus ça change*. His son was also to be a consistent spokesman for religious toleration, including protestant dissenters, and to carry with him throughout life a reputation for honesty and upright-ness. Though both men were considered shrewd and eloquent speakers, neither was ever called witty. Unfortunately, the boy grew up in a house where wealth and a surfeit of servants to meet one's every whim were considered quite normal and, once brought up in this manner, it was hard for him later to reconcile his own situation and reduced circumstances. Thus he spent money all his life, like his father before him, ignoring the financial implications.

If William Pitt's father was an extremely difficult man to please, he was nevertheless satisfied with his son, whose precocity he early recognised and abetted. Later young William was at his father's side when he collapsed in the House of Lords on 7th April 1778. With all eyes upon him, the boy helped carry his dying father out of the Chamber, a sight many were not to forget.

After reading law at Cambridge and at Lincoln's Inn, William passed the bar examinations in 1780 and was elected to Parliament the following year at the age of twenty-two. If ever a man was destined for a career, it was Pitt in the House, where one friend described his debating voice as 'full of melody and force', a sentiment echoed by the often irritable Lord North, who acknowledged his 'amazing eloquence'. Although his somewhat withdrawn attitude never permitted him to become a party man, it did not prevent him from becoming a true son of the House and, indeed, perhaps the leading representative of British parliamentary democracy. He was to rise to the top like a rocket. By the age of twenty-four, he had kissed the King's hands for the first time, as First Lord of the Treasury, and Prime Minister, a post he held continuously for nearly eighteen years, until 1801.

At the same age as Pitt was assuming office as Prime Minister, Henry Dundas, some seventeen years older than Pitt, was appointed Solicitor-General for Scotland (a position his father had held before him), no mean feat in a country where respect for authority and one's elders was more deeply imbued than in England. Like Pitt, the young Henry Dundas (later first Viscount Melville, as he will be referred to hereafter), the fourth son of Robert Dundas (Lord of Arniston and President of the Court of Sessions), was a brilliant child whose academic qualities were quickly perceived and developed in his native Edinburgh, where he was to read law and become a member of the law faculty by the age of twenty-four.

Although never enamoured of his legal calling – 'a dull and laborious profession', he once called it – he quickly gained a large and influential law practice, resulting in his decision to delay his entry into national politics until he was thirty-two, first sitting in Parliament in 1774. The following year he was appointed the Lord Advocate of Scotland, or the King's representative in Scotland, the highest legal post in the land and thus a singular honour.

If his public life and work were unusually successful, his early marriage to the wealthy, beautiful and erratic Elizabeth Rannie (who brought him a £100,000 dowry) was not, although they had three daughters and a son. Unfortunately he lost that £100,000 in the major investment of his youth, as a share-holder in the Ayr Bank upon its unexpected collapse, which forced him thereafter to live on his own earnings. The failure of the bank was followed by that of his marriage, when his young wife suddenly disappeared with an army captain, leaving behind her husband and four children, never seeing them again. Melville promptly divorced her but, always a hard drinking man, he now drank more than ever, lost in a misery he could not understand, for he loved his wife deeply. 'I feel nothing upon my mind but a settled gloom and melancholy', he lamented to a close friend in November of that same year, 1778, a few months after the event.

Lady Arniston, Melville's mother, once commented to her son, reflecting an era in which honour and a sense of public duty were predominant, 'My usefulness in life must be determined by the opinions of others, not my own.' With that apparently in mind, and in spite of his financial problems and the shambles of his marriage, he pursued his political career and, after securing the prestigious sinecure of Keeper of the Signet of Scotland, he finally made plans for a future in Parliament. He was always known to his friends as a just and loyal companion and Sir William Gordon, who knew him well, described him as 'a very brilliant figure; he is really a fine manly fellow, and I like a decided character. He speaks out and is afraid of Nobody.' As a man with definite views on the badly needed reforms of his age, it is not surprising that Melville, once in Parliament, acquired a reputation as a forthright and most competent orator. It was here that he met William Pitt for the first time.

Melville called for major reforms both in Parliament and in the administrative organisation of India, and espoused the cause of Catholic emancipation in Ireland – all of which drew him and Pitt together, despite the great differences in their ages and social background. Several months after his initial meeting with Billy Pitt, Melville wrote to his children a most revealing letter, the essence of which remained true throughout the years to come:

> My attachment to Mr Pitt personally grows more and more unbounded every day, and of course to fight by his side when he is annoyed from so many enemies gives me more heartfelt pleasure than I ever enjoyed since I was in Parliament. I feel him to be sent from Heaven as a saviour to his country.

It was an extraordinary declaration of feeling and loyalty for a mature man hardened through his experiences in the law and the political world. As for Pitt, he was to remain devoted and loyal to Melville to the very end.

If William Pitt was intellectually and politically a child prodigy, emotionally he never properly matured. He drank heavily from early youth, finding it essential for good fellowship and a release from the pressures of work and the unpleasant aspects of his life. In public he was considered a cold, aloof and forbidding gentleman, which no doubt was simply his own way of keeping the world at bay, as among his Wimbledon friends in the 1780s he was just another rollicking, free-drinking chap. Even though he started imbibing at breakfast and came to the Houses of Parliament equipped with a flask, he was only once noted – and then humorously – as being a bit under the influence when addressing that distinguished body.

Many of his neighbours at Wimbledon were lawyers by training, gentry by breeding and politicians by inclination. If not all members of this bucolic colony of mansion-holders were political allies, most were on surprisingly friendly terms with Pitt now and later, including Addington, Spencer, Rockingham, Fox, Grenville, Wilberforce and Horne Tooke, to name some of his more eminent neighbours. Indeed, the Wimbledon Common of those days, though only seven miles from Hyde Park Corner, seemed a rustic paradise of sorts, with its 'fine old trees . . . bright green common . . . and shining ponds glistening in the turf', extolled by Lord Jeffrey, another neighbour.

Heavy drinking and unabashed whoring were common enough in the late eighteenth century and it was hardly frowned upon to see Billy Pitt, Melville and others, singing and staggering across the Common in the wee hours of the morning. William Wilberforce, an idealistic young member of Parliament, Melville and Pitt, with similar political leanings although with often divergent desires for reform in their society, were extremely close in those days. Just as Wilberforce crusaded to end slavery (which Pitt did not endorse), Melville fought to have criminals removed from 'the hulks', or prison ships, to be transported instead to Botany Bay, while espousing on behalf of minor criminals a stint in regiments serving in the colonies. Although Wilberforce gradually distanced himself from Pitt politically, they nonetheless remained close personal friends and were frequently found in each other's houses, as was Henry Addington, even when he had replaced an exhausted William Pitt as Prime Minister in 1801. Indeed, curiously enough, it was in Addington's house in Wimbledon that Pitt sought refuge on occasion, where 'Mr Pitt's bedroom' was always ready and waiting for him. Similarly, Melville and his second wife always kept a room available for him, even when they were away in Scotland for months at a time. The social world in the last decades of the century was still extremely small and very inbred and even though people were bitter public enemies who might denounce opponents, such as Fox, in the House of Commons, they could still be found drinking together cordially that same evening. (This was one aspect which Bonaparte never appreciated when he attempted to assess the British political climate for, even before the destruction of aristocratic circles during the Revolution, the French gentry and upper classes had never associated in this way – French political opponents usually remaining bitter social enemies as well.)

It was Melville who first took William Pitt seriously as a candidate for Prime Minister, describing him as a man 'who perhaps has no fault but too much virtue'. It was due to Melville's persistence that Lord Shelbourne had presented and advanced Pitt's case before a most reluctant King George who, however, finally gave in.

Pitt differed from most of his friends in that he never married and, with one or two fleeting exceptions, never seemed interested in women. Was Pitt a homosexual? It is possible, and this possibility was often discussed quite publicly, Sheridan going so far as to compare him with James I's Duke of Buckingham, while Captain Charles Morris of the Life Guards, a gambling crony of the Prince of Wales, lampooned him mercilessly in the bawdy refrains of his popular song *The Virgin Minister*. That he was impotent as a result of years of heavy drinking also seems likely. One thing, however, is certain: Pitt, perhaps because of his unsatisfactory relationship with his mother and sisters (whom he rarely saw or even mentioned), invariably preferred the company of men to women.

That William Pitt was absolutely dedicated to his work as Prime Minister there is no doubt. He spent many long hours working and took very few holidays despite the increasing number of occasions when he was ill through sheer exhaustion and the advice his doctor gave him to rest.

There was, however, yet another side to William Pitt, when as Warden of the Cinque Ports he resided much of the time at Walmer Castle on the Kent coast near Deal, where his niece, the twenty-seven-year-old Lady Hester Stanhope, the daughter of his late sister, Harriet, joined him permanently in 1803. 'Henceforth she sat at the head of his table,' a table that had been singularly masculine for over twenty-five years. Indeed, the vivacious and impetuous young woman did take charge of the ex-Prime Minister and his affairs. Despite her blue eyes, fair complexion, 'a very fair figure, and the air and gait of a queen', and perhaps because of her height (she was nearly as tall as Pitt himself, who was over six foot) and a brilliant if erratic mind (she later moved to the deserts of Syria where she lived in an isolated castle and became known to one and all as 'the recluse of Mount Lebanon'), she never married. She considered herself unattractive – 'I am not handsome', she insisted, to which friends, such as Sir William Napier, concurred.

If Pitt had at first baulked at the idea of having Lady Hester in the house, he soon found her, as her brother put it, 'a light in his dwelling'. She was a brilliant conversationalist, excelling in repartee, her wit and mimicry winning the adulation of the army officers and politicians who sat at Pitt's often boisterous table several times a week. 'I am an aristocrat, and I make a boast of it,' she once declared. 'I hate a pack of dirty Jacobins, that only want to get a people out of a good place to get into it themselves.' That Lady Hester increased the warmth of Pitt's homes (at Walmer Castle and his new house now at Putney), could not be denied and, for once, he looked forward to returning to a home no longer empty. Although she continued to say and do the most outrageous things, she genuinely loved her uncle and felt a real responsibility and admiration for him. Indeed, she spent her final years recounting these days, which proved to be the highlight of her life.

When Pitt returned home after an all-night session in the House, or from a party, he was a different man, very informal, very relaxed. The difference between this atmosphere and that of Napoleon's circle at St Cloud or the Tuileries could not have been more marked, and certainly reflected opposing philosophies and values as Hester Stanhope pointed out: 'He [Pitt] did not pretend to despise wealth, but he was not a slave to it,' she noted. Yet his personal finances were so out of control that his indebtness would have landed anyone else in debtor's prison. Melville, greatly worried by his friend's total disregard of his personal affairs, asked the King to intervene. George offered Pitt £30,000 from his privy purse, which the proud man refused. Melville himself managed to raise £10,000 to help alleviate the situation – providing a fair amount himself – but then again Pitt also declined £100,000 offered with 'no strings attached' from four rich City merchants. 'He very politely thanked them, and returned the present,' Hester recorded in her diary, also adding Pitt's succinct comment after they had left the room: 'There are no public philanthropists in the City.' He had to be under no obligation to representatives of special interests, in order to retain his political integrity of action.

Hester Stanhope provides an intriguing insight into the life of Pitt in 1804 after his return to office: 'During the sitting of Parliament, what a life was his! Roused from his sleep (for he was a good sleeper) with a despatch from Lord Melville; then down to Windsor; then, if he had half-an-hour to spare, trying to swallow something; Mr Adams with a paper, Mr Long with another; then Mr Rose: then, with a little bottle of cordial confection in his pocket, off to the House until three or four in the morning; then home to a hot supper for two or three hours more, to talk over what was to be done next day: and wine, and wine! Scarcely up next morning, when tat-tat-tat – twenty or thirty people one after another, and the horses walking before the door from two 'til sunset, waiting for him. It was enough to kill a man – it was murder!'

Although Lady Hester's remarks about people were sometimes outlandish, at times they were also both amusing and even remarkably adroit, as when she described her uncle: 'Mr Pitt had nothing remarkable in his appearance. Mr Pitt's was not a face that gave one the idea of a clever man. As he walked through the park, you would have taken him for a poet, or some such person, thin, tall, and rather awkward; looking upwards as if his ideas were in air, and not remarking what was passing round him; there was no expression in him at such a moment.'

The usual picture of William Pitt as the arrogant aristocrat with his 'up-turned nose', as he addressed his colleagues in the House, was simply a protective façade. He could sit and talk with anyone, from 'vulgar sea captains, and ignorant militia colonels' – as Hester put it – to princes and kings. 'He was careful to cheer the modest and the diffident, but if some forward young fellow exhibited any pertness, by a short speech, or by asking some puzzling question, he would give him such a set down that he could not get over it all the evening.' Once, 'a respectable commoner, advanced in years' came to stay at Walmer as Pitt's guest, arriving at about the same time as a young duke, but he gave the last remaining free bedroom in the rather small castle to the commoner, finding a place for the young gentleman in the village, 'for it is better . . . that these young Lords should walk home on a rainy night, than old men; they can bear it more easily'.

Pitt was also a genial man, capable of disarming a potential enemy using old-world charm and courtesy. For instance, General Sir William Napier, the scion of a traditional Whig family and hence one with an almost inbred hatred of Pitt and his party, relates how, as a nineteen-year-old officer, he and Hester Stanhope's brother, Charles, dropped in without warning on Pitt at his house in Putney: 'Arriving rather late, the great man [this was in 1804 just after he had assumed office as Prime Minister] was at dinner when I entered the room; he immediately rose, and giving me both hands welcomed me with such a gentle good nature that I instantly felt . . . that I had a friend before me, with whom I might instantly become familiar within the bounds of good breeding . . . Brought up amidst Whigs, and used to hear Mr Pitt abused with all the virulence of Whigs, I looked upon him as my enemy of all good government . . . Thus, primed with poison, I endeavoured to sustain my mind's hatred against the Minister, but in vain; all feelings sank, except those of surprise and gratification, at finding such a gentle, good-natured, agreeable and entertaining companion.'

That Pitt missed not having a family of his own, he revealed only to his closest relatives. He would romp and play as if in the nursery, as the following tale from Lady Hester illustrates: 'We [Lady Hester and two of her brothers, Charles and James Stanhope] were resolved to blacken his [Pitt's] face with burnt cork, which he most strenuously resisted.' Suddenly they were interrupted by an embarrassed servant who announced that Lords Castlereagh and Liverpool had come to see the Prime Minister on business. ' "Let them wait in the other room," he replied, and the great Minister instantly turned to the battle, catching up a cushion and belabouring us with it in glorious fun. We were, however, too many and strong for him, and, after at least ten minutes' fight, got him down and were actually daubing his face, when, with a look of pretended confidence in his prowess, he said, "Stop, this will do; I could easily beat you all, but we must not keep those grandees waiting any longer." ' After his nephews and niece had cleaned him up, 'the grandees' were shown into that very room. 'For some time they spoke; he made now and then some short observation and, finally, with an abrupt, stiff inclination of the body, but without casting his eyes down, dismissed them. Then turning to us with a laugh, caught up his cushions and renewed our fight.' Is it any wonder then that even the inscrutable Talleyrand could never fathom the man who was to wage war as Napoleon's foremost opponent in 1804 and 1805?

'I never trust a Corsican or a Frenchman', Admiral Lord Nelson told his old friend the British Minister at Naples, Hugh Elliot, upon receiving news of Napoleon's assumption of the Imperial purple. 'I would give the devil all the good ones, to take the remainder.' When *The Times* first announced the official resolution by the French Senate on that 18th day of May – 'That NAPOLEON BONAPARTE be declared Emperor of the French' – the Editor referred to it as 'this extraordinary change' in the French Government.

Some, including the political cartoonists and punsters of Fleet Street, laughed, the scathing broadsheets calling Napoleon 'the tyrant', 'that Corsican upstart' and 'the Corsican ogre', among other things, while *The Times* showed a little more restraint, simply referring to the title as 'this new-fangled honour'. But once John Bull's ale had settled a bit, the scornful laugh of reddened faces had eased, and quaking bellies had returned to a more equilibrious state, the impact of this latest piece of news could only spell gloom, if not despair. 'We can assure our readers, on the best authority', wrote *The Times*' Editor, 'that nothing can be more uncertain or undecided, than the state of Europe at this moment . . . That Buonaparte entertains some schemes of aggrandisement of a stupendous magnitude we know for certain, [however] how far he will be permitted to realise them is the great question'. The answer came on 12th May when a Portsmouth newspaper revealed what political and military leaders had long feared: 'It appears that the information communicated to the Government induces it to believe that the French [war] preparations are in such a state for execution that an immediate attack from the French coast may be expected'.

'I am going into this war with regrets and a feeling of horror', the newly acknowledged French Emperor had told the Russian Ambassador before his departure for St Petersburg, 'because, speaking as a European rather than as a Frenchman, I would be as distressed as yourself if, upon waking one morning, you were to learn that England no longer existed.' However, earlier, in the privacy of his study, he had dictated a letter to General Augereau at Brest, where he was inspecting bustling military preparations: 'I have reason to hope that I shall soon attain the end which Europe awaits. We have six centuries of insults to avenge.'

Pilots, spies, smugglers and sea captains from the Dutch coast to the Bay of Biscay were interrogated by British naval agents. Admiral Lord Keith, the Commander-in-Chief of the Home fleet, had informed Admiral John Markham several months earlier that, 'it seems evident an expedition of some extent' was being prepared once again at the Dutch island of Texel and another '300 boats and vessels' with some 21,000 troops already aboard were sighted in the basin at Flushing. More were expected from Rotterdam and other Dutch ports. 'It never was [my] opinion', Captain Owen of the *Immortalité* told Keith back in December of 1803, 'that anything more was intended on the side of Boulogne than a feint to draw a large [British] military force to this part of the country.' Lord Keith, Owen's superior, disagreed, however: 'Boulogne is undoubtedly the place'. That most of the Dutch preparations were intended for an attempt on Ireland (not England) – as in two past unsuccessful efforts – could not be doubted, though some of the ships and men could also pass down to the Channel to supplement the principal French attack far to the south. However, Captain Owen could not explain away the impressive statistical evidence he himself had just gathered along the Channel. He had found at least thirty brigs and schooners lying in three divisions, along with some 200 luggers at Boulogne alone when pre-

viously it had been a half-deserted harbour fit only for a few fishing
smacks. 'They are as close alongside each other as they can be stowed',
he admitted from his post off the French coast. The enemy had recently
erected numerous new batteries and mortars on Point d'Alpreche and
elsewhere. 'The new works . . . proceed night and day with the basin and
entrance of Ambleteuse', he confirmed, where '2,000 men' were
constantly at work, while 'huts have been erected for the soldiers, and the
extent of the camp increased.' At Boulogne proper another 2,400 men
were observed working on the harbour and forts. 'At Wimereux, about a
mile north of Tour d'Ordres, or Cropie, they have begun to form another
basin and batteries to protect it, at which they work incessantly, and have
a camp adjoining which has latterly increased much and an additional
1,900 men were seen at work there as well, hundreds of torches alight at
the new works far into the night. The camp on the heights north-east of
Boulogne appears also increased in extent, and several wooden houses
for superior officers are erected.'

The entire coastline from Brest to Holland was now linked by a new
semaphore 'telegraph', set on high wooden towers along hundreds of
miles of coast, which meant that news of the sighting of any British ships
of war approaching France could be reported to all other French and
even Dutch ports and batteries within five hours, making a surprise or
unopposed attack or landing much more difficult.

Despite all this evidence, Captain Owen closed his report with the words
that, in his opinion, the real invasion attempt 'will be made elsewhere'.

After being informed of the large numbers of new cannon and mortars
along the northern coast of the Channel, including 61 very large pieces
recently installed at Cape Gris Nez alone – that is, half-way between
Boulogne and Calais – Keith acknowledged that he was more than ever
convinced about where he could expect an attack from. As he confided to
Markham, 'I think the plot begins to thicken on the other side [of the
Channel] . . . I never saw a shore so covered with artillery in my life . . .
We are all alert here. I have the secret orders: everything is as ready as
possible, and myself too. I have ordered all the ships to their stations as
fast as possible.'

Crusty Admiral Lord Keith, with his shock of grey hair, arthritis, gout,
and a much wrinkled brow, had decades of experience gained at sea
stations across the world, giving him a decided advantage over young
Owen in assessing the current threat, and he considered Boulogne the
prime place for the launching of Bonaparte's much-vaunted armada,
despite its small, half-dry harbour, which naturally weakened its strategic

value. Only a Napoleon, a soldier, would have insisted upon centring his naval activities at such a place, without even taking into consideration such basic navigational considerations as shoals, currents, tide, wind patterns, or sailing accessibility, but then he never did understand ships or the sea. Nor did he maintain a consistent interest in the Navy, only turning to it when an immediate project necessitated it, as in this case in order to transfer an army from one point to another.

Diplomatic and naval intelligence reports informed the Admiralty where Napoleon was, whom he was seeing and what he was spending most of his time doing, including his recent tours of inspection of naval and military installations along the coast from Le Havre to Dunkirk and even as far north as Flushing. Napoleon went on numerous excursions, studying coastlines and possible sites for harbours, basins and army camps. He studied freshly prepared ordnance maps to co-ordinate the road networks so that the sites he had selected could be reinforced with supplies from the provincial capitals and Paris, routes which could also accommodate numerous regiments, thousands of artillery horses and an unending column of transport wagons. The Emperor had one thing on his mind, the Boulogne invasion of England; nor was he a man to waste his precious time (and he was spending many weeks in the field), men and resources now that hostilities had been resumed. When France received the 54,000,000 francs[3] from the young American Republic for the sale of Louisiana in 1803, that money had been earmarked for one general purpose, a renewed European war of expansion, and much of it, at least one third, for the invasion of England, though ultimately it would take a great deal more than the entire sale price of Louisiana or any other colony to cover the cost of those vast preparations.

Timber, canvas, hemp and supplies of all kinds had to be brought from as far away as the Baltic and Black Seas. That required time and planning, especially in an age where all long-distance transport was by sail, each journey frequently requiring many weeks, sometimes months. Thousands of workers had to be hired from the public sector, or seconded from the army, to build ports, boat basins, harbour installations, coastal batteries and immense new army camps at St Omer, Bruges and Montreuil. The enormous amount of work all this meant for Bonaparte and his administrators, Admiral Lord Keith well appreciated and it was hardly surprising therefore that his anxiety increased: 'I think the plot begins to thicken on the other side'.

The British Government was under pressure to take more decisive action than Prime Minister Addington was willing to, or capable of, executing in the continuing struggle with the French, begun some fifteen years earlier when news of the fall of the Bastille had reached an incredulous England. Henry Addington now accepted that he had to go and secret negotiations were being carried out by the King with various leaders, though it quickly became apparent to political insiders that it was Pitt who was leading the pack. By the beginning of May 1804, Pitt and George III were in almost daily contact and on the 5th William Pitt received the following note from the King (who wrote in the third person):'Before he could consent to Mr Pitt forming an Administration he should expect he would agree to make an explicit declaration that he would *never*, at any time, agitate or support the question of Catholic Emancipation or the repeal of the Test Act.'

Pitt had received a similar request from the King in 1801 that he could not comply with, which was one of the reasons for his resignation then. Times and priorities had now changed and Pitt, already considerably weakened by declining health, acquiesced. Five days later George Rose[4] noted in his diary that Pitt would 'definitely' accept the posts of First Lord of the Treasury and Chancellor of the Exchequer and that the issue was as good as settled.

'Yesterday [Tuesday 15th May], Mr Addington had an audience with the King', reported *The Times*. 'At 3 pm a Privy Council was held', and the new Government appointed, excluding the egregious Charles Fox whom George III utterly detested. Some of the principal figures of the day kissed his Majesty's hand and were sworn into office: Lord Harrowby, as Secretary of State for the Foreign Office, Lord Hawkesbury (whom Napoleon loathed) at the Home Office, Earl Camden in the War Office, George Canning as Treasurer of the Navy and William Dundas as Secretary of War. The official bulletin was issued from Whitehall the same day: 'The King has been pleased to constitute and appoint the commissioners for executing the office of Treasurer of his Majesty's Exchequer', which of course was to be led by the First Lord of the Treasury, William Pitt, nominated by a most reluctant King who had always preferred Henry Addington. It was ironic that Pitt – as we have seen, now so heavily in debt himself that even his close banker-friends were unable to extricate him – should now direct the Treasury of millions of his fellow countrymen.

It was a foregone conclusion that the ailing Prime Minister should be re-elected to his usual seat for the University of Cambridge on Friday 18th May, and that thus he should officially accept office at the head of the Government on that same day, despite the illness which was destroying him and would in less than two years lead to renal failure and cirrhosis of the liver. A forty-six-year-old alcoholic was now to have to come to grips with the renewed outbreak of war and confront the greatest war machine seen in Europe since the days of the Roman Empire.

The Navy had been so emasculated under the dilatory leadership of the peace-loving Addington and the thrifty stewardship of Lord St Vincent at the Admiralty (despite the Admiral's outrageous public protests to the contrary: 'I do not say the French cannot come. I only say they cannot come by water') that drastic action had to be taken. Even the diplomatic Horatio Nelson, long on close and friendly terms with St Vincent, admitted that Addington's First Lord of the Admiralty 'has been led astray'. And indeed, in Paris two months earlier, on 14th March, First Consul Bonaparte had informed Admiral Bruix that the conquest of England was now his main objective and that he was drafting plans to raise a force of 120,000 men and an armada of 3,000 vessels. It sounded incredible, but for a Napoleon nothing was impossible, as William Pitt was shortly to discover.

Aided by instinct, fresh intelligence reports from France and friends' knowledge of the state of the Royal Navy, William Pitt MP had addressed the House of Commons the following day, 15th March, insisting that the nation must arm, increase the military budget and initiate a crash ship-building programme, not to mention increasing the number of seamen and officers to man those vessels. Pitt coolly claimed that the Navy could no longer defend British shores (which so infuriated the Earl of St Vincent at the Admiralty that he later inelegantly referred to Pitt's supporters in the House as 'those animals of offal of Pitt'). Ignoring an enraged George Tierney, a friend and defender of the First Lord and an old adversary of Pitt (they had once fought a duel), who now dramatically accused Pitt of trying 'to obstruct the defence of the country' and of engendering 'suspicion and despondency' in the British people regarding the capabilities of the Navy, 'on which they prided themselves', Pitt pointed out that only twenty-three gunboats had been built over the previous fifteen months of Addington's administration, while the French had been producing hundreds.

Dozens and dozens of ships had to be found or built if they were going to begin to match the numbers Napoleon had projected the year before. Press gangs once again would have to harass and waylay wayfarers and the unsuspecting, from Penzance to Gravesend and Newcastle (where one wretched man trying to escape such a gang under a hail of musket balls, drowned while attempting to swim the Tyne). Indeed the reports reaching the Admiralty, from spies and neutral sea captains, were disturbing to say the least. That 'adventurer', 'Little Boney', as political caricaturist James Gillray now dubbed him, was surely up to no good, as the sharply increased naval activity in the Channel had been indicating for some months now.

'About six o'clock last evening,' a report from Folkestone announced, 'we could observe from the hills several of the enemy's flotilla and the harbour of Boulogne. We could count about 130 sail, and among them were five brigs.' Such reports were reaching the Admiralty several times a week. The Royal Navy had been shadowing and occasionally engaging the newly formed French units. But did the Sea Lords fully appreciate the gravity of the situation, what the French were really up to, just how enormous their naval effort was? Were men like Keith being taken seriously? Pitt felt they were not.

Nevertheless, one thing was finally clear, even to men such as St Vincent, that preparations of some sort by Bonaparte for the invasion of England were already well under way. On Wednesday, 16th May, with a determined new Prime Minister and the industrious and energetic Lord Melville appointed by him to replace St Vincent as First Lord, the Admiralty Board issued new orders to the ships at the secured anchorage off Spithead, to prepare for hostile action, and as *The Times* related, they were 'of more serious expectation than any that had been known since we were first threatened'. The fleet at Spithead were to have slip buoys added to their cables to permit a rapid departure, the top-gallant yards – for the highest sails of the huge wooden ships – were to be kept reefed to enable the immediate hoisting of sail when necessary. All ships facing the Isle of Wight and the sea lanes to France were 'to clear for action every evening at sunset'. To speed things up further, the signal for slipping their cables was also 'to be considered the signal for action' and in general they were 'to keep in momentary readiness for putting to sea, as that instant it may be expected to engage with the enemy.' Already there was a new spirit in the navy, a new feeling of firm and decisive resolve. With Pitt back in Downing Street and Lord Melville's steady hand at the tiller of the Admiralty the recent years of lassitude were a thing of the past.

Emperor Napoleon was feverishly manning the ports and support camps along the coast, as he faced a phlegmatic but equally determined British Prime Minister. The political and military battle lines were being drawn as the two adversaries carefully studied each other in preparation for the escalating hostilities that were soon to shatter the tranquillity of Europe for years to come.

At the War Office, Earl Camden (John Pratty) was just as decisive and fully committed to the rapid re-armament of a most inadequately defended island and his orders for the review of ten new volunteer regiments at Blackheath on Friday 18th May 1804 were just one instance of the zeal he was to bring to his office. Forts had to be built and volunteers raised, cannons had to be cast, troops had to be trained and new camps established.

Just across the Channel at a tavern in Calais, some French army officers celebrating the growing strength of the impressive invasion force that they had just joined were concluding with toasts: 'To the barrack-master who shall issue the first billets at Dover', and 'To the first review of French troops in St James's Park!'

That same evening, the 18th day of May, the Lord Mayor of London was giving a reception at the Mansion House for the Commander-in-Chief, Frederick, Duke of York and the commanding officers of the latest volunteer regiments even as a weary Horatio Nelson was being piped aboard his new flagship, the *Victory*, in the western Mediterranean.

Also upon that same day in May, Napoleon, dressed in his green uniform as a Colonel of the Guards, received the official delegation from the Senate in the Grand Salon at St Cloud. The Senators, led by Jean-Jacques Cambacérès, bore a document asking Napoleon to assume the Imperial title, and his signing of it marked the first act of his Imperial reign: 'I accept the title [of Emperor] which you believe useful to the glory of my country'. Once they had withdrawn, he gave orders for the striking of a medal to commemorate his invasion plan which was to read: 'Descent Upon England', on one side, 'Minted in London, 1804', on the other, and discussed the details of the invasion with Admiral Ganteaume, including a projected eight-hour night-crossing of the Channel, a crossing, the Emperor declared, which would 'decide the fate of the universe'.

'Our King! Our Country!
And Our God!'

Victualling Office, 24th April, 1804

The Commissioners for Victualling his Majesty's Navy do hereby give Notice, that on Tuesday, the 22nd of May next, they will be ready to receive Tenders in writing, (sealed up) and treat for 500 tons of LYMINGTON or NEWCASTLE SALT, or SALT of equal goodness; and for 400 tons of ENGLISH BAY SALT, of the largest grain, of which the persons who make the Tenders are to produce samples. To be delivered into His Majesty's Victualling stores at Deptford, one half by the 31st of July, and the remainder by the 30th of September next, free of all charge and risk to his Majesty (except that the Contractors will be allowed 2s. 11d. per Ton for Porterage of the Salt from the Wharf to the Stores) and to be paid for by Bills payable with interest 90 days after date.

I return the List of [Army] Commissions which having all met with my approbation I have signed . . . The arrangements for the Volunteers and Lieutenant-General to be called for in the case of actual Invasion meet with my fullest approbation.

George III to Frederick, Duke of York, 10th September 1803

May the Gallic Cock never roost on the British Oak; but should he land, may the Severn Corps do their duty, while the Stanley remains in the rear looking on.

Volunteer regimental rivalry during the threat of invasion
Severn Riflemen vs. Royal Stanley Sharp-shooters

If the French carry out the expedition [against England], all their movements are sure to be abrupt. Eight days will decide the fate of the war.

General Dumouriez

We shall never have a solid Peace until the Invasion is tried and found to fail.

Nelson, 11th April 1804

FROM WINCHESTER, PORTSMOUTH, nearby Southampton, Salisbury, Bournemouth and Lymington, 10,000 spectators had come – men, women and children – converging on the River Beaulieu at the south Hampshire hamlet of Buckler's Hard. Villagers from the coast along Southampton Water, the Solent and Poole Bay had made their way during the previous two days, some of them past the gates of 'Newlands', Admiral Cornwallis' splendid estate, over the paths and roads of the New Forest and across Beaulieu Heath, from Brockenhurst, Lyndhurst and Dibden Purlieu. Despite the exorbitant cost of one shilling per vehicle along the turnpike from Southampton to Beaulieu Abbey, there seemed no end to the carriages bearing visitors of distinction – famous naval captains, retired admirals, aristocrats and the inevitable politicians. Those who stopped to rest at Beaulieu Abbey before completing the last stage of the journey to Buckler's Hard would have found the graves of shipwrights and craftsmen who had been building the King's ships here for nearly sixty years – the top and bottom sawyers, blacksmiths, copper riveters, canvas makers and, of course, the men who created the ingenious variety of wooden forms from the 2,000 oaks required to build a 74-gun ship of the battle line, its keel, hull, decks, masts, spars and bowsprit.

On this clear day, 6th June 1803, many admired the half-completed *Swiftsure*, being built at a cost of £35,787 and which would mean yet another festivity in less than a year's time. Ever since Admiral Lord Nelson had begun his career aboard the *Agamemnon*, launched here back in 1781, this hamlet with its couple of dozen houses seemingly lost along the forested banks of this small Hampshire river, had become renowned, every naval captain familiar with its name and that of its shipwright, the sprightly eighty-nine-year-old Henry Adams, who was still in charge this day.

Veterans of the seven seas had come for a close inspection of Adams' latest work of art, which he had built in less than two years at a cost to His Majesty's Government of £15,568 16s, the 36-gun frigate, *Euryalus*. Among the crowd of senior naval officers, a bright young captain, the Honourable Henry Blackwood, studied intently the ship he would soon command.

The carriages were parked helter-skelter in the hamlet and along the road between the two terraces of houses built far apart to leave room for logs to be rolled down the slope, and for the high stacks of timber fresh from the saw mill or destined for the kiln. Everywhere the smell of wood and tar filled the air. After waiting nearly two years for this launching on the Beaulieu, it seemed only fitting that the sun should shine after months of bad weather, for nothing was more typical or more festive in England at the turn of the nineteenth century, than the launching of a ship. All social classes mixed freely – naval officers in their smart uniforms, farmers and shopkeepers in their best suits, children playing games and a navy band entertaining everyone, as the aroma of hot and cold cooking wafted over them from nearby stalls.

But now the specially raised scaffolding was filled to capacity. Officers who had come from Portsmouth for this occasion made speeches praising the workers, the navy and national patriotism. All attention was focused on this frigate, which towered on its stocks, as everyone awaited the signal announcing that the incoming tide had brought the river up to its maximum depth of eighteen feet, swelling the waters to the other shore some eighty feet away. Here along the miniature grey stone quay, just two miles north of the Solent, across from the Isle of Wight, at long last the order boomed out and mighty hammers knocked away the dog-shores as the *Euryalus* slid into the clear waters. The 10,000-strong crowd cheered as the band played a jubilant 'Off She Goes' and then a resounding 'God Save the King', followed in turn by a special dinner for the 150 invited guests. Dozens of craftsmen watched with pleasure and pride as the graceful frigate, the newest vessel of the Royal Navy, was moored to the quay, where a proud Captain Blackwood was also to be observed. Soon he would be taking her to foreign shores where, two-and-a-half years later, the *Euryalus, Swiftsure* and *Agamemnon* – the three sister ships of Buckler's Hard – would participate in the nation's greatest naval battle.

England had been at war with France since May 1803 but no major successful landing had taken place, even though rumour of a possible French invasion of the British Isles (including Ireland) had been circulating off and on for several years. Therefore, when fresh rumours spread through the realm early in the blustery autumn of 1803, there should have been no untoward anxiety, yet there was. Speculation that up until now had been restricted primarily to the market place and discussed in the same breath as the weather, now swelled in intensity taken up by gentlemen in the clubs in Pall Mall and of course, in the corridors of Westminster. The threat was real enough this time: the Admiralty released reports to the newspapers from English naval officers of concentrations of warships, transports, supplies and troops in French-occupied Holland and along the north-western Channel coast of France facing the Straits of Dover, where less than twenty-five miles of sea separated the two ancient foes.

Momentum was building up from a level of mere awareness and anxiety to one of near panic, such as had rarely been seen in London. To be sure, the last significant successful invasion of England had taken place in the eleventh century. That single invasion, though, had been by the French and had led to the subjugation of Britain! Could it happen again?

Prime Minister Henry Addington, a cautious man, had been slow to act, but he had taken a few of the basic steps required to defend the isles and to put the considerably reduced army and navy on a war footing, but they could hardly be called adequate. The harm had already been done. The contrary First Lord of the Admiralty, the Earl of St Vincent, had reputedly cut the nation's dockyard workers from 130,000 to 70,000 – defying the vehement protests of Pitt's parliamentary opposition – while Addington had previously reduced the army and militia to a total of 143,000 men prior to the resumption of hostilities. Furthermore, long years of war had weakened the economy, and major shortages had occurred, including wheat, resulting in widespread bread riots in England. These led Addington to abolish William Pitt's income tax in order to alleviate the burden, though the value of the pound sterling continued to fall on the Continent by between thirteen and sixteen per cent annually. And yet there was more than economics involved here, for even if Addington had had a full treasury and granaries, he was dedicated to fighting a 'defensive war', as opposed to Pitt's more realistic policy of taking the war to the enemy and openly subsidising the allies and garrisons in Europe to the tune of £8,250,000 a year (which is one of the reasons why he had originally introduced an income tax).

Despite maintaining his overwhelming parliamentary support at this time – 230 as against 58 Pittites – circumstances were now forcing Addington to take more vigorous measures and a 5 per cent income tax was reluctantly reintroduced; the Royal Military College (as it was originally called) was created to train officers; the Militia Act of 1802, intended to raise 51,500, was bolstered by a similar act the following year, adding another 25,000 men – who could be eligible for a bounty of £7.12s.6d upon joining up – to the roster for five years' service. Calls for volunteers left the local volunteer regiments, existing or about to be created, suddenly inundated by a few hundred thousand men, numbers they simply could not begin to cope with. But the number of professional soldiers – as opposed to sunshine patriots – did not increase appreciably under Addington's administration and the nation's forts and artillery batteries were improved only grudgingly at minimal levels as late as April 1804, leaving the country, in the words of historian J Steven Watson, in a state of 'suspended animation'. Although Pitt declined attacking Addington's destructive apathy until March 1804, none the less his former Secretary at War, William Windham, had taken that task upon his own shoulders through the previous spring.

With the arrival once more of Pitt at the head of Government that May, a new feeling of optimism and energy rose in the land, as redoubts and batteries of guns began to ring the coast, and the way was paved for expanding the military through the Additional Forces Act. 'It is time for England to cut the thread that holds the sword of Bonaparte above her head', *émigré* General Charles François Dupérier Dumouriez, a former army commander and foreign minister under the French Revolutionary government, and now military adviser to the crown, warned the British, 'Nothing is so demoralising as an everlasting defensive . . . Let it be clearly understood that if from this year [1804] an attack [on France by England] does not supersede a defensive policy, then his [Napoleon's] chances [of invasion] will be very much increased', – words Pitt very much took to heart.

In the King's Speech of 31st July 1804, the new Prime Minister proclaimed this very policy, of prosecuting the war vigorously, increasing the numbers of troops and sailors, expanding the existing army camps, creating new ones and greatly enhancing coastal fortifications:

> The benefits to be derived from our successful exertions will not be confined within ourselves but that, by their example and their conse- quences, [it is hoped] they may lead to the re-establishment of such a system in Europe, as may rescue it from the precarious state to which it is reduced; and may finally raise an effectual barrier against the unbounded schemes of aggrandisement and ambition which threaten every indepen- dent nation that yet remains on the Continent.

Pitt was willing to offer substantial subsidies to future allies in order to encourage Continental opposition to Napoleon, which he hoped would ultimately take the form of a Third Coalition involving Austria, Russia and Prussia.

Within a week of Pitt's taking office, *The Times* was more optimistic, reflecting a new spirit in the land: 'It must be allowed that there never appeared a more favourable period than the present for overthrowing the pernicious tyranny under which France has fallen, and restoring Europe as to something like its ancient balance.'

Great Britain was now divided into sixteen military districts under the overall command of the Duke of York, each with a commanding general – the Earl of Harrington in the case of London (which was a separate district), and General Sir David Dundas for the district comprising Kent,

Surrey and Sussex. Middlesex, Berkshire and Herefordshire formed one district, Bedford, Northampton, Oxford and Buckingham another, Essex, Norfolk and Cambridge another, Hampshire, Wiltshire, Dorset and the Isle of Wight yet another.

It is difficult to say what received top priority now, for everything seemed to be happening at once. The number of regular army regiments was brought up to 94 and the strength of each expanded from 700–800 men per regiment to 1,000. To attract such numbers, the Exchequer had to provide substantial incentives, for the differences that existed between the standing army on the one hand and the militia and volunteers on the other meant not only that the professional soldiers had to undergo more rigorous training and greater discipline but were also likely to have to serve abroad, which was singularly unpopular. Therefore, bounties of £40, £50 and £60 were offered to entice regular army recruits. Between 1803 and the beginning of 1805, fully effective army strength went up by perhaps 25,000 men, reaching a total of 99,411 (including 19,274 cavalry), and eventually some 116,000 in Great Britain (excluding 55,000 men stationed in Ireland), at an annual cost of £3,774,562.[1] However, great as the popular appeal was to prove one's loyalty to King and Country, in reality there were many who did not appear willing to do so. The army, for example, lost large numbers of able men in two ways: first, the system permitted the purchase of substitutes for those called upon to serve; second, men deserted. Between 1803 and 1804, of 45,492 conscripts, 40,998 were replaced by substitutes and another 8,106 men already serving in the army deserted.

The militia, which was to have raised another 76,500 men between the ages of 17 and 45, had an effective strength of only 61,235 (at a cost of £1,731,857 annually) by the beginning of 1805. Meanwhile, the volunteers who had inundated recruiters throughout the British Isles brought rosters up to some 480,000 in number, whereas their maximum effective armed force, that is, properly armed for combat, was closer to 250,000 infantry and another 25,000 cavalry, which did not include some 20,000 Hanoverian mercenaries. Pitt's Additional Forces Act of June 1804 was intended to shore up the Defence Act of 1803 and the nation's reserves, but there was bitter debate as to how effective was the investment (of manpower and money) in any military unit not connected directly with the regular army.

Nor did the Royal Navy escape Pitt's vigilance: one of his first acts was to raise its strength from 100,000 sailors and marines to 120,000. At the same time, he took steps to increase the number of warships in service from 469 to 551 over the next 18 months – an astonishing feat that he achieved, thanks to the energetic support he was given at the Admiralty by Lord Melville. Such a colossal increase in the navy naturally cost a great deal of money, its budget going up from £12,350,600 in 1804 to £18,864,000 by the end of 1805, and that did not even include the expense of building or otherwise acquiring new warships. In addition, the number of sea-fencibles – the volunteers manning some 800 gunboats (often armed fishing boats with a cannon, howitzer or mortar) guarding the nation's shores (divided amongst twenty-eight coastal districts, from as far west as Swansea and Hartland Point, along the entire southern coast from Land's End to Dover and Sheerness, up to Yarmouth, Whitby, Berwick and the Firth of Forth) – was increased from 14,000 to 25,000 men.[2] Pitt was intent on making Great Britain a well-defended land.

'The capture of London is no doubt the chief object of Bonaparte's dreams . . . The English must never relax their defences', General Dumouriez admonished Frederick, Duke of York. The threat facing them was real enough. 'My dear son', George III wrote to the Prince of Wales in the autumn of 1803, 'Should the implaccable enemy so far succeed as to land, you will have an opportunity of showing your zeal at the head of your regiment . . . and I shall certainly think it mine to set an example in defence of everything that is dear to me and my people.' Everyone, of every station, was arming and preparing and that October even Colonel William Pitt, still a private citizen, thought it too risky to leave Walmer Castle to attend a social event given by his close friend, George Rose: 'I do not like at present to go so far from my post . . . Before the long nights we hope to be very well prepared to receive them [the French], both afloat and ashore . . . [and] I am much more inclined than I have ever been hitherto to believe that such an attempt will be made soon.'

'I have ordered all the ships to their stations as fast as possible', fifty-seven-year-old Admiral Lord Keith informed Admiral John Markham on 5th November 1803, as intelligence reached him that large divisions of French and Dutch boats were attempting to put to sea. 'Preparations, vast and various, are going forward in every quarter to repel the invasion', Keith continued. 'On the coast every officer is at his post . . . Lord Cravan, in the Isle of Wight, ordered them not to sleep out of the Island. No military officer is for the future to be permitted to leave his camp or barracks for more than two hours on any pretext.'

'Letters from the military headquarters of Kent and Sussex mention that almost every regiment in those districts is on the eve of taking the field', *The Times* reported in May 1804, even as Pitt was moving into Downing Street. 'The first regiment of the Royal Surrey Militia . . . marched from Margate and encamped on the Western Height over Dover', the paper noted. Large military camps at Beachy Head, Southbourne, Brighton, Bexhill, Hastings, Winchelsea and Rye were bursting with activity, most roads leading to and from them cluttered with military traffic. In addition, the army was also drafting plans for damming sluices for the flooding of Romney Marshes and similar orders were given for marshes in Essex and Suffolk, along with instructions for breaking up all the roads, except one or two turnpikes, in the event of a French landing. Pitt issued orders for the forts, castles and batteries along the southern coast in particular to be seen to at once. Plymouth's citadel was reinforced as new redoubts were built along the heights above that port, and nearby Fort Monckton was given more powerful cannon. Old forts at Portsmouth, Weymouth, Gosport and the Scilly Islands were fortified. Devonport, Sandown Castle (on the Isle of Wight), Walmer Castle, Gravesend, Tilbury, Chatham and the Isle of Grain were improved or received new batteries; nor were Milford Haven, Little-hampton, Blatchington and Seaford forgotten, along with the Channel coast including Dover, Landguard Point, Harwich, Great Yarmouth, Lynn, Hull and Berwick.

While he was still at the Admiralty, Lord St Vincent had designed a 'triple line of barricade' to protect British shores. This included a first line of defence along the Dutch and French coasts where squadrons of ships of the line, frigates and gun vessels were deployed with the intention of maintaining a strict blockade, literally locking the enemy navy in port. Another force of large warships, the second line of defence, was stationed off the Downs to protect the approach to English coastal waters, while the final line was manned by the sea-fencibles' 800 gunboats.

Closer to London, breastworks extending all the way to Battersea were begun behind the Greenwich Naval Hospital at Blackheath, supported by a formidable assemblage of artillery overlooking the Thames and the immediate approaches to the capital. On the Thames itself, many dozens of gunboats patrolled the waters, including those furnished by the great houses of commerce, the East India Company, for instance, donating, arming and manning twenty of them.

With the resumption of war, and the King's proclamation of a national day of prayer, the Dean of St Paul's conducted a 'prayer of consecration' for the sets of colours presented by the Lord Mayor and the City of London to ten new volunteer regiments:

> Thine, O Lord, is the praise that we, strenuously contending for everything dear to man in society, have hitherto stood alone among the Nations; and, inasmuch as the War is just and necessary, so cause it to be finally crowned with success. As there has already infused into the heads of our Voluntary Defenders, a zeal even surpassing all expectations, so grant that, should the Enemy effect a landing on our shores, these banners, now to be presented as a further encouragement to Loyalty, may prove such inspiring rallying points that there may be formed around them impenetrable ranks . . .

Although this was the age in which the Royal Navy was performing spectacular feats at sea, bringing to Britain great glory, it was the volunteers who now seemed to come in for the greatest public attention. The Lord Mayor of London applauded 'those gallant and patriotic Bands, who, roused by the voice of honour, yield their pleasures and their preoccupations, a willing sacrifice at the shrine of their country'. The King himself, as sincerely patriotic as any of his subjects, attended by members of the French Royal family – including the future monarchs, Louis XVIII and Charles X – reviewed 17,000 troops in Hyde Park on 19th October as an estimated 200,000 people looked on, a spectacle repeated at another great review of volunteers at Blackheath the day William Pitt took office. The roll of drums and files of thousands in splendid uniforms marching before them, naturally brought forth flocks of fresh recruits. Men between the ages of sixteen and sixty formed more than four dozen volunteer regiments in London alone. Young boys playing soldier with blackened broomhandle muskets chased after them, trying to identify all the new units as the troops drilled from Camden Town to Shoreditch. The regimental names were as colourful as their new uniforms: Loyal London Volunteer Cavalry, 1st Regular Royal East Indian Volunteers, St George's-in-the-East Volunteers, Bethnal Green Volunteers, Southwark Troop of Yeomanry, Bloomsbury and Inns of Court Volunteer Infantry, Loyal North Britons Volunteer Infantry, Loyal British Artificers Volunteer Infantry – and so the honourable list continued.

King George was delighted with this overwhelming response, as the Commander-in-Chief, Frederick, Duke of York, informed the people of Britain:

His Majesty perceives, with heartfelt satisfaction, that the spirit of Loyalty and Patriotism, on which the system of the *Armed VOLUNTEERS* through the Kingdom was originally founded, has risen with the exigencies of the times, and at this moment forms such a Bulwark to the Constitution and *Liberties* of the country, as will enable us under the protection of Providence, to bid Defiance to the unprovoked Menaces of our Enemies and to *Hurl Back* with Becoming Indignation the Threats which they have presumed to vent against our Independence and even our Existence as a Nation.

Each volunteer joined a separate, independent unit of part-time soldiers drilling twice a week in time of peace but daily when under threat and, though basically subject to the same discipline as any regular soldier, and even to heavy fines, they were administered, not by the War Department directly, but rather by a Military Committee. A small bounty of a few guineas was offered upon joining and volunteers received a small stipend during hostilities but were unpaid in time of peace. Each reservist signed a 'Declaration' upon joining his unit and that of the Saint James's Loyal Volunteers was typical:

We declare that we will, at our own Expense, provide ourselves with uniform cloathing, according to the Pattern agreed on, and will not accept Pay for our Service . . . That we will be in Readiness to assist the Civil Magistrates in suppressing all Tumults and Riots . . . or any other hostile force within the Metropolis, and to act with other Volunteer Corps as Occasion may require.

'The Great Terror', as the period of impending invasion from 1803 – 1805 was known, caught everyone up in its wake. 'My friends and Neighbours, where our duty calls us, I will be with you,' the Duke of Clarence assured his regiment of volunteers at Bushey, while the Prince of Wales, also a mere colonel of a volunteer regiment, and deeply jealous of his younger brother, the Duke of York, badgered the King relentlessly for higher command and more gold braid. The King, tiring of giving the same negative reply, finally answered that, should the French indeed land, and hence the 'necessity arise', he would personally assume command of the armed forces, without adding, however, what he would do with the prince. The King himself proffered his own suggestions about defending the country but was overruled: 'I cannot deny, I am rather hurt', George III wrote to the Duke of York, 'that there is any objection made to forming so large an Army of Reserves in Dorsetshire or Cornwall', where, he predicted, the full brunt of the French invasion would be felt.

'If you have qualities for a soldier,' the editor of the *Bath Herald* declared, 'you are imperiously called upon, by everything valuable to a man, to be a soldier . . . Your country demands your exertions': while to the north, the 2nd Regiment of Liverpool Volunteers, in the pages of the *Liverpool Chronicle*, addressed 'the manhood of this Town, to awaken the insensible to the present exigency, and to demand, publicly, whether any man can remain an inactive spectator of the tremendous preparations of the enemy, now ripe for execution? Need any more be said to those who labour under no disability?' Apparently not, for the nation responded generously, perhaps a bit too generously in some cases, as when Pitt's old political foe, the ineffable Charles James Fox – whom the King adamantly refused permission to partake in any government – waddled up, enrolling as a private in the Chertsey Volunteers! Even the peace-loving, if dilatory, Henry Addington appeared in Parliament one day in full military attire, sword and all, much to the amusement of the other side of the House (and not a few of his own supporters).

Political punster and caricaturist George Cruikshank later conjured up the spirit of London at this time, recalling how youth learnt the 'tattoo' on the drum, or practised 'some march or national air' on the fife, accompanying the recruits, 'and every morning at five o'clock the bugle horn was sounded through the streets, to call the volunteers to a two hours' drill, from six to eight, and the same again in the evening.' Sergeants bellowed, 'Give them the bayonet!' and one could hear 'the pop, pop, pop, of the single musket or the distant thunder of the artillery' in Hyde Park. Not everyone found this degree of patriotism quite so marvellous, however. The celebrated *émigrée* portrait painter Madame Vigée-LeBrun (who had executed the miniature of Emma Hamilton that Nelson always wore round his neck), residing in London at this time, viewed the valiant recruits 'who were forever marching about with drums beating, making an infernal din' a bit less sympathetically!

And there were those who did not march steadfastly to the patriotic beat, some placing personal gain before national honour, others simply indifferent to the needs of a land preparing to defend itself. Along the Straits of Dover Admiral Lord Keith had received complaint after complaint about lack of patriotism on the part of the civilian pilots needed to navigate the local coast and harbours for the navy. 'These Deal pilots', he grumbled, 'it is time some measure was taken to punish their insolence and ingratitude. They are far too rich, and abandon the interest of their country at a moment their services are required, in order to [carry out] an illicit commerce [in smuggling]'. While on a tour of naval yards, Admiral

Lord St Vincent found just as much to criticise. 'The picture I sent you of the total want of vigour, discipline and subordination at Portsmouth is much heightened at this port [Plymouth]', he informed a colleague, 'where nothing is thought of but contrivance to delay equipment and to frustrate the orders issued by superiors . . . ', or to remove Government stores that found their way to the public market.

Shirkers and deserters were sought out energetically and public servants failing in their duty, or those leading them astray, were now prosecuted with equal vigour, as *The Times* reported on 18th December 1804, when several night watchmen were found asleep on the job in wartime London:

> Yesterday, at Marlborough-street, a publican, in the parish of St George's, Hanover Square, was fined ten shillings, and costs, for suffering night-watchmen to tipple in his house, after the setting of the watch.

The war had to be fought on the home front as well and protecting the country was everyone's business.

'It will be good policy to show the world that we are virtuously rancorous against the French,' Vice-Admiral Russell insisted to a friend, advice with which the Church of England apparently concurred, as it instilled its own brand of patriotic fervour. 'You will not, I think, be guilty of betraying Christian charity,' the Bishop of Llandaff instructed in an address to the clergy of his diocese, 'in the use of harsh language when you explain to your congregations the cruelties which the French have used in every country they have invaded. [Should they do so here] the nation will be ruined by exorbitant impositions – our naval policy will be destroyed – our commerce transferred to France – our land will be divided . . . amongst French soldiers . . . contempt, pillage, rapine, beggary, slavery and death' await English citizens at their hands and 'no language', the indignant bishop insisted, 'can reach the atrocity of the fact.'

Although some of the younger clergymen literally joined up, others saw their role in a more traditional light, as for instance the sedentary Bishop of Chester, who advising clergymen that after performing their most important function – of 'protecting property, women and children' [in that order!] – reminded them that 'if the enemy effect an invasion . . . [clergymen] would then be most actively and suitably occupied . . . [by maintaining] that ascendancy over the minds of the people, which is of so much importance to the effectual discharge of the Sacred Office they have sworn to execute.'

By October 1803 anxiety had given way to panic, further fuelled by journalistic speculation. 'Rumour of a forthcoming invasion appeared to be given credit and even to be confirmed', London's *Morning Post* declared in the first week of October, and continued 'It was stated confidentially that the First Consul's preparations were almost finished and that the great undertaking [the invasion] was to take place some time this month'. Sir Walter Scott personally witnessed the fire beacon being lit at Hume Castle, warning the people of Berwickshire of the arrival of enemy ships – in error as it turned out. 'Do not be alarmed, but the French are landing, and the drum on the quay is beating to arms,' a native of Aldeburgh wrote in haste to his son [in October 1803], while in Essex, despite the proximity of a large army camp, fear also affected local inhabitants, viz Thomas Twining: 'I suppose you will ask me why I leave Colchester. I leave it because I am afraid to stay in it. Many have left, more are preparing to leave it; though I myself think there is very little danger, yet I should be very uneasy to stay here and run the risk. And if I stay 'til the moment of alarm upon the coast, I may not be able to get away at all unless I walk away with [just] a knapsack on my back.'

It was not only lives that were at stake, but property, and many dozens of wagons left such towns laden with furniture, crockery, silver and bedding. But 'there must be no thought of denuding [evacuating] any counties threatened with invasion', advised an anxious General Dumouriez, for it would have both 'fearful and ruinous' results for the nation.

In addition to direct 'telegraph' links in the form of naval messages signalled by shutters from towers and buildings from Portsmouth and Chatham, to alert London of an invasion, hundreds of signal beacons had been prepared all along the coasts of England, Wales and Scotland. These beacons – many of the prominences upon which they were built still bearing the name 'Beacon Hill' – were connected with a series of other bonfires, which the army required to be visible from a distance of at least four miles. Eight wagon-loads of faggots and wood and three or four barrels of tar were prescribed for each at night, while moist hay was to be added during the day to provide a visible column of dark smoke. 'As it is most desirable and essential on the near approach of the expected enemy, or his actual landing on the coast of Kent . . . it is judged expedient, to establish fire beacons on the fifteen or sixteen most conspicuous and elevated points of the country', General Sir David Dundas instructed the commanders of his military district.

Seventy-four Martello towers were also built along the coast during

1803, 1804 and 1805, providing not only look-out stations, but rallying points for defence and, more importantly, magazines for powder, arms and munitions. Thirty feet high, with solid brick walls six to nine feet thick, these squat, round, two-storey towers were built to withstand a long siege, though the only armament they actually boasted was to be found on a four-foot parapet encircling a flat 'bomb-proof' roof – a swivel gun, and one or two howitzers. In some cases the towers were built in clusters of two or three, especially in strategic places along the entrance to the Medway and Thames between Chatham and Tilbury.

'The cardinal points of the defence [of Great Britain] or . . . pivots of communications . . . must never be allowed to fall into enemy hands', urged General Dumouriez, pointing first to the Isle of Sheppey (which controlled the Medway Estuary), then naming all the important ports and rivers along the English coast as far north as Berwick. Dumouriez, whom Nelson had helped entice to England, had one of the best military brains of the day and had studied the overall strategic situation as well as the specific defences of the country in considerable detail, addressing memorandum after memorandum on the subject to the King, the Duke of York and Pitt's Government. He devised a 'checker-board' system of army camps along the southern coast of England in which to ensnare any French troops that might reach those shores. He also analysed the best locations for artillery, explaining the most effective means of deploying guns in each and every location, and concluded finally that a maximum of 200,000 well-trained troops could easily defend the entire country.

Dumouriez urged the building of coastal redoubts (as opposed to Martello towers) capable of providing refuge for up to 500 men and of supporting battle lines along either side. He called for the deployment of large numbers of coastal batteries (just as Napoleon was now doing), but mounted on naval carriages (which were easier to maintain and less costly). He next developed plans for three different kinds of coastal batteries: open batteries with a simple parapet for use before seafronts and army camps; closed batteries (placed in redoubts with flanks, pallisades and dry moats) for coastal headlands some distance from camps; and finally, isolated batteries (closed with flanks and palisades and surrounded by a moat of water) that would be ideal in expanses of marsh or country cut by canals (along the Pevensey coast between Rye and Hythe, for instance, in the Blackwater in Essex, and the Wash), inside coves and at the heads of rivers 'to prevent the descent of the enemy and his deployment should he manage to land . . . Mortar batteries can be placed at the inner ends of bays and coves or on side headlands in a parallel line to the anchorage'.

There would also be three types of army camps: medium-sized camps, serving as the first line of defence, within eight miles of coasts and harbours; camps of the second line, much larger, from which greater concentrations of troops could be launched; and finally, camps along a third line of defence, or, rallying points for inland troops taking up positions for a stubborn stand.

Although Dumouriez did not expect the full French invasion flotilla would ever reach southern England, nothing could be left to chance: 'London must be strongly fortified as to leave the enemy fearful of ever attempting a successful disembarkation at the mouth of the Thames,' he urged. 'In no case must the foe be allowed to penetrate higher [on the Thames] than Tilbury, which protects the shipyards, the powder-stores, the arsenals and the metropolis [London] itself – it must be defended to the last extremity. . . . it is clear that if a descent upon England is feasible, it will be by means of small, shallow draught boats', he predicted in 1803, later managing to convert William Pitt to the idea as well. If a major landing were somehow effected, Napoleon would launch his armies in *Blitzkrieg* fashion, the like of which the English had never before witnessed. 'Eight days', Dumouriez insisted with almost apocalyptic solemnity, 'will decide the fate of the war . . . '

Some of General Dumouriez's advice was heeded. The coasts of Essex and Kent were well fortified; batteries, forts and entrenched strongholds were also undertaken along the River Stour, Mersea Island and the left bank of the Thames as well. A first line of defence was developed simultaneously on the Isles of Sheppey and Grain, and along the coast either side of Deal and Dover, taking advantage of natural obstacles, such as Romney Marsh, continuing along Hythe Turnpike, at Aldington Knoll, with strong camps at Oxney, Challock and Coxheath, also at Broomhill, Fairlight, Bexhill, Hollingsbury Castle (Brighton), Highden Hill (Shoreham), Arundel and Chichester. Pitt and Dumouriez could not have been in more complete agreement.

IN PARIS, NAPOLEON was kept abreast of most of these defensive measures, chiefly by French army and naval officers living in England and information passed on by one or two 'anonymous' British traitors. They provided advice as to the best possible locations where large-scale landings could be made and what sort of resistance should be expected. Before leaving London, French Ambassador Louis Guillaume Otto managed to send Foreign Minister Talleyrand a memorandum entitled, 'Political Considerations on Ireland and the Means Required to Separate it from England', in which Otto strongly supported the feasibility of being able to 'start a revolution in that country'. Another secret report, by one Dupont Derval (bearing no date, but probably written in late 1803), informed the War Ministry that, at this stage, there were 'very few strongly fortified places in England' along the coast, and 'none at all in the interior of the country . . . Some cities are encircled by ancient walls, but their ramparts are too weak and in any event too cluttered with merchandise and wares to withstand an attack by our grenadiers'.

There were exceptions, however, particularly along the coast, including Plymouth, which was well protected, Portsmouth with 'its numerous and well-manned batteries' and whose 'citadel is also very strong' though that port 'could not withstand a long siege from an attack by land'. The Isle of Sheppey and Sheerness were well defended, but worth taking as a major landing site, and though it was true that the fort at Tilbury, opposite Gravesend at the entrance of the Thames, was ringed by powerful batteries, 'none the less, for the victors of Lodi and Marengo, this should not present a problem'. Once it was in French hands they could then take the dockyard and arsenal at Chatham where 'we could find all the materials necessary with which to build and equip a large fleet, if the English had not burnt them first'. Upriver just 'four leagues from London, is the great artillery depot of Woolwich . . . with all its enormous *trains de guerre*. There I saw with sadness all the cannons stored which had been taken from French warships . . . ', but, he assured Paris, 'it is not at all fortified', and would be easily captured. London, on the other hand, was well defended, by the Tower of London in particular. It was 'an old walled fortification flanked by smaller towers' covered with cannons, but would soon collapse after 'a bombardment by us, that is, if the Governor even attempted to defend the place' and where the French would find stored, in addition to dozens of powerful cannons, some 100,000 muskets.

Nevertheless, some aspects of this report also verged on the ridiculous. It was noted that in London 'there are rich bourgeois brilliantly equipped with all the trappings, for instance the London regiment called the City Horse Volunteers [a regiment composed of bank clerks and others of the same ilk] who would much prefer to be at their counters than fighting against the people whose cannons from atop the Alps now control Europe. At least two-thirds of the soldiers in England have never been under fire', Derval added, as he closed his nebulous report with such a grandiosely absurd assessment of the English as to make even the desiccated cynic Talleyrand emit a gentle titter of astonishment. 'I have noticed', concluded this unique secret agent, 'that a large part of the English people love, esteem and honour the First Consul even as much as do the people of France. His portrait', he solemnly reported, 'is in almost all their houses, praise of him coming from almost every mouth.' In brief, the English would greet the French on the beaches as their saviours!

A variety of other spies, chiefly army officers, suggested launching flotillas from the Meuse and Rhine for landings at Exeter, Dorchester or Harwich. 'Having been employed [as a high British officer or perhaps as a French émigré spy attached to the British general staff] to prepare the means for the defence of England', one anonymous report read, 'I know the best means of attack'. He then recommended several different landings, including Ireland, deploying no more than 15,000 men at any one point. The report concluded 'I believe there are many Englishmen who would join and support the invaders.'

It was no doubt because of these numerous optimistic reports that Napoleon continued to feel so confident about the outcome of his intended invasion, especially when this information often included astonishingly accurate data. For instance, one 'Report by an agent in England', sent to Talleyrand in the summer of 1804, listed the eight largest English army camps – at Harwich, Lowestoft, Colchester, Canterbury, Chichester, Winchester, near Weymouth and at Launceston (in Cornwall) – and reported some 206,000 army, cavalry, Hanoverian and militia troops then on active duty. This report also provided very precise information on each army and artillery unit. The situation it described at Yarmouth was typical: the harbour installations there were 'not very strong', comprising three batteries, each with eight 16-pounders, and a nearby garrison with a maximum of 1,500 men to guard the coast and beach that would be ideal for a French landing, while the roadstead off Yarmouth was 'very badly guarded' for such an important place, usually with just two ships of the line, two or three corvettes and some luggers.' With detailed reports like this reaching Paris, the French invasion forces under Marshal Soult soon had a fairly complete idea as to what to expect, and where their landings would be most effective. 'In spite of these defensive forces', the report stated, 'I believe that if but a single French division of 40,000 men reached England, it would meet only fairly light resistance' upon landing. This same, very professional observer included disparaging comments on the volunteers and militia, depicting them as too soft and too elegant, 'requiring carriages, then morning coffee, afternoon tea and a warm bed at night.' As for the volunteer cavalry, most of their horses 'are hired by the day out of livery stables'. Nor was 'one of the best volunteer units', the Saint James's Dragoons, in for better treatment, manned as it was by the richest young men, including the nobility, each dragoon being attended by half a dozen servants to carry wine, liqueurs and civilian clothes.

Another spy in England, one Badini, also disparaged the presence of the volunteers 'who are, for the most part, shopkeepers incapable of any discipline and who, when coming under fire the first time, would no doubt simply turn and run, just adding to the general confusion'. 'Since the union of Belgium with France and the Dutch alliance, the English Government has not been able to recover from the shock of having to face a foe capable of landing forces easily along its open 200-mile-long shoreline.' Still other reports accurately pointed out weaknesses in coastal defences, confirming complaints by Pitt himself about the lack of fortifications north of the Humber, and that most rivers, with the exception of the Thames and Medway, were either totally undefended or inadequately provided for. The Thames, however, generally had six ships of the line, some frigates and cutters available, while the most heavily fortified areas were to be found between Tilbury and Sheerness, and then between Beachy Head and Folkestone.

A final report reminisced about the days of earlier successes, declaring what a coup it would be for French history, not to mention the Emperor's personal glory, if he could execute an invasion between Hastings and Beachy Head. 'As we all know', it concluded, 'it was along this coast that William the Conqueror effected his landing.'

ALTHOUGH DURING THE day sailors plied the waters of the Thames and soldiers paraded through St James's and Hyde Park, in the evening they flocked to Piccadilly, Drury Lane and the Strand, for the advent of

war had once again revived London's night life, each theatre vying with
the next to outdo and amuse a nation under arms.

Britons Strike Home was billed as a 'patriotic entertainment' at the Sans
Souci Theatre in the Strand in the autumn of 1803, while at the Theatre
Royal, in the Haymarket, *King Henry the Fifth, Or, the Conquest of France*,
followed by 'All Volunteers', and two new songs, 'The Country Squire A
Volunteer', and 'The Chapter of Volunteers', were attracting large
crowds, as did *The Surrender of Calais* later at that same theatre. Nor was
the nearby Theatre Royal in Drury Lane to be denied its share of the
events, offering a comedy, *The Ship Launch* to the men in uniform,
though many preferred the more feminine attractions of 'the Grand
French Spectacle' *The Female Hussar*, playing at the Royal Amphitheatre
at Westminster Bridge. The great beauty of the day was the Duke of
Clarence's mistress, the appealing Dorothea Jordan, whose anti-Gallic
songs – 'Flat-bottom'd Boats', 'The Strutting Emperor' and 'Albion will
Govern the Sea' – always drew rousing throngs to Drury Lane as well as
to the private entertainments given at Bushey Park.

The good citizens of London always liked to laugh, as much now as in
Samuel Pepys' day, a characteristic that the threat of invasion in no way
diminished. An old form of amusement became nearly as popular as the
music halls, namely theatre bills for imaginary spectacles.

> Some dark, foggy, Night, about November next, will be attempted by a
> strolling Company of French Vagrants, an old Pantomimic Farce, called
> HARLEQUIN'S INVASION, or THE DISAPPOINTED BANDITTI.
> Harlequin Butcher, [played by] Mr BONAPARTE, from Corsica (who
> performed that Character in Egypt, Italy, Switzerland, Holland). The
> other parts by Messrs Sieyes, LeBrun, Talleyrand, Murat, Augereau and
> Massena.

Specialist printers in Fleet Street produced a variety of posters for a
penny each (or a dozen for nine pence), including the very popular
'Twenty Thousand Pounds Reward'.

> MIDDLESEX
>   To all Constables, Headboroughs, Tithing-Men, and other Officers of
> the County of Middlesex,
> *Whereas* a certain ill-disposed Vagrant and common Disturber, commonly
> called or known by the name of NAPOLEON BONAPARTE, alias Jaffa
> Bonaparte, alias Opium Bonaparte . . . by the instigation of the Devil, and
> with malice aforethought, hath lately gone abroad swindling and defraud-
> ing divers Countries, Towns and Villages, out of their Rights, Comforts,
> Conveniences and Cash; . . . hath been guilty of divers Outrages, Rapes,

and Murders, . . . WE DO hereby will and require . . . that NAPOLEON
BONAPARTE . . . may be forthwith sent to our Jail for WILD BEASTS
. . . and that he be placed in a certain IRON CAGE, with the Ouran
Outang, or some other ferocious and voracious animals like himself . . .

Not to be outdone by the crude punster printers, patriotic poets recited
their works (such as they were), exhorting audiences at social events – or,
in the case of W. T. Fitzgerald, before a meeting of the Literary Fund on
14th July, reminding those present that 'The cause of George and
Freedom is your own!', while an address by R. B. Sheridan entitled 'Our
King! Our Country! and Our God!' was also delivered before a large
London crowd:

> They [the French] call on us to barter all of the Good we have inherited
> and proved, for the desperate Chance of Something better which they
> promise. – Be our plain Answer this: The Throne we honour is the
> People's Choice – the Laws we reverence are our brave Father's Legacy –
> the Faith we follow teaches us to live in Bonds of Charity with all Mankind,
> and die with the Hopes of Bliss beyond the Grave. Tell your Invaders this;
> and tell them too, we seek no change – and, least of all, such Change as *they*
> would bring us.

Even as William Pitt was assuming his new duties as Prime Minister once
again in May 1804, the popular song, 'The Invasion', was being cheered
in Piccadilly.

> Bright honour now calls each true Briton to arm,
> Invasion's the word which hath spread the alarm,
> Bonaparte, and his legions, they threaten us hard,
> Yet their threats and bravados we ne'er need regard.
>
> ### *Chorus*
>
> Then stand up, bold Britons, for children and wives,
> In defence of Old England to venture your lives.
> Subscriptions now rise thro' the country at large,
> To King and to Country their duty discharge;
> For freedom we fight, and our cause it is just,
> On our army and navy we place our whole trust.

With coastal batteries being installed and manned in harbours and on
clifftops, with squadrons of warships and hundreds of gunboats guarding
them by sea, and nearly 500,000 men under arms, the people of England
felt they would soon be ready to meet any French threat, even from 'the
wretch reeking in blood', as a *Times* editorial described Napoleon, and,
in the words of the Lord Mayor of London, eager to prove their

'. . . devotion to the sacred cause of freedom and independence'. And yet, little did they suspect – not even General Dumouriez or Prime Minister Pitt himself – what extraordinary invasion plans the French Emperor was concocting, with a singleness of purpose and concentration of effort and national resources such as England's democratic Government in 1804 could not even have begun to match . . . in preparation for the greatest joint army–naval operations Europe had ever witnessed.

Building an Armada

Some day or other, that Buonaparte, if he lives, will attempt the invasion and conquest of Great Britain.

Nelson

Tell me, what do you think of the Boulogne expedition? Things will go badly with the English, you know, if Napoleon gets across the Channel.

Pierre Bezuhov, War and Peace

Only Achieving the impossible is admired in France.

Napoleon

LIKE ALL SAILORS, Rear-Admiral Denis Decrès was an early riser. Arriving at the Ministry of the Navy and Colonies at the crack of dawn and spending the entire day in meetings or dictating reports and letters, he could still be found at his desk as dusk fell and lamplighters returned to the Place de la Révolution (the former Place Louis XV of Decrès' youth, where another king, Louis XVI, had been guillotined just eleven years earlier), that immense square extending all the way to the River Seine across from which the Palais Bourbon stood barely outlined against the sky. The dingy oil lamps grew brighter as darkness descended once again over the wartime capital of the newly proclaimed French Empire.

After many hours at his desk studying the reports of the seven maritime Prefects (whose districts extended from Dunkirk to Brest and Toulon), authorising victualling tenders, considering the promotion of new officers, and the dismissal of incompetent colleagues, Admiral Decrès needed his customary drink at the end of the day in the unaccustomed silence of his immense and elegant office. Turning from the window and the clatter of the changing of the guard he would sink into a chair as exhaustion – mental and physical – set in. Somehow, at sea, he was never this tired, not in this way, not so early. In contrast the Emperor of the French, as Napoleon had been called this past fortnight, never seemed to rest, but was always thinking, creating, changing, doing and undoing. He was a human whirlwind and, though Decrès was two years younger, he could barely keep apace of the man and his mind.

Like the Emperor Napoleon, Admiral Decrès was a little man with a tough reputation. He may have been born an aristocrat at Château Villain in Champagne, but a career in the French Royal Navy, which he had joined at the age of seventeen, quickly taught a young man that one must either be decisive and able, or fail. Life in a fighting navy was very hard indeed, and a fighting navy it was, as he soon learnt, becoming a veteran of several battles against the British in the Caribbean by the time he reached his twenty-first birthday.

Denis Decrès, forty-three years old in May 1804, had earned his reputation, as his subordinates could well attest. There had been no place in his brilliant naval career for an aristocrat with elegant manners, beautiful women and social poses. Decision and action were what was required of this still relatively young man. No philosopher he, just a sailor, a hard, practical man, who knew how to accept orders – all orders without question – and carry them out as expeditiously as possible. Napoleon liked that in a 'soldier' (and a French admiral continued to hold the rank of 'general' as well). His naval career had been exemplary, thus, when in February 1794 he had reached Lorient after an arduous voyage from the Indian Ocean with a special report for the Naval Ministry, he was suddenly arrested by gendarmes and whisked off to Paris to be held like many officers who had served under the Bourbons without rhyme or reason as a 'suspect', a danger and threat to the society he had been defending at sea for half his life, he was both astonished and bewildered. There had never been the slightest complaint recorded, officially or unofficially. Fortunately within a matter of months his superiors at the Admiralty Office had successfully intervened and he was back on active duty again, and by the age of thirty-six in 1798 had been promoted to the rank of rear-admiral. In March 1801 he was appointed Maritime Prefect, ironically at the very Lorient where he had been arrested.

His relationship with his Emperor was rather unusual. Napoleon as a rule knew surprisingly few naval officers and liked even fewer of them. He had neither an abiding interest in the Navy nor an understanding of it and the sea, notwithstanding the fact that France had two strategic coastlines and that he was in the process of building the largest naval force Europe had ever seen. He treated Decrès as a subordinate, to be sure, and, like most of the other ministers time and again dealt him a great deal of abuse. But which other cabinet minister would ultimately be able to boast of an unbroken career with Napoleon, in the same ministerial post, for nearly fourteen years? It was not just that Decrès was hard working – Pierre Forfait before him in this very office had worked reasonably hard – nor was it just because Decrès could take orders and could bend when Napoleon's will required it of him (as it often did). Decrès had been appointed as Naval Minister at the age of forty in 1801 because of his very special qualities, borne out by his career.

First and foremost, despite his junior standing amongst his fellow officers, he was promoted above other rear-admirals, vice-admirals and admirals, in part because of his long years at sea. Unlike numerous colleagues who had many years seniority over him but who had spent most of their careers in snug berths ashore (indeed, some of whom had not commanded a squadron at sea for fifteen or twenty years) Decrès had been at sea most of his life since 1778. Not unlike Napoleon himself, who had risen to the rank of general, despite his heavy Corsican accent, not so much because he had friends in high places – though he was not without influence – but rather as a result of his own hard work and astonishing accomplishments. It was ability and talent that counted. Promotion had brought Napoleon command, which he had assumed so successfully, not only achieving his objectives, but also gaining the respect of the common soldier, not to mention that of his fellow officers (despite their frequent bitter envy).

Denis Decrès also had that experience as a leader of men. As a young naval lieutenant he was given command of a schooner, then advanced to frigates and finally to a ship of the line, the *Formidable*. His career proceeded fairly quickly after 1796 when he was promoted to *Chef de Division* enabling him to command a 'division' of ships (usually comprising a variety of vessels, a squadron or fleet being divided into two or more divisions as the situation dictated) and he had commanded a squadron under Admiral de Brueys, successfully attacking the British at Malta in 1798. He understood men, ships and strategy, putting all to good and effective use. He had worked in various theatres of operations – the Caribbean, off the American coast, the Channel, the Mediterranean, and even the distant Indian Ocean. He knew the charts of foreign seas from first-hand experience (and how inaccurate they could be) and the problems stemming from lengthy military expeditions. He could be placed in any situation, at any time, and always manage to succeed.

Decrès' personal bravery and initiative in battle had been recorded on numerous occasions. He obtained the rank of ensign in 1782 after he had practically single-handedly recaptured a French frigate, the *Glorieux*, from the English in the Antilles, coming under such withering fire that all masts were reduced to shredded stumps. Later he seized a British vessel, the *Argo*, under dramatic conditions. He had shown bravery, perseverance and initiative, as when he had landed French troops in Malta in April 1798 under extremely heavy British fire from the fortress at La Valetta. Following the defeat at Aboukir, commanding some of the remaining vessels, Decrès limped back to Malta where the French were under attack from a combined British, Russian and Neapolitan naval force. After seventeen months the rest of Malta surrendered to the British, but Decrès, once again seizing the initiative in March 1799, managed to break through the British blockade on board the *Guillaume Tell*, with some 1,000 soldiers and crew, not to mention 200 evacuated wounded from the island. Even while escaping he seized the chance to attack the British frigate, the *Penelope*, which he boarded for a while until he was in turn attacked by the 64-gun *Lion* and the 86-gun *Foudroyant*. The precision of British gunnery was famous world-wide and, in this instance, forced Decrès to release the *Penelope*, which soon trained its guns on the *Guillaume Tell* as well. With fire pouring in from three different angles, the French ship was trapped, unable to escape, greatly hampered by congested decks where many of the wounded lay, but Denis Decrès continued to fight for hours in a miniature battle that went down in French and British naval history. The French crew was decimated and Decrès lost over half his men to British gunfire as all three masts were blasted to bits, bringing down the ship's rigging, spars, canvas, and masts. Admiral Decrès had personally taken part in the fighting and, after suffering several wounds, finally collapsed. He was taken prisoner by the British and removed to Syracuse to await an exchange of officers. The British, who rarely had much praise for the French navy, published a report of this battle in the *Naval Chronicle* of 1799, describing it as 'perhaps the hottest action that any enemy vessel ever brought to bear against ships of His Majesty.' It was these and other exploits that led to Denis Decrès being one of the few naval officers Bonaparte really respected, as witnessed by the First Consul personally awarding Rear-Admiral Decrès his 'sword of honour' in Paris on 1st March 1801.

Having suffered serious wounds while in action, Decrès was forced to relinquish sea command, but the First Consul could not allow such a valuable man simply to retire and so tested his administrative abilities by naming him Maritime Prefect of Lorient in March. Could the man organise forces, men, materials and ideas on land as well as he had done at sea? Perhaps the severity of his wounds, the protracted convalescence and the shock of the battle had taken some of the spirit and initiative out of him, as they had in so many others? Decrès, a remarkably resilient man, seemed more active if anything, however, despite the occasional pain from his wounds. His authority now extended from Brittany to Holland, carrying out major works at the ports of Cherbourg, Nieuport and Flushing. He created new shipyards and, at Anvers, an arsenal, while fitting out an expedition for San Domingo – all this within less than six months.

Studying the reports on Decrès' career at St Cloud in 1801, reports prepared for him by Pierre Forfait, Minister of the Navy and Colonies, First Consul Bonaparte read them with special interest. He was pleased that his extremely favourable first impressions of Decrès had been correct. Now he studied his entire dossier, covering a career of nearly twenty-three years. He had rewarded Decrès that March for that single battle in the *Guillaume Tell*, but now Bonaparte read of his other exploits, of his rapid rise in rank through sheer hard work and unusual ability. He was twice as effective as any naval officer he had ever met. He could organise ports and shipbuilding and fit out major expeditions involving thousands of men quickly and efficiently. Denis Decrès was definitely the man for him and he was summoned to Paris where, on 1st October 1801, Pierre Forfait was fired and dispatched to the coast as Inspector General of the new flotilla, while Rear-Admiral Decrès was named the new Naval Minister, much to the astonishment of nearly everyone as, outside the navy, his name had hitherto been quite unknown for, unlike Forfait, Decrès was no politician. Decrès was to remain with Napoleon – despite the ups and downs of his career – until 1814, a captain who stayed loyally with his ship until the very end.

Decrès would sit in his darkened office, the large maps and charts folded or rolled up and put away, as he tried to understand the full impact of recent events. First Consul Bonaparte, to whom Decrès owed everything, was now Emperor Napoleon. He was a difficult man to work for, of course, and when one accepted such a promotion as this, one knew that it was necessary to be on call twenty-four hours a day, frequently having to work into the small hours or missing the usual respite offered to lesser individuals on the tenth day of the revolutionary calendar. He was sometimes summoned by the Emperor in the middle of the night (like the War Minister Alexandre Berthier who was once called from his bed *seventeen times* before dawn) and Napoleon insisted that his ministers always appear in full dress, spurs and all, regardless of the hour! In brief Napoleon now owned him, as he did everyone round him. It was as simple as that. The Emperor was as unrelenting with himself as he was with all his subordinates, but he did not treat all of them in the same manner. Police Minister Joseph Fouché, for instance, was a crafty fellow who knew a great deal, indeed far too much, and who had to be handled a little more carefully than most. No one could ever complain that *he* was lax, indeed the man seemed to work twenty-four hours a day, nothing escaping his notice. As for his supercilious Foreign Minister, Talleyrand, he was at once the most difficult and complex man Napoleon had ever known, one whom he could never quite fathom. Indeed the Emperor was far more wary and circumspect when dealing with *him* than he ever was even with the Emperors of Austria or Russia. Everyone else, however, had to approach Napoleon most carefully, as he treated his other subordinates with a careless derision that he scarcely attempted to conceal and this often extended to his brothers and sisters as well. It was one great chess game and Napoleon was moving all the pieces just as he pleased.

The ministers did also have their private lives, of course – at least occasionally. In the case of Decrès, for instance, who had not yet married at this time, there was the fleeting affair or liaison, as time permitted and for as long as the patience of the woman of the hour lasted. Ambition, however, remained the one permanent mistress of his life.

Decrès' egotism, a conspicuous fault in his character, became more accentuated in his new role as Naval Minister, working in the shadow of the Emperor, the greatest egotist in French history, barring none. Yet, with this unpleasant trait, which was apparently accepted along with his new-found powers and personal wealth (for Napoleon gave Decrès a peerage, making him a duke and heaped riches on him) came his equally growing reputation for injustice. His servants resented his arrogance and overbearing attitude and frequently stole from him and, indeed, many years later, one of them blew up the admiral while he was asleep in his own bed! Many of his subordinates at the Ministry not only disliked him, but feared him as well. Denis Decrès had reached the highest political office a naval man could hold (although he was yet to attain even higher naval rank) and he was not about to compromise or relinquish his new position as a result of mediocre young officers, or indeed as a result of anyone else's incompetence anywhere in the Imperial Navy, as it was now called. The admiral worked like a demon and expected no less of everyone else. If his lieutenants lagged for a moment, he was merciless. Emperor Napoleon often demanded the impossible of his ministers, and Decrès, perhaps more than any of the others, sometimes even managed to accomplish just that. Yet, for all the praise Napoleon bestowed upon him, Admiral Decrès was not a fellow soldier – one who had campaigned by his side – and no sailor, no matter how good, could ever become

Napoleon's 'favourite'. Jean–Jacques Cambacérès, the Emperor's newly named Arch-Chancellor of the Empire, was tolerated and useful politically over the years; Fouché was an evil necessity given all the plots constantly being hatched against the Emperor; Talleyrand was as unbearably arrogant as he was indispensable, both in matters of state and foreign affairs, but it was Alexandre Berthier at the War Office who came as close to being a favourite as anyone in the army or government.

Berthier had served with Napoleon during every campaign since the invasion of Italy as his Chief of Staff and had proved invaluable as such, even in the field, and as a loyal friend – one of the few with whom Napoleon allowed the informal 'you'. In 1805, Berthier was raised to the rank of Major-General of the *Grande Armée*. His superb organisational and administrative abilities for the army matched those of Decrès for the navy and Napoleon needed both men to succeed.

Decrès had always been able to think for himself, but now, at Napoleon's side, subject to both his good will and his malicious whims, the Admiral gradually became less adventurous. He learned quickly that if he did not have Napoleon's written authorisation for nearly every action he took, things could easily backfire.

Decrès had never met such a brilliant man as the Emperor before. He was capable of doing a dozen different things – in amazing detail – at the same time and the man's feverish brain never seemed to rest, nor even needed to do so. His detailed knowledge of every aspect of government, even of the navy, including the names of middle-ranking officers, ships, their locations, the number and types of armament they carried, their individual assignments – was really quite staggering, but Napoleon could easily change plans as the mood of the moment took him, leaving his subordinates bewildered, stranded and dismayed. It was virtually impossible to anticipate what the Emperor was thinking or doing, though many ambitious men tried. When he was gloomy or displeased about events or operations – and he was a most difficult man to please – the Emperor could be very hard indeed on the nearest scapegoat, for he always needed one. There was not a soul who worked closely with the Emperor who did not know the wrath of that tongue. Napoleon's tirades – whether directed at generals, ministers or foreign ambassadors – were legendary, as were his rare bouts of subsequent remorse, apologies invariably being made in the form of gold coin. Gold, to Napoleon, was always the easy answer, the balm to soothe anyone – even the illustrious Talleyrand, though admittedly he required much more than anyone else.

The Imperial Navy was very different to that of Great Britain where a completely independent Admiralty Board, headed by its First Lord and his Sea Lords, decided everything about the management of the Royal Navy, totally independently of the King and quite independently of any prime ministers, with few exceptions. Lord Melville, First Lord of the Admiralty, for instance, though himself politically appointed, gave general direction to the navy free of interference from Prime Minister William Pitt and, in any event, considered him a friend and equal, not a distant superior. Melville delegated a great deal to the Admiralty Board, including the First Sea Lord who was responsible for the organisation and distribution of the fleet. The Admiralty Board comprised the best generally retired admirals that could be mustered. No one – not even Pitt – could pretend to match their knowledge of the Royal Navy and no one was foolish enough to try. In Paris, however, the situation was entirely different. Admiral Decrès, as Naval Minister, headed the French Admiralty Board, or *Conseil de la Marine* as it was known, but also, in reality, dictated to the Board, delegating very little initiative or authority to its members, quite unlike the British equivalent. Decrès in turn took his orders directly from Napoleon. Pitt would never have dreamed of challenging the authority of the Admiralty Board concerning ships' complements, anchorages, armament, stating which ships were to train where or sail when, except in the course of general geo-political demands and even then only in general terms. How it was to be done and who was to do it, with orders for the commanding officers, was all left in the hands of the Admiralty. In Paris, Napoleon directed almost every movement of every vessel – just as he directed the movement of every regiment and artillery battery – the Emperor's orders being handed to Decrès who, in turn, passed them on to both the commanding officer concerned and the Admiralty, and then to the Maritime Prefect involved. Bonaparte had complete confidence in no one and was wary of the delegation of power. Thus, for him, no detail was too unimportant, too trivial, as he was to point out to his commanders time and again. Indeed, the Emperor frequently bypassed Naval Minister Decrès, writing directly to his squadron commanders, giving them orders or asking information of them, not always informing the Naval Minister of what he was doing. Decrès, a man with a strong ego, but also with great personal abilities – abilities he wished to show the world and apply – had to tread very warily indeed.

Napoleon needed help, there was no doubt about it, help that Denis Decrès in particular was well suited to provide. Even before the last efforts to revive the Treaty of Amiens in the late spring of 1803, Napoleon began mobilising his forces along the Channel.

Back in 1798 the Government had placed General Bonaparte in charge of a premature invasion force of some 50,000 men destined for England. Although the General had held that command for only a few months, it was long enough to plant the seeds of the idea of a real, full-scale Channel operation against the English some time in the future. At the same time, learning from the mistakes made by the Government then, General Bonaparte realised the importance of long-term planning where a naval operation was concerned and the necessity of putting all the nation's efforts behind such a scheme. If the idea of an invasion was often in Napoleon's thoughts thereafter, it was only in 1803, some five years later, that the opportunity to create such an invasion force presented itself. French armies were not needed elsewhere, as peace had been established through treaties with the rest of Europe, and when the Amiens accord collapsed, there would be only one country to face initially – Britain – and should Britain bring in fresh allies through her usual system of military subsidies, those subsidies (and any subsequent coalitions) would disappear once Britain was invaded and crushed, and so all resistance to the French would simply evaporate overnight.

Although Napoleon was a genius, and he had long mulled over the idea of an invasion, he had not prepared a general master plan. Curiously and irrespective of the obvious need, he was not much good with pen and paper. He could think quickly on his feet, but not seated at a desk. It was all in his head. He was going to attack the problem piecemeal, as he often did, although ultimately the plan included four basic aspects: building a flotilla large enough to ferry men, horses, equipment and supplies across the Channel; providing large enough port facilities to accommodate those vessels and supplies from which to launch that attack; the preparation of major port and channel fortifications to protect the invasion preparations; and the building of a large special invasion force of army troops. Despite his rather haphazard approach, by May 1804 the newly acclaimed Emperor was to have in hand impressive war preparations, though the British government for many long vital months seemed unaware of just how powerful a force was being built.

It had all begun tentatively with orders concerning the initial work on the port of Boulogne and the creation of the National Flotilla. In fact the plans for this new flotilla, designed and promoted by Pierre Forfait – 'he who has never even stepped aboard a warship, nor heard the whistle of shells falling round him,' as Decrès scathingly referred to him – were only accepted because Napoleon, through his ignorance of the sea, had liked them. Almost every seasoned naval officer had thought the design and use of the flat-bottomed boats quite mad (though only a few of them had the courage to say so), Admiral Laurent Truguet for one predicting that 'half of these skiffs will be lost during the crossing', arguing instead for the construction of 'true transport vessels [of traditional design]'. Admiral Ganteaume considered the whole venture as 'extremely chancy'. Naval Minister Decrès was even more outspoken in discussing the subject with the First Consul, denouncing 'the absurd paradoxes' of Forfait's 'monstrous ideas . . . which are as wrong as they will prove to be disastrous.' Indeed, Decrès insisted, Forfait was guilty of 'attempting to deceive you concerning matters of the highest national importance.' But Bonaparte turned a deaf ear to all logic and overruled the Naval Minister. Thus forced to continue working on the project very much against his will, Decrès informed the First Consul in his early report of 3rd March 1803 that he could have the first order of 150 such vessels built, 50 *chaloupes canonnières* and 100 *bateaux canonniers* – 'a heap of precious baubles', a disgruntled Admiral Bruix described them – at a cost of 2,000,000 francs. Over the next two months plans, provisional needs and cost estimates were being prepared for war in the Channel even before the British Ambassador Lord Whitworth concluded his final talks in Paris with Napoleon and Talleyrand. Indeed, on 18th May 1803, Admiral Decrès duly authorised a shipbuilding programme for the invasion flotilla that involved the actual orders for the first forty-one *chaloupes canonnières*.

On 23rd May 1803 Pierre-Antoine Daru, a future Intendant-Général of French forces in Austria and Prussia, officially addressed the Tribunate and the French nation in the First Consul's name, preparing them for an invasion of England:

> If, as I speak here now, you were to be informed that the English had carried out a landing on our shores, who amongst you would not have been greatly disturbed . . . Imagine then how alarmed they would be in England upon learning of the arrival of a French army, whose passage there would no doubt be more difficult to carry out, but the effect of which would be even more terrible. We are already masters enough to be able to conquer the King of England's [German] states on the Continent, and once we land on his island, we will have broken all English power once and for all.

The nation – and the world – had been put on notice, publicly informed of the First Consul's intention of invading England, and the following day Napoleon named 'Citizen Forfait' as Inspector-General of the National

Flotilla (later to be called the 'Imperial Flotilla') to oversee its construction and the administrative structure required for its execution. Finally, on that same day, Napoleon awarded the first major contracts for flotilla vessels, involving some 1,050 boats, delivery of the first 310 vessels set for 23rd December 1803!

It was a tall order and typical of the way in which Napoleon worked. Once he made up his mind about something, he wanted to see it accomplished immediately, that very instant, or, in this case, requiring within seven months' time the building of more vessels than Britain had built (of a comparable size) in the last seven years – all this in addition to the regular building programme for the replacement fighting ships for French squadrons round the world. Full-scale prototypes of newly designed vessels had to be built, seasoned timber for spars, masts, hulls and decks had to be acquired, along with large quantities of tar and hemp (all of which had to be ordered from abroad, chiefly through Holland), shipyards had to be made ready and Napoleon even ordered Decrès 'to requisition all the labourers in Belgium and along the Rhine' to help build these craft. At the same time he ordered fellow Consuls Jean-Jacques Cambacérès and Charles-François Lebrun, as well as Foreign Minister Talleyrand, to seek out wealthy acquaintances who could donate at least one vessel each, which would then be named after them.

Five days later, a most impatient Bonaparte changed his mind: the first boats must be ready not by 23rd December, but by 23rd September! Forfait now had only *four* months in which to produce and deliver the first few hundred vessels, and as if this were not maddening enough, it was to happen time and time again over the next year and a half. Initial boat orders, which were difficult enough to complete, were repeatedly replaced by even more impossible demands. For instance, Napoleon wrote to Inspector-General Forfait reminding him of the minimum number of vessels he must have completed by the end of September but added 'try to have twice that number . . . Speed up all boat construction . . . there will be no shortage of money . . . just keep in mind that every hour is precious.' Napoleon was not an easy man to work for.

Boats of all sizes and types were to be constructed everywhere: not only in the traditional naval yards, such as at Cherbourg, Brest, Rochefort, Nantes, Marseilles and Toulon, but now throughout the French hinterland and beyond – cities were to be transformed into shipbuilding centres wherever there were rivers from which boats could be launched, as far east as the Rhine, and in Bruges, Ghent, Liège, Namur, Lyons,

Compiègne, Strasbourg, Lille, Amiens, Versailles, Toulouse, Grenoble, Rouen and dozens of other cities. The French capital already had two small naval yards, but that did not suffice: 'It is my intention Citizen Minister [Decrès], that the shipyards of Paris become much more productive', Napoleon ordering an additional sixty boats to be built there by the end of September. He suggested creating two more shipyards, one at Vincennes, another in the Champ de Mars, and soon barges were unloading stacks of timber and hemp along the quays and boat builders and craftsmen tramping in large numbers before the gates of the Ecole Militaire. Thousands of skilled men were required to meet the deadlines and anyone who knew how to use a hammer and saw was called up, literally drafted: 'let all the workers living along the banks of the river in the Départements of the Seine, the Seine-et-Oise, the Oise, and the Seine-et-Marne be summoned to the works in Paris'. It had not occurred to Napoleon that not everyone might *want* to do this work, work forced upon them at bayonet point. Yet even this tremendous effort was not sufficient, and one month after the very first boat orders were tendered, Naval Minister Decrès informed Forfait at Boulogne that, 'It is the First Consul's wish that every possible means be used to accelerate the formation of a flotilla . . .' which could also be augmented by the purchase (between Anvers and St Jean-de-Luz) of '300 of the best commercial vessels' capable of holding at least 90 to 100 men each.[1]

No sooner had First Consul Bonaparte issued orders for the construction of the first 300 boats and the purchase of another 300 merchant vessels, than on 5th July he increased the orders, requiring immediate completion of 50 *prames*, 300 *chaloupes*, 300 *bateaux canonniers*, 50 *caïques* (long-boats), 10 *bombardes* (bomb vessels), 700 *péniches*, 1,000 *chasses-marée* (coasting luggers), for a total of 2,410 further vessels. Then without warning and reflecting Bonaparte's still undefined policy, Decrès informed State Counsellor Forfait that 'The First Consul has formally notified me that he wants a [second] flotilla prepared in the Mediterranean', though what the precise purpose of this one was to be remains a mystery to this day, unless perhaps it was meant simply as a decoy for Admiral Nelson. The orders emanating from St Cloud did not always make sense, they often did not include explanations, and frequently were never again referred to. Meanwhile, however, more boat orders were authorised for construction at Ostend, Dunkirk, on the Escaut, at Boulogne, Calais, Saint-Valéry, Dieppe and Honfleur.

For the most part the various orders concerned four classes of vessels, all specially designed, or re-designed, to draw very little water as they were intended simply to be ferrying and landing craft with enough armament to protect each vessel upon reaching the beach. Unfortunately, although models of each class were requested, they were frequently built and tested only after large-scale orders for them had been placed and most classes quickly proved to have drawbacks, sometimes most serious ones, which resulted in many cancelled orders later and continued requests for modifications, not to mention subsequent experiments with artillery to find the type and calibre best suited to each vessel.

The largest craft designated for this armada was the *prame* – a 110-foot vessel with a 25-foot beam and corvette-type rigging, but *no real keel*. It had instead only three very shallow 'keels', like those found on small coastal fishing boats, to support the boat when beached. This shallow draught vessel – it drew just over eight feet of water – with its three masts and heavy rigging soon proved to be most unstable in heavy weather – with or without its full complement of 38 sailors and 120 soldiers. For armament, most *prames* initially carried twelve 24-pound guns on their single deck!

The other three classes of landing craft included the first class, or *chaloupe canonnière* – a 76- to 80-foot vessel with a slender beam of just 17 feet, its rigging of brig design, drawing six feet of water, armed with three 24-pounders and one 6- or 8-inch howitzer, capable of carrying some 152 men (including a crew of 22). Again, designed as a landing vessel, it had no keel.

The next two classes of boats proved to be the most numerous. First, the lugger-rigged *bateau canonnier*, with its three small masts, was 60 feet long and of 14 foot beam, drawing 4½ feet of water. This slender vessel carried one 24-pounder, 1 howitzer and 1 piece of field artillery, in addition to 112 men (which included a crew of 6) and 2 horses. Again, like the preceding vessels, it was more or less flat-bottomed, having no proper keel to stabilise it while navigating.

The 'third class', or *péniche*, was the smallest of the landing craft, also designed with lugger-rigging, three abbreviated masts and 60 feet long, but with only 10 foot beam, drawing a mere 3½ feet. As it lacked a deck of any kind, it was really one long, enormous open-hulled surf boat, designed to carry 71 men (including a crew of 5) with two guns – usually one 6-inch and one 4-inch howitzer (or instead, sometimes a 'Prussian howitzer', or an 8-inch mortar). The boat had no keel.

These four classes of boats were the backbone of the flotilla intended by Napoleon to provide defensive gunpower upon landing (all vessels bearing guns fore and aft) and maximum ferrying abilities, capable of

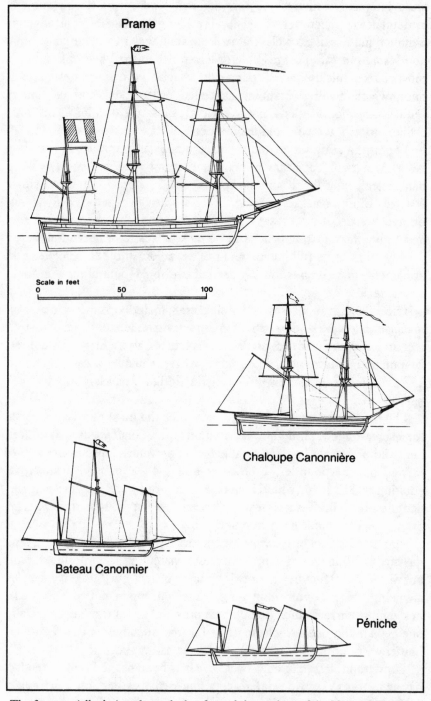

The four specially designed vessels that formed the nucleus of the National Flotilla.

landing in very shallow water. Despite their large numbers (and the figure constantly varied), all told by the end of 1803 orders had been placed for a total of 1,301: *prames, chaloupes, bateaux canonniers* and *péniches* (plus 180 older vessels already in existence), exclusive of other types.

The cost of this flotilla was far greater than Napoleon had reckoned on – a total of 29,917,500 francs was required just for the boats and their basic rigging, exclusive of all armament, supplies and modifications to civilian craft bought as transport vessels to make them suitable for military purposes.[2] Napoleon may have been taken aback by this figure, but if he did not look visibly shaken, it was perhaps because he had already devised other means of payment. Indeed, he continued to place new boat orders for the flotilla, though it must also be kept in mind that the figure of 29,917,500 francs did not include any costs of the regular naval warships also being built at this time.

These boat orders, impressive as they were, with continual reminders by General Bonaparte that they must be done on time, were nevertheless somewhat misleading and the actual numbers ordered or available were constantly fluctuating, at times even in doubt. Meanwhile, as the first boats were launched, fitted out and armed, then tested in the Channel, various problems were revealed, most of which could never be solved without completely re-designing each class of boat. The *prame* design in the words of one French officer, proved to be 'disastrous'. This 110-foot vessel with no proper keel held the wind badly, that is, could not be steered properly to maintain a straight course and, as the Channel ports were notorious for frequently heavy seas and contrary winds, Admiral Decrès was obliged to reduce the order for fifty *prames* to eighteen and ultimately just a few were in actual use. A boat was not much good if it would not go in the direction required, while the excessive weight of the twelve cannons meant that these single-deck boats were constantly going aground long before leaving the French coast, often not even getting out of harbour.

As for the *chaloupe canonnière*, it was not much better. Without a keel it navigated badly and was certainly far too narrow to remain stable under its immense square sails. Also, being of shallow draught, it lacked holds for both proper ballast and equipment. The hull was not nearly strong enough to withstand damage sustained from frequent groundings, not to mention the shock of heavy artillery discharges. Even the weight of the artillery was far in excess of what such a fragile craft could reasonably be expected to support.

All craft, whatever the type, suffered as a result of being built from unseasoned timber used because of the need to meet the rushed orders, resulting in warping and major leaks in many vessels. The upriver shores of ports were soon littered with newly built and even more recently discarded boats in need of caulking or re-building.

The *bateaux canonniers* also had weak hulls, incapable of supporting their complement of men in addition to their artillery, and too little freeboard – the distance between the gunwale and the sea – leaving them 'unable to sail in heavy seas'. Even when these craft were moored in the roadstead of a port, they were constantly being swamped by waves, requiring continuous pumping and bailing. What should happen even close to port in the event of a full-scale gale, Decrès feared to think, little realising that he and Napoleon were soon to see this for themselves. As for crossing the Channel in high seas . . . The partial answer, of course, was to reduce the armament and number of troops and not carry horses – but at this stage Napoleon was adamantly against the very suggestion.

The *péniches* – the smallest class of boats – did sail well, at least in calm seas. Although Napoleon insisted upon arming these sixty-foot boats with a couple of small howitzers, despite the remonstrances of sailors, they completely lacked accuracy with even the slightest pitch of the boat and, indeed, most of the armament of all four classes lacked accuracy and range and were, to all intents and purposes, of little real value.

The above vessels were considered the 'armed flotilla' as opposed to the seven hundred-odd 'transport boats', which had been bought and which at least were solid sailing vessels, designed for fishermen and the sea – far more reliable than any of the vessels of the new flotilla.

Each vessel was to be considered fairly self-sufficient so far as supplies were concerned, from the point of departure until reaching Britain and thus the most common combination of boats – a *chaloupe canonnière* and its *péniche* – carried:

> 197 men (including 3 cart drivers and 8 surgeons)
> 27 muskets or rifles
> 20 bayonets
> 27 axes
> 12,000 cartridges
> 1,200 flints
> 1,200 biscuits
> 150 pints of eau-de-vie
> 4 sheep

At this stage it was estimated that 12 divisions – or 324 *chaloupes* and 324 *péniches* – could transport up to 36,000 men. The *bateaux canonniers* and their accompanying *péniches* originally carried two horses but fewer men, while the largest of these armed ferrying vessels – the *prame* – was assigned eighty men, rations, supplies, six sheep and ten horses. In fact, just about all these calculations were to vary completely over the next several months and the few remaining *prames* were no longer designated to carry horses, resulting in feverish attempts later to find more stable-ships – another problem that was never resolved satisfactorily.

It would seem Napoleon sometimes lived in a world of fantasy, and not only boasted to foreign powers of what he could or would do, but deluded himself as well. For example on 22nd August 1803 he informed the newly appointed Commander-in-Chief of this flotilla, Admiral Bruix, that this was 'the composition of the flotilla as it appears it must be definitively decreed', while on a dozen different occasions he was to say precisely the same thing, 'definitively', but each time involving major changes. By August 1803, theoretically, there were approximately 2,008 vessels ready for the flotilla, including 172 former fishing boats for transport, but when Admiral Bruix made a tour of inspection, taking a tally of the actual boats in port, he found only 1,026 vessels. Napoleon had overestimated flotilla strength by some 982 boats, nearly 100 per cent![3] How the First Consul calculated 2,008 vessels remains an unresolved mystery.

The construction programme could only be as good as the man designated to build and supervise it. If Napoleon considered Pierre Forfait a rather ineffective Naval Minister, he thought him an excellent Inspector-General of the National Flotilla.

A native of Rouen, the fifty-one-year-old Pierre-Alexandre-Laurent Forfait had an interesting background. The son of a Rouen cloth merchant he received a good education in mathematics and science at the Jesuit-run *Académie de Rouen* and, upon completion of his studies with honours, he accepted a commission in the Royal Navy as a student-engineer at the age of twenty.

Although he was called an engineer, in reality he was both an engineer and naval architect, occasionally serving on board ships as well. He early created his own practical and economical system of excavating canals and, as a result, was named a member of the *Académie de Marine*. He designed and supervised the construction of merchant ships destined for use in the Antilles, created a new type of naval transport ship, the *Normandie* being the first prototype to be launched, and was finally sent by the government of Louis XVI to England to study the organisation of British arsenals, with the full co-operation of the British, his report on this unusual subject attracting much attention in Paris a few years later. A man with political interests as well, he was elected briefly as a Deputy to the Legislative Assembly in the new Revolutionary Government where he specialised in naval affairs, soon returning however to the navy where he designed and built flat-bottomed luggers capable of bringing supplies up the Seine to Paris. It was on these successful vessels that later designs for the National Flotilla were to be based. In 1798 he, Admiral Rosily and Admiral David were named Principal Commissioners for the Navy, *Commissaires Principaux de la Marine*, and sent to study the possibility of naval construction in Belgium and Holland. With such a background as this, Pierre Forfait seemed the logical choice for the new post of Director-General created in 1798 with the task of preparing a fleet and flotilla under the orders of General Bonaparte: theoretically for the invasion of England, whereas in May of that year its destination was suddenly changed to Egypt.

First Consul Bonaparte was to reward Forfait in November 1799 (immediately following his *coup d'état*), naming him Minister of the Navy – a post he held until he was replaced by Rear-Admiral Decrès in October 1801. His stint as Naval Minister was not altogether unsuccessful, for he reorganised completely the Naval Construction Services, created the Commission for Naval Prizes, drafted and created the Maritime Prefectures, whose administration encompassed the nation's coastline, created the Naval Health Service, and finally the Naval Artillery Service.

In 1803 Bonaparte officially named Forfait Inspector-General of the invasion fleet – a post that he, more than any other man in France, was best qualified to fill – and he was awarded various State honours as well, including being named a State Counsellor and Commander of the Legion of Honour. He was soon at Boulogne organising the first camp there and attended the First Consul on various inspection trips. Although he was to prove most effective in this post, some of the plans he personally submitted to Napoleon (such as his enormous, 60-gun 'floating artillery platform') were hardly feasible at that time and, in the summer of 1805, he was sent as Maritime Prefect of Genoa. This was clearly a demotion, a post from which he was soon to be fired when a ship in his district was sabotaged. He ultimately was to leave office in disgrace, dying of a heart attack a couple of years later. However, now, in 1803, he was still a man of power, in a most influential, indeed critical position as Inspector-General, under the orders of Admiral Decrès, with personal access to Napoleon himself.

Admirals were required to sail the flotilla and warships, however, and, unfortunately for Napoleon, there was only a handful of men who could even be considered for posts of high naval command, among them Admirals Latouche-Tréville, Villeneuve, Bruix and Ganteaume. The person named on 21st July 1803 to head the immense invasion flotilla had to be an extremely unusual and energetic man and it was not surprising that this post fell to the forty-four-year-old Admiral Eustace de Bruix.

Although born in the colony of San Domingo, Eustace de Bruix was one of those rare naval officers who had been well-educated in Paris and had come from a long and distinguished line of army officers. Unlike his ancestors, however, his first love was the sea and he joined the French Royal Navy in 1776 at the age of fifteen. Shortly afterwards he saw action in the Caribbean where he constantly distinguished himself both as a man of action and science, resulting in a series of promotions and honours. He was named a member of the *Académie de Marine*, promoted to the rank of Major-General, made Director of the Port of Brest and Commander-in-Chief of its large fleet, subsequently serving as Naval Minister for a year. Although he next headed an ill-fated expedition against Ireland in 1797, nevertheless, two years later he was successful in breaking the English blockade of the principal French Atlantic naval port of Brest, leading the large fleet with its badly needed supplies to a blockaded Genoa and then boldly returning through the Straits of Gibraltar to Cadiz (where he was joined by some Spanish vessels), finally returning safely to Brest. In November 1799 Bruix aided Bonaparte in his *coup de'état* overthrowing the last Government of the French Revolution and consequently it was hardly surprising that on 21st July 1803 First Consul Bonaparte should have appointed him Commander-in-Chief, with the title of 'Admiral of the National Flotilla' which was assembling at Boulogne for the projected invasion of England. Yet what a man to name at this time for this position, who, though insistent on the role of science in naval tactics, privately practised alchemy and somehow even found time to compose the lyrics to L'Unionville's opera, *La Chasse au Loup*!

It was only on 10th September 1803 that the First Consul finally ordered a first series of charts to be prepared for himself, Admiral Bruix and Inspector-General Forfait – charts listing the number of boats required and the number of men they could transport for an invasion of Britain. The figure arrived at was 114,000 troops (exclusive of the navy) and some 7,000 horses for both cavalry and artillery.

One calculation, as we have seen, that proved surprisingly elusive – both now and later – was the number of vessels ready to transport troops. Bonaparte was to be anxious about this to the very end, although it was he alone who was directly responsible for the many constantly changing facts and figures and subsequent contradictions and confusion. For example, on 4th October 1804, Bonaparte wrote to Decrès about the deficiencies in the flotilla: 'included in the figure of 536 *péniches* are 100 to be built at Lille, but which have not yet been begun. It is most imperative that these *péniches* be completed for active service. Let me know what measures must be taken to begin construction immediately for the *prames*, *péniches* and *caïques* we are still short of.' Yet a week later Decrès received the following contradictory note from him: 'It seems to me that the naval building programme in the ports is coming along so nicely now that I think it is quite unnecessary to continue with any more in the interior. Have a full report ready for me by Friday.'[4]

Despite his orders to the naval authorities to rush through a massive building programme, with assurances that there was plenty of money available and that everyone would be paid promptly, Napoleon was, in fact, having a most difficult time finding the financial resources. With demands for payment flowing in, he hit upon the simple solution of employing national loyalty. He would ask not only rich individuals to donate boats and funds for the proposed flotilla, but cities, associations, provincial administrative bodies and, indeed, the French army itself: 'Prepare a report for me . . . on the full scope of the boatbuilding programme that the various communes and citizen associations have offered to provide, that I might issue a decree as to where each group should deposit those funds, it being quite useless allowing construction to begin if it can never be finished.' Promising the money was one thing, fulfilling that promise was another and the very practical First Consul, who had stolen millions of francs as war booty during his conquests, did not trust human nature – cash first, then the laying down of the hulls.

Although most 'offers' to provide boats or funds came from France itself, others came from allies. 'The Italian Republic has offered us twelve *chaloupes canonnières*,' Bonaparte informed the Naval Minister on 29th August 1803, while in occupied Belgium, the cities of Ostend, Bruges and Liège offered to build some more flat-bottomed boats. 'I think it would be useful to accept the offer by the Dutch and to prepare a contract for thirty completely outfitted *chaloupes canonnières*', he informed Decrès. (Little did the Dutch realise that this 'offer' was but the beginning.) As for the Italian proposal, it came because Napoleon had forced himself upon that Republic as its President and had *demanded* that a war contribution be made.

After the French Government had obtained a 20,000,000-franc bank loan for 'naval munitions', public war contributions, or 'patriotic offers', as they were called, began to flood the desks of both Decrès and the First Consul. For example the *Département* of Seine-et-Oise pledged 1,200,000 francs for naval construction, with the following note attached: 'Our legions have crossed the Alps, a narrow body of water cannot prevent us from conquering Albion. They can reach the shores of the dismayed English in a single day.'

Large ships were offered by other *départements*, including Seine-Inférieure, Nord, Ourthe and Eure. Needless to say the Prefect of each *département* was appointed and named directly by Bonaparte and it was he who sometimes had to put considerable pressure on the local provincial governments to meet his demands.

Individual towns and cities were not to be denied their place of honour in the lists of loyal citizens, among them Pont-Audemer, Louviers, Evereux, Bernary, Beauvais, Le Mans, Avranches and Montauban; and expressions of loyalty came in from every province of the land: Deux-Sèvres, Oise, Meuse, Haute-Marne, Lot-et-Garonne, Mayenne, Loir-et-Cher, all offered either money for the flotilla or boats. Ultimately a total of some 24,000,000 francs or the equivalent was pledged by the people of France and their allies.

Military units also expressed their loyalty by making 'patriotic contributions', the Corps de la Garde donating 20,000 francs towards the cost of one *chaloupe canonnière*, while many regiments gave up one day's pay, the general-staff of the 11th Division offering two days'.

Along with the flow of money into the capital came the thousands of workmen and hundreds of barges filled with naval supplies as two new boatyards were established at Les Invalides and at La Rapée, plus others at St Germain, Compiègne and Meaux. Thirty students from the Ecole Polytechnique were assigned to study boat construction and then to travel throughout the provinces to inspect and direct the work there. Indeed, so great were the offers of money and vessels that on 11th October General Bonaparte finally stopped accepting any more patriotic pledges. Even for Bonaparte 24,000,000 francs seemed enough.

It was hardly surprising that so much frantic military activity should attract a great variety of enterprising individuals seeking fame, fortune and power. The results of the great questioning and scientific curiosity aroused by the Enlightenment were now to be reaped and seen as inventors in particular laid siege to the antechamber of First Consul Bonaparte. New ideas for weaponry and transport seemed to pour in weekly. For instance, one suggestion was to tunnel beneath the English Channel and launch a 'surprise attack' on the unsuspecting British. There was also the more visible development of warfare in the air, or to be more precise, the use of observation balloons, already evident in Paris and all along the Channel coast. But when Jean-Charles Thilorier presented his new plans at the Ministry of War, even the most jaded officials stopped in their tracks temporarily. This elegant gentleman produced a drawing of a gigantic 'montgolfière' hot air balloon capable of transporting 3,000 troops and their equipment by means of a single platform capable of supporting 600,000 pounds! Of course, the brave inventor could not produce a working model a quarter of the size required, as any physicist could have told him, and his colourful plans for the 'Thilorière' were quietly filed with hundreds of other unfeasible plans in the archives where, perhaps, in another distant time, some genius might better work out the practical problems involved. Yet, for all that, the idea of transporting tens of thousands of troops in a massive airlift was breathtaking, and it certainly would have taken Lord St Vincent by surprise to find these balloons descending all round him as he crossed St James's Park! Other inventors were much more practical, though their ideas were often no less fantastic. Among these one gentleman in particular rose higher than any Thilorière.

With the most unlikely professional background as a jeweller, then portrait and landscape painter, a restless twenty-nine-year-old American by the name of Robert Fulton came to England in 1794 to try his hand at the one subject that really fascinated him, engineering, although his first attempts at inventing had brought him little attention and even less reward. Fulton emigrated to the one country thousands were trying to flee in 1797. When he got to Paris he immediately contacted Naval Minister Pléville.

Fulton now presented his plans for a three-man, twenty-one-foot submarine, 'a diver', the French called it, while asking the Directory to cover its development costs and to give his officers commissions in the French Navy. In February 1798, the Naval Minister replied that he would consent to subsidise up to half the costs, but there would be no naval commissions, nor would he allow the use of naval personnel 'for this sort of undertaking'.

Pléville's successor as Naval Minister, Admiral Eustace de Bruix created a commission in July 1798 to study the possibilities of the use of the submarine, and its chairman, Admiral Rosily, handed in a generally favourable report. However, although the Naval Ministry felt that Fulton's promise to block the Thames and greatly harm London commerce was good in theory, they were not yet prepared to sanction the means of accomplishing this, for if they did indeed produce this new underwater vessel, 'the English, so ingenious in creating destructive machines, would soon be doing the same thing, and this would thus result in the elimination of the accepted punishments [to captives] hitherto assured by the War Code for those who would otherwise normally be inclined to carry these out in a vicious manner.'

The main reason, complained the American inventor, that the French Directory turned down 'Citizen Fulton's request to build the machine at Paris he has invented with which to strike at our enemies', was 'based on humble humanitarian considerations, as if they would ever make any claims against the use of a means destined to avenge humanity and deliver it from France's most implacable enemies, by annihilating the insolent despotism of the English Navy.' Though he met one effective rebuff after another by the French authorities now, Fulton refused to give up.

If the Government would not give him the 20,000 francs he needed to build the first submarine, he would build it himself. On 30th July 1800, Robert Fulton duly wrote to the new Naval Minister, Pierre Forfait, that the boat, the *Nautilus*, had been successfully launched on the Seine at Rouen on 10th April 1800. 'Its tests succeeded perfectly,' Fulton informed Forfait, and described the new invention. 'It is a veritable under-water vessel, six and a half metres long and two metres wide', that rose or fell in the water according to the amount of water pumped in or out of its compartments. 'It has two rudders, one vertical and the other horizontal, a cupola with windows for directing its course, a barometer for establishing the depth of the machine, and a compass for navigation, all of which work perfectly under water. It is built entirely of wood. A small mast and sail can be raised or lowered at will to permit the vessel to sail on the surface.' It could ascend or descend with the assistance of two men cranking two stabiliser-like wings. 'The three men operating the machine used candle light below and could remain under water for three hours at a time.' It contained two hand-turned propellers that could give it a speed of one and a half knots. During the initial test it towed a torpedo at a distance of one hundred metres, which when in contact with the enemy ship, 'was detonated by a timed battery'.

The Naval Ministry and the Commission were finally impressed: 'The weapon created by Citizen Fulton is a terrible means of destruction, because it works in total silence and in a manner whose results are almost inevitable. It is especially suitable for the French people, because having a navy which is weaker than that of their adversary, it is advantageous to have the means by which to annihilate their opponents. This weapon is no doubt imperfect, but it is only the first model developed by a man of genius'. Then came the words Fulton had been waiting for for nearly three years: 'The Committee invites the Naval Minister to give Citizen Fulton the authorisation necessary for producing the machine based on his model'.

Despite this official enthusiasm, however, Fulton did not receive much financial support – a mere 10,000 francs instead of the 60,000 francs requested and then only on 30th March 1801. Nevertheless that had not prevented him from continuing to develop both the vessel and its torpedoes. It had sunk one target ship with thirty pounds of powder at Le Havre back in October 1800 before continuing on to the naval yard at Brest where the rest of the experiments were carried out. There in the roadsteads not far from Spaniards' Point on 3rd July 1801, taking the *Nautilus* down to a depth of twenty feet, Fulton and a crew of three fired a torpedo at their target. 'The gunboat jumped into the air, broken into a thousand pieces by a torpedo with a charge of only twenty pounds', an admiring naval observer reported to Paris, but when the American engineer then asked to take his *Nautilus* out beyond St Matthew Point in order to sink two nearby English frigates, Admiral Villaret-Joyeuse refused permission, Naval Prefect Caffarelli explaining to Paris, 'The Admiral and I both decided against this for a most important reason, namely that this manner of waging war against an enemy will be considered so reprehensible, that should those persons carrying out such an attack later fall into enemy hands, they would be ignominiously hanged. That certainly is not the way soldiers should die!' However, Admiral Latouche-Tréville disagreed completely with his colleagues, strongly urging the Naval Ministry to develop and use the submarine as he declared it to be the ideal weapon with which to kill 'Nelson, a tyrant whose punishment both justice and mankind have for such a long time demanded'.

Nevertheless between the summer of 1801 and 1803, a preoccupied French Government showed very little further interest in Fulton's inventions and it was not until 2nd September 1803 that Robert Fulton finally had an interview with Naval Minister Decrès, the minister then reporting the results to the First Consul: 'By your orders I have seen M.

Fulton, the American inventor of a diving boat. He seems very much disposed to try fresh experiments and assures me that he is confident of success; but he makes one condition without which he will not work; it is to have a short interview with you. He has, he says, political views of the greatest importance to impart.'

Fulton was not granted an appointment, however, and instead wrote personally to the First Consul on 6th September explaining his plans. 'The diver [submarine] is a concealed artillery battery. With three of these machines, we could force the British to surrender. Each diver carries twenty to thirty torpedoes. We could advance to the very entrance of the British naval ports and either release the torpedoes with the current carrying them into the port, or leave them [like stationary mines] at the entrance of Portsmouth, Plymouth, Torbay and at the mouth of the Thames'. Fulton then went on to describe the two types of 'torpedoes' he had invented:

> The first type is fixed with a mechanism like that of a clock which works automatically by means of an alarm [setting off a detonator], over a period of time from as little as 4 minutes up to 4 hours. The Second type is held beneath the submarine and explodes upon contact with the enemy vessel, striking at a depth of between five and six feet beneath the surface. There is not a pilot in the navy who could avoid these unseen blows, which can thus close the enemy's ports, and at very little expense.
>
> The only sure means of subjugating that country is by interrupting all commerce on the Thames, for it would be cutting off the traffic which is vital to – indeed the life blood of – the court of Saint James.

Napoleon rejected the idea of attempting to close English harbours in this manner, however, though it is not clear why, even refusing to purchase the *Nautilus* from Fulton for 40,000 francs.

However inventors are optimistic by nature and an undiscouraged Fulton persisted, drafting plans for a new larger submarine, one large enough to carry a crew of eight, provisions for up to twenty days, and capable of descending to a depth of 100 feet. In addition he achieved very real success on his first steam engine during the summer of 1803. Curiously enough it was the steam engine, not the already working submarine, that really caught Napoleon's attention. On 21st July 1804 he ordered the Institute to set up a special commission to study it. 'Try and have the whole thing determined within a week, as I am impatient', the new Emperor demanded. The report was delayed a bit, but none the less the Emperor's reaction was inexplicable. 'I have just read the report on the project of Citizen Fulton, the engineer, which you have sent me, sent

me, I might add, much too late, since it is one that may one day change
the face of the world.'

And thus Robert Fulton finally admitted defeat, crossing the Straits of
Dover to Britain with his inventions, to make one last offer to the British
Government.

Meanwhile, Napoleon had other things on his mind. Though he kept
abreast of events in the rest of the rapidly expanding French Empire
throughout the year 1803, by far his greatest preoccupation was with the
National Flotilla and its preparations. Years later, however, after its
failure, he consistently denied both its importance and the time he had
spent on it, frequently claiming he had never really intended to invade
Britain at all, just scare the British. As was often the case with Napoleon,
the truth was quite different. He spent nearly every spare hour – indeed
entire weeks in his green and yellow travelling carriage or in the saddle –
surveying possible new port or camp sites, shipyards, ports under
construction, locations for artillery batteries or inspecting the training of
men along the Channel, not to mention diverting most of the French
annual budget to his celebrated invasion project. When he was not
actually in the field on inspection tours, he was corresponding with the
various naval personnel in charge of flotilla preparations, in particular
with Inspector-General Forfait and Vice-Admiral Decrès. He frequently
went over the heads of officials, including Decrès, the Naval Minister,
who would then later have to consult Bonaparte as to what naval reports
had been given directly to the First Consul but not shown to him.
Napoleon's letters went into extraordinary detail about port activities and
construction problems, but, despite the splendid offers of the French
people to provide ships and money, the shortage of boats – *chaloupes
canonnières* and *péniches* in particular – continued and Bonaparte's
provisional order to stop accepting any more boat orders after 11th
October 1803 was to prove overly optimistic.

The continuing boat shortage could sometimes be blamed on the
construction firms themselves. In some cases they gladly accepted
Government orders and money to build vessels, but did little more than
lay down a hull then abandon the effort. In most instances, however, it
was simply the lack of money. What had happened to the 24,000,000
francs pledged for shipbuilding and the 20,000,000-franc bank loan?
Immense profit-taking and corruption on a vast scale (military, administrative and civilian) no doubt were the answer.

Admiral Decrès was only too well aware of some of these problems and he complained to the First Consul about dishonest men running shipyards and the lengths they would go to in order to tap Government funds for work they never intended completing. 'There are three shipyards at Calais [where] they have begun construction on 108 boats, but have failed to complete even one of them . . . We have been spending money left, right and centre and now we do not even know when we'll ever have anything to show for it.' And it was the same story at Dunkirk and at St Omer for, as Decrès acknowledged, 'the builders are more interested in receiving the first [government] payment for them, than in really building boats or ever getting them to us within a reasonable time.' Also, by delaying production, the contractors felt the government would panic and be forced to pay higher prices to rush them through completion.

General Bonaparte however, had an answer for such war profiteers, announcing that all boats had to be completed by the contracted date and 'once that has expired, all construction already undertaken will have to be completed at the expense of the contracting shipyard', and there would be no further payment by the Government. In brief, the builders themselves would either have to assume the costs to complete the boats or abandon them.

Pierre Forfait was at odds with his superior on this subject however. 'The First Consul is convinced that a large number of vessels have been started simply in order for the builders to receive the first Government instalment', but he argued that this was not generally true. If there were contractors out to dupe the First Consul and take the public treasury for all they could get, there were many more contractors – the vast majority – who fulfilled their contracts and rendered perfectly honest accounts and yet were not paid – in part or whole – sometimes for a very long time. This resulted in them being unable to buy more materials and complete their work. For the Government to cancel their orders pre-emptorily like this was intolerable, Forfait continued in an outraged letter to Decrès: 'I find that this disposition is simply unconscionable [therefore] I have *not* informed the contractors of the Government's threat to make them assume any production costs for vessels that remain unfinished after that fateful deadline . . . You can rest assured of one thing, your administration is not a creditor to any of the shipyards, quite to the contrary, it is in debt to them all . . . I ask of you, not indulgence for them, which they do not need, simply justice, and it is your department which is responsible for this, for it has lost all credibility as a result of the measures which have been taken by it, to the extent that it is no longer considered trustworthy either by the navy . . . or by the war contractors whom everyone now considers to have been duped by the Government, indeed, sacrificed by it. General, it will cost you nothing to correct this injustice; all you have to do is what I propose to you in the attached report. The financial interests of the State demand that it be done, moral interests demand it even more so – let the boats that have been undertaken be finished and allow them a reasonable amount of time in which to do so and you will then put an end to the outcries, unfortunately too well founded, by the detractors of the naval administration'. In fact, Decrès had recommended not making further payment to perfectly honest contractors when it was discovered that the Government had ordered too many of certain classes of vessels. The Naval Minister recommended to the First Consul that they get out of this unhappy situation simply by cancelling these contracts midstream – something Bonaparte was to do time and again with army victuallers and suppliers as well. Pierre Forfait's strong language and persistence apparently paid off, however, Decrès reversing his position and asking Napoleon to give the contractors another two months in which to complete construction. Nevertheless Napoleon was not a man to accept defeat and lose face before his subordinates and thus he compromised, extending the deadline by a mere twenty days. 'All the contractors at Fécamp, Dieppe, Saint-Valéry-en-Caux, Le Tréport, Saint-Valéry-sur-Somme, Etaples, Calais, Boulogne, Dunkirk and St Omer who have not completed their orders by 20 pluviôse (10th February 1804), will now have until 10 ventôse (1st March), as these places are close to the delivery ports.'

Whether Napoleon lost face or not, threatened to cut off funds or cancel contracts without compensation, his construction programme, though perhaps one hundred times superior to anything being done in Great Britain, was still well below the projected goal of 2,008 vessels launched and fully armed. In fact, by the spring of 1804, just before William Pitt took office and Napoleon was proclaimed Emperor, France had 1,273 vessels of all classes completed for the flotilla, though only 149 of them were in fact ready for action with full crews and all their armament. Realising far in advance this would be a problem, Napoleon put pressure on those who could not talk back, his 'allies' in Holland.

The Dutch, a subjugated people, were in no position to complain to the First Consul, or attempt to evade the unceasing list of demands which Napoleon described to the French people as 'patriotic offers' towards the war cause. With a French bayonet at their throat the Dutch had seen their country transformed into the Batavian Republic in 1799, accompanied by French military occupation as well as control of their economy, restricting Dutch trade severely and imposing new forms of taxation. But it was the Batavian-French Convention of 25th June 1803 dictated by Napoleon that made the Dutch full-time military partners with the French in their war with Great Britain. Holland was important to Napoleon for several reasons: long a major importer and transporter of British goods, the closure of those markets could harm Britain immensely, as indeed it did. Strategically, Holland's frontiers lay next to northwestern Germany and would be an ideal place from which to launch an invasion against those northern states, as was later the case. What the Convention of 1803 really did for Napoleon, however, was provide Dutch naval support against the British Royal Navy, not to mention all the naval supplies required for shipbuilding. In fact, the Convention specifically required the Dutch to organise two expeditions: for one they had to provide five ships of the line, five frigates and enough transport vessels to carry 25,000 men and 2,500 horses; for the other expedition they were required to provide 100 *chaloupes canonnières* and 250 *bateaux canonniers* intended to transport 36,000 men, their artillery and equipment, and 1,500 horses. Then, facing up to the grim realities of the time, Napoleon reduced these requirements to 54 *chaloupes*, 216 *bateaux canonniers*, and 110 transport vessels (half of them for horses). But by 30th November 1803, however, the pressure was mounting as Napoleon changed his mind again, naming the new Dutch naval commander while restoring the initial flotilla cuts. Foreign Minister Talleyrand informed the Dutch Government that 'The First Consul has placed Rear-Admiral Verhuell in charge of that expedition [against Britain] . . . The decisive moment is approaching and the First Consul has calculated his projects based on the full execution of the Convention signed by the Batavian Government.' Bonaparte insisted on the Dutch providing immediately an extraordinarily large amount of war material for a nation of just 2,000,000 people, that is, for another nation of 28,000,000, especially when in reality this would require the Dutch to provide more than half of the first and second types of *chaloupes* and *bateaux canonniers* of the entire French flotilla. It was an outrageous demand and although thirty-nine-year-old Admiral Charles Henri Verhuell protested, he argued in vain. Nor did these fresh demands yet include other vessels, such as fishing boats and stable-ships to be used for transport.

Rutger Jan Schimmelpenninck, the senior Dutch foreign affairs spokesman, replied to the French on behalf of his Government – which he was shortly to head as Grand Pensionary – that his country was sending the French 150 boats (including 108 or 110 stable-ships), not to mention some 20 or so *chaloupes canonnières*, but, he added, 'we can only provide these at the greatest hardship to ourselves'. (Translated into reality, the phrase 'greatest hardship' meant that the minuscular Batavian Navy would practically disappear, leaving the Dutch coast and ports almost entirely unprotected.)

Napoleon also insisted that the Batavian Republic completely fit out these vessels, quite contrary to the Convention, but, replied Schimmelpenninck, 'given the present extraordinary and pressing circumstances, as good and true allies, we are executing what duty does not legally prescribe', and his Government would 'use all the means within its power to provide crews and outfit at least a part of these boats'. The First Consul also demanded a great number of Dutch naval officers but this he said was 'quite impossible' as 'the entire officer corps of the navy consisted of only 280 individuals', few of whom had ever commanded a vessel.

Napoleon further insisted that the Dutch provide and pay for all provisions for this flotilla while it remained in Dutch territory. Again, as Schimmelpenninck pointed out, this was 'absolutely contrary to the Paris Convention' that held the French Republic responsible for this. Nevertheless, he said, the Dutch would like to be able to provide cannons and food, 'but we have now exhausted all available means'. As for the First Consul's request for a large number of 24-pounders for this new flotilla, he stated 'that apart from what the navy has remaining in service, we do not possess one-tenth of the cannon required' and he added that the structure of the *chaloupes* and *bateaux canonniers* would not bear the weight of such heavy and powerful guns which Dutch naval construction requirements specifically forbade because '[according to] our navigation regulations, they are not capable of either carrying any cannon of that calibre or of supporting the recoil of their discharges' (which is precisely what some French naval officers had been trying to point out). Regarding the problem of transport vessels, as the Batavian Republic did not own enough to carry all the men, horses and equipment required by Bonaparte, they did the next best thing – leasing 30,000 tons of shipping for a period of six months.

Summing up the situation, Schimmelpenninck noted that, 'Nevertheless we shall spare neither time nor trouble in order to comply with your needs and in this great crisis my Government will put no limits to its devotion and zeal for the common cause; in a word, it will do all that it is physically and morally possible to do . . . My Government wants to be convinced, however', he then concluded, 'to be assured that the First Consul does indeed appreciate the efforts sustained by a country exhausted by such long and enormous sacrifices. It expressly enjoins me to represent to him once more that the financial situation of my unfortunate fatherland is truly heart-rending and that soon, in order to prevent its ruin, it will be forced to call upon the help of its magnanimous ally. Never perhaps will a people so faithful and worthy of something far better, have solicited the kindness of a great nation and of an even greater man'. It was a most extraordinary plea by a proud but exhausted Dutch nation, and showed Napoleon's announcements that the Dutch had *freely* given vessels and war aid of all kinds were completely fictitious.

Bonaparte, however, was neither sympathetic nor satisfied; instead he rapaciously demanded more and more again. He refused to be hood-winked by the sentimental Dutch pleas, and told Talleyrand they were just holding out on him.

The First Consul sometimes followed a whim or arrogantly pushed on with his ideas as to what he perceived a navy capable of doing, sometimes relying on reason, albeit 'reason' fashioned to substantiate his rationali-sations and justify his objectives. To the Dutch argument that the *bateau canonnier* was too light to carry guns of any sort, but particularly heavy artillery, Napoleon replied, 'We have armed a *bateau canonnier* in the harbour of Boulogne with a 24-pound gun. It performed perfectly well. Therefore there should be no difficulty whatsoever in arming all the Dutch *bateaux canonniers.*' And he informed them that it should be 'very easy indeed to find two hundred 24- and 18-pound cannons in Holland'. The boat tested in Boulogne, however, had only one gun on board, it sailed on a calm day in the protected waters of Boulogne where the *bateau canonnier's* perennial problem of swamping presented no problem, and after two or three shots naturally did not reflect any fatigue on the light hull or the effect of the after-shock forcing the boat backwards and deep into the water. Indeed, had there been several boats behind it, it would have recoiled backwards into them. Furthermore, each *bateau canonnier* was intended to carry and fire an additional howitzer of considerable power and weight as well as another piece of artillery, but these had not been placed on board the vessel being tested, nor was it laden with its full complement of men and supplies. As usual, Napoleon saw and heard what he wanted to, and he believed he had proved any objection by the Dutch regarding their shipbuilding regulations could be completely disregarded. He also thought that the Dutch were lying to him about the cannons and that another two hundred could indeed be found in Holland.

Admiral Decrès knew the truth, however, as did Admiral Verhuell, the highest-ranking Dutch naval officer, but who could argue with a Napoleon?

Charles Verhuell was a conscientious man and certainly did his best to comply with Napoleon's thinly disguised threats – 'The First Consul has counted on the strict execution of the Convention, and the failure to carry out all or part would greatly delay the combined projects aimed at ending the war, which would in turn have unfortuante consequences *for both our countries*,' Talleyrand reminded the Dutch allies. The very next day an impatient Bonaparte himself wrote again, directly to Verhuell: 'I have demanded an explanation from Schimmelpenninck about this [the failure to send all the boats and munitions he wanted].' By the end of 1803 as a result of Napoleon's demands the entire Dutch Navy was reduced to a mere three armed vessels: 1 old *chaloupe canonnière*, the *Grondeur* (crew of 60); 1 lugger, the *Triton* – 20 guns and a crew of 12, and 24 soldiers; and 1 cutter, the *Fortitude*, 6 guns. If the Dutch Navy no longer existed, this still did not satisfy Bonaparte.[5]

Following his return from a tour of inspection in mid January 1804 Naval Minister Decrès, certainly not renowned for being a sympathetic or understanding person, informed the First Consul that he had found only nineteen *chaloupes canonnières* in Holland, and these had now been transferred to the French. Eighteen of these were of very old construction 'and armed with every conceivable variety of gun', the nineteenth being of recent construction, however, was being dispatched to Boulogne forthwith. 'In order to provide these eighteen *chaloupes* of older construction, the Batavians have left all the points of their coast where these boats were needed completely defenceless. Now there is nothing left.' It was an utterly damning report so far as Napoleon's war aims and rapacious methods were concerned, but nothing could move the remorseless First Consul. Decrès praised the Dutch war effort and Admiral Verhuell in particular: 'No one could have been more zealous, more energetic or have shown more perseverance', though the Dutch naval officers on his flotilla, out on manoeuvres, constantly had a most difficult time with French troops and officers 'who refused to take orders from them on board Dutch ships'.

What is more, he added, the Batavian government now had another thirty-four *chaloupes canonnières* under construction, seventeen of which would be ready for delivery shortly, and thus the Dutch were certainly doing their best.

The one real obstacle, one that could not be overcome by Verhuell's zeal or Napoleon's threats, said Decrès, was that of the 'lack of crews'. This was to become such a major problem – in Holland as much as in France – that many newly built vessels of all kinds and classes ultimately had to be beached. And thus Napoleon had clearly underestimated this aspect. In January, for instance, the 44-gun frigate, *La Furieuse*, one of the few ships brought in by the French to replace the denuded Dutch Navy, and protect the coast, had in turn to be stripped of her crew and guns and put in mothballs in order to use the experienced sailors in the new flotilla. This was just the beginning of perhaps the most serious problem Napoleon was to face over the next twenty-two months.

As for the First Consul's demands that the Dutch provide 200 24-pound guns, Admiral Verhuell had to strip and dismantle five of the larger remaining Dutch ships (the *Chatam*, the *Victor-Polus*, the *Hertzeller*, the *Zoontmorn*, and the *Wreker*) whose combined total of 142 24-pounders was to be distributed among 68 flotilla vessels.

After reading the Naval Minister's January 1804 annual report for the year's activities, Napoleon had Talleyrand inform the Dutch of his 'great disappointment in noting that none of the contractual engagements' had been fulfilled. He pointed out that, although the Batavian Republic had been ordered to furnish 100 armed *chaloupes canonnières*, it had only delivered nineteen, 'all in the worst possible state'[6]; furthermore, only 109 *bateaux canonniers* had been produced and even these were 'without crews or artillery'. As for the stable-ships to transport 1,500 horses, nothing was yet prepared. Talleyrand, who conveyed Napoleon's message, added, 'It has been most painful for the First Consul to have to stop and think about such an unfortunate state of affairs and to have to have these views transmitted to the Batavian Government', and he then ordered 'Citizen Schimmelpenninck to use all his influence in having the present situation fully appreciated [by the Dutch Government] as well as the harm that the passions and lack of forethought by certain men might cause'. The Dutch needed 'an impetus and activity that would result in their executing their contractual obligations forthwith'.

Such letters were being received by the Dutch at least once a fortnight, in addition to Napoleon's own personal correspondence to Verhuell. Less than a week after sending the preceding letter, Talleyrand wrote that the First Consul was 'deeply upset' by the continued failure on the part of the Dutch to fulfil their engagements. It was sheer harassment of course and maddening for both Schimmelpenninck and Rear-Admiral Verhuell as the pressure mounted, literally week by week, despite the slow means of communication of the day. The Dutch were not only to build ships and supply larger numbers of vessels than was physically possible, but to do so immediately or suffer the consequences! They also had to produce crews and guns that they had not got! By the second week of February, Bonaparte was notified by the Dutch Ambassador that, 'Every means within the power of the Government has been used to provide sailors, boats and guns for you . . . The [Dutch] Admiralty attempts to reject, at least in part, however, your reproaches by enumerating their continuing efforts to execute every clause of the Convention'. He further announced that they were providing 63 *chaloupes canonnières* and 120 completely finished *bateaux canonniers*, not to mention 108 leased stable-ships, and were in the midst of building the remaining boats, including 80 more *bateaux canonniers*.[7] It was a remarkable achievement. As for Admiral Verhuell, he had performed miracles, mainly by sheer persistence (and no doubt threats) in the face of constant opposition from within the Dutch Government and by loyal naval officers who often did all they could to impede his progress, to stop Napoleon becoming more powerful and remaining in control of their land and lives. Verhuell was both a realist and an opportunist (some considered him a traitor) and so successfully did he manage the construction and organis-ation of the Batavian flotilla that, when it was assembled at Ostend (destined to be transferred to the final embarkation point, Dunkirk), Napoleon named him as its commanding officer – he would command nearly one-third of the entire invasion force.

With the orders for the boats in and Admirals Decrès and Bruix there to keep a close eye on the delivery of those vessels, as well as the training of their crews, First Consul Bonaparte could turn his attention to the next critical phase of operations – the preparation of the Channel ports and an expeditionary force.

Invasion Preparations

On entering a war, a general's first duty and consideration must be the achieving of glory and honour in arms. The health and safety of his men is only secondary . . .

Napoleon

SO FURIOUS WAS the pounding of waves battering the dozens of vessels and crashing against the shore along the foot of the cliffs at Boulogne, that it almost completely drowned out the peals of thunder, howling gale-force winds and the cries of several hundred sailors and soldiers floundering in the surf or clamouring in helpless confusion on the beach. Although it was a midsummer's day (20th July 1804), except for the repeated flashes of lightning, the sky was as black as night, matching Emperor Napoleon's mood as he stood watching in consternation – surrounded by admirals, generals and his personal staff – drenched, stunned and motionless before this terrible spectacle for which he alone was responsible.

Then, as more faint pleas for help from drowning men were heard through the din, the Emperor suddenly leapt into the nearest surf-boat and ordered the crew to row him out to help the others, but his command was barely heard even by the aides at his side as he and the boat were swamped by mountainous waves, the boat tossing about literally like a cork. Tumultuous sheets of water knocked Napoleon to his knees and nearly overboard, and those near him could barely hold on to him as his hat disappeared in the swirling foam. Soon, thousands of spectators from the cliff above swarmed down on to the beach and, following the Emperor's lead, attempted to save at least a few lives, as broken bodies were hurled ashore amid the dangerous flood of broken timber. Was this to be the result of over a year's very hard work to build a flotilla and ports for his celebrated invasion? Napoleon, soaked through, remained on the shore for several hours, no doubt trying to keep thoughts of his orders that morning out of his mind.

It was the Emperor's faithful valet, Louis Constant, who alone was brave enough to publish this account many years later. Napoleon had come from Paris in order to inspect troops, naval units and the nearly completed new port at Boulogne. The following morning, 20th July, as he stepped from Pont de Briques, the villa serving as his headquarters, he sent one of his ADCs to Admiral Bruix with an order to have him remove the sixty or so boats moored in the roadstead to join the other divisions of boats with their full complement of troops and artillery, for a naval review of all types of flotilla vessels. He wanted to see the new port facilities in use and the flotilla in action. However, an embarrassed ADC returned with the Admiral's refusal. Napoleon was furious and summoned Bruix, the Commander-in-Chief of the Imperial Flotilla, to appear before him immediately.

'Monsieur l'amiral, why haven't you carried out my orders?'

'Sire, a terrible storm is brewing. His Majesty can see for himself,' he said as he looked up at a grey, overcast sky, hearing the rumbling of thunder far out at sea. 'Do you want me to risk the lives of so many brave men needlessly?'

'Monsieur, I have given you an order. Once more I am going to ask you why you have not executed it? The consequences concern me and me alone. Carry out this order!'

'Sire,' replied an erect and defiant Admiral Bruix, 'I shall not obey it.'

'Monsieur,' snapped an angry Emperor, 'You are insolent!' and he stepped forward raising his riding crop as if to strike the Admiral.

'Sire, mind what you do!', Bruix replied, taking one step back and placing his right hand firmly on the hilt of his sword. The aides and staff officers froze in their tracks, exhilarated no doubt by the extremely rare sight of someone contradicting and defying Napoleon Bonaparte. Only Alexandre Berthier had ever done so, and then not in public.

Moments passed and then, flinging down his riding crop, the Emperor said, 'Rear-Admiral Magon, you will carry out this order this very instant. As for you, Monsieur', he said, turning to Bruix once again, so angry that he could barely speak, 'you will leave Boulogne within twenty-four hours and retire to Holland. Go!'

Even before the departure of Bruix, the consequences of Napoleon's lethal whim was being seen all along the coast, as shattered boats and twisted bodies, along with the Emperor's hat, were washed ashore. Broken hulls, masts, spars and rudders of dozens of recently launched *chaloupes canonnières, bateaux canonniers* and *péniches* were hurled on to the beaches of Boulogne and northwards for many miles. Constant said that staff officers estimated that some 200 corpses were washed ashore over the next 24 hours, while a more accurate report made by coasting British vessels, which had observed both the incident and the aftermath, put the figure at about 400.

Napoleon was clearly shaken by this event and his closest advisers were afraid to look him in the eye. The Emperor had lost his temper again, unfortunately before dozens of witnesses, including his own general staff. He had not only made a complete fool of himself, but had caused the needless deaths of hundreds of brave French soldiers and sailors. Everyone was aghast, the sight so terrible that soldiers feared even discussing it, while in the taverns of Boulogne, the previously pro-Bonaparte townspeople now spoke of him and the tragedy with loathing. To erase this memory from the minds of the good burghers and soldiers alike, Napoleon resorted to his usual solution to problems – gold and large amounts were handed out by his aides over the next couple of days. Silence must be bought. As for Napoleon, shattered for the moment, he had however regained his usual composure by the following day when he related the day's events to Josephine:

> The wind freshened during the night, and one of our gunboats dragged its anchor, but we managed to save everything. The spectacle was grand: the alarm guns, the coast a blaze of fire, the sea tossed with fury, and roaring . . . At 5 am it cleared up, everything was saved and I went to bed with all the sensations inspired by a romantic and epic dream.

Yet the destruction of a few dozen new boats in no way diminished what Napoleon had accomplished – the flotilla was a reality and army recruits were training on board the various vessels in the designated ports.

The ports themselves were another achievement. As the coast between Dieppe and Dunkirk offered no large natural or sufficient existing harbours or ports, this very coast from which Napoleon intended launching his armada, he ordered new ports to be created. Although this idea made his naval engineers and admirals wince, there was no other option. For the Emperor's invasion to work, 2,000 to 3,000 flat-bottomed boats were needed to transport an armada of over 150,000 troops, exclusive of naval personnel, and they needed to be able to do this in the shortest possible time in order to catch the English by surprise. As he was considering a night crossing, one which would not take more than six to eight hours, this automatically meant eliminating the larger existing harbours at Brest, Rochefort or Toulon – at least for the landing craft.

The possibility of building new ports along the stretch of unsheltered coast extending from Dieppe to Dunkirk was nothing new – a whole file of engineering reports on this subject had been accumulating for several decades. After a study of the primitive port facilities at Boulogne in 1776, one Engineer de Briche noted that, 'The entrance to the port is always dangerous when a westerly wind is blowing . . . The river has no real current and sandbanks are constantly forming. It is one of the worst ports of the Channel.' This conclusion was reinforced by the reports of other port officers and engineers including that of one M. Sauvage. 'In its present state', he noted, 'it is as difficult for boats to enter as to leave it, and even then this can be carried out for a short while only. The force of the tide is the first obstacle hindering any vessels leaving.' During the first two hours of high tide the force of the current is so great 'that neither caution nor manoeuvring skill can succeed in getting boats out'. Added to this was the problem of contrary winds, which were notorious at Boulogne in the age of sail power. Even mild winds out of the west-south-west, or out of the east-south-east meant 'the port is completely closed to all shipping wishing to enter it.' He concluded 'that this situation could only be changed by the installation of locks and barrages'.

In the summer of 1803 Napoleon was preparing his first general set of plans for the invasion flotilla and the Channel ports. He had already decided that Boulogne would be his principal port, but it still had neither locks nor barrages – indeed it had only two small, ancient breakwaters extending from the quayside on either side of the mouth of the River Liane, which did nothing to raise, lower or alter the course of the river or control the tidal flow in any way. One key factor in his plans for the ports was how many vessels could leave port during one tide. As many, many hundreds of vessels were involved, at least two tides would be required for all the vessels to leave most ports, and perhaps three. This meant the crossing would involve twenty-four hours at least, *not* six or eight. Napoleon had obviously forgotten his own conclusions regarding the feasibility of the port back in February 1798: 'It would be useless to carry out long and costly works at the port of Boulogne in order to increase the number of boats it could hold unless they could all get out during one tide.' Now, on 21st July 1803, he drew up tentative plans for all the channel ports: Flushing was to have 100 *chaloupes canonnières* and 200 *bateaux canonniers*. The right wing or flank of the flotilla was to be moored or anchored at Ostend and Nieuport, and to contain at least 300 vessels (enough to transport 30,000 men). The centre was to consist of the ports of Dunkirk, Gravelines and Calais, where another 300 vessels (the larger ones) were to be held. The left wing of the flotilla Napoleon decided tentatively to station at Wissant (which he was shortly to exclude completely), Ambleteuse, Boulogne and Etaples – to hold a total of 2,380 vessels capable of transporting 100,000 men and 3,000 horses.

Napoleon made numerous inspection trips along the cliffs and beaches of the Channel between Dieppe and Ostend and it was he who had determined to make a port of Wissant. Naval engineers quickly eliminated it, however, as an utter impossibility, given the two elements uppermost in Napoleon's mind – time and money. He wanted ports but he did not want anything really permanent, just something capable of being used for a year or so, after which he was not interested.

As in everything he did, he now had to find one man in whom he could have complete faith as far as the engineering projects and costs were concerned. He settled upon an engineer in the Department of Bridges and Highways by the name of Sganzin. However, even this man, hand picked by Napoleon, could not always give him the good news he wanted, as the practical engineer now reported on Boulogne:

> Most of the port (three-fifths of it) has a depth greater than four metres, and thus boats drawing six feet of water can remain afloat for about four hours when the tide is coming in, and thereafter for another three and half hours. But it must also be pointed out that close to half the lower basin and almost the entire upper basin are not deep enough to keep *chaloupes canonnières* afloat during low tide.

This stated the position when boats were not moving, but there were also problems of sandbanks at the entrance, contrary winds, lack of moorings, loading facilities, and the shallow narrow channel.

An initial 305,000 francs authorised in June 1801 to repair and lengthen breakwaters had accomplished little. It was only in the spring and summer of 1803 when talks with Lord Whitworth over Amiens were in their final stage that, immediately following the ambassador's departure for London, Napoleon authorised the first extensive works on the Liane and the proposed port development at Boulogne, including one kilometre of new quays, the excavation of a large artificial basin on the south bank of the river, capable of containing 100 *chaloupes canonnières*, the redirecting of the river bed, and the building of a retaining dyke with locks to control the water level, though still failing to deal with the navigational problems resulting from the narrow, hazardous port entrance.

The initial work on the port project for the extension of the quays, the sinking of pilings and the excavation of the basin, began on 1st May 1803, and as the British Channel Squadron was soon to note by mid-May, some 3,000 labourers were at work, Sganzin estimating the completion of this port by 8th October.

In the course of this development, however, just about every estimate, both as to the amount of time required to accomplish a project and the cost, were inevitably over-optimistic. For instance, the original estimate for the work on the basin was set at 286,846 francs, and 1,840,000 francs was budgeted for all the work on the ports of Boulogne, Ambleteuse and Wimereux, but Sganzin was soon re-calculating that Boulogne alone was costing 393,000 francs *a month* (and that included the very cheap labour of troops). Even a completed basin, though, would not begin to solve their problems at Boulogne as a sceptical Inspector-General Forfait informed the Naval Minister: 'When speaking to qualified individuals about the port of Boulogne, their first observations are: how do you expect to launch 800 vessels from that port? How can you promise the port and city that they will be protected from a bombardment? . . . This work simply cannot be carried out while we are at war.' They *were* at war, however, and the initial designs for the port did not provide nearly enough room for the flotilla to be stationed there.

Forfait now submitted his own plans for the new port. 'Before I left Paris I spoke to the First Consul about a floating fort . . . He liked the idea very much.' Nevertheless it was only towards the end of August 1803 that Bonaparte began to consider Forfait's idea seriously. 'He [Forfait] thinks that we could begin work on the fort and that it could be finished by the end of November', Bonaparte wrote to Bruix and continued, 'Before going ahead with such a plan, which to me seems quite an extraordinary one, I should like you and Citizen Sganzin to study the possible sites for this fort to see if you think this project is feasible.' Just a week later the First Consul authorised work for the new 'floating fort' to begin with a completion date set for 7th November 1803. It was all being done piecemeal, most unprofessionally, and it is surprising that Napoleon of all men was to delay consideration of the basic fortification problems so long after an unprotected port had been begun.

The floating fort (which did not actually float) became known as Fort Rouge and was to protect the centre of the harbour and the mooring line. Two more forts – Fort de l'Heurt and Fort de la Crèche – situated 4,800 yards apart, were authorised to cover the flanks of the harbour entrance. These forts were absolutely necessary for the protection of all vessels entering and leaving Boulogne, but Decrès was most pessimistic about Forfait's estimates that they would be ready within a few months, informing Bonaparte in June 1803 that he thought the three forts would cost at least 3,000,000 francs and take close to three years to complete! The work involved in their construction was time-consuming, and ramps, for example, had to be excavated from the cliffs to the beach to enable men and equipment to reach the sites and the foundations for these alone were to take several months.

The First Consul had worked out his invasion plan in a fairly general way, realising only in part what would be involved. He completely failed to make allowances for all the engineering work that they required, their general complexity, time and costs – all of which soon became an unrelieved nightmare for him.

Forfait's fears of possible British bombardment of both Boulogne proper and the new port projects were only too well founded. The First Consul himself witnessed one such attack by three British ships on 29th June 1803, the main purpose of the attack being to destroy the new installations. This was followed by another attack a fortnight later. What really infuriated Napoleon was that the British could anchor off the coast and fire with impunity for as long as they wished as the few artillery batteries that were in place were totally ineffective. These events only served to reinforce Forfait's argument for the three major new forts.

In the first two weeks of July 1803 the First Consul began trying to solve the question of batteries to protect not only Boulogne, but the entire coastline. He set about installing long-range mortars as well as 24- and 36-pound cannons in ten new batteries between Boulogne and Calais alone, a distance of forty-two kilometres.

The Royal Navy took these new batteries and gun emplacements along jetties and clifftops most seriously, and between 8th and 19th August 1803 bombarded both Boulogne and the coastline heavily on five different days. The *Moniteur* acknowledged only one such attack, nevertheless admitting, 'At this time the enemy fired from a distance of 2,100 yards on the pilings prepared for the construction of a fort, with the purpose of preventing the continuation of this work.' In fact this was just the beginning of a series of deadly attacks by the Royal Navy that were to impede the port and defence construction work over the next several months.

Needless to say, Bonaparte did not like the British pointing out just how vulnerable his projects were, as he informed Admiral Bruix on 22nd August 1803: 'I was greatly grieved to learn, and could not find justified in any way, that your lack of artillery and naval support has left the English free to attack our fort [Fort Rouge].' He also chided the Admiral personally for living safely inside Boulogne: 'I recommend that you set up your tent at the Tour d'Ordre [on the cliffs overlooking the new works in the port], for you can accomplish nothing so long as you remain within the city walls. In matters of this kind it is hardly unusual for the commanding officer to be obliged to do everything himself', and he concluded, 'I intend to have the work continue on the fort. Regardless of the cost, it must be done. Have fires lit [for the lighting of firing devices] all night long at the end of jetties and in the batteries and have our naval forces spend every night out of doors, ready to man their stations at a moment's notice.'

As a result of this reprimand, by the beginning of September 1803 massive temporary floating platforms supporting over thirty cannons and mortars were placed at the foot of Fort Rouge, which, in its turn, was being built upon a spit of land artificially extended by rock and pilings. Despite these precautions, bombardments during the first half of August successfully disrupted all work on this principal fort until 17th September. In his end of the month report that November, the Deputy Director of Fortifications, Dode, acknowledged the poor results thus far, reiterating the effect of Admiral Lord Keith's Home Fleet's artillery fire on men and projects: 'The labourers are afraid and their fear has spread, disrupting all work ... The short-range mortars along the coast have permitted the British ships to get close to our forts, their artillery reaching them and even beyond, while our batteries could not even begin to reach them in return.'

There were two other elements that were even more instrumental in slowing down all work in the port – weather and lack of money.

Gale-force winds, often lasting many days at a time, powerful enough to whip up enormous waves, lashed at the new pilings and rock foundations and, with the equally powerful high tides, destroyed much of the newly finished stone emplacements. These storms kept delaying work on all three major forts at Boulogne throughout the summer, autumn and winter of 1803 and the beginning of 1804 – only the Fort de la Crèche being a little more protected by the cliffs.

The lack of funds influenced things to a great extent even as early as mid-August 1803 and again one wonders what happened to the tens of millions available through bank loans, public contributions and the national budget. For instance Dode reported: 'By the end of Thermidor [17 August] all wages were six weeks in arrears and the workers began to lose confidence in us and their work and gradually began deserting the various projects.' None of this would have happened 'if the zeal of the officers charged with carrying out these works had been seconded by the regular payment of sufficient funds with which to pay the workers and contractors.'

The three forts were especially affected by all these problems and the British also kept up their attacks in an effort to prevent them from becoming operational. This was hardly surprising – from a structural viewpoint they were formidable. The two flank forts, L'Heurt and La Crèche, required massive stone foundations to support an emplacement with a circumference of 151 metres and a diameter of 48 metres, large enough for more than two dozen artillery pieces, including 36-pound cannons and 12-inch mortars. Each required the work of 150 stone-masons and 430 manual labourers, not to mention another 100 men and women to carry the stone from the 70 heavy quarry wagons and 15 barges assigned to each fort. The Fort Rouge, a much more difficult engineering feat, required a far greater number of masons and labourers.

To counter the British attacks, every possible means of defending the harbour had to be taken and Bonaparte felt that the navy had to bear its share of the burden as well. In a confidential letter to Admiral Bruix dated 4th September 1803, he ordered the first of the newly built *chaloupes canonnières, bateaux canonniers*, bomb vessels and *caïques* to be brought into a mooring line close to the forts under construction, believing that their guns would provide an extra degree of protection. In fact, incessant attacks by the Royal Navy revealed just how vulnerable the port still was, as Bonaparte now pointed out:

> Even at low tide there is twenty-two feet of water, thus making it possible for the enemy to attack with a large number of double-decked vessels, bomb ketches and flat-bottomed boats. Supposing, for example, that your line were thus attacked by twenty 74-gun ships or ten or twelve bomb ketches, do you think it could hold? Now the objective of the English is to force us to withdraw from Boulogne and therefore they think nothing of sacrificing three or four vessels to seize or destroy a part of our flotilla.

He then went on to suggest naval strategy to the Admiral, advising him 'to place two or three [*caïques*] between every two *chaloupes canonnières*, and thereby present a greater mass of fire'.

Napoleon was also making plans for the development of other ports. 'I have found an important place for a new port in a swamp', Bonaparte wrote with great enthusiasm to Cambacérès in July 1803. This was at about the closest point for crossing, which unfortunately was Wissant. Although it was also close to the nearby site of Camp César at Boulogne, it was, in fact, a naval engineer's nightmare and a costly one at that, as

Engineer Sganzin quickly indicated, rejecting Bonaparte's great find out of hand.

Another site for a port – at Etaples – drew more serious attention, although Admiral Latouche-Tréville had earlier rejected it because of the smallness and shallowness of the River Canche. Sganzin's report on Etaples was scarcely more encouraging, pointing out as it did that there were constantly shifting sandbanks at the mouth of the river, while at low tide there was no more than three feet of water left in the riverbed: 'The bay is completely exposed to ocean winds . . . no mooring is possible for vessels drawing 12 to 14 feet of water . . . the boats along the riverbanks will be on dry land twenty days out of every month . . . It would be dangerous to station a division of *bateaux canonniers* there . . . There are neither quays nor cables [for mooring] and even small boats are aground during low tide'. Although physically a 'port' could be designed to hold up to 350 *bateaux canonniers*, that is to say, on sandbanks and dry shores, it would be difficult to launch them. He concluded in his special report to the First Consul that 'It is quite obvious that the bay of Etaples offers neither facility nor safety for the stationing of a part of the expedition', although he thought that with a great deal of work and money, the port and part of the River Canche could be used. On 3rd September 1803 an impatient First Consul officially notified Admiral Bruix, 'We must now take up the matter of Etaples. I have ordered that a road be built from Neufchâtel to the sea that we may go from Boulogne to Etaples without having to go along the beach. Has this work begun? Has a Maritime Committee been appointed and have the sites been selected for the various army and naval services there? See to it that everything required is done to prepare this new port.' Bonaparte concluded by stating that he had finally decided on the use of Etaples because the Royal Navy, under Admiral George Byng, had landed sixty troop transport vessels there in 1708! Was it any wonder that most of Napoleon's associates could rarely fathom his thinking?

Ambleteuse was definitely another new port he wanted built. Napoleon referred to an engineer's report dated 2nd February 1794 recommending the creation of a roadstead there (at a cost of 35,000,000 *livres* in 1794!) and more recently in 1801 Admiral Latouche-Tréville had submitted similarly favourable findings. On 21st July 1803 the First Consul issued a decree formally authorising work to begin on this port and the River Slack for an initial anchorage of forty to fifty vessels. Engineer Sganzin's plans to expand this new port to allow for 250 to 300 boats was then accepted that September, although these involved the excavation of a

large lateral basin. As with Etaples and Boulogne, the initial estimates for
the work at Ambleteuse proved totally inadequate, based as they were on
Sganzin's recommendation to hire only 600 workers at a cost of 180,000
francs per month, whereas after work actually began the 43rd Regiment
brought that work-force up to 1,200 men per day, and costs skyrocketed.
Even so the First Consul was not content with the rate of progress and
ordered an additional 500 troops brought in. Although the rate of serious
illness at Ambleteuse proved higher than at any other port (with the
exception of Ostend), and the death rate as well, General Bonaparte now
increased the work-force once again bringing it up to 3,300 men, and yet
by the end of January 1804 the basin was still not completed despite all
the calculations by engineers to the contrary and the incessant proddings
by the First Consul.

In mid-September 1803 General Soult was asked to look into the
possibility of building 'a refuge for some vessels of the flotilla' near the
Tour de Croy just north of Boulogne and, within a fortnight, Soult had in
hand a favourable report from Brigadier-General Bertrand indicating that
at the mouth of the Wimereux, the riverbed was '6 feet deep for a stretch of
900 feet, though only 4 feet wide at its mouth, but that with just 200 men
working daily, it could be deepened and widened sufficiently for use
within a month'. That satisfied Bonaparte for the time being as he
informed Soult, 'If we could only manage to shelter forty to fifty vessels
from the enemy there, that in itself would be a great conquest', and,
although Sganzin's report then contradicted Bertrand's, Bonaparte, who
was expecting the delivery of several dozen newly commissioned boats,
ordered the creation of the new 'port' of Wimereux on 21st October 1803.
The first article of this decree read as follows: 'A port will be opened at the
mouth of the Wimereux, capable of holding 150 vessels of the National
Flotilla', to be built at a cost of 250,000 francs, charging army engineers
with the execution of this project by 7th December 1803. Thus, within a
month of Sganzin's unfavourable report and Bonaparte's own declaration
of the need of a port holding up to fifty boats, the First Consul had decided
on building the port anyway, one now capable of holding three times that
number. As usual the projected date of completion was not met, by several
months, as the labour force once again increased rapidly to complete the
640 metres of new breakwaters, the excavation of a 420-metre stretch of
channel for the inadequate river, as well as a boat basin, all of which finally
opened for the first boats in mid-March 1804.

Another seemingly likely port of real importance was Calais. However,
although it already had some existing facilities, including eight hundred

metres of quays and excellent, empty warehouses, its small port held only twenty vessels and a fully armed frigate could not be accommodated. The obvious place for flotilla vessels, therefore, would have been the roadstead just outside the port, but it was totally unprotected from both enemy bombardment and strong winds, added to which was the problem of constantly shifting sandbanks and riverbed and hence the engineers concluded that Calais 'offers nothing that could in any way warrant the enormous expense that this would cost the military establishment today . . .' and no major work was carried out there.

Nieuport was also under consideration, but its small port was practically dry at low tide (having only three feet of water then) and, although it was a fishing community and therefore had many trained seamen available, the French found no one willing to serve aboard warships! In fact, the report reaching St Cloud concluded, 'This population is scarcely French at all', while pointing out that its roadstead lay unprotected from a sea attack and therefore recommended that no major work be carried out there. A similar decision eliminated Gravelines as well.

Travelling further northwards into occupied Belgium, French naval engineers then considered the possibilities of Ostend. To begin with they found problems with the people, 'difficulties arising from their ignorance of our language and hostility to French aims'. The existing port facilities were good, however, capable of coping with up to 200 commercial vessels, though the port was nearly empty, as Naval Minister Decrès informed the First Consul that June, for 'Ostend is paralysed by the effects of the war'. The twenty-eight vessels found there were seized by the French navy and stripped of their rigging for use on the flotilla, which did not endear the burghers of Ostend to a war effort that had shattered their economy. If the port was good, not so the large road-stead, which lay entirely unprotected. 'Here,' Decrès acknowledged, 'the dominant feeling is that of fear, fear of bombardment'. The Naval Minister's general conclusion was nevertheless favourable because of the good deepwater port and so he ordered major new gun emplacements (for 36-pounders) on the east and west jetties and others along the dyke.

The final port of interest to Bonaparte so far as the invasion of Britain was concerned was that of Flushing in the Batavian Republic. Napoleon's policy of stripping countries of most of their coastal defences was now applied here. Consequently, Denis Decrès wrote to St Cloud at the end of June 1803 asking for men, artillery and gunboats to help protect a most vulnerable port. The existing troops there included Dutch conscripts who were '. . . constantly deserting, as they have been called up from conquered territories' (Bonaparte, of course, never referred to Holland – theoretically an independent republic – as a 'conquered' country). The Naval Minister added, 'The provinces of Zeeland have been completely disarmed by us and have no troops whatsoever.' As for the port of Flushing itself, Decrès was most enthusiastic: 'With very little work we can use it to receive twenty-four ships of the line of any size'. The only drawback was that, as in the case of Rochefort, these large ships could only enter without their armament and full crews as the harbour was not deep enough.

The ports Napoleon could employ in his plans for the great armada against the British extended from Dieppe in the south to Flushing in the north. The engineering problems involved in the development of the new ports, Boulogne in particular, but also, as we have seen, at Etaples, Ambleteuse and Wimereux, were to prove far more protracted and enormously more expensive than Napoleon had ever dreamed, mainly due to the storms. Continuing bad weather also rendered it nearly impossible for Admiral Bruix to find enough decent days in which to send out divisions of his flotilla for training operations or even to convoy the many hundreds of new vessels from the northern rivers and ports to their embarkation points.

Naturally both ports and vessels required protection at all times and, as very little was to be offered by the geological structure of the coast, this meant that the burden fell upon artillery units, forcing Bonaparte to search far and wide for large mortars, howitzers and guns for new batteries all along the coast. The number of cannons ultimately placed there was to prove staggering, some several hundred, a figure not matched again in number and equivalent power until the German occupation of France during the Second World War. Even that did not suffice, however, for, inevitably, there were places along the coast where passing convoys remained unprotected from Admiral Cornwallis' ubiquitous Channel Squadron. In fact, aggressive British measures not only resulted in the destruction of a considerable number of new enemy boats, but the landing of raiding, sabotage and intelligence-gathering units. They also seized boats, many of which were successfully taken back to England for inspection by Prime Minister Pitt and then added to the British coastal service.

In an effort to stop these constant attacks by Admiral Keith, whose squadron had virtually sealed off the entire English Channel from

Flushing to Ushant, Napoleon hit upon the idea of creating mobile or flying artillery units. These consisted of horse-drawn units to accompany each division of boats as it left one port and slowly made its way say to Dunkirk or Boulogne, the artillery travelling along newly created roads over the cliffs and sand dunes. Bonaparte was very good at improvising and, although elaborate, this improvisation was to prove most effective by 1804 in fending off the English. The first six such 'mobile artillery batteries' were created at the beginning of September 1803 and stationed at Le Havre, Fécamp, Saint-Valéry, Dieppe, Le Tréport and Saint-Valéry-sur-Somme. Each battery initially consisted of four artillery pieces, fifty horses assigned to each unit, while cavalry units of fifty men each were in turn assigned to protect each battery (and any boat or beach threatened by a British landing party). It was Naval Minister Decrès who announced the creation of these units to General Berthier, who was then responsible for providing them where needed. 'The purpose of these new emplacements,' Decrès explained, 'is to protect coastal navigation and in particular, that of the vessels of the National Flotilla as they pass from one port to another.' Similar mobile batteries were established north of Boulogne up to the Dutch border, and south of Le Havre all the way to the Spanish frontier.

The permanent artillery emplacements that had so startled Admiral Keith were most impressive indeed. It was not simply a question of those round the immediate coastal positions of the flotilla at the ports, however, for on 28th May 1803 First Consul Bonaparte issued a sweeping decree calling for the creation of 100 companies 'of coastguard artillerymen to man and service the batteries established along the coasts of the Republic and French islands in Europe', which included the cities and ports of Bruges, Lille, St Omer, Le Havre, Cherbourg, Brest, Nantes, La Rochelle, Perpignan, Montpellier, Toulon and Corsica.

Even as late as May 1803 General Bonaparte had not yet decided on making Boulogne the centre of invasion activities, however, despite some tentative projects in that region, and thus initially most of the new batteries were sent to Le Havre, Cherbourg, Brest, Nantes, La Rochelle and Toulon. Nevertheless, even after the formation of these 100 companies (made up by transferring men from existing army and navy artillery units as well as from former coastal defence units), numerous positions along the coast, in particular, difficult island defences, remained vulnerable and necessitated the First Consul's calling up of 'national guards' (that is, local inhabitants of coastal villages), men between twenty-five and forty-five years of age, for a renewable five-year period, who were to form an additional twenty-eight 'stationary companies' at Belle Ile, Ouessant, Ile de Groix, Ile Bréchat, Ile de Batz, Sept-Iles, Ile d'Yeu, Noir Moutier, Ile de Ré, Ile d'Oleron and Elba.

All coastal defences were initially placed under the authority of War Minister Alexandre Berthier, who on 4th June 1803 ordered some 60,000 troops from five army divisions to man coastal defences from Anvers to Lorient, these troops being totally independent of, and unrelated to, the invasion force under the command of General Soult. In theory the basic coastal defences were completed throughout the month of June and, although all control of such positions remained in the hands of the army, there were inter-ministerial and inter-service disputes between the navy and army about many of these issues, particularly where port installations were concerned.

When Napoleon began inspecting these new sites and found many of them less than satisfactory, he frequently blamed the army even where the navy and naval engineers had some responsibility, as, for example, at Boulogne. Unfortunately for War Minister Berthier, Napoleon was an artillery officer, he often spending many hours at just one battery, studying it for efficiency and accuracy. In one instance when Berthier replied that the failure to execute an order establishing one such battery at Boulogne was not his fault but that of the Naval Minister, Napoleon snapped 'It is not the naval engineers who are at fault, it is army engineers and the Minister of War!'

As soon as an order was issued, especially where military units were concerned, Napoleon expected a clicking of heels followed by the immediate execution of that command. Artillery units were to be in place and fully operational within a couple of weeks of the orders being given for their creation.

He read many of the reports of junior artillery officers, occasionally to their later consternation, and for example on 9th July after inspecting a battery at the end of one of the jetties at Boulogne, he dictated a note to Berthier: 'The engineering officer's report is not at all correct [when he said this unit was in operation]. I spent four hours at that battery which was unable to fire a single round.' For the most part, however, it was his good and close friend, Alexandre Berthier, who came in for a deluge of complaints and even abuse: 'It is indeed curious that four months after receiving the King of England's message [regarding the declaration of war], I find the coasts undefended, there being no protection for our commerce,' or, after another unsatisfactory inspection of an army battery, 'How is it possible that the artillery perform their profession so badly?'

Napoleon frequently went into considerable detail explaining how and why a particular port was not being effectively protected by artillery and what was needed. Writing from Namur that August, the First Consul informed the War Office:

> According to the report you sent me from Le Havre, it appears that the enemy was only 2,400 yards from that place [during a recent attack] . . . I am therefore fully justified in asking why there are small mortars there with only a range of 1,600 yards? The coastal batteries firing at an angle of 10 degrees must be able to reach a distance of 2,400 or 2,600 yards; and if the artillery commander had even the slightest degree of intelligence he would have placed some artillery pieces on old transport boats, thereby allowing him to fire at an angle of 45 degrees and covering a range of 3,600 yards. I am writing now to ask you to prepare batteries whose artillery can fire at an angle between 43 and 45 degrees.[1]

As has already been seen, conflicting inter-service interests and authority sometimes caused problems and this was especially so when it came to works carried out in port areas. The army was generally responsible for most engineering works as well as coastal artillery batteries, but so far as the growing flotilla was concerned it was the navy that knew best *where* the big guns were needed to protect passing vessels and naval activity in general. Thus even before ten additional batteries were ordered for the coast north of Boulogne, Admiral Decrès issued orders to the army to build the initial six batteries between Boulogne and Calais. If this procedure as a rule worked reasonably well, it was because Napoleon was there to stop any bickering in the guise of general decrees or personal remonstrances. The most common way Decrès gave Berthier an order was to state that he was simply relaying Bonaparte's orders, as in the case of the six gun emplacements:

> Citizen Minister, as a result of his inspection tour and whom I had the honour to accompany, beginning at Saint-Valéry-sur-Somme, the First Consul has ordered the establishment of six new batteries between Boulogne and Calais . . .
>
> On the orders of the First Consul I sent a naval officer to examine the armament of the coast there, so far as navigation was concerned, and he has drawn up a report in which he specifies some changes needed in the operation of the existing batteries as well as the necessity for some new ones.

On 30th July 1803, the Naval Minister informed War Minister Berthier that Bruix had just been named Admiral, Commander of the National Flotilla and would now be responsible for 'taking the war to English territory which that power wanted to carry to that of the Republic'. He closed this message with the formal important notification that, hereafter, the navy had command over 'all army batteries overlooking the sea'. This was also the first time that the basic invasion ports were actually named by Napoleon through the intermediary of Admiral Decrès. The right wing of the armada was placed at Ostend and Nieuport, the centre at Dunkirk, Gravelines and Calais and the left wing tentatively at Wissant, Amble-teuse, Boulogne and Etaples. Before this announcement, Bonaparte had concentrated most of the new heavy artillery overlooking the ports and coast between Brest and La Rochelle and, while this plan of 30th July was not final (Wissant of course was never used and the concentration at Ostend was to be moved southward to Dunkirk) it was in its essentials the one that was developed over the next two years. The principal decision was that of moving the troops and boats of the invasion force to be within closer striking distance of Britain.

Sometimes Napoleon intervened directly, issuing orders to Decrès on how and where to move just a few ships or to Berthier on where to move even small military units. At other times the orders received from St Cloud involved larger military units, orders accompanied by very detailed instructions as seen in the following one to Berthier:

Here are the definitive dispositions which I have decided upon for the artillery service: The artillery company of the 1st *Régiment à pied* now at Ostend, that which is at the island of Cadzaud, the two companies on the coast near Bruges, shall all proceed to Boulogne . . . The companies of the 1st *Régiment à pied* at Boulogne as well as the other four are to remain there until the artillery service at Etaples is organised, at which time they will furnish the units required there . . . The eight companies of the 5th *Régiment à cheval* which have been ordered to proceed to Boulogne will join the seven of the 1st Regiment, which will make a total of fifteen companies for Boulogne.

Have all transport battalions meet at Douai, with the exception of the one at La Fère; have them bring there all the harnesses they can provide and have the detachments of the baggage train which are in the provinces now to collect horses, bring those horses to Douai and La Fère . . . Thus I conceive of the distribution of the companies to take part in the expedition in the following manner: the 1st Regiment must furnish ten companies: seven will be stationed at Boulogne, one at Dunkirk, one at Calais, which makes nine, and one at La Fère, along with the ten other companies of that regiment.

This order was typical of the many dozens issued throughout this period and reflects Bonaparte's personal administration of the army as well as his determination to prepare for a successful invasion of Britain. During the first week of September 1803 Generals Soult and Davout were made responsible for the supervision of the northern coastal region including all land defences between Boulogne and Le Havre. When, after making such extensive arrangements for the protection of the new flotilla, the First Consul was informed that British vessels were *still* successfully attacking French vessels under the very noses of existing artillery units, he was understandably furious. 'Citizen General Davout, a French sloop has been captured between Nieuport and Dunkirk by an English *chaloupe* and fourteen men. Therefore contrary to orders, you do not have cavalry patrols along with mobile batteries established along that coast'. If there was one thing Bonaparte did not like, it was being humiliated before his

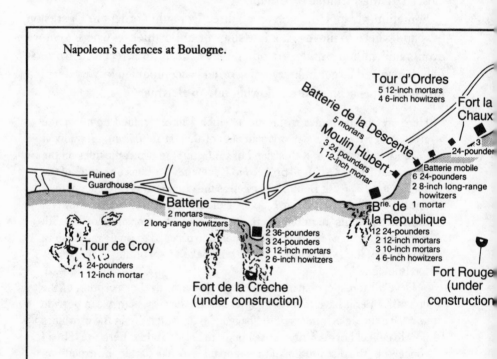

Napoleon's defences at Boulogne.

people by the British. General Soult came in for an even greater hiding: 'I simply cannot understand how your regiment of hussars was not there ready to help. Do you not have them stationed all along the coast to provide just such emergency help when needed?' The First Consul then ordered patrols 'to be in the saddle night and day'. When St Cloud was informed that a newly created coastal battery failed to hit attacking British vessels, Bonaparte sent a special courier to Soult: 'Your mobile battery at Wissant is not powerful enough. You must have 12-pounders with all artillery units.' He also ordered more intensive artillery practice.

The First Consul's preoccupations with the invasion defences included the southern half of the Atlantic coastline as well, from Brest to Bayonne, with a special emphasis on a more systematic deployment of mobile, or flying, artillery along the Loire, at Sables, Noirmoutiers, Aiguillon, La Conchette and along the Charente and Gironde.

The result of a more intensive effort to protect the coast between Boulogne and Ostend was felt by the British Navy by the time William Pitt returned to Downing Street in May 1804. Dozens and dozens of new

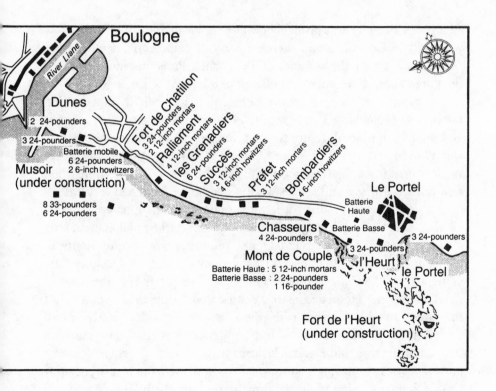

gun emplacements and batteries lined the clifftops and projected from all
the ports designated for flotilla activity, the most intensively protected
port naturally being the principal invasion port, Boulogne (which Captain
Owen tried to convince Admiral Keith was simply 'a feint'). By the
summer of 1804 that new port alone was protected by 180 guns,
howitzers and mortars (see map pages 114–115), covering the area from
the Tour de Croy to the Fort de l'Heurt, a distance of less than three
kilometres. Included in this number were 16-, 24- and 36-pounders as
well as a variety of howitzers and mortars ranging from six to twelve
inches. This figure did not include the various mobile artillery units on
either side of the port, nor the naval guns on the hundreds of vessels in
and near the port. The British Navy was soon to learn that it could no
longer easily come within a mile or so of Boulogne with impunity.

There was a final part of the invasion preparations, however, which
First Consul Bonaparte had yet to concern himself with, for with all the
boats, ports and coastal defences in the world, there could be no invasion
without a large, well-trained landing force, nor without the man
responsible for that army, General Berthier.

Alexandre Berthier was probably never happier than during the last few
years of the Consulate and the beginning of Napoleon's new Empire,
particularly during the summer of 1801 when Paris was more resplendent than at any time since the collapse of the reign of Louis XVI. There
was a happy atmosphere and riches abounded, seen in the growing
number of fashionable carriages, the exquisite fashions of society ladies
and their even more dazzling array of fine gems. That General Berthier
was War Minister again for First Consul Bonaparte and already a very
wealthy man (though as yet nothing to what he was soon to become when
new titles, privileges and estates were heaped upon him) had very little to
do with the reason for his supreme happiness at this moment in mid-
June, as some 1,200 carriages formed a traffic snarl five kilometres long
all the way to the Porte Saint-Denis, requiring over twenty hours in
which to discharge their elegant owners in the spacious cobblestone
courtyard at 72, rue de Varenne. This enormous property in the heart of
Paris, the former Hôtel de Castries confiscated during the Revolution (of
the same Duke de Castries with whom as a young officer Berthier had
served in the American War of Independence) was an elegant mansion
famous for its splendid Louis XV furnishings – in an age when Consular
glitter was fast replacing good taste. Nor was the War Minister happy
simply because First Consul Bonaparte himself had accepted his

invitation (one of his very rare appearances at a private gathering) nor indeed because General Berthier was entertaining – amongst his three thousand guests – the entire diplomatic corps, including Russian, Austrian and German ambassadors and ministers. And it was not even because he was giving this ball and festivities in honour of the King and Queen of Spain's son, the newly acclaimed King of Etruria (Tuscany) and his young wife, who had just arrived from Madrid. No, Alexandre Berthier was even more genial and beaming tonight because of the stunning brunette at his side, his mistress of several years, indeed, the love of his life. Giuseppa Visconti, the wife of the Marquis Visconti, former president of the Cisalpine Republic, now lived openly here with Berthier, she whom Napoleon's Josephine so adored, 'his beautiful Italian', as Madame de Staël referred to her, whom the celebrated portraitist of Marie-Antoinette, Madame Vigée-LeBrun pronounced 'so remarkable for the beauty of her face and figure'. And this was an age when phenomenal women vied for the favours of the salon and public opinion, competition including such beauties as the superb Madame Regnault de Saint-Jean d'Angély and the sensuous Madame Tallien. Berthier had remained surprisingly free and unattached to any woman for so long, indeed, until his early forties, when he first met the Marchioness Visconti. Even the caustic Madame de Staël acknowledged this very special Giuseppa 'whom Berthier loves with all his heart,' a most unique admission and compliment coming from the lips of one of Napoleon's most bitter critics. The General was to love her the rest of his days, despite their permanent separation a few years later.

Alexandre Berthier was considered a most unusual man in this age of rogues, adventurers and upstarts, when working-class men appeared in salons awkwardly bedecked in lace with the recently awarded gold braid of generals, but lacking the polish and culture of officers of a former age. 'Berthier', remarked a startled Prussian emissary formerly of Frederick II's court, 'is a Frenchman both in education and manners . . . He has in his demeanour something of that well-bred amiability of another era which I do not find in any of his ministerial colleagues. He expresses himself well and fulfils his role as master of the house with the greatest charm . . .' Although not a handsome man, General Berthier, because of his slender build, looked taller than his average height indicated. As his guests were announced upon reaching the ballroom, he greeted them with an unaffected geniality that would have astonished Denis Decrès, his winning smile heightened by the blue-greenness of his eyes and offset by the shoulder-length youthful chestnut hair. With '*sa belle italienne*' at his side, they made a couple all of Paris was talking about, their '*soirées dansantes*', given every ten days, being the envy of many a hostess.

Tonight was unlike so many others, when one talked, whispered and gossiped about the beautiful women, splendid gowns and outrageously magnificent jewellery (so much of it recent Italian war loot). Tonight the War Minister – this man who had accompanied a young General Bonaparte to Egypt as his Chief of Staff, who had prepared the organisation which permitted an even younger Bonaparte to seize Italy and was closer to the First Consul than any other during his long reign – had prepared the largest gala in recent Parisian history with a magnificence that was to please even a Bonaparte, with its astonishingly different military theme: a sort of silk-bound bivouac. As guests passed through the glass doors into the garden, they found themselves under an immense silk marquee 120 feet long and 42 feet wide supported by twelve columns of golden cannons, draped with flags and garlands of flowers and crowned by olive branches, each bearing the inscription of recent French military victories. Between the columns stood suits of glistening armour reflected in huge mirrors, heightened by hundreds of candles in dozens of silver candelabra. It was oriental pomp *à la Parisienne*, for the military theme did not end there, as the host's bevy of aides-de-camp, in velour uniforms of scarlet and white appeared everywhere, co-ordinating events. Soldiers in red, white and blue uniforms danced to the music played by an impeccable military band. There were fireworks, fusillades and even cannonades, followed in turn by a play starring the two most celebrated actors of the day, Francis Joseph Talma and Mademoiselle Mars (Anne Boulet). Then came the ball where the lovely women became the centre of attention as they danced their quadrilles. Later, in the middle of the night, with the strains of music still in the air, the guests gladly returned to the enormous Arab-style tent in the garden where small military camp-fires had now been lit round twenty gorgeous tables, laden with a lavish display of exotic delicacies for the constantly changing guests over the next several hours. Indeed, so long was the queue of carriages outside, that by six o'clock the next morning some guests were still arriving. By then, however, the late-comers had missed Berthier's final spectacular surprise – the launching of a gigantic hot air balloon from the end of the garden that, once above the city, traced out in fireworks the letters of Berthier's recent great victory, Marengo. It is said that even the blasé Foreign Minister Talleyrand was impressed by the evening. The soldiers of the day, Davout, Ney, Soult, Lannes, Marmont and Junot with their rows of ribbons and medals mingled with the guests, lost amidst a glittering

William Pitt, Britain's Prime Minister 1783–1801 and 1804–1806. (*Inset*) Hundreds of thousands of British citizens responded to the 'Great Terror' of invasion by joining volunteer units, including Pitt, Colonel Commandant of the Cinque Port Volunteers.

(*Top*) The Admiralty, London, whose officers controlled the Royal Navy.

(*Above*) An Admiralty Board Meeting.

(*Top*) Henry Dundas, Viscount Melville, appointed by Pitt as First Lord of the Admiralty in 1804.

(*Above*) Melville instituted a crash warship-building programme to strengthen the Royal Navy, seen here at Blackwall naval yard in London.

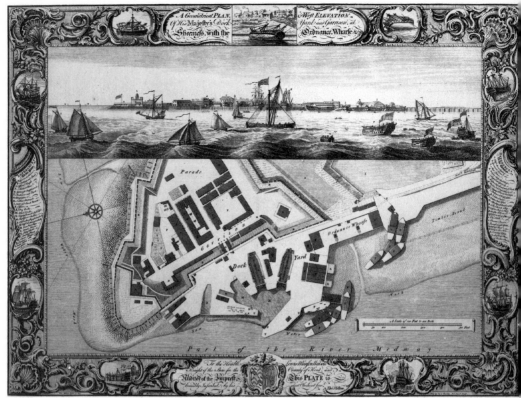

War preparations 1803–1805. (*Top*) Sheerness dockyard and fortifications, (*above*) Chatham dockyard.

The Earl of St Vincent, who
served as First Lord of the
Admiralty under Addington.

Henry Addington, Viscount Sidmouth,
Prime Minister 1801–1804.

Frederick, Duke of York, Commander-in-Chief of
Britain's defences during the French invasion threat.

General Orders

HORSE GUARDS, October 29th, 1805.

His Royal Highness the Commander in Chief has received the King's Command to convey to the several Volunteer and Associated Corps, which were reviewed in Hyde Park on the 26th and 28th Inst. His Majesty's highest Approbation of their Appearance, which has Equalled His Majesty's utmost expectation.

His Majesty perceives with heartfelt satisfaction, that the spirit of Loyalty and Patriotism, on which the System of the ARMED VOLUNTEERS throughout the Kingdom was originally founded, has risen with the exigencies of the times, and at this moment forms such a Bulwark to the Constitution and Liberties of the Country, as will enable us under the Protection of Providence to bid Defiance to the unprovoked Malice of our Enemies, and to Hurl Back with Becoming Indignation, the Threats which they have presumed to vent against our Independence, and even our Existence as a Nation.

His Majesty has Observed with peculiar Pleasure that amongst the unprecedented exertions which the present circumstances of the Country have called forth, those of the CAPITAL of His United Kingdom have been eminently Conspicuous, the Appearance of its numerous and well regulated Volunteer Corps, which were reviewed on the 26th and 28th Inst indicates a degree of Attention and Emulation both in Officers and Men which can proceed only from a deep sense of the important OBJECTS for which they have enrolled themselves, a just Estimation of the blessings we have so long enjoyed, and a firm and manly determination to defend them like Britons, and transmit them unimpaired to our Posterity.

The Commander in Chief has the highest satisfaction in discharging His Duty by communicating these His Majesty's most gracious sentiments, and requests that the Commanding Officers will have recourse to the readiest means of making the Same known to their respective Corps.

Frederick, Commander in Chief.

GENERAL RETURN of the Volunteer Corps reviewed by HIS MAJESTY in Hyde Park.

On Wednesday the 26th October.

Corps	Commanders	Effective in the Field
LOYAL LONDON VOL. CAVALRY	Lieut. Col. ANDERSON	217
HON. ARTILLERY COMPANY	Colonel LE MESURIER	904
1st REG. ROYAL EAST INDIA VOL.	Colonel Sir L. DARELL	640
2d Dº. Dº.	Colonel Sir H. INGLIS	£86
3d Dº. Dº.	Colonel J. ROBERTS	565
1st REG. LOYAL LONDON VOL. INF.	Lieut. Col. BIRCH	752
2d Dº. Dº.	Lieut. Col. J. SMITH	647
3d Dº. Dº.	Lieut. Col. KESSINGTON	804
4th Dº. Dº.	Lieut. Col. PRICE	790
5th Dº. Dº.	Lieut. Col. T. SMITH	501
6th Dº. Dº.	Lieut. Col. WIGRAM	647
7th Dº. Dº.	Lieut. Col. SHAW	404
8th Dº. Dº.	Lieut. Col. CANNING	772
9th Dº. Dº.	Lieut. Col. Sir W. CURTIS	651
10th Dº. Dº.	Lieut. Col. COMBE	587
11th Dº. Dº.	Major NESBON	295
1st REG. TOWER HAMLETS Dº.	Lieut. Col. MELLISH	556
WHITECHAPEL Dº.	Lieut. Col. CRAVEN	445
MILE END Dº.	Major LITTHAP	353
St. GEORGES IN THE EAST Dº.	Major SPLSHT	230
RATCLIFF Dº.	Major DOULOT	185
SHOREDITCH Dº.	Major MARSHALL	294
BROMLEY St. LEONARD'S Dº.	Major STOVARD	175
BETHNAL GREEN Dº.	Major CARRICK	106
St. CATHARINES Dº.	Captain JENKINS	121
CHRIST CHURCH VOLUNTEERS	Major STEVENS	184
		12,461

On Friday the 28th October.

Corps	Commanders	Effective in the Field
LONDON & WESTMIN. LIGHT HORSE VOL.	Colonel HERRIES	727
WESTMINSTER REG. VOL. CAVALRY	Lieut. Col. ELLIOTT	725
SOUTHWARK TROOP OF YEOMANRY	Captain COLLINGTON	46
CLERKENWELL CAVALRY	Captain VALLAN	46
LAMBETH Dº.	Captain WATSON	80
St. GEORGES REG. VOL. INFANTRY	Colonel Earl of CHESTERFIELD	663
St. JAMES Dº. Dº.	Colonel Lord AMHERST	524
BLOOMS & INNS OF COURT Dº.	Colonel COX	972
ROYAL WESTMINSTER Dº.	Colonel ROBERTSON	991
PRINCE of WALES'S Dº.	Colonel M. P. ANDREWS	540
St. MARGARET'S & St. JOHN'S Dº.	Hon. Lieut. Col. EDEN	662
LOYAL NORTH BRITONS Dº.	Col. Sir. E. Lord BEAT	366
MARY-LE-BONE Dº.	Colonel Lord DUNCANNON	905
LAW ASSOCIATION Dº.	Lieut. Col. Hon. T. ERSKINE	555
DUKE of GLOUCESTER'S Dº.	Colonel Lord CHETWYND	462
SOMERSET PLACE Dº.	Colonel TIERNEY	360
St. CLEMENTS & St. GEORGE'S Dº.	Lieut. Col. Sir J. NICHOLL	366
CLERKENWELL Dº.	Major MACNIAC	591
LOYAL BRITISH ARTIFICERS Dº.	Lieut. Col. BURTON	242
LOYAL BRITONS Dº.	Lieut. Col. BAYSTON	242
St. ANDREW'S & St. GEORGE'S Dº.	Lieut. Col. READER	177
ST. ANDREW & St. QUEEN'S ROYAL Dº.	Colonel Lord HOGART	314
KNIGHTSBRIDGE Dº.	Major EYRE	109
St. CLEMENT DANES Dº.	Major BLAKE	122
1st TRUST Dº.	Lieut. Col. GAITSKILL	715
St. SEPULCHRE'S Dº.	Major FORD	343
St. MATHEW'S Dº.	Major POTTS	174
LOYAL SOUTHWARK Dº.	Colonel TIERNEY	141
LAMBETH Dº.	Lieut. Col. EDWARDS	555
CHRIST CHURCH Dº.	Major TOULMIN	171
St. OLAVE'S Dº.	Major KING	135
SIDNEY'S Dº.	Major SLOAN	110
ROTHERHITHE Dº.	Major WELLS	185
DUKE of CUMBERLAND'S CORPS of VOLUNTEER SHARP SHOOTERS	Captain BARKER	54
GRAF & INN CORPS OF VOL. RIFLEMEN	Captain J. K. COOKE	51
		14,676

HARRY CALVERT, Adj. Gen.

To the Volunteers of the Metropolis, this Transcript from the London Gazette is inscribed, By their most obliged humble Servant, Samuel Dunbar Neely.

London, Published Mar 8, 1806, by S. D. Neely, Bird in hand Court Cheapside, at the Shakespeare Gallery Pall Mall, & at Mess. Clay & Sons, Ludgate Hill.

(*Top*) 74 Martello Towers ringed Great Britain, providing look-out stations, rallying points for defence and magazines for powder, arms and munitions. (*Above*) Walmer Castle on the Kent coast, where Pitt lived as Warden of the Cinque Ports, ready for war.

(*Opposite page top*) George III reviewing his troops in Hyde Park. (*Below*) General Orders to the Volunteer Units reviewed in October 1803.

(*Right*) A printed poster of 1803 with instructions to the British public in the event of a French invasion.

(*Below*) As Napoleon amassed his invasion force across the Channel, beach defences were erected along the Sussex coast.

In cafe of actual Invafion.

The Deputy Lieutenants and Juftices, acting in Chefter Ward, defire to recommend to your Parifh of the following Plan for the Removal of Women, and Children, and the aged, and infirm, and requeft you would call a Meeting of your Parifh, as fpeedily as poffible, to take into your Confideration the faid Plan; and apply it (if neceffary) as far as Circumftances will admit.

To leffen as much as poffible that Confufion which muft necceffarily take Place in cafe of Alarm on the landing of the Enemy,—the following PLAN for the more eafy Removal of the Women and Children, and the aged and infirm, from Villages near the Sea Coaft to the Place of general Military Rendezvous, is recommended.

The Village to be nominally divided into Stations, where Carts fhould be appointed to receive the people.

STATION. No. 1. *The Parfonage.*
No. 2. *The Poor-houfe.*
No. 3. *The Common Pump*
No. 4. *The Pinfold* } or as the Names of Places may be.
No. 5. *The Common Pond*

The Stations to be in fuch Parts of the Village as are moft known and confpicuous; and interfere as little as poffible with the Turnpike-road, fo as not to prevent the March of Troops, &c.

The Carts to attend at their refpective Stations immediately on a Signal given, in the following Order—

CART.—No 1. To attend at Station No. 1. there to wait and receive the People from thence, to the Houfe of A. B.
No. 2. To attend at Station No. 2. for the People of the Poor-houfe only.
No. 3. To attend at Station No. 3. for the People from the Houfe of C. D. to the Houfe of E. F.

and fo on, a Cart for each Station. The No. of Carts will of courfe vary in Proportion to the Size of the Town.

Each Cart thus properly numbered, and the Names of the Owner, and Driver, and the No. of the Station marked thereon, fhould be provided with two Horfes, a Truf of Hay, fix Battins of Straw, with a winnowing Cloth, which, by the Help of Poles, may ferve as a Covering at Night.

Thofe who wifh to receive the Benefit of this Conveyance, being previoufly furnifhed with a Ticket (fee the Form) defcribing their Names, and the No. of their Children, are expected, on Alarm given, to be at their proper Stations, there to wait till the Cart appointed for that Station arrives—To carry there their Blankets, and a Change of Cloaths, bound up in the Coverlid of their Beds, with a Direction on the fame defcribing their Name, and the Parifh to which they belong.

All Women (except thofe who are fick, or near being confined) who ufually go out to work at Hay or Corn-harveft, will be confidered as able to walk by the Side of the Carts; and Children above 7 Years of Age will not be fuffered to ride in the Carts, unlefs fick or tired.

A Cart to be provided with extra Provifions for a few Days, till the firft Struggle is over—to attend at the Station No. 1. as the neareft the Road to S........ the general Rendezvous.

Carts with tilted Covering made of Hoops and Sail-cloth, for thofe who cannot fecure other Carriages for their Families, and are able and willing to fubfcribe to the Expence of the fame. Thefe Carts are intended for the Ufe of the upper Set of People—but for the helplefs fick Poor a Cart of fimilar Convenience and Comfort fhould be provided at the public Expence of the Parifh, to be paid out of the Poor's Rate—

The whole to be under the Direction of the Clergyman of the Parifh, as Superintendent, affifted by twelve of the principal Farmers, armed, cloathed and mounted at their own Expence, who are to attend as an Efcort Corps, not fo much to fhew a good Face againft the Enemy, as to protect their Convoy againft domeftic Plunderers.

If the Rules of this PLAN are punctually obeyed with common Alacrity, the whole of the Women and Children, aged, fick, and infirm may be removed out of the Town in an Hour's time, after the Alarm is given. Every thing depends upon Regularity, Sobriety, and Subordination to the Superintendent and his Affiftants.

FORM OF THE TICKET. *No.* 1.

A. B. You and your three Children belonging to Cart No. 4.—Driver G. D.—Station No. 4.—as foon, therefore, as the Alarm is given, do you pack up your Blankets, and a Change of Cloaths for yourfelf and Children, in the Coverlid of your Bed, and fix upon the Bundle this Direction—

No. 1. *A. B. Cart No.* 4.—*Driver G. D.*
Station No. 4—*of the Parifh of N* - - - -

Carry alfo what Meal, and Meat, and Potatoes (not exceeding one Peck) you may have in the Houfe at the Time; but on no Account will any Article of Furniture, or heavy Baggage, be allowed to be put into the Carts.

crowd, including such personalities as the writer Laharpe and a royalist of another age, Adrien de Montmorency and Louis de Narbonne (the bastard son of Louis XV), not to mention certain favoured English guests, Charles Fox and his brother and sister-in-law, Lord and Lady Holland, whose pro-Bonapartist sympathies were especially appreciated.

Although these magnificent balls and festivities celebrated throughout 1801, 1802 and 1803 were hardly to be outshone by those of the Empire, though they were sometimes to match them in splendour and even ceremony, giving the last few years of the Consulate and the early years of the Empire a reputation for frivolity and unsated limits of wealth, they almost completely hid from view, even from the probing eyes of dozens of foreign ambassadors and spies, the military activities that were now afoot throughout France.

Alexandre Berthier, however, perhaps more than any other man, apart from Napoleon and Naval Minister Decrès, spent very long hours, days, weeks and months, on this single war effort. Not only was Berthier capable of working for very long periods without sleep or even rest, he was also perhaps the most spectacular military administrator in recent French history. Indeed, Napoleon would not even consider a major campaign without Berthier serving as his chief of staff. In that capacity he set down the organisational and administrative rules, procedures and objectives for the army that made it so successful in campaign after campaign, rules followed by the French army right into the twentieth century. It was he who stressed that the general staff should concern itself with four basic administrative services: one responsible for the efficient movement of troops, another providing all material and provisions for the entire army (as well as hospitals and military courts), a third concerned with intelligence-gathering and, of course, the fourth, with communications.

So great has been the interest shown by historians in Napoleon that the key man who made Napoleon's amazing success possible year after year has generally been overlooked, reduced in history books to a footnote or, at best, a paragraph. That Napoleon Bonaparte was a brilliant military tactician cannot be denied, but without a handful of good, reliable military commanders in the field as well as Alexandre Berthier as his chief of staff and always at his side, many of Napoleon's celebrated victories would, perhaps, never have taken place. It is hardly surprising then that no man was closer to the General Bonaparte who was to become First Consul and then Emperor, than General Berthier. Berthier above all was solid and reliable and, unlike so many of Napoleon's commanders,

surprisingly honest and objective in his judgement of men and situations
and almost invariably right, as history was to attest. These were very rare
qualities indeed, as Napoleon Bonaparte was quick to realise.

Berthier, nearly sixteen years older than Bonaparte, was forty-two
years old and the newly named commander of the Italian Army, only
twenty-six, when they first met at the sixteenth-century fortress in the
harbour of Antibes on 25th March 1796. From the very start these two
men, so utterly different in background and character, seemed to take to
each other immediately, understanding one another and, in particular,
appreciating each other's special unique qualities, again so utterly
different as military men. No sooner would Napoleon sketch out an idea
for a campaign and the main objectives, for instance, than Berthier would
grasp it all almost intuitively without further explanation, setting to work
to make that campaign and those objectives realities in the most efficient
manner possible, as Napoleon's aide, Lejeune, relates:

> Napoleon's genius gave birth to those conceptions, creating, improvising
> the means, inflaming men's hearts thus making anything possible . . .
> Berthier identified himself with his chief's thoughts completely, establish-
> ing for each commander what he had to do as a part of the entire picture, as
> he ironed out any difficulties, seeing to it that everything needed was there.
> His solicitude, ever anxious, his ceaseless activity and his unstinting co-
> operation did not relax until after success had been achieved . . . During
> his early years of mathematical studies his mind had reached such a degree
> of integrity and directness that his later writings and orders were drawn up
> and reduced to their simplest form, with a lucidity and mathematical clarity
> that permitted him to explain the most complex military movements in a
> few well-chosen words.

Napoleon Bonaparte for his part had never met such an extraordinary
military administrator before. He seemed to have been placed on this
earth specifically for his personal needs and the young general quickly
arranged to have the Directory transfer Berthier from the staff of General
Scherer's division to his own for that initial invasion of Italy. Italy was to
prove just the beginning of the long succession of victories over the next
few years – Arcola, Lodi, Rivoli, Montebello, Marengo – that were to be
closely associated with Napoleon's meteoric rise to power, providing him
with a reputation for victory unmatched by any man in French history.
Thanks to his new association with Alexandre Berthier, Napoleon found
that armies were in place, supply depots provisioned and ready, encampments prepared, communications established, military commanders in
receipt of lucid, comprehensive orders, along with the requisite logistical

information and reports on the terrain that lay before them. All this thoroughness and efficiency was totally new to a French army of the Revolution and made it possible for Napoleon's special genius simply to deploy army corps and war material when and where they were needed, and, of course, the victories ensued. The successful young general was not unappreciative of what General Berthier had made possible for him and, for instance, following the victories in northern Italy in 1796, he reported to the Directory in Paris: 'From the outset of this campaign, the Chief of Staff, General Berthier, has spent every day on the battlefield and every night at his desk; it is quite impossible for anyone to have shown greater activity and good will or to have been more courageous or better informed'.

Although Berthier did occasionally differ with Napoleon (he bitterly opposed the kidnapping and execution of the Duke d'Enghien, for example), this never detracted from his complete admiration of Napoleon's military genius. After returning with General Bonaparte from the Italian campaigns, he accompanied him to Egypt, later sailing with him on the frigate *La Muiron* to Fréjus in 1799 to help carry out the famous *coup d'état* on 9th November of that year which ended the Directory, placing the thirty-year-old Bonaparte at the head of the newly created triumvirate of consuls.

If Berthier was present at every major campaign Napoleon ever fought (with the exception of Waterloo), he was also present during many of the major events in the administration of the country, joining the Government as War Minister two days after the fateful 18th Brumaire when the Directory had been overthrown. In September 1800 First Consul Bonaparte dispatched him to Madrid as his special envoy to supervise the negotiations with the court of Carlos IV and Queen Maria Luisa that resulted in the transfer of the Louisiana Territory in America to the French Republic, as successfully as he had earlier transferred Pope Pius VI from the Vatican to a French prison, if a regal one. Berthier seemed always to be there, and on 19th May 1804, one day after Napoleon had been acclaimed Emperor of the French, Berthier was created the first of fourteen Imperial Marshals of the realm, and needless to say he was also the first to be awarded the Grand Aigle – Grand-Croix, of the newly created Legion of Honour. In December of 1804 he attended the Imperial Coronation in Notre-Dame Cathedral in his new court uniform of blue velour, embroidered in silver, with his red cordon of the Legion of Honour, and carried the ceremonial golden Orbe on a scarlet cushion to the altar. Just as he had been named the first Marshal of the new régime, following the successful defeat of the Austrians and Russians at Austerlitz, in March 1806 he would be named the first 'hereditary prince' of the Empire, with the title of Prince of Neuchâtel, thereby allowing the Emperor to address him as 'My Cousin'. After being given his own private domaine in occupied Switzerland, along with his own private 1000-man-strong army, in 1808 he became Vice-Constable of the Empire, and then Prince of Wagram following that great victory in 1809. So far as Napoleon was concerned, no honour was too great, no mark of gratitude prestigious enough for his 'cousin', the most loyal soldier in France. Ultimately Berthier held the post of 'Major-General' of the Imperial General Staff and received enormous outright gifts of hundreds of thousands in gems and coin of the realm. Apart from the wealthy principality of Neuchâtel, Napoleon gave the faithful Berthier immense estates in other occupied lands – Hanover, Westphalia and Poland – making him perhaps the richest man of the Empire, second only to Napoleon himself.

In addition to the plans to provide the vessels required for the invasion flotilla, and prepare the ports to serve as embarkation points as well as a massive wall of artillery to protect the entire coastline, there was one final element that needed to be considered and on the face of it, it was probably the easiest to accomplish – the gathering of the invasion troops. However, just as there had been uncertainty about the flotilla vessels and the ports, what the army now was to consist of and where it was to be stationed or deployed preparatory to the invasion was the subject of varying thought and many different plans.

The earliest study carried out by the War Ministry was completed on 18th April 1803, General Berthier announcing the first tentative project on 23rd May. It involved five major encampments, including one in Holland, a large one at St Omer, another at Paris, a fourth at Coblenz and the fifth near Brest. Less than a fortnight later, however, after further discussions with the First Consul, War Minister Berthier informed General Mathieu Dumas that the original project had been scrapped in favour of three large camps, one at St Omer, another at Arras and a third at Compiègne. Ten days later, however, Napoleon told the War Minister that he had changed his mind again! 'Here is the definitive plan that I intend to adopt. Six camps will be formed comprising seventy-eight battalions,' to be located in Holland, at Ghent, St Omer, Compiègne, St Malo and Bayonne. Berthier then drew up an entirely new set of orders for the camps and for the complex problem of transport to them only to learn on 28th August that Bonaparte had shelved these 'definitive plans', reducing the number of camps to four at St Omer, Bruges, Compiègne and Bayonne. The camp at Bayonne was originally created in the event of war with Spain, but by the end of August the First Consul informed the War Minister at the Rue St Dominique that agreement had been reached with the Spanish royal family (in the form of a secret Franco-Spanish Treaty signed on 19th October[2]) and that these troops were no longer needed for their original purpose, Berthier in his turn informing General Pierre Augereau on 29th August 1803:

> The corps which you command now [at Bayonne] is to be a part of those assembling along the Channel and which are to carry to English territory the very war which that nation wanted to wage against the Republic.

With that, the Bayonne camp was dropped and between 29th August and 4th September three army corps were established as they were to remain: General Davout was to head a corps of three divisions at Bruges, General Soult, who was to have the overall command of the entire army of three corps, was ordered to his new headquarters at St Omer where another corps of four divisions was stationed, while General Ney was soon at Montreuil preparing the three divisions of the third corps. Although in London coffee houses in the autumn of 1803 talk was rife of a pending French invasion of southern England, in fact the three army corps intended for that expedition were only at their respective camps by the middle of January 1804, and then still only totalled 70,000 men. At the same time General Augereau's troops were ordered to three camps, one at Brest, another at Saintes, while the remainder proceeded to Toulon.

Augereau's troops assembling at Brest were to prepare for a co-ordinated descent on Ireland as Napoleon appealed for fresh volunteers: 'All the Irish who are in Paris and who wish to take part in this expedition are to proceed to Morlaix', their numbers to be reinforced by a second unit of Irish volunteers forming at Rochefort. Their grand total when added to the nucleus of troops coming from the Spanish frontier would give General Augereau some 25,000 men there.

In order to form the three principal army corps plus reserves of infantry and cavalry, army units were transferred to the Channel from Cologne, Brussels, Strasbourg, Mézières, Nancy, Besançon, Schlestadt, Agen, Dôle, Belfort, Gray and Lyons, to mention just a few of the major garrisons affected. While most of the troops were destined for the three main camps, dozens of smaller units were also maintained at such camps as Ath, Tournay, Arras, Mayence, Meaux, Compiègne and Amiens.

It was not until 12th December 1803, however, that Napoleon officially announced 'The Organisation of the Great Expedition', confirming the creation of the three army corps at St Omer, Bruges and Montreuil. At the same time he also proved just how serious he was about the imminent invasion by naming War Minister Berthier as his Chief of Staff, giving him a staff of forty-three officers who were to be responsible for preparing the entire Anglo-Irish expedition.

Despite the First Consul's impatient orders and the superb organisational skills of the inexhaustible Berthier, the War Minister had to acknowledge in his report of mid March 1804 that he could only muster some 71,336 men at Bruges, St Omer and Montreuil, bringing that total up to 100,233 *only* after including the reserves. At a pinch he could also muster another 37,240 men, by withdrawing the troops occupying Batavia, but scarcely 16,000 of them were French. However, the number of army recruits was the least of the War Minister's worries so far as the principal invasion camps were concerned. The problems experienced at St Omer and Bruges are just one example of the difficulties he had to face.

As troops were to be kept in these camps for many months, suitable housing had to be prepared. Entirely new 'cities' were built, streets were laid, supply depots established and fuel and food contracts negotiated. Housing over 30,000 men at St Omer alone proved a major operation and by the end of June 1804 the newly created Marshal Alexandre Berthier could report to St Cloud that some 2,750 barracks and huts had been built or were planned. Therefore, when British naval officers occasionally reported seeing just a dozen or so of these buildings going up, they were greatly misled as to the actual situation. Reports on food, discipline, heating and supply depots were generally good at St Omer and Boulogne, although providing fodder for thousands of horses proved a serious problem from the very beginning.

While artillery men, cavalry units and infantry were constantly receiving instructions in the field or practising on manoeuvres, other troops – perhaps as much as a third – were on various special assignments. Marshal (he too had now been promoted) Nicolas Jean de Dieu Soult (to give him his full name) assigned 3,862 men to labour battalions to work on various engineering projects, including roads, warehouses and arsenals, though most of them were employed on port and harbour installations, such as work on the new forts and batteries at Boulogne, Wimereux and Ambleteuse, and others were assigned to the navy. The port facilities and engineering projects for Boulogne were never fully completed, the work still in progress on the Fort de l'Heurt and the Fort de la Crèche in July 1804 while the rest of the labour corps stationed at Wimereux and Ambleteuse were working in shifts night and day to prepare those harbour facilities. In addition, each month 7,126 men were assigned to garrison duty on the newly built flotilla vessels where they were required to live, often in the roadstead, for several days at a time, when the sailors then taught them how to swim, row, rig sails and carry out elementary navigation for, as Napoleon boasted, there was nothing a French soldier was incapable of doing.

Berthier's report stated that the newly established artillery units were now practising six hours per day on manoeuvres, in association with infantry units and in battle practice, and 'the greatest vigilance was being exercised by patrols night and day while in the artillery batteries, order and discipline have been maintained and that service has carried out its duties to the letter'.

On the other hand, Berthier's report on building and engineering works was mixed. To be sure, the new barracks for Napoleon's Imperial Guard, located near his headquarters at the Pont de Briques in Boulogne, had been completed and the port facilities at Wimereux were proceeding nicely at long last, although admittedly many months behind schedule. The Fort de l'Heurt in the Boulogne harbour was now provisioned for battle, but because of 'the violent and almost continual gales throughout the month' the Fort [de la Crèche] was 'now two or three feet lower than it was at this time last month.' Berthier had to report other problems as well. 'The absolute lack of funds and three months of unpaid debts have halted all work on military communications' which resulted in numerous roads, old and new, remaining unprepared for the movement of heavy military units and wagons. Although troops' pay was up to date there were some 129 desertions by French sailors and workers during this month alone and the military prisons held another 60 men on a variety of charges, mainly soldiers arrested for fighting, including rather fierce sabre skirmishes by the Imperial Guard, although only one prisoner was executed, one 'Monsieur Franqueville' of Boulogne 'who has been found guilty of communicating with, and spying for, the enemy.' The longer the invasion was put off, the more problems there were in the three principal camps arising from boredom and rebelliousness. As for the state of the flotilla now situated in the ports along the Boulogne coast, Berthier reported a total of only 1,196 boats ready for use (including 648 transport vessels).

A second report Napoleon now received from General Mathieu Dumas concerning the 'Camp de Bruges' listed many problems,

problems which worried the Emperor very much. If 'there were some complaints by the 1st Division about the quality of the bread and vinegar,' which could be remedied quite easily (for soldiers' stomachs had to be assuaged), the bitter tone of the report could not be ignored, as when he complained about the defenceless state of the coast from which Marshal Davout had removed 'all the mobile batteries' to the south. But at least army and naval instruction was 'improving day by day . . . and all the troops have already been aboard vessels several times, frequently supplying pickets aboard the *péniches*.' Here too, though for the first time, were alarming observations stemming from troops being contained in the same place month after month, the problems becoming increasingly prevalent from now on. General Dumas acknowledged that a 'decline in discipline, inevitable disturbances and theft have been recorded through-out the Corps, as well as extreme difficulty in having all variety of orders executed.' There was also the problem of 'desertion by conscripts from these neighbouring provinces, in addition to excesses of every kind by soldiers held in one place for a long time, as well as their disgust at having to remain in these camps during the winter, and of course the growing danger of serious illness . . .' As a good general, Bonaparte had to think very carefully about these problems, the seriousness of which he could not ignore, although, apparently, he was willing to do so, as these troops remained where they were for yet another year.

The final part of Dumas' report dealt with a problem that was more or less unique to the army corps stationed at Bruges and about which something could be done. It was illness. It affected units near Ostend, resulting in thousands of men being sent to sick bays and hospitals. Indeed, so great was the increase of illness caused by the stagnant ponds, the cold and damp, that five new hospitals (averaging from 300 to 400 beds) had to be created, including the conversion of one of the local schools to contain another 1,000 beds. However, vigorous action was taken almost immediately to overcome this problem, including the rotation of troops to healthier camps every twenty days and the maintenance of clean, well-aired living quarters.

Of all three camps created specifically for the invasion of England, only Bruges presented a generally negative situation, but even then all three could report continuous training exercises for infantry, cavalry and artillery units, including stints aboard flotilla vessels so that, by the summer of 1804, Napoleon already had the nucleus of a large, well-trained army. He knew that he would have to act soon, however, to take advantage of this high state of readiness if he were not to jeopardise the entire, enormous war effort that he had demanded of the French people. Three army corps, totalling some ten divisions, or forty regiments, were prepared and ready to cross the Channel. With the expedition proper now well in hand, Napoleon was free to concern himself with the last vital factor of this operation – co-ordinating the fleets of the fighting navy, for so long as Britannia ruled the seas, there could be no successful invasion.

'The Safety of the Country Will Never be at Hazard'

My Lord, as it appears essentially necessary that some plan should be adopted for defeating any projects the enemy may form of a descent on that part of the coast within the limits of your Lordship's command during the winter months, my Lords Commissioners of the Admiralty have deemed it advisable that I should transmit to your Lordship for your consideration a general outline of the plan which they conceive to be best adapted to that purpose . . . first, that of having an active force on the enemy's coast for the purpose of keeping a vigilant and constant look-out on their proceedings, and preventing, as far as may be practicable any considerable number of boats or craft from leaving their ports unmolested; and, secondly, to fix such stations on our coast as may be best calculated to operate against the enemy in case they should elude the vigilance of our cruisers on their coast . . .

Secret communication from Sir Evan Nepean to Admiral Lord Keith,
Admiralty Office, 11th October 1803.

When the Colonel of the Cinque Port Volunteers [Pitt] gave as a toast, 'A speedy meeting with the French Army in the Island of Great Britain', it is to be hoped, for the credit of his intellect and the sanity of his mind, that he was only guilty of a little bragging and vapouring . . . if he really thought as a Member of Parliament, that the Earl [St Vincent] had left one single hole or cranny unmasked and unguarded, for the enemy to pass out and realise these vain and puerile wishes.

St Vincent

ON 15TH MARCH 1804, William Pitt gave the bitterest speech of his career, and singled out First Lord St Vincent, for the brunt of his attack with the intention of bringing down Addington. The First Lord had emasculated the navy, reducing its strength – now, in time of war – both in men and ships. Moreover, those few ships he *was* building were ships of the line, frigates and cruisers, not the many hundreds of gunboats that were desperately needed to meet the very real menace of a French invasion.

This man whom he was accusing in his humourless old age was still at the height of his naval career. He looked somewhat like the unhappy combination of a tortoise and an owl, with his head sunk grimly upon his stubborn shoulders into which his neck receded without leaving a trace.

Long an enemy of William Pitt, he seemed to be unhinged by Pitt's criticisms of Addington's government, and in particular by that venomous attack against himself, Admiral of the White, Lieutenant-General of Marines, and First Lord of the Admiralty. How else could his furious diatribes to his colleagues at the Admiralty against Pitt – 'hollow, treacherous and base' – and 'the laches of his Administration', be interpreted?

When John Jervis, Earl of St Vincent, had exchanged command of the Channel Fleet in February 1801 for the position of First Lord, little did Prime Minister Addington realise what he was letting himself in for. For, however unbalanced and outrageous were St Vincent's fulminations at meetings within the panelled chambers of the Admiralty, or before his ailing wife in the privacy of their home, what he produced in the 84 pages of his *Memoirs of the Administration of the Board of Admiralty* which he had privately printed in 1805, following the collapse of Addington's government in May 1804, when Pitt named Melville to succeed him as First Lord, proved so utterly shocking that, upon his death, the whole impression was destroyed by Mr Justice Jervis – all, that is, except for one copy left upon a dusty shelf deep in the British Museum library.

He had assumed office back in February 1801, 'when all was danger and when all was dark', these *Memoirs* began, and if 'there was in all the State, at home or abroad, a post of fatigue and peril, of exertion and responsibility, it was the Admiralty', claimed St Vincent, which he alone had been capable of, and willing to, assume. There had been mutiny in the fleet (the remains of which were not yet dead) by seamen unhappy with the brutal conditions at sea under certain captains or by Irishmen bent on fomenting trouble to avenge the English occupation of their country. There was also 'a most dangerous sedition and confederacy amongst the workmen in the Royal-yards', where incompetence and outright theft were the accepted norm and yet these workmen had the audacity to demand 'to have the permanent rate of wages doubled!' Ships were rotting on the stocks, left unfinished due to supplies and stores which, though long ordered, paid for and indeed delivered, never reached the Royal Naval or merchant yards for which they had been intended. Incompetent commissioners of the navy, thieving Royal suppliers and yard personnel, crooked contractors in victualling, stores and supplies were everywhere so deeply ensconced that many of their positions were passed down from father to son, and this was so not only in Great Britain but abroad in British yards in Antigua, Jamaica and Gibraltar. Yet it was the workers in these very yards, especially in

England, who were protesting, refusing to work. At Plymouth in particular where 'rebellion was ripest . . . the Infantry, Cavalry, and Volunteers, had been called out, [and where] cannon had been pointed at the insurgents down the Fore-street'.

The situation in the docks and Royal naval yards was clearly out of hand. Only a most extraordinary man could have brought order out of this chaos, obedience out of such insurrection. 'Upon *one* temper, the constitution of a *single* mind, and the firmness of a single wrist, depend sometimes the fate and glory of an Empire. The Earl of St Vincent demanded, and the King's Cabinet consented, to measures of vigour and decision' and thus he had saved the day, he acknowledged. Thanks to 'the great Chief's . . . unwearied efforts', he continued in the third person, rebellion was quashed as a Baltic fleet was prepared and dispatched to fight and break 'the formidable confederation of the North, by the glorious battle of Copenhagen, [on 2nd April 1801] and this is the Victory, the credit for which Mr Pitt has the incredible candour and modesty to claim for his own!' The battle of course was won thanks to the great efforts of St Vincent himself, no one else, though in fact 'the great Chief' had nearly *lost* that battle by appointing as Commander-in-Chief of the British fleet the irresolute and utterly incompetent Admiral Sir Hyde Parker who, fortunately, had under his orders the celebrated if insubordinate Vice-Admiral Horatio Lord Nelson, to whom St Vincent really owed this great naval victory. It had also been thanks to that same Nelson who, by disregarding the orders and battle plans of the then Admiral Sir John Jervis (as St Vincent was still called at that time) and acting on his own initiative, that the Royal Navy had finally won the Battle of St Vincent, for which Jervis received his earldom and a small fortune in gold, while Nelson had to content himself with another medal and the title of Viscount, though he had expected an earldom too.

Addington's former First Lord of the Admiralty, fresh out of office in the summer of 1804, now lost all control whenever Pitt's name was mentioned. How could anyone take seriously Pitt's various de-nunciations, 'the perishable infamy of the fifteenth of March . . . Mr Pitt's most contemptible notions,' when compared to the views on these same subjects by himself, the Earl, 'the greatest seaman that ever existed'? St Vincent talked about the crooked merchants who provided victuals, ropes, stores, timber and canvas for the Navy as Pitt's special friends whom he was protecting through self-interest, as a result of 'the debt he owed to the Contractors, to whom no name is so dear, so welcome and so honoured, as the Right Hon. Gentleman's . . . Let him vindicate this [his] foul connexion with the Shipping interest, the ruin of the King's [naval] yards . . . let him explain this corrupt preference for Contracts and [private] Contractors [as opposed to the Royal naval yards] . . . Audacious Minister, criminal perversion and double guilt!' Indeed, it almost sounded like the witches' incantations from *Macbeth*!

As far as naval strength was concerned, he considered it no more than rubbish when Pitt stated the number of gunboats the Royal Navy had available 'fit to repel the actual attempts of the enemy, is at this moment more immaterial, and less adequate to the exigency of the danger, than at any period of former times', claiming that 'the enemy possessed an increased power of effecting an invasion beyond any former period'. He further disputed Pitt's notion that the best means of meeting this particular challenge was by providing a large force of gunboats to defend Britain and his charges that the Admiralty were guilty of 'delay and gross neglect, in not preparing a quantity of this craft to meet the enemy in his own way'. The Earl was outraged. As for the importance of flat-bottomed gunboats, he said, 'we will be bold enough to tell the Colonel [of the Cinque Ports, Pitt], that the boasted thousands of Bonaparte's craft could not approach a single ship of the line, or even a frigate, without inevitable destruction'. Pitt, however, was talking about *defending* the English coastline with flat-bottomed boats similar to those which had been built for a different purpose as part of Napoleon's *offensive* strategy. St Vincent now rightly contended that it was ships of the battle line, frigates and cruisers, which were going to have to meet, stop and destroy any enemy flotilla long before it ever reached English shores. Pitt's new flotilla would not only have been incapable of doing that, but would 'literally have taken men out of the ships of the line to man this craft', as indeed Admiral Decrès was already learning at Boulogne. Unfortunately, St Vincent then claimed the government would have to buy hundreds of these gunboats from merchant yards for Prime Minister Pitt 'was too much a friend of the Contractors to think of building them in the [royal] dock-yards' where it would have been cheaper. In other words St Vincent accused Pitt of doing this as a favour to monied interests, his friends. St Vincent, however, neither knew the real Pitt nor cared to do so. He could be as ruthless as Pitt when it came to a fight to the finish – no holds barred – describing Pitt's small-craft proposal as nonsense that would end in 'folly and inevitable ruin'. 'We pledge the triple laurel of his [St Vincent's] victories over *all* the enemies of England, over the foe in arms, over mutiny, and over corruption – we pledge all the hard earned glory of Lord St Vincent's name', to support this evaluation justified by half a century's experience at sea and 'the acquirement and exercise of all the knowledge of all the branches of the naval profession' [that] 'the safety of the country will never be at hazard.'

St Vincent attacked Pitt's policies on the grounds of efficiency and cost and this time he was on very solid ground. During his three-year stewardship at the Admiralty he had carried out painstaking inquiries into all phases of operations, both at the Admiralty and at all the naval yards which he personally inspected – including those spheres related to the Naval Board – and gathered an immense amount of detailed information and statistics to provide all the evidence he needed. For example, although William Pitt claimed that it was much cheaper to build a 74-gun ship of the line through private contract at a merchant's yard than at one of the King's yards, St Vincent established that this was not so. Admiralty books in fact put the cost of a 74-gun battleship at £41,875 in a merchant's yard in January 1803, while it cost only £36,668 for the identical ship on the stocks in a Royal naval yard. As for Pitt's wild accusations against St Vincent's office, the admiral parried in turn calling the Prime Minister 'a false, a factious, and a calumniating accuser . . . a wilful enemy and opponent of the wisest and justest counsels'.

Pitt had stated that St Vincent had greatly reduced the number of men working at the King's shipyards. The former First Lord countered this accusation saying that he had, after careful investigation and analysis, simply eliminated the number of non-productive workers which had been 'scandalously and fraudulently swelled' and in reality had fired only 514 of the 3,877 dockyard workers, and those for being rebellious, blind, infirm, or incompetent. As for Pitt's claim that the number of seamen had been decreased drastically by St Vincent, 'the Noble Earl' stated that this was utterly false. For instance, Parliament had allowed the number to rise from 41,040 seamen in 1803 to 78,000, and with the marines serving on board, this brought the total to 100,636 men. Thus the First Lord 'had exceeded the bounds of his duty, having raised by his unparalleled energy, a greater number of men than the vote of Parliament' had called for 'and 14,636 more than Mr Pitt thought proper to state'.

The real cause of the poor state of the Royal Navy in 1801, when St Vincent had assumed the post of Commissioner for the Admiralty, was, he claimed, the Navy Board. The political appointees to the Board were incompetent and lacked vigilance. It was to them that most of the Navy's annual budget (£12,350,606 in 1804[1]) had been entrusted and they who decided how that money was to be spent without any further audit. They alone ran the navy yards and, though told time and again of the corruption there, did nothing 'while the officers of one of the yards were quarreling like banditti for their plunder, and daily accusing and criminating each other, to the manifest danger of subordination and discipline'. And although the Navy Board's own investigating committee duly confirmed major malpractices the Board 'immediately consented to bury all the past in oblivion'.

Finally St Vincent approached a subject of special importance to him, involving in the process an admixture of fresh accusations, some of which were intentionally misleading, slanderous and low, while others, unfortunately for the nation, were very true indeed. In order to pay the inflated bills for goods never received and services never performed or, if performed, done badly, the admiral stated that, 'The flagitious hands of the Minister have invaded and usurped the powers and privileges of Parliament!' by bypassing the proper agent to raise and approve the naval budget. 'The very sanctuary of the Constitution has been profaned and rifled by the sacrilege of the Treasury! . . . The Navy-Board has conspired with the King's Minister to raise FOUR MILLIONS of money [in addition to the annual budget], without the knowledge of Parliament, in contempt and defiance of it' in order to pay 'bills for NAVAL SERVICES never performed, made payable to [the Scottish contractors] Messrs. Donaldson, Glenny, and others, who had performed no service . . .' Melville, too, he said was directly involved in this bias in the placing of contracts through 'the Scots coercion' resulting in the value of contracts to merchants north of Hadrian's Wall increasing a dramatic 'five times' above what it had been under Addington.

Then St Vincent went for the jugular of Pitt's administration by attacking the 'partial, unjust, and despotic influence of Lord Melville'. He continued: 'We denounce and proclaim the high crime and misdemeanour of the Viscount Melville, formerly Treasurer of the Navy, in withdrawing from the Bank of England, contrary to the law (st. 25 of the King, c. 31), the money issued from the Treasury for the service of the Navy; and in converting the use of it to his own profit, at the hazard of his personal solvency.' It was an amazing accusation, most of it quite senseless, and one which was to shake both veterans at the bar and the Pitt establishment. Napoleon was to follow the proceedings with glee.

He further claimed, 'We are prepared and desirous to prove, that the Noble Viscount could not have obtained possession of any part of the public money voted for the naval service, without a wilful violation of the law, and a systematic breach of his duty, coupled either with fraud upon the Bank of England, or collusion with the Lord of the Treasury', and that ultimately 'the sum of one hundred thousand pounds sterling, and to the full amount and extent of all the gain, profit and emolument, he shall hereafter be proved to have derived from the said iniquitous and illegal traffic, hazard, and conversion.' He went on to denounce 'the high misdemeanour and delinquency of the LORDS OF HIS MAJESTY'S TREASURY; and the high breach of duty and violation of the law committed by the Comptroller of the Navy, in conniving at, and permitting these illegal and criminal abuses. The Lords of the Treasury we make publicly responsible to the law for participating in the crime of the VISCOUNT MELVILLE, and for actually receiving loans and accommodation from the funds of the Navy, which they knew him to have illegally withdrawn from the Bank, and of which the law expressly prohibited him or his executors from ever, by any means, obtaining the possession and disposal', – all this the much incensed St Vincent concluded, from monies that 'were actually wanted for the Navy of Great Britain!!!'

This accusation was the keystone of St Vincent's *Memoirs*, a vicious attempt using lies and distortion combined with very real facts and evidence, amid summaries of the important and valuable work which he himself had accomplished as perhaps one of the finest administrators of the Admiralty during its long history, an attempt to get back at Pitt and bring down his government. Politics were politics, war or no war, and personal animosity was as biting as sulphuric acid. Jealousies were rife, even among naval commanders as they vied with one another for commands and ships. It was under this intense pressure that both Pitt and Melville now worked. Despite these accusations and defamations, perhaps as great as any new Government had hitherto had to sustain, Pitt settled in at Downing Street and Melville at the Admiralty with a disinterestedness, maturity and calm that no doubt amazed friends and enemies alike. When the chips were down, regardless of what St Vincent and others might say, it was a surprisingly efficient Admiralty Board that assumed its proper role. Equally, superbly trained naval officers, far from the din of Parliament and smoke-filled panelled rooms in Pall Mall, manned the ships and, once at sea, broke the seals of the orders issued by Admiral Sir William Cornwallis.

Secret [on board the] *'Culloden'*, in Torbay, 25th April 1803,
*George Campbell, Esq., Rear-Admiral of the Blue, to Captains
Searle, Ferrier, Bedford, Winthrop, and Pearson.*

Whereas it is intended that a general impress of seamen should take place at
the different ports and places along the adjacent coast [Dartmouth,
Paignton, Brixham, Torquay, Teignmouth and Salcombe], and that preparation should be made with the utmost secrecy and caution to perform that
service with promptitude and effect, you will, immediately on receipt of
these orders, select from the crew of his Majesty's ship under your
command a sufficient number of trusty and well disposed men to man three
boats, with as many marines and petty officers as you may judge necessary to
send in each, under the orders of a lieutenant, to whom you will deliver a
press warrant accordingly . . . You will endeavour to have previous
communication with one of his Majesty's Justices of the Peace for the
district, applying to him to back the warrants, taking especial care to cause as
little alarm as possible.

*Dispatch – Sir William Cornwallis, Admiral of the Blue, to Rear-Admiral
George Campbell*, 25th May 1803. *'Dreadnought'*, at sea.

The Right Honourable Lord Hobart, one of his Majesty's principal
Secretaries of State, having signified his Majesty's pleasure that all ships and
vessels belonging to the French Republic should be seized or destroyed by
any of his Majesty's ships that may fall in with them; you are, in consequence
therefore hereby required and directed to seize or destroy all ships and
vessels belonging to the French Republic . . . All ships or vessels belonging
to the Batavian Republic are to be detained and sent into port . . .

Dispatch – Sir William Cornwallis, Admiral of the Blue, to Captain Wilkinson,
26th July 1803 [regarding secret signals to be used by the British
squadron when identifying each other off Brest].

BY DAY

The first ship making the signal shall hoist a flag *RED*, over a flag *WHITE*
with a *BLUE CROSS*, at the main top-gallant mast-head. To be answered by
a flag *YELLOW*, at the same place. The ship first making the signal should
then hoist a flag quartered *RED* and *WHITE* at the *fore top-gallant mast-head*.
Then the ships shall each show their respective number upon the list of the
Navy.

BY NIGHT

The ship first making the signal is to show *two lights, one over the other*, and
burn *one false fire*. To be answered by *three lights of equal height, where best seen*
and burning *two false fires*. The ship first hailed shall answer 'King George';
The ship which hailed shall reply 'Whom God'; Then the ship first hailed
shall say 'Preserve'.

I desire that my Body if I die at sea may be sewed up in an old cot or canvass, and thrown from the gangway into the sea in the same manner as the seamen are buried.

Last Will and Testament of William Cornwallis

ENGLAND WAS AGAIN at war with France and the new First Lord of the Admiralty, Henry Lord Melville, had seen fit to confirm the appointment of Sir William Cornwallis as Commander-in-Chief of the Channel Fleet (or Western Squadron as it had been formerly known) made by Lord St Vincent under Prime Minister Addington's administration. Indeed it had been about the only thing those two bitter rivals, Melville and St Vincent, could agree on. Admiral Cornwallis was the best man to ensure the safety of the British Isles by commanding the first line of defence in the form of a fleet extending from Brest in the north to Gibraltar in the south. It was the French fighting navy, the ships of the line and frigates stationed in those deep-water harbours with which he was principally concerned, rather than the flotilla of gunboats and transport vessels in the northern Channel ports, for there could be no crossing without a powerful naval escort.

Yet on the face of it, Cornwallis was an extraordinary choice for those two hard-bitten opponents; the only senior admiral (out of the seventy-three admirals and vice-admirals of the Royal Navy) who not only had never commanded a fleet or squadron in a major action (though in his earlier years at a lower rank he had participated in many battles) but who had also been court-martialled and censured for having refused to take up a new command in the West Indies in 1798. What is more, he was an aristocrat in a navy where the vast majority of senior officers, that is, rear-admirals and above, such as Collingwood, Pellew, Hardy, Calder, Louis, St Vincent and Nelson, were all men of middle class background.

He was a surprisingly quiet and retiring gentleman for a high-ranking naval officer in an age when such men were still often known for their *bonhomie* and loud, gruff orders. The son of Charles, fifth Lord and first Marquess Cornwallis and six years younger than his brother, the recently created first Earl, the Admiral jokingly told an editor of the *Naval Chronicle*, interviewing him after he had been named to his new post in the Channel, that he would not be found at court or at the select balls to which he had been invited prior to going to sea again, preferring instead his secluded country estate, Newlands (situated three miles from Lymington and ninety-three miles from London) where the only society he would be enjoying would be that of his cabbages. And when, in the early months of 1805, he was forced to return to Cawsand Bay for new tillers and received a 17-gun salute from the ships at anchor, he returned these, as the *Naval Chronicle* noted once again, 'drily observing there was not any occasion for all this fuss and ceremony on his being obliged to come into port to refit'. Nor at that time did the Admiral think it the moment to enjoy a little leave. 'He will not accept any invitation on Shore, as the Service requires his attention on board his Ship.' He was a sailor and the Royal Navy was his family.

Unlike his elder brother (the celebrated General Cornwallis who had fought in the American War of Independence and who had then twice accepted the post of Governor General of India) and, indeed, unlike most of his fellow officers, William Cornwallis had never married. It was a lonely sort of existence, although when he was on one of his extremely rare visits ashore he did take a keen interest in horses and his library. Cornwallis was a relatively warm-hearted chap, however, once one got to know him. Somehow one could never be jealous of this rather plump aristocrat with the red face (though a relatively abstemious partaker of spirits) whom the seamen and midshipmen affectionately referred to as 'Billy go tight' and 'Mr Whip'. Another nickname well known throughout both the fleet and the navy was 'Blue Billy', referring to the blue pennant hoisted from his flagship to inform the captains of other vessels that they were to be ready to weigh anchor and get under way at the first opportunity, which always seemed to be flying since his new command over the Channel Fleet. Indeed, Cornwallis could never wait to get at the French, whom he had been fighting off and on now for nearly twenty-five years. Ironically, if any admiral in the navy looked like the caricature of John Bull, it was Cornwallis – right down to his paunch and perennially red face. Unlike John Bull, however, the Admiral was a man of very few words and of surprisingly quick and decisive action. The nation was at war and Sir William was in command of the number one fleet whose job it was 'to seize or destroy' all French vessels of war once and for all.

It was no accident that both the present and previous First Lord had requested this particular admiral, 'the veteran Cornwallis' as the *Naval Chronicle* referred to him. Although St Vincent, as we have seen, considered himself 'the finest seaman in history', he begrudgingly conceded Admiral Cornwallis a respectable second place. Cornwallis had first gone to sea in 1755 at the tender age of eleven and never regretted it, even now, fifty years later. He had served in North America and the West Indies, off the west coast of Africa, in the Mediterranean and in the Far East. His bravery in numerous naval actions had not gone unnoticed by commanders under whom he had served. He knew the French and knew them very well indeed.

One exploit in particular attested to his gallantry. In June 1795 he commanded a squadron of seven ships off the Brest coast, which was being pursued by thirty French vessels under the command of Admiral Villaret-Joyeuse. Cornwallis, at great personal risk to himself, turned his flagship back to protect a much damaged vessel – the *Mars*, commanded by Sir Charles Cotton – which was lagging far behind and surrounded by two divisions of French ships. The French admiral, perhaps thinking Cornwallis had been reinforced by the rest of the British fleet, suddenly retreated and Cornwallis thus saved that ship, escorting it back to Plymouth.

Cornwallis also had a good knowledge of men, ships and the sea that no one would or could contest. He always demanded the finest officers in his squadrons and expected nothing less than the best from them. Either they were good officers or they were transferred to a different theatre of war. Cornwallis had spent less time on land during his long career than the vast majority of his fellow officers and only a handful of senior officers could even approach this record.

If Nelson often fumed among his colleagues about the rich enemy ships that had eluded him, about the injustice of the distribution of prize money when, on the rare occasion, he did capture valuable enemy vessels (and he spent years in court suing St Vincent on this very account) or about a less than able Commander-in-Chief he had to serve under, such as Hyde Parker, he could never complain about 'Blue Billy'. Nelson respected Cornwallis as a sailor as much as he admired him as the good friend he had been for over two decades, going back to those perhaps better earlier days when they had shared a mess at Jamaica. Nelson claimed that it was Captain Cornwallis who, in 1780, had brought him aboard his ship and back to England, enabling him to get the medical help that had saved his life. 'It is my pride and pleasure to boast of your friendship', Nelson was to write to him at the end of the century, while describing Cornwallis privately to Collingwood as 'a very good officer and an aimiable character'. A perfectly modest man, Nelson and his band of brother officers could only admire and respect him, but most British historians, through sheer ignorance no doubt, have disparaged him, referring simply to the years 1801-1806 as those when he served 'without any opportunity of distinction' while Admirals Lord Hood, St Vincent and Nelson, to name a few, clearly stole the limelight.

In fact, it was Cornwallis, the unobtrusive hero, not the more flamboyant and charismatic Nelson, who was to be named to the most sensitive, critical and, indeed, difficult post, commanding the seas off the coast of France, Spain and Portugal. It was to be *his* decisions as to tactics, strategy, objectives and commands that were to be responsible for controlling most of the powerful French fleet – and very powerful it was, regardless of St Vincent's emotional antics – sheltered in the harbours at Brest, Rochefort, Lorient, El Ferrol, La Coruña and Cadiz.

Sixty-one years old in May 1804, the *Naval Chronicle* of that year described him as being 'of the middle size, stout and portly, with a certain degree of prominence before, which may be supposed to add dignity to a Commander-in-Chief'. He was in good health most of the time for a man of his age – sixty-one being the equivalent of perhaps seventy-five today – especially as he had served very long stretches at sea in damp vessels, within the cramped quarters of ships never over 190 feet long. His love for the navy and respect for the service and duty imposed upon him by his nation made Cornwallis, a relatively wealthy gentleman in his own right, continue at his station off the coast of Brest and the island which gave that station its name, Ushant. There were younger men who could have assumed that wearying command, with its reputation for more terrible and more prolonged storms and unremitting cold, grey weather than any other, but Cornwallis demanded nothing more of life or his nation than the privilege of commanding his Majesty's Navy in the Channel, despite the aches and pains of old age, including more serious eye problems now, and a growing physical fatigue that he could not always disguise.

Two other commands were nearly as important as that of Cornwallis – Admiral Lord Keith's off the Downs and Admiral Lord Nelson's off Toulon. In addition, another fleet was stationed off Jamaica to protect British West Indian colonies and shipping, while yet another served in the Indian Ocean to protect increasing British interests from continuing French harassment. Smaller naval units could be assigned to the African coast or South Atlantic possessions and trade routes, while three or four British warships were detached and assigned to protect immense merchant convoys averaging eighty or more heavily laden ships between the West Indies and Great Britain and convoys of well over 100 ships plying the seas between England and India. Although the total number of vessels of the Royal Navy in 1804 seemed substantial – 88 ships of the line, 128 frigates and another thirteen 50-gun ships (in the fourth-rate category)[2] – these were widely dispersed over the seven seas. It was rare indeed, for instance, for any admiral to actually have under his immediate command more than 20 ships of the line (that is, the largest battleships of 64 to 120 guns), which is why history relates very few major naval encounters at this time. Aboukir Bay, Cape St Vincent and Copenhagen were very rare battles indeed.

Admiral Lord Keith, whose flagship was stationed off the Kent Downs, had a total of twenty-one ships of the line and twenty-nine frigates under his command, eight of these under Admiral Thornborough off Texel, Heligoland and Helvoet. The colourful if frequently disobedient Commodore Sir Sidney Smith had eight smaller vessels off Flushing. Although Lord Keith's command also included the entire coastline of Holland and what is now Belgium as well as the French coast where the National, or Imperial, Flotilla was gathering, he did not keep any battleships stationed there permanently off Dunkirk, Etaples, Boulogne or Le Havre. Instead, the Admiral maintained smaller vessels there which could approach closer to shore even in shoal water to harass the flotilla or bombard harbours. Off the Downs, Admiral Keith kept under his immediate orders five ships of the line, one 50-gun ship, four frigates and numerous smaller vessels to protect the southern coast of England, with another seven ships of the line in port being repaired or within easy call. Altogether he commanded a fleet comprising some 176 vessels of all classes. His initial orders from the Admiralty, received back in October 1803, did not change much during the ensuing months of that first year of resumed hostilities, though, with the growing awareness of new activity in the French coastal ports, Admiral Thomas Louis' small squadron off the coast of Boulogne was gradually being strengthened.

Off Toulon the Commander-in-Chief of the Mediterrranean Fleet, Admiral Lord Nelson, had under his command thirteen ships of the line and one 50-gun fourth-rate, eleven frigates, ten sloops of war and eleven smaller vessels.

Admiral Cornwallis' fleet for its part comprised a total of thirty-three ships of the line, ten frigates and numerous smaller vessels, while in the West Indies, Sir John Duckworth and Commodore Sir Samuel Hood had another eight battleships and a dozen frigates. The former North American command had, since the establishment of peace with the new American Republic, been reduced to a handful of frigates.

Only two other smaller commands are worth mentioning. Some eight frigates or so were stationed off Guernsey and Jersey, under the temporary orders of Sir James Saumaurez, and another six frigates defended the Irish coast under Lord Gardner's pennant.

As impressive as Cornwallis' fleet strength at first appears, in fact, not all these vessels were available at any one time, as a rotation of ships was constantly taking place between the Channel and their principal dockyard and victualling port of Plymouth for supplies and brief refittings or longer ones when substantial damage had to be repaired, usually caused by the violent storms. Others sometimes were not 'on station' because of the storms, having been blown hundreds of miles away. The remaining ships were then divided into squadrons appointed to different substations, watching and blocking ports along hundreds of miles of very rugged French and Spanish coast. Cornwallis kept a small squadron of at least six ships of the line off Ushant, which was his personal station and 'headquarters' for the fleet, while the main inshore squadron of another half-dozen vessels stood off the entrance to Brest itself. One squadron was responsible for Rochefort, while yet another was to be found far to the south, off Finisterre and the north-west coast of Spain, to watch El Ferrol and La Coruña. As his fleet was so dispersed, it was hardly apparent that he did in fact have over sixty vessels of all types and classes at his command.

In May 1804, the entire Royal Navy comprised 405 vessels, including all the fleets at sea (excluding ships assigned to harbour service, lighters and some 624 very small armed boats temporarily on duty protecting England's coastline). The number of ships of all classes actually built for King George's navy was not particularly impressive when compared to Napoleon's herculean undertaking. Between 1st January 1803 and 1st January 1804 only five 74-gun ships had been built in the United Kingdom (one in the King's naval yards, four by private contract in merchants' yards) and one had been captured from 'the enemy'. What was particularly distressing to fleet commanders, however, was that, by 1st January 1804, in the category of ships of the line, only two more 74s were on order to be built. Equally, during 1803 no cruisers had been built in the King's yards and only four in merchants' yards, although forty-eight could be added to this number as private vessels were purchased or captured from the French, and others went to sea privately with letters of marque and were known as privateers. The term 'cruiser' referred to naval vessels (sometimes two or three) employed on detached operations – away from the main fleet – and could be anything from 50-gun fourth-rates and frigates (which ranged from 28 to 44 guns), to sixth-rate vessels (postships of 20 to 24 guns), sloops of war (not to be confused with the single-masted pleasure craft of the 20th century) mounting between 14 and 28 guns, bomb vessels, fireships, gun-brigs and cutters.

The real problem, however, was that there were not enough ships of the badly needed frigate-class (fifth-rates) and every fleet commander was crying out for them. Only three had been built in 1803, another seven added to this number (chiefly captured from the French) and a mere seven more were on order to be built the following year, despite the fact that four British frigates had been 'captured, destroyed or wrecked'. Thus, protest as St Vincent might, there were indeed excellent reasons for William Pitt's accusations against the navy under St Vincent and Addington, reasons why men such as Cornwallis, Keith and Nelson were in despair.

The figures for 1804, however, showed some changes, including the greater toll of British vessels. Twenty-one ships had been lost to the newly reinforced French coastal batteries and appalling weather conditions. The seemingly defiant aggressiveness on the part of British captains to challenge the French often under the most adverse conditions to themselves, exhibiting an almost foolhardy gallantry, led to the toll being heavier than it might otherwise have been. No doubt, Napoleon and Decrès greatly envied the British 'foolhardiness' when compared to the general mediocrity of French naval captains and their at times almost pusillanimous attitude toward their adversaries. It was therefore inevitable that the British lost more warships under the category of 'captured, destroyed or wrecked', than the French who rarely even ventured from their own ports to challenge the British, to the great chagrin of French Naval Prefects.

Thus by January 1805 the Royal Navy had 83 ships of the line actually commissioned and at sea (including six more first-rate vessels, i.e. ships of between 100 and 120 guns). Surprisingly though, most of these had only 18-pounders, and indeed only eight 74-gun vessels out of the total of 83 ships could boast 24-pounders, (unlike the more powerful armament on French Imperial battleships). To these could be added another theoretical forty ships of the line not available for service, chiefly due to being in a state of total disrepair. The active list also comprised 17 three-deckers within this number (ships of 90 to 120 guns), and 66 two-deckers (third-rate ships of the line carrying 64 to 80 guns), and then 13 fourth-rate vessels of 50 to 56 guns (and two more not in service) which were more powerful than frigates, but not quite ships of the line; and finally 101 frigates, with another 18 removed from service.

These January 1805 figures showed an increase of eight ships of the line brought into service during 1804 and of an additional fifteen frigates, despite the ever-rising toll on these vessels from war and weather. By now there were 473 vessels in commission, including fourth-rates, frigates, (fifth-rates), postships (sixth-rates), sloops of war, bomb- and fireships, gun-brigs and cutters,[3] thanks to the extraordinary efforts of the new

First Lord of the Admiralty, Melville, and Pitt's administrative support. Furthermore, Lord Melville announced that twenty-six ships of the line were either on order or being built (as opposed to nineteen under St Vincent). Only another fifteen of the badly needed frigates were under construction, but to this figure could be added ten more purchased or captured, thereby bringing the total up to twenty-five. An additional thirty-nine smaller vessels of all classes were also being built or under order now. During 1804, Britain lost three ships of the line, (captured, destroyed or wrecked), four fourth-rates but only three frigates. That same year Pitt built or purchased forty-five 12-gun gun-brigs and thirteen 18-gun brig-sloops, thus reflecting the Prime Minister's decision *not* to build the many hundreds of shoal-craft and gunboats the very lack of which he had so sharply criticised St Vincent's navy for in March 1804. However, the naval budget had been increased by a few million and between January 1804 and January 1805 the First Lord built or purchased an additional 119 vessels of all classes, whereas St Vincent, the previous year, had increased these numbers by a mere twenty-nine. Complain and vituperate as the despotic St Vincent might about the invincible strength of the Royal Navy during his three-year stint in office, the figures speak for themselves, reflecting a much less complacent and altogether much more vigorous attitude by the Admiralty under Lord Melville to gird the nation's loins. William James, for one, willingly gave credit to him when he acknowledged this in his *Naval History*: 'At no former or subsequent time[4] have eighty-seven British ships of war been launched within the year . . . Nothing can better demonstrate the exertions made by the new lord of the admiralty [Melville] . . . to recover the British navy from the low state into which it had previously fallen [under St Vincent].'

It was all very well to increase the number of ships and vessels – as indeed Napoleon was now doing – but they required well-trained officers to command them, an obstacle Napoleon could never seem to overcome. In time of war a reserve corps had to be activated to expand the officer cadre as greatly as possible. Most surprisingly Melville enlarged the naval officer corps by only 20 men during the period when he had commissioned 87 new warships and purchased another 32, bringing the total number of officers up from 3,662 in January 1804 to 3,682 by the following January! It was most extraordinary and has never been explained. Whereas the number of admirals and vice-admirals had not changed much – there were 9 more admirals in 1805 making a total of 50, and 4 more vice-admirals, or 36 in all – while the number of promotions from the rank of post-captain to rear-admiral had been increased by 13, bringing the figure up to 63 in January 1805, thereby preparing the way for a partial expansion of the much needed senior officer command at the squadron level by well experienced men. Decrès for his part was forced to put hundreds of newly launched vessels into mothballs for want of officers and crews. The Royal Navy, if not pushed to such extremes thanks to Pitt's decision not to build a large number of gunboats similar to those being built in France, nevertheless was very often short of officers and crews. Many Royal Navy warships, therefore, put to sea with inadequate ships' complements and frequently stopped even friendly merchant vessels at sea, including East Indiamen, in order to press trained sailors.

Naval administration was an extraordinarily complex, even antique, affair, which had emerged with true Darwinian evolution over the past few hundred years. In fact 100 years earlier the Royal Navy had been in a most deplorable state, and one shudders to think what a St Vincent would have said had he been named First Lord at the beginning of the eighteenth century. In reality the Georgian navy had built on the superb job quietly done over a period of several years by one of the greatest reformers in the history of the Royal Navy, Admiral Lord Anson, who while serving as First Lord of the Admiralty from 1751 to 1762, transformed this service into the effective fighting machine it now was. Amongst other steps he replaced the combination of part-time aristocratic admirals and an abundance of ill-educated rough captains and admirals, with the sea-going career officer, which had attracted and made way for the educated middle-classes as well as the serious aristocratic officers, such as Cornwallis and Rear-Admiral Alexander Cochrane.

The Royal Navy was administered through several organisations and, in theory, by the Secretary of State. In reality, however, the navy was run by the Admiralty Board, the Navy Board, and the Victualling Board, though the Admiralty and Navy Boards were the keys to the organisation. The First Lord of the Admiralty was always a political appointee, usually someone with a specialised knowledge of the navy, such as an admiral, though someone like Melville, or, later, Churchill, could also be brought in. The First Lord was a part of the cabinet and sat in on cabinet meetings concerning the navy and he, the Secretary of State for War and the Prime Minister would co-ordinate policy.

Lord Melville was a good choice in this respect because, as a senior member of the party and a long-time friend of Pitt and the other key political figures of the day, he had an unusual degree of political independence and authority. He was, in fact, the political head of the Admiralty Board, but the man holding this post had to be *able*, unlike so many other political posts of the day. Melville made no pretence about being an expert in naval affairs, but he did take his new appointment in May 1804 most seriously and worked diligently at it, in spite of some criticism.

Melville headed his fellow 'Commissioners' of the Admiralty Board, each of whom had a special task. The First Lord was in charge of the general direction of all business, the First Sea Lord had to oversee all organisation in the event of war as well as the distribution of the fleet, the Second Sea Lord was responsible for personnel, the Third for material; the Fourth for stores and so on, while the two civil Lords oversaw works, buildings, hospitals, contracts and dockyard business, and a parliamentary secretary dealt with financial matters. But second to the First Lord, perhaps the most powerful and influential man, was a civilian, bearing the title First Secretary, or Permanent Secretary. In 1804 the post of First Secretary for the Admiralty Board was held by a Pickwickian character by the name of William Marsden.

Sixty years old when he accepted this position, Marsden, the son of a prosperous shipping agent and bank director, had served as secretary to the East India Company in Sumatra for nine years where he established his reputation as a scholar of linguistics and the history of Malaya, producing a *Dictionary of the Malayan Language* and later a grammar.

Although he had established upon his return from the East Indies a most profitable import-export business, William Marsden joined the Admiralty in 1795 as Second Secretary to Sir Evan Nepean, whom he replaced as First Secretary in 1804 at a salary of £4,000 a year (nearly three times what the average vice-admiral was earning). There he managed both the Admiralty's administrative business and its complicated political affairs, and was, as Rodger notes, 'the channel by which many promotions and appointments were arranged' as well as being 'the only official eyes and ears of the Board'. It was to him alone that all Admiralty correspondence was addressed (at least in theory) and who in turn was responsible for issuing all correspondence. Thus when Admirals Keith, Cornwallis or Nelson received fresh orders it was through the aegis of Secretary Marsden, to which were appended the signatures of three Lords Commissioners of the Admiralty.

*

If the Admiralty was naturally the instrument by which the Royal Navy was controlled, it fell to a totally separate body of men to manage the dockyards, the supplying of every type of naval stores and the construction and repair of all naval ships. This was done by the Navy Board. This Board's members were officially entitled the Principal Officers and Commissioners of the Navy, including the Controller (who served as Chairman of the Board), the Surveyor (responsible for all ship design and construction), the Clerk of Acts (who supervised the Board's secretariat), and the civilian Controllers of Accounts (who managed all financial transactions). A final member of the Navy Board, though in fact entirely independent of it, was the Treasurer of the Navy (a post formerly held by Lord Melville). He was responsible for all navy finances, including the paying of all officers and men through monies voted by Parliament.

The Admiralty and Navy Boards were totally separate entities, however, and, to confuse matters more, there also existed a body of men known as the Commissioners of the Dockyards who were, in theory at least, all members of the Navy Board, but, in reality, a detached service. Although these Commissioners ran and managed the dockyards, they received their orders from the Navy Board or from one of the Principal Officers. These Commissioners, therefore, could only report, warn, advise or supervise the dockyards, but were not entitled to initiate and issue orders to them. If, for instance, Admiral Cornwallis arrived at Plymouth and wanted to have one of his ships docked or repaired, in theory he could only do so by requesting the Navy Board to arrange this, but, in fact, he could sometimes go directly to the Commissioner for that dockyard and its master shipwright to arrange this without awaiting the Navy Board's approval.

Each dockyard was a world unto itself, headed by its own internal senior officer, a master shipwright, the master(s) attendant – responsible for the ships afloat, moored or in reserve, and all pilots – the storekeeper, the clerk of the cheque, and the master ropemaker.

What Admiral Lord St Vincent greatly criticised, however, was the Navy Board's system of issuing its own Navy Bills, without any means of surveillance or authorisation from either the Treasury or Parliament. The use of its own debt instruments permitted the Board to finance its own projects, which, during Pitt's new administration, St Vincent claimed to have risen to well over £4,000,000. Indeed, it was the Navy Board and the Treasurer of the Navy who came in for such heavy censure from St Vincent.

Naval stores were administered by the Navy Board, but not so victuals, which were regulated by the autonomous Victualling Board. It was second in size only to the Navy Board, managing both the victualling yards as well as stores at the dockyard ports. Then there were the Commissioners for Sick and Wounded Seamen (or Sick and Hurt Board) who supervised the navy's hospitals and saw to the prisoners of war. Last, but not least, there was the Ordnance Board – again totally independent of the Navy Board – responsible for providing the navy with its guns and ammunition and supervising all fortifications as well as the artillery and engineering corps.

Certainly a complex, if not mystifying, system for the French and Spaniards – indeed, to many a British politician or landsman not associated with the navy. However, for all the enormous theft, abuse and incompetence claimed by St Vincent, these organisations did generally keep three-quarters of the ships of the navy either at sea or ready for sea service, and between 1804 and 1805 they were to be put to the test as never before.

The Politics of War

The world powers are dying of indigestion.

Napoleon

WILLIAM PITT'S FINAL term as Prime Minister and Chancellor of the Exchequer of Great Britain had been difficult from the outset. King George III had refused to allow Charles Fox into the Government, which in turn led Lord Grenville and his cohorts to remain in the opposition as well. Only Pitt's winning over of Addington at the beginning of 1805, when the latter accepted the title of Viscount Sidmouth and the position as Lord President of the Council, permitted him to manage a working majority in Parliament, leading George Canning to comment acidly that Addington was like the measles, everyone having to have him once. If Pitt was never able to put full confidence in his new ally (Addington tendered his resignation more than once before withdrawing permanently that summer) there were three other factors which caused the Prime Minister even more anxiety, tapping his last reserves of strength: the precarious state of his health itself, the Melville Affair, and finally the necessity to create a new, third coalition against the French Emperor.

'I really think Pitt is done: his face is no longer red, but yellow; his looks are dejected; his countenance I think much changed and fallen, and every now and then he gives a hollow cough. Upon my soul, hating him as I do, I am almost moved to pity to see his fallen greatness', the Prime Minister's staunch Whig opponent, Thomas Creevey, MP, had recorded in his diary as early as May 1803. The death of Pitt's mother, Hester, the Dowager Countess of Chatham, the month before, was but one reason, however, for his ill health. 'He could retain nothing on his stomach, nor could he sit down to dinner without being sick,' his physician, Walter Farquhar, acknowledged. And, as his old friend John Ward related to a colleague, 'His physical powers are, I am seriously concerned to remark, perceptibly impaired . . . his lungs seem to labour in those prodigious sentences which he once thundered forth without effort.' Even the fresh sea air at Walmer could not revive a forty-five-year-old man who was slowly, painfully dying of alcohol poisoning. His skin was indeed turning yellow and his lungs often gasped for the oxygen they lacked, and yet he carried on, much to the amazement of the egregious Creevey, who described him when addressing Parliament at this time thus: 'Then came the great fiend himself – Pitt – who, in the elevation of his tone of mind and composition, in the infinite energy of his style, and the miraculous perspicuity and fluency of his period outdid (as it was thought) all former performances of his.' 'Detesting the Dog as I do,' Richard Sheridan acknowledged to Lady Bessborough, 'I cannot withdraw this just tribute to the Scoundrel's talents.' Quietly determined, Pitt was not to be denied his last few months of life, at the head of his Government.

Praise from both friends *and* enemies indicates just how remarkable Pitt was at a time when a lesser individual would have withdrawn from all public life. Instead he met with his cabinet frequently, personally carried out Government business, including most of the transactions for both the Foreign and War Offices, formulating national policy and answering attacks in the Commons throughout 1804 and until December 1805. That he was frequently suffering not only from gout and growing weakness, but from back and chest pains, not to mention his inability to hold down his food, was self-evident – it was not something Pitt could readily disguise. None the less he maintained a remarkable pace during these months, Government business suffering very little.

Troops were being raised and trained, coastal defences and the new Martello towers ringed the island and the navy's budget and manpower were increasing, thanks to Pitt's persistence and the able hand of Henry Lord Melville. Nevertheless the First Lord of the Admiralty was now having problems as a result of attacks by Pitt's bitterest foes, problems that were beginning to consume the Prime Minister as well by the opening months of 1805.

Melville was 'learning the conduct of the navy', Lord Grenville commented caustically, 'by studying the manoeuvres of the bathing machines at Worthing', while Lord Minto (Gilbert Elliot) more accurately thought him 'as likely to repair the evil [created during St Vincent's stint there] as any man that could have been placed at the head of the Admiralty'. St Vincent disagreed, of course, and his ill-measured attacks continued as he gathered more information with which he was to supply the Commission now carrying out an inquiry. Under Addington's previous administration Admiral Lord St Vincent had launched his own intensive inquiry into the administration of the Royal Navy covering the ten-year period from 1791 to 1801 and, in particular, into the actions of the Paymaster of the Navy, Alexander Trotter.

The Commission's report was finally released in February 1805 and came as a blow to Melville and Pitt. Among other things it was found that Paymaster Trotter had speculated with public funds to the tune of millions of pounds, but had repaid every penny. Unfortunately Lord Melville, as Henry Dundas, had been Treasurer of the Navy from 1782 to 1801 and, although that post was essentially a sinecure, he holding more important time-consuming cabinet posts during this same period as Home Secretary and Secretary at War, nevertheless was legally responsible for supervising the actions of the Navy Paymaster. Under the aegis of St Vincent, the Commission's report went a step further, accusing Melville himself of having been a party to Trotter's speculation and indeed of having profited from it. To make matters worse, Melville had, in fact, borrowed very large sums from the Paymaster during this same period (up to £30,000 at a time) which the First Lord openly admitted, though disclaiming any knowledge of where the money originally came from. What was worse still, Lord Melville, when questioned, now refused to say where the money he had borrowed had gone, which simply damned his position in the eyes of the general public. 'It was obvious that the funds diverted to other public services', Pitt's biographer Robin Reilly states, in fact 'had been used to finance the secret service'. 'It was clear', Reilly continues, 'that he had been culpably negligent in his supervision of the navy accounts', but had done nothing illegal himself.

As seen earlier, St Vincent was after Melville's scalp, regardless of the cost to individuals, the nation or even to his beloved navy, and he now pressed the attack, bringing all his considerable influence to bear in Parliament where he urged for impeachment. On 8th April 1805, the radical Whig and brewer, Samuel Whitbread, addressed a full House, moving eleven resolutions of censure against Viscount Melville, charging him with corrupt use of public funds. Pitt was simply staggered and, though his friends advised him to abandon Melville, to his credit he resolutely refused to do so. In order to avoid impeachment, Pitt moved for a Select Committee of Inquiry, while Charles Fox, George Ponsonby, Lord Henry Petty (the son of Lord Shelbourne, the Marquess of Lansdowne) and William Wilberforce went in for the kill, as George Canning, Viscount Castlereagh and Attorney-General Spencer Perceval attempted to defend a much shaken First Lord. When the House divided a few days later and the votes were tallied, it was discovered that there was a tie. The speaker, Charles Abbott, then cast the deciding vote – in favour of censure, in an attempt to bring down Pitt's administration. Utter pandemonium broke out in Westminster accompanied by the ebullient and pervasive fox-hunting politicians' shouts of 'view-halloo' resounding through the ancient structure, with cries for Pitt to resign.

Lord Malmesbury's son, Lord Fitzharris, who was present at this time, recorded the effect on the Prime Minister: 'I sat wedged close to Pitt himself the night when we were 216 to 216; and the Speaker, Abbott (after looking as white as a sheet, and pausing for ten minutes), gave the casting vote against us. Pitt immediately put on the little cocked hat that he was in the habit of wearing, when dressed for the evening, and jammed it deeply over his forehead, and I definitely saw the tears trickling down his cheeks . . . A few young ardent followers of Pitt, with myself, locked their arms together, and formed a circle, in which he moved, I believe, unconsciously out of the House.'

Melville's resignation was tendered and accepted forthwith, but the story was not yet finished. The self-righteous Samuel Whitbread moved for impeachment on 11th June and, although the motion was rejected by the House then, it was adopted a fortnight later. This resulted in the impeachment of Viscount Melville, followed by a trial in 1806 when he was acquitted on all charges. By then, however, it was too late for his old friend, William Pitt, who had died at the beginning of the year. The Wimbledon days long a thing of the past, Melville, of whom Admiral Cornwallis' brother had once said 'I can truly say that I never met a more fair and honourable man', withdrew to his estates in Scotland embittered and disillusioned.

Returning once more to 1805, Napoleon, who had been following the English Parliamentary proceedings with ill-concealed malicious delight, now wanted to take full advantage of this scandal which had shaken the British Government: 'Have a little pamphlet prepared on the Melville Affair', he ordered the Finance Minister, 'to show the immorality of the English Government', which was all the more ironic coming from the man who had ordered and executed the rape and occupation of several countries, filling his personal coffers with untold loot.

Before the month of April 1805 was out, the Royal Navy was without a leader and, with large French and Spanish fleets manned, armed and ready to sail, or already at sea, the English Prime Minister had to find a very special replacement for Lord Melville.

Everyone was expecting a man of the sea to be appointed, a seasoned veteran, a man who had commanded large squadrons during major naval engagements, someone who understood the situation off the coasts of France and Spain as well as the problems of navigating in those seas, a man in robust good health who could act vigorously. When however,

William Pitt selected a sailor who did not know the coasts of France and Spain well, indeed, who had not been at sea for decades, since he was a young officer, and who had achieved flag rank on land in London as a result of his administrative abilities in the navy, in fact, a man who not only had never commanded a squadron against the enemy, but who had never even commanded one in peacetime, the talk at the Admiralty, at the Chatham yards, at Portsmouth and Plymouth, was one of amazement and consternation. To make matters worse, Pitt had chosen a man who not only was not a gentleman born, nor even a member of the Church of England, but who was imminently due to celebrate his eightieth birthday! Pitt's friends and enemies alike were incredulous, for the newly appointed officer was none other than Sir Charles Middleton, a relative of Melville's, whom Pitt now raised to the peerage with the title of Baron Barham.

George III was not at all pleased, and St Vincent, jealous, while Thomas Creevey – for want of anything sensible to say – referred to the new appointee as 'the superannuated Methodist'. 'I deplore the choice you have made', Sidmouth informed the Prime Minister on 22nd April (he having two members of his own family in mind for that very post). 'It will, I fear, have the effect of weakening and lowering the Government, at a time when it is peculiarly important to give it additional strength and to raise its character', which sounded very strange indeed coming from this particular ex-Prime Minister. Generally, however, the feeling in the clubs of St James's was one of bewilderment, even of stupefaction. Bonaparte, too, was as astonished as he was delighted (at least initially), for like most Englishmen, he thought William Pitt was clearly losing his grip.

A result of the Melville Affair and Pitt's nomination of Barham as successor to the post of First Lord did indeed involve a further weakening of the British Government, threatening to bring it down, as both Viscount Sidmouth and Lord Hobart (the Earl of Buckinghamshire) resigned in the summer of 1805, Lord Camden now becoming President of the Council and Viscount Castlereagh, Secretary of State for War.

In September, a most anxious Pitt, physically weaker than ever before, his gout adding to his troubles, was forced to follow the King to Weymouth to implore him yet again to include in his Government, if not Charles Fox and Grenville, then at least prominent members of their parties fearing that otherwise the new Budget would not be passed by Parliament. King George remained as implacable as ever, apparently willing to risk political mayhem rather than admit Fox or one of his party to his councils; and so, in the words of Holland Rose, 'thus ended Pitt's last effort to form a national administration'. Disappointed though he was, Pitt returned to London and Downing Street to resume his duties, and the King to the esplanade.

Although the Prime Minister did on occasion make major mistakes in his appointments, his choice of Lord Barham was not one of them. Barham, as Charles Middleton, may have never served afloat in flag rank, but he had, instead, proved his rather unusual abilities ashore as Comptroller of the Navy. In this position he gave continuity and meticulous attention to the needs of the Royal Navy. As honest as he was hardworking, preferring a sea of ink to the vagaries of the oceans, he was a man with many enemies within the navy and without.

As Comptroller he had been responsible for ship design and building between 1778 and 1790, while also representing Rochester in Parliament. He later was named to the Board of the Admiralty where the main preoccupation then, as now, was the execution of the naval war against the French. Barham therefore knew every senior naval officer and his abilities, in addition to having a detailed working knowledge of the Admiralty itself. Nor was he a stranger to Pitt, whom over the years he had advised on a variety of naval matters. Pitt thus knew precisely what he was doing, and what to expect from his new First Lord.

Barham's naval policy was simple, maintaining strong Home and Channel Fleets for the protection of the country in time of war. Upon the return of Admiral Lord Nelson to England in August, the new First Lord, with a bookkeeper's wariness of the extraordinary actions taken by the Commander-in-Chief of the Mediterranean Fleet ever since abandoning his assigned station on the other side of Gibraltar, immediately ordered that the *Victory*'s journals be brought to the Admiralty for his personal scrutiny. After reading them, however, he conceded that the iconoclastic Nelson had indeed justified his acts and was worthy of an even higher command in the future.

Anxiety over his own failing strength or no, the approaching débâcle in Parliament over the 'Melville Affair' notwithstanding, Pitt had other matters as well to see to in governing the nation. Fortunately, the Royal Navy – unlike Napoleon's – could take care of itself, thanks to a variety of institutions tested by history and experience, particularly the Board of Admiralty and Navy Board. Due to a serious accident late in 1804, the Earl of Harrowby had to relinquish the portfolio of foreign affairs to a less talented gentleman, Lord Mulgrave, and, as a result, Pitt gradually took on the onerous problems relating to this post himself. His objective in this sphere was not merely to put an end to Napoleon's catastrophic interference in commerce, and his armies rampaging across international frontiers, but to bring about a sound, lasting European peace.

If the French Emperor were to be restrained, and indeed stopped, Great Britain would require firm allies on the Continent once again and a third coalition based on 'barrier treaties'. Pitt was to spend much time and effort in trying to create and then shore up these treaties. A restored balance of power had to be established with Austria controlling Northern Italy and Prussia the Low Countries, and Russia, Eastern Europe and the Near East. Pitt's aim, however, was not to establish or restore European 'national' justice – and hence Italian and Polish sensibilities were excluded from his analyses – but simply to raise effective military barriers against the present or any succeeding Napoleon.

Austria was certainly an important key to much of this. Francis II, the last Holy Roman Emperor, had seen Austria's *real* power in the lands of the Empire nearly spent as a result of the Treaty of Lunéville of February 1801 and a treaty with Austria, France and Russia in December 1802. Jealousies and acrimony now festered in many a princely heart, whether in southern Germany, Prussia, Austria or Russia. The possibilities of continuing instability and renewed hostilities were numerous, with Napoleon's continued expansion abroad in Holland, Switzerland and Italy (both in the Cisalpine or Italian Republic and Piedmont) destabilising the political and military situation of most of Western Europe.

Prussia, too, had lost in the process, including her domination of Northern Europe and, like Austria, by 1803 was also in a state of flux. Frederick William III found himself required to maintain an alliance with England because of Hanover – ironically the very property he so coveted but that could only be his by renouncing his ties with London and joining forces instead with the French. On the other hand, Frederick William had met with the Russian Tsar at Memel in June 1802 and, as a result, a growing if nebulous bond between the two empires appeared to be emerging, thanks in part to the prompting of the Prussian King's wife, Queen Louise, with her strong pro-Russian bias.

Great Britain's relationship with France had begun changing in October 1802 when Napoleon had annexed Italian territory and intervened in Switzerland, at a time when Talleyrand was favouring the creation of a 'Gallic Empire' or 'Empire of the West'. France's aggression on the Continent had forced Lord Hawkesbury (under Prime Minister

Addington's regime) to accept a complex and costly solution that he did not particularly like. 'Our policy must seek to use these aggressions to build a defensive system of alliance for the future, together with Russia and Austria', he insisted. Russia, like Prussia, was wavering at this time, declining a formal alliance with Britain, while at least supporting the Ottoman Empire against France in Egypt, which she wanted to remain under her sole influence.

With the resumption of war between France and Great Britain in May 1803, the great chess game resumed, France making the first move by securing a convention with Holland on 25th June 1803, the Dutch agreeing, under duress, to furnish France with many ships and 16,000 troops. On 19th October 1803, likewise under duress, Godoy signed an agreement with France under which Spain was to contribute 6,000,000 francs a month to Paris, Portugal later agreeing (under great pressure) to add another 16,000,000 francs.

The British could not even begin to match such moves, but, on 27th July 1803, Parliament at least called for all men between the ages of seventeen and fifty-five to drill and train to defend the nation. For Pitt to obtain new allies on the Continent, he had to demonstrate British military strength and determination as he organised army volunteers under state control, united militias, increased the strength of the regular army and created new coastal defences, while Lord Melville continued to devote his efforts to the navy. All this required the restoration of the much detested income tax, for everything, including subsidies to allies, depended on the availability of a full Treasury at a time when permanent taxes were only bringing in annually about £15,000,000.

Until 1803, accord with Russia had been the keystone of Napoleon's foreign policy, but then all changed. Much of the change was blamed on the unstable character of the new Tsar, Alexander I, who proved to be an unpredictable mixture of pro-liberal and staunch autocrat, though the liberal German element among his advisers tended to predominate. Alexander wanted to see good ties established with Germany, but even more than this, Russian expansion southwards in and beyond the Caucasus. He would take as much of the Ottoman Empire as he could get, including Constantinople if possible, hence his apprehension about French motives and moves in Ottoman Egypt. The Tsar had vacillated between negotiations with London first and then Paris, much of this initially pivoting round the question of who was to control Malta as Russia, too, wanted this strategically situated island. If the Tsar had then been angered by England's announcement in June 1803 that she

intended to retain her Maltese conquest, he was even more disturbed by
the First Consul's seizure and occupation that same summer of Hanover
and the Neapolitan ports, followed by the abduction and murder of the
Duke d'Enghien, which led to his decision to recall Russia's Ambassador
Oubril and to break off diplomatic relations with Paris.

William Pitt quickly got things moving on the diplomatic front in the
summer of 1804 when, on 29th June, he proposed an Anglo-Russian pact
for the purpose of taking Belgium and the Rhineland away from France.
Ambassador Nikolai Novosiltzoff was then sent to London – ostensibly
on a scientific mission – to negotiate personally with Pitt. Meanwhile, the
King of Sweden seemed to be moving almost as fast, Gustavus IV signing
a secret convention with Pitt's Government on 3rd December 1804,
giving England two military bases in the north in exchange for a subsidy
of £80,000. This was followed by a Swedish treaty of alliance with Russia
in January 1805. Even as England and Russia were reaching agreement
about the use of Russian troops in Corfu (as part of the strategy to rescue
Naples) and signing the Anglo-Russian treaty at Downing Street on 11th
April 1805, Pitt was preparing to dispatch General Sir James Craig with
an expeditionary force to Malta and Sicily.[1]

As usual England had to foot the bill for the allies and agreed to pay an
annual subsidy of £1,250,000 for every 100,000 men contributed by the
Continental powers in the struggle against France, while Holland was
secretly assured of acquiring Belgium, and Prussia the northern stretch
of the left bank of the Rhine. Russia and Great Britain would reinforce
Gustavus' army in Pomerania, which was set for the invasion of Hanover
and Holland. The gears were beginning to mesh at last and, although
Napoleon had forced Queen Maria Carolina of Naples to dismiss her
British Prime Minister, Sir John Acton, back in May 1804, and Naples
could never be counted on by the allies for real military help – as Nelson
for one could easily attest – Britain had yet to form alliances with Austria
and Prussia.

As seen earlier, Prussia and Russia had formed a defensive alliance on
24th May 1804 when Frederick William III and Alexander I had finally
reached agreement, Russia promising 50,000 men in the event that
Bonaparte strengthened his forces in Hanover or engaged in fresh
aggression east of the Weser.

Even as late as the spring of 1805, Tsar Alexander was uncommitted
either to France or Great Britain. Although the Anglo-Russian Treaty
was signed in London on 11th April of that year, it took other events to
decide the Tsar on its ratification at St Petersburg on 28th July, namely,

Napoleon's seizure of both the crown of Italy on 26th May and the Ligurian Republic of Genoa on 4th June. Indeed, news of the fall of Genoa in the first week of June was the proverbial last straw so far as Tsar Alexander was concerned: 'That man [Napoleon] is insatiable! . . . He is the scourge of the world. He wants war, he will get it, and the sooner the better!' And on 17th June he finally ratified the new alliance with Austria (which had been held up in limbo since 6th November of the previous year).

Count Simon Vorontzoff, the Russian minister at Vienna who was preparing the treaty that would co-ordinate efforts of the forces of Great Britain, Russia and Austria, explained Russia's view of the new alliance: 'As for the motives and justification of a coalition against Bonaparte, this can be recognised as just and necessary as a result of his violation of the treaties of Amiens and Lunéville, his assumption of the crown of Italy, the usurpation of Genoa, and, finally, all that may be expected in the future from his audacity and the enormous base of power that he has formed and with which he now threatens the whole of Europe'. The Austrians were convinced and four days later, on 9th August, signed the treaty, thereby completing the coalition against France. Nevertheless King Frederick William refused to join the Tsar (in spite of the alliance of May 1804) and, in mid July 1805, had also refused to allow Russian troops to cross Pomerania – alliance or no. This did not stop Austria, however. Buttressed by Russian military help and British gold, Francis II was to invade Bavaria, France's ally, on 11th September 1805 . . . little realising that Napoleon had already made the first move.

Historians have long debated the question of Napoleon's real military and political intentions for France in 1805 and, in particular, if he *really* did want to invade Britain and Ireland. Edouard Desbrière felt that the French Emperor's views fluctuated considerably and that this could be seen in the variety of plans he drew up over the period from 1803 to 1805. Was he simply buying time – as he later declared – in order to prepare the army for the launching of yet another great Continental war? 'There can be no question that the French could have occupied London without firing a shot', historian Georges Lefebvre has solemnly pronounced, among other statements of similar rarefied nonsense[2], although at least he was correct in describing the French leader as 'an incorrigible improviser' of tactics, which alone most accurately explains his 'method' of achieving his war aims.

In fact Napoleon Bonaparte was perhaps the supreme military juggler of all time. Of the many balls he seemed to keep suspended in perpetual motion, several concerned a variety of naval actions, such as direct attacks on Britain and Ireland, on South America and the Antilles, expeditions to the West Coast of Africa under the command of his brother Jérôme, others to the South Atlantic, to Egypt or even as far as India, and many of them involved the frequent major changes discussed in these chapters. Other balls involved mounting offensives on land, including full-scale Continental warfare. What Napoleon generally did as 'an incorrigible improviser' was to keep all the balls in the air at once, waiting for the precise moment when one was needed. If, for example, the French Mediterranean Fleet managed to combine with the squadrons at El Ferrol and Brest and, the weather and British permitting, reached Boulogne, he could launch the armada. After all, no one had conquered Britain since the 11th century! It would be a great coup! On the other hand, if the Austrian or Russian Emperors attacked and, in so doing, laid themselves open to an easy defeat, Napoleon could move in that direction. Between 1800 and 1812 he was to call up some 1,300,000 Frenchmen and they, added to the hundreds of thousands of troops furnished by his Continental allies, gave him the armies required to support almost any combination of plans that he might put together in his incessant juggling act.

One of these balls included a surprise letter, dated 2nd January 1805, addressed to 'Monsieur mon Frère', the King of Britain, calling for peace between the two countries. France and Britain, he said, 'may struggle for centuries' resulting in 'so much blood spilled to no real purpose', and though he, Napoleon, was now calling for an end to hostilities – 'Peace is my heart's desire' – he would resume the war if forced to do so, for after all 'War has always added to my glory'. What more did Britain possibly hope to achieve by continuing the fighting? 'In the past ten years your Majesty has gained more territory and riches than contained in all of Europe. Your country is at its most prosperous right now. What then do you expect to gain from a war?' The French Emperor then tried to anticipate some of King George's thoughts by asking what he hoped to achieve: 'To form a coalition with some of the Continental powers? The Continent shall remain calm; such a coalition would only enhance French preponderance on the Continent. To stir up internal dissension in France? Times have changed. Destroy our finances? A national economy based on a good agricultural foundation can never be destroyed. Take away France's colonies? Our colonies are of only secondary importance to us; and in any case does your Majesty not already possess more colonies than he can cope with?' In short, Napoleon was arguing

that, so far as Britain was concerned, the continuation of such a war was
'. . . pointless, utterly without reason . . . The world is quite large
enough to hold both of us and reason tells us that we can find the means
of overcoming all our differences if both parties wish to do so'. Napoleon
wanted a special treaty with Britain now, to forestall a general peace treaty
with all the major European powers, or to prevent Britain's financial and
military support and co-operation in the formation of a third coalition.

King George, who utterly detested the French (including the surviving
members of the House of Bourbon) and Napoleon in particular,
instructed Pitt to reply to 'the head of the French Government', on 12th
January. George III wished for peace for his subjects, Napoleon was
informed, but 'This can only be achieved by arranging for the future
peace and tranquillity of Europe, in other words, by guarantees which
would prevent the renewal of the dangers and miseries such as we now
face'. The British Government, therefore, found it impossible to
acquiesce with a favourable response without a peace treaty in concert
with 'the Continental powers and especially with the Russian Emperor'.

For Napoleon the offer of peace was just another ball to juggle with,
another ploy, but as Miot de Mélito commented, 'the significant step he
had taken with the King of England . . . was undertaken to prove that, in
the event he was caught up in a fresh war, he could say he had done
everything in his power to avoid it'. The truth was, as Miot, a close friend
and confidant of the Bonapartes, rightly pointed out, that 'the Emperor
. . . strongly desired a rupture of relations that would result in war in the
very theatre where French arms had achieved such great success in the
past', that is, on the Continent.

Stepping up Operations

With the same unprecedented energy and exertion, upon the breaking out of the present war, they [the Admiralty Board] dispatched Admiral Cornwallis with the squadron for Brest, WITHIN FORTY-EIGHT hours after it was known that hostilities would commence. They held that port of France in an uninterrupted blockade from almost the instant of the cessation of the peace . . .

St Vincent

When I contemplate all the difficulties which surround the extensive and complicated task I have undertaken, you will not suppose me insensible to the obstacles I have to surmount, and the exertions which the country has a right to expect from me. Under these circumstances I cannot pretend to be perfectly at ease.

Melville to Cornwallis, 4th June 1804

THE VAST NUMBER of intelligence reports reaching Admiral Cornwallis' flagship, the 110-gun three-decker, the *Ville de Paris*, at its sea station several leagues to the west of Ushant, not to mention the seemingly endless number of orders the Admiral was issuing himself to his half-dozen vice- and rear-admirals, were all a part of the daily routine for a commander in charge of a fleet of over forty-three battleships and frigates, dispersed in far-flung squadrons off the coasts of France, Spain, Portugal and Ireland. The operation was extremely complex when it came to communications, victualling, watering, supplies and ship repairs. Although there were no major naval battles involving powerful squadrons of ships of the line throughout this period, nevertheless British frigates and cruisers were involved in weekly skirmishes with the French. Inland squadrons of smaller vessels were posted off Brest, Lorient and Rochefort where they were required to venture as close as possible to those ports several times a week for surveillance purposes. They were to report on the number of vessels of every class in port, the specific state of readiness of each one, whether or not they had their full complement of men, what ships and vessels were still in the dockyards, what kinds of ships were receiving the most attention in those yards, what sort of armament the ships were fitted out with, the state of the harbour and coastal defences, what difficulties the French might be having in obtaining supplies or in manning their vessels and, finally, any information about troop movements to those ports and how many troops were actually on board ships ready to depart. It was a tall order and one man alone was responsible for co-ordinating it all – Admiral Cornwallis.

Although French warships rarely hauled out of Brest to challenge the British, despite Naval Prefect Louis de Cafferelli's orders to do so, new batteries were being installed overlooking the main sea approaches, guns powerful enough to sink vessels more than a mile away. If English warships could still easily approach much of the coastline, not so the main harbours, making it more and more difficult for Cornwallis to obtain the information he needed, which sometimes was limited to counting the masts protruding over the slate roofs of warehouses or the shallow hilltops. Guns or no guns, though, he was absolutely adamant about getting a *precise* count of French ships and, often as not, this meant getting dangerously close to French guns. Occasionally a British naval officer or spy would be put ashore to provide this data when all other means failed, a boat being sent to collect him several hours later – if he had not been caught in the meantime. Neutral merchant vessels – American, Danish, Swedish and Spanish – were also boarded upon leaving French ports, to confirm the information they had and to provide any additional news. When, on the rare occasion a few French warships would put to sea or a convoy of coastal freighters or gunboats were spotted, the Royal Navy invariably gave chase immediately like a pack of hounds after a fox.

Great Britain may not have been at war with Spain at the beginning of the year 1804, but, as an allegedly neutral country in time of war, Spain was openly succouring the French navy, offering them safe harbours and dry-docks for repairs. In fact, however, and unknown to Britain, a Franco-Spanish Pact had been secretly signed on 19th October 1803 calling for Spain to provision and repair French warships, while paying the French some 6,000 *livres* monthly (to be provided by treasure ships coming from America). Nevertheless, Spain continued to claim her rights as a neutral country, while Admiral Cornwallis for his part took a distinctively pragmatic attitude to any country – 'neutral' or not – engaged in aiding and abetting the elusive French.[1]

Alert as ever to fresh problems, even as early as the spring of 1804, Cornwallis could not discount the seemingly marginal role played by the Spanish, and in particular, that of the strategically situated, spacious twin ports of El Ferrol and La Coruña, on her northwestern Atlantic coast, close to Cape Finisterre. Thus when on 7th January 1804 Commodore Sir Edward Pellew reported from his recently launched flagship, the

Tonnant, that the situation did not look good, enclosing a detailed report on the growing enemy activity there, it received the Admiral's full attention.

Cornwallis suspected that if Spain were to be drawn into the war on behalf of the French within the near future, she could strengthen the enemy navy considerably. The French had four ships of the line and two frigates at the twin ports ready to put to sea now, two more in dry dock completely stripped for repair or condemnation, and another battleship at Cadiz, all of which had returned under the command of Rear-Admiral Jacques Bedout from the ill-fated San Domingo expedition. Spain for her part had eight ships of the line at El Ferrol and La Coruña, two of them nearly ready for sea, along with sixteen gun- and mortar-vessels. What worried Cornwallis now was that Sir Edward Pellew's small squadron of half a dozen vessels could shortly be facing not four or five, but twelve or thirteen battleships should the tide and fortunes of war change yet again.

Upon the resumption of hostilities with France the previous year, Admiral Cornwallis had assigned Sir Edward's squadron to Cape Finisterre with orders to prevent the ships and vessels at El Ferrol and La Coruña from joining with other naval units in the French Channel ports and from participating in an expected expedition against Ireland and/or Britain, or from returning to Toulon. At the same time Pellew was to prevent any other French vessels from putting into the Spanish ports, a difficult task, not made any easier by the frequent gales that had begun to whip that coast as well as the Channel ports to the north late in 1803 and which were to continue well into the spring of 1804. Indeed, because of the need for protection offered by a safe anchorage and to prevent them from being blown far off station, Pellew had selected nearby Betanzos Bay as a haven. It turned out to be a wise choice, if an irritating one for both the French and the Spanish. His squadron could put into neutral La Coruña for food supplies *and* gather intelligence on port activities in El Ferrol, located just across the small peninsula separating the twin ports.

Rear-Admiral Bedout's warships had put into El Ferrol and La Coruña by accident, due to Bedout's illness (he was shortly to be replaced by Gourdon) and the poor state of his vessels. They had come, too, to replenish totally exhausted supplies and to seek hundreds of seamen to replace those lost in battle, at sea and during the great yellow fever outbreak in San Domingo where some 25,000 French soldiers and sailors had died.[2]

In the first week of January 1804, Admiral Cornwallis had informed

Commodore Pellew that the French were embarking 38,000 men at Rochefort and Brest and that the Royal Navy must be prepared for just about anything as this expedition could move north or south, to Ireland or Egypt, and Cornwallis for one was not yet sure, while Pellew's report that the Spanish were now beginning to man the fort's batteries only confused the picture more. Was this sheer coincidence or were the two nations already co-ordinating their efforts? Time would tell. The British Minister accredited to Madrid, John Hookham Frere, former Under Secretary of State for Foreign Affairs, confirmed to Pellew that the Spanish King had indeed authorised an expedition of *at least* 6,000 men to be prepared at El Ferrol, while British intelligence reports noted further large-scale ship and troop movement between Bordeaux and Brest. Fresh reports of feverish naval and port activity at both Rochefort and Lorient led Admiral Cornwallis to remind Captain Elphinstone off Lorient 'to be very vigilant upon this service, using your utmost endeavours to obtain information on their [French] proceedings and designs . . .' and advising Sir Robert Calder at Rochefort that it was 'of the utmost national importance that the port should be as closely watched as possible'.

Cornwallis was a curious sort of hero for, unlike the gruff St Vincent and the ubiquitous Nelson, he was almost never seen where the action was taking place, much to his own consternation. Being the ideal Commander-in-Chief, he was to be found instead sitting quietly in his cabin, carefully analysing the data reaching him and almost invariably arriving at the correct conclusions, without the aid of a large staff or complicated technology. He would then draw up fresh orders and directives for his far-flung fleet, co-ordinating their actions with such a persistently deft hand that the *Naval Chronicle* that year acclaimed him 'the indefatigable naval hero'.

Rear-Admiral the Honourable Alexander Cochrane duly arrived off Cape Finisterre in March 1804 to relieve Commodore Pellew of his Spanish command, while to the north, Admiral Cornwallis was reporting to London that the French Admiral Truguet in Brest water now had twenty-nine ships and frigates seemingly ready to put to sea, and insisted that he be provided with more ships of all classes if he were to be able to control a situation that was clearly becoming more and more ominous. On that same 17th May, further still to the north, Commodore Smith was sending a signal to Admiral Lord Keith off the Kent Downs of his encounter with Rear-Admiral Verhuell and a large Dutch flotilla.

*

If ever there was a sailor in the Royal Navy who could be described as an inveterate buccaneer, a gentleman buccaneer at that, who belonged more to the age of Drake and Hawkins than to that of stuffy St Vincent, it was Commodore Sir Sidney Smith, whose small squadron of five vessels and a few scattered gun-brigs guarded the ports of the Batavian Republic.

The very evening that William Pitt was in London meeting with the new members of the Government he was in the midst of forming on 15th May, across the Channel a weak sun was beginning to set over the shallow waters off the coast of Ostend where the 16-gun sloop, *Rattler*, rolled gently at anchor. Extending his telescope, Captain John Hancock suddenly noticed unusual activity at the port as a series of single-masted gun-vessels started to leave the harbour. First five, then ten, then finally seventeen armed vessels, followed by a schooner, rallied outside the port, taking up an anchorage off the lighthouse and close to shore.

The excited young captain signalled to his sister ship, the 18-gun brig-sloop, *Cruiser*, and his good friend, Captain Francis Mason. While he was waiting for the *Cruiser* to come alongside, Captain Hancock dispatched the hired armed cutter, *Stag*, to sail immediately and inform their squadron commander, the ineffable Commodore Smith, who was with the three remaining vessels of the squadron – the 50-gun *Antelope*, the 36-gun frigate *Penelope* and the 32-gun *Aimable* – at their station at least nine leagues to the west of Flushing. At the same time he tried to signal for help, in vain it would seem, to the four gun-brigs far to the south, which were communicating with another squadron. It was soon dark, however, and all the *Cruiser* and *Rattler* could do until daybreak was to move in as close as possible in order to prevent the division of Dutch gunboats from escaping, though they were well protected by the newly installed harbour batteries.

The *Cruiser* was still at anchor at 9.30 the following morning, waiting for the tide to change and for the appearance of Commodore Smith, when the *Rattler* signalled that more Dutch vessels could be seen approaching from the east-south-east where they had just left their anchorage in the inner Wieling. Indeed this new division, when finally counted, came to another fifty-nine sail – bringing the total of Dutch gunboats to eighty-two under the command of Rear-Admiral Verhuell himself, apparently bound for Ostend. Their division included two newly launched *prames*, the *Ville d'Anvers* with twelve long 24-pounders and the *Ville d'Aix*, similarly armed, the remaining fifty-seven vessels armed with 36-, 24- and 18-pounders, not to mention brass carronades, mortars and the 4,000 troops they were also carrying!

If young Hancock was disconcerted, he certainly did not show it, though he was now caught between two strong divisions of enemy gunboats. Instead, the two British vessels, the *Cruiser* and *Rattler*, did the only thing warships of the Royal Navy could possibly do under such circumstances – they got underway to face Rear-Admiral Verhuell and his 59 vessels with their 150 to 160 guns and mortars!

As the two sloops got closer, the wind shifted in their favour to the south-west, greatly facilitating their approach. Much to the consternation of both Captains Hancock and Mason, however, Rear-Admiral Verhuell gave orders for the Dutch flotilla to put about in order to try to return to the safety of Flushing. Verhuell, who had finally completed the number of vessels demanded of him by Napoleon, and then only after the most extraordinary efforts on his part, was not about to see such a fine division of gunboats jeopardised by two spirited young English captains!

An hour later, Commodore Smith, with the *Antelope*, *Penelope* and *Aimable* finally sailed into sight, or rather appeared as specks on the horizon, just as the *Cruiser* and *Rattler* were closing fast on the hindmost vessels of Verhuell's division. 'At 2 [o'clock] observed the *Rattler* and *Cruiser* commence firing on the enemy's flotilla', Smith recorded in the log of the *Antelope*, though he was still two hours' sailing distance from the scene. A fierce battle ensued between the *Rattler* and *Cruiser* and the vessels under Verhuell's command. The two British vessels 'attacked this line with the greatest gallantry and address', Smith wrote, 'attaching themselves particularly to the two *praams*, both of them of greater force than themselves, independent of the cross-fire' from the other fifty-seven gunboats. If it was madness on the part of the British captains, it was a madness expected of them by their superiors. 'For a period of two hours the fighting was extemely hot', the Dutch Admiral wrote afterwards, the Dutch 24-pounders causing the English many casualties and much damage to their rigging.

Seeing Smith's three ships approaching, Verhuell signalled from the yards of the *Ville d'Anvers* to break off action and come about once again in order to reach the safety of Ostend if that was still possible. Smith got there first, however, the *Aimable* going to the aid of the *Cruiser* and *Rattler*, while the frigate *Penelope* attacked a swarm of gunboats at the rear of the flotilla 'as near as the shoal water would allow' and Smith, on board the *Antelope*, manoeuvred to the van or head of the flotilla. Due to the great skill of Smith's pilot the *Antelope* was able to safely sail through the shallow waters of the Stroom Sand and bring her broadside to bear on the foremost schooners before they were able to reach Ostend. The leader immediately struck her colours, surrendering, as her crew deserted her, though, as Smith reported, she remained under 'the constant and well-directed fire . . . of the artillery from the town and camp, and the rowing gunboats from the pier. Our shot, however,' he continued, 'which went over the schooners, going on shore among the horse artillery, interrupted it in a degree. Still, it was from the shore we received the greatest annoyance, for the schooners and *schuyts* crowding along could not bring their prow guns to bear without altering their course . . . In this manner the *Penelope* and *Antelope* engaged every part of their long line from four until eight, while the *Aimable*, *Cruiser* and *Rattler* continued to press their rear.'

Verhuell's *prame*, the *Ville d'Anvers*, had by now been driven aground and was soon joined by eight more Dutch gun-vessels. 'At eight, the tide falling, and leaving us in little more water than we drew, we were reluctantly obliged to haul off into deeper water to keep afloat; and the enemy's vessels that were not on shore or too much shattered were thus able to reach Ostend.' Smith added, 'It is but justice to say the enemy's Commodore [Admiral Verhuell] pursued a steady course notwithstanding our fire, and returned it with spirit to the last', only ceasing upon reaching the safety of the Ostend basin.

Summing up the battle report, noting the losses and damage sustained, Commodore Smith noted that, 'The *Rattler* and the *Cruiser* have, of course, suffered the most . . . The smoke would not allow us to see the effect of our shot on the enemy; but their loss, considering the number of them under our guns for so long [four to six hours] must be great in proportion. We see the mastheads above the water of three of the schooners and one of the *schuyt* which were sunk.' The British casualties were thirteen killed and thirty-two wounded – unusually high figures for a minor action of this kind, clearly reflecting the intensity of the battle – and, though the *Rattler* and *Cruiser* incurred considerable damage, the British lost no vessels, whereas it was estimated that the Dutch probably lost up to twenty per cent of their craft (destroyed or so badly damaged as not to be salvageable). The Dutch and French casualty figures were also proportionately higher.

Among the seemingly endless problems First Lord Melville had to cope with upon taking office was one that had persisted ever since the troubles of 1797 – mutiny. Off the Brest coast in 1803, the cruiser, *Pickle*, had proved a hotbed of intrigue and now in 1804, also off the same coast, the crew of the *Montagu* plotted another mutiny and the murder of their officers, with the aim of handing over that warship to the French Imperial Navy. Melville had to act and swiftly.

Rear-Admiral Sir John Sutton, second-in-command at Plymouth and President of the court-martial board, sat in his heavy blue full-dress uniform at the centre of a long mahogany table along with nine distinguished naval captains, their medals attesting to every major naval battle won by Great Britain over the past twenty years. The Deputy Judge Advocate, Robert Liddell, addressed the board in the great cabin of the *Salvador del Mundo* as it rolled almost imperceptibly at anchor, accusing James Dunn, Patrick Gorman and Edward Plunkett, seamen of the *Montagu*, 'of having made a mutinous assembly and seditious conduct tending to excite the discontent of the ship's company'.

Seaman John Ryan had prepared a deposition stating that these three men planned to kill four of the ship's officers and then with the assistance of fifteen or sixteen companions swearing 'to be true and loyal an [sic] die together' in their attempt to seize the ship and hand it over to the French in Brest harbour.

An informer among them notified Captain Otway in time, however, and all the men concerned were put into irons before their plan went into effect. The accused claimed before Admiral Sutton that they were completely innocent, and 'threw themselves on the benevolence and humanity of the Court', though witness after witness came forward to confirm their guilt.

Deputy Judge Advocate Liddell then reported the findings of the court-martial board. After hearing and weighing all evidence and testimony, 'the Court . . . was of the opinion that the charges had been proved against the prisoners . . . and, in consequence thereof, adjudged the said James Dunn, Patrick Gorman, and Edward Plunkett to be severally hanged by the neck until dead at the yard-arms of such of his Majesty's ships and at such time or times as the Right Honourable the Lord Commissioners of the Admiralty shall direct'. The Admiralty duly confirmed this finding and issued warrants for the execution of the three men. Admiral Young at Plymouth was to see to that of James Dunn, while to Admiral Cornwallis fell the unhappy charge of appointing a date for the other two. On the morning of 9th July 1804, off the coast of Brest, Captain Otway had the entire crew of the *Montagu* mustered before Admiral Cornwallis as Gorman and Plunkett were hanged from the yards high above the deck. No doubt the solemn Cornwallis would have preferred to be with his books and horses.

*

With a long naval career already behind him, having served with distinction in the Mediterranean and Egypt and off Brest, the forty-year-old Rear-Admiral Cochrane now hoisted his flag aboard the *Northumberland* as he assumed command at El Ferrol. If Commodore Pellew, with his fluent Spanish, had maintained relatively calm and gentlemanly relations with the Spanish naval authorities before him, not so Cochrane. A man of immense energy and little patience, he was, nevertheless, a most thorough and effective squadron commander. While the mutineers Dunn, Gorman and Plunkett were being condemned, Alexander Cochrane was informing his Commander-in-Chief off Ushant that the French were making every effort to complete the refitting of their small squadron at El Ferrol. Clearly something was in the air.

For over a year now the enemy's feverish activities had been matched by Sir William Cornwallis' unrelenting hold over the Channel and the Bay of Biscay, managing to contain the French Navy admirably in every major port between Brest and El Ferrol. This achievement the Corporation of the City of London now gratefully acknowledged, thanking Cornwallis and his fleet 'for the very eminent services rendered their country, for their great zeal and uncommon exertions by which our enemies have been kept in a constant state of alarm, not dared for a moment to show themselves upon that element which has so often been the scene of their defeat and disgrace'.

The question uppermost in everyone's minds was, what were the French up to? Tens of thousands of troops were reported to be boarding ships and vessels now at every important naval port, even the Spanish manning guns at El Ferrol. With the few ships at their disposal, the British could ill afford to make a mistake. No doubt Cornwallis and the Admiralty Board would have been staggered to learn that Napoleon had in fact only prepared his first overall strategic invasion plan at the end of May 1804!

Part of the plan involved Admiral Latouche-Tréville assuming command of the fleet and operations at Toulon. Latouche had a good naval record and had briefly succeeded Admiral Villaret-Joyeuse as Commander-in-Chief of the fleet off San Domingo in the spring of 1803, but by July of that year he too had succumbed to the yellow fever outbreak there and was invalided home.

'Think most carefully about the great undertaking', Napoleon counselled on 2nd July 1804 as he laid his plan before the new commander – and what a plan it was! With his fleet of ten battleships and eleven frigates, Admiral Latouche was ordered to put to sea from Toulon before

30th July. After evading the British fleet ('if you fool Nelson, he will go to Sicily, or Egypt or Ferrol'), and slipping through the Straits of Gibraltar, he was to sweep up the Spanish coast (while avoiding Cochrane's squadron off Finisterre) making his first rendezvous off Rochefort, where another half dozen ships were to join him and, with that combined force, head for Cherbourg where Napoleon himself was to give him his final briefing for the approach to Boulogne. There 'the flotilla would be ready to carry an army of 125,000 men to Britain', this by the end of September at the latest.

In order to dispose of the troublesome Cornwallis, the Brest squadron – numbering some twenty-three vessels or so – was to break out, sailing *away* from the direction of Boulogne, expecting Cornwallis to follow in hot pursuit. Latouche meanwhile would be escorting some 2,000 flotilla vessels across the Channel to the coast of Kent, less than 30 miles away. It was the simplest plan to be devised regarding a descent upon Britain, but what is truly surprising is that it took Napoleon so long to develop it, well over a year after first preparing the flotilla.

If Lord Melville was to remain in ignorance of this current invasion plan, the French Emperor was to have a little surprise in store himself, for on 19th August, while still aboard the *Bucentaure* in Toulon harbour (where he had remained, too fearful of encountering Nelson to slip out), Admiral Latouche-Tréville died suddenly. This was reportedly due to the strain put on his heart by frequently climbing the 'telegraph-tower' above the port, although no doubt his constitution had been greatly weakened by the yellow fever he had contracted just the year before.

Meanwhile Melville wrote to Admiral Cornwallis privately on 14th July, suggesting some of the possibilities occurring to him if all or part of the Brest squadron should escape. 'Our whole intelligence certainly tends to the idea of their Brest force being intended for some part of the United Kingdom, and I am disposed to believe that to be the object most at heart'. Naturally there were other possibilities as well, depending upon whether all these vessels were used in a sortie and whether or not they were accompanied by a large number of troop transports. Melville suggested that, among other ploys, they could possibly be aiming to seize the Cape of Good Hope or the British colonies in the West Indies or carry out a major attack on the British squadrons blockading Rochefort and El Ferrol to release all French warships there prior to reinforcing the fleet at Toulon. He then went on to make a very interesting statement indeed: 'I am free to confess that I conceive any of the objects I have mentioned would be more likely to annoy this country, in some of its most essential [commercial] interests, than any desperate attempt they may meditate of an attack on any part of the United Kingdom, against such a superiority at sea as we possess'. Melville concluded, 'I thought it my duty, in this private, unofficial form, to suggest to you what has occurred to me and I should be glad to hear from you in what light the suggestions I have thrown out appear to you.'

Did the Royal Navy really command the degree of 'superiority at sea' that the First Lord claimed, however? Not every admiral would have been so assured on that point and, within a matter of months, by mid-January 1805, that superiority was to be greatly diminished by two elements that the Admiralty had not taken into consideration at that moment: the weather and Spain. As for attacks on British global commercial interests, Napoleon was already drafting plans for a new expedition with that very thought in mind.

Throughout the month of July 1804, both the Admiralty and Cornwallis remained very much concerned about a possible French breakout from one or more of their ports, as the Admiral reminded his Second-in-Command, Sir Charles Cotton, then cruising off Brest. 'A considerable force' was ready to put to sea and certain basic strategic and tactical steps had to be kept in mind should that occur. If foul weather forced them to abandon Brest, he was to wait it out at Torbay. Should the French decide to use this fleet as a decoy to lead Cornwallis away from the primary objective of a Channel invasion, Blue Billy directed Sir Charles Cotton 'not to follow them, unless you can be very sure of the route they have taken, or leave the mouth of the Channel unguarded, as the enemy might in that case take the opportunity to push up the Channel for the purpose of aiding the threatened invasion of His Majesty's dominions', and, in conclusion, Cornwallis reminded Sir Charles that protection from just such an invasion was, after all, 'the principal object of the force placed under my command'. The Admiral was too old a seahand, and too good a Commander-in-Chief to be lured away from his duties and to be taken in by an old ruse such as Napoleon was now plotting.

The summer months naturally brought an improvement in the weather, which helped Napoleon as far as his invasion plans were concerned. Throughout July, August and September, Admiral Cornwallis and his squadron commanders off Brest, Rochefort, Lorient and El Ferrol, therefore, remained particularly alert. They continued to bombard and harass French ports and coastal shipping, meeting a response from artillery batteries but rarely the challenge of a French man of war.

They even planned complicated fireship attacks to destroy large concentrations of flotilla vessels at Boulogne and Brest.

The French were by now feeling the full brunt of this tight blockade imposed by the Channel Fleet which, added to the news of the unexpected death of Admiral Latouche, soon forced Napoleon to reassess his strategy, producing a second, totally new plan later in September.

Meanwhile, French Naval Prefects along the Channel were trying to cope as best they could with increased British harassment. 'The enemy have re-appeared, anchoring at their usual post' before the port of Boulogne, thereby putting a halt to most French naval activity, Admiral Eustace de Bruix complained again to Naval Minister Decrès. 'The English are constantly along our coast', Naval Prefect General Caffarelli moaned at Brest, 'several vessels are always off Ouessant, four or five anchor during the day off the Black Rocks', while other smaller vessels maintained this watch closer to the harbours or nearby islands. 'What is more, the English have landed at Béniguet. They asked if at Conquet there was not a convoy consisting of fifteen coastal freighters which has just arrived from the north, and what their cargo was. He [the Frenchman being interrogated] replied that he knew nothing about it. They [the English] responded that there were an additional ten boats there as well, making a total of twenty-five. An English officer then made a wager with the wife of this Frenchman that within a matter of days they would have captured some of them. The wager being ten louis against one of her cows!' It was outrageous, it was humiliating, but would continue to happen time and again up and down that coastline.

Complain as Decrès or Caffarelli might about the ever-present proximity of the British, they did little or nothing about it and Napoleon for one was again in a sour mood. 'I see with the greatest regret that, in spite of my very real intention that the vessels in the roadstead of Brest weigh anchor every day', he wrote in May 1804 to Vice-Admiral Laurent Truguet shortly before dismissing him, 'that the crews get the essential practice they need in their work, and in order to harass the enemy . . . that not a single vessel has put to sea since the beginning of the year, which has resulted in the enemy blocking an impressively large squadron with just a handful of ships.'

Nevertheless Napoleon was trying to build up the courage of his naval commanders, including that of Vice-Admiral Honoré Ganteaume, who now succeeded the unfortunate Truguet at Brest. 'Your sortie [on 24th August when they ventured out of the harbour for a few hours] instilled great terror among the English', and if he could now land 16,000 men and 500 horses in Ireland 'the results will be calamitous for our enemies.' At long last 'the Brest Squadron finally seems to be in a position to do something . . . Be perfectly honest with me: how many [vessels] do you have with seasoned crews really capable of putting to sea? . . . Let me know how many I can really count on'.

In fact, Ganteaume was greatly disappointed by what he had found upon assuming command at Brest. If the ships were good and often far superior to what the British had – several of them having just recently been launched – the great problem of inadequate crews to man them remained. Ganteaume informed Naval Minister Decrès, 'On that particular point we are in a pitiful state . . . It's terrifying to think what a very small number of well-trained men we have with which to put to sea'. He noted that the men were given 'much gunnery practice' and would no doubt perform well enough in calm seas, 'but if it came to sailing in bad weather, we would be very embarrassed indeed'. These crews 'all lack the will, strength and courage to succeed', and, to aggravate matters still further, Ganteaume stated that even so he was 4,369 men short to man the fleet and transports! It was a damning admission, but explained to a great degree why this powerful French fleet rarely ventured forth or attempted to escape the British during the frequent periods of bad weather. After reading this correspondence between Decrès and Ganteaume, the frustrated Emperor replied to the latter 'Don't expect to get what we do not have [trained crews]; I cannot perform miracles'.

Caffarelli's complaints also continued to reach the Naval Ministry with alarming regularity throughout the rest of 1804 and well into 1805. As a result of the British blockade at Brest, coastal trade had fallen drastically and Naval Prefect Caffarelli was to write to Decrès by 4th February 1805: 'My experience of the difficulties encountered, so far as navigation between St Malo and Bayonne is concerned, have forced me to put a halt to all free [unescorted commercial] navigation, even so, what defence can one possibly expect from a few boats whose armament [is poor] and whose crews [are] composed of invalided artillerymen? . . . It is well known that the enemy assiduously maintain cruisers round the Chausey Isles, Béhat, Perros and Batz Island; that the Passage du Four, Iroise and of Audierne Bay are all closely guarded by them; that the English have light cruisers capable of approaching very close to our shores and that they frequently land expeditions to capture our ships and vessels that lie at anchor. Many enemy cruisers abound in the waters off Quiberon, Belle Ile and Rochefort, and it is only by luck and under the most favourable conditions, which are rare enough, that our vessels succeed in getting through. Our boats sailing without any escort invariably fall into the hands of the enemy . . .

'To these already formidable considerations is added yet another danger we must be aware of; it is that of communication with the enemy, which has already resulted in a variety of attempts to stir up trouble inland, and which have been checked finally only as the result of the greatest vigilance.'

As usual, Napoleon had complaints of his own, informing Ganteaume that trained crews – that is *thousands of sailors* – were in short supply, that, worse still, good officers, in particular, top brass to lead those men into battle were also lacking. 'I do not have enough admirals [Latouche had just died, Bedout and Bruix were both seriously ill]. I want to create some new rear-admirals . . . but without consideration to seniority. Send me a list of a good dozen officers.' The British warships often did not possess full complements of men – especially the squadron off Cape Finisterre, which had been assembled in great haste – but those they had were, as a rule, well-experienced men, capable of sailing for long months at sea, often under the worst possible weather conditions, thanks, in part, to a plentiful supply of extremely able and diligent naval officers *at every level*.

When news of the death of Admiral Latouche-Tréville reached St Cloud, Admiral Decrès once again felt the full fury of the Emperor's temper. All his plans were in jeopardy once more because of the navy – always the navy! He had to come up with a replacement for Latouche and quickly. Although he considered Admirals Rosily and de Bruix in September, he finally made a choice that was to have dire consequences in the long run: Vice-Admiral Pierre-Charles-Jean-Baptiste-Silvestre Villeneuve, a forty-one-year-old Provençal aristocrat. Latouche was dead and the season of relatively good weather already behind them. Napoleon now summoned Rear-Admiral Missiessy (who was to succeed to the command of the Rochefort squadron) and Vice-Admiral Ville-neuve to Paris, briefing them personally of his new plans, replacing those issued earlier to Latouche–Tréville, and on 29th September 1804 the French Emperor ordered the Naval Minister to put these instructions into effect.

By 12th October Villeneuve, with at least ten sail of the line, was to haul out of Toulon harbour, hopefully unseen by the ever-watchful Nelson and his Mediteranean Fleet, coming round Spain to collect one ship at Cadiz and then to sail westwards to the northern shore of South America and Surinam where they would land 5,600 troops and where

Rear-Admiral Missiessy (who was to have set sail from Rochefort by 11th November) would join them with half a dozen vessels after having first proceeded to Martinique, thence to take possession of St Lucia and Dominica with 3,500 men under the command of General Lagrange.

Meanwhile, a third, smaller expedition of 1,500 men was to be sent from Toulon to take the strategically situated island of St Helena, then to concentrate on the west coast of Africa in particular, landing reinforcements at Senegal and re-taking neighbouring Gorée, with specific orders from Napoleon to attack 'every English establishment along the coast of Africa, which will then pay us a war indemnity before being burned to the ground'.

Napoleon certainly felt very confident about this new plan: 'The English will find themselves attacked in Asia, Africa and America . . . Unaccustomed as they are to feeling the real impact of war, these successive shocks at the main points of their [global] commerce will make them realise at long last just how weak they really are' and, after these three operations, they 'will certainly not be expecting anything else; it will be easy to surprise them'.

Surprise them he would with Villeneuve's combined squadron from the Caribbean, which would then quickly return to Europe, arriving first at El Ferrol to raise Cochrane's blockade, thereby gaining an additional five battleships, and sailing northwards to Rochefort and up to Boulogne with at least twenty ships of the line to protect the crossing of the invasion force – 'la grande armée de Boulogne' – of 125,000 men, which will 'then enter the county of Kent'.

As for Vice-Admiral Ganteaume's squadron of twenty-one ships of the line and several frigates, he was to sail from Brest water by 22nd November at the latest with another 18,000 troops (the number having been increased) under the orders of General Augereau, circling Ireland and landing in the north at Lough Swilly Bay where all those troops were to disembark and 'march straight for Dublin', to quote Napoleon. Ganteaume would then return to the Channel to join the main invasion force, bringing the number of French battleships between Boulogne and Dover to over forty!

Hopefully, several British squadrons would already have been sent from the Channel to the aid of the colonies attacked in Africa and the West Indies. Upon learning of Ganteaume's escape, 'Lord Cornwallis will go to wait for him in Ireland', Napoleon predicted and, 'When he realises that he has already landed in the north, he will return to Brest to await his return'. So much for the British Channel Fleet he thought, little suspecting that Cornwallis had given specific orders never to leave the Channel unguarded.

The final part of this scenario involved General Marmont's 25,000 French and Dutch troops now aboard the flotilla at Texel, Holland, about which Sir Sidney Smith had already reported in considerable detail to Admiral Lord Keith. This separate expeditionary force was to sail on seven ships of the line and several transports to reinforce the initial Irish landing, bringing the total there to over 40,000 men!

'One of these two operations must succeed', Napoleon told Decrès, 'whether I am in England or Ireland, in either event we will have won the war.'

It was a most daring plan of many dimensions, with several different means of striking at Britain, as Napoleon rightly pointed out. It affected British colonies and trade (which of course was something Lord Melville was most anxious about, though not knowing where precisely to expect attacks) and involved major French landings in Ireland and Britain. It was most complicated and sweeping in its strategy and logistics for its day, involving landings of some 173,000 men on both sides of the Atlantic. It had the distinct advantage, however, of having separate aspects succeed even if others failed, and Napoleon could not see how the British Government could possibly cover all these bases at once. Yet, even if the Caribbean and Mediterranean Fleets were not available in home waters, Lord Melville could muster the combined fleets of Keith and Cornwallis against the major thrust aimed at Kent, with a few ships to spare for Ireland. However, unlike the French vessels, which had suffered little from the elements as a result of their long stay in ports, the British Navy had already suffered considerable storm damage by the end of November when this invasion was due to take place, and how it would have fared only a Napoleon or St Vincent would have been foolish enough to predict.

Alas for the French Emperor, this second invasion plan, like the first one, went awry most unexpectedly. These orders dispatched to Vice-Admiral Ganteaume were intercepted by the British and never reached him, and thus the entire, extraordinary project was cancelled.

Forewarned by Napoleon's own orders, Cornwallis was now prepared for anything and reminded his squadron commanders to maintain 'the utmost vigilance'. Rear-Admiral Cochrane had already reported to Cornwallis and the Admiralty on 14th September that Captain-General Texada was beginning to arm the Spanish warships in El Ferrol harbour. He, Cochrane, had taken the bull by the horns, however, and immediately ordered the Captain-General to desist, which, after some hesitation and a formal exchange of correspondence, the Spanish commander did in part – disarming them and returning the ships to the arsenal.

Off Ushant on 21st September, Cornwallis notified Cochrane that not only must he stop the five French battleships from leaving that port, but likewise any of the Spanish ships of war sailing from El Ferrol. Great Britain was *not* at war with Spain, but this was tantamount to just such a declaration and marked a serious escalation in a very dangerous game. The following day, Admiral Cornwallis sent a 'secret' dispatch to Captain Graham Moore of the *Indefatigable*, ordering him to proceed to Cadiz 'with all possible despatch, and use your best endeavours . . . to intercept, if possible, the two Spanish frigates expected with treasure from South America', treasure it was feared that would otherwise fall into the hands of Napoleon. As it turned out, these two orders to Cochrane and Moore were to alter the naval war considerably because, if British ships did indeed seize Spanish treasure ships, the Kings of Spain and Great Britain would no doubt inevitably soon be at war, thereby making the Spanish Navy openly available to Napoleon's war effort. Their combined might would outnumber that of the Royal Navy as well as extend the theatres of operation which had already stretched British naval lines almost beyond their effective capabilities.

As a result of these fresh orders (although Cornwallis' formal order 'to seize or destroy' Spanish vessels would not come until mid January 1805) events were now set in motion that were to resolve the issue of who ruled the seas once and for all.

Captain Moore, the younger brother of General Sir John Moore, had distinguished himself on numerous occasions during his twenty-seven years at sea and was well regarded. He was not only brave but able to maintain a cool head at times of crisis, qualities which were ultimately to help him rise to the rank of full admiral. Taking command of three other frigates – the *Medusa, Amphion* and *Lively* – Moore scouted the waters of the Atlantic between Cadiz and Gibraltar for the treasure ships and on 6th October 1804 he reported back to Admiral Cornwallis: 'Sir, I have the honour to acquaint you that I have executed the service you did me the honour to charge me with . . .

'Yesterday morning, Cape St Mary bearing N.E. nine leagues, the *Medusa* made the signal for four sail W. by N.; I made the signal for a general chase; at eight A.M. discovered them to be four large Spanish frigates, which formed the line of battle ahead on our approach . . .' Some time later the four British vessels came alongside them. 'My orders were to detain his [the Spanish Rear-Admiral's] squadron . . . it was my earnest wish to execute them [his orders] without bloodshed . . . After hailing to make them shorten sail without effect, I fired a shot across the rear-admiral's fore-foot [foremost sail], on which he shortened sail, and I sent Lieutenant Ascott of the *Indefatigable* to inform him that my orders were to detain his squadron . . . After waiting some time, I made the signal for the boat [Ascott's] to return, and fired another shot ahead of the admiral. As soon as the officer returned, with an unsatisfactory answer, I fired another shot ahead of the admiral, and bore down close on his weather bow. At this moment the admiral's second astern fired into the *Amphion*; and the admiral fired into the *Indefatigable*; and I made the signal for close battle, which was instantly commenced with all the alacrity and vigour of English sailors. In less than ten minutes, *La Mercedes*, the admiral's second astern, blew up alongside the *Amphion*, with a tremendous explosion.' Within half an hour two of the Spanish frigates struck their colours, surrendering to Captain Moore, while the remaining ship, the *Medusa*, fled, pursued and captured later that day by the *Lively*.

'As soon as our boats had taken possession of the rear-admiral, we made sail for the floating fragments of the unfortunate Spanish frigate which blew up; but, except [for] forty taken up by the *Amphion*'s boats, all on board perished.' Rear-Admiral Don José Bustamente and his officers were taken prisoner and his flagship, the 42-gun *Medea*, the 36-gun *La Fama* and the 36-gun *La Clara* were sent to Gibraltar. As for the 'treasure', it did indeed exist and, although 1,111,940 silver dollars, 1,627 bars of tin and 203 pigs of copper were lost with *La Mercedes*, Moore still brought back a rich haul.[3]

The British had no prior knowledge of the civilians on board, and, in fact, had been expecting only two vessels, not four. Captain Moore's aim was 'to detain' the treasure ships, for which, according to British maritime law, he and his men were to receive a portion of prize money, and the explosion of *La Mercedes* caught him, as well as the Spaniards, by surprise and meant a considerable personal financial as well as human loss.

To be sure the fat was now in the fire. Neutral Spanish ships had been attacked on the high seas by the Royal Navy, one had been sunk, 240 Spaniards (including friends of the Spanish Royal family) had been killed and very valuable treasure (approximately one-third of which belonged to the King of Spain) had been seized or lost. Admiral Cornwallis' orders of 22nd September 1804 had changed the complexion of the war. It was almost inevitable now that Spain, once learning of her loss and humiliation, would declare war on the United Kingdom and join Napoleon in his future naval undertakings. Was the British move a wise one in the long run?

It was only two days later, on 8th October, that the French Emperor actually realised that the British had intercepted his latest invasion plans of 29th September – those involving England, Ireland, Surinam, the West Indies and Africa. He wrote to Admiral Decrès immediately, informing him that he 'must change all the expeditions', and once again a most frustrated French Emperor had to re-think all his plans, though the seizure of the Spanish treasure ships had certainly proved an unexpected coup in his favour. The English had accomplished what all his previous bullying and cajoling had failed to do – bring the Spaniards in on the side of the French.

In fact it was the First Lord of the Admiralty who had issued the original orders to Admiral Cornwallis authorising the attack on the Spanish vessels, and now that it had been carried out, Melville knew that the British force on active duty between Brest and El Ferrol would have to be greatly extended. Accordingly, on 27th October 1804 he ordered Vice-Admiral Sir John Orde to form and take command of a new squadron not far from Gibraltar at Cadiz, with orders to 'seize any Spanish treasure or warships'.

Cornwallis did not appear to have any private or professional objection to the change of British naval policy, but where were the Royal Navy to find the ships and men for this extended war? He knew full well that Orde was to be given half a dozen ships from his own fast depleting fleet off Ushant, however, and pleaded with Lord Melville for more replacement ships, but an unusually testy First Lord snapped back on 2nd November 1804, 'You know perfectly how many of the ships I found in commission when I came into office [and which] have been sent in such a [decaying] condition as to require [them] to be broken up or put into [dry] dock . . .', nevertheless, he added, 'I cannot shut my eyes against the *certainty* of what we must experimentally know, that you have not the means of sustaining the necessary extent of naval force, if your ships are to be torn to pieces by an eternal conflict with the elements during the tempestuous months of winds', though 'no exertion shall be omitted, and I hope with success, to bring forward additional ships of war; but, 'til that can be done, it is necessary to make the most of those we have'. He reminded Cornwallis that he expected 'the system of unremitting blockade' off Brest to be maintained, regardless of the cost in men and ships.

Meanwhile, the reports reaching the Admiralty from Spain were almost daily becoming more and more serious. 'Here the Spaniards are engaged in mounting the guns on their batteries [once again], and all the gunboats in the arsenal are getting ready for service', Rear-Admiral Cochrane reported from El Ferrol on 13th November. Less than a fortnight later he warned that the Spaniards had two more ships ready 'to be masted', the 114-gun *Príncipe de Asturias* and the 74-gun *San Juan Nepomuceno*, and that 'Troops are marching in from the country to reinforce the garrisons at Ferrol and Corunna'. Four days later it was revealed that orders had been received from Madrid 'to seize all English vessels . . .' The following day the British Vice-Consul at Santander informed Cochrane that 'a Cabinet courier arrived here [yesterday] . . . with orders to assemble the regiments of militias . . .' and added that a French merchant had 'lately contracted with the Spanish Government for two million *fanégas* [bushels] of wheat to be imported into the different ports of Spain [for the military]'. 'We expect war', wrote British Vice-Consul Fernandez from El Ferrol. 'Reprisals on English property have taken place already . . . They say that M. Gravina, who was in Paris, is to come here to take charge of this department.' Tension and activity were increasing in Brest, Lorient and Rochefort, on the one hand, and in Spanish ports on the other, keeping the lights burning even longer than usual at the Admiralty offices in London and at Melville's home in Wimbledon. On 22nd December 1804 Rear-Admiral Cochrane, writing from his flagship, the *Northumberland*, off Cape Finisterre, notified the Commander-in-Chief that his squadron was 'now denied all species of supplies from shore . . .' Finally, on the first day of the new year, 1805, Cochrane sent an urgent 'secret' dispatch to Cornwallis: he had just learned 'that war was actually declared [on 12th December 1804] by Spain against Great Britain.'

As if the mounting anxiety over maintaining the blockade of French and Spanish ports were not enough to preoccupy Admiral Sir William Cornwallis aboard the *Ville de Paris*, the reports of storm damage reaching him off Ushant throughout the early months of 1804, from the captains of his much dispersed fleet, only added to his worries. Even sheltering in Douarnenez Bay off the coast of Brittany, or Betanzos Bay at La Coruña, did not seem to spare them from the extraordinary violence of the elements. 'The excessive bad weather' had ushered in the new year with three disastrous gales in January leaving five major warships – the *San Joseph*, the *Impetueux*, *Foudroyant*, *Boadicea* and the *Louis* – badly damaged, crippling Cornwallis's effectiveness off Brest for the next few months as those vessels limped back to Plymouth for repairs. Other storms continued to lash the entire length of the Channel, letting up only at the end of April to give the haggard fleet a much needed respite till late autumn. But by November 1804 the raging Atlantic was once again taking its toll. From Betanzos Bay on 5th November Cochrane reported the resumption of the 'most severe blowing weather', the 74-gun *Malta* having 'lost her main topmast and suffered in her sails', while the *Spartiate* was in such desperate straits that 'I am now forced to keep her at anchor' permanently. Off Rochefort by mid-November, Collingwood had to acknowledge that so much water was pouring into his flagship's (the *Dreadnought*'s) magazine 'that I fear there is very little serviceable powder' remaining but, although no longer in a position to challenge the French squadron there in battle, he was determined to keep his station, as there was not a single ship to spare! Even in home waters, however, British ships were not safe from some of the most horrendous gales of the century as the *Venerable* was driven against the rocks and sunk right off Paignton!

The weather was just as unrelenting on New Year's Day 1805, when Admiral Cochrane informed Cornwallis that, although the badly needed *Illustrious* had finally reached him from Britain, she had 'suffered severely in the different gales' *en route*, having 'lost main and foretop masts, with all the sails and rigging' and was in a useless state upon her arrival. Some of the other ships of his squadron were in a similar state and 'will be forced to return to Plymouth, for the gales here are both frequent and severe'.

If it took a great deal to make Cochrane complain about his plight, it took even more to raise a complaint from Admiral Cornwallis and thus, when Secretary Marsden received his letter of 6th January 1805, he knew the situation in the Channel was very bad indeed: 'Hard gales', Cornwallis informed him, had continued for a fortnight 'and we were seldom able to carry *any* sail', the ships were suffering from 'a very great sea' and constantly being driven far to the west. The *Plantagenet* had a 'defective' mainmast, four other ships had 'shifted topmasts' while the *Prince George* was 'leaky', that is, shipping so much water in her holds her pumps could barely keep her afloat. 'It has blown exceedingly hard since that time [23rd December] . . . Both the *Ville de Paris*' tillers have given way and Captain Guion of the *Prince*, has reported the same'. Two days later, Cornwallis had to acknowledge further major storm damage and that Vice-Admiral Collingwood's flagship, the *Dreadnought*, which had just joined him, was 'the only ship of the line I have seen since the 15th of last month, when I put to sea from Torbay with *eleven* sail of the line'. His ship 'labours most exceeedingly' in 'a great deal of sea or swell', which in fact was literally tearing ships apart.

The result was that, by the middle of January 1805, Cornwallis admitted to Lord Melville, 'I am very sorry to say that there is very little dependence to be placed in these vessels keeping to their stations at this season' and that he, therefore, had no choice but to return to Plymouth and Cawsand Bay with nine ships and vessels of his fleet – a tenth to join them shortly – all of which required immediate major repairs. The Royal Navy had lost a total of fourteen warships in 1804, chiefly as a result of storms, from the 74-gun *Magnificent* off the Black Rocks near Brest, to the 12-gun *Sterling*, off Calais, and to this statistic a fifteenth was now added with news that the *Doris* had just sunk, yet another storm victim.

The coast of Brittany had been swept almost entirely clear of Admiral Cornwallis' fleet of over fifty vessels and, while he was supervising the repair of ten warships in dry dock at Plymouth that 24th January 1805, far to the east, in London, a declaration of war against Spain was being read before a gloomy Parliament. St Vincent might boast of the great 'superiority at sea' of the Royal Navy over that of the French, but at moments like this it seemed a very poor joke indeed. Not only was the blockade off the French coast more or less totally non-existent that January, but the shores of Britain itself remained virtually undefended at sea.

'As Many Tricks as a Monkey'

For the past two years France has made the greatest possible sacrifices anyone could have asked of her, and she has borne the burden. The outbreak of a general war on the Continent, such as the one I am now anticipating, requires no less of her. As a result, I now have the strongest army and most complete military organisation in Europe, and thus am in the same state of preparedness I would have been in had we already been at war. But in order to gather such a military force in time of peace, to have 20,000 artillery horses harnessed and all their gun-crews ready, one must find a pretext to create and assemble just such a structure without alarming the Continental Powers. We have found this very pretext by letting them think we are going to invade Britain.

Napoleon before the Conseil d'Etat, 17th January 1805

I am here watching the French squadron in Rochefort, but feel that it is not practical to prevent their sailing if it be their intention, and yet, if they should get past me, I should be exceedingly mortified.

Collingwood, 4th November 1804

Perhaps none of us would wish for a West India trip; but the call of our Country is far superior to any consideration of self.

Nelson to Captain Keats, 8th May 1805

EVERY BRITISH NAVAL officer commanding a squadron off a French port had acknowledged the impossibility of preventing the French from sailing and escaping should they really be determined to do so. London politicians, however, failed to grasp this point. Rear-Admiral Collingwood lamented in a letter to a friend in February 1805, 'Their idea is that we are like sentinels standing at a door, who must see and may intercept all who attempt to go into it . . . little considering that every one of the blasts which we endure lessens the security of the country.'

Nevertheless the Channel Fleet had done remarkably well since the resumption of hostilities in May 1803. Not a single squadron had escaped from a French Channel port, no doubt to the astonishment of seasoned naval veterans who knew just how nearly impossible it was to guard a port, any port, twenty-four hours a day, 365 days a year, without some opportunities (including those provided by the numerous Channel storms) allowing for a break-out. Indeed, given the odds such an escape was absolutely inevitable, because in the winter of 1804 and into 1805, of course most of the British Channel Fleet were frequently either far out at sea – having been blown off station by harrowing gales – seeking shelter at Torbay, or else in Plymouth for repairs. Even so, did British commanders expect the French to make a break for it now given such harsh weather conditions?

The news they had all been dreading came on 17th January 1805, in a dispatch sent by Rear-Admiral Sir Thomas Graves in the *Foudroyant*, at anchor in Quiberon Bay. He reported that the enemy squadron was sailing from Rochefort, comprising one three-deck and five two-deck ships, two frigates and two brigs. 'I instantly hauled my wind under close-reefed topsails and reefed courses, but finding it impossible to weather the shore on either tack, and it being then half-past four o'clock in the evening, blowing a gale of wind, I was compelled to anchor here with the squadron.' The look-out frigate, *Felix*, had first sighted Rear-Admiral Missiessy's squadron off the coast on 12th January and had apprised Graves five days later, but given the brief hours of daylight and the foul weather it was hardly surprising that the French had been able to slip silently past the few remaining British sentinels in the Channel and into the mists of a grey, enveloping Atlantic.

Where did Missiessy go? Cornwallis was as much in the dark as anyone else and on 3rd February thought that the Rochefort squadron had no troops aboard and that they had 'either put into Lorient or returned to Rochefort'. Other guesses included their putting in at Brest to join that fleet, but for once he was completely wrong. Ten days later, an intelligence report suggested the possibilities of either the Mediterranean or the West Indies as their destination. In fact, it was another fortnight before it was finally spotted by a Swedish packet 'in latitude 40°, in the longitude of Teneriffe, steering south-west', whereupon Cornwallis immediately dispatched Admiral Cochrane from El Ferrol with five ships of the line in pursuit.

The new year, which began with battering storms resulting in much damage to British ships and the disclosure of the first major escape of a French squadron, now brought further disturbing news. From Brest, the Admiralty was informed that the French had three three-deck and eighteen two-deck ships of the line, along with some frigates, manned and ready to put to sea. Two days later an intelligence report stated that at El Ferrol five French ships of the line were also 'ready for sea, having been refitted and provided with new masts, sails &c', and that four

Spanish ships of the line were also ready. 'They intend going over to Corunna the first easterly winds, when our squadron is out of the way, from there they go to the West Indies.' There was considerable fresh activity in the naval yard there where men were seen 'rattling down the rigging' of three more Spanish battleships as well, for, as one frigate captain put it, 'The Spanish are very inveterate against and will do everything in their power to annoy England.'

Such was the situation at the beginning of March 1805 and Sir William Cornwallis was as mystified about French intentions as anyone else, in some cases as much as the French themselves, which was hardly surprising considering the major changes in the French naval plans beginning that January.

In fact the orders Rear-Admiral de Burgues Missiessy was following had been given on 26th October 1804 and then modified on 23rd December 1804, when Napoleon personally instructed the Rear-Admiral to sail to the West Indies 'to conquer several of the English islands in the Antilles, and in particular, Dominica and St Lucia, and to reinforce our colonies of Martinique and Guadeloupe that they will no longer be threatened', Villeneuve's fleet at Toulon was to sail to the tip of South America to seize Cayenne, Surinam, Berbice and Demerara. After landing a few thousand troops in Martinique together with tons of supplies and ammunition, Missiessy was 'to really ravage English commerce' at Antigua, Montserrat, St Christophe and other British possessions. Afterwards they were all to return together to the Channel ports. In short this operation was intended to harm British commercial interests as much as it could and hopefully draw some British ships away from the Channel in the process. This, at least, was the plan Missiessy had with him when he sailed on 10th January.

But Rear-Admiral Missiessy's unseen departure from Rochefort had not gone off as well as the British had thought. Although the complement of 3,429 troops had already embarked, their commanding officer, General Lagrange, and his staff only reached the port and boarded the flagship (the 118-gun *Majestueux*) in the roadstead off the Ile d'Aix just before it sailed. Close by, four 74-gun ships in mint condition had just been fitted out for the expedition and lay at anchor: the *Jemmapes*, *Magnanime*, *Suffren* and *Lion*, in addition to three frigates and two brigs.

But then complications arose, as Missiessy later reported. 'The weather was ominous and it was snowing . . . the tide being favourable at one o'clock in the afternoon, the *Majestueux* set sail, the rest of the squadron following suit, with the exception of the *Magnanime* as it could not weigh anchor. I had to wait an extra hour-and-a-half 'til that was done'. Then, once at sea the real problems began, for the squadron was caught up in an unexpectedly fierce gale, indeed so fierce that it swept the sea clear of the Royal Navy, which was seeking shelter as best it could. Several of the French vessels suffered major damage. The flagship *Majestueux* lost her mainmast and a topmast, while the *Suffren* one of her topmasts, as the *Jemmapes* saw her mainyard shattered and two other vessels reported similar damage. Fortunately Missiessy did not encounter the British and, with the aid of jury-rigged masts, limped across the Atlantic to the West Indies.

The vessels reached Fort de France on 22nd February where Rear-Admiral Missiessy met with the Captain-General of Martinique, Vice-Admiral Villaret, and laid plans to attack British forts, settlements, 'factories' and shipping. This included the siege of Dominica by the French who were to be surprised by the vigorous defence they encountered there causing them to withdraw. Over the ensuing weeks Missiessy captured a total of thirty-three British merchant vessels. Though by now he was quite ill, this did not seem to prevent him from pushing on with his mission as best he could with his squadron in its weakened condition.

On 12th March, however, Missiessy received fresh orders from Admiral Decrès, informing him that 'the combined operations [were] cancelled' and that there was to be no meeting up with other French vessels because 'Vice-Admiral Villeneuve had been forced by gales to return to the port of Toulon'. Instead, Missiessy was to return to Rochefort because 'it is likely the enemy will no longer be there in force'. The Naval Minister concluded by congratulating him, informing him of the Emperor's 'satisfaction with the first part of your campaign'.

After leaving reinforcements and supplies at Martinique and San Domingo, the Rochefort squadron set sail for France on 28th March with the same ten vessels it had started out with, but now manned by only 3,937 sailors! In addition to the captured shipping at St Christophe, Nièvres and Montserrat, they had added 886,384 francs in booty to the French Treasury, which at least paid for their salaries and wages.

After reading the final reports of the expedition, however, far from appreciating Rear-Admiral Missiessy's feat – for a feat it was with a crippled squadron, skeleton crews, untrained men and an ailing skipper –

the Emperor informed the unfortunate commander upon his return of his great disappointment in him, thanks in part to a highly critical report he had received from Vice-Admiral Villaret, who had been upset at the sudden departure of the squadron before it had accomplished everything he wanted it to. It was only upon his return to Rochefort that Missiessy learned that Napoleon had, in fact, issued an entirely new plan (his *fifth* invasion plan) on 27th February, which had never reached him in Martinique, that required him to remain there after all and await Villeneuve!

Missiessy returned a broken man, broken in health and in spirit. 'I find it extremely painful to learn that he [Napoleon] is not satisfied with it [the results of his mission]', he informed Naval Minister Decrès in the first week of June, 'after I had acted most vigorously and used all my experience, all my intellectual faculties and the last ounce of my strength to carry it out.' He then struck his flag, although he was the only French admiral so far willing to, or capable of, carrying out his orders without excuses and, indeed, with great valour and distinction. The Emperor was not always an easy man to deal with, but in fact the real reason for Napoleon's frustration in this instance was probably his own failure to get the change of plans out to Missiessy in time.

The Secret Convention that Spain had signed and exchanged with France on 19th October 1803 had upset the British and made a mockery of Madrid's claims to neutrality. As seen earlier, it required Spain to provide, in addition to a large 'subsidy' to France, all ship repairs and armament demanded by French warships in Spanish ports, as well as allowing French soldiers and sailors to cross by land from France into Spain to reinforce French vessels in those harbours. French guns, or to be more precise, the threat of General Augereau's army poised at Bayonne for an invasion of Spain, had ensured a reluctant Spanish signature. However, all the guns in France could not force the Spanish to live up to every clause, and when less than half of the first six-month 'subsidy' instalment of 36,000,000 francs demanded by Napoleon was received on 21st February 1805, Foreign Minister Talleyrand immediately informed the Spanish Ambassador that the First Consul could not accept such conduct, but was assured of the 'effectiveness of the efforts you will make to ensure the execution of the engagements contracted by your court'.[1] In short, at this stage the relationship between France and Spain could hardly be described as either enthusiastic or even amicable. French ships in Spanish ports would receive help, gradually, and subsidies would be sent from the depleted Spanish Treasury, in part, but then only under continued threat.

The British, in turn, complained constantly about the special consideration and preference given to the French in all their relations with Spain, leaving an unhappy Spanish Government caught between two powerful foes. Indeed, the British Government officially stated later, after learning about the October 1803 Convention, that they considered it in itself 'sufficient reason for a state of war to exist between England and Spain', claiming that Spain 'now found herself identified with the republican government of France and was entirely under its control'.

Spain remonstrated with Bonaparte over the legitimate criticisms by Great Britain concerning the contravention of the laws of neutrality by arming French ships. Bonaparte replied on 1st March 1804, agreeing in theory to desist from further requests to the Spanish to arm his vessels or, as he put it, the demand 'not to arm [French vessels] in the ports of Spain is in keeping with the concept and obligations of neutrality', but he nevertheless reserved the right to have his vessels repaired 'in the ports of Spain which find themselves there as a result of untoward circumstances'. Naturally this meant that French vessels would continue to be both repaired and armed there. What was even more galling to the British, and Cochrane for one was repeatedly bringing up the matter, was that the French were also selling their prizes in Spanish ports, that is, British vessels seized at sea, while their crews were detained in Spanish prisons and considered as 'prisoners of war'.

It was these actions that Prime Minister Pitt's Government found so blatantly offensive and that finally led to Admiral Cornwallis being authorised, as seen earlier, to seize Spanish treasure ships in the autumn of 1804 and prevent Spanish warships from leaving harbour to aid the French.

By mid-July 1804, Foreign Minister Talleyrand had some observations of his own to make about the presence of the enemy. 'The English squadron [off El Ferrol], as a result of its proximity to the coast and by constantly maintaining its station without let-up within view of land, indeed almost always within cannon-shot of land, seems to be more of a littoral establishment for attack and defence than a means of mobile naval warfare', he observed to Admiral Gravina, adding that it was responsible for intercepting communications between ports and preventing French vessels from entering or leaving. Therefore, he continued, this 'part of the Spanish coast which is continually threatened by the presence of an enemy squadron must deprive them [the British] of such advantages as can now be derived from the official state of neutrality'. Unlike the French squadron, which had entered El Ferrol in a state of distress, the British had established themselves there 'with hostile intent' and, consequently, Spanish neutrality no longer applied and must cease forthwith.

Month by month the French Government were putting more and more pressure to bear on Spain. The French certainly made no bones about the situation and, immediately after receiving the news of Captain Moore's seizure of the Spanish treasure ships, employing the same heavy-handed means he had used earlier when forcing full co-operation from the conquered Dutch, Talleyrand ordered General Beurnonville to proceed to Madrid as the new French Ambassador. 'A state of war having broken out most unexpectedly between Spain and England, as a result of one of the scandalous violations of the law of nations, perpetrated by the usual means employed by England for more than a century now when beginning all her quarrels, His Majesty has decided that you must go to Madrid without delay' to make the most of the situation and urge the Spanish to make a formal declaration of war against Britain. He pointed out to the Spanish Prime Minister 'that this war is not a subject of doubt or deliberation, but an established reality. Spanish blood had flowed. The audacious attack by the English squadron was a barbarous act'. Further, that, in consequence, France and Spain must draft a new treaty, one providing for joint military action against the enemy or, as the elegant Talleyrand concluded on 30th October 1804, 'The Spanish Government must freely unite its efforts with ours in a cause that is one we both share.'

Within a month Beurnonville was able to report complete success to Talleyrand following intensive talks with the Prince of Peace, Manuel de Godoy. Godoy, as Prime Minister, had agreed to acknowledge 'the existence of a state of war' and to the immediate arming of all major naval ports, while assuring that 'all English vessels, ships or boats' would be seized by the Spanish military authorities. Furthermore, an embargo would be placed on all ports, 'all English property will be sequestered' and all English citizens arrested. Finally, Admiral Gravina (who was still in Paris) had been 'authorised to prepare a plan of Spanish naval action in concert with the French, based on the views and special projects of His Imperial Majesty'. Clearly this was to be a French show. By 27th November, Napoleon had what he wanted and a formal agreement would follow shortly.

It is curious, if not ironic, that the two principal Spanish links with France were those established through the good offices of the Prime

Minister Manuel de Godoy, who was to die a French subject, and Admiral Gravina, born an Italian.

Don Federico Carlos Gravina came from an old Sicilian family and was born in Palermo in 1756. Thanks to their close ties with the Royal family, young Federico was invited to accompany Carlos III (whose bastard son he was reputed to be) to Spain, at which time Gravina began his career in the Spanish Navy. Unlike his French counterpart Pierre Villeneuve, Federico Gravina had distinguished himself in numerous naval actions, showing 'bravery and resolution'.

An intellectually restless man, at the age of thirty-two he went to Constantinople to study the more refined aspects of astronomy and later was sent by his Government to Britain for several months to study the Royal Navy. He afterwards distinguished himself again in battle, this time in taking Toulon, then in the defence of Rosas and later at Cadiz against the British, where his conduct was described as 'brilliant'.

By the turn of the century he had already demonstrated his kinship to French ideas and values and a general antipathy to things British. It was hardly unexpected, therefore, that he was dispatched in 1801 to the Spanish section of San Domingo in the West Indies to co-ordinate efforts there with the French Navy. Nor was it surprising that, upon the creation of the new Empire in France in 1804, the Spanish King, Carlos IV, dispatched him to Paris as his Ambassador and asked him to represent the Spanish Royal family at the Emperor's coronation that December.

It was, in fact, during the last six months of 1804 in Paris that Admiral Gravina had the opportunity to meet Naval Minister Decrès and Napoleon, whom he took to immediately and greatly respected. The meeting between Gravina and the stony Vice-Admiral Pierre Villeneuve was not quite so felicitous, however, and from the outset the two men, so very different in character, did not get on at all well together. The swarthy Gravina, who was short and stout, with a long, thick nose, emphasising all the more a receding mouth and chin, always had the look of energy and action about him, whereas Villeneuve, with his large, thin nose, high forehead, arrogant chin and almost snarling lips, looked the effete caricature of the smug French naval officer of the *ancien régime* he was. Be that as it may, Fate and History had brought the two men together for the remaining months of their lives.

*

As General Pierre Beurnonville had stated in November 1804, the signing of a military pact between France and Spain was merely a question of time. Following Spain's declaration of war against Britain in December 1804, and a few weeks after attending the Emperor's coronation in Notre-Dame Cathedral, Admiral Gravina wrote an official but cordial letter to Admiral Decrès stating that, 'given the violence and hostile acts committed by English warships against Spanish frigates [the treasure ships]', the King of Spain had declared war against England and 'at the same time deigned to confer upon me the command of his fleet', which would necessitate the Admiral's return shortly to Spain to take up that new position. He made it perfectly clear that he was completely in accord with his King and added that, 'I believe it suitable and in conformity with the instructions I have received from my Court and in our meetings that I had the honour of having with Your Excellency, to make some observations about the subjects under discussion and to refer them to Your Excellency which, if you find them useful, you may then present to His Imperial Majesty . . . in order that the two Governments may reach a consensus and inflict the greatest amount of damage on our common enemy'. He then went on to discuss Spanish naval strength, conditions in Spanish ports and the possibility of expeditions against British possessions in the Caribbean and the Indian Ocean. It must be emphasised that Gravina was now introducing this subject freely and offering his fullest co-operation in executing them. In both regions the two nations had mutual interests and could be of considerable help to one another in joint or co-ordinated naval exercises. 'I should be charmed if, before my departure for Madrid, Your Excellency might communicate to me, in writing or verbally, His Imperial Majesty's views on these matters, that I might in turn inform the Minister of the King, my Master.'

One week later, on 4th January 1805, Don Federico Gravina signed the Franco-Spanish Pact of eight articles, which now permitted complete military co-operation between the two countries or, to be more precise, put the entire Spanish Royal Navy at the disposal of the French Emperor. It was everything Napoleon could have hoped for, comprising the elements that General Beurnonville had mentioned on 27th November, including the invasion flotilla gathering at Texel, Ostend, Dunkirk, Calais, Boulogne and Le Havre, in addition to the other expeditions preparing at Brest, Rochefort and Toulon, where a combined total of 188,000 French, Dutch and Irish troops were now assembled.[2] These squadrons 'are destined for expeditions that His Majesty the Emperor will himself explain to His Catholic Majesty within the next month'.

The King of Spain 'will have armed immediately at the port of Ferrol' eight ships of the line and four frigates, which were added to the French force of five ships and two brigs already there, along with 4,000 Spanish troops. Another twelve to fifteen Spanish battleships were to be prepared along with 24,000 troops at Cadiz and another six ships at Cartagena.[3] All ships and men were to be ready in all ports by 30th March at the latest. Carlos IV had expressed his anxiety about possible British retaliatory expeditions against Spain and her possessions in the Caribbean and Latin America and, in Article Six of the agreement, Napoleon 'guarantees to His Catholic Majesty the integrity of his territory in Europe and the restitution of any of his colonies should they be seized in the course of the present war', the Emperor also promising his good offices in negotiating the return of the island of Trinidad to Spain. The Spanish Government, of course, were constrained from entering into a separate peace with Britain. Altogether Spain would be adding between twenty-nine and thirty-one ships of the line to the French war effort and thus this treaty was a major coup for Napoleon. If ever he could pull off his invasion plans, now was the time.

After congratulating Admiral Gravina on his new appointment by Carlos IV as Commander-in-Chief of the Spanish Fleet, Naval Minister Decrès then informed the Admiral that Napoleon 'wishes you to leave as quickly as possible in order to hasten the preparation of your fleet. Time is flying and His Majesty is determined to strike the major blows that he has been preparing for so long.'

The Spanish Ambassador left Paris in the first week of January 1805, making great haste, reaching Madrid on the 31st of that month where the French Ambassador, General Beurnonville, was busy co-ordinating events between his Government and the Spanish naval ministry. Admiral Gravina was as good as his word, setting to work at a tempo rarely seen before in the dignified Spanish capital: 'The day before yesterday he went to Aranjuez to receive his orders from the King: yesterday (4th February) we had a conference together with the Prince of Peace, and today the Admiral sets out for Cadiz'. In fact, 'the greatly increased activity that will be caused there by his presence now makes him hope to have instead of twenty, thirty-one vessels ready for sea (at the three ports): sixteen at Cadiz, nine at Ferrol and six at Cartagena.'

Before the month of February was out General Beurnonville was able to confirm to Talleyrand that 'the sole purpose towards which the Spanish Government is today directing its efforts and attention, is the rapid preparation and arming of their squadrons. They continue to work towards this goal with unceasing effort . . .' A new estimate now found that El Ferrol would soon have eight battleships and four frigates ready, Cadiz another twelve ships and Cartagena six, for a total of twenty-six ships of the line.

Writing from his new headquarters at Cadiz that February, Gravina privately informed Admiral Decrès that he did indeed think that the twelve ships at Cadiz would be ready by the end of March, but he now acknowledged for the first time that he was encountering two most serious problems. 'I very much doubt that the number of sailors required to complete the ships' complements will be found by the time required', nor would there be nearly enough provisions and supplies. In closing he asked Decrès 'to present my humble respects to H.M. the Emperor. For my part I shall do everything I possibly can to have everything ready'. Gravina's French grammar and spelling may not have been up to par, but there could be no complaints about his optimism and his intention to succeed at his formidable new task.

Spain was indeed short of experienced sailors, many thousands having died or been invalided as a result of epidemics ravaging the southern Spanish ports, Cartagena in particular. 'I shall continue to endeavour with all the zeal and activity possible to fulfil the orders of my Government', Gravina nevertheless assured Decrès on 5th April, and though he was bringing about minor miracles in the preparation of ships and their armament, he could not do the impossible and create trained sailors where they did not exist. If to the north Admiral Verhuell was also doing everything in his power to meet the incessant demands of Napoleon, it was to further his own career, for the success he personally expected to achieve. Gravina, on the other hand, an equally capable man, gave as much devotion to Napoleon as he did to the King of Spain himself.

The first week of April found the Spanish Admiral aboard his new flagship, the 80-gun *Argonauta*, in the roadstead at Cadiz directing all phases of the preparations, for if all went well and Villeneuve did successfully evade Nelson's ships, he would soon be appearing there. As it turned out, Gravina's letter of 5th April was to be the last he was to write to Paris prior to putting to sea.

The first inkling of a real plan of strategy and objectives involving a major joint Franco-Spanish naval effort emerged late in February 1805 as Prime Minister Godoy awaited the imminent visit of Colonel-General Andoche Junot from Portugal, who was to present Napoleon's instructions on this very subject. 'There is only one thing I expect from the Prince of Peace', Napoleon had informed Junot on 23rd February, 'that the Spanish fleets be ready for the great expeditions that I am contemplating . . . I require his taking effective measures that, between 20th and 30th March, we will have six ships of the line and two or three frigates at Cadiz [and] six ships and two or three frigates at Ferrol' each of which was to carry about 1,000 troops. These would then join French squadrons as they appeared off those ports, though 'it is my intention that my squadrons do not enter either Cadiz or Ferrol, that, instead, the junction take place just outside while still under sail' once the British blockades had been broken. 'This will be the year of our great operations!' Thus it was that the French Emperor now approached the critical period, 27th February to 2nd March, when he would formally draw up these new plans for the '*grandes opérations*'.

Napoleon next checked with the flotilla and army units round Boulogne, to co-ordinate their efforts with his new blueprint. 'Let me know the precise situation of the army', he wrote to General Soult on 27th February, 'for the time is not very distant when we shall finally begin our operations'. He also demanded 'a very detailed report on the state of the wooden fort (Fort Rouge), on the basin and ports of Boulogne, Wimereux and Ambleteuse and the situation of the various divisions of the flotilla'.

On the same day, Naval Minister Decrès dispatched a change of orders to 'General Missiessy' at Martinique, informing him of the new plans, that his squadron remain in the Antilles until the end of June, and that further instructions were to follow soon. As we saw earlier, however, these orders only reached Martinique *after* Missiessy had set sail for the return journey to Europe. On 16th January, Napoleon had authorised another plan (his fourth invasion plan) involving the French squadrons at Brest, Rochefort and El Ferrol (including a small Spanish contingent) to sail to the West Indies where they would be joined by Villeneuve's Toulon fleet with some 26,000 men, the main purpose being to ravage and destroy British colonies throughout the Caribbean, but, eleven days later, the French Emperor rescinded that order in favour of the sweeping new plan he was to develop between 27th February and 2nd March, which now, for the first time, included an important role for the Spanish Navy.

Even as he was preparing his latest set of plans, however, he was meeting a most unexpected obstacle. It was not from British blockades, the lack of crews or provisions, nor even from the weather, but from the newly named fleet commander at Toulon, Vice-Admiral Villeneuve, ordered to serve as Ganteaume's Second-in-Command, who was now having cold feet.

A highly emotional boy, Pierre-Charles-Jean-Baptiste-Silvestre Ville- neuve, a native and aristocrat of Valensoles in Provence, had entered the navy of Louis XVI at the age of fifteen. His early zeal and apparent capacity had brought quick promotion, he reaching the rank of rear- admiral by the age of thirty-three.

He had fought against Nelson at the battle of the Nile at Aboukir Bay and had narrowly escaped in the *Guillaume Tell*, instilling in him an intense fear of that English admiral for the rest of his life. The remainder of his career seemed surprisingly colourless for a sailor, lacking the many clashes at sea with the enemy that were so characteristic of the backgrounds of his British counterparts, which nevertheless did not prevent him from being promoted to the rank of vice-admiral in 1804, and assuming the command at Toulon later that year. Ironically, he was an outspoken opponent of Napoleon and thought most of his naval concepts and plans utter madness.

Villeneuve had reached Toulon on 19th December 1804 when he hoisted his flag over his new flagship, the recently launched 80-gun *Bucentaure*. There he found sealed orders waiting for him, which he duly promised 'to execute to the letter'. On 21st December he warned the captains of his fleet that they would suffer the worst consequences if 'any commanding captain . . . is not at his post in the heat of battle' when they eventually met with the British, though even to them he acknowledged that he 'did not propose to go out looking for the enemy, in fact I even want to avoid him if necessary, in order to reach my destination'.

The bad weather beating the Channel now also reached across the French heartland, keeping Villeneuve in harbour, followed by suddenly shifting winds preventing him from getting under way. 'All is ready for our departure', he insisted. 'If yesterday's winds had continued, I should have set sail', but the winds were contrary. Each successive report included a note on the position of the British: 'Admiral Nelson's fleet was sighted the 5th [26th December] by the coastal look-out stations . . . their number put at eleven ships and two frigates . . . The entire Mediterranean is aware that the [French] squadron is about to depart. Nelson certainly knows it and it will not be easy to escape his look-outs', he informed Decrès on 30th December. A week later he notified him that, 'The number of enemy vessels has increased along the coast;

according to reports I have received, the English fleet, though out of sight, is very close at hand', and he estimated Nelson's strength now at fifteen ships of the line. In a second letter the same day, the agitated vice-admiral advised Decrès that the situation required 'great caution' on his part if he were to escape, but on 2nd January 1805 the Naval Minister, who was by now feeling the full brunt of Napoleon's blistering tirades, sharply reminded Villeneuve once again that he must depart forthwith. Paris had had enough of his excuses. None the less, on 14th January he was *still* sending those excuses to Decrès from Toulon harbour, acknowledging that the weather was improving, and that the 'enemy cruisers have not appeared'.

Finally the long awaited event occurred – Villeneuve hoisted the signal from the *Bucentaure* to the other ten ships of the line and seven frigates, carrying some 6,333 troops, to get underway. But as he sailed out of the harbour on 18th January, he was struck immediately and battered by powerful north-westerly winds which soon separated some of his vessels from the fleet and damaged others.

'I have some sad news to relate to you about the squadron and its return to Toulon', he informed the Naval Minister on 21st January 1805. As every vessel had suffered some damage and 'there being no possibility of raising a full press of sail with vessels under such difficult conditions', which could sail neither well nor quickly, and noting that two British frigates had already spotted them, Vice-Admiral Villeneuve had signalled his ships to return to port. 'Had I been seen by the English squadron, it would have been quite impossible to escape from it', he pleaded. So ended his first attempt to carry out his orders and leave Toulon and the Mediterranean. Needless to say, Napoleon was not much pleased with his performance, and ordered General Lauriston, the commanding officer of the troops on board the *Bucentaure*, to report back periodically on the actions of the unreliable Villeneuve.

With the Spanish entry into the war and the problems arising from Villeneuve's continued inability to escape from Toulon, Napoleon once again decided to revise all plans for his naval expeditions, and devised his fifth invasion plan, which resulted in fresh orders to Admirals Ganteaume, Gourdon (at El Ferrol) and Villeneuve. On 2nd March 1805 Vice-Admiral Henri Ganteaume was informed of this latest move to invade Great Britain by Napoleon himself, who ordered him to sail at once with his fleet of twenty-one ships of the line and six frigates, though still forbidding him to attack Cornwallis' blockading ships. Time and again Decrès and Napoleon had ordered Ganteaume to sail over the past several months in order to make a rendezvous with another squadron, but every time he, too, had an excuse for not doing so: the weather, lack of supplies or trained sailors, the presence of Cornwallis' fleet just off Brest. Thus Napoleon now wrote again: 'You are to put to sea as quickly as possible' along with the 8,768 troops on board. 'You will first go to Ferrol' where he was 'to attack and take the seven or eight vessels of the English squadron' at the same time releasing Rear-Admiral Gourdon's long-pent-up squadron (then estimated at four ships and two frigates), as well as the Spanish division, both of which were to join him. 'Having thus rallied these squadrons, you will take the most direct route to our island of Martinique [where] you will find our squadrons from Toulon and Rochefort, which have orders to sail under your flag.' Meanwhile, the troops he was bringing were to be landed to reinforce French holdings there. 'God willing, if all goes well, we hope that you will find you have a fleet of more than forty ships of the line under your command.'

Vice-Admiral Villeneuve's orders had been issued the same day: 'Having resolved to assemble the largest part of our naval forces at our island of Martinique, it is our intention that you proceed at once to Fort de France, Martinique, with our squadron at Toulon and the ships we have in the roadstead at Cadiz' and then to land 3,140 troops there under the command of General Lauriston. If he did not find Vice-Admiral Ganteaume and Rear-Admiral Missiessy waiting for him upon his arrival, he was to wait for up to forty days, but if during that period they did not arrive, he was 'to return to Europe via San Domingo while doing all the harm you can possibly do to the enemy'. He was to stop *en route* at Santiago Bay, in the Canaries, for another twenty days before continuing on to Cadiz where he was to receive orders for his 'final destination'.

If all went according to plan, all three squadrons meeting at Martinique, Vice-Admiral Ganteaume, at the head of this combined fleet, was commanded 'to return to Europe without losing a moment', arriving at Ouessant, near Brest where 'you will attack the English vessels you find waiting there and then continue in a direct course for Boulogne where our person will be and where we will inform you of your final destination'. Napoleon expected the Franco-Spanish fleet of some forty or so battleships to arrive at Boulogne 'within the month designated, between 10th June and 10th July [1805]'.

In fact, there were several other variations to the plan in the event that all or part of the other squadrons did not rendezvous with Ganteaume at Martinique and these included his continuing on to Boulogne 'with at least twenty-five ships' if he thought he was in a favourable enough position *vis-à-vis* the British to do so. Napoleon concluded his orders to Admiral Ganteaume with his usual best wishes. 'In confiding the command of an army [*armée*] as important as this, whose operations will have so much influence over the destinies of the world, we count on your devotion, your talents and your attachment to our person.'

Even without Rear-Admiral Missiessy, however, who as has been seen was already *en route* back to his home port, Ganteaume's powerful fleet, including the squadrons at El Ferrol, Cadiz and Toulon, could still muster some forty-three battleships[4] if all went well, and it was with that in mind that Napoleon dispatched General Junot, the French Ambassador to Portugal, on 3rd March to Spain to arrange for complete co-operation from the Spanish Navy in this enterprise.

Nevertheless, the long months of waiting, of inaction, were equivalent to failure in the eyes of many of Napoleon's men and commanders, and towards the end of 1804 reports began reaching the Tuileries of desertions, growing problems of drunkenness and lack of discipline, and some of his officers were far more honest in their appraisal of the situation than he was himself.

'I beg Your Majesty to permit one of your most devoted subjects to discuss some of his thoughts on the present state of public opinion', began an extraordinary letter from Naval Prefect Forfait at Le Havre on 13th November 1804. 'It seems quite evident that the army no longer plans on invading England. I hear this view expressed every day, indeed expressed in such a way as to make me despair, because I think otherwise and I expect to see Your Majesty master of the World before this year is out.' However, he knew, too, that officers and troops were worrying about 'the difficulties involved in the flotilla making this crossing and, alas, appear to have very little confidence in this force'. Even as memories of the Coronation celebrations were dying out in January 1805 Naval Prefect Bonnefoux echoed similar reservations at Calais. 'So long as the Government wanted to maintain the threatening attitude of the flotilla, to let the enemy think that it could at any moment be launched to carry out the invasion, and so long as everyone was openly declaring the imminent departure of this flotilla, it was absolutely necessary that all the vessels were constantly ready, their sails on board, full provisions of food and supplies and every other characteristic sign of a forthcoming sailing . . . But when the political curtain which conceals a major operation is removed and one sees that a postponement has been declared, and this known by everyone, then there is no longer any inconvenience in taking

the measures required to execute certain wise practical economic steps'
and he then advised withdrawing many dozens of flotilla gunboats from
service at Calais, removing their ammunition, sails, supplies and food.
And just to bring home the reality of the deplorable state of the vessels
now he informed Decrès that at Calais alone the gunboats had suffered
such damage from storms and British bombardments that they required
'2,072 days of repairs' to put them in sailing order while the transport
vessels required another '2,894 days work'.

As if this were not bad enough, now in this amazing year of 1805,
startling new problems arose involving Villeneuve, who wanted to resign
his commission and abandon the fleet at Toulon, following his abortive
sortie on 18th January. 'You will be so good as to recall that I have not
asked for the command of this squadron. What is more, to the contrary, I
have always sought a practical and useful career, as opposed to one filled
with glory', Villeneuve declared to Decrès on 22nd January. 'I should like
to point out to you that *about all one can expect from a career in the French
Navy today is shame and confusion*,* and anyone who denies this I declare
to be presumptuous, utterly blind, and incapable of straight thinking, for
such men are as ignorant about their own situation today as they are of the
real situation concerning our enemies.'

The fact is that Villeneuve had been promoted too quickly and to a
rank whose duties he was incapable of performing and now, in a moment
of sheer frustration, clearly at his wits' end, he was in no mood to bandy
the usual polite thrusts with either the Naval Minister or the Emperor.
None the less, much of what he had to say was indeed true.

He continued, 'It is my most ardent wish that the Emperor decide not
to commit any of his squadrons to the hazards of these events, for if he
does *the French flag will be seriously compromised*.* In reality *it is utterly
impossible for us to defeat the enemy when both sides are equal, indeed, they will
beat us even when they are a third weaker than we are*.'* It was shocking, to
say the least, the like of which had probably never been seen in the entire
annals of the French Navy. Pierre Villeneuve continued that his health
had suffered from his career and that in consequence, 'I should view it
with the greatest pleasure if the Emperor would replace me in this
command . . . I have only one wish remaining and that is to see my
conduct in this affair justified, but under no circumstances do I intend to
become the laughing stock of Europe by being involved in further
disasters'. He pointed out that he had just returned to Toulon 'with

*Author's italics.

half the vessels dismasted' and that, although the squadron had seemed splendid enough at anchor and the crews looked quite smart when they were turned out, 'they had had no experience at sea, in stormy weather' and when they finally did sail for the first time, they did not know what to do and panicked. 'Thus it was impossible to manoeuvre the ships properly', which led to the extraordinary amount of damage suffered, a situation compounded by 'the inferior quality of supplies provided by the arsenals and Naval Yards'. Ropes, canvas and timber were of substandard quality (a claim echoed by Lord St Vincent as a result of his own investigation into the Royal Navy, and later by Rear-Admiral Missiessy at Rochefort). Under such circumstances a disaster such as they had suffered was hardly surprising, indeed, it was almost inevitable.

Denis Decrès no doubt was absolutely horror-struck when he received this letter and would have had to summon up the courage to bring it to the Tuileries for Napoleon's attention. What was surprising, however, was that both the Emperor and Decrès avoided censuring or castigating Admiral Villeneuve (at least officially), but instead tried to mollify him. Napoleon, though, wrote privately to General Lauriston, the commander of the troops aboard Villeneuve's ill-fated fleet, confiding, 'I really believe your Admiral does not know how to command. The separation of a few vessels was nothing at all. We would have to renounce ever putting to sea, even during the finest weather, if we always worried about losing a few ships'.

In the end Villeneuve neither resigned nor was dismissed because Admiral Decrès simply had no one else of his rank and experience with whom to replace him at this moment. Pierre Villeneuve, therefore, remained at Toulon, preparing for the next attempt to put to sea, supervising the repairs of the fleet, while venting his spleen against Rear-Admiral Emériaux, Naval Prefect of Toulon, for 'the lack of good sailors [and] the defective quality of the sails, rigging and masts furnished by the port of Toulon' and condemning a severe decline in discipline and lack of faith by local officials and crews, though acknowledging that 'It is quite impossible to prevent desertions when the ships are in this harbour'.

It was in that unsettled and grudging half-hearted state of mind that Vice-Admiral Villeneuve remained at his post, though at this stage under the orders of Vice-Admiral Ganteaume once he reached Martinique.

Dispatch – Sir Robert Calder, Vice-Admiral, to Mr Marsden, Admiralty
'Prince of Wales', off El Ferrol, 2nd March 1805.

Sir, – I beg to acquaint you for the information of the Lords Commissioners
of the Admiralty, I arrived here this day in pursuance of orders from the
Honourable Admiral Cornwallis, and took upon me the command of the
ships stationed off this coast . . .

REAR-ADMIRAL ALEXANDER Cochrane had been serving off El Ferrol
and La Coruña for the past year, where he had maintained a successful
blockade, preventing a total of ten French and Spanish ships of the battle
line from escaping independently or from forming a rendezvous with
other squadrons off the coast. However, Sir Robert Calder, who now
assumed command of the El Ferrol squadron, unlike Cochrane, or
Pellew before him, was to prove a handful for Admiral Cornwallis. An
inordinately ambitious, even ruthless, gentleman, it was rumoured
among Admiralty Board Commissioners and in the fleet off Brest, where
he had been serving under Admiral Cornwallis since 1803, that, upon
returning from the great victory off the Cape of St Vincent in February
1797, Calder had deliberately omitted Nelson's major role in that success
from the official reports he brought to London.

Having been promoted from rear- to vice-admiral the year before, on
Admiral Cornwallis' recommendation, this new appointment off Cape
Finisterre at El Ferrol seemed only fitting. Yet Robert Calder was a naval
officer who respected no one else's authority and therefore had to be
watched. For instance, he soon began bypassing Admiral Cornwallis,
sending long reports directly to the Admiralty, requesting that his
squadron be reinforced by another two frigates and two smaller vessels in
addition to the seven vessels already under his command (the *Prince of
Wales*, *Repulse*, *Terrible*, *Impétueux*, *Montagu*, *Malta* and *Indefatigable*), with
two more, the *Hero* and *Defiance*, which in fact were already *en route* to join
him. This he argued was necessary 'if this squadron is to be kept in a
proper state to be enabled to oppose the Combined Squadron of the
enemy if they should escape from Ferrol . . .' Nevertheless, his efforts
upon assuming this critical post were certainly vigorous to say the least –
hardly endearing him to the already overtaxed officers and men of the
squadron. On 2nd March he informed London that, despite previous

reports to the contrary, he found the French and Spanish ships 'in bad order, not half manned, nor provisioned', which though good news now, was a situation that was to change dramatically over the ensuing months.

Meanwhile Cornwallis, who since refitting had been at sea throughout a long tempestuous winter and spring, now requested two months' leave on 3rd March 'in order I may have an opportunity of using some exercise on shore during that time for the benefit of my health', while reporting that the *Ville de Paris* was once again in need of substantial repairs, 'her stern frame . . . very much shaken' as a result of 'the very severe gales of wind and remarkably heavy sea' they had been experiencing for many weeks. At this time he was in the midst of preparing an entirely new, separate squadron, initially of five ships, for Vice-Admiral Collingwood (including the *Dreadnought, Tonnant, Mars, Illustrious* and *Minotaur*) and a foreign destination shortly to be named. With the detachment of these ships from service off the coast of Brittany, the Channel Fleet would of course be greatly weakened, but Cornwallis was following an Admiralty order and it was no good questioning it.

While seeking shelter in Torbay on 14th March from another gale, Cornwallis was informed that his request for leave had been granted, and that Admiral Lord Gardner, currently on station off the Irish coast, would replace him during his absence. Before going ashore, the Admiral informed Lord Melville that he was already beginning to find Sir Robert Calder a bit of a prima donna and quite irksome. For one thing it rankled that Calder had been continuing to communicate directly with the Admiralty, bypassing the chain of command. 'If he meant to write to their Lordships . . . he might, I should think save himself the trouble of sending long dispatches here' to him as well. As for the question of extra vessels, 'If the Vice-Admiral has two frigates stationed with him, there must be fewer looking off Cape Finisterre and farther to the westward for any squadron of the enemy which might be passing on to obtain intelligence. The small vessels, if we had them to send at the moment, might be very useful, and I have no doubt that the Vice-Admiral would find them very convenient', he quipped caustically, observing that 'Neither Sir Edward Pellew nor Rear-Admiral Cochrane had more than one, nor did they apply for a reinforcement'. With that Admiral Cornwallis returned to his estate at Newlands for a few weeks of badly needed rest where the only prima donna he would have to come into contact with was a recently purchased horse for his stables.

There was much more behind Cornwallis' peevishness, however, than Calder's demanding behaviour. The fact was that he was now an old man, by naval standards of the day, and Calder for one knew he would soon probably be having a new Commander-in-Chief, and thought he could irritate old Cornwallis with impunity. As long as Melville remained First Lord of the Admiralty, however, Cornwallis knew that he need not worry about being ordered to strike his flag and go ashore permanently. But the parliamentary manoeuvring to remove Lord Melville through the act of impeachment mentioned earlier was in full swing. Once he was out of the way, Cornwallis could be removed, against his will, and yet, in spite of deteriorating health, he liked his command off Brest and wanted to remain there. Lord St Vincent, however, was making it clear to all who would listen that he wanted Cornwallis out in order to replace him personally, now that he was without a berth himself! Understandably Admiral Cornwallis became more and more touchy about 'slights' he received from London from this moment forward and not without reason. Within less than a year he would be back at Newlands permanently, while St Vincent was occupying his quarters on board the *Ville de Paris* off Ushant.

Throughout the spring of 1805 another battle of wills was taking place, between Paris and Brest, where a fidgeting French Emperor was still trying to prod a seemingly unco-operative Vice-Admiral Ganteaume to leave the nest, to sail out of Brest water and carry out the apparently endless variety of plans he was sending him. 'I wish . . . to be informed, by return courier, of the time when you will be ready [to sail]', Napoleon wrote. 'It is already 15th March – there is not a moment to lose. Do not lose sight of the great destinies you hold in your hands. If you are bold enough, success is inevitable'.

The truth of the matter was that Napoleon's orders had left Ganteaume in a quandary. At first Napoleon had wanted him to sail out of Brest frequently and fight Cornwallis' squadrons in order to clear the blockade. More recently, however – even when Ganteaume had enough well-manned vessels to carry this out and, indeed, repeatedly requested permission to fight the British – Napoleon had forbidden it, informing him instead that he must keep all twenty-one ships of the line in perfect form and to escape with them from Brest *unseen* by Admiral Cornwallis in order to make the rendezvous with Villeneuve at Martinique. Their combined forces, at full strength, would be required upon their return if they were to plough through Cornwallis' ubiquitous fleet and then escort an army of some 167,000 men safely across to the shores of Kent.

Vice-Admiral Ganteaume replied on 24th March by telegraph to the

Emperor: 'The naval army is indeed ready and can set sail tomorrow night, but there are fifteen English vessels in the Iroise Passage [off Brest], and it is quite impossible to leave without risking a fight. Our success in such a fight, however, is not in doubt. I await Your Majesty's orders'. Unlike Villeneuve, Ganteaume was quite willing to have a go at the British, or so he said. Napoleon's reply was short and sweet: 'A naval victory under these circumstances serves no purpose. You have but one objective, that of fulfilling your mission. Sail without fighting', a message the Emperor was to repeat frequently over the ensuing weeks.

Vice-Admiral Honoré Ganteaume was fifty years old, in fairly good health (apart from his gout) and one of the very few senior French naval officers willing to take on the British. He had seen much fighting during his thirty years at sea, which included service in the West Indies during the American Revolution. In 1793 he had been captured by the British near the Gulf of Suez and dispatched to a prison in England, which hardly endeared his present enemies to him. Later, he had been wounded in action while commanding a squadron that successfully released other French vessels in Smyrna. Time and again he proved a skilful naval tactician and served for a long time in the English Channel. He was chief of staff to Admiral de Brueys at the ill-fated Battle of the Nile in Aboukir Bay, from which he, like Villeneuve, had escaped. In August 1799, Bonaparte had ordered Ganteaume to bring him from Alexandria, Egypt, to the small port of Fréjus, near Toulon, enabling the ambitious general to launch his successful *coup d'état* and become First Consul. Ganteaume, a loyal sailor, was not forgotten by Napoleon. It was at his personal request that Ganteaume had been promoted to the rank of rear- and later, vice-admiral. A few years later, after retiring from the navy, Napoleon appointed him to the *Grand Conseil d'Amirauté*, the French equivalent of the British Admiralty Board, which the Emperor had just created.

Now, however, it was a question of whether or not Ganteaume could follow orders and escape from Brest without engaging the enemy. In fact, his squadron was at this time the most powerful fleet possessed by France.*

On 28th March, Sir Charles Cotton, acting Commander-in-Chief pending the arrival of Lord Gardner, informed the Admiralty that

*See appendix 3

twenty-seven sail (including twenty-one sail of the line, four frigates and two brigs) had come out of Brest and anchored in the roadstead, 'from every appearance all of them ready to put to sea'. This was enough for Lord Melville who, on 31st March, directed Lord Gardner to make all haste and 'proceed to sea immediately'.

Gardner's flagship, the *Hibernia*, reached Ushant by 3rd April, where he joined the seventeen British sail of the line, only to discover that Admiral Ganteaume's entire fleet had left Bertheaume and Camaret roads to retreat to the safety of Brest Harbour on 29th March. It was a most frustrating business for British naval officers who wanted to come to grips once and for all with this powerful, if elusive, fleet. The French had declared war, but now refused to fight.

Calder had to report that, due to storm damage at El Ferrol, 'this squadron is now reduced to only five sail of the line, one frigate and a cutter' remarking a significant change beginning to take place there, the combined enemy force 'increasing and getting ready for sea very fast', including ten French and Spanish battleships and five frigates. Lord Gardner immediately detached three more sail of the line – the *Ajax*, *Malta* and *Terrible* – to reinforce Calder.

Vice-Admiral Collingwood returned aboard his flagship, the *Dreadnought*, on 8th April, following his first meeting with Admiral Lord Gardner since his assuming command, and was deeply distressed by what he had found: 'I saw him yesterday for an hour or two, and was sorry to find him altered for the worse – old, and out of spirits; yet, I think, if he were established he would recover again and be as active as ever, for there is no officer a more perfect master of the discipline of the fleet than he is'. Collingwood also confirmed that the French ships at Brest 'are perfectly ready for sea . . . We stood with our fleet, 17 sail of us, close up to their 21; but they did not show any disposition to come from under their batteries' – little suspecting the restraining nature of Ganteaume's personal orders from Napoleon.

From Paris the French Emperor was even now instructing Ganteaume that he was pleased with the state of preparedness and that he would find another eleven warships waiting for him when he reached Spain. 'The essential thing now is not to lose any time before Ferrol, and once your orders have been sent to them, that squadron will come out and join you.' As for the situation at Cadiz, 'Admiral Gravina is ready to join the French squadron [from Toulon]', with 8 ships and 2 frigates, though Napoleon had to acknowledge with some anxiety that he had 'no news at all yet from my Toulon squadron' but that, should all go well, 'I therefore expect you to be leaving the rendezvous [at Martinique after collecting all squadrons and returning to Europe] with more than 50 ships of the line'.

The moment was tense for all sides, with the renewed port and naval activity up and down the French and Spanish coasts and most ships appearing to be manned and ready to sail. What the Admiralty Board were now asking themselves was who was to move first – Brest, Rochefort, El Ferrol, Cadiz or Toulon, or a combination of them, and what the strategy was? Would the Brest fleet finally break out? Would the Toulon fleet ever put to sea and try to reach the Atlantic? There were a great many questions by the first week of April and few solid answers.

The earlier plans (27th February – 2nd March) which Napoleon had issued for a fresh attempt on England were finally rescinded by the Emperor on 22nd March, but it was only *after* Villeneuve's eventual departure from Toulon on 30th March that Napoleon formed his sixth invasion plan. These new plans now omitted the West Indies altogether and replaced that journey with one round Ireland and an appearance in the Channel before Dunkirk and Boulogne. Nevertheless two weeks later, on 13th April 1805, the French Emperor changed his mind *yet again*, now reverting to the previous plan, calling for a major expedition to the West Indies.

This seventh invasion plan would involve Villeneuve's fleet of eleven ships and six frigates stopping before the port of Cadiz where they would be reinforced by one French ship and Admiral Gravina's squadron of five ships of the line (the other Spanish ships being left at Cadiz in order to attract a large British naval presence). Now, with a total of perhaps nineteen ships (if two more joined them from Rochefort), Villeneuve was to sail for Martinique where Ganteaume, now reduced once more to Second-in-Command, would join him, hopefully with another twenty-one ships of the line. Their initial task once there was 'to expel the English from all their colonies in the Windward Islands', and conquer 'some English possessions or at least carry out expeditions that will utterly destroy the prosperity of the establishments belonging to the enemy for a long time to come'. This included seizing the islands of St Lucia and Dominica, to name just two, while strengthening the French positions on San Domingo, Guadeloupe and Martinique with the 12,400 troops under the command of General Lauriston.

But it was indeed ironic that these new plans involved a major shift of emphasis away from the Brest fleet to that of Toulon, naming Villeneuve the Commander-in-Chief of the most important naval operation of the war. It seems quite inconceivable that Napoleon, a soldier first and foremost, could have possibly placed a man who had declared categorically his doubts about the ability of the French Navy ever beating the British at sea in a command of such critical importance.

Contingencies always had to be anticipated, however, and if, for some reason, Vice-Admiral Ganteaume did not make the rendezvous at Martinique, after waiting a total of thirty-five days from the time of his arrival, Villeneuve was to return 'by the most direct route' to El Ferrol where he was to break the British blockade, freeing the 'fifteen French and Spanish ships'. They were then to join him, increasing his fleet strength to a total of about thirty-four or thirty-five ships. 'With this force', Napoleon instructed him, 'you will appear before Brest (but without entering that port) where you will execute your junction with the twenty-one ships under Admiral Ganteaume's command, and with that great naval army you will enter the Channel and advance to Boulogne' where the Emperor would personally give him his orders 'for the last phase of these operations'.

It was finally beginning to take shape and, for the first time since conceiving the invasion plans, Napoleon was also authorising the French Navy to confront large numbers of British ships by ordering Villeneuve to clear the Royal Navy before El Ferrol and Brest in order to release the squadrons there. Napoleon now wanted to remain 'master of the seas for forty-five to fifty days'. His ruse of leaving a large naval presence at Cadiz to attract the British was enforced by ordering the Spanish squadron at Cartagena to sail for Toulon where it was to give Nelson the impression that a fresh expedition was being prepared against Sicily and Sardinia. The French Emperor was now spending the better part of every day directing the French Navy while co-ordinating plans with Marshal Berthier for the army of Boulogne and the Imperial Flotilla – this time it had to work.

Vice-Admiral Villeneuve's first attempt at leaving Toulon, as has been noted, had ended in near disaster, utter humiliation and a blunt, if unexpected dissertation as to why the whole plan was doomed to failure. Yet Villeneuve's rather tarnished flag had continued to fly from the masthead of the *Bucentaure* and on 30th March, it happened. With favourable winds and, for once, even the British frigates completely out of sight, the coast was clear.

'I am leaving, my dear General', he finally informed Admiral Decrès as thousands of men scrambled up the rigging and along the yard-arms of the seventeen vessels just before he gave orders to the squadron to weigh anchor. 'May fortune smile upon me, for I badly need it . . . In the name of our long friendship, I confide to you all that I hold most dear in the world. I have not been very happy with several of your decisions concerning me, but I attribute that solely to the difficult position in which you find yourself. I pray that the future will treat me more kindly.'

On the face of it the Admiral's squadron was powerful enough, including as it did four 80-gun ships (*Bucentaure, Neptune, Formidable, Indomptable*), seven 74-gun ships (*Pluton, Mont-Blanc, Berwick, Atlas, Swiftsure, Scipion, Intrépide*) plus six 40-gun frigates (*Cornélie, Rhin, Hortense, Hermione, Sirène, Thémis*) and two gun-brigs. The crews of many of these ships, so sparse and so poorly trained, were beefed up at the last minute with several hundred troops, all of whom were given a crash-course in basic seamanship. It was hardly surprising under the circumstances that Vice-Admiral Villeneuve and his thirty-five-year-old Second-in-Command, Rear-Admiral Dumanoir le Pelley, felt little enthusiasm for what, to them, seemed an ill-starred venture. With some 3,332 troops, including infantry and artillery units under the command of General Lauriston, the Toulon fleet set sail at four pm with a north-westerly wind, 9th Germinal of the year XIII (30th March 1805).

Successfully avoiding Nelson's fleet, they hugged the Spanish coast, reaching Cartagena on 7th April, where Villeneuve was apparently offered the six Spanish ships of the line at anchor there, but, for reasons which have never been fully explained (perhaps the fear of serious epidemics which had recently ravaged that port), General Beurnonville reported to Napoleon that Pierre Villeneuve had refused to accept them under his command. Napoleon simply did not believe that Villeneuve was the sort of man who would ever turn down help under any circumstances, however, and told Admiral Decrès that he could not understand how 'an intelligent man like this ambassador [Beurnonville] could permit himself to speak such rot.' Whatever the reason, when the French fleet hauled out of the Spanish harbour, it was without the Cartagena squadron, and by 9th April Villeneuve was able to report, 'I passed through the Straits [of Gibraltar] today . . . and am approaching Cadiz.'

Reaching Cadiz at 8 pm the same day, Admiral Villeneuve dispatched an officer to Admiral Gravina's flagship 'to inform him how precious every moment was and that the enemy squadron in the Mediterranean [Nelson's] must already be in pursuit of me and could be expected to be joining the British squadron which has been blockading Cadiz thus far, and that therefore it was absolutely essential to set sail for our destination

immediately. Admiral Gravina replied that he was as impatient to leave as
I, that I could hoist the signal to put to sea and he would then repeat it to
his squadron'. At two o'clock on the morning of 10th April Villeneuve
sailed out of port. However, the next morning he discovered only one
small Spanish vessel in sight. Gravina had indeed kept his word to set sail
immediately, but, due to the tangled cables of some of his ships, his
departure was delayed by hours and therefore the two squadrons sailed
separately, only joining forces again at Martinique on 26th May, with a
combined fleet of some seventeen ships of the line (six of them Spanish),
and 5,262 troops (including 1,930 Spanish soldiers).

Vice-Admiral Sir John Orde, aboard the 98-gun *Glory*, the flagship of his
squadron of six ships stationed off Cadiz (including the *Renown*, *Defence*,
Polyphemus, *Agamemnon* and *Ruby*), was the first to report what had
transpired: 'I was induced to quit my station [on 9th April] . . . with the
squadron under my command by the sudden appearance of the Toulon
fleet . . . of 20 or 24 sail . . . which joined the Spanish force in Cadiz the
same evening . . . With colours flying at every masthead [they] were
apparently received with great joy by all description of people, flags being
hoisted on every house; 7 or 8 sail of the line are in readiness to join them
from Cadiz. Where their destination may be after this junction (which I
am not astonished at) I cannot tell, but I judge it westward'. As for the
British Mediterranean fleet, 'Where Lord Nelson is I cannot hear, but I
am told he is likely to return to Egypt on hearing of the French fleet being
at sea'. Sir John said he expected a combined fleet of '19 or 20 sail of the
line' and '10 or 11 frigates' to depart shortly, though he claimed he was
helpless to do anything about it, other than provide a detailed list of the
Spanish vessels, their armament and officers.
  What the British had long feared had now happened, a major French
force had at last escaped from port, unscathed, and with no British force
in pursuit. (And yet had it been Nelson there with those six ships, it is
most likely he would have attacked regardless of the odds against him.)
  Admiral Lord Nelson was indeed far away in the Mediterranean at this
very moment, but not *en route* to Egypt, as Napoleon had hoped and
rumour had indicated. Instead he was sailing between Sardinia and Sicily
at the time when Villeneuve's fleet hauled out of Cadiz harbour under a
full press of sail to Martinique for the rendezvous which would begin the
final phase of the operations that had so preoccupied Cornwallis and
Decrès these past two years. If the remainder of the Spanish fleet at
Cadiz and El Ferrol could meet Villeneuve's Franco-Spanish fleet of

some seventeen ships, as well as Ganteaume's Brest force of twenty-one ships, England and Ireland could indeed expect the very worst, even if only part of the great Boulogne flotilla managed to sail.

Long before receiving the disastrous news from Cadiz at his sea station off Ushant, Lord Gardner realised how critical the situation could become at any moment, as he informed the Admiralty in a dispatch of 19th April. Because Sir Robert Calder's squadron off El Ferrol was running dangerously low on fuel, food, water and also needed reinforcement against the pending threat of the combined enemy fleet, Gardner had dispatched the *Ajax*, *Terrible* and *Malta* with emergency stores to permit Calder to maintain his station there. None the less this was just a stop-gap measure, for Gardner knew Sir Robert would have to send at least two of his ships back to Britain shortly thereafter for more supplies and 'his force will then be so reduced and inferior to the enemy, that I am humbly of opinion his remaining off Ferrol, unless he is reinforced, will answer no good purpose if the enemy should escape from Brest, which I by no means think improbable, and should form a junction with the squadron at Ferrol . . . Sir Robert Calder will then be very unpleasantly situated.'

Napoleon, like Gardner, was expecting the imminent break-out of Ganteaume's powerful fleet from Brest, and now, with the known departure of Villeneuve's fleet for the West Indies, all eyes were fixed on Brest and Vice-Admiral Ganteaume. 'The non-departure of Ganteaume upsets me very much', Napoleon snapped at Decrès on 21st April. 'Monsieur Decrès,' he wrote two days later, 'a letter which I have just received from Admiral Ganteaume . . . informs me that he is ready to leave. I await this news with the greatest impatience . . . Tell General Villeneuve to do as much damage as he can to the enemy [in the West Indies] while awaiting the arrival of Admiral Ganteaume . . . He should take St Vincent, Antigua, Grenada and why not Barbada as long as he is there?' The Emperor went on to praise what he had heard thus far of Missiessy's success in the Indies, then asking what precisely was the problem at Brest? 'It only remains now for me to learn of your [the navy's] departure there . . . I find it difficult to express to you just how very impatient I am about this whole affair, for all our plans are based on the departure of the Brest fleet and its junction with that of Ferrol.'

Because of the great distances and slow communication it was not until 26th April that Lord Gardner learned at Ushant of the appearance of Villeneuve's fleet off Cadiz and he was still in the dark as to their destination. If they sailed northwards, however, he thought that they would certainly be going to El Ferrol, which would give the French thirty-one sail of the line. Meanwhile, as seen earlier, Lord Melville was ordering Vice-Admiral Collingwood to prepare a squadron of five ships immediately 'for foreign service', that is, to pursue Villeneuve.

At St Cloud Napoleon's phenomenal 'impatience' was nearly out of control. 'I am surprised to learn that Brest is not yet ready to leave', he wrote again on 2nd May. 'Many very well informed people assure me that Ganteaume has missed a perfect opportunity to sail, because he delayed it by twenty-four hours as a result of his captains not being aboard their ships'. This message to Decrès was brief and its very brevity was indicative of just how much anger the Emperor was holding back. To have all jeopardised now, because of Ganteaume in particular, was simply more than he could bear, however, and on 8th May he reluctantly notified the Naval Minister that 'Villeneuve will have to start moving [from Martinique] on 10 Messidor [29th June] at the latest if he is to arrive at Ferrol on schedule. As for Ganteaume, if he has not left by 30 Floréal [20th May], then he must not be allowed to leave at all', but instead remain in port, all men still on board, awaiting further orders for his rendezvous with Villeneuve off Ushant between 9th and 19th July. 'Finally, I reiterate that this is our final and definitive set of operations. I shall be along the coast [at Boulogne] on 25 Messidor [14th July], and on 10 Thermidor [29th July] I shall be awaiting the return of my squadrons.'

Meanwhile, Vice-Admiral Collingwood's new squadron was increased to seven ships in number and ordered 'to proceed with them . . . with all possible dispatch to the southward and westward of Ushant' where he was to break open his sealed instructions. Before he could put these orders into effect, however, on 15th May Lord Gardner informed him of a change of plans that he had just received at one o'clock in the morning from the gun-brig *Swinger*. 'In pursuance of an order from the Lord Commissioners of the Admiralty, dated the 10th inst [May], you are required and directed to proceed in his Majesty's ship *Dreadnought*, together with such ships as have been placed by me under your command . . . without a moment's loss of time to Barbados' where he was to put a halt to French ravages there.

A dispatch from Vice-Admiral Calder off Cape Finisterre at this time confirmed reports from La Coruña 'that the Cadiz squadrons are gone to the West Indies', adding that the Spanish squadron at El Ferrol was ready to sail with seven ships of the line (two of which were French) and two frigates. On the same day as the Admiralty was issuing fresh orders to Collingwood, it was also instructing Sir John Orde, who was still at Cadiz, to return to Cawsand Bay, Plymouth, where he was to strike his flag, though not yet naming his replacement. That day also, another vessel bearing naval dispatches, this time a French frigate, the *Didon*, set out from Lorient to bring up-dated instructions to Admiral Villeneuve about Ganteaume's inability to carry out his orders and their new rendezvous off Ushant.

The well-laid plans of Admiral Cornwallis involving a fairly close blockade of all French and Spanish Atlantic ports, plans which he had conveyed to Admiral Lord Gardner when he went on leave, were, in fact, to be abandoned by the ailing Gardner, perhaps as a result of slackening discipline and control over events. Squadrons from Rochefort, Toulon and Cadiz had all successfully escaped from ports theoretically under British surveillance, Villeneuve's fleet of seventeen ships of the battle-line disappearing into the mists of the Atlantic as effectively as Missiessy's had earlier, while Sir John Orde, upon sighting the enemy, had simply fled panic-stricken in the opposite direction, not even leaving frigates behind to follow the enemy or to inform Nelson, who he knew would be in hot pursuit, thereby permitting his long-pent-up personal jealousy of Nelson to distort sound professional judgement.[5]

Admiral Lord Nelson had been taken as much unawares as Lord Gardner by the news of Admiral Villeneuve's escape from Toulon on 30th March. In fact, Nelson was making for Pulla Bay off the south-western coast of Sardinia and passing the island of Toro when, at 8 am on 4th April, the cruiser *Phoebe* emerged out of a thick morning haze and drizzling rain and worked its way through the maze of vessels to the *Victory* where an excited Commander-in-Chief was told of this event. The enemy fleet was last seen sailing in a southerly direction. It was not much to go on, but for Nelson, who had been waiting many months for this opportunity, it was more than enough.

After hoisting signals from the *Victory* informing the fleet of this news, they set sail immediately, reaching the coast of northern Sicily off Palermo on 7th April, where they remained until 9th April. At that very moment, hundreds of leagues to the west, Vice-Admiral Villeneuve was scattering Sir John Orde's squadron and entering the spacious protection afforded by the harbour of Cadiz.

It was perhaps one of Nelson's greatest limitatons that he, like

Napoleon, was held and captivated by the classical mystique of the Mediterranean, which he considered to be the centre of the naval universe, despite his own long service in the Far East and West Indies. He could not always, therefore, readily perceive important objectives which lay beyond his own bailiwick. Thus he had set sail for Sicily in hope of obtaining news about the Toulon fleet, to confirm perhaps what he had long suspected it would one day do, make for Egypt again. Nevertheless there was no intelligence to be found in any of the ports of northern Sicily, and Nelson reluctantly turned westward – although Napoleon was counting on his continuing on to Egypt[6] – sailing now in the direction of Sardinia, where on 18th April he finally learnt that Admiral Villeneuve's fleet had successfully cleared the Straits of Gibraltar nine days earlier. 'I feel vexed', Nelson confided to Admiral Lord Gardner, 'at their slipping out of the Mediterranean, as I had marked them for my own game.'

Writing from the *Victory*, on 19th April, at a position some ten leagues to the west of Toro Island, Sardinia, Nelson informed Lord Melville of his intentions. He was about to take the greatest risk of his career, one already filled with an ample number of such exploits. He could hardly conceal the movements of his large fleet, with thousands of men under his command, and thus he now informed London: 'The enemy's fleet having so very long ago passed the Straits and formed a junction with some Spanish ships from Cadiz, I think it my duty which must be satisfactory to their Lordships, to know exactly my situation'. He explained that he had decided *to abandon the theatre of operations assigned to him – the entire Mediterranean Sea* – in order to give chase to Admiral Villeneuve's fleet. If at first it sounded outrageous, in reality there was no other important French squadron remaining in the Mediterranean to worry about. 'The circumstance of their having taken the Spanish ships which were ready from Cadiz satisfied my mind that they are not bound to the West Indies nor probably the Brazils, but intend forming a junction with the squadron at Ferrol, and pushing direct for Ireland or Brest, as I believe the French have troops on board.' Consequently, he was now charting a course for the Atlantic 'to take my position fifty leagues west from Scilly' from which point it would be 'equally easy to get to either the fleet off Brest or to go to Ireland should the fleet be wanted at either station. I trust', he concluded, 'this plan will meet with their Lordships' approbation.' Meanwhile, writing privately, he told Lord Melville, 'I am not made to despair, what man can do shall be done. I have marked out for myself a decided line of conduct and I shall follow it well up [in spite of serious problems with his health] . . . I shall pursue the enemy to the

East or West Indies, if I know that to have been their destination, yet if the Mediterranean fleet joins [under the command of] the Channel [Fleet], I shall request . . . permission to go on shore'. It was, of course, a not very subtle hint to the First Lord not to impinge upon Nelson's freedom of action.

Once again, however, fate seemed to be against the irrepressible Horatio Nelson, for, after setting a full press of sail on 19th April, he found himself becalmed. 'Dead foul! Dead foul!', he agonised that day in a state of utter exasperation. 'I cannot get a fair wind, or even a side wind . . . My good fortune, my dear Ball, seems flown away . . . But my mind is fully made up what to do when I leave the Straits, supposing there is no certain information of the enemy's destination', he confided to his old friend Sir Alexander Ball, Governor of Malta. 'I believe this ill-luck will go near to kill me [because of the extra physical stress on his poor health], but as these are times for exertion, I must not be cast down, whatever I may feel.' Indeed, because of contrary winds and the necessity to stop for supplies at Mazari Bay, near Tetuan, he only reached Gibraltar on 7th May.

Continuing up the west coast of the Iberian Peninsula, Nelson received news from Rear-Admiral Donald Campbell, employed in the Portuguese Navy, that Villeneuve was believed to be sailing for the West Indies after all, which confirmed his own suspicions, aroused even before leaving Tetuan on 5th May. On the 10th, the Mediterranean Fleet put into Lagos Bay, Portugal, to complete their stores with five months' provisions, enough for a transatlantic crossing to the West Indies and back, a wise precaution as it turned out. Their departure was delayed unexpectedly, however, by the arrival of a convoy of naval transports from England with some 5,000 troops, which requested protection. When, after detaching the 100-gun *Royal Sovereign* to fulfil that duty, leaving him with only ten ships and three frigates, on 12th May Nelson 'crowded sail to the westward, in chase of an enemy's fleet' of seventeen battleships, 'My lot is cast', he confided to Alexander Ball, 'and I am going to the West Indies where although I am late, yet chance may have given them [Villeneuve's fleet] a bad passage, and me a good one: I must hope for the best.' It was not until 3rd June, however, one day out of Carlisle Bay, Barbados, that Nelson received a report confirming that the combined Toulon-Cadiz fleet was indeed there.

In the Channel on 19th May, Lord Gardner had found himself in a bind, stymied by Nelson's abrupt appearance in the wrong sea (and now probably somewhere between Cape Finisterre and the Irish coast) – an action he would never have dreamed of. Addressing the Admiralty Board he appealed for guidance, for, as he put it, 'I do not consider myself authorised to send Lord Nelson any orders either to join me, to go to Ireland, or to return to the Mediterranean'. Poor Gardner, of course, did not yet know that Nelson had already made that decision for himself, selecting a fourth alternative, the West Indies.

Earlier, on 14th May, when Sir Robert Calder received news at El Ferrol of the sighting of Missiessy's squadron on its return voyage from Martinique to Rochefort, he 'instantly bore up with all sail with the squadron and pushed for Cape Ortegal [Spain]', he reported to Lord Gardner. 'Not seeing the enemy at break of day . . . I now concluded they must have kept farther to the northward. I therefore made all sail with the squadron and stood to the N.N.E. with the hope of crossing upon the enemy provided they were running down the latitude of Rochefort as I have every reason to think it is the Rochefort squadron who are upon the return from the West Indies to that port.' However, the westerly wind suddenly veered in a southerly direction, abruptly ending the possibility of Calder's continuing, and thus he was to be denied the perfect moment to surprise Missiessy's battered and exhausted squadron, for it was indeed those ships and he was right on course to meet them, but they later slipped past his position and into the safety of their home port.

Despite his rather egotistical sense of command, which so put up Cornwallis' hackles, Calder was for all that an intelligent officer capable of making fast decisions. Lord Gardner, on the other hand, who had also been informed of the sighting of that squadron, had declined to act. 'I certainly should have detached a squadron in quest of them did I conceive myself justified in doing so', he informed the Admiralty, but with just twenty sail of the line he felt he could not afford to weaken his fleet by several vessels to such an end.

The Royal Navy, and in particular the Channel Squadron under the temporary command of Admiral Lord Gardner, were clearly in a state of confusion at this time, having two elusive enemy squadrons flitting about the Atlantic, with no precise knowledge of their ultimate objectives. One of the men the Admiralty held primarily responsible for a major part of this problem was Sir John Orde and his fiasco at Cadiz. Although Orde's successor had not yet been named, it was Vice-Admiral Collingwood, whose orders to pursue Villeneuve were changing almost every week or so this May, who was shortly to find himself before Cadiz with his own squadron, without having been first named to that post.

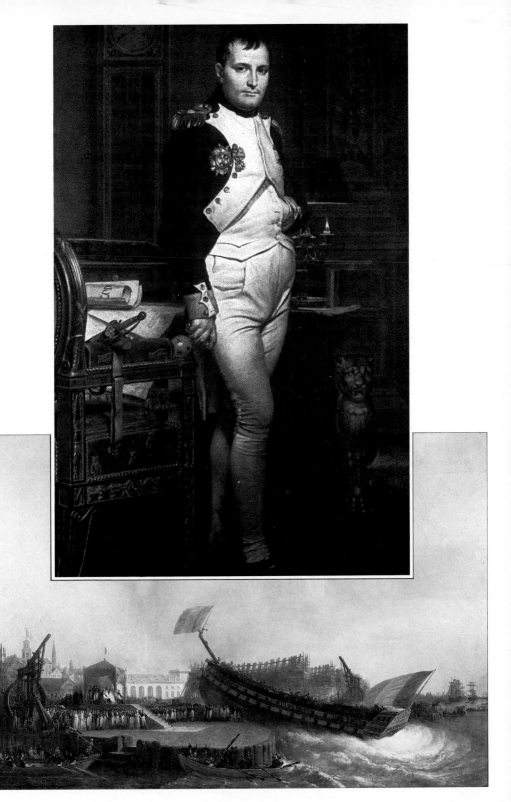

(*Top*) Napoleon Bonaparte in his study.

(*Above*) Napoleon took immense personal interest in the details of the invasion preparations.
Here he launches a ship.

Pierre Forfait, Inspector General of Napoleon's National Flotilla, was responsible for designing the unseaworthy flat-bottomed boats that made up the fleet.

Marshal Soult, who was placed in command of the French troops massing at the invasion headquarters Boulogne.

Despite the primitive facilities there, Napoleon was determined to launch his invasion armada from Boulogne, and ordered extensive work to improve the port.

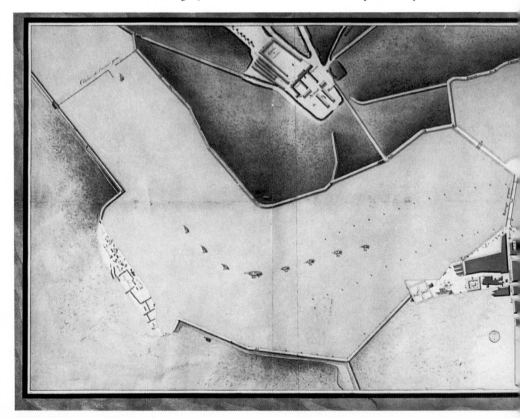

Napoleon inspecting his army and flotilla at Boulogne, 1805.

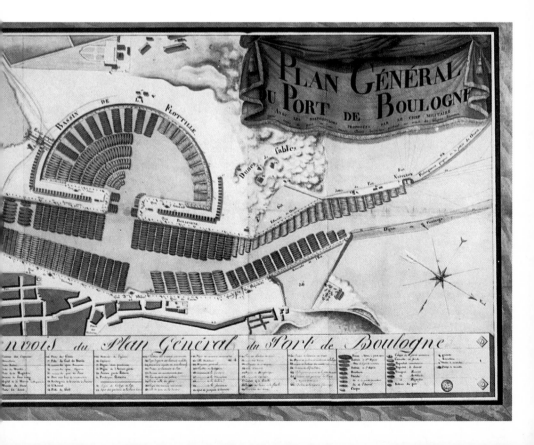

Admiral Denis Decrès, France's Naval Minister 1801–1814, in charge of invasion operations.

Marshal Berthier, Napoleon's War Minister, responsible for coordinating all aspects of the invasion army.

The National Flotilla poised at Boulogne in 1805.

(*Left*) Admiral Eustace de Bruix, Commander-in-Chief of the invasion flotilla. On his death in March 1805 he was replaced by Admiral Lacrosse (*right*).

Napoleon and Admiral Bruix surveying 'Britain's watch-dogs', the Channel Fleet blockading the French coast under the command of Admiral Cornwallis.

(*Above*) General Beurnonville, French ambassador to Madrid, 1805.

(*Right*) Admiral Verhuell of the Batavian Navy.

Marshal Davout, commander of the invasion force at Bruges.

Marshal Ney, commander of the invasion camp at St Omer.

(*Left*) Vice-Admiral Ganteaume, commander of the
French fleet that Cornwallis' Channel Fleet kept
blockaded in Brest, and (*below*) the town and
harbour of Brest with his sheltering fleet.

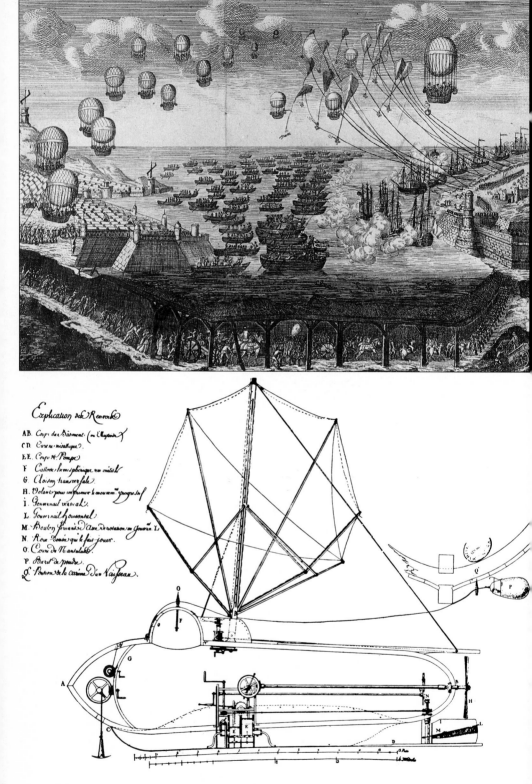

Napoleon was besieged with inventors' plans for the invasion of England, (*top*) by balloon, ship and tunnel, and (*above*) by submarine; the *Nautilus* was Robert Fulton's first operational submarine, which he failed to convince either the French or the British governments to commission.

The adventures of the French Rochefort squadron, small as it was, were not yet over, for scarcely had it put into port on 20th May, than it was ordered to be ready for another sortie. With news of its arrival and feverish activity to prepare for another destination, London would soon have yet another mystery to solve. Indeed, Lord Gardner was disturbed enough about this fresh spate of work to do something about it and, in the first week of June, informed the Admiralty, 'I have ordered Rear-Admiral Sir Thomas Graves, K.B., in the *Foudroyant*, to take under command the ships named in the margin [six ships of the line: *Barfleur*, *Windsor Castle*, *Repulse*, *Triumph*, *Warrior* and *Raisonnable*, as well as the frigate *Egypt-ienne*] to proceed without a moment's loss of time off Rochefort', Gardner then remarking that this left him 'with only 15 sail under my command.' The entire Channel Fleet was being reduced gradually as a result of newly created squadrons and detachments and nearly all were low on supplies and required repairs. Clearly the fleet was over-extended and Gardner was probably counting the hours until there would be news of Cornwallis' return.

The situation in Spain was no less tense, especially at El Ferrol where the Spanish and French force looked very menacing indeed. On 1st June Sir Robert Calder saw with delight the arrival of Rear-Admiral Sir Richard Bickerton with three months' supplies for his squadron of six ships, and though Bickerton's ships – the *Royal Sovereign*, *Queen* and *Dragon* – were to remain attached now to Calder's command, Sir Robert's vessels, the *Indefatigable*, *Prince of Wales*, *Hero*, *Defiance*, *Malta* and *Terrible* (with the exception of the latter two, which had just joined him from Ushant), had been at that station for many months and needed more than temporary supplies – 'bullocks and vegetables' – and his exhausted crews and officers many weeks rest ashore.

Exhaustion, lack of supplies and badly needed repairs after two years of continuous service were having a serious effect on the efficiency of the much dispersed Channel Fleet by the summer of 1805. More and more frequently, the French squadrons at Brest and Rochefort were to find entire days during periods of fine weather when there was not a British warship in sight or even over the horizon. Admiral Ganteaume was quick to note this and reported precise daily figures on the decline of British naval strength.

And once again he requested permission to attack the blockading squadron off the coast with Napoleon refusing yet again, 'I really do not see what Admiral Ganteaume hopes to achieve. What good would a battle be to us? Nothing at all.'

The last thing Napoleon wanted to do now was to draw British attention away from the Melville Affair to the expeditions he was about to dispatch, which a major naval action by Ganteaume off the Brest coast now would do. 'I want to keep the English sleeping as long as possible, so far as the Brest squadron is concerned', he told Decrès on 22nd June.

As for the Rochefort squadron, let it 'be prepared to leave momentarily, for the English will not maintain this blockade'. 'There is nothing much to worry about from the English Government, with its internal political wrangling [a reference to the Melville impeachment proceedings] which can only be bothered to look up when a particular problem arises.' Meanwhile Sir Robert Calder was reporting to London that, 'the enemy [had] thirteen sail of the line, five frigates and three corvettes . . . perfectly ready for sea' at El Ferrol.

London might have had its political problems and an ailing Prime Minister as well, but the Royal Navy was not asleep; quite the contrary, they were champing at the bit, Rear-Admiral Graves reporting to Lord Gardner on 28th June that he was 'extremely anxious to make your Lordship acquainted with the rapid progress of the equipment of the enemy's ships at Rochefort'. Rumour had it, he said, 'that the squadron is bound for the West Indies and will sail as soon as ready', and that there had just been 'a very hot press, and people of every age and description were taken' to man this squadron. The only thing that report lacked was the news that Rear-Admiral Missiessy, having fallen ill, had now been replaced on 25th June by a new, more vigorous commanding officer, Captain Zacharie Allemand.

Meanwhile Admiral Gardner seemed content with the news of Collingwood's arrival at Cadiz, for if there was one man he could always rely on it was that admiral. Cuthbert Collingwood had served throughout the Mediterranean and off Toulon and, following two vigorous years blockading Cadiz, had displayed courage and leadership at the Battle of St Vincent. He then served another two and a half years in the Channel blockade off Brest up to the signing of the Treaty of Amiens in 1802. A rather severe and unwelcoming man to strangers, to a few chosen acquaintances, such as Cornwallis and Nelson, he was a stable and loyal ally, 'the last to leave and the first to join me', as Cornwallis put it. The bluff Collingwood was a sailor's sailor.

The orders and counter-orders Collingwood had received over the preceding weeks had been confusing to say the least, but he managed to explain the whole thing quite clearly to an old friend. 'The sailing of the Toulon Squadron and their joining the Spaniards here [Cadiz] put me in motion. My ships were increased to 14 sail to pursue them, unless I received certain information that Lord Nelson had, and then I was directed in my conduct by the best intelligence I could get of the enemy.' As noted earlier, he was dispatched first to a position fifty leagues off Ushant and from there he was to launch a search in the West Indies, Barbados being named specifically in one set of orders. Then, however, the appearance of Nelson had altered the situation. 'Lord Nelson was at this time supposed to have taken a station west of Ireland, convinced from the style of their preparation that the enemy was destined for that quarter. In my way south I met Sir Richard Bickerton, who first informed me of the real state of things', that the Franco-Spanish fleet had, in fact, sailed to the West Indies. 'Finding the Spaniards here and at Cartagena had a considerable force ready to sail, I determined to come here [instead] where I found them on the eve of departing, waiting only for the Cartageneans, who actually did sail on the very day I arrived here', but then immediately returned to their port. After sending two ships to reinforce the West Indies, Collingwood had stood guard at Cadiz. 'But I think it is not improbable that I shall have all these fellows coming from the West Indies again before the hurricane months, unless they sail from thence directly for Ireland, which I have always had an idea was their plan'. Then Collingwood came closer than most in assessing the situation: 'I believe their object in the West Indies to be less conquest than to draw our force from home. The Rochefort squadron seems to have had nothing else in view'. If with the Spaniards they can 'cause a great alarm, and draw a great force there [to the West Indies] from England, they will have so much less to oppose them in their real attack, which will be at home in harvest time'. He for his part was not going to be deceived by this Bonaparte who, as he put it, 'has as many tricks as a monkey'.

Further to the north at El Ferrol, Calder, too, felt the growing tension, reporting that the combined force of thirteen sail of the line and several frigates were ordered to shift southwards from the port and arsenal at El Ferrol to the more open waters of La Coruña bay where they could catch more varied winds and have better access to the Atlantic. 'In any case, once the enemy take up their anchor at Corunna', Calder apprised Gardner on 5th July, 'it will behove me to alter my present plan of the blockade, by which I have hitherto had the good fortune to have thus far succeeded in, by preventing all their attempts to escape from Ferrol. I am sorry to say it will become a much more difficult task to keep them in at Corunna'.

A general pattern was now beginning to take shape as Cornwallis resumed his command of Ushant on 7th July. Two days later he received information relayed from Lord Nelson's fleet, including 'an account of the combined squadrons of the enemy being on their way home from the West Indies', he informed London. 'I instantly detached the *Colpoys* to Vice-Admiral Sir Robert Calder, off Ferrol, communicating this intelligence to him, and at the same time I sent the *Nimble* with the information to Rear-Admiral Stirling (who had replaced Graves) off Rochefort'. Fortunately for Britain and the Channel Fleet, the deft hand of its Commander-in-Chief was at the helm again.

There could be no doubt in the mind of William Cornwallis that the moment in history, so anxiously awaited these past two hazardous years, was shortly coming, when Napoleon would at last make his great play, for if ever he was to launch his expeditions against Ireland and Britain, it would be now in the summer of 1805. The combined Franco-Spanish fleet under Villeneuve was sailing eastward to Europe, Ganteaume was poised to haul out of Brest with twenty-one sail, Allemand with five more at Rochefort, a combined Franco-Spanish force of another thirteen sail of the line at El Ferrol and another ten or so at Cadiz. Depending upon how many of these separate squadrons could break the British blockade, it was possible that Cornwallis would be facing upwards of fifty-eight French and Spanish sail of the line under the command of Villeneuve. Refreshed and in good spirits, the Admiral no doubt felt that, at long last, he was at the right place at the right time for what promised to be one of the most important naval battles in the history of modern Europe.

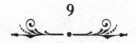

Phantom Fleets

I believe that all my men will remain at their posts, but no one will be fighting wholeheartedly. I foresaw all this before leaving Toulon.

Villeneuve to Decrès, 6th August 1805

All Europe says that English ships cover the seven seas. In the Mediterranean we did not encounter any, in the Atlantic we found only one, and none in the West Indies.

Lauriston to Decrès, 26th May 1805

Mine [his fleet] is compact, theirs must be unwieldy; and although a very great fiddle, I don't believe that either Gravina or Villeneuve know how to play upon it.

Nelson to Lord Seaforth, Governor of Barbados, 8th June 1805

What a race I have run after these fellows . . .

Nelson to Sir John Acton, 18th June 1805

'I FLEW TO the West Indies without any orders, but I think the Ministry cannot be displeased,' Viscount Nelson wrote from the *Victory* to his old friend Simon Taylor on 10th June 1805. 'I was in a thousand fears for Jamaica, for that is a blow which Buonaparte would be happy to give us . . . I was bred, as you know, in the good old school, and taught to appreciate the value of our West India possessions.'

Much to his consternation Nelson found that Cochrane had only two vessels waiting for him at Carlisle Bay, Barbados, bringing his fleet strength up to a mere twelve ships, and not the sixteen he had been expecting, for Rear-Admiral Dacre at Jamaica had detached four powerful vessels from Cochrane for his own use. That was not the worst of it, for though rumours abounded in Barbados as to the position and strength of the French, no one could attest to actual sightings though some claimed to possess second-hand information of a reliable nature, including Brigadier General Brereton who wrote from the island of St Lucia to Lieutenant-General Sir William Meyers, 'I have this moment received a report from the Windward side of Gros Islet [between St Lucia and Martinique] that the Enemy's Fleet, of 28 sail in all, passed there last night. Their destination, I should suppose, must be either Barbadoes or Trinidad.'

Nelson was in an almost feverish state to act, his long voyage in pursuit of the elusive Villeneuve apparently not dampening his spirits. Nevertheless this information did not seem to ring true. He had expected to see his French adversary sailing in a northerly, perhaps a north-westerly direction towards the prosperous British possessions of Antigua or Jamaica, not heading for the southern end of the chain of the Windward Islands. Lieutenant-General Sir William Meyers, as Commander-in-Chief of the forces at Barbados and the Leeward Islands, assured Nelson that General Brereton could indeed be relied upon, however, and even insisted on embarking 2,000 of his own troops with which to assist in the anticipated campaign.

Admiral Nelson had left Europe weeks after Villeneuve's escape from Toulon and evidently felt he simply could not sit in a harbour, calmly awaiting more precise news, perhaps pointing in a different direction. Reluctantly, he gave orders for his Mediterranean Fleet to weigh anchor at 9.30 am on 5th June, less than twenty-four hours after their arrival, and they made all sail for the *south*, despite continuing nagging thoughts about the wisdom of that course.

Upon reaching the southern tip of the archipelago and the harbour of Mud Fort, Tobago, at 6.10 pm on the 6th, he received two different reports from coastal schooners, one of a sighting along the west coast of St Vincent, another at Trinidad. Although Nelson had barely set foot ashore after his 3,227-mile transatlantic crossing, he again sailed to the south-west, reaching the Gulf of Paria, near the western entrance of the Bocaz at Trinidad, at 5.30 pm on 7th June. His ships were ready for action before daybreak and Nelson anticipated 'a second Aboukir [Egypt] in the Bay of Paria', alas, in vain.

'The information from St Lucia of the Combined [Franco-Spanish] Squadron having been off that Island to the Windward, must have been very incorrect', a furious Nelson informed Lord Seaforth, Governor of Barbados, on 8th June. Indeed, that very day Admiral Villeneuve's fleet was sailing *north* – just as Nelson had surmised – and at that moment was between the islands of Antigua and Barbuda. No one knew this at the time, of course, and all the frustrated Admiral could do was assure the Governor that his island was in safe hands: 'My Lord, powerful as their force may be, they shall not with impunity, make any great attacks'.

Admiral Nelson received a seventeen-gun salute as he next put into St George's Bay, Grenada on 9th June to seek further information. He

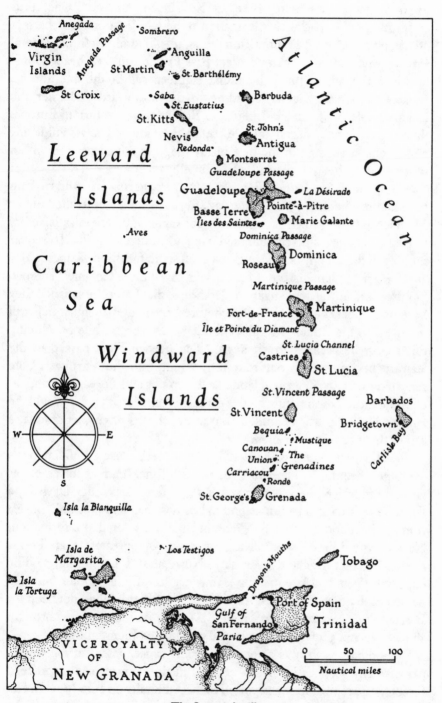

The Lesser Antilles.

learned that all was safe there, at St Vincent and St Lucia, thus confirming 'all our former information to be false'. At one o'clock that afternoon he received a report from the island of Dominica from General Prevost who 'saw the Enemy's Fleet pass Prince Rupert's head [Dominica] on the 6th of June', including eighteen sail of the line and six frigates 'under the Saints, standing to the northward. Whether the Enemy's object is to attack Antigua, or St Kitt's, or to return to Europe, time must show,' Nelson told Secretary Marsden. 'I shall guide my movements according to the best of my judgment, for I have too often unfortunately, been deceived by false intelligence.'

Sailing out of St George's Bay, Nelson swept northwards and by 12th June had reached Antigua. 'Yesterday afternoon the Fleet fetched under Montserrat, from which Island I only got vague and very unsatisfactory intelligence', he said, rumour referring to Antigua again. 'If I hear nothing of the Enemy from Antigua, I shall stand for Prince Rupert's Bay and form my judgment; but, I feel, having saved these Colonies, and two hundred and upwards of sugar-loaded Ships, that I must be satisfied they have bent their course for Europe before I push after them, which will [then] be to the Straits' Mouth [Gibraltar].' But even while concluding this report he received fresh news: 'The French Fleet passed to the leeward of Antigua on Saturday last, standing to the Northward', he reported excitedly. They had landed a few troops and stores there and, in consequence, Nelson informed Secretary Marsden that he would be landing his 2,000 troops immediately at St Johns, Antigua, 'and hope to sail in the morning after them'.

For the first time he realised just how very close to Villeneuve's combined fleet he had been on 4th and 5th June. 'I am as miserable as you can conceive,' he was afterwards to write to Alexander Davison, a Canadian who was a wealthy London businessman and Nelson's closest friend and confidant. 'But for General Brereton's damned information, Nelson would have been, living or dead, the greatest man in his Profession that England ever saw. Now, alas! I am nothing'. The opposing fleets had been within a few leagues of one another, but had passed each other blindly. Nelson also claimed that if it had not been for Brereton's incorrect report from St Lucia, he could have brought Villeneuve and Gravina to battle and annihilated them on 6th June.

'My opinion is firm as a rock, that some cause, *orders*, or *inability* to perform any services in these seas, has made them resolve to proceed direct for Europe', Nelson reported to the Admiralty on 16th June. In fact upon hearing of Nelson's arrival, Villeneuve and his twenty ships of the line hastily dropped all their immediate plans, disobeying Napoleon's orders to remain there for thirty-five days waiting for Ganteaume's arrival on 22nd June, and, instead, headed for Europe as fast as they could go. 'I am, as you may readily believe, very, very unhappy at not having got at the Enemy . . . but I shall be close after them in Europe, and when I have housed them, I shall certainly instantly return to England: I want rest . . . I think we cannot be more than eighty leagues [240 miles] from them at this moment', he wrote hopefully, noting he was 'carrying every sail' and using his 'utmost efforts' to catch up with them. But that was as close as he got to Villeneuve, who was following a slower course along a more northerly latitude towards the coast of El Ferrol and La Coruña, while Nelson, far to the south, was making for Cape Spartel.

Nelson reached the southern tip of Spain on 18th July where he met the phlegmatic Collingwood, who, though without information about the French fleet, was nevertheless overwhelmed at seeing Nelson again. But this was no time for friendship for a completely exhausted Nelson, who had just travelled another 3,459 miles. Now proceeding to the Straits, the Admiral wrote to London from Rozia Bay, Gibraltar on 20th July: 'I have to acquaint you that I anchored in the Bay yesterday morning without having obtained the smallest intelligence of the Enemy's Fleet', but that once he did have specific information, 'I shall embrace their Lordships' permission to return to England for a short time, for the re-establishment of my health.' He had now been aboard the *Victory* for two years 'wanting ten days' and felt nearly broken. 'I am, my dear Mr Marsden, as completely miserable as my greatest enemy could wish me . . .'

Worn out he may have been, but his fleet had twice traversed the Atlantic without docking to take on fresh stores and was in need of supplies. After stopping at Tetuan, Morocco, to re-victual and to catch up on his sleep, Nelson sailed for Ceuta where, on 25th July, he was informed that, ironically, his own sloop, the *Curieux*, which he had dispatched from the West Indies to Europe with signals for London, had spotted Villeneuve far to the north on 19th June! The Mediterranean Fleet now pushed through the Straits of Gibraltar again, following the Spanish coast. But the winds were either weak or contrary, frustrating their attempt to sail northward quickly in the direction of Admiral Cornwallis at Ushant, to whom Nelson wrote on the 27th, 'I shall only hope after all my long pursuit of *my* Enemy, that I may arrive at the moment they are meeting you.'

Once again, however, Nelson was to be foiled. Having missed

Villeneuve off Finisterre by a few days, and after learning that it was Sir Robert Calder who had finally stopped the combined Franco-Spanish Fleet, if only momentarily, a very sad Horatio Nelson sailed north to Ushant. There, on 15th August, he stopped briefly leaving his fleet with Admiral Cornwallis, then continued on to England and a dubious welcome. On the evening of 19th August a weary Nelson stepped on English soil and boarded the coach to Merton where Emma Hamilton and his daughter, Horatia, were waiting.

THIRTEEN DAYS AFTER dropping anchor in the warm translucent green waters of the harbour of Fort de France (formerly Fort Royal), Martinique, on 29th May, Vice-Admiral Villeneuve was still safely ensconced there, immobile under the protection of the fort's guns. Dinners were given on shore in Captain-General Villaret-Joyeuse's Government house, amid the spacious tropical gardens engulfed in overwhelming heat and humidity, where a chamber orchestra played, ladies dressed in Parisian fashions and officers in Imperial military uniforms. Apparently, Pierre Villeneuve did not find these *soirées* very agreeable, however, as he wrote to Naval Minister Decrès on 21st May: 'It is with the greatest impatience that I await the arrival of the Brest Fleet, and am ready to follow them at their first signal . . . There is nothing more disconcerting than the state of inaction which the nature of my orders now requires of me,' and his current orders failed to give him authority to do anything but wait for the rendezvous with Admiral Ganteaume.

Nevertheless, Admiral Villaret had done all in his power to induce the reluctant Villeneuve to put an end to this state of inaction, requesting him to carry reinforcements to the French garrisons of Martinique and Guadeloupe (where Governor Ernouf had also requested his help), and from there to launch attacks against British-held islands scattered throughout the Windward Islands. As Villaret was discovering, however, Villeneuve was in an unfathomable, if not bizarre, state of mind and not an easy man to influence. He was, in fact, determined to remain inert at Fort de France until he was joined by Ganteaume's twenty-one ships – or as late as 22nd June, if Ganteaume did not show up – when he would return to Europe, as his orders of 2nd March had specifically stated.

On 30th May the frigate *Didon* finally arrived with Napoleon's new set of orders issued on 13th and 14th April, instructing Villeneuve (as we saw in Chapter 8) to land all his troops there, to beef up the garrisons of Martinique and Guadeloupe and then to capture nearby British possessions. If Ganteaume did not make his rendezvous he was to return directly now to El Ferrol where he would be joined by fifteen French and Spanish ships, then to 'proceed with this force to Brest and execute a junction there with the 21 ships under Admiral Ganteaume's command', and sail with them up the Channel to Boulogne.

It was quite a change of plans, both in Europe and at Martinique. Villeneuve was suddenly catapulted from a passive role to one of unceasing activity.

At Villaret's request, he now reluctantly agreed to assault and capture HMS *Diamond*, no doubt the only rock ever to have been commissioned a vessel in the history of the British Royal Navy (presumably for administrative purposes) that the Royal Navy might arm and man 'her'. The islet of Diamond Rock was situated strategically outside the entrance of Fort de France, from which it was possible to observe every ship entering or leaving that port and launch attacks against all French naval operations to the south of the harbour's entrance. It was hardly surprising that Admiral Villeneuve finally captured the 128 British sailors in possession there after three days of heavy fighting. The Union flag was lowered on 2nd June.

Both Napoleon and Decrès assured Villeneuve that Nelson was still far away in the Mediterranean where 'he is running after you to Egypt', adding that the only British force in the Indies now was Admiral Cochrane's six vessels, which hardly posed a threat. Villeneuve was to begin reinforcing the garrisons on Martinique and Guadeloupe immediately. Napoleon's plans of 13th and 14th April (including appended modifications on 23rd April) specifically ordered him to capture Dominica, St Lucia, Trinidad and Tobago. He was also 'to take St Vincent, Antigua and Grenada, and why not Barbados as well?' with the 12,440 troops he was to land. If for some reason he could not accomplish that, he should 'at least carry out expeditions against the enemy's possessions so as to effectively destroy their prosperity for a long time to come'. All this in the three weeks remaining from the time Villeneuve received these orders at the end of May! Napoleon reiterated, however, that he must leave by 22nd June at the latest, if he were to get back to El Ferrol on time . . . and these were the last instructions he was to receive until August (when he was informed of still further changes).

It was with these orders in mind, now, that Villeneuve embarked extra troops, gathered from garrisons at Martinique and Guadeloupe, to conquer the Windward Islands, while General Lauriston privately assured Admiral Decrès that he thought there was no need to worry about any possible British naval threat, which in any case he felt to be overestimated, given their nearly complete invisibility since leaving Cadiz. Only a ghost fleet could possibly appear out of nowhere.

'I told you how upsetting I found the previous orders which had not permitted me to act', Villeneuve explained apologetically to Decrès on 1st June. Since the arrival of these new orders, however, the situation had changed: 'Everything is different today. The enemy is on his guard, having been warned by the *Mercury* [sent by Orde].' Now it was quite impossible. 'I cannot undertake the operations prescribed without at least two and one-half months' food and supplies for the return journey', which he would not have if he left Martinique to lay siege to the British islands. Even now his supplies were low. 'The Spanish squadron is in the same plight,' Gravina having already reduced their rations by one quarter. Therefore the Naval Minister should not be surprised if their fleet sailed for El Ferrol far sooner than expected.

With Diamond Rock taken, and despite the food shortage and his considerable protests to the contrary, Admiral Villeneuve reluctantly announced the imminent sailing of the fleet. 'We are leaving to attack either Antigua or Barbados.' The ever-indecisive Villeneuve had now rationalised this change, after much pressure brought to bear by General Lauriston – 'The instructions I received make it perfectly clear that I must accede to the Captain-General's wish to employ all the means at my disposal to enhance the safety and commercial interests of the colony.'

In the meantime, as a few fresh supplies were being stowed aboard the fleet on 4th June, Rear-Admiral Magon and his two 74-gun ships, *Algésiras* and *Achille*, arrived from Rochefort with orders to reinforce Villeneuve. Several miles away to the south-east of Martinique, that same afternoon, Vice-Admiral Nelson was entering Carlisle Bay, Barbados, after travelling all the way from Sardinia.

At four o'clock on the morning of 5th June, with a high tide and a freshening breeze, the Combined Franco-Spanish Fleet (composed of fourteen French vessels – now including Magon's ships – and six under the Spanish flag, making a total of twenty ships of the line) finally hauled out of Fort de France twenty days after its arrival, quite unaware of Nelson's appearance at nearby Barbados, one of the two ports Villeneuve was planning to attack. Having already embarked an additional 796 men from the Martinique garrison, the Admiral was first sailing in a northerly direction for Guadeloupe where he was to pick up further troops (to give him a total of 1,476 men, in addition to the 12,440 marines he had brought with him) before commencing operations.

Villeneuve bypassed the large British-held island of Dominica, then the Saints, reaching Basse-Terre, Guadeloupe, at 3 o'clock in the afternoon on 6th June, where he embarked the final contingent of 700 troops and local pilots, sailing at 9 o'clock that same evening. Instead of heading south to attack nearby Dominica or Barbados, however, he charted a *northerly course* in the direction of British Antigua.

Admiral Villeneuve explained the reasons for this move. When he sailed from Martinique he had 'the intention of going to attack Barbados' he later stated in his report of 11th June, but first he wanted to land the Guadeloupe garrison 'between Antigua and Montserrat', evidently intending to sail southwards after that. Then, at 10 am on the 7th, while sailing round Antigua, he spotted a convoy of fifteen British merchant-ships – as it turned out fully laden with coffee and rum – which had just set sail for Europe from Antigua. The two small Royal Navy vessels escorting them fled at the sight of the Combined Fleet and Villeneuve secured all fifteen ships, worth some four to five million francs, without a struggle.

From some of the prisoners he interrogated, the French Admiral learned for the first time that 'the English Mediterranean Fleet, some twelve or fourteen strong and with several frigates' had just arrived at Barbados. Nelson's force, he also found out, 'joined with Admiral Cochrane's . . . would suffice to equal our own strength, if not exceeding it . . . Under the circumstances, not only an attack on Barbados, but any undertaking against enemy possessions here would now be impossible.' What choices remained? 'All we could do would be to return to Martinique, where our enforced immobility and period of waiting until our appointed date of departure, would prove both humiliating as well as detrimental to our crews' health.' The wind out of the east being unfavourable at this moment, 'it would take us ten days in which to reach Martinique, not to mention *incurring the risk of a fight** [with Nelson]'. In the event of staying longer they would consume the last of their dwindling supplies (which apparently Martinique could not replace) and in the event of a clash with Nelson, they could not repair their vessels properly, 'and even should we be victorious, it would be quite impossible for the fleet to return to Europe' – presumably because of repairs needed – and

*Author's italics

thus would be forced to remain at Martinique indefinitely. 'Given this perplexing situation, I decided to confer with Admiral Gravina' (whose ships were suffering from much illness and desertion) who agreed with him 'as to the necessity of our returning to Ferrol forthwith in order to execute our junction with that fleet thereby permitting us to fulfil our primary objective'. He could not wait a moment longer for Admiral Ganteaume. 'Therefore, with the greatest interests of the state in mind, I have decided to return to Europe immediately.'

On 9th June, Villeneuve sent the fifteen captured ships under a frigate escort to Martinique and ordered four other frigates to land the 1,496 men of the local garrisons at Guadeloupe (which was closer than Martinique), those vessels later to rendezvous with him in the Azores. After signing this report to Decrès on 11th June, Admiral Villeneuve gave orders to sail for El Ferrol, but he did so in such haste that *he failed to land the 12,440 troops he had brought from Europe for the protection of these very islands.* This he neglected to mention in this or in any subsequent report!

General Reille, a member of General Lauriston's staff, recorded his own view of the situation in his Journal of 10th June:

It seems we have some information about Nelson having arrived in the Antilles with 10 or 12 ships and that the Admiral [Villeneuve] intends to avoid any fight with them. Time will tell what the results of this prudent planning will achieve. We have been masters of the sea for three weeks . . . but have only captured a single islet [Diamond Rock].

Shortly after leaving Antigua, the frigate escorting the prizes ran into two British sloops, which the French frigate apparently mistook for Nelson's look-outs, and fearing British reinforcements, burned all fifteen ships and fled. Villeneuve's few triumphs were disappearing before his eyes.

Captain-General Villaret, who was only informed of the disappearance of Villeneuve's entire fleet several days later, wrote an angry report to Decrès on 8th July, complaining that Martinique found itself 'in a dangerous position' and that he was extremely anxious, for in addition to Villeneuve's abrupt departure with arms, and supplies intended for the islands as well as General Lauriston's troops, the colonies were left in a weaker state than before, due to desertions and illness (yellow fever now killing an average of five men a day). He was left with only 2,800 men under arms, with another 469 in hospital. 'I shall let the colonial prefect fill you in regarding the details of the painful situation we have been left in as a result of the visits of the Toulon and Rochefort squadrons . . .'

Meanwhile Villeneuve was sailing in a north-easterly direction, heading for the Azores, the Canaries and then the Spanish coast.

Nelson having anticipated just such a precipitous flight by Villeneuve, had left the Indies to pursue the Combined Fleet, although following a more southerly course, which would take him eventually to Cadiz and Gibraltar. Luck it would seem was still on the French admiral's side, if just barely, while Nelson's controversial decision to leave the Mediterranean to follow the French fleet, weeks after discovering its destination, had proved correct after all and his conduct justified. He was, however, to be denied his battle (a battle that might have made the one fought at Trafalgar five months later unnecessary) as a result of the false information given him by General Brereton, whose name he cursed in every letter he wrote during the return voyage.

Admiral Villeneuve has been asked to establish a concerted effort and harmony between you and him which will enable the two naval forces to operate with a unity of spirit, will and action which the success of our operations requires.

Decrès to Gravina, 17th April 1805

Dispatch – Sir Robert Calder to Admiral Sir William Cornwallis, 'Prince of Wales', off Ferrol, 15th July 1805

Rear-Admiral Stirling has joined me with his squadron, and I am going to bear up for my station 30 leagues west of Cape Finisterre, agreeable to your last order, received this morning . . . I shall endeavour to prevent the combined [French and Spanish] squadrons expected from the West Indies from making a junction with those now at Ferrol, which I have little doubt is their intention . . .

Dispatch – Admiral Gravina to Admiral Decraise [Decrès], 'Argonauta', 3rd August 1805

As you can see, though I hold the rank of Admiral, that did not prevent me from ordering my ships to form the vanguard, nor from personally taking the lead position in that line during that fighting, as if I were just an ordinary captain . . .

'LATITUDE 43°34' NORTH, longitude 16°13' west, from Paris.' Fifteen ships of the line, two frigates, a lugger and cutter were barely moving in the light breeze out of the west-north-west, frequently invisible to each other in a thick mist which varied from an almost blinding haze to an impenetrable fog, broken only occasionally. Captain William Cumming, commanding Vice-Admiral Sir Robert Calder's flagship, the 98-gun *Prince of Wales*, recorded his position to be east-south-east of El Ferrol by thirty-nine leagues (about 117 miles) at 11 o'clock that morning, 22nd July 1805. The sea was great with swell, Admiral Calder's flag fluttering almost imperceptibly in the hot, humid air as the look-out sighted three columns of vessels to the west-south-west, before they disappeared again.

Admiral Don Federico Gravina, on board the *Argonauta* and whose six Spanish sail of the line formed the vanguard of the twenty ships of Admiral Villeneuve's Combined Franco-Spanish Fleet, was the first to sight the British force.

No sailor likes fog and, to some at least, it must have been quite eerie that morning as the phantom fleets approached each other, the voices of thousands of seamen in a dozen different languages, shouting excitedly, their human efforts muffled by the fog that enshrouded them. With but fleeting glimpses of one another, it was understandable that each side overestimated the other slightly, Gravina putting the British at twenty-one sail originally when they had twenty, counting the frigates, cutter and lugger, and Calder calculating Villeneuve's force at twenty sail of the line, three 50-gun ships, five frigates and three brigs when, in fact, there were seven frigates and no 50-gun vessels. Given the thickening veil round them by noon, it was a miracle that any sort of accurate count could be taken, but enemy counts they needed and enemy counts they would have.

'I immediately stood towards the enemy with the squadron,' Calder later reported. At noon the *Prince of Wales* made the signal to prepare for battle, as two columns were formed, followed by the order to form a single battle-line. This initial jockeying into position, which frequently took many hours to achieve with such unwieldy ships under sail, was today completed by 1.15 pm when another signal was given to keep in close order. Finally *Defiance*, which had come within two miles of the approaching enemy, then returned at 3 pm to take her place in the line. *Hero* was now in first position, then *Ajax*, *Triumph*, *Barfleur*, *Agamemnon*, *Windsor Castle*, *Defiance*, *Prince of Wales*, *Repulse*, *Raisonnable*, *Dragon* (shortly to join the line), *Glory*, *Warrior*, *Thunderer* and *Malta* in that order, most with their topgallantsails set, and on the starboard tack.

Meanwhile, Villeneuve's fleet of twenty sail of the line and seven frigates, which had been cruising in three columns, issued similar signals, and formed an immense battle line, Admiral Gravina's Spanish squadron still in the van and closest to the enemy, with *Argonauta* leading them, *Terrible, America, España, San Rafael, Firma,* followed by fourteen French ships – the *Pluton, Mont-Blanc, Atlas, Berwick, Neptune, Bucentaure* (in twelfth place), *Formidable, Intrépide, Scipion, Swiftsure, Indomptable, Aigle, Achille* and *Algésiras.* By 3.30 pm the Combined Fleet, which had hove to for a long time before deciding to meet the British challenge, their topsails set, stood on the larboard (or port) tack in a well formed line, preceded by a frigate, while in the rear another frigate was towing a recently captured treasure galleon worth some 15,000,000 francs. The remaining five frigates formed a second line on the windward side of the centre. The two fleets were nearly abeam at this stage (or parallel to each other), but still about seven miles apart.

These great wooden giants were moving painfully slowly in the slight breeze like a herd of ancient elephants lazily loping across some immense savannah, occasionally slipping into thicker bands of fog and haze. Clearly the lack of a strong wind to permit good manoeuvrability matched by even poorer visibility were to prove the most difficult problems for the two fleets to cope with as their battle lines closed almost imperceptibly.

At 3.20 pm Calder made the signal to engage the enemy, followed by other orders to tack, to make all possible sail in a south-south-westerly direction, and to form the line of battle now in open order. As the distance between the two fleets decreased, the foggy patches tended to thicken, making it difficult if not impossible to see each other's movements, indeed even to see the ship before them. Admiral Calder issued the order to turn, tacking sharply to cut off the Spanish ships' escape route, but Gravina, who was now within three miles of the British fleet, wore, bringing his ship round to protect the rear of the fleet, including the treasure galleon. The British frigate *Sirius* following in the wake of the Combined Fleet then darted forward, making a bold attempt to cut off and board the treasure galleon, but was forced to withdraw by Gravina's ship, *Argonauta.*

'With a forebearance highly honourable to Admiral Gravina', commented the historian William James, 'the *Argonauta* passed the British frigate without firing, and so did the *Terrible* and *America.*' As the foremost British ship, the 74-gun *Hero* with her royals set approached the Spanish line at 5.15 pm, the Spanish ships hoisted their colours and fired the first shots of the battle, the 80-gun *Argonauta* raking the *Hero,* the 64-gun *España,* the *Sirius.* At this moment, from the *Prince of Wales,* Calder issued several signals, manoeuvring his fleet to engage the French ships in the enemy's centre and to engage the enemy as closely as possible. Without orders, however, the *Hero* alone had suddenly tacked, when through the fog she saw that the Combined Fleet had just come about, changing direction, followed slowly by the other British ships doing the same, which in a diagram would have shown the two fleets each making a zigzag to enable them to approach each other in the same direction and abeam. But manoeuvring those wooden vessels was a cumbersome process, and it was only at 5.45 pm, thirty minutes after the *Hero* had tacked and begun returning the fire of the *Argonauta*, that the second British ship, the *Ajax*, followed, but then left the battle line to inform the commander of the change of tack – the *Ajax* then dropping back behind the *Glory*, in twelfth place. The firing was soon quite general and, by 6 pm, all the British ships except the *Dragon* had altered course and were firing at the enemy.

The visibility, which had been so poor that Admiral Calder had not even been able to see the *Hero* tack before him earlier, now worsened. In the clearest of weather conditions, without any haze whatsoever, the smoke produced by the hundreds of 18- and 24-pound cannons generated an almost suffocating bank of cloud, rendering opponents just a couple of hundred yards away only partially visible at best. Today, however, the initial fog and haze were compounded so effectively by the smoke of these guns that their targets were rendered quite invisible and merely a matter of surmise and guess-work, despite the unending bright flashes of their cannons. Chaos was soon general and sometimes resulted in several ships all attacking a single opponent. The three-deck, 98-gun *Windsor Castle*, under Captain Charles Boyles, suffered especially from this on the English side, as did the Spaniards, and in particular the 80-gun *San Rafael*, the 70-gun *Firma* and 64-gun *España*, the majority of the French vessels not being directly involved in the battle most of the time.

So battered were both the *San Rafael* and *Firma* that they fell out of the battle line to the leeward as the British relentlessly went in for the kill, with only one other ship, the 74-gun *Pluton*, attempting to protect her Spanish allies, until she was driven off. The *España* now came under extremely heavy British fire as well and was barely saved by two French 74s, the *Mont-Blanc* and *Atlas* (the latter herself being badly mauled). Admiral Gravina's six leading ships were certainly in a desperate situation now, four of them badly damaged and no longer an effective fighting unit.

By 8 pm with the fog, haze and smoke darkening the failing sea light, the thirty-four-year-old *Firma*, all her masts shot away and perfectly helpless after a magnificent struggle, surrendered to the British, followed a few minutes later by the fifty-one-year-old *San Rafael* which was equally dismasted. By 9.25 pm Calder's fleet, like Villeneuve's, was completely scattered and disunited, the night enveloping them. The British fleet held off just to the windward, barely within gun-shot of their opponents, as the *Windsor Castle* limped past the *Prince of Wales* and was taken in tow by the 74-gun *Dragon*. In fact, by 8.25 pm, because of the thickening opacity, Calder had decided on making 'the night private signal' to the fleet to discontinue the action. Many of the ships did not see or hear it, however, and thus fighting had continued for another hour. Calder then brought his ships to a new course, heading west-south-west, from which position he tried to assemble them and issued orders for them to lay to for the night.

Of the British vessels, the *Windsor Castle* had suffered the most damage, having had her fore-topmast and a great part of her fore-top shot away; next came the 64-gun *Agamemnon*, which also lost a mast, and the 80-gun *Malta*, with top- and mizenmasts damaged, while the 74-gun *Ajax* had lost a main yard. Surprisingly, considering the intensity and duration of the battle, only 39 British officers and men were killed and another 159 wounded in the engagement.

Villeneuve's combined fleet suffered more grievously, with two Spanish ships completely dismasted and in British hands by the end of the day (though their captors quickly discovered just how ancient and worthless they really were). Another five vessels (including one frigate) were so badly shot up, most of them having lost at least one mast, that upon reaching the Spanish coast later they were put into dry dock for major repairs, keeping them out of action in some cases for several months. The Combined Franco-Spanish Fleet lost 149 officers and men killed and 327 wounded, making a total of 476, 337 of whom were Spanish. Approximately 1,200 prisoners were taken by the British from two Spanish vessels. Three of the sixteen French ships had fought with distinction, the *Mont-Blanc*, *Atlas* and *Pluton*, they accounting for 89 of the 139 French casualties. As for Admiral Villeneuve's flagship, the *Bucentaure*, she, like most of the remaining French ships, saw very little action and later reported just six casualties.

The Spaniards had shown themselves to be very brave men indeed, their six ships taking on the entire British line of fifteen ships. Admiral Calder had gained a nominal victory of sorts, but certainly not a decisive one.

At daybreak on 23rd July, all parties remained in about the same position as the day before, though, instead of confronting one another, each side stood back, Calder even more so perhaps. They sheltered in an unrelenting fog, neither side willing to renew the fighting or to withdraw from the battlefield. In fact, Calder refused to attack on the 24th as well, though there was a change for the better in the winds. Calder, in the words of William James, 'would neither attack nor retreat'; indeed, he was apparently more concerned with convoying the crippled *Windsor Castle* and his two ancient Spanish prizes beyond the reach of danger, than renewing hostilities. It was only on 25th July that the two enemy fleets, now many miles apart, silently acknowledged their mutual decision to declare the battle over by sailing off in different directions. The Admiralty Board was to accept this for the humiliation it was, and Sir Robert Calder – so vehement in speech, but so slack in action – was later to appear before a court of inquiry to account for himself. The French never bothered to do the same, however, or Admiral Villeneuve would not have been in command at Trafalgar three months later.

Villeneuve's report on the battle was very sketchy indeed, more typical of a diplomatic assessment than of a naval summary of events, deliberately giving little indication of the real roles he, Gravina and their fleets had played. Indeed, Villeneuve intentionally distorted the situation by concealing the fact that Gravina's six ships led the battle for the full duration of the fighting, took the greatest risks and punishment and incurred the greatest number of casualties, not to mention a greater part of the Combined Fleet's damage. Nor did Villeneuve state or even hint that it was Gravina's squadron that had inflicted the greatest damage to Calder's fleet. Likewise he failed to mention that only three French ships (out of fourteen) made a real attempt to get into the fighting and come to the aid of the beleaguered Spaniards, and that he, the Commander-in-Chief, was almost never personally at risk, indeed almost never under fire throughout the entire battle. Never once did he praise Admiral Gravina's distinguished role in the day's events, to which Villeneuve remained more or less a bystander.

In his report to Admiral 'Decraise' (he never could spell Decrès' name correctly) on 28th July, Gravina informed him that 'this fight began very well, the vanguard (consisting of my ships) and M. Villeneuve's centre, and some of his rearguard ships fought the Enemy with the greatest Courage, but then a thick Fog and night fell which paralysed our operations, to the extent that we could no longer distinguish either signals or movements and that is why I was not able to see (until the next day) that we had lost the *San Rafael* and *Firma*'. In a second report to Prime Minister Godoy, Gravina acknowledged that 'fire was always very lively and sustained', only ending around 9 pm 'when the enemy withdrew from the fight'. That night Villeneuve had sent up rockets every half hour to try to locate his fleet, and to give them his position, but they were scattered over a few miles and the fog remained almost impenetrable. The following day, he continued, 'it was still very foggy when we realised we were missing two ships from my squadron'. He then said something which no one has been able to corroborate, that on 23rd July, 'We continued to pursue them throughout the day, though to little effect, because the enemy instantly manoeuvred to avoid a second engagement . . . The same thing happened on the 24th,' while on the 25th, 'under heavy seas we lost sight of the enemy' and they headed for Vigo.

In Calder's defence (it is not worth even trying to defend Villeneuve's pathetic performance) he argued that he feared Villeneuve's fleet joining with other French squadrons – including Captain Allemand's five ships (which were close by) and the fifteen ships at El Ferrol – which would have put him at an even greater disadvantage. But Sir Robert was evidently more interested in protecting his own damaged ships and keeping his two Spanish prizes than engaging the enemy a second time and deliberately withdrew several miles away while remaining within sight of the Franco-Spanish fleet. Villeneuve's report would indicate that this was not necessary as his Combined Fleet really made no serious effort to pursue Calder and most certainly did not chase him off the battlefield, despite Napoleon's claims to the contrary at a later date. Indeed, Villeneuve's journal in this instance would indicate that Gravina was playing with the truth when saying he pursued the British, stating that on 23rd July the visibility was extremely poor and he was forced to stay put. Thus he gave no orders to pursue Calder. His preparatory order late that night to prepare for battle on the following morning of the 24th was rescinded because of the fog. The day after that, however, it was contrary winds that made it impossible for him to advance, in addition to the prevailing fog. On 25th July he made a decision: 'As there seems to be no break in the weather, and fearing the dismasting of several of my vessels any moment now, in particular those that were heavily damaged during the battle, and as several of our poorly sailing vessels require repairs as well . . . after having conferred with Admiral Gravina, I have decided to sail to Cadiz'. Contrary winds then making *that* impossible, he instead charted a course for El Ferrol, only fifteen miles away, and when even that course did not prove feasible, the exigencies of his fleet requiring him to put into the first possible port, he sailed for Vigo.

Having accepted Calder's explanations for failing to renew the battle on the subsequent days, one can merely close the subject with a 'but if' – but if Nelson had been in Calder's shoes. The fact is that the brash Sir Robert, who felt no qualms about complaining about the small number of ships under his command off El Ferrol, and continually going over Admiral Cornwallis' head when wishing to communicate directly with the First Lord, was better at talking and complaining than acting when he was face to face with the enemy, even though he had a fleet of fifteen sail of the line (five more than Nelson had when pursuing that same fleet across the Atlantic to Martinique). Indeed Sir Robert's failure to resume the battle on 23rd and 24th July resulted in a 'severe reprimand' from a court-martial held in the last week of December.

To return, though, to 25th July 1805. Villeneuve's situation was deteriorating rapidly, due to battle and storm damage and dwindling food and water supplies, aggravated by a considerable number of ill and wounded on board – not to mention the shattered state of his mind that his correspondence was to reveal – and he made for Vigo Bay, arriving there on 27th July, where he took a brief respite and left two battered ships before proceeding to El Ferrol on 31st July.

Calder meanwhile accompanied his two prizes and the lame *Windsor Castle* until 26th July, when he dispatched them under escort to Plymouth while he, with his remaining fourteen sail of the line, returned to a rendezvous point off Cape Finisterre where he hoped to join Nelson. Not finding him there, however, he pushed on for El Ferrol on 29th July to resume his duties, while reluctantly parting with a second vessel, the *Malta*, which had also suffered considerable damage.

On 2nd August, he detached Rear-Admiral Stirling and his four ships, ordering them to return to their former station off Rochefort, leaving Calder in the uncomfortable situation of having just nine ships of the line before a major enemy port. Much to his consternation, upon returning to El Ferrol on 9th August, following a storm that had blown him out to sea, he found Villeneuve's Combined Fleet already safe in harbour, having completed the junction that he had so dreaded with the squadrons of Rear-Admirals Grandallana and Gourdon, now giving them a force of twenty-nine sail (though only twenty-seven would sail with the fleet). 'In this state of things,' James commented, 'Sir Robert, with his nine sail of the line abandoned the blockade and on the 14th [August] joined Admiral Cornwallis off Ushant.'

You are to proceed to Cadiz . . . I want you to rally the Spanish ships you find there . . . without staying . . . more than four days at most, and then sail to Ferrol where you will add the fifteen French and Spanish vessels to your fleet . . . whereupon, with all these forces now under your command you will proceed to Brest and thence to Boulogne where, if you put me in full control for three days . . . and with God's help, I shall put an end to the destinies and existence of England.

Napoleon to Villeneuve, 26th July 1805

HE HAD MORE tricks than a monkey, Collingwood had said of the French Emperor, who on 26th July dictated the above orders which Commander-in-Chief Villeneuve was to receive at La Coruña, several days after his arrival there on 1st August. Of course, having come to this port directly, common sense would dictate cancelling the part of the order concerning Cadiz, where the remaining squadron was, in any case, insignificant. At this time Villeneuve was already preparing a fleet of twenty-seven sail of the line (nine of them Spanish), six frigates (including one Spanish) and several corvettes and brigs to sail within a few days' time.* He also learned that Allemand had left Rochefort with a squadron of five ships on 17th July 'for the purpose of carrying out raids along the coasts of Ireland, in order to draw the enemy there and weaken their force before Brest', after which he was to join Villeneuve off El Ferrol 'between 29th July and 3rd August'. As it turned out however, confusion in the dates set for that rendezvous issued by Decrès, followed by the capture of the *Didon*, the ship bearing final instructions to that effect, by the British *Phoenix*, led to the failure of that meeting. Allemand was left cruising aimlessly for the next several months, but not harmlessly, as he destroyed or captured numerous British merchantmen and warships.[1]

Foreign Minister Talleyrand, who was conveying most of the diplomatic correspondence to the Emperor, had never been enthusiastic about the entire Channel operation and the intended invasion of Great Britain – indeed, he had done everything in his power to dissuade the Emperor

*See appendix 3

from continuing with it. He now quickly took advantage of the news of Nelson's return, pointing out to Napoleon that, with that fleet, the British now had 'a line of 54 or 55 ships' off the Spanish and French coasts. 'This unforeseen gathering of forces no doubt renders any plans for a descent quite impracticable for the moment' which meant that two-thirds of the entire British navy would soon be converging on Boulogne. None the less Napoleon continued with his personal preparations at Boulogne for the launching of his 2,000 vessels, and met with his army and naval commanders on a daily basis throughout the first half of August.

It was during a tour of inspection on 8th August that he finally received news of the battle of 22nd July between the Combined Fleet and Calder and at first he seemed content enough with the reports reaching him from both El Ferrol and Madrid. 'The Combined Fleet has been in a battle off Ferrol', he informed Arch-Chancellor Jean-Jacques Cambacérès that same day, 'It has fulfilled the mission's objective, which was its junction with the Ferrol squadron . . . It [also] chased the enemy fleet away and for four days remained master of the battlefield', or such was his view of the event. One British ship was sunk, he claimed, and two others completely dismasted, whereas the French fleet had received very little damage. He complained bitterly, however, that Gravina had 'lost' two ships as a result of the Spanish 'probably fighting very badly'. He concluded, 'I feel that we can consider this affair a success'. To Treasury Minister François Barbé-Marbois, Napoleon was even more scathing of the Spanish role at the battle off El Ferrol. 'It went well enough, but it could have been quite splendid, *had it not been for Spanish blunders . . . You know how very little one can ever count on them . . .*'*

Never in his reports to Decrès or the Emperor had Pierre Villeneuve indicated the full scope of his own failings, whether at Toulon, in the West Indies or now at El Ferrol, and Napoleon, who had even fewer scruples than Villeneuve when it came to the suppression of the truth or distortion of events, both for war propaganda purposes and the historical record, now added his deft touch to the business. In this instance he stated that the British fleet had suffered far more grievously than was the case. 'Have it made known and understood [in the press and throughout the country] that this affair has been in our favour', he informed Police Minister Fouché on 9th August. The British fleet, he would have it, had 'fled' from Villeneuve, albeit the Spanish had let them down of course. 'But as all this will be rather unpleasant for the Spanish, you had better

*Author's italics

praise Gravina . . .' The British squadron, he concluded, had suffered 'some twenty million francs worth of damage.'

This was typical of Napoleon's handling of the situation. He had no reports as to what the *real* role of the Spanish and Gravina had been in that battle, nor had he specific details on damage incurred by the British, and therefore had no means of even beginning to estimate the cost of damage suffered by Calder's fleet – he literally plucked a figure out of thin air. Indeed, Villeneuve was never even to give him a detailed report on the damage his *own* fleet had suffered, but this lack of facts did not deter the French leader. 'Write to the Prince of Peace to let him know how distressed I was to learn of the loss of the 2 Spanish ships,' he instructed Decrès caustically on 10th August, while stating privately that 'the two Spanish vessels *were lost through incompetence; but they are such poor soldiers that, in reality, it is perhaps preferable not to have them with us any longer.*'* Napoleon then gave his own version of events to Marshal Berthier at Boulogne, who, in turn, issued an Order of the Day to the 'Army Along the Coasts of the Ocean', announcing Villeneuve's great victory over the British, closing with the good news that the Combined Fleet '*had suffered no major damage. The number of dead and wounded has been negligible*'.*

Napoleon, who had been waiting for some good news – any good news – for over two years, ever since preparing for this invasion of England, now took full advantage of the situation. He made use of any and all propaganda available and when it did not exist, he created it. 'It may be useful for you to make known to the Amsterdam Stock Exchange', he informed the head of the Dutch Government, 'that Admiral Villeneuve has defeated Admiral Calder.'

The Emperor had up to 167,000 men and a flotilla of nearly 2,000 boats ready to land in Britain, but an army and navy – according to private reports he had received – that were demoralised and no longer believed in the invasion. He needed Villeneuve's 'victory' to counter this serious problem (not to mention critical financial ones) and he was to leave no avenue unexplored. He dictated fabulous reports that subsequently appeared in the official Government organ, the *Moniteur*. When the British version of that naval battle was finally quoted in Batavian newspapers, however, Napoleon was furious, informing French Ambassador Serurier at Amsterdam to have the Attorney-General of the province of Holland 'give a firm order to all the newspaper editors of the country, to desist from publishing anything on this subject'.

*Author's italics

It was only between 11th and 13th August, however, that the more accurate reports of the battle between the Combined Fleet and the British began reaching Napoleon and the real extent of the distortions and omissions by Villeneuve became patently clear. Villeneuve may have 'a little talent', the Emperor said, but he was too indecisive. 'On the other hand, that damned Gravina is all genius and action in battle . . . If only Villeneuve had those qualities . . . How does he have the nerve to complain about the Spanish? They have fought like lions!'

At this very moment Napoleon also received news of what had really transpired in the West Indies, though his reaction was surprisingly mild. 'Why is it that Admiral Villeneuve never said anything about this in his reports?' The 12,440 troops had never been landed after all. None of his orders had been carried out and, indeed, 'at one time my islands of Martinique and Guadeloupe were in jeopardy', when he fled before Nelson. 'All thanks to this incredible Villeneuve', which just proved that he 'is a man with double vision', that is, he saw twice the number of enemy and problems there actually were and 'who has far more intelligence than he does character, or guts'.

In the meantime, General Reille was writing privately of these events, which he had witnessed, to Prince Murat, the *Grand Amiral de l'Empire*, and of course Napoleon's brother-in-law. 'Here is this Navy, which could have done so much harm to the English, which has returned having accomplished nothing . . . I must confess I simply cannot conceive how the Minister [Decrès], who has personally served under our Admiral's [Villeneuve's] orders [earlier in his career], and who knows him far better than most, could have possibly recommended him to His Majesty to head an important expedition.'

In spite of the Emperor's rapidly declining estimation of Vice-Admiral Pierre Villeneuve – who, along with his twenty-seven ships of the line, was now snug in the harbours of El Ferrol and La Coruña – and his shock upon receiving the first accurate reports of Spanish gallantry and French apathy, he was apparently ready to keep him on, at least for the moment. He still had no one else to replace him, for during the early years of the French Revolution most of the really competent officers in the navy had been executed or dismissed. In his first letter to the Commander-in-Chief of the Toulon fleet, written from Boulogne on 13th August after receiving this devastating news, Napoleon began by saying he was pleased 'with the gallantry shown by several of my vessels', but nevertheless he, Villeneuve, should have captured the two British ships he said he had disabled. That would 'have given us the real victory we so badly needed', but as it was, unfortunately the admiral had been 'too indecisive'. Just as he had been in the West Indies when he had left those possessions 'in a weaker state than he had found them'. Be that as it may, now he, the Emperor, and the entire invasion army were waiting at Boulogne *for him*. Napoleon hoped that this letter would *not* reach him still at El Ferrol, that the admiral had in fact already sailed northward and made a rendezvous with Captain Allemand, when 'you must sweep away all that you find before you and *come up the Channel where we are awaiting you most anxiously*.* March straight at the enemy.' Now was the time to act – 'Never will a fleet have run such risks, and never will my soldiers and sailors have spilt their blood for a greater or more noble purpose. We should all of us gladly give our lives in order to help bring about an invasion of that power which has been suppressing France for six centuries. Such are the sentiments which ought to animate my soldiers.'

Villeneuve, therefore, had to discard the previous instructions to go to Cadiz and then El Ferrol. From El Ferrol he must *now* sweep directly up the Channel with his armada, joining the five of Allemand's squadron and with those thirty-two ships sail to Brest where Ganteaume's twenty-one ships were to join him giving him *fifty-three ships of the line*!

'Nelson and Collingwood are off the battlefield,' Napoleon assured Decrès on 14th August, 'Cochrane's and the West Indies Squadrons as well; 12 [English] ships are at Texel; 12 . . . at Helvet-Sluys . . . Well now, really, what a splendid opportunity we should be missing! . . . What a perfect occasion, *if I only had a real man there*.'* But 'Villeneuve is one of those men who needs more spur than bridle . . . Is it truly impossible to find a single enterprising man in the Navy, someone who has real blood in his veins?'

Villeneuve's pathetic outbursts at Toulon prior to weighing anchor could at very best have been attributed to a temporary attack of nerves, as a result of overwork, perhaps, but all his actions since that time had proved that not only was he totally unfit for the post but was undergoing some sort of mental breakdown and was almost out of control, as a letter he sent during August to his old friend, Denis Decrès, clearly demonstrated: 'I cannot pull out of this deep depression into which I have fallen.' This expedition, he felt, was a mistake from the outset. 'But the sailors in Paris [Napoleon and his cohorts] and elsewhere in the provinces who have been interfering in this are indeed blind, reprehensible and stupid.' He had already told Decrès that the French and

*Author's italics

Spanish were not capable of executing joint manoeuvres, indeed, 'they
are not even ready enough to put to sea separately . . . Because,' he
continued, 'of the lack of experience by my officers and sailors, because
of my captains' lack of wartime experience, and as a result of everything
put together', this fleet is incapable of sailing and is doomed to failure. As
if this were not bad enough, General Lauriston had been making life hell
for him in the fleet, on board his flagship, indeed at his own dinner table,
this man who 'criticises me every day, even before my own naval officers'.
Lauriston was humiliating him, though 'I have exhausted every effort to
treat him well . . . It is awful for me to have to be continually in his
presence, seated at the same table with a man I can but consider a
declared enemy . . . It is quite impossible to have been unhappier than I
have been since the moment of our departure . . . *I cannot conceal my belief
that we have no chance of winning** . . . My Lord, put an end to this
situation.'

Despite his grave misgivings, on 10th August Vice-Admiral Villeneuve
informed the Naval Minister that he was finally weighing anchor. 'The
[Spanish] squadron at Ferrol is making its junction [with his in La
Coruña]; I am leaving, and depending upon the circumstances am
heading for Brest or Cadiz. The enemy can observe us too easily to be
able to deceive them about our destination, however.' In fact, in spite of
Napoleon's most recent categorical and implicit instructions that the
Combined Fleet meet him now at Boulogne, Pierre Villeneuve finally
decided to sail *south*, to the safety of Cadiz.

Receipt of this fateful news left the Emperor simply stunned. 'What a
Navy! What an admiral! All those sacrifices for nought!' he exclaimed to
his secretary, Count Daru.[2] In fact Pierre Villeneuve's unilateral decision
to sail for Cadiz on 11th August clearly made any further attempt to
launch the invasion quite impossible. Napoleon was left standing on the
cliffs of Boulogne with an army of 165,000 men.

*Author's italics

The Last Homecoming

We trust, that we shall yet have to announce the total discomfiture of the Combined Squadron. It should be in vain to conceal, that the public has experienced a severe disappointment that the enemy were not brought to action a second time [by Calder]. We have been so habituated to triumph over the fleets of France and Spain, that our expectations become immoderate, through success.

The Times, 6th August 1805

I only wish to stand upon my own merits, and not by comparison, one way or the other, upon the conduct of a Brother Officer.

Nelson to Captain Fremantle, 16th August 1805

We should regret if Lord Nelson were deprived of the chief honours of a victory [against the Combined Fleet] which his extraordinary sagacity and unparalleled activity have well deserved.

The Times, 10th August 1805

THE BUST OF Vice-Admiral Lord Nelson standing on Napoleon's mantelpiece was the only one of an enemy the French Emperor had ever commissioned for himself and, curiously enough, Nelson, the one military genius he respected next to himself, as a sailor, would never face Napoleon on a battlefield.

Both men were extremely egotistical, but each in a different way. Whereas Napoleon's vanity excluded the existence of everyone else, indeed, all mankind, Nelson, though he never made an effort to conceal his belief that he could always defeat any French or Spanish admiral or fleet and plastered every wall and corridor of his house at Merton with his own portrait and war trophies, did not exclude humanity. Unlike Napoleon, he was close to many of his fellow officers and their families and went out of his way to help them when they were in difficulty or to make their lives more comfortable while they were serving under him. He was of course a religious man, unlike Napoleon, and yet even he – the supreme scoffer of all time – could not laugh at the sailor who got down on his knees every morning and night to pray to his Lord.

It was hardly surprising that Horatio Nelson remained a devout man all his life, he who had been born at, and spent his formative years in, the parsonage of Burnham Thorpe, Norfolk, while both of whose grand-fathers, two great uncles, eight cousins and, later, two brothers, were Anglican clergymen.

Nelson's God was a strict one, enforced by a Cambridge-educated father who considered it slothful and disrespectful even to let one's back rest against a chair when at table. He was nine years old when his mother died (after bearing eleven children, some of whom had already preceded her to the graveyard) and was not to experience a woman's love, warmth and generosity again until the last decade of his life, when he met Emma Hamilton.

In a world where seagulls wheeled over fens and fields of corn, where wafts of sea air carried the tang of salt marshes some four miles away, from shores where mammoth tusks were still occasionally washed up after Channel gales, it was hardly surprising that the mysterious world over the horizon would entice an imaginative young boy. But in young Nelson's case, family tales of the exploits of his uncle, Captain Maurice Suckling, also played a share in events. Time and again he was told of his uncle's defeat of a superior French squadron off Cape François, as captain of the mighty three-decker, the *Dreadnought*, on 21st October 1757 (a date Nelson was to remember until the day he died). What sort of future lay before him in this flat, well-cultivated land? For a gentleman there was not much choice: a military career or the law. He certainly had no intention of taking religious orders like his brothers and, for an impoverished family, there was nothing for him here.

Whatever the reason, it was an inordinately mature twelve-year-old who finally persuaded a most reluctant father to let him go to sea on 1st January 1771 as a midshipman on board his uncle's man-of-war, the *Raisonnable*, which was destined for hostile Spanish shores. By the age of fourteen he had been to the West Indies and on an Arctic expedition and by seventeen had nearly died of malaria in the Indian Ocean, an illness that greatly undermined his health for the rest of his life, his light auburn hair and ruddy complexion changing permanently after many months in bed. Youth and drive, however, were on the boy's side and he quickly rose in his profession, serving many years in and near the Caribbean, and, by the age of twenty-one, he was promoted to post-captain of a 28-gun frigate, years in advance of most of his peers.

It was while in the West Indies and sharing a mess with the then thirty-six-year-old captain of the *Lion*, a man who was to remain a friend the rest of his days, that Sir William Cornwallis had instilled into him something he never forgot: 'You can always beat a Frenchman if you fight him long enough. The difficulty of getting at them is sometimes more fancy than fact . . . People never know what they can do until they have tried . . . When in doubt, to fight is always to err on the right side'.

During the American War of Independence, Nelson not only fought the Americans and their French allies, but also escorted large convoys of merchantmen (sometimes numbering between 200 and 300 ships) to Britain and others back to St Johns, Newfoundland and Jamaica, not to mention taking part in an occasional military expedition, including one to Nicaragua, the latter resulting in a particularly serious recurrence of malaria. He detested St Johns, just as he later found the Downs station off the south-east coast of Britain 'a horrible bad one'. As well as all the experience he was gaining in nearly every aspect of seamanship and from commanding vessels in a fighting navy, however, he also had the good fortune to have been born in the age of the giants of British naval and exploratory history, a fact which the perceptive young man himself was quick to appreciate.

It was late in 1782 that he first served under, and made the acquaintance of, Admiral Lord Hood, stationed at that time off Staten Island in New York harbour. While there he met, and got to know quite well, a seventeen-year-old midshipman who was to crop up every once in a while throughout his career – Prince William Henry, later the Duke of Clarence and ultimately King William IV. It was also during these early years that he came to know Alexander Davison, who remained his closest friend all his life. A great many of Nelson's friendships were made in his twenties, especially in the West Indies, including the Collingwood brothers, Cuthbert in particular. He was to meet the remainder of his naval friends a few years hence when serving in the Mediterranean.

It was in the West Indies, too, that he made the acquaintance of his future wife. In March 1785 he met Fanny Nisbet, the attractive young widow of a local doctor, whom he married when he was twenty-eight, acquiring at the same time a stepson, Josiah, who was to become the proverbial albatross around Nelson's neck practically until the day he died, which made the boy resent him all the more. Later in Nelson's career, after losing an arm and an eye in battle, which caused him considerable difficulty whenever he had to be hoisted aboard ship when at sea, Josiah Nisbet, then a captain of a frigate, laughed at one such spectacle, loudly proclaiming his wish that his stepfather would fall backwards and kill himself. Naturally this quickly got back to Nelson, who wrote to Fanny: 'I have done *all* for him, and he may again, as he has done before, wish me to break my neck, and be abetted in it by his friends, who are likewise my enemies', and he asked to be rid of him once and for all and 'to be left to myself'. But all that lay in the future.

Nelson was one of those rare sea officers who occasionally became embroiled in controversy, but who nevertheless managed to extricate himself professionally. His motto at this time seemed to be 'a uniform course of honour and integrity seldom fails of bringing a man to the goal of Fame at last' and it was to see him through thick and thin, indeed, to that very goal – albeit failing to help him achieve wealth, which seemed to escape his grasp with a maddening regularity throughout his colourful career, though he sometimes came close enough to it. His personal standards of integrity did indeed enable him to get through some sticky situations, and in a letter to Fanny he once summed up his attitude and philosophy: 'My character and good name are in my own keeping. Life with disgrace is dreadful', and in that spirit he always acted.

Following the close of hostilities with the Americans, French and Spanish, Nelson found himself grounded in Norfolk with his wife for a few winters, not to be recalled to service again by Lord Hood until January 1793 when he was given command of his first ship of the line, the 64-gun *Agamemnon*. If after this his career never looked back again, his marriage was already proving a failure. His neurotic and chronically ill wife apparently refused to have children by him – though he longed for them – and her frigidity assumed such proportions as to make a sailor happy to flee his hearth on a blustery January day, and only return for rare short spells in the future. Indeed he never once visited Roundwood, the house he bought for Fanny, and which she finally abandoned in despair. By 1800 Nelson had had more than enough between his stepson, Josiah, and his histrionic wife, Fanny. At a performance of the play *Pizarro*, at the Theatre Royal in Drury Lane in November 1800, she suddenly stood up, screamed and fainted, to the enormous embarrassment of Nelson, who never again appeared in public with her. On 23rd April 1801 he reminded Alexander Davison (who was the unfortunate middleman in this affair) that 'sooner than live the unhappy life I did when I last came to England, I would stay abroad for ever . . . My mind is as fixed as fate . . .'

While serving under Admiral Lord Hood in the summer of 1793, during a respite of international peace, Nelson landed at Cadiz where he carefully inspected the harbour and defences, which somehow inspired this ever-perceptive sailor to remark at the time, 'The Dons may make fine ships – they cannot, however, make men [that is, good sailors] . . . Long may they remain in their present state'. The year 1793 proved of special importance in another respect, for it was that autumn he sailed with his thirteen-year-old stepson (whom he referred to as his 'son-in-law'), Josiah Nisbet, to Naples for the first time, marking the beginning of both his career in the Mediterranean and the one passionate love affair of his life, as it was here that he met Lady Emma Hamilton, his future mistress.

Between July 1794 and July 1797, Nelson's life was greatly altered. Earlier in his career he had received a few negligible wounds, but, on 12th July 1794, in his twenty-fourth year in the Royal Navy, Horatio Nelson was struck sharply in the face and chest by splinters and stone from an enemy battery while laying siege to a fortress outside Calvi, in Corsica. At the time he simply informed the Admiralty that his left eye was 'a little hurt this morning: not much', though his eye was never the same again. Hereafter he could only distinguish between light and dark, all ability to focus in the left eye having been lost completely. However, Calvi was captured and Corsica came under British rule as Nelson's friend, Sir Gilbert Elliot (the future Lord Minto) assumed the new office as viceroy of that tormented island, after lowering the French flag that had been first hoisted there just prior to Napoleon's birth.

Though in great pain off and on for years to come because of the injury to his eye, and the growing strain it placed on his remaining good right eye, Nelson was not one to complain in public. Most naval officers suffered rather savage wounds in that age of primitive and brutal warfare, when swords hacked through bodies and cannon balls blew off arms and legs. Three years later, at the age of thirty-eight, on 25th July 1797, a few months after the successful Battle of Cape St Vincent, Nelson was wounded severely again, when grape-shot nearly severed his right arm at the elbow during the siege of the Spanish capital of the Canaries, Santa Cruz, necessitating its immediate amputation aboard ship. By the time he reached London that September, he was still in excruciating pain, as he was to be for many months to come. This was only alleviated at night by opium. In public he was always to make light of his suffering, as when he appeared at Surgeons Hall for his eye check-up prior to being awarded a pension for its loss. Asked the purpose of his visit there he replied, 'Oh! this is only for an eye: in a few days I shall come for an arm: and in a little time longer, God knows, most probably for a leg'. By now his naval career had already included four fleet actions (three with frigates), six engagements against batteries, ten cutting-out expeditions and the capture of three towns. With those achievements to his name he celebrated his thirty-ninth birthday on 29th September.

Nelson is an oft-quoted gentleman, but perhaps the most important principle or precept of his life he appears never to have articulated. That one had to be honourable, do one's duty, give one's life if necessary to protect Britain, be loyal to fellow officers – all these he talked about and took for granted. Above and beyond these things, however, he learned from Cornwallis, Hood and others and the examples he found in the rectory of Burnham Thorpe, that every responsible person had to think for himself. To be an outstanding naval officer one had to analyse all orders given and occasionally ignore a few (and there were not that many) 'for the good of the Service'. In the West Indies he got into trouble with British colonial merchants, ironically, for enforcing the Navigation Laws against merchant ships, American ones in particular, that restricted their trading rights with the British establishments. As most of his colleagues gave in to the pressures exerted by the large planters, Nelson's wilful defiance of their demands made him the odd man out. This translated into threats and then substantial law suits, filed against him by numerous powerful trading interests there. Admiral Lord Hood had taught him to stand up for what he believed in when, in his opinion, it served the best interests of the Royal Navy and Great Britain and, as a result, Admiral Hood himself was eventually ordered by London to strike his flag permanently. 'Oh, miserable Board of Admiralty!', Nelson exclaimed upon hearing this news, but Nelson was to match Hood time and again, especially after entering service in the Mediterranean. When, for instance, he was later Second-in-Command under Admiral Sir William Hotham, Admiral Lord Keith and Sir Hyde Parker at Copenhagen, he deliberately ignored orders which he felt were detrimental to his job. At the Battle of Cape St Vincent he had disobeyed Admiral Sir John Jervis' tactical orders, and had thereby made a brilliant victory out of one that would otherwise have been merely acceptable; Jervis cheered him on, once he realised what Nelson was doing. Because of this rather unusual instinctive approach, which permitted him to survive and improve his position in the navy, Nelson gained some foes – such as Keith, Gardner, Hotham and Hyde Parker, not to mention several among his peers including Sir John Orde and Sir Robert Calder – but at the same time developed a powerful reputation for himself among British seamen and his fellow officers. Hood already respected Nelson and apparently expected great things of him, though he had still not seen any of his remarkable accomplishments before leaving the service.

The devious Sir John Jervis who, as we have seen, took for himself the glory of the battle off Cape St Vincent on 14th February 1797, playing down Nelson's part, and became the Earl of St Vincent as a result, would on occasion tolerate extraordinary laxity in Nelson for which he would have court-martialled any other officer. In fact, St Vincent was never a popular man in the navy, as his harsh discipline and grim view of life included his frequent condemnation of sloppy and unhealthy ships as well as the '. . . indiscreet, licentious conversations of the officers'. This once led to his captains, at a dinner with their wives, proposing a whispered toast 'That the discipline of the Mediterranean never be introduced into the Channel Fleet', to which a bitter naval wife added, 'May his next glass of wine choke the wretch!'

Although Nelson, too, was often extremely irritated by St Vincent, he at least ventured to do what no other man would have dared – to break rules or disregard certain instructions. This he did, however, only when his own intelligence, experience and judgement told him it had to be done, and never just out of spite or as a puerile lark. St Vincent understood this and Nelson – who greatly disliked any sort of restraints – accepted him and his sometimes outrageous demands, because Nelson generally respected St Vincent's judgement, and there were very few men who fell within that élite category.

Nelson did argue with him sometimes, however, and, indeed, ultimately even had to go to court against him when St Vincent, already a very wealthy man as a result of the many sea prizes he had taken over the decades, claimed prize money that Nelson felt was rightly due to him. Greed and jealousy were always two of St Vincent's several great weaknesses, as Nelson was beginning to find out, as, for instance, when First Lord St Vincent refused to order a medal to commemorate Nelson's great victory at the Battle of Copenhagen on 2nd April 1801.

Admiral Lord Keith, who served as Commander-in-Chief in the Mediterranean following St Vincent's assumption of his Admiralty post, was constantly at odds with Nelson, and though he was an effective commander later when placed in charge of the Home Fleet in the Channel, his actions were not always that wise in the Mediterranean, which Nelson felt bound to point out.

No naval officer found it smooth sailing throughout a long career, and perhaps Nelson's occasional problems seemed relatively mild in comparison. Indeed, he rose quickly in his profession, being promoted from captain to the nominated rank of commodore at the age of thirty-six in March 1796 (at the insistence of St Vincent), then, just after the great naval victory at the Battle of Cape St Vincent in February 1797, was promoted to flag rank, as Rear-Admiral of the Blue (yet again at the insistence of St Vincent) and, following the battle, was knighted and personally invested with the prestigious Order of the Bath (the first of four such orders he was to receive) by a grateful George III. Although following the Battle of the Nile on 1st August 1798 Nelson went up only one step in seniority, still as a rear-admiral, nevertheless he was raised to the peerage as a baron, thereby becoming the 'Lord Nelson' who was soon to appear on many a pub sign.

However, rapid promotion and unique distinctions did not alter the good-natured admiral, his fellow officers discovered. Sailors sometimes have a curious sense of humour, but this at least was mutually understood and appreciated by their colleagues, and thus, following the great Nile victory when Captain Ben Hallowell presented Nelson with a unique gift, his own coffin made from the mainmast of *L'Orient*, the forty-year-old Nelson was delighted. Thereafter he kept the coffin in his day-cabin behind his Windsor chair and, noting day after day that his fellow officers tended to stare at it with a combination of amusement and curiosity, Nelson would smile mischievously: 'You may look at it, gentlemen, but depend upon it, none of you shall have it.'

Horatio Nelson was finally gazetted Vice-Admiral of the Blue on 1st January 1801, at the age of forty-two, which he celebrated that same month along with the announcement of his legal separation from Fanny. This was followed on 2nd April 1801 by the new vice-admiral's staggering victory at the Battle of Copenhagen, he directing the entire operation, while under the nominal command of old Hyde Parker, whose orders, fortunately, Nelson ignored for the most part. Because Nelson was only Second-in-Command, however, he was merely made a Viscount that June, rather than an Earl. Nevertheless the King and Queen of the Two Sicilies had already made a Duke of him (which included a large, if worthless estate in Sicily), which resulted in him signing himself Nelson and Brontë.

With strong intimations by the end of 1801 that peace would be re-established at last between France and Great Britain, Nelson knew that there would be no more opportunities for a major confrontation with the enemy and for the defeat, nay, the destruction, of the French fleet, which is what he not only desired, but felt was absolutely necessary to put an end once and for all to any talk of a French threat against Britain or her colonies and a truly lasting peace.

By the year 1799 one woman had come to dominate Nelson's mind and life, and this of course was Emma Hamilton. Their love affair had

blossomed at Naples, literally under the roof of the Hamiltons, to which
the elderly Sir William Hamilton, the British Minister accredited to that
court, appeared to acquiesce. The love of Horatio and Emma never
flagged, despite Nelson's great anxieties over her possible infidelity to
him – especially after 1801 when the Prince of Wales began displaying an
undue interest in her – Nelson knowing only too well the weaknesses of
her strong, sensual nature.

Friends and enemies both resented her growing role in his life and
Lord Keith's cutting remark, 'Lady Hamilton has had command of the
Fleet long enough!' no doubt got back to him. Both St Vincent and
Thomas Troubridge now refused to cross his doorstep, and again later
refused invitations to Merton as well. Even Nelson's close friend of many
years, Lord Minto (as Sir Gilbert Elliot was now called), found returning
the admiral's visits at Merton a somewhat excruciating experience,
indeed one his wife declined to share. 'The whole establishment and way
of life [at Merton Place],' Minto related to his wife after one dinner, 'is
such as to make me angry, as well as melancholy . . . She [Emma] going
on cramming Nelson with trowelfuls of flattery, which he goes on taking
as quietly as a child does pap . . . he thinks her quite an angel, and talks of
her as such to her face and behind her back, and she leads him about like
a keeper with a bear'. Nor did he approve of her socially, not only as the
working-class girl who had risen too far above her rank, but as a gambler
and whore to boot. This is how most of Nelson's friends also looked upon
Emma who had been the mistress of three men before marrying her last
lover, Sir William Hamilton. 'He does not seem at all conscious of the
sort of discredit he has fallen into, or the cause of it . . . But it is hard to
condemn and use ill a hero . . . for being foolish about a woman who has
art to make fools of many wiser than an admiral.' Nevertheless some of
Nelson's fellow officers did maintain close relations with Nelson and
Emma, including young Thomas Fremantle (a future vice-admiral) and
his wife, whom Nelson invited to a party aboard his flagship thus: 'My
dear Fremantle. If you don't come here on Sunday to celebrate the
Birthday of Santa Emma, Damn me if I ever forgive you.'

If she was unpalatable to many of his colleagues, she was equally so for
the Admiralty and Government, which, without her complication in his
life, no doubt would have done even more for him, including promoting
him to the rank of full admiral, which he never attained. Although she was
equally distasteful to the Nelson clan, including his sisters, now Mrs
Bolton and Mrs Matcham, they all finally accepted her presence, for they

loved their brother and his fame, and with such a sibling in the family greater honours and wealth were no doubt in store for them all.

No one could deny Nelson's complete infatuation with, and devotion to, Emma Hamilton, as his correspondence with her attests: 'If I could tell when to begin a letter to my dearest, beloved Emma, I could never tell when to stop . . . Dear wife, good, adorable friend how I love you . . . My own dear wife, for such you are in my eyes and in the face of heaven . . . I love, I never did love any one else . . . My longing for you . . . you may readily imagine. It setts me on fire.' The thought of their last meeting, Nelson wrote in August 1803, 'makes the blood fly to my head . . . Not all the wealth of Peru could buy me for one moment, it [his love] is all yours.'

With such intensity of feeling, it is hardly surprising that Horatio Nelson was also a very vulnerable lover, fearful either that Emma would deceive him or leave him for another. 'I own I sometimes fear you will not be so true to me as I am to you,' he wrote, but then tried to reassure himself and stop his growing anxiety concerning her relationship with the Prince of Wales. 'I know you too well not to be convinced you cannot be seduced by any prince of Europe.' But then all pretence gives way to sheer anguish: 'I am so agitated that I can write nothing. I knew it would be so, you can't help it . . . I am in tears, I cannot bear it . . . I am almost gone mad . . . *no one, not even Emma*, could resist the serpent's flattering tongue . . . Oh! I could thunder and strike dead with my lightning'. Then the lover, jealous and fearful, pleads with her with such a passion: 'I am calmer . . . Tears have relieved me . . . Only tell me you forgive me; don't scold me, indeed I am not worth it . . .' This was an insecure Nelson, needing a woman's love, a man very different from the one his closest friends thought they knew, this man who daily commanded the lives of thousands of men. By the last two years of his life, however, Emma was able to reassure him more or less completely.

Nelson's love for Emma remained as strong for the rest of his life and was undeniably touching. One year before his death he was writing, 'I want and wish to tell you all my thoughts and feelings, but that is impossible; for thoughts so rush upon thoughts, that I cannot, as I said before, know where to begin . . .' and, 'Dear wife, good, adorable friend, how I love you'. Regarding the post he was sending her, which might be intercepted by the enemy or read by the Admiralty, '. . . I don't chuse to say anything more than I care for all the world knowing, that I love you more than anything in the world and next my d[ea]ʳ H[orati]ªʼ.

Nelson was a most devoted father to their illegitimate daughter, Horatia, born to Emma at the beginning of 1801. He had longed to be a paterfamilias and to hold his own child in his arms – the one thing he envied about his brothers and sisters – and it was hardly surprising to see him become a most doting father. He was constantly sending instructions for her care, accompanied by anxious questions as to her health and actions, and whether Emma was taking good enough care of her. 'How I long to hear her prattle!', he wrote from a warship in the Mediterranean, 'I dreamt last night, I heard her call "Papa".'

Nelson's love for Emma was clearly reflected in his giving her permission to select and purchase an estate for him. Sir William Hamilton was simply appalled. 'I have lived with our dear Emma for several years', he told Nelson. 'I know her merit, have a great opinion of the head and heart that God Almighty has been pleased to give her; but a seaman alone could have given a fine woman full power to chuse and fit up a residence for him without seeing it himself'.

Nevertheless, Nelson, who, as a vice-admiral, was earning just under £1,000 a year (exclusive of another £3,000 in disability pensions and investments), was rarely in Britain to oversee his business affairs and, even when he was there understood or cared little enough about such matters. Alexander Davison invested his small savings for him and paid his bills, automatically advancing the perenially impecunious admiral money whenever he required it – a subject that preoccupied Nelson none the less, a man who did not like owing a farthing to anyone. To make matters worse, he was, by nature, generous and anyone with a tale of woe rarely left him empty-handed. Ironically, although he knew little enough about his own expenses and bills, he paid very close attention to these – down to the last penny – when it came to the navy, and no detail ever escaped his attention. He was, therefore, furious when British manufacturers supplied his ships and men with shoddy goods. For example, after inspecting a batch of new clothes for the crew of his fleet, he wrote back angrily to the Admiralty, 'The contractor who furnished such stuff ought to be hanged'.

Out of his salary and pension he gave his estranged wife, Fanny (whom he categorically refused ever to see or communicate with), a most generous £2,000 a year and lesser sums to Emma and members of his family, including £200 a year to a brother's widow and £150 '. . . to assist in educating my Nephews'. Other debits included the enormous invisible expenses incurred for entertainment on a lavish scale in his role as a senior naval officer – the sums were sometimes staggering. For example, during the brief period when he was Second-in-Command of the fleet off Copenhagen in 1801, he spent nearly £2,000 out of his own pocket, which was just under a quarter of the purchase price of his estate! It is hardly surprising, therefore, that he was more or less perennially in debt.

Emma Hamilton was just as bad when it came to understanding the necessity of balancing the accounts, not only regarding clothes and furnishings for the house, but architectural work she had done as well. If the bills she submitted often shocked him, for Nelson in love Emma could do no wrong, and he could never be angry with her. 'Your purse, my dear Emma, will always be empty, [but] whilst I have sixpence, you will have five-pence of it . . .' Little wonder that Emma was passionately devoted to her one-eyed, one-armed Nelson. Once faced with the reality of Emma's choice of Merton Place, exclusive of the thousands more she spent on major structural alterations, improvements to the grounds, the purchase of furnishings, not to mention additional neighbouring acreage, a somewhat humbled Nelson walked round his new estate for the first time and acknowledged, 'my soul is too big for my purse'. Yet, it was because of this warm, generous trait – or at least, in part – that Nelson was so different from most of his fellow officers and why he was so universally loved, admired and respected, from the most humble seaman to the highest admirals and politicians – among them William Pitt.

There is again a great bustle on account of [the threatened French] invasion, but there is a general hope in the possibility of Nelson's getting *a knock* at the combined fleets.

Lord Minto to his Wife, 8th August 1805

The alarm of Invasion has increased in proportion as the probability of a Continental War has been multiplied. Since the abrupt termination of the Russian Mission, the preparations of the enemy for making a descent on this country have been such, that Government has found it necessary to summon all its energies to meet the shock with which we are menaced.

The Times, 12th August 1805

Depend on it, Blackwood, I shall yet give Mr Villeneuve a drubbing.

Nelson to Captain Blackwood, 2nd September 1805

BY AUGUST 1805, having twice missed his great opportunity of getting at Villeneuve's fleet (first off Toulon, and then in the West Indies) and with the knowledge that the premature clash of Calder's force with the Combined Fleet the month before had at best merely stunned the Franco-Spanish force, a weary and, for the moment, stymied, Nelson had been ordered home for a well-earned rest after spending more than two years at sea. For the first time in his naval career of nearly thirty-one years, however, he was returning home without having accomplished his task, indeed, having failed in some respects.

It was a most wary Admiral Lord Nelson who stepped ashore at Portsmouth at 7 pm on 19th August, not knowing what sort of reception lay in store and, as he told Emma Hamilton, 'I have brought home no honour for my Country, only a most faithful servant.' Realising just how unforgiving the Admiralty Board could be when it came to failure in a senior officer, Nelson even thought he had possibly ended his career in the Royal Navy and he warned Emma to be prepared: 'There will be so many desirous of the Mediterranean Command, that I cannot expect they will allow me to return to it. I may, very possibly, be laid on the shelf', although one friend ('Mr Bulkeley') admonished him for such thoughts: 'Look into your own acts and read the public papers for the last four months, then judge if John Bull will consent to give up his sheet anchor.' Indeed, if he had any real doubts they were quickly dispelled upon his arrival at Portsmouth, *The Times* reporting the event in glowing terms: 'As soon as Lord Nelson's flag was descried at Spithead, the ramparts, and every place which could command a view of the entrance of the harbour, were crowded with spectators. As he approached the shore, he was saluted with loud and reiterated huzzas, as enthusiastic and sincere as if he had returned crowned with a great naval victory.'

Nelson may have been bewildered momentarily, but no doubt greatly relieved to find John Bull – who could be ruthlessly unforgiving, as Calder was shortly to discover – completely on his side. The London press also boasted how the French attempt on the West Indies had been 'baffled by the sagacity of Lord Nelson', a sentiment heartily endorsed by the West India Merchants and Planters who moved that 'his bold and unwearied pursuit of the Combined French and Spanish Squadrons to the West-Indies, and back again to Europe, have been very instrumental to the safety of the West-India Islands in general, and well deserve the grateful acknowledgements of every individual connected with the Colonies.'

An exhausted Admiral Viscount Nelson arrived at his estate at 6 am on 20th August 1805 in the mud-splattered post-chaise after driving all night in the rain from Portsmouth. The dishevelled, white-haired gentleman looked quite gaunt and frail and at least a decade older than his forty-six years. He little realised, of course, that this would be his last homecoming. 'Thank God, he is safe and well', wrote Sarah Connor, one of Emma Hamilton's relatives. But 'timid widows and spinsters are terrified at his foot being on shore', she insisted, for clearly Britain was no longer safe without Nelson at sea mounting guard.

His twenty-five days of leave, for that was all he had before him, were busy ones from the outset, allowing little time for rest or 'refreshment ashore'. The whirlwind began the very next day when he went to London (an hour's drive by carriage from Merton), leaving his bags at Gordon's Hotel, 44 Albemarle Street, then setting off on his rounds for, as he was wont to say, 'Duty is the great business of a Sea-officer'. A *Times* reporter, as anxious as everyone else in the capital to follow the footsteps of the great admiral, traced him to the Admiralty at ten o'clock that Wednesday morning where he paid a courtesy call on Lord Barham – who was 'all but a stranger' to him – to discuss briefly the current situation, including the disposition of the British and Franco-Spanish squadrons, agreeing to return later in the day for a fuller briefing. He next went to see his prize-agents in Norfolk Street, then over to the Navy Office at Somerset House, his rapid strides followed by 'an extremely numerous concourse of persons' as he crossed the Strand. Later in the day 'this distinguished Commander' walked back to the Admiralty for a longer meeting with the Admiralty Board and thence across the Horse Guards to Downing Street to see the Prime Minister, Pitt, with whom he spent some time.

Nelson's intensive activity in London now hardly constituted the 'rest and refreshment' one would have expected of an admiral who had been at sea some twenty-seven months and had just sailed, more or less non-stop, from Sicily to the West Indies, back to Gibraltar, then up to Britain, averaging 120 to 150 miles per day! Nevertheless the tireless reporter found Nelson to be 'in the best health and spirits, and as anxious as he has ever been for immediate employment of his country.' Thus he now met with the newly nominated Secretary of State for War and Colonies, Viscount Castlereagh, 'who has only sat one solitary day in his Office, and of course knows but little of what has passed' (though, unknown to Nelson, he was very much one of his admirers), Lord Mulgrave at the Foreign Office and George Canning, 'a very clever, deep-headed man' recently appointed as Treasurer of the Navy (and also a firm supporter of the admiral), but more importantly, the Right Honourable George Rose, President of the Board of Trade and Pitt's closest confidant and adviser.

The Prime Minister's welcome was warm and sincere as always. Nelson for his part had long admired Pitt, saying once, 'I think him the greatest Minister this country ever had and the honestest man', while an observant George Rose remarked in his diary the surprising resemblance of character he found in the two men. They had taken to each other immediately when Pitt had dined on board ship with Nelson back in 1801, when he was stationed off the Downs following an unsuccessful bombardment of Boulogne. Nelson now spent more time at Downing Street over the remaining few weeks than with Lord Barham at the Admiralty, apparently finding it much more congenial and practical to discuss naval policies and aims with William Pitt, who ultimately provided the nation's money for such enterprises and at this stage even took a hand in giving fleet orders to Barham.

Although Nelson had little time for 'pen and ink men', as he referred to diplomats, it was with just such pen and ink that he now prepared a top-priority memorandum concerning the strategic significance of Sardinia. The British Government could not afford to allow the French to seize this strategically situated island for several reasons as he now pointed out: it would deny a major source of water, cattle, fruit and vegetables, as well as good shelter and secure anchorages for the British fleet, and, as Malta was simply too distant to be effective here, it would mean 'our Fleet would find a difficulty, if not impossibility, of keeping any Station off Toulon'. The French fleet there would then be capable of eluding the Royal Navy with extraordinary ease, while French possession of Sardinia would permit them to control, harass, destroy or prohibit British commerce with Italy or the Levant. Needless to say, this would also allow them to interfere more easily in the military affairs of that region as well. Nelson felt very strongly indeed about this question and brought it up whenever he could.

Despite the warm welcome given to him and his tremendous public popularity, not all his ideas were equally acceptable at Downing Street. However, if some of his memoranda on the Mediterranean were not acted upon, at least they were all given a sympathetic hearing.

Of more pressing concern, Nelson found considerable anxiety in London about possible moves by the French Imperial Navy acting in conjunction with that of Spain, a feeling echoed by Lord Minto in a letter to his wife on 24th August: 'The sailing of a great hostile fleet . . . created no small uneasiness here [London] . . .' The imposing army at Boulogne still remained poised, only awaiting Napoleon's signal, despite military rumblings beyond the Rhine. So far as Downing Street was concerned, there could not only be naval attacks anywhere throughout the eastern Atlantic and the Channel, but one or more invasion attempts on British soil, whether in southern England or northern Ireland. Another topic discussed round the fireplaces of Lloyd's Coffee House was the possibility that the combined Franco-Spanish fleet – perhaps with the added force of Ganteaume's Brest squadron – could attack the vast homeward-bound convoys of merchantmen heading for the British Isles from the Far East, the West Indies and Newfoundland, not to mention those about to make the return voyage. Richly laden convoys from both India and Jamaica were already overdue. 'All the outward-bound fleets, which lately sailed from Portsmouth, are ordered . . . to put into Falmouth, until positive information is received respecting the Combined Squadron', *The Times* announced on 27th August. In particular, the enormous convoy returning from India – involving hundreds of vessels – was of special concern, for the loss of it could perhaps result in the bankruptcy of the East India Company itself and shake the very foundations of the City. Lord Minto for one, as a close observer of the daily scene, now acknowledged in private what as a diplomat he could not possibly venture to admit aloud, that 'There has been the greatest alarm ever known in the city of London since the combined fleet sailed from Ferrol . . . The question is beginning to arise whether our naval superiority is still sufficient to guard all these points at once against such numerous fleets. If not!!'

With Nelson's return, however, and the 'hearty welcome' he received from the Admiral, Minto acknowledged that he found 'his conversation . . . a cordial in these low times.' Indeed, Nelson remained fully confident about the Royal Navy's ability, and his own, to destroy the Combined Fleet if they could ever get their hands on them, even if they were greatly outnumbered. To be sure, *The Times*, usually well-informed, was boasting on 3rd September of an additional fifty-two ships of the line for the navy planned or being built at Pitches's dockyard at Northfleet, at Jacobs's in Milford Haven, at Buckler's Hard, at Chatham, Plymouth and Woolwich, but that was for the future, and what was needed now were such ships off the Spanish coast.[1]

Nelson had by this time developed some new battle tactics which he humbly called 'the Nelson touch', a plan of attack that he first disclosed to Captain Keats during his visit to Merton and which he would be using for the first time off Trafalgar. 'It will bring forward a pell-mell Battle', an excited Nelson exclaimed, and that was what was needed. He exuded conviction and felt warmly confident, all of which had a magical, indeed infectious effect on everyone. A gloomy London, belaboured by fears and rumours of a renewed Continental war, was quickly transformed wherever the dapper admiral appeared, even in the street. 'I met Nelson to-day in a mob in Piccadilly', Lord Minto related to his wife, 'and got hold of his arms, that I was mobbed too. It is really quite affecting to see the wonder and admiration, love and respect, of the whole world' he receives.

His presence had the same effect at Downing Street, on George Rose and William Pitt, who had considerable anxieties of their own about the possible depredations of the Combined Fleet. The exuberant Nelson insisted that, given half a chance, the Royal Navy would do the job once and for all and there would be nothing more to fear, at least not for a very long time to come. On the other hand, Pitt's great relief and belief in the admiral's own optimism frightened Nelson a bit. 'I am now set up for a Conjuror', he lamented to Captain Keats, 'and God knows they will soon find out I am far from being one. I was asked my opinion [by the Prime Minister], against my inclination, for if I make one wrong guess, the charm will be broken; but this I ventured without any fear, that if Calder [who was still in charge of the largest portion of the British fleet off the Spanish coast at this time] got fairly alongside their twenty-seven or twenty-eight Sail, that by the time the Enemy had beat our [smaller] Fleet soundly, they would do us no harm this year.' It was a magnanimous opinion of Calder's merits, considering what had transpired on his previous meeting with Villeneuve and Gravina in July.

In fact, Calder was then the subject of much talk, rumour and conjecture, but when he was compared unfavourably with Nelson, the hero of the Battles of the Nile and Copenhagen was genuinely upset. He very much disliked the idea of pitting one officer against another, making them vie for the public's seal of approval. The newspapers had been all but crucifying Calder throughout the latter part of August and then well into September, expressing their 'severe disappointment' in him as a commander, criticism that was heightened by the news that Vice-Admiral Calder had permitted the Combined Franco-Spanish Fleet to slip past him into the safety of El Ferrol and La Coruña, which they called 'the disgrace and mortification of that great national disaster'. It was hardly surprising that the British public had turned against him when they had a Nelson in their midst, even Lord Minto referring scathingly to 'Calder's puny, half-begotten victory!' 'As to Sir Robert Calder', Lady Malmesbury confided to Lady Minto, 'he will never catch anything but crabs if he attempts to row about. He puts me in mind of the clown in a harlequin farce, who always lets harlequin slip in and out, and then comes staring about to look for it till he runs his head against a post.'

Pitt asked Nelson what he thought Villeneuve's next move would be, though Nelson was mistakenly under the impression that Admiral Decrès himself had now superseded Villeneuve as Commander-in-Chief at Cadiz. Nelson frankly admitted that he simply did not know. The Combined Fleet could sail north to Brest to join Ganteaume's squadron, he pointed out, or, given a good wind, might escape to the west once again, this time to prey upon the major merchant convoys. Being Mediterranean-oriented in strategy, however, he perhaps gave a little more weight to the possibility of the fleet escaping through the Gut at Gibraltar and into the Mediterranean, the Spanish leaving their squadron at Cartagena while the French returned to their home base at Toulon or went on to Genoa.

In this latter view he was not alone, even *The Times* supporting the opinion that the Mediterranean was the most likely goal, Malta and Egypt being primary French objectives, and Lord Minto privately concurred. George Rose, too, felt it was France's 'undisguised intention of seizing upon Egypt', including the Isthmus of Suez and the Red Sea. 'If they should succeed', he contended, 'they would effectually bring the trade of India to Marseilles . . . carrying the commodities of that country [India] through Egypt, for probably one half the expense of our freight by the Cape of Good Hope.' This would prove '. . . ruinous and destructive . . . to us in various points of view, affecting our manufactures, commerce, navigation and revenue, not to mention the strategic military implications now and in the future. If . . . Buonaparte is to be allowed to possess himself of those [Egypt and Malta] . . . and we are consequently to lose India, or, at least, all important advantages from it, what a situation we are in!' – Britain, he lamented, would end up 'crippled, discredited, [and] dispirited'.

Nevertheless, whatever the intention of the Combined Fleet, merely bringing them to battle would not suffice, as Calder had already established. 'It is,' Nelson explained, 'as Mr Pitt knows, *annihilation* that the Country wants – and not merely a splendid victory of twenty-three to thirty-six – honourable to the parties concerned, but absolutely useless to the extended scale, to bring Buonaparte to his marrow-bones . . .' For, argued Nelson, a combined fleet of thirteen to sixteen ships of the line escaping unscathed from such a battle would leave yet another menace to contend with, especially if they re-combined, say, with Ganteaume's twenty or so ships at Brest, and, with insistence, Nelson repeated the

word which seemed more in tune with the twentieth century than his own
– 'annihilation'.

William Pitt was also considering another means of achieving these
ends, however, for, since Robert Fulton's return to England the previous
year, when the American inventor had had an audience with both Pitt and
the then First Lord of the Admiralty, Lord Melville, there had been
considerable talk about the use of submarines, steamships and torpedoes
against the French. Pitt was intrigued enough to convene a Commission
of seven men to consider the merits of the case: Lord Mulgrave and Lord
Castlereagh – both Government ministers – Sir Joseph Banks, Mr
Cavendish, Major Congreve (the inventor of the Congreve rocket), Sir
Charles Rennie, and Admiral Sir Home Popham (who had devised the
signalling system now in use in the Royal Navy). They, too, found
Fulton's inventions to be intriguing and authorised tests for two of them –
the submarine and the spar torpedoes, which simply infuriated Admiral
Lord St Vincent, who called Fulton a 'gimcrack'. In fact, scheming
behind the scenes, St Vincent had a great deal to say about, or rather,
against, both Fulton the man and his inventions and used all his influence
to dissuade Pitt from considering the use of such weapons, for, in so
doing, claimed St Vincent, 'he was laying the foundation for doing away
with the Navy, on which depended the strength and prestige of Great
Britain'. The vision of sailors paddling about beneath the seas was simply
too much for him to countenance. Nevertheless, Pitt did indeed authorise
the tests, St Vincent immediately calling him 'the greatest fool that ever
existed to encourage a mode of war which those who commanded the
seas did not want, and which, if successful, would deprive them of it'.
Curiously enough, although two torpedoes successfully destroyed the
brig *Dorothea* in October 1805 as the Prime Minister viewed the event
from Walmer Castle, both the submarine and torpedoes were rejected,
perhaps in part as a result of the news from Trafalgar and the efforts of St
Vincent. As for Robert Fulton, he returned to America, where the first
steam-driven warship, the *Demologus*, was launched nine years later.

Meanwhile, if at Merton Place Emma Hamilton now tried to avoid the
reality of the times, and the fact that 'her Nelson' had not really come
home for a respite and to begin putting down roots, but rather as a sailor
on temporary leave, she did try to ignore it, despite his refusal of all but a
couple of dinner invitations and receptions. Emma, however, had been
preparing for his home-coming and she was not to be denied her hour.
She was determined to show off the costly new drawing room, the
splendid silver in the dining room and, of course, the home she had made

for her hero, and her special family invitations quickly went out. 'We have Room for you all', she wrote to the Nelsons, Matchams and Boltons, 'so come as soon as you can. We shall be happy, most happy'. Soon the fifteen bedrooms at Merton were chock-a-block as carriages disgorged nine adults and seven children, Nelson taking a special fancy to his nieces and nephews. His four-and-a-half-year-old daughter, Horatia, however, stole the show as he presented her with her own fork, knife and spoon set, which he had just had engraved with the words 'To my much-loved Horatia' at the London silversmiths, Salters.

Enormous amounts of food were delivered to the kitchens of Merton – frequently costing more than £100 per week, in an age when workmen earned less in a year – along with haunches of venison from friends, while children and family were found throughout 'the farm', as Nelson called his estate. He saw his head gardener, Thomas Cribb, every morning at 6 o'clock to discuss the day's work for his crew of twenty men and to inspect what had already been done to date. Later he would occasionally pass an hour with Emma and Horatia in 'the Poop', the round, white, classical-style summer house in the large garden. Even as early as 29th August, however, just nine days after reaching Merton, Pitt had privately intimated that Nelson's services might soon be required yet again.

Referring to this in a letter to Alexander Davison, he explained, 'My time and movements much depend upon Buonaparte. We are at present ignorant of his intentions and whether the Squadron from Ferrol are coming to join the Brest Fleet, going to the Mediterranean, or cruising for our homeward-bound Fleets'.

And then it happened. At 5 o'clock in the morning on Monday the 2nd of September, the tremendous clatter of an unexpected post-chaise and four horses was heard coming quickly up the gravel drive of Merton Place, and Captain Henry Blackwood of the frigate *Euryalus* (stationed off Cadiz) appeared at the door. Nelson, who was already dressed, had him shown in immediately. An excited Blackwood quickly informed him that he could not stay, for he had just returned to England with important dispatches for the Admiralty from Admiral Collingwood who had finally sighted the Combined Franco-Spanish Fleet in Cadiz harbour! The long, agonising period of uncertainty was over. The time to act had come at last.

Shunning protocol and without awaiting an official summons, Nelson arrived at the Admiralty offices later that same morning where he had a long meeting with Lord Barham, who informed him on the spot that he was to have the *Victory* manned, provisioned and ready to sail as soon as possible. The First Lord then handed him his orders along with the Navy List of officers available for service, from which he was to choose his commanders. At an earlier meeting with Pitt, Nelson had already been informed that the newly reconstituted Mediterranean Fleet off the Spanish coast would need a new Commander-in-Chief and asked for a recommendation. Nelson suggested Collingwood who was already there on the spot. 'No, that won't do', a thoughtful Pitt replied. '*You* must take command', and then informed him he must be ready to sail in a few days' time. 'I am ready now', an alert Nelson replied. Privately, however, a more subdued Nelson confided to George Rose, 'I hold myself ready to go forth whenever I am desired, although God knows I want rest: but self is entirely out of the question.'

When Nelson returned to Emma Hamilton's house in Clarges Street, he informed her of the outcome of the meetings and the news that his luggage had to be ready to be shipped to Portsmouth within forty-eight hours. She was simply shattered. 'My dear Friend', she wrote to Susanna Bolton, Nelson's sister, later that day, 'I am again broken-hearted, as our dear Nelson is immediately going. It seems as though I have had a fortnight's dream and am awoke to all the misery of this cruel separation.'

Four days later the *London Gazette* commented that, 'Lord Nelson's new appointment is very extensive and in some degrees unlimited. Lord Nelson's new command comprehends not only the whole of the Mediterranean but extends also to Cadiz'.

When General Dumouriez heard this, he could not resist a brief note sending Nelson his best wishes, ending with the words 'Sail in the *Victory* to Victory'. A letter from Kensington Palace, in the handwriting of Edward, the Duke of Kent, however, went beyond a formal expression of best wishes on his forthcoming campaign and, after referring to Nelson the sailor as 'a colleague', he stated that 'it would be a great satisfaction to me to know that your Lordship would not be averse to having me with you', and closed with the acknowledgement that 'it will be a subject of real pride to me to be considered one of your warmest friends and admirers', something he had never said to his father, the King.

Writing in a more reflective mood, after having safely dispatched his trunks to the *Victory*, Nelson did a little thinking aloud in a note to Alexander Davison. 'I hope my absence will not be long, and that I shall soon meet the Combined Fleets, with a force sufficient to do the job well: for half a Victory would but half content me . . . But I will do my best . . . I have much to lose, but little to gain: and I go because it's right, and I will serve my Country faithfully'. He then went over to his upholsterer in

Brewer Street, leaving him with the order to prepare and engrave the coffin which Captain Hallowell had given him six years earlier, 'for, I think it highly probable that I may want it on my return'.

Emma's late husband, Sir William (who had died in April 1803), had always found life at Merton a whirlwind of madness – 'nonsensicall' he had called it – but now it was even worse, as servants scurried to make up the list of last-minute items Emma had prepared, while the Admiral dictated a batch of letters to friends, solicitors and business acquaintances.

Following a gloomy, nearly silent farewell dinner on Friday 13th September, the post-chaise collected Admiral Lord Nelson to drive him to Portsmouth, via the Guildford road, where he arrived before the George at 6 o'clock on the following morning. After breakfasting, and writing a quick message to Emma, he went to the dockyard to pay his respects to the yard's commissioner, Sir Richard Saxton. He then met the captains of three ships which were due to follow him shortly, the *Royal Sovereign*, *Defiance* and *Agamemnon* (the first ship of the battle line he had ever commanded, which now lay at anchor off Spithead), while two more were refitting at Plymouth. Treasurer of the Navy, George Canning, and George Rose had come down to see Nelson off, and a large crowd had gathered outside the George, some enthusiasts cheering him on, others simply falling to their knees on the rough cobblestone to pray. The crowd re-formed along the parapet at the Southsea beach and even sentries with drawn bayonets were unable to control them. A deeply touched Nelson acknowledged: 'I had their huzzas before. I have their hearts now.' Nelson, Canning and Rose were rowed out to the *Victory* which lay at single anchor at St Helens, and Nelson invited them, along with Captains Blackwood and Hardy, to a final, most elegant dinner.

The *Victory* weighed anchor at 8 am on Sunday 15th September, accompanied by Blackwood's frigate, the *Euryalus*. Though England was still in sight, Nelson's mind was already on the sun-burned shores of a distant Spanish port he had last seen in 1797 with St Vincent, and the ships and men he would find there waiting for him.

Having left five ships behind, *Thunderer*, *Ajax*, *Royal Sovereign*, *Defiance* and *Agamemnon*, which were due to join him as soon as they were ready, Nelson's last act before sailing was to send each the following orders:

Victory, *at Sea*, 15th September 1805

Secret Rendezvous.

Off Cape St. Vincent, where a Frigate will be stationed to give information where I am to be found. In the event of not meeting the said Frigate, after cruizing twenty-four hours, the Ship in search of me must call off Cape St. Mary's and Cadiz, approaching them with the utmost caution.

Nelson and Brontë

'WHEN THE PROBABILITY of the enemy making a speedy attempt upon our shores is officially announced by Government . . . we cannot be accused of exciting improper alarms, in calling the attention of our readers to the subject', a *Times* editorial proclaimed in mid-August 1805. The war was certainly on everyone's mind and the subject frequently occupied entire pages of the country's newspapers. War on the high seas was not the only concern now, however, as Nelson found upon his return. The invasion hysteria of 1803 and 1804 gathered fresh momentum towards the end of summer 1805 when it was said that there would be attempts to land French troops on British soil. 'We have never doubted, from the moment Buonaparte uttered the threat', *The Times* persisted, 'much less since the commencement of his preparations, that the menace was serious, and that the attempt would at some time be made . . .'[2]

Prime Minister Addington's initial reaction to the renewal of hostilities in 1803 had been at best negligible, whether on land or at sea, but with Pitt back at Downing Street in May 1804, everything had changed dramatically so far as the navy was concerned, as Nelson for one was happy to attest, though it never went far enough. On land the results were even more immediately visible, with the activation of militia and volunteer corps throughout the land with special emphasis along the coasts. No one doubted the perfidy and cunning of the French Emperor who was cursed almost daily in the London papers: 'his Corsican Majesty', 'the Usurper of France', 'the Imperial boat-builder', 'the Chief Highwayman of the Empire' (the *double entendre* referring to his international 'thievery' as well as to the new military highways he was constructing throughout the country).

Although Pitt had initially mobilised tens of thousands of regular troops and volunteers, a year later in the autumn of 1805 the Additional Forces Act called forth another levy of thousands of young recruits, as new fortifications continued to appear. There was now an even more acute sense of impending, renewed warfare on the Continent itself, with the increasing reports of Russian and Austrian troops mobilising, not to mention many a wild rumour, including one about the break-out of the Brest squadron, the appearance of Villeneuve's Combined Fleet off the coast of Ireland and, of course, those '5,000 vessels' now gathering at Boulogne, a port that could not even hold 1,000. News of Napoleon's arrival at Boulogne on 4th August 1805 was a confirmed fact, however, and it naturally received prominent notice as the London press kept track of his every move.

Nevertheless the situation along the coast Napoleon found upon his arrival was hardly encouraging from his viewpoint. In his report of 31st December 1804, Naval Minister Denis Decrès had informed the Emperor that the Imperial Flotilla comprised '889 French warships' (including *prames, chaloupes canonnières, bateaux canonniers* and *péniches*), which, added to the Dutch transport vessels, gave them a total of 2,054 vessels gathered at the six ports of Ostend, Dunkirk, Ambleteuse, Etaples, Wimereux and Boulogne, capable of carrying only 127,000 men and some 15,764 horses. By 25th March 1805 Decrès had informed 'The Commander of the National Flotilla at Boulogne' of a further reduction in invasion vessels leaving a total 'war flotilla of 804 boats'[3] – 108 boats short of the 912 required by earlier estimates, to accompany the several hundred transport vessels. There were 906 boats available in the six invasion ports, but, he added, '234 require such basic repairs as to leave only 672 actually available for service'. Constant British attacks along French ports, despite the impressive array of coastal artillery, the toll taken by storms, and the lack of money to maintain these vessels, were monthly *reducing* the invasion force.

At times Napoleon Bonaparte appeared to live in the world of illusions, abetted it would seem by officials in his service, including the 'Chief of the General Staff of the National Flotilla', Lafond, who on 8th August informed an amazed Naval Minister and the Emperor that the Flotilla now comprised 1,016 'war vessels' in addition to some 1,058 transports of all types! Lafond further maintained that this fictitious fleet could launch 167,500 men and 9,149 horses on 2,343 vessels (including a few more held in reserve)!

To be sure, Marshal Berthier had at an earlier date built up a splendid body of troops – over 167,000 strong at Montreuil, St Omer and Bruges alone and there were well over 10,000 horses ready for boarding – but the number of flotilla warships was obviously much inflated, that is to say, falsified, probably some 300 above what really existed, and thus capable of embarking perhaps no more than 130,000 men. But by now, due to illness and recent troop reassignment, there were no longer even *100,000* men ready to embark by August 1805, reports varying between 90,000 and 112,000 men.

Both Marshals Soult and Ney had studied the official reports during the previous months and compared them with the reality of the situation they found along the coast and confronted Berthier with their disquieting findings. The upshot was that War Minister Berthier castigated Ney for pointing out these irregularities and refused to pass on his report to the Emperor. Napoleon himself, however, occasionally discovered the discrepancies and was furious when he did so. When he learned that Decrès was concealing the truth, as well as doctoring the figures that the War Minister had sent him, Napoleon said bluntly 'that the figures were statistics according to what should be, but not what in fact exists'. When he also discovered that hundreds of transport vessels were on the books but not in the water, the Emperor commented drily, 'It seems . . . that these ships are in no condition to put to sea . . . Take the appropriate measures to have this situation rectified immediately . . . For these administrative matters there is only one person I hold responsible, the Minister'. If on the other hand he discovered that this was happening because the Naval Prefect was 'squandering' funds and supplies, he added, 'I will no longer be complaining, but punishing the guilty ones'. He concluded, 'If the budget I set is followed, the flotilla can be maintained properly; but, if for various reasons you spend those funds on provisions and other items, it is obvious that I will not have a single ship left. See to this at once!'

This then was the background to Napoleon's thoughts when he arrived at Boulogne in the first week of August, before receiving news of Villeneuve's contrary actions (going to El Ferrol and not Brest as ordered) and of happenings in the rest of Europe.

MEANWHILE GREAT BRITAIN continued to arm. Three squat Martello towers outside Folkestone were nearly finished, 'intended as a protection to East Wear Bay, the most exposed and assailable point of any on the coast of Kent', these added to the dozens of other such structures now ringing the coasts of England including those at the mouth of the Thames, and at Chatham.

Enormous bonfires were stacked within sight of these towers along the coast often advancing well inland to the nearest army camps. Even in far away Devon, bleak Dartmoor was pierced with a couple of dozen such signal fires reaching down to Torquay and sweeping westward across Cornwall to Falmouth and Penzance. Cavalry units were evident everywhere, making preparations for a possible French landing, traversing coastal cliffs, familiarising themselves with their newly assigned outposts. Local populations, though, were seldom informed of their movements in advance, sometimes resulting in near panic. On Tuesday 13th August Lord Paget, at the head of his brigade of cavalry, manoeuvred along the coast between Hoseley Bay and Aldeburgh, and 'the sudden and unexpected appearance of three regiments equipped for actual service, and galloping towards the coast, caused a great consternation . . . It was immediately concluded, that the enemy had effected a landing to the coast of Suffolk, and several persons, in consequence, prepared to quit the neighbourhood of Ipswich.'

On not quite such a clamorous note, coastal artillerymen and volunteer sailors were equally diligent. There were numerous reviews, too, involving the testing of new weapons. One such event took place on the Thames in the presence of William Pitt and War Minister Castlereagh, demonstrating a type of catamaran landing vessel just created by Sir Sidney Smith (from which Lord Castlereagh was knocked overboard and nearly drowned in the murky waters). At a display of artillery at Brighton the Prince of Wales witnessed the testing of 'a newly-invented species of howitzer shells . . . The experiments were made from the Valley, at the foot of Race-hill, and several of the shells were thrown against the slope, at the distance of 300 yards, when they burst, and threw their contents, chiefly musket balls, to a distance of 40 yards in all directions. This instrument of destruction,' it was noted, 'is calculated to produce dreadful havoc amongst close bodies of men.' The new exploding shells – as opposed to the traditional solid cannon balls – would soon be causing a revolution in modern warfare, on land and at sea.

With the news of fresh troop movements in Eastern and Central Europe, and given Napoleon's well-established reaction to such events, 'Can it be expected, that Buonaparte will defer the commencement of hostilities until the Russian and Austrian armies shall be drawn up in battle-array upon the Italian frontier?' as *The Times* put it. This expectation of a large-scale clash of troops on land, in addition to those already taking place at sea, led to fresh appeals for volunteers. And if most young men throughout the land did their duty once signed up – and their newly created units were accompanied everywhere by the appearance of

'Volunteer Inns' – there were some who simply signed, accepted the few guineas offered as enticement for that signature, and then promptly disappeared, if they could. One such private in the South Gloucester Militia was captured, however, and promptly sentenced to receive five hundred lashes for his desertion, the punishment administered before his entire regiment, while a more fortunate soldier in Liverpool, who had failed to attend the prescribed number of Corps drills, was fined £274.4.0.

To a great extent Admiral Lord Nelson's last homecoming was overshadowed by the growing uneasiness over the rapidly deteriorating situation in Europe. From Gibraltar news had just been dispatched that the Spanish had been 'busy . . . landing shot, shells and [building] fascines at the Orange Grove', their camp of 10,000 men shortly to be increased with the expected arrival of 16,000 French troops, prior to a major siege of this British stronghold. In St Petersburg and Vienna, the situation was unsettling and becoming ominous.

> St Petersburgh, Aug. 21.
> The preparations for war are carried on here with a quickness and activity of which we know no parallel in the Russian military history. To-morrow the three regiments of grenadiers . . . besides the regiments of Guards will commence their march . . . Two Russian armies are [now] approaching Vienna . . . A division of Russian troops is already arrived at Brody, in Gallicia.

From Austria came news that the 'regiment of infantry of the Archduke Charles marched from Vienna for Italy' on 26th August. 'The regiment of Prince Auersperg is also gone from hence to Italy . . . The whole Austrian force for the protection of the frontiers is estimated at 200,000 men, besides bombardiers, cannoniers, sappers and pontooniers.' The Archduke Charles was to command the army in Italy, and the Archduke John that in the Tyrol, while another thirty battalions of Austrian infantry were already '. . . in and about Venice'.

Meanwhile, Napoleon, who was now indeed delighted with the prospects of dealing with a Continental war – the one situation that could liberate him from his invasion enterprise – fed the *Moniteur* with the propaganda he wanted the world to hear: 'She [Britain] now places no limits to her violence. Nobody hereafter shall navigate but upon her account and to sell her articles alone', while making Great Britain the chief force and influence behind Austria, 'whom she is precipitating into war by inducing her to make in the Tyrol and Italy armaments that cannot but be considered as a commencement to hostilities . . .' He also blamed

Britain's 'corrupted intriguers' in the Court of St Petersburg for the
Russian signature to an Alliance with Britain and Austria.

The news bulletins continued and, within a short time, the Austrian
Emperor, Francis II, named Field Marshal Lieutenant Baron Mack
Commander-in-Chief of the Austrian forces (a fatal nomination Nelson
felt presaged doom for the allies) and the more able General Kutusow
holding the equivalent post in the Imperial Russian Army, which already
had some 180,000 men along the western frontiers.

In fact, Prussia's Ambassador to Paris, the Marchese di Lucchesini,
for one had long been convinced that Napoleon had only one thing in
mind: 'War on the Continent is, and I cannot emphasise it enough, the
First Consul's secret desire', he had reported back in May 1804. 'It clears
his honour for the setback he has suffered in the too well publicised
announcement of his celebrated invasion plans; it offers fresh opportunities for glory and in particular for new wealth, for his generals currently
serving along the [Channel] coasts . . . a continental war which ruins the
other Powers, eases France's financial burden in maintaining her armies,
and this consideration, combined with the embarrassment the public
treasury finds itself in as a result of its inability to pay them . . . must make
us more and more apprehensive, that they will in fact seize the slightest
pretext to use their armies in easy conquests, these armies which are
dying of boredom along the Channel as a result of the prolonged wait for
a naval expedition which is always on the point of sailing, but then
continually postponed.'

Ambassador Lucchesini had certainly assessed the French position
correctly. According to French historian Georges Lefebvre, Napoleon
only fully recognised how critical this state of affairs was by 23rd or 24th
August 1805, but he had, in fact, been drawing up contingency campaign
plans long before, seeking 'the slightest pretext' to launch seven army
corps, which alone would extricate him from the embarrassment of his
unsuccessful invasion plans and a failing economy.

If Britain was suffering from the consequences of the Melville Affair,
Napoleon's own financial difficulties were of a far more serious nature by
1805, threatening the great new French Empire as no allied army could
possibly do at this time. In fact, Treasury Minister Barbé-Marbois was
unable to find the funds with which to pay for the unwieldy wartime army
and naval apparatus that Napoleon had created in 1803. The situation
was critical everywhere. The *Département* of Pas de Calais, with its heavy
share of the invasion costs, could meet payment of neither bona fide
Government contracts nor the Government payroll, a similar situation at

Strasbourg only being averted by last-minute borrowing. François Barbé-Marbois continued to discount bank notes to such an extent that public confidence was undermined, giving way to a very real sense of panic. Bankruptcies ensued and queues lengthened at banks where Frenchmen demanded gold in exchange for dubious paper notes, the recently created Banque de France itself unable to cope with the situation as private houses, such as the Banque Récamier and the Banque d'Hervas, closed their doors to angry unsatisfied depositors. Nor were even the most powerful army contractors, such as Després and Vanlerberghe, immune – Napoleon owing the latter alone some 147,000,000 francs. It was all very reminiscent of the situation in the late 1790s when no solution for a tottering economy seemed apparent, apart from a young Corsican General's plan for conquest and loot beyond the Alps.

In the last days of summer 1805, the 'subsidies' from Spain were in arrears, although Prime Minister Manuel de Godoy, who had been threatened by Talleyrand back in December of the previous year, had already been forced to assign their payment to Napoleon's financial *bête noire par excellence*, the maddeningly ingenious Gabriel Julien Ouvrard. This financial manipulator was to pay Spain's monthly subsidies now and be reimbursed from the Spanish Treasury in Mexico (where some 52,500,000 piastres in gold and silver were awaiting shipment for him), through an arrangement of Byzantine complexity with Peter Labouchère, of the Banking House of Hope of Amsterdam, who in turn was to attempt to arrange for this transfer from Mexico through the intervention of the London offices of Baring, the City banker (who just happened to be Labouchère's father-in-law) with the consent of William Pitt himself![4]

In August 1805, however, time was indeed running out for the fifteen-month-old French Empire, with the Banque de France over-extended to the tune of at least 92,000,000 francs in notes and linked with a Spanish currency that had already lost 58 per cent of its value. Given Villeneuve's strange behaviour and these financial storm clouds threatening at home, Napoleon's response to them was not difficult to anticipate, though it did not prevent him from first celebrating his thirty-sixth birthday on 15th August (which had become St Napoleon's Day) with a *Te Deum* in the church at Boulogne, double rations for the troops and reviewing of General Oudinot's division of grenadiers at Wimereux. At 6 am on 22nd August, he made his final review of the entire Boulogne flotilla.

Standing on the cliffs of Boulogne for the last time, looking out to sea for any sign of the ineffable Admiral Villeneuve, Napoleon's great juggling act of possibilities had, at last, been reduced to a mere two: either he could go to war or lose his throne. Discounting the second, he needed not only a little war, but a full-blown Continental war because lightning victories, rich war tribute and wagonloads of booty alone could ensure full French vaults once more. Napoleon had no choice in August 1805, if he were to survive, but to unleash his legions on Europe.

The French Emperor now ordered Bernadotte's troops to withdraw from occupied Hanover, even as he was signing hurriedly drafted agreements with Bavaria on 25th August 1805 and Württemberg on 5th September to secure his south-eastern flank and gain additional troop contingents for the great war effort he was now envisaging against Austria. On 26th August 1805, Marshal Soult's invasion force at Boulogne – comprising the three army corps at Montreuil, St Omer and Bruges, hereafter known to history as the *Grande Armée* – broke camp and set out on its three-week forced march to the German frontier and beyond that would culminate in great victories and conquest for the French (including those at Ulm and Austerlitz), resulting in the dissolution of the Holy Roman Empire and the creation of the Confederation of the Rhine.[5]

Almost immediately a rumour spread through the clubs of Pall Mall 'that Government has received certain intelligence, that a very large part of the troops which were encamped at Boulogne, has marched for the interior, and that the camps along the coast are all breaking up', the inference being drawn that their destination was the Rhine. 'It is said that the enemy [at Boulogne] are dismantling the flotilla', while similar news came from Holland, where it was reported that 'the troops embarked on board the fleets of the Texel and of Helvoetsluys, have received orders to disembark and to march to Mainz . . .' Indeed, even before the final news had reached London, Lord Minto told his wife, 'The Continent war seems on the point of breaking out . . . which might set the world on its shanks once more . . .'

With most of his *Grande Armée* on the march, and after a final meeting with Berthier and his commanders on 2nd September, Napoleon himself left his Channel headquarters at Boulogne in great haste. 'It seems the lot for war is already cast,' *The Times* announced bleakly, quoting the following bulletin:

Hamburgh, Sept. 20.
The Austrians have entered Munich, Raisborn, Augsburgh and are advancing into Suabia, and toward the Rhine, in great force.

Although all the news items only reached London over the next three weeks, the War Office had in fact anticipated such moves it seems, and on 7th September it was announced that, 'Orders have been given to several regiments to prepare for immediate embarkation for foreign service', including 12,000 cavalry.

What had so far been limited basically to a naval war was now bursting into a full-scale land war as well, due to the continued territorial claims and expansion by Napoleon, one indeed which was to reach from the Iberian Peninsula to the golden domes of Moscow, enveloping the whole of Europe in its wake.

But life at Weymouth went on, despite the deteriorating international scene, or to be more precise, life and death, for the long-expected demise of the King's brother, Prince William, the Duke of Gloucester, on 27th August resulted in the court going into mourning, imposing constraints on the daily routine at the Royal Lodge, now limited largely to quiet promenades along the Esplanade and visits to the large army camp just outside Weymouth. The Lord Chamberlain's office proclaimed the appropriate change of wardrobe for the Royal family and the nation. Ladies were to wear black silk, plain muslin, or long lawn, crape or love hoods, black silk shoes, black glazed gloves and black paper fans, while gentlemen 'black cloth without buttons on the sleeves or pockets, plain muslin or long lawn cravats and weepers, and black scabbards and bucklers', though the Admiralty Office announced that 'His Majesty doth not require that the Officers of the fleet or Marines should wear any other mourning for the present melancholy occasion . . . than a black crape round their left arms, with their uniforms', and thus Admiral Lord Nelson added a black band round his one remaining arm. But as the Duke of Gloucester was not an immediate heir, his death meant only a limited curtailment of activities for the nation. Indeed, scarcely a week after the interment of the Royal Duke, life was returning to normal, *The Times* reporting:

> Weymouth, Sept. 10
> The Royal Family did not land from their [daily] cruize till six o'clock last evening. Their return to shore was announced by the ships in the harbour firing a Royal Salute. They prepared to go to the Theatre, and went to see the Comedy of the *Poor Gentleman*, and the Farce of *Peeping Tom* . . .
>
> At the conclusion of the Farce, Mr Kemble [who played the part of Sir Robert Bramble in *Poor Gentleman*] delivered a Cento, to the Army and Navy, on the threatened invasion of the country . . .

Nor was the King alone in wanting his amusements, however, for on the very evening Nelson was piped aboard the *Victory*, the lovely Mrs Jordan, 'ever gay and ever young', was playing the role of Miss Peggy in *The Country Girl* to a packed house at the Drury Lane Theatre, where the even lovelier Mrs Siddons was to appear shortly in *Romeo and Juliet*.

As the King refused to leave the rustic charms of Dorset, a fortnight later a much weakened William Pitt rode out for consultations with George III in the hope of converting his way of thinking to allow for a wider, more powerful range of political personalities in his Government, as the only means of saving his wobbling ministry. Although he found the King in good health and spirits, he was as unbending as ever during a long early morning ride on 23rd September, and the disillusioned Prime Minister made the long, tortuous journey back to a capital now well on a war-footing. As *The Times* had proclaimed, 'It seems the lot for war is already cast' . . . and indeed it was.

Cadiz

Our voyage [from El Ferrol to Cadiz] was quite uneventful. We pursued three of Admiral Collingwood's vessels as far as the Straits [of Gibraltar], but we were not able to close with them by nightfall and their speed saved them.

Villeneuve to Beurnonville, 21st August 1805

Let me know every movement [made by the Combined Fleet at Cadiz]. I rely on you, that we can't miss getting hold of them, and will give them such a shaking as they never yet experienced: at least I will lay down my life in the attempt. We are a very powerful Fleet, and not to be held cheap.

Nelson to Blackwood, Victory, 10th October 1805

I have no intention of seeking out the enemy, indeed, I want to avoid them in order to be able to reach my destination. But if we do meet them, there will be no shameful manoeuvres, for that would demoralise our crews and result in our defeat.

Villeneuve to Commanding Officers of the Combined Fleet, in his Final Instructions, 20th October 1805

ADMIRALS CORNWALLIS, VILLENEUVE and Nelson, and Fate decided there was to be a battle of Trafalgar. The myth that it was Barham who made Trafalgar possible should now be laid to rest once and for all. Six days after the inconclusive clash between the British Fleet and the Combined Franco-Spanish Squadrons on 22nd July, a stunned Vice-Admiral Pierre Villeneuve had limped into the Spanish port of Vigo (just north of the Portuguese frontier), where he landed several hundred ill and wounded and abandoned three battered ships. Continuing on his way again on 31st July, he sailed north along the jagged coast strewn with innumerable inlets and bays, past Santa Eugenia and on to Cabo Fisterra (or Cape Finisterre), gradually working his way to the north-east and into the safety of the large twin ports of La Coruña and El Ferrol, at the entrance to the Bay of Biscay, anchoring at La Coruña at 10 am on 2nd August 1805. Admiral Federico Gravina's Spanish squadron had earlier separated from the French and put in at nearby El Ferrol where it was quickly landing wounded men, ordering repairs and calling for provisions, which they badly needed following their long journey from Martinique and their infelicitous encounter with Vice-Admiral Calder.

Napoleon was still waiting for the Combined Fleet at Boulogne eight days later when Villeneuve wrote to Naval Minister Decrès on 10th August that he was ordering the fleet to weigh anchor that day, thereby beginning one of the biggest guessing games of this naval campaign, for Villeneuve had said that he might be sailing to 'Brest or Cadiz', depending upon the circumstances. For the next eleven days, until Villeneuve's fleet was finally sighted again on 21st August as it reached the southern port of Cadiz, the French were as much mystified as to the whereabouts of the Franco-Spanish Fleet as were the British, Decrès privately advising an incredulous Napoleon that he felt there was only one chance in four of Villeneuve's making for Brest.

Meanwhile Calder, having found himself with a mere nine ships now at El Ferrol before a superior enemy force some four times larger than his own, had made sail for Ushant, and reached Cornwallis' Channel Fleet on 14th August. At 3 o'clock the following afternoon Admiral Lord Nelson, then *en route* for England after his non-stop journey from the West Indies, joined Cornwallis for a few hours, leaving most of his Mediterranean Fleet with him.

Once again events were moving very quickly and Admiral Cornwallis, who had so carefully prepared and executed a most successful blockade of the French coast for more than twenty-seven months – only the small Rochefort squadron escaping – now had to make a quick decision, which was to prove perhaps the most important one of his entire career. Vice-Admiral Ganteaume with his twenty-one battleships still lay under the guns of Azenor Tower and the Château de Brest on the Penfeld River, successfully immobilised (apart from one or two skirmishes just outside Brest within the confines of Bertheaume, Camaret and Douarnenez waters) and, though Captain Allemand's squadron of eight ships and frigates was cruising most destructively in the Channel, it was none the less isolated, far from the larger more strategically situated French squadrons. But Calder's critical news of the return to European waters of Villeneuve's Combined Fleet of over forty sail to a Spanish harbour required an entire re-evaluation of Cornwallis' plans.

Sir William's primary concern at this moment was to ensure the safety of British shores and shipping by preventing Vice-Admiral Villeneuve from sailing northwards or westwards and to destroy or disable his mighty force before it did any real damage. Without calling for a war council with Nelson (while he was still there), Calder and the other senior officers under his command, Admiral Cornwallis prepared his own assessment of the situation and the strategy to cope with it. Thus Lord Nelson continued on his way to England without ever knowing that the decision to prepare the fleet he was eventually to command at Trafalgar was drafted while the *Victory* was just a couple of cables' distance from Cornwallis' flagship, the *Ville de Paris*.

For Sir William Cornwallis, who had been waiting off Ushant for over two years to get his crack at his French opponents, the atmosphere by mid-August 1805 was both very tense and frustrating. For him, a patient player of naval chess, sitting with his large Channel command just a dozen miles from Brest and the largest standing French war fleet had seemed an ideal position, as surely such a powerful fleet was bound to venture forth and sail sooner or later. However, the wait of 'a few weeks' had turned into 'a few months' and he was now in his third summer there. It seemed the English admiral was to be denied the opportunity he had been preparing himself for for more than four decades – the big battle, the one which had escaped him so consistently time and again, while falling to most of his colleagues including 'young' Nelson, that pathetic Hyde Parker, Lords Hood and St Vincent, and even Calder – there seemed to be no justice in the world.

Thus the decision Cornwallis was to take now on 15th August was to prove the most important one of his career, for it meant acknowledging the fact that the real battle he had so ached for with which to cap his long career, would be fought elsewhere, by others, although with his help and his ships. Indeed, he would be reduced to fifteen sail of the line for a few weeks, not all of which would even be on station with him off Brest. Consequently, if Ganteaume did finally weigh anchor and put to sea, although nothing in the world could prevent Cornwallis from challenging him, probably even establishing a technical victory over him, with his own inferior numbers, there would be little likelihood of his destroying or capturing more than a few of his vessels. Yet, squarely facing the situation now before him, Cornwallis made his decision, as painful as it was, to detach *twenty ships of the line* (of the thirty-five then with him), placing them under the command of Sir Robert Calder (the senior commanding officer under his orders). He was, however, too old and too able a sea hand not to face the reality of the moment. A combined Franco-Spanish Fleet of twenty-nine to thirty-three ships of the line was about to sail, or perhaps had already done so, and it was imperative that he, the Commander-in-Chief of the Channel command, met that challenge – a good officer could not do otherwise.

On the following day, 16th August, William Cornwallis signed the orders creating Calder's new fleet:

Secret
The French and Spanish squadrons from the West Indies having arrived at Ferrol, you are hereby required and directed to proceed off that port immediately with the ships in the margin.

   You are to endeavour, as soon as possible, to get information of the enemy's force and situation, and to use your utmost exertion to prevent their sailing, or to intercept them should they attempt it.

If he found upon his arrival at El Ferrol that the Combined Fleet had sailed and he felt he could overtake them, he was ordered to do so. On the other hand, if he had 'no prospect of overtaking them', he was to keep some ships off El Ferrol and to return the remainder to Ushant. Cornwallis then informed London: 'I request you will be pleased to acquaint the Lords Commissioners of the Admiralty that I detached on the 17th instant Vice-Admiral Sir Robert Calder, and under his direction, Rear-Admiral the Earl of Northesk, Rear-Admiral Louis and the ships named in the margin', and thus the nucleus of the fleet that was to be sent to Trafalgar was created, it including eight of Nelson's Mediterranean Fleet*. It was a bold move of course and Cornwallis acknowledged this: 'I have left for the service here at present but a few ships [15 plus two more to join him shortly . . . nevertheless] I have thought the step I have now taken might meet with their Lordships' approbation . . .' And they officially confirmed this a few weeks later.

Two days after Calder's separation from the fleet, on 19th August, Admiral Cornwallis sent a most urgent, if disturbing, dispatch: 'This morning the *Naiad* brought me accounts of the combined squadrons of the enemy having sailed from Ferrol . . . I immediately sent Captain Dundas to Vice-Admiral Sir Robert Calder with this intelligence, and . . . I have directed him to go in pursuit of the enemy . . .'

Due to the reduced British presence, Captain Allemand continued to go more or less unchallenged, he even capturing two warships – the 16-gun *Ranger*, and the 54-gun *Calcutta* – off the French coast right under Cornwallis' nose. In fact on 22nd August, Admiral Ganteaume – with news of the depleted strength of the British fleet and under threats from the Naval Minister and Napoleon's headquarters at Boulogne – left the safety of the powerful guns of the sixteenth-century Château (protecting the entrance to the narrow Penfeld River) with twenty-one ships, four

*See appendix 3

frigates, a brig and a corvette, and sailed through the Goulet, or channel between Pointe du Diable (on the north shore) and the guns high on the cliffs of the south shore at Pointe des Espagnoles, in the westerly direction of Pointe de St Mathieu, but then stopped at the entrance to the narrows giving him very little room in which to manoeuvre. From here he suddenly saw Admiral Cornwallis fast approaching Pointe de St Mathieu and 'the whole of the Squadron [now] seventeen sail of the line'. 'I thought at the time there was a prospect of being able to get at them', Cornwallis later reported to Secretary Marsden of the Admiralty. Ganteaume now did continue briefly, 'but when their headmost ship had advanced off Pointe de St Mathieu, and nearly within gunshot of our sternmost ship, she fired at her broadside and tacked'. Turning tail, Ganteaume's entire fleet hastened to the safety of the Goulet Channel and the inner roads, Cornwallis being stopped from chasing them by 'the immense quantity of shot and shells thrown from their batteries' and, apart from a few casualties, including Cornwallis himself who was struck by some ricocheting fragments, he reported 'no mischief of any consequence happened to the ships of the squadron'. Little did he realise that this would be as close as he would ever come to the great encounter with the foe.

On 5th September, Admiral Cornwallis finally received a dispatch from Vice-Admiral Collingwood, dated 21st August and sent to Ushant via James Gambier, the British Consul-General at Lisbon, that proved to be the final piece of the puzzle which had begun to take shape several months earlier at Toulon: 'This morning the combined fleet of 36 ships came down upon me when I was before Cadiz with three, and obliged me to abandon my station'.

In the freer scope of a personal letter to his wife, Cuthbert Collingwood described 'what a squeeze we had like to have got yesterday. While we were cruising off the town [Cadiz], down came the combined fleet of 36 sail of men of war; we were only three poor things with a frigate and a bomb, and drew off towards the Straits, not very ambitious, as you may suppose, to try our strengths against such odds . . .'

With this latest piece of news before him, Admiral Cornwallis wanted to act, but, with his much reduced force, there was little he *could* do, as he informed the Admiralty: 'I have only 17 sail of the line. Otherwise I should have hoped to have been approved by their Lordships if I had sent all the ships that could have been spared instantly to join our squadron off Cadiz'. Collingwood simply had to be reinforced if the Franco-Spanish Fleet were to be kept there until an equal British force could join him. On the other hand, if they had good luck for once, perhaps Calder would be hot on their heels. Two days later, 7th September, Cornwallis received confirmation that Sir Robert had indeed been sighted off Cape St Vincent, *en route* to Cadiz with a force of eighteen ships and two frigates (having detached two cruisers). If all had gone well since, Calder should already be at Cadiz with a combined force of twenty-six sail of the line, for Rear-Admiral Knight had just joined Collingwood with his five ships as well. Things were looking up.

Admiral Cornwallis was also most anxious about the overdue convoys of merchantmen from India and the West Indies, and thus it was with a sigh of relief that on 17th September he received a report from Captain Parker of the *Amazon*: 'I beg to acquaint you we fell in with the homeward-bound Jamaica fleet at sunset on August 31 during a gale.' Although some of the vessels had been separated by the storm, the convoy was basically intact, making its way to the Thames estuary, and would be escorted *en route* by a squadron mustered under Rear-Admiral Stirling.

Finally, news came from Calder himself, that he had indeed reached Cadiz on 21st September, as Cornwallis had anticipated and prayed, and thus on 28th September Cornwallis decided 'to stretch over to the Lizard with the squadron to go off Falmouth', leaving Sir Richard John Strachan 'to remain there [at Brest] to watch the enemy . . .' First, though, he would seek out Captain Allemand's marauding squadron and keep an eye out for more merchant convoys. Less than a fortnight later Cornwallis duly received authorisation to return to England where he would be found a few weeks hence on a fateful day in October.

GENERAL ORDER

Victory, off Cape St Vincent, September 27th, 1805.

To all Junior Flag Officers, and the Captains or Commanders of any of His Majesty's Ships or Vessels, ordered by Admiralty under my Command.

Pursuant to Instructions from the Lords Commissioners of the Admiralty, you are hereby required and directed to put yourself under my command, and follow and obey all such signals, orders, and directions as you shall from time to time receive from me for His Majesty's Service . . .

Nelson and Brontë

Saturday, September 28th, 1805

Fresh breezes at N.N.W. At daylight bore up, and made sail. At nine saw the
Aetna cruising. At noon saw eighteen sail. Nearly calm. In the evening
joined the Fleet under Collingwood. Saw the Enemy's Fleet in Cadiz,
amounting to thirty-five or thirty-six Sail of the Line.

Nelson's Diary

I verily believe the Country will soon be put to some expense for my account,
either a Monument, or a new Pension and Honours; for I have not the very
smallest doubt but that a very few days, almost hours will put us in Battle; the
success no man can ensure, but the fighting them, if they are to be got at, I
pledge myself, and if the force arrives [from Great Britain] which is intended
. . . I want for the sake of our Country that it should be done so effectually as
to have nothing to wish for; and what will signify the force [*en route* from
Britain] the day after the Battle [if they arrive late]? It is, as Mr Pitt knows,
annihilation that the Country wants . . .

Nelson to George Rose, 6th October 1805

'THE RECEPTION I met with on joining the Fleet', Nelson wrote to a
friend, after a surprise party on 29th September to celebrate his forty-
seventh birthday and to welcome his arrival, 'caused the sweetest
sensation of my life. The Officers who came on board to welcome my
return, forgot my rank as Commander-in-Chief in the enthusiasm with
which they greeted me'. A sentiment echoed by Captain George Duff of
the *Mars* who found his new Admiral to be 'so good and pleasant a man,
that we all wish to do what he likes, without any kind of orders'.

'I got fairly into the fleet yesterday', Nelson informed his old friend, Sir
Alexander Ball, Governor of Malta, on 30th September, 'and under the
circumstances I find them as perfect as could be expected . . . The
[British] force is at present not so large as might be wished', he admitted,
'but I will do my best with it; they [the Admiralty Board] will give me more
[ships] when they can, and I am not come forth to find difficulties, but to
remove them.' He found himself off Cadiz with twenty-nine ships of the
line, six of which were destined shortly to be leaving on revictualling duty
at Gibraltar, thus leaving him with an effective force of twenty-three
ships.

To London he reported finding the fleet in 'very fair condition',
assuring them that 'every exertion of mine shall be used to keep it so, and
in a state to meet the Combined Fleet in Cadiz', while to Brigadier
General William Steward, he did acknowledge an edginess, even
uneasiness, in finding 'thirty-six Sail of the Line looking me in the face'
and preparing to put to sea in a few days. 'The sooner the better', he
hastened to add, 'I don't like to have these things upon my mind . . .'

Clearly the British force was outgunned, which simply meant they would have to be all the more vigilant and determined. 'In our several stations', he informed Rear-Admiral Alexander Knight, 'we must all put our shoulders to the wheel, and make the great machine of the Fleet intrusted to our charge go on smoothly.' The new Commander-in-Chief was not one to be easily daunted.

Admiral Lord Nelson was an emotional man who enjoyed his 'huzzas', but he had specifically forbidden the seventeen-gun salute due to him upon his arrival, or for his colours to be flown from every mast as this would have alerted the timid sailors snug in Cadiz Bay that the most feared and dreaded of their enemies had arrived, bringing more ships with him. The last thing Nelson wanted was to have another Ganteaume on his hands, refusing to clear port; everything possible had to be done now to induce Villeneuve and Gravina to venture forth from behind the batteries of guns at Cadiz. Horatio Nelson had a great deal on his plate as he now assumed command.

Although he had described the fleet as being in 'very fair condition' physically, it was dangerously low in every type of provision, including bread and water. Rectifying this would be an immediate priority, but in addition signals had to be arranged, look-out squadrons had to be placed between his fleet and Cadiz, battle plans prepared, distributed and explained to his commanding officers and, of course, there was the inevitable amount of administrative paperwork to clear out of the way, and one entire day would have to be set aside just for that. He was also praying desperately that Lord Barham would be as good as his word and send more warships to reinforce him *before* the Combined Fleet sailed.

Alas, it had also fallen to his unfortunate lot to have to deal with Calder, personally relaying orders from London – it was not always pleasant being a commanding officer.

On 29th September Calder learned from London newspapers, which Nelson and his officers had brought with them, of the great public outcry growing against him. At first taken aback, his surprise gave way to anger as he wrote to the Admiralty Board: 'Having learnt with astonishment yesterday by the ships just arrived, and by letters from friends in England, that there has been a most unjust and wicked endeavour to prejudice the public mind against me as an officer, and that my conduct on the 23rd of last July in particular has been animadverted on in the most unjust and illiberal manner . . . I must therefore request you will be pleased to move the Lords Commissioners of the Admiralty to grant an inquiry into my conduct . . .'

Nelson had brought with him special orders from the First Lord 'suggesting' that under the circumstances it would be to Calder's benefit to submit himself to just such a board of inquiry, though privately Nelson had advised Sir Robert to drop the request for a hearing, in the light of what he had witnessed at several other similar proceedings. He pointed out how harrowing and destructive it could be. As he related to Admiral Collingwood afterwards, he '. . . has an ordeal to pass through which I fear he little expects'.

Calder, however, was also in a painful position here at Cadiz, having not only been superseded as the Commanding Officer, but even bypassed (by Collingwood) as Second-in-Command, all of which was aggravated when, pursuant to orders from the First Lord, Nelson instructed Calder to strike his flag and shift his belongings from the three-deck *Prince of Wales*, and prepare for his return voyage. Calder was startled and appalled and, in a private letter to Nelson, said that his orders had 'cut me to the soul at the thought of being turned out of my Ship . . . My heart is broken'. But Calder knew Nelson's reputation as a soft touch and pleaded with him, and Nelson finally relented, permitting Vice-Admiral Calder to return to England in his own powerful flagship, though Nelson knew it was desperately needed in Cadiz. Indeed, Nelson's decision to part with the three-decker was quite irresponsible. Calder was an egotistical and selfish man, however, who could not see beyond the end of his own nose, though in this instance he did appreciate Nelson's face-saving generosity, promising to come and see him before leaving, 'to thank you in person for all your kindnesses to me since I have been under your command, and to wish you every possible success.'

The removal of the *Prince of Wales* not only weakened the fleet, but left Nelson in a most awkward position *vis-à-vis* Lord Barham and the Admiralty Board. For weeks he had been begging London for more ships, pointing out how understrength the British force was in comparison to that of the mighty Combined Fleet, and here he was doing what no seemingly intelligent naval commander would do just before the great battle he was anticipating. 'I fear I shall incur the censure of the Board of Admiralty,' for having done this, he confessed to Barham. 'I may be thought wrong, as an Officer, to disobey the orders of the Admiralty, by not insisting on Sir Robert Calder's quitting the *Prince of Wales* . . . and for parting with a 90-gun Ship . . . but I trust that I shall be considered to have done right as a man, and to a Brother Officer in affliction' who otherwise would have had to have been removed 'from his Ship which he commanded, in the face of the Fleet . . . My heart could not stand it, and so the thing must rest'. Finally, on 14th October, Calder sailed for England in the ship that, had it been present a week later, might have saved several British lives.

Nevertheless Admiral Calder's plight was not the only thing concerning Nelson now, and even before he had made all the proper preparations for his fleet, his mind was turning to the forthcoming encounter with the enemy. Indeed, no sooner had the *Victory*'s anchors been released, seeking a secure hold off Cadiz, than a very anxious Nelson wrote to Alexander Davison that he was 'expecting the [enemy] Fleet to put to sea – every day, hour, and moment; and you may rely that, if it is within the power of man to get at them, that it shall be done . . . I must think, or render great injustice to those under me, that, let the Battle be when it may, it will never have been surpassed'. This anticipation of an impending battle was reflected in almost every letter he wrote, whether privately to friends abroad or to fellow officers, while to Abbé Campbell he also managed a bit of humour, indicating his brother's hopes for a great battle, 'that somehow or other he may be a *Lord*'! He would do anything in his power, and use any tactic, to coax the Combined Franco-Spanish Fleet out of Cadiz, including the use of Colonel Congreve's rockets and fireships and carrying out a bombardment of the town and fleet, all of which he was considering.

Although keeping most of his fleet about fifty miles or so to the west over the horizon from, and thus well out of sight of, Cadiz, he maintained a very close watch on that harbour with some fast-sailing frigates under the command of Captain Blackwood in order 'to lure them out'. Another small squadron, this time of ships of the battle line under the command of Captain George Duff, was stationed between Blackwood and the main fleet, to convey signals and be able to sail in quickly with heavy gunpower if needed. Nelson stressed to Blackwood 'the importance of not letting these rogues escape us without a fair fight, which I pant for by day, and dream of by night . . . [but] I am confident you will not let these gentry slip through your fingers, and then we shall give a good account of them, although they may be very superior in numbers'.

Rogues or gentry, they had to be dealt with and, unfortunately, indeed astonishingly, by 5th October Nelson still had only *two frigates* with him to give to Blackwood and was eagerly awaiting a reinforcement of both frigates and ships of the line. 'I am most exceedingly anxious for more *eyes* [frigates]', he explained to Secretary of State for War Castlereagh. 'The last Fleet [Villeneuve's at Toulon] was lost to me for want of Frigates: God forbid this should be'. Then, in a more anxious vein, to the

Admiralty, 'I am sorry ever to trouble their Lordships with anything like a complaint of a want of Frigates and Sloops [but without them] . . . services must be neglected to be performed' and, as a result, the enemy could escape. He required 'never less than eight Frigates and three good fast-sailing Brigs' to cover the large area for which he was responsible, as the present untenable situation with just two 'makes me very uneasy'. He wanted to post five frigates at Cadiz (including one off Cape St Mary's), two frigates and two sloops for duty between Cadiz and Gibraltar, others at Cape Spartel, off Cabo Blanco and the Salvages and more for Malta and General Sir James Craig's expedition to the Mediterranean. He recommended a bare minimum of ten frigates for his widespread command.

On 5th October he wrote excitedly to Lord Barham, 'It looks like a junction . . . The French and Spanish Ships have taken troops on board . . . and it is said they mean to sail the first fresh Levant wind' to meet the Cartagena squadron, which was also reported to be ready to sail. 'I have twenty-three Sail with me, and should they come out I shall immediately bring them to Battle. But although I should not doubt of spoiling any voyage they may attempt, yet I hope for the arrival of the [additional] Ships from England, that as an Enemy's Fleet they may be annihilated.' This was to prove the first of several false alarms, however, though the Cadiz lighthouse had been lit as a guide for the expected squadron from the Mediterranean. In fact, that squadron *did* set out from Cartagena, but, upon learning of Nelson's arrival, turned round and returned to port. Their real purpose, apparently, was not to join Villeneuve, but to act as a diversion in order to draw off some of the British fleet blockading Cadiz, in turn permitting the Combined Fleet to escape.

As Captain Blackwood was stationed about three miles from Cadiz and within view of it, all depended upon his signalling when Villeneuve's fleet finally weighed anchor. Fortunately, the process of communicating had been revolutionised in 1800 with the introduction of Sir Home Popham's new method, which replaced the former ideogram flags used to transmit a limited list of specific words and ideas. Admiral Popham's genius lay in having devised the first alphabet system using sets of coloured flags hoisted from the masts of a ship. As individual flags, or combinations of them, represented individual letters now, any word could be transmitted, indeed entire sentences, some 3,000 of which were included in the fifty new navy signal books distributed to the British fleet at Cadiz. The system, brilliant as it was, nevertheless relied on reasonably good weather, co-operative winds and daylight, in the absence of which other more primitive methods had to be substituted, including the firing of guns and rockets and the use of coloured lamps on the mastheads.

In early nineteenth-century naval warfare it was still the individual and commander who counted in the final analysis, however, and not a particular signalling system. In this situation Captain Blackwood of the *Euryalus* was the ideal man for Nelson. He was intelligent, energetic and completely reliable and accomplished a great deal with his two frigates until 8th October when Nelson signalled good news: 'I send [the frigate] *Naiad* to you, and will [the frigate] *Phoebe* and [schooner] *Weazle*, as I can lay my hands upon them. I am gratified [at Blackwood's determination to get the enemy] because it shows your soul is in your business . . . I see you feel how much my heart is set on getting at these fellows, whom I have hunted so long . . . ' And Admiral Nelson was as good as his word, Blackwood shortly having an inshore squadron comprising five frigates and two schooners with which to continue his reconnaissance work, the most Nelson ever used for such an operation, so keen was he on not losing Villeneuve a second time.

Initially Nelson also wanted to have at least three fast-sailing 74-gun ships between Blackwood and the main force and on 4th October appointed Captain Duff to see to this task, with the *Mars*, the *Defence* and *Colossus*. 'As the Enemy's Fleets may be hourly expected to put to sea from Cadiz, I have to desire that you will keep . . . from three to four leagues [nine to twelve miles] between the Fleet and Cadiz, in order that I may get the information from the Frigates stationed off that Port, as expeditiously as possible'. If, because of the weather or hour, Popham's flags could not be used or seen, alternative signals were arranged. 'Should the Enemy [at Cadiz] move, I have desired the Vessels coming with the information, to fire a gun every three minutes and burn a rocket from the mast-head every half hour . . . In thick weather the Ships are to close within signal distance of the *Victory*; one of the Ships to be placed windward, or rather to the Eastward of the other two, to extend the distance of seeing; and I have desired Captain Blackwood to throw a Frigate to the Westward of Cadiz, for the purpose of an easy and early communication'. Although Nelson was sometimes wrongly accused of maintaining poor communications and too loose a watch on enemy ports, he was, in fact, most alert about this matter, personally insisting upon daily contact with his 'eyes' immediately off shore.

Nelson now decided to stay at least sixteen to eighteen leagues (forty-eight to fifty-four miles) west of Cadiz for two reasons: he did not want Villeneuve (though he thought Decrès had assumed command there) and

Gravina to know exactly how many ships he had (ironically, as a result they were later to overestimate the strength of Nelson's force) and, more importantly, to prevent himself and his larger more cumbersome three-deckers from being blown off station and into the Straits of Gibraltar by westerly gales. 'In fresh breezes Easterly, I shall work up for Cadiz, never getting to the Northward of it; and in the event of hearing they are standing out of Cadiz, I shall carry a press of sail to the Southward towards Cape Spartel and Arrache, so that you will know where to find me' and in order to cut off their escape through the Straits of Gibraltar, he told Blackwood, closing with an informal, 'I send you two [news]-papers, I stole them for you.'

There was a constant bustle of ship movement, not only within the fleet, as the result of local manoeuvres or the shifting of positions due to wind changes and by transports and tenders loading and unloading supplies and provisions as best they could in these Spanish seas so infamous for their enormous swells, but also by frigates on their fortnightly journey to and from England with news and dispatches, not to mention the constant coming and going of various warships. There was nothing boring about these early October days as Nelson fretted impatiently for the enemy to oblige him and haul out of port.

Before leaving London in mid-September, the Prime Minister himself, while accompanying Nelson to his carriage in Downing Street, had assured him that he would have the First Lord send him every available warship he could spare, and Nelson was counting on him keeping his promise. Whether Barham would have done all for Nelson that he eventually did do, without Pitt insisting upon it, will perhaps never be known. The First Lord did approve of Cornwallis' decision to create and dispatch a large fleet to El Ferrol and Cadiz (which Pitt himself had also privately suggested), thereby creating the force that made the meeting with Villeneuve and Gravina at Cadiz and Trafalgar possible. In so doing, however, Barham was simply carrying out Pitt's orders (he could hardly have remained at his post had he not done so) and from now on Horatio Nelson could do no wrong and was given almost *carte blanche* whenever possible. Thus, when he later informed the Prime Minister of the number of ships needed at Cadiz, Pitt concurred and promised to provide whatever could be spared. Unlike most politicians' promises, Nelson knew he would be as good as his word.

The *Zealous* and *Endymion* had joined the fleet by 1st October, but both had badly decayed or sprung mainmasts and had to be sent on to Gibraltar for repairs. By 8th October, *Naiad*, *Phoebe* and *Weazle* had arrived (shortly to be followed by *Juno*, *Sirius* and the *Niger*), which were then attached to Blackwood's inshore squadron. Later that same day three more ships of the line joined the fleet: the 74-gun *Leviathan* (returning from Gibraltar), the 74-gun *Defiance*, and the 100-gun *Royal Sovereign*, which had been designated as Collingwood's replacement flagship for the *Dreadnought*, while the *Aetna* was being detached for repairs in Gibraltar as well. By 9th October the *Hydra* and the ubiquitous schooner with a colourful name, the *Pickle*, also joined Blackwood's squadron.

The next day, as Captain William Hoste was in the act of replacing an ailing Captain Sutton on board the *Amphion* and Sir William Bolton was replacing Hoste on the *Eurydice*, the long-expected 74-gun *Belleisle* arrived from England, followed by the *Acasta*, *Renommée* and *Aimable*. When Sir Edward Berry finally arrived with the *Agamemnon* on 13th October, after a harrowing crossing from England, a jaunty Nelson, flapping his 'fin' (his empty sleeve), exclaimed: 'Here comes Berry; now we shall have a Battle!' and then in a more sober mood, said goodbye to Calder and the *Prince of Wales*, as they set out on their fateful journey home.

The fleet was definitely beginning to shape up, and though *Amphion* was sent on a mission to Algiers, and the 74-gun *Donegal* to Gibraltar for a supply of casks, the 64-gun *Africa* joined the fleet on 14th October, while the 74-gun *Defence* and 64-gun *Agamemnon* were sent to beef up Duff's small squadron half-way between Cadiz and the fleet. By 15th October the British fleet had reached its full strength – twenty-seven ships of the line and five frigates – as the force which would meet the Combined Fleet a week later.*

But ships alone do not make a powerful fleet. Provisions of every nature had to be found - from wood for the stoves to canvas, rope and food - to keep it operating efficiently. On 2nd October, Nelson had informed Marsden that, 'The Ships are getting short in their water and provisions', including bread, water, meat and vegetables. 'I shall there-fore send Rear-Admiral Louis with Six Sail of the Line [including the *Queen*, *Canopus*, *Spencer*, *Zealous*, *Tigre* and *Endymion*] immediately to Gibraltar and Tetuan to complete in everything . . .' When Louis protested that he would miss the great show and 'have no share in the Battle', Nelson replied, 'I have no other means of keeping my Fleet complete in provisions and water . . . The enemy will come out, and we

*See appendix 3

shall fight them; but there will be time for you to get back first.' (In fact Louis would have had time in which to return for the great battle, but while at Gibraltar was then ordered on temporary convoy duty, taking him into the Mediterranean instead.) No sooner was Louis gone than Nelson was already designating the next six ships to replace them upon their return, for he was not one to procrastinate. Arranging for these supplies and transports now proved a daunting and time-consuming job during the first couple of weeks of October, Nelson delegating much of the supervisory work to Collingwood.

The few supplies which reached them from England were distributed not according to the seniority of the officer, but rather according to need – those longest out and most needy receiving them first. The most immediate source of fresh food had been Portugal since the closure of Spanish ports, this arranged by victualling agents, Nelson reminding them 'not to be *penny wise* and *pounds foolish*', the cheapest not necessarily always being the best for healthy crews and sound ships.

When the supplies started arriving, all was bustle.'As the Transports have stores in which you sent for, do call the Ships about you, and make the arrangements', Nelson instructed Collingwood. Fresh meat was always welcomed after months of salt provisions, and transports of bullocks – for cattle were kept alive on board till needed – were a welcome sight on 7th October. 'Chests of lemons will be most acceptable for the fleet,' Nelson informed the British Consul General in Lisbon, James Gambier. Portugal, though a neutral country, was making it difficult for Nelson to obtain provisions, but the Portuguese were not the only obstacle. When Gambier asked Captain James Dunbar of the warship *Malabar*, who was then at Lisbon, to ferry urgently needed provisions to the fleet, and Dunbar refused to do so, Nelson – preoccupied with the preparations of a fleet anticipating a major battle – called Dunbar's conduct 'very reprehensible' and wrote to the Admiralty Board asking them to censure him. But the next day the Admiral was informed of some 392,000 pounds of 'bread' awaiting them at Gibraltar, which was very good news.

Loading and unloading provisions, however, was a cumbersome process. Once brought on board, salted meat and other supplies had to be re-weighed with an officer present to witness the transaction in order to prevent theft and fraud, which were often rife in British fleets. Unloading was made all the more difficult by the 'bad swell' so common in these waters, causing the smaller boats conveying supplies from transports to warships to bob like corks and smashing many an arm and leg in the process. 'At half past four or five pm make a signal for all Boats to be repaired on board, and to keep the wind under three topsails and foresail for the night', Nelson instructed his Second-in-Command, 'and direct the ships with Transports in tow, to keep to the Windward this clear night . . . Should the swell get up before the evening, telegraph me, and the Boats shall be hoisted in.' 'I wish I could go on board the Victuallers', a frustrated Collingwood replied, 'for they go exceedingly slow.' Finally, at the end of the day, as the 'empty wine-pipes, hoops, staves, and condemned provisions' were rowed out to the now empty transports, an exhausted Collingwood sighed gratefully with the thought that 'this transport business', as he called it, would soon be finished, once the medicines from Gibraltar had arrived.

The Combined Fleet had problems with supplies as well, and in their case the situation proved just as critical, which the British were willing to exploit. 'We have a better chance of forcing them out by want of provisions', Nelson insisted in a letter to Lord Castlereagh at the War Department shortly after reaching Cadiz. 'It is said hunger will break through stone walls – ours is only a wall of wood.' Only just before the battle did the French begin to send provisions from Nantes, Bordeaux and small ports in the Bay of Biscay in neutral Danish vessels through to Spanish ports close to Cadiz and thus the British had to maintain a tight watch on all coastal freighters to prevent such supplies from getting through. 'There never was a place so proper to be blockaded, at this moment, as Cadiz', Nelson acknowledged, and with an effective blockade 'the Enemy must soon be in distress, and consequently be forced to come out.' This was his aim and hope. Though the people, sailors and troops in the port of Cadiz were not actually starving, their situation was quite desperate and Nelson intended to keep the pressure up. He simply had 'to provoke or lure them out', if that is what it took to bring them to the battle he was 'panting' for. 'We shall have those fellows out at last,' a sanguine Collingwood assured his Commander-in-Chief. 'I firmly believe they have discovered that they cannot be subsisted there . . . I really think these people in Cadiz are about to move.' Fortunately Nelson had other things to keep himself occupied, and his mind off the enemy: the enormous amount of paperwork. This included the necessity of preparing the monthly disposition of the fleet for the Admiralty Board – a particularly complex report for this busy period.

He also had to rest, and when weather and work permitted, he managed to have all the fleet's captains at his dinner, an occasion most of them looked forward to. During one of these repasts he first mentioned his new plan for attacking the Franco-Spanish Fleet, the 'Nelson Touch', which stunned them 'like an electric shock', he related to Emma Hamilton. 'Some shed tears, all approved. It was new, it was singular, it was simple!' His new strategy and tactics were indeed unusual, only Rodney having first devised and executed the method, successfully defeating a surprised French Admiral de Grasse off Martinique on 12th April 1782.

Until this time there were only a couple of traditional methods of attack where two large fleets were concerned. They would approach each other in two long, enormous battle lines, manoeuvring to gain the advantage of the wind, then either one side (having the wind advantage) would back their topsails to await their opponent, or both fleets would sail past each other in two close parallel lines, lambasting each other with their broadsides preparatory to boarding.

Nelson found that these traditional tactics left individual captains too reliant upon their commander's signals (which they often could not see) and were far too time-consuming, sometimes taking an entire day just to form and approach the enemy before commencing hostilities, and Nelson never had much patience for minuets, in the ballroom or on the high seas. He wanted battle, and one of obliteration at that, and hence he devised a method (obviously based in part at least on Rodney's concept) as a more lethal short-cut, involving the cutting off and surrounding of sections of the enemy's fleet.

On 9th October, Admiral Lord Nelson finally composed his famous Memorandum in which he set forth his new battle plan: 'Thinking it almost impossible to bring a Fleet of forty Sail of the Line into a Line of Battle in variable winds, thick weather, and other circumstances which must occur, without such a loss of time that the opportunity would probably be lost of bringing the Enemy to Battle in such a manner as to make the business decisive, I have therefore made up my mind to keep the Fleet in that position of sailing (with the exception of the First- and Second-in-Command) that the Order of Sailing is to be the Order of Battle.' In the approach to the enemy, the fleet would be divided into three separate lines, re-formed into columns sailing directly and perpendicularly at the long line of the combined enemy fleet, permitting them to pierce it like three spears. There were to be two major lines of sixteen ships each, accompanied by 'an advanced squadron of eight of the fastest-sailing two-decked Ships'. This squadron was to serve as a type of mobile reserve, to be attached to either of the two larger lines when directed, thereby ultimately giving one of them a tactical unit of twenty-four ships of the line.

Nelson was to have command of the centre line of sixteen ships and Collingwood 'to have the entire direction of his Line to make the attack upon the Enemy and to follow up the blow until they are captured or destroyed'. Collingwood's line would lead through the enemy battle line at about their twelfth ship from the rear and thus cut off and encircle the entire rearguard – very much the tactics American Indians used when attacking wagon trains. 'My Line would lead through at about their Centre, and the Advanced Squadron to cut two or three or four ships ahead of their centre', the objective being to divide the last half of the enemy battle line into two separate units. 'The whole impression of the British Fleet must be to overpower from two or three ships ahead of their Commander-in-Chief, supposed to be in the Centre, to the Rear of their Fleet'. This would leave upwards of twenty sail of the Combined Fleet untouched, but Nelson could not create ships he did not possess, and in any event 'it must be some time before they could perform a manoeuvre to bring their force back to attack any part of the British Fleet engaged, or to succour their own Ships . . .' He acknowledged that, of course, 'something must be left to chance; nothing is sure in a Sea Fight beyond all others. Shot will carry away the masts and yards of friends as well as foes', but he had no doubt as to the outcome: 'I look with confidence to a Victory before the Van of the Enemy could succour their Rear' and, by that time, the British fleet would have succeeded in controlling, capturing or destroying enough of the Combined Fleet to be able to cope with and 'receive their twenty Sail of the Line, or to pursue them . . .' There were to be alternative tactical approaches depending upon the direction of the wind, but the ultimate strategy and objectives remained the same – a plan of the greatest simplicity. 'Captains', he closed, 'are to look to their particular line as their rallying point. But, in case Signals can neither be seen or perfectly understood, no Captain can do very wrong if he places his ship alongside that of an enemy.'

Unlike Napoleon's celebrated proclamations before major battles, there was no waffling, no false promises here of glory and booty, no histrionics. Even with a somewhat inferior number of warships, Nelson knew he could defeat the Combined Fleet, but what really disturbed him was the realisation that, for want of at least another dozen ships of the line (if he faced forty enemy ships) he could not possibly capture or destroy or annihilate the *entire* enemy force. Being a practical man, however, he accepted the constraints placed upon him and would do the best he could with what he had. The major drawback of this plan was that the British ships spearheading the two or three columns approaching the Combined Fleet would come under intense fire for up to half an hour before they would be in a position to return it with their own broadsides as these ships carried very little forward artillery. That notwithstanding, Nelson's flag-officers and captains liked the plan and apparently endorsed it whole-heartedly, and no doubt, with him leading them – Nelson had never lost a battle – they had full confidence in the outcome as well.

By 9th October, the basic provisions were being transferred from transports to warships, and the battle plan circulated among the commanding officers. Nevertheless that did not allay Nelson's impatience over the failure of the enemy to haul out of Cadiz and, in almost every letter to friends, he invoked the gods of war to grant him this wish – 'From my soul, I hope they will soon come forth'. A few days later, Nelson signalled Collingwood excitedly, 'The Enemy's Fleet are all but out of the harbour, perhaps this night . . . they may come forth . . . I shall lay to all night', just in case.

With the bulk of the transports temporarily out of the way, Nelson now drafted plans for the creation of a new Mediterranean Fleet of ten sail of the line and two frigates to be dispatched to Toulon and Genoa once the battle was over to cover British armies in that region and to save Sardinia from the French. He was also occupied with dictating and drawing up fleet orders and memoranda all day on 10th October, while arranging Vice-Admiral Collingwood's transfer from the *Dreadnought* to the faster and better equipped *Royal Sovereign*.

Before tackling the formidable list of administrative tasks which lay before him, Nelson had a touching exchange of letters with Cuthbert Collingwood, who acknowledged his gratitude for Nelson's 'kindness to me, and the full confidence you have reposed to me', this in a letter to his commanding officer, junior to him by some eight years in age. He continued, 'I hope it will not be long before there is an opportunity of showing your Lordship that it [his confidence] has not been misplaced.' Nelson insisted that he wanted Collingwood to remain 'perfectly at ease' in the forthcoming battle 'and to give full scope to your judgment for carrying them [the battle plans] into effect. We can, my dear Coll, have no little jealousies. We have only one great object in view, that of annihilating our enemies.'

While captains of the fleet were busy painting their ships 'à la Nelson', as George Duff called it (which included yellow lower masts with large black rings – in sharp contrast to the black hoops round the enemy's masts – and black strips between the yellow of the gundecks and black ports, giving the English ships a chequered appearance when the gun ports were closed), on 10th October Admiral Lord Nelson was drawing up a list of orders and memos addressed 'To the respective Captains,' covering a variety of subjects he had left for a rainy day:

> It is my positive directions that the Pursers are obliged to purchase vegetables for the Ships' soup when it is possible to procure them; and that the Government onions are not used for the soup, if the Purser has the power of obtaining onions or other vegetables [elsewhere], as he is bound to do . . . but the onions, for the account of Government, are not to be purchased without my orders.

> As gales of wind increase so suddenly in this Country, the Ships of the Fleet are directed, particularly in the night, to shorten sail without waiting for the Admiral's motions.

> It is my particular directions that the name and family of every Officer, Seaman, and Marine, who may be killed or wounded in Action with the Enemy, on board any of His Majesty's Ships and Vessels under my command, be returned to me as soon after the circumstances happens, in order that I may transmit it to the Chairman of the Patriotic Fund at Lloyd's Coffee-house, that the case of the relations of those who may fall in the cause of their Country may be taken into consideration.[1]

Thus with enough temporary provisions finally on board and stowed away – though Louis' squadron had not yet returned, most of the other ships assigned to the Fleet having arrived, Calder dispatched on his return journey to England, and Vice-Admiral Collingwood's move to the *Royal Sovereign* safely effected – the wait for the enemy fleet's appearance became more onerous, only relieved by Nelson's sumptuous feasts on board the *Victory* and endless speculation on the enemy's next move.

'The Combined Fleets are all at the Harbour's Mouth', Nelson informed Alexander Ball on Tuesday 15th October, 'and must either move up again, or move off, before the winter sets in', but adding, 'I trust we shall be able to get hold of them.'

'Fine weather, wind Easterly,' Admiral Nelson recorded in his diary on Friday 18th. 'The Combined Fleets cannot have finer weather to put to sea.' 'It is very extraordinary the people in Cadiz do not make some movement', Collingwood later echoed irritably from his new cabin in the *Royal Sovereign*.

'What a beautiful day!' Nelson greeted Collingwood early the next morning, 19th October. 'Will you be tempted out of your Ship [for dinner]? If you will, hoist the Ascent and *Victory*'s pendants.' Before Collingwood could reply, however, just after 9.30 am the look-out shouted that Captain Duff on board *Mars* was relaying a message from Captain Blackwood on the *Euryalus*: 'The enemy are coming out of port'. An eager Nelson then signalled: 'General chase, S[outh] E[ast]'. Finally, at 3 pm, the longed-for signal reaching the *Victory*, still some fifty miles west-south-west of Cadiz, 'The enemy's fleet is at sea'.

I have the greatest satisfaction in hastening to announce to Your Excellency the safe arrival in this port of the Combined Squadron. This brings the total force, including the vessels brought from Ferrol, to 29 ships of the line, 6 frigates and 4 corvettes.

Commissaire Général des Relations Commerciales à Cadix Le Roy,
to Foreign Minister Talleyrand, 3 Fructidor An XIII (21st August 1805)

VICE-ADMIRAL VILLENEUVE'S long report of 22nd August 1805 reached Denis Decrès in Paris early on 2nd September, and brought with it the very news he had been secretly dreading ever since Villeneuve's disappearance from El Ferrol. 'I shall refrain from informing you of the impression it made on him [Napoleon],' the Naval Minister replied after having already received the first of several fulminating notes and letters from St Cloud.

'This Villeneuve business is heart-breaking for me', Decrès confided to Napoleon. 'I went on my first naval campaign with him, and with him I share twenty-five years of ties and friendship . . . I do not believe it is a question of cowardice, but rather, simply of his having lost his head.' Needless to say Napoleon saw it differently: 'It is out and out betrayal . . . There is no name for . . . That Villeneuve is the worst possible sort of wretch . . . He would sacrifice anyone and anything in order to save his own hide!' Nothing Decrès could say could possibly mollify an embittered French Emperor who was at the end of his tether and determined to remove the Naval Minister's old mentor and comrade in arms as quickly as possible. 'You never really believed he would come to Brest. Until such time as you can find something plausible to say [to justify Villeneuve's actions], I beg of you not to mention a word to me about *such an humiliating business*, nor remind me of the very existence of that miserable coward . . .'

Adding to Napoleon's problems Vice-Admiral Ganteaume – who previously had been so anxious to fight but had been prevented by Napoleon's orders – now, when Napoleon *was* ordering him to quit Brest, consistently failed to do so. Moreover he was insisting on being relieved of his command, 'temporarily', reporting to Decrès that his health was 'in a pathetic state . . . his gout has risen to his stomach; his doctors repeat the necessity of his arranging for an immediate change of air', which, coming at the worst possible of times, hardly endeared the navy and its amazing admirals to an Emperor in a state close to despair.

With the disastrous news that the Combined Fleet had sailed in the wrong direction and his armies already marching across France prepara-tory to launching strikes across the Rhine, Napoleon issued fresh instructions on 16th September for the Combined Fleet. Villeneuve and Gravina were to sail from Cadiz at the first opportunity and return to the Mediterranean, disembarking the troops they were carrying at Naples and capturing whatever enemy ships and convoys – Russian, Austrian or British – they could lay their hands on. They were to remain in that area 'so long as they could remain masters of the sea', before going to Genoa and Toulon to collect some newly launched vessels.

Napoleon had indeed had enough of Villeneuve and the next day (17th September) Decrès informed Admiral Rosily that he was to replace Vice-Admiral Villeneuve as Fleet Commander and 'to proceed to the port of Cadiz with the greatest possible speed'. In his long-pent-up exasper-ation, Napoleon was replacing Villeneuve with the one admiral in the French navy who was even less resourceful and more incompetent than himself! But in fact Decrès did not write to Villeneuve that day – he simply could not bring himself to do so – and the next two days were perhaps the most anguished of his life. Napoleon, however, who was waiting for confirmation, could be put off no longer, and on 20th September a grim Naval Minister sat down to write a single, inevitable sentence: 'H[is] M[ajesty] the Emperor and King has just named Vice-Admiral Rosily to assume command of the naval army at Cadiz, and has commanded that you return to Paris to render account of the campaign which you have just concluded.'

The act was done, but as it turned out it was to take a good month, even by special courier, for the news to reach the other end of Spain . . . and much could happen in the meantime.

During this interval there was one slight diversion, as Decrès presented the Emperor with another variation on the invasion theme. On 11th September, as Napoleon was meeting with his general staff in preparation for his big push through the German states, Decrès delivered a 'Secret Project' calling for an equally fast push by the navy, but in the opposite direction. 'England believes she has been relieved, at least for the moment, of the fear of an invasion', began the project drawn up by a naval officer by the name of Lescallier. 'This is precisely the moment to strike our great blow against her.' The plan in theory was simple. Without detaching any warships from Brest, Rochefort or other ports or squadrons, using instead those few already at the Channel ports between Dunkirk and Flushing, they were to embark 80,000 troops (taken from coastal camps in France and Holland) on board 500 transport vessels and gunboats, launching the whole enterprise on one tide. 'They must all set sail simultaneously' during one of the long winter nights 'at a time when the English believe the Emperor to be occupied elsewhere . . . We will enter the Thames rapidly in force under cover of night' with the purpose of causing as much destruction as possible all within a specific period of just a few hours. 'At the very least we can be certain of setting the ports of Chatham and Sheerness ablaze', and, if all went well, they could 'travel quickly right up to London, to burn down the entire dockyards area including some six miles of works at Greenwich, Deptford, Blackwall and Woolwich', after which they could retreat quickly on the outgoing tide under the protection of French warships. 'Its success, if only partial, will do incalculable harm to England.'

A most impatient Napoleon, impatient in particular with anything and anyone connected with the Imperial Navy at this moment, dismissed the whole thing out of hand, almost as quickly as he had done the 'Thilorière'. By now, however, there were no longer 80,000 men remaining along the Channel and it would already be difficult to prepare, re-arm and re-man 500 transports and gunboats. Even if such a force ever *did* reach the Thames, no sailor – in the age of sail, and in his right mind – could expect to be able to get to the London docks sailing up a crowded river few Frenchmen had ever navigated, past large gun emplacements, military camps and numerous warships, all within a short span of time, and then, unhindered, burn at will six miles of dockyards, warehouses and naval works in the very heart of the enemy capital *and* return to sea on the next tide! Thus the final proposal for a descent upon British shores, while the last vestiges of the invasion armada were still partially intact, was shelved.

Napoleon had, in fact, washed his hands of the whole affair and his attitude towards the fleet now was clearly reflected in his correspondence with Decrès. If the Combined Fleet ever completed its new mission at

Naples and reached Genoa and Toulon – where new ships were waiting to join it – well and good, but if, on the other hand 'it did not return . . . according to plan, I'll assign it to a cruise, it does not much matter where, any destination will do'. Napoleon's sudden disdain for the Navy did not make the plight of the Combined Fleet at Cadiz any more tolerable. Indeed, as Admirals Villeneuve and Gravina now discovered, they had been all but abandoned by Paris, for when they ordered supplies and provisions preparatory to putting to sea, they quickly found that there was neither money nor credit with which to purchase them. None the less, food was available, if one searched carefully enough in neighbouring Seville, Cordoba and Malaga and, if needs be, one could press for help from Granada as well, where no doubt six months' provisions could be found . . . but at a cost.

Upon receiving Decrès' new sailing orders at the end of September, orders destined to take the Combined Fleet to Naples, Villeneuve responded maddeningly, 'If the Imperial Navy only had a little character and backbone, I believe I could assure Your Excellency that the present mission would be crowned by a brilliant success', which coming from Villeneuve of all people, was simply too much for Bonaparte. By now Admiral Villeneuve knew that the British squadron off Cadiz comprised at least twenty-seven ships and frigates and by 16th September had discovered that Nelson himself was *en route* to assume command. Villeneuve complained that he had only thirty-two French and Spanish ships of the line and even they could do nothing for want of basic supplies.

Before Gravina sailed to America and right up to the time of his return to Spain in August 1805, the Spanish arsenal at Cadiz had prepared and armed fifteen ships, thereby exhausting its resources before the arrival of the Combined Fleet. Most of the ships now needed numerous repairs and 'the frigates lacked all their sails'. The French squadron's muster rolls listed over 1,700 men ill or AWOL – one-tenth of the entire force – and Spanish hospitals, where they existed, were poor and could not begin to cope with such numbers. With only a little more than 17,000 men with which to man the entire French squadron of eighteen ships, five frigates and two brigs, obviously some ships' complements were incomplete – Villeneuve claiming that he was at least 2,060 men short – and there was not enough food even for them, Government warehouses and depots remaining dank and empty. With the Spanish naval force totalling another 11,817 men, the Combined Fleet had some 30,000 men to feed and clothe.[2]

Admiral Villeneuve, who was willing to lower his sights and agree to a mere three months' supply of all provisions, rather than the original six demanded, persisted in reminding Paris of the current situation. 'The lack of funds, the impoverished state of the port, the great shortage of crews for the Fleet', he wrote to Decrès on 2nd September, 'have brought all activity to a halt . . . I have impressed on M. Le Roy the need to hasten the procurement of all resources . . . I know that he is most zealous, honest and motivated by the most ardent desire to do well, but unfortunately he is not endowed with a personality that invites one's affection and willingness to co-operate in these matters. I must also point out that he has almost no financial resources whatsoever and, as a result, our victualling and outfitting suffer accordingly. I am writing to the Ambassador [General Beurnonville] to request his assistance', for even 'daily subsistence requirements' were about to be cut off 'because of local businessmen's anxiety about not having been paid to date.'

Admiral Nelson and Collingwood had rightly reckoned on the critical lack of supplies and provisions for the Combined Fleet, but had incorrectly assessed its effect on them. 'Starvation' and the lack of the most elementary staples did not drive them out of that port, but on the contrary forced them to remain there, immobile.

Decrès had failed to act promptly upon the news of the fleet's arrival at Cadiz and it took a series of frantic demands from exasperated naval officers, diplomats and victuallers at Cadiz and Madrid, to get the Naval Minister to act. Le Roy, as General Commissioner for Commercial Affairs for the French fleet at Cadiz, had taken Villeneuve's pleas to heart – though victualling the fleet was not his usual job – agreeing to see to these needs. On 16th September, the French Naval Minister replied to Le Roy's letter of 21st August, informing Le Roy that he had written to Admiral Villeneuve, ordering him 'to press on with the repairs and provisioning of H[is] M[ajesty]'s fleet' and ordered Le Roy to do everything in his power 'to speed up the operations required to put that fleet in a state of readiness that will permit it to set sail as quickly as possible'.

The man answering to the Naval Minister in charge of supplying all the fleets was the 'Victualler General of the Navy'[3] in Paris. On 15th September he finally appointed a 'Director' to assume control of the entire victualling operation at Cadiz, ordering him to leave at once for that port. Decrès directed the Victualler General 'to procure everything that Admiral Villeneuve requires, whether in food supplies, sails or rigging, anything which H[is] C[atholic] M[ajesty]'s warehouses are unable to provide' and letters of credit (bills of exchange) were to be 'drawn on me [Decrès]' for expenses incurred.

The authority had been established, delegated and re-delegated, and the appropriate structure started to function to carry out this operation, but, as Le Roy already sadly knew, Spanish Government warehouses were as empty as French coffers in Cadiz and Madrid. Indeed, so remiss were the French in the matter of paying past debts, apparently, that official French Government letters of credit were no longer being honoured and Le Roy appealed to anyone and everyone for help, including the French Ambassador in Madrid (who was himself reduced to paying part of his rent out of his own pocket). To be sure, when writing to Admiral Gravina, Decrès asked him to use his considerable influence with the Spanish authorities, reminding him that 'the interests of the two Powers are one and the same and therefore one must not hesitate to share whatever means are available'. Ambassador Beurnonville informed Decrès that the Prince of Peace, Manuel de Godoy, had promised his help and they were hopeful of finding three months' supplies of food and naval provisions, while at the same time closing with a surprisingly undiplomatic nudge that reflected the navy's reputation for not paying its bills – 'but I must beg of you to honour his [Villeneuve's financial] engagements'.

Nevertheless it was weeks before anything significant was done in Spain to alleviate the situation. Drastic action had to be taken. Normal Government channels were failing and, as a last resort, General Beurnonville contacted the one man who – although detested by Napoleon as much as any Englishman – had always found a solution in the past, a man who had money and the highest reputation in Spanish ruling circles, the man who had already undertaken to meet the Spanish war subsidy to France – Gabriel Julien Ouvrard himself. As it turned out, however, even the illustrious Ouvrard was currently without resources, not having been paid for his past services by either the French or Spanish Governments. And when he appealed to former associates, the old firm of Segalas, Lovato and Hemas, to arrange for the credit necessary to produce the flow of supplies needed, those gentlemen replied from Cadiz on 13th September that 'It was our sincerest wish to be useful to you in this present situation, but all our efforts have proven unavailing'. That same week Ambassador Beurnonville was informing Foreign Minister Talleyrand that '. . . everything Commissioner General Le Roy has done will scarcely provide the bare minimum of food and munitions required for the French squadron'. Yet there was, in fact, no real shortage of food, simply no faith on the part of war contractors that they would ever be paid.

Villeneuve's fleet was at least two thousand men short – despite the fearsome efforts of press gangs – and this problem, added to the lack of supplies, found the Combined Fleet still immobile in the last week of September (five weeks after its arrival). It was then that Villeneuve received Decrès' new orders to sail to Naples. 'It would be useless on my part to reiterate how wretched things are here', General Beurnonville informed Decrès in the first week of October, 'suffice it to say that even if you provide M. Le Roy with 20 million francs credit, he will not be able to sign a contract for a single barrel of lard' without cash in hand.

It was Ouvrard of course who, despite his own financial problems, finally came up with the first instalment of 100,000 francs (not Decrès), thereby enabling Le Roy to draw up and sign forty-nine contracts, which he then forwarded for endorsement to Ambassador Beurnonville, who was greatly miffed by this action. 'He had the audacity to send them to me, as if my position as ambassador empowered me to counter-sign business contracts!' None the less by 10th October the situation had changed for the better and General Beurnonville could inform the Naval Minister that Julien Ouvrard was now arranging everything 'and you can now count on it all being done just as you wished'.

By the time Decrès' 'Director' – Monsieur de Limeux – finally reached Madrid on 9th October, much of his work had already been done for him and by the 14th, a more sanguine and less irascible Beurnonville could assure Decrès 'that I have no doubt that the Navy will be completely outfitted and provisioned for up to five months . . . M. de Limeux is now travelling with his agents to arrange it'. All was finally under control and the fleet would soon be able to sail, once Admiral Rosily reached Cadiz. Thus ended the supplies crisis which had paralysed thirty-three ships of the line in Cadiz Bay since late August. Four days later Admiral Villeneuve was to announce his intention of weighing anchor.

Back on 16th September Villeneuve had sent his monthly disposition of the fleet (including eighteen ships of the line, five frigates and three brigs) to Paris, noting that at least six to eight of the largest ships were bad sailors, needing numerous important repairs or suffering from untrained crews, or were greatly undermanned, stressing that the fleet was simply in no condition to sail – quite apart from the lack of basic provisions, but all eventually sailed on time.[4] The Spanish had twelve ships of the line ready and another three in dry dock, all of which were to join the Combined Fleet on 19th October.

Villeneuve received his new instructions dated 16th September, ordering him to Naples, just twelve days later. Despite the lack of provisions and the state of unfinished repairs, he began embarking the expeditionary force immediately, as Nelson had noted. By 2nd October, Chief of Staff Prigny found Villeneuve a seemingly much rejuvenated, even optimistic, man as a result of these fresh orders to return to the Mediterranean. Added to this there had been the welcomed recall to Paris on 30th September of Villeneuve's most critical messmate, the scowling General Lauriston, but not before that general dispatched a final report to Napoleon, lambasting Villeneuve's 'haughty pride and aloofness', chiding him on his 'indecisiveness . . . [and] fear of Nelson' which had left Lauriston feeling 'truly humiliated' to have been a member of such an expedition. The upshot was that Villeneuve was hastening preparations to sail, claiming he had nearly three months' food supplies. 'I really do not think the enemy can remain here before us with such a considerable force for much longer', he informed Decrès. 'I intend to take advantage of the first favourable opportunity in which to sail with the entire combined force and join up with the Cartagena squadron . . .' In reality his new-found energy and determination to sail stemmed from news of a different nature, that of 'the arrival here of Admiral Nelson with four ships of the line and some major projects for attacking, bombarding and burning the Combined Fleet at Cadiz.' Just a week later Villeneuve was beginning to have second thoughts, sounding like his old self once again, complaining about 'the inferiority of our forces compared with those of the enemy who now have 31 to 33 ships of the line [in fact they had twenty-seven], eight of which are three-deckers [actually seven], along with a large number of frigates' [they had the same number as the French!]. The three Spanish ships which had just come out of dry dock (the 110-gun *Santa Ana*, the 100-gun *Rayo*, and 74-gun *San Justo*) were not yet armed and manned, though he stated for the first time that he felt 'a battle was indeed inevitable the very moment we leave port'.

Given the growing might of the British fleet and the presence of Admiral Lord Nelson and, subsequently, the growing uneasiness among Spanish naval commanders, Gravina requested, and Villeneuve consented to, holding a '*Conseil de Guerre*' on board the *Bucentaure* the following morning, Tuesday 8th October. The purpose of this gathering of navy brass was the need to reassess the situation *vis-à-vis* the Royal Navy. The tension in the air, if not overt animosity, was unmistakable, as

Villeneuve summed up in the minutes he prepared for Decrès later that same day: 'Everyone acknowledged that the ships of our two allied countries are for the most part badly armed and manned [and] that several vessels and their new crews have never been to sea', therefore the Combined Fleet was in no condition to meet a superior enemy force of at least thirty-one ships. 'All our observations . . . led us to recognise unanimously that the enemy fleet . . . is much stronger than ours, which, nevertheless, would be forced to fight it at the most unfavourable of moments, just as we were leaving port . . . [and hence] everyone agreed as to the necessity of waiting in port until a more favourable occasion presented itself . . . The officers of both countries attending this meeting, however, expressed their wish to go and fight the enemy, regardless of the size of its force, whenever His Majesty requests it . . .'[5]

The minutes of this extraordinary meeting, witnessed and signed on 8th October by all fourteen officers of the French and Spanish navies present, meant that they were *formally refusing to obey Napoleon's order* of 16th September to leave port *immediately* to sail to Italy and that they would only do so in the future when they received a confirming order to this effect! The officers made this official by taking a formal vote, thereby declaring *a mutiny of sorts of the entire combined fleet*, though they probably did not consider it to be such. The fact is that they now decided to remain in port perhaps indefinitely and, if necessary, await Nelson's attack *there* rather than meet it out on the high seas.

As usual, Villeneuve's report was full of half-truths and omissions, and this included, most notably, his failure to disclose that while some of the French officers had wanted to put to sea at once, they met with stiff opposition from fellow officers, including Villeneuve himself and his Chief of Staff, Prigny, who were supported in turn by most, if not all, the Spanish naval commanders, Prigny reinforcing his argument by pointing out that, while the British had been at sea 'without intermission since 1793', their own navy had 'scarcely weighed anchor for eight years!' and therefore simply could not compete.

This was followed by a heated scene between Rear-Admiral Charles Magon, who insisted upon their following the Emperor's orders, and Captain Dionisio Galiano (acting as spokesman for Rear-Admiral Antonio de Escaño) who advocated remaining in Cadiz and defending that port against an anticipated attack. Magon, a hot-headed young man, lost his temper and said things to the Spaniard that no officer or gentleman would dare have said to another, especially in the presence of colleagues, and swords were almost drawn. It was only after considerable arm-twisting that Magon apologised, no doubt thereby avoiding a later duel. By now Rear-Admiral Escaño was quite fed up with Villeneuve and the French, and in a private letter to Commodore Enrique MacDonnell he lamented their 'conflicting views' and 'the excitability one expects from those people'. On the other hand, none of the Spanish officers had uttered what they really felt, which was that it would be foolhardy to sail with a weak fleet under an incompetent commander for the sole benefit of a foreign government against a superior enemy.

In fact, despite the reinforcements Nelson had been receiving since his arrival, the Franco-Spanish force still outnumbered his twenty-seven ships with their thirty-three, or, in terms of 'rated firepower' – that is, the officially designated number of guns per ship – 2,568 Franco-Spanish guns against Nelson's 2,148, giving Villeneuve an advantage of 420 guns.[6] Nelson never knew that there had been a virtual mutiny in the enemy's ranks and that he had narrowly missed not having his great battle later that month, and then it occurring only as a result of some most disagreeable news that reached Cadiz on 18th October.

But what then had happened on 10th October, when Pierre Villeneuve suddenly ordered the fleet to prepare to sail? What tergiversations! Rear-Admiral Magon was probably as bewildered as Admiral Gravina and Captain Galiano. Why this faint-hearted attempt (for he did not seriously push these preparations), only to cancel it immediately, giving as a reason the approach of stormy weather? Or was it faint-heartedness? Was it rather a feint, for Nelson or, more likely yet, for the French Naval Minister and Emperor, to deceive them into thinking that he was still on the job? Or was he fighting a subconscious battle with himself, tormented as he was? In any event the fleet made no serious attempt to put to sea that day after all, which was followed by a week of thick and dirty weather of the kind they had been hoping for during their 'war council' on 8th October – weather which would clear the British from the area – but alas, Nelson did not budge.

Following the gales, however, on the afternoon of 18th October, everything had changed yet again, Villeneuve leaving his lieutenants, Spanish and French alike, simply staggered by his frantic and most insistent order that the Combined Fleet prepare to sail forthwith, indeed that very day. The reason for this sudden, contradictory rush to action stations was revealed in Villeneuve's confidential letter of the same day to Naval Minister Decrès: 'I have just been informed that Vice-Admiral Rosily has arrived in Madrid; it is rumoured that he has come to take command of the fleet.' It was shattering news for the hapless and bewildered admiral. 'I should be delighted to cede my place to him', he continued, with a proviso, 'if the position as second-in-command is kept for me . . . but it would be too awful for me now to lose all hope of being able to show you that I was worthy of a far better fate.' It was quite outrageous of course, an admiral challenging such orders, saying that he deserved to be given yet another opportunity to show what a splendid commander he was!

In fact the 53-year-old François-Etienne, Comte de Rosily-Mesros, who had just been promoted to the rank of full admiral, had arrived at Madrid on Thursday 10th October after a most arduous three-week journey from Paris via Bayonne, though he was unable to set out for Cadiz until the 14th because of damage sustained by his carriage. Ambassador Beurnonville, who had for some days prior to this been privy to the news of Rosily's appointment superseding Villeneuve, told Decrès ' . . . I did not feel it was incumbent upon me, Monsieur le Vice-Amiral, to notify M. Villeneuve of M. Rosily's arrival at Madrid', nor the reason for his presence. As Rosily himself had not yet informed Villeneuve, 'I felt it was wiser to follow his example.' Villeneuve's histrionics were too well known, and no one – least of all General Beurnonville – wanted to risk a scene with him. Rosily himself wrote to the Naval Minister from Madrid on the 12th, stating he would be leaving once the coach was repaired and a sufficient guard found to accompany him on the seven- to ten-day journey along brigand-infested roads between the capital and Cadiz.

It was under these circumstances then – with Admiral Rosily now *en route* to Cadiz to relieve him of his command, and realising that orders to this effect were on their way and could arrive momentarily – that Pierre Villeneuve abruptly ordered his fleet to weigh anchor, though the weather was hardly suitable with scarcely a breeze in the harbour. Meanwhile, he had found another more feasible pretext for his departure, having just received intelligence that very day that a detachment of Nelson's ships under Admiral Louis was now in or near Gibraltar, and thus he argued – 'This force of six ships removed from the English fleet seems to offer me a favourable opportunity in which to put to sea. Accordingly I have made immediate signals to prepare to sail, bringing on board our barges and weighing anchor . . . if I have a land breeze during the night or tomorrow morning, I intend to sail.' And Commissioner General Le Roy, who was in Cadiz directing some of the provisioning of the fleet at this time, reported these fresh preparations to General Beurnonville in Madrid. Although some of the key correspondence regarding Villeneuve's sailing has been removed from the archives (it is not clear for instance when

Rosily actually reached Cadiz, though it was perhaps while a defiant Villeneuve was still in sight of land), fragments remain to give an outline of events and the reactions of those involved.

'Upon my word, my dear Minister', a bemused Beurnonville reported to Decrès, ' Vice-Admiral Villeneuve has flown the coop!' and, upon his arrival at Cadiz, Admiral Rosily will find that 'the nest is empty'. While some of Rosily's correspondence, too, has disappeared from Spanish archives, his later reactions were succinct: 'I cannot begin to express to you the bitterness and humiliation I felt upon reaching Cadiz', he fumed in a brief letter to the Admiralty in Paris. Little did the ill-fated Rosily suspect that this was just the beginning of a series of disastrous events in this port.[7]

After a week of thundering storms, Friday 18th October proved to be a clear warm day and, although the breeze was unco-operative, out of the west-north-west, after writing to the Naval Minister, Villeneuve gave the orders for the fleet to sail. The weak wind prevailed, however, immobilising them so that only a few vessels had weighed by 10.30 that night. Although Villeneuve again hoisted the signals from the masts of the *Bucentaure* for the entire fleet to put to sea at 5 o'clock the following morning, there was still so little wind that only a handful of the most forward frigates and ships actually managed to clear the harbour.

Sighting these ships, however, the ever vigilant Captain Blackwood immediately signalled from the *Euryalus* the eagerly awaited news, while dispatching one of his frigates to Gibraltar to fetch Admiral Louis and his squadron. 'What think you, my dearest love?' an excited Blackwood wrote hurriedly to his young wife. 'At this moment the Enemy are coming out, and as if determined to have a fair fight . . .'

'A Pell-Mell Battle'

I shall go at them at once, if I can, about one-third of the line from their leading ship . . . I think it will surprise and confound the enemy . . . It will bring on a pell-mell battle, and that is what I want.

Nelson

The enemy will not limit their tactics to forming the usual battle line parallel to ours . . . [rather] they will endeavour to surround our rear-guard, and cross through in order better to envelop and defeat us, carrying away those of our vessels they will have isolated.

Villeneuve, 'Final Instructions'

A man should witness a battle in a three-decker from the middle deck, for . . . it bewilders the senses of sight and hearing. There was the fire from above, the fire from below . . . the guns recoiling with violence, reports louder than thunder, the decks heaving and the sides straining. I fancied myself in the infernal regions, where every man appeared a devil.

Second-Lieutenant Rotely, Royal Marines

SOMETHING WAS WRONG, indeed, nothing was going right as the forty-year-old, 100-gun *Victory* gradually approached closer and closer to the formidable enemy of thirty-three mighty ships of the battle line . . . the enemy that Nelson had been longing to give '. . . such a shaking'. The seven big British three-deckers manoeuvred clumsily in the light westerly breeze, finding before them not the single battle line Nelson had been expecting, but, instead, groups of French and Spanish ships, two, three and even four abreast, clumps of sail clearly in no specific battle formation, simply cruising in 'natural order'. What was worse, the English admiral could not discern which ship was the French Commander-in-Chief's. Nelson's own white flag flew brazenly from the main masthead of the *Victory* and every British ship would soon be hoisting their colours but, with the exception of occasional signals, not a single flag or pennant of any type fluttered from the ninety-nine masts of the enemy battle line. Nelson had not counted on any of this.

It had all started earlier when Captain Edward Berry had nearly been caught, while dawdling in his ship the *Agamemnon* just outside Cadiz harbour on 20th October, towing an American merchantman prize he had just captured and obstinately refused to release, this despite Captain Blackwood's repeated orders to do so if he were to save himself the ignominy of capture before the enemy's ports by several of Rear-Admiral Magon's ships. There was always the unexpected.

Now, as he neared the enemy line extending before him some five miles long, Nelson, if not confused, was at least undecided. It appeared he would have to abandon his much vaunted plan of attack, at least in part. He would go for the van, the head of the fleet, to cut it off from Cadiz, and forget the centre and the seemingly non-existent French Commander-in-Chief who insisted on cloaking himself in anonymity. Furthermore, it would not be a matter now of simply piercing the enemy line. First, he did not have the reserve division of at least half-a-dozen ships he had initially planned on, for though Nelson had scanned the southern horizon time and again, Admiral Louis had not yet returned with his squadron from Gibraltar. Second, he could not slice through a thick, irregular enemy line and encircle the French and Spanish ships. Indeed, in some places he could not even find room enough to pass between the enemy ships at all, so closely were they bunching up, bowsprits practically brushing the stern of the preceding vessel, like so many elephants, trunk to tail.

As was tradition, Nelson liked to make a jaunty quip before his officers and men as he approached the enemy, but today everything was different. Nelson simply could not decide what to do. At first he thought the Combined Fleet, which was no more than a dozen miles from the Spanish shore at Cape Trafalgar, might wear and return to Cadiz, for they had altered course, sailing in a northerly direction, which would allow them to do this. Now, however, as the British fleet approached them, Nelson with his northernmost division of twelve ships, and Collingwood a mile-and-a-half away to the south, on his lee side, with fifteen ships of the line, it seemed more and more possible that Vice-Admiral Villeneuve was going to stand and fight. Nelson, of course, did not know that Villeneuve was determined never to return to Cadiz, where only humiliation lay in store for him with Admiral Rosily *en route* (if not already there) to replace him and orders calling him back to Paris to face the even greater humiliation of a dressing down by Napoleon before the entire court. This, after all, was his usual procedure when dissatisfied with the performance of one of his officers and no officer had ever humiliated him as much as Villeneuve! No, Villeneuve thought it better to stand and fight and die here, at the head of this immense fleet. He did not delude himself into thinking that he would defcat Nelson and survive.

Nor had it begun well for the French admiral. Early on Saturday morning, 19th October, when Blackwood had signalled the appearance of the French ships at the entrance of the port, there had been so little wind that several of these vessels had lowered their boats to tow them out past the lighthouse. Villeneuve was practically beside himself. He *had* to sail, yet even what little breeze there was, was coming from the wrong direction. No doubt he had had a hard time convincing the allied commanders to put to sea with him after the 'mutiny' of 8th October when they had voted *not* to sail. Apparently it was Admiral Federico Gravina who had once again stood so faithfully by his dubious French colleague, somehow convincing recalcitrant officers to weigh anchor, despite the evident folly of doing so when the British were waiting just outside the harbour, even if their fleet had been considerably reduced to perhaps twenty-two or twenty-four as Villeneuve now insisted. What is more, the Franco-Spanish force would not even have a reasonable chance of escaping a battle, for want of a good wind, *any* wind, with which to fill their sails. In fact Admiral Gravina did not find it easy to convince some reluctant Spanish ships to put to sea and, until the very last moment, even after he and Villeneuve had cleared the port, Commodore Enrique MacDonnell's ship *Rayo* had not weighed anchor.

By leaving now with so much dissension among his fleet commanders, Admiral Villeneuve was of course taking the considerable risk of finding part of his fleet separating from and abandoning him even if they all did put to sea – he could not *force* them to fight with him. Indeed, French officers reported that not all Villeneuve's orders were being obeyed, Captain Prigny, his most loyal Chief of Staff, trying to coerce and co-ordinate in the face of this unsettling reality. Even those apparently more than willing to fight, such as Rear-Admiral Charles Magon and Captains Jean-Jacques Lucas and Gabriel Denieport (of the *Redoutable* and *Achille* respectively), were disobedient (everyone by now having heard the rumour that Villeneuve was about to be replaced and sent back to Paris),

Magon himself arrogantly and flagrantly ignoring some of his commander's orders. (What would the French Commander-in-Chief do if he did indeed find himself with a fleet suddenly reduced in numbers, ships literally abandoning him at sea?) No, this was one battle which did not bode well for Vice-Admiral Villeneuve, as he retired to his day cabin to prepare his final instructions for the Combined Fleet. 'I have no intention of going out to seek the enemy; I even want to avoid them in order to arrive at our destination', he informed his commanders in these instructions, reminding them of 'the necessity of concealing the fleet's course . . . But if we do indeed meet, I shall tolerate no shameful behaviour which could in turn discourage our crews and bring about our defeat'.

If Vice-Admiral Villeneuve was extremely overwrought and no hero, nevertheless he was an intelligent, perceptive, officer, now even *anticipating* Nelson's battle plan. They 'will not restrict their tactics to forming the usual battle line parallel to ours and opening the normal artillery duel . . . [rather] they will endeavour to surround our rear-guard, and cross through in order better to envelop and defeat us, carrying away those of our vessels they will have isolated'. It was quite uncanny. How well Villeneuve understood his foe, whom he had studied so closely. Nelson himself would have been utterly astonished to see his 'secret plans' on Villeneuve's desk! Villeneuve was to be neither 'surprised' nor 'confounded' as the English admiral had boasted.

If it ultimately did come to a show-down with the Royal Navy, Villeneuve continued, he expected a great deal from his officers. Each commanding officer was to rely upon his own 'courage and love of glory' rather than on the Admiral's orders. To further inspire his men now, just hours before the battle itself, Villeneuve was sending his captains books of naval regulations and special signals, which also contained 'some excellent maxims which you should contemplate and with whose spirit you should imbue yourselves . . .'

In the final analysis, 'maxims' alone would not suffice, however, for it was bravery and the will to fight that counted. 'Should it come to a battle, any commanding officer not under fire will not be considered to be at his post, and a signal from me pointing this out will be taken as a stain upon his honour', he added. He declared that the British 'are not braver than we are and have much less enthusiasm and love of country than ourselves. They are skilful sailors, but in another month we will be their equals' and thus he had confidence in their 'achieving the most glorious success, and the beginning of a new era for the French Imperial Navy'.

Admiral Sir William Cornwallis, commander of the Channel Fleet and creator of the fleet Nelson was to command at Trafalgar.

Vice-Admiral Sir Charles Cotton, second-in-command of the Channel Fleet blockading Brest, 1803–1805.

Vice-Admiral Lord Nelson, the victor of Trafalgar.

Vice-Admiral Cuthbert Collingwood, Nelson's second-in-command at Trafalgar.

(*Left*) Thomas Hardy, captain of Nelson's flagship the *Victory*.

(*Below*) The *Victory* in Portsmouth, 1805.

Vice-Admiral Sir Robert Calder, who
relinquished his command of the
British fleet off Cadiz to Nelson.

Captain Henry Blackwood of the frigate
Euryalus, whose squadron alerted Nelson
that the French fleet had put to sea.

Vice-Admiral Pierre Villeneuve, commander of the Combined Franco-Spanish fleet at Trafalgar.

Admiral Gravina, commander of the Spanish squadron.

Villeneuve's flagship, the *Bucentaure*.

Rear-Admiral Charles Magon, who insisted on fighting at Trafalgar despite Spanish reluctance.

The fiery Captain Lucas of the *Redoutable*.

The *Redoutable*, surrounded during the battle of Trafalgar.

(*Opposite page*) The log of the *Victory*, recounting the battle and the death of Nelson.

Tuesday 22nd   N87W 24   36°11'   6:30h   N28°6' 8 Leags   Cadiz

Remarks &c Victory

Mod[erate] W[inds] at 11:40 the Action commenced between the Wt. Leeward
and the Rear of the Enemy's Line at 11:50 the Van of
the Enemy's line opened their Fire on us all sail set
at 12:15 opened our fire at 12:20 in attempting to break
through the Enemy's line fell on board the 10th and 11th Ships
the Action became General with the Van Ships of both
Columns, at 1:15 the Right Honble Lord Viscount Nelson was
wounded, at 1:30 the Redoubtable having Struck ceased
firing our Starbd Guns, the Action continued on the Larbd
side with the San hsima Trinidada and some other Ships
at 3:0 all the Enemy's Ships near us having Struck ceased
firing, observed the Royal Sovereign had lost her Main and
Mizen Mast, and several dismasted Prizes around her;
at 3:10 4 of the Enemy's Van Jack'd & stood along our line &
engaged us in passing at 3:40 made the Sign for our ships
to keep their wind, for the purpose of attacking the Enemy's
Van at 4:45 the Spanish Rear Adml Struck and one of
the Enemy's Ships Blew up, the Right Honble Lord Viscount
Nelson Departed this life. at 5 the Mizen Mast fell, our
Ships employd in taking possession of the Prizes, Vice Adml
Collingwood hoisted his Flag on board the Euryalus, employd
securing the Mast's & Bowsprit. sounded occasionally
from 19 to 13 fms observed 14 Sail of the Enemy standing
to the Northward and three to the Southward AM Struck the
Fore Top Mast to fish the Fore Masts at Noon the Fleet
& Prizes in company but not having communication
with any of our ships remain ignorant of the No. taken
our loss on board the Victory is as follows

6 Officers and 48 Seamen & Marines Killed
7 Officers and 74 Seamen & Marines Wounded

(*Top*) Nelson's funeral procession on the Thames, 8th January 1806. (*Above*) The cortège reaches St Paul's, 9th January 1806.

After drafting these orders Pierre Villeneuve, in the dark blue full dress uniform of the French Navy's Vice-Admiral, with its stiff, high collar edged with gold lace, heavy gold epaulettes, his chest laden with the large ribbons and medals representing the history of his entire naval career, appeared on deck accompanied by the commanding officer of his expeditionary force, Major-General Théodore Contamine, and the ship's Captain, Jean-Jacques Magendie, preceded by drummers and two teenage midshipmen, Donadieu and Arman, carrying a resplendent white flag bearing the Imperial eagle. As they carried out the final tour of inspection of crews standing smartly at their guns, cheers of 'Vive l'Empereur!' and even of 'Vive l'Amiral Villeneuve!' reverberated through the *Bucentaure*. 'It is impossible, Monseigneur, to have shown greater enthusiasm and desire to fight than did the officers, sailors and soldiers of the *Bucentaure*', Magendie later reported to Admiral Decrès, 'everyone swearing again before the admiral and the eagle given us by the Emperor, to fight to the death'. With the mighty cheers ringing in their ears, 'we climbed back to the quarterdeck and went to our posts, and the Imperial flag was placed at the foot of the mainmast'. Like some ancient Egyptian god, the golden eagle beheld a fleet ready to meet its enemy and to die for that Imperial bird if needs be. 'The signal was given at nightfall to weigh anchor, and the entire navy was immediately moved by the greatest desire to fight. Those soldiers and sailors who were ill in hospital, deserted it, a large crowd of them gathering on the quayside to embark . . .' wrote Contamine to Naval Minister Decrès.

THE *SIRIUS*, ONE of Captain Henry Blackwood's four frigates (including *Euryalus*, *Phoebe* and *Naiad*) and two schooners (*Pickle* and *Weazle*) now comprising the inshore squadron reconnoitring Cadiz, was the first to spot movement in the Spanish harbour at 6 am on Saturday 19th October, and immediately signalled: 'Enemy have their topsail yards hoisted', followed in another sixty minutes by signal number 370, that the enemy's ships were coming out of port. Fifty miles to the south-west and two and a half hours later, upon receipt of this message, a much keyed-up Admiral Lord Nelson immediately gave the order for 'General chase, south east', followed by 'Prepare for battle'.

Nelson's actions were, nevertheless, a bit precipitous, for only two French frigates, the *Hermione* and *Thémis*, managed to clear the harbour at 7 o'clock that morning, with instructions to reconnoitre the strength of Blackwood's squadron. By one o'clock Villeneuve's frigates had been joined by part of Rear-Admiral Charles Magon's second division of the Observation Squadron, including the *Algésiras*, *Achille*, *Argonaute*, *Neptune*, *Héros*, *Duguay-Trouin* and *Bahama*, and a third frigate, the *Rhin*. However, unlike the composition of the fleet on 22nd July when they had met Admiral Calder, the Combined Fleet today had intermingled the French and Spanish ships (as a precaution no doubt against disloyal units) comprising four squadrons in all: the Observation Squadron of twelve ships under the command of Admiral Federico Gravina, the First Squadron of seven ships under Admiral Báltasar Hidalgo de Cisneros, including Villeneuve's flagship, *Bucentaure*; the Second Squadron under Admiral Ignacio María de Álava y Navarrete, also of seven ships, and finally the seven remaining vessels of the Third Squadron under Rear-Admiral Pierre Dumanoir Le Pelley. The failure to follow orders by resentful French and Spanish captains, compounded by feeble or contrary winds, rendered useless Villeneuve's impetuous plans for their immediate formation however, and the ships continued to come straggling out as best they could at any hour.

By six o'clock that evening, Magon's division was located some six miles west-south-west of the Cadiz lighthouse, when the rear-admiral deliberately refused to follow Villeneuve's order to anchor for the night, preferring to remain under sail and ready for action, as he kept an eye on the movements of Blackwood's squadron – which was following his own – neither party wandering far from the port of Cadiz throughout the night.

Daybreak on Sunday 20th October found an overcast sky, the wind out of the south-south-west having freshened considerably, as Admiral Magon reformed his division and at 6.45 am ordered a 'General chase' after three of Blackwood's squadron, the *Sirius*, *Euryalus* and the newly attached *Agamemnon*, which was forced to release its American merchantman as the British scurried off. At about the same time, Villeneuve was signalling the rest of the fleet to put to sea as the wind continued to freshen, accompanied by heavy rain and thickening fog. Perhaps he thought that with a bit of luck he might be able to lose the British after all.

As the entire fleet – with the exception of the *Rayo* – finally assembled outside the harbour, it was the first time several thousand of its 'sailors' had ever ventured beyond a beach. The ships were in no order whatsoever, and in the ensuing chaos one French seaman from Ville-neuve's flagship fell overboard, an embarrassing event for an irritable French admiral already despised by half the French fleet and most of the Spanish. It was not until 3 o'clock that afternoon that the Commander-in-Chief at long last had his fleet arranged in three columns, his own squadron – including the *Bucentaure, Redoutable, San Leandro, Neptune, Mont-Blanc, San Francisco de Asis, Duguay-Trouin, Formidable, Scipion, Santísima Trinidad, Héros, Neptuno* and *San Agustín* – in the centre, with Admiral Álava's second squadron – including *Pluton, Monarca, Fougueux, Santa Ana, Indomptable, San Justo* and *Intrépide* – off his port beam (to his left), and Federico Gravina's Observation Squadron to his starboard (or right-hand side) – the *San Juan Nepomuceno, Berwick, Príncipe de Asturias, Achille, San Ildefonso, Argonauta, Swift-sure, Algésiras, Montañes, Aigle* and *Bahama* – and *Rayo* would soon be trailing after them as they steered to the south-west in the direction of the Straits of Gibraltar.

At six o'clock on that evening, *Achille* signalled to *Bucentaure* with the news that eighteen sail of the British fleet had been spotted tailing them. The Combined Fleet, now eight to ten miles south-west of Cadiz, was ordered to prepare for battle while maintaining their south-westerly course. At this stage Admiral Gravina, on board the *Príncipe de Asturias*, as on 22nd July, was the senior commanding Spanish officer, leading the entire Combined Fleet with his Observation Squadron. At 11 pm Villeneuve gave the order for the three columns to converge into one to form a battle line. He did not want any nasty surprises during the night.

Dawn the next day, Monday, 21st October, 29 Vendémiaire of the Revolutionary year XIV, found the Combined Fleet under a cloudy sky and 'light airs' in a scattered formation nine miles long, a dozen miles from Cape Trafalgar (close to the entrance of the Straits) maintaining its southerly course. Meanwhile Nelson's entire fleet, now thirty-one sail strong, including the four frigates, reappeared on the horizon to the north-west, some dozen miles or so behind them, with the wind astern. The news that the British force was now much stronger than the one he had been expecting after the previous night's sighting, greatly agitated Admiral Villeneuve. He would have to re-think the situation. He needed time.

Having ordered his fleet to resume three cruising columns just forty minutes earlier, at 7 am he hurriedly signalled them to re-form into a single battle line, again in sailing order, and to man their action stations, but stay on the same course. The result was another sprawling display of naval ineptitude several miles long – hardly 'a line' at all, despite the

French commander's orders to straighten it and to close to one cable's distance (or 200 yards) between ships. By now they were just a few miles from the entrance to the Straits of Gibraltar. They had escaped from the British at Toulon and slipped past them in the West Indies when they were nearly this close, with a bit of luck they could do so again.

The moment Villeneuve had so dreaded, yet knew was inevitable, had come at last. He would finally have to make the decision . . . to stand and fight or run. Napoleon had issued orders for him to sail to Naples and, theoretically, the French Commander could use that excuse for fleeing and, as Decrès could well attest, Villeneuve was a past master at providing supremely logical excuses for his failings. Yet, even if he arrived at Naples he would be replaced immediately and sent to Paris to report and justify his most remarkable behaviour over the past several months. What is more, it was he who was always quoting the 'naval maxims' found in the signals book, spouting forth on honour, patriotism, duty and glory - what would everyone think if he now continued on his way, escaping instead of turning to face the enemy? For the next sixty minutes Pierre Villeneuve pondered on his dilemma while maintaining the course set for the Straits, which were now in sight, the decision he must make seemingly escaping him like the long white wake disappearing into the waters of the Atlantic.

Then at 8 am Villeneuve summoned the flag lieutenant, giving an order which was to astonish his Chief of Staff, Captain Jean Prigny, the ship's captain, Jean-Jacques Magendie, and Nelson himself: 'To wear together' – and thus turn back. The irrevocable step had now been taken and the fleet altered its southerly course slowly swinging round to a northerly one taking them back to Cadiz and on a near collision course with the Royal Navy. At the same time, this literally reversed the sailing order of the entire Franco-Spanish fleet, as each ship remained in the same position – as opposed to 'turning in succession' – but reversing its direction. Thus Rear-Admiral Dumanoir Le Pelley's division, formerly in the rear, now found itself in the van, and Admiral Gravina's Observation Squadron now the rear-guard, though the inexperienced captains and crews, with an unco-operative wind, found it impossible to form a traditional battle line as ordered. Indeed, temperamental winds were causing navigational problems for both fleets, as it veered to the south-west, then jumped suddenly to the north-west and then to points between. It was another hour and a half before the Combined Franco-Spanish fleet had executed Villeneuve's order.

By 10 am the Combined Fleet had finally changed direction, but formed an irregular, angular crescent, with some ships bunched together, others separated by enormous spaces, as they hauled slowly upwind in a northerly direction, the French frigates and brigs now sailing to the lee of the fleet, between them and the Spanish shore. If the two naval forces continued on their courses, a clash seemed inevitable.

Villeneuve could no longer escape the consequences of his decision. As he had been telling Decrès ever since leaving Toulon that the French navy could never defeat the British in an equal battle, nor even if the Royal Navy were one-third weaker than the French, he must have considered this almost a suicide mission. Perhaps he even preferred a quick (hopefully) and noble death at the hands of a worthy opponent such as Nelson, to returning home in ignominy to be stripped of both command and rank. He was a proud man who could not bear such humiliation. As Colonel Desbrière so succinctly put it, 'Given the situation in which he now found himself, it was perfectly clear that Villeneuve could not avoid a battle, even if he wanted to do so.'

It was not until 11 am that Admiral Villeneuve himself was finally able to see Nelson's entire fleet for the first time, the fleet which had harried him round half the world. It was now deployed before him in two columns and they would be within range of one another's guns before the hour was out. It was all happening just as he had expected. Although the wind remained very weak, the swell continued to grow, an ominous sign of a severe storm and high winds far out to sea. Dumanoir in the van was steering generally to the north-east as the order to close haul reduced the speed of the foremost vessels in an attempt to consolidate the battle line. Nevertheless, the slower ships in the rear now began falling to leeward, slowing down even more, while Gravina's rear-guard swung out in the wind to the west in an unwieldly fashion. Villeneuve was most intent upon tightening this straggling line, particularly in the centre where in some places ships were separated by hundreds of yards.*

Although in terms of gunpower the British were inferior – 2,148[1] as opposed to 2,568 for the Combined Fleet – in tactical terms they certainly were at an even greater disadvantage, the Franco-Spanish Fleet boasting an additional six ships of the line (which later greatly enhanced the effectiveness of their cross-fire), not to mention the numerically superior (albeit less well trained) manpower – nearly 30,000 strong compared to Nelson's force of a little over 17,000.[2]

*For their formation see appendix 3

Finally, at 11.30, with the fleets only minutes apart and converging irresistibly, Villeneuve ordered the combined squadrons to commence firing when the British came within range. The gods of war had won again.

After having received the signal from Captain Blackwood at 9.30 am on Saturday 19th October that the Combined Fleet had put to sea, the British Mediterranean Fleet of twenty-seven ships of the line, four frigates, one schooner and a cutter had sailed towards the south-east to cut off Villeneuve's anticipated escape, reaching the mouth of the Straits of Gibraltar at daybreak the following day. Finding no sign of the enemy (whom they had lost during the night), Nelson took advantage of a fresh southerly breeze wearing to the north-west where he felt sure he would find them. At 7 am on 20th October, *Phoebe* signalled excitedly to the *Victory* that she had just sighted the Combined Fleet to the north-east of them, sailing on a southerly course for the Straits. Nelson was right after all.

Lord Nelson pushed ahead under a press of sail, determined not to permit the elusive French Commander-in-Chief to slip away unscathed this time, and by noon the British fleet found itself some twenty-five miles south-west of Cadiz, standing to the west-north-west. Villeneuve's force was not yet in sight, however, which meant that there would be no confrontation on this day. By five o'clock that afternoon Blackwood telegraphed that the enemy fleet now appeared to be sailing in a more westerly direction, Nelson instructing him to keep a close eye on them during the night and, whatever happened, not to lose them. It was not until 8.40 pm that he brought the fleet round on a new south-westerly course to close the distance with the Franco-Spanish armada. Finding that he was advancing too quickly by 4 am the next morning Nelson, who had not been to bed at all, altered their course once again, bringing them round to the north-east. He was determined to remain in the tactically superior position of having the wind behind him, so as to be able to sweep down (if possible in those ill-assorted breezes) upon the Combined Fleet which, as it turned out, he judged with his usual remarkable skill.

At 5.40 am Lord Nelson gave the order for his fleet to alter course from the southerly direction it had been following parallel to the Combined Fleet, to the east-north-east, then to the east-south-east. This brought the immense war machine round, closing the gap between them and their opponents, as Nelson had signal number seventy-two hoisted for the British fleet to deploy in two battle columns. When they were about twenty-one miles north-east of Cape Trafalgar, the Combined

Fleet was spotted half-way between the Cape and themselves, still heading for the Straits. Twenty minutes later, at 6 o'clock exactly, with the fleet now making a top speed of three knots, Nelson gave signal number thirteen, 'Prepare for battle', as the gun crews – twelve men to each pair of guns, 14,000 men altogether – opened their ports and ran their artillery out. The decks were washed down and covered with sand (to prevent the possibility of fire and to absorb the flow of blood and reduce the slipperiness), all fires were doused, loose furniture and equipment stowed in the main hold or simply thrown overboard (along with any live cattle that remained on board). Meanwhile the powder magazines were opened and readied and the bulkheads separating different compartments removed throughout the ship or lifted up and hooked to the beams of the above deck, and replaced by heavy, water-soaked, felt fire curtains. The arms lockers were opened and muskets, pistols, cutlasses and pikes issued to the crews and troops. When all was in readiness the men were piped below for a hurried last dinner of cold meat, cheese, wine or grog. They were to need all the energy they could muster.

At 7.40 am Nelson ordered the captains of his four frigates to come aboard for special instructions – a fifth one having been dispatched to fetch Rear-Admiral Louis. He greeted them in his usual, everyday, threadbare blue frockcoat with its four weather-beaten orders of knighthood across his chest (making a perfect target for marksmen, Blackwood pointed out). Collingwood already had his orders, namely to form his column in the line of bearing, that is to say, like Nelson's one-and-a-half miles away to the windward, one ship following in the wake of the preceding one, though Collingwood was to remain under Nelson's orders until they actually came within range of the Combined Fleet's guns, an order Collingwood was to disregard.

At half-past eight one of Collingwood's ships signalled the unexpected news that the Combined Fleet was suddenly altering its course and heading straight for Cadiz and the British fleet! An astonished Nelson stood speechless and puzzled. No one, least of all Nelson, knew what Villeneuve had in mind. Was he trying to make for the safety of Cadiz or was he about to face him, man to man, at long last?

Puzzled or no, the business of the fleet had to continue and further signals were ordered hoisted by Nelson and, after 8.45 am, chiefly by Collingwood, who unilaterally assumed command of his column now, ordering some ships to change places in order to speed up their approach to the enemy's line. It was part of the Nelson magic that men who were normally limited and cautious, such as Collingwood, under Nelson's infectious presence felt suddenly freed of their usual diffidence and inhibitions and were now capable of anything. Nelson for his part seemed to understand intuitively this effect he had on his men and refrained from reprimanding them for most wayward actions, at least directly. Therefore, when Collingwood ordered his lee column of fifteen ships to form a tauter line by hauling to the wind, Nelson overrode this action silently and simply by sailing faster himself. The little tug-of-war between the two admirals was not over yet, however, Collingwood now putting on more sail intent on being the first to cross the enemy's battle line. 'See how that noble fellow Collingwood carries his ship into action!' Nelson laughed. This, though, did not prevent Nelson from showing Admiral Collingwood his disapproval, and when at 9.30 am Collingwood ordered Captain Hargood of the *Belleisle* to come up from fifteenth place to second, immediately astern of him, Nelson countered by ordering Captain Duff of *Mars* to take that same position behind Collingwood in the *Royal Sovereign*! Nelson was still boss and Collingwood was not to forget that, while the signals officers of both flagships no doubt enjoyed the little esoteric skirmish, though it was *Belleisle* who did indeed ultimately take second place.*

Now sailing in formation, they were, however, missing their third column, the Advance Squadron, which had been a part of the original Nelson plan and which was to have included *Mars, Colossus, Defence, Ajax, Agamemnon* and *Belleisle* (most of which ultimately went instead to Collingwood). Nelson of course had been counting on the reappearance of Louis' squadron of six ships, but they had been detained near Gibraltar, thus requiring some last-minute changes.

British ships were now ordered 'To interchange places in the line or order of sailing', 'To take a station astern of the ships whose distinguishing signal will be shown', 'To keep in close order' but, more frequently than all the others, 'To make more sail', followed by an even more imperative, and Nelson's favourite, 'Make all sail possible with safety to the masts' – or put on every sail in the locker! So far most of Nelson's signals had been standard ones for arranging a fleet as it approached the enemy, and were simply referred to by number.

Like Villeneuve, Nelson had encountered some manoeuvring problems due to the feeble wind as his two columns were nearing their opponents, the lack of order among his fleet being nearly as irritating to him as the Combined Fleet's was to Villeneuve. In some instances both the *Victory*

*For the formation of the two columns see appendix 3

and *Royal Sovereign* had ordered certain ships which were sailing too slowly and holding up the advance to fall back to a later place in the line, but this was sometimes only achieved after a spate of impatient signals.

A true Northumbrian, Collingwood was pushing ahead with no eye to the finesse required in leading his men, a finesse that came so naturally to Nelson. Indeed Collingwood's column started to disintegrate much too soon, well before coming under French and Spanish gunfire, whereas Nelson's more or less maintained its formation as a proper unit, sweeping down on the enemy as he ordered, though even he had problems with three vessels. One, the 64-gun *Africa*, found herself separated from the fleet during the night and was now far north of the battle line, rather than in her assigned sixth position, while another, the 74-gun *Orion*, was too far to the south, nearly half-way to Collingwood's column. Then there was Rear-Admiral Lord Northesk's ship, the 100-gun *Britannia*. It had fallen out, and remained out, of Nelson's column early on, though it had, in theory, been assigned to lead the second division of six ships. Indeed, Northesk, with almost Villeneuvian skill, managed to remain not only out of the battle line, behind Nelson, but out of most of the subsequent battle as well, when both the *Victory* and *Royal Sovereign* were nearly overwhelmed in the heat of fighting, surrounded and badly in need of her support. Because of the fortunate outcome of the battle, however, no inquiry was ever launched into Northesk's most peculiar behaviour that day.

An unscheduled race now developed between the ship second in Nelson's column, the *Téméraire*, and the *Victory* as they approached the enemy line, a race to be first to engage the enemy. But there was more than just sport involved here, for Nelson's officers rightly felt it was both foolhardy and dangerous for the commanding officer – upon whom the entire fleet depended – to expose himself needlessly by being the first ship crossing the hostile line, which would soon be receiving the full brunt of enemy gunfire for up to thirty minutes before any effective help could be expected from supporting vessels. Captain Blackwood was selected as spokesman for the concerned officers and he duly broached this delicate subject with his chief during the last half-hour before the fighting began. Blackwood suggested that he might want to direct the battle from his ship, the *Euryalus* as, from a distance, he could get a more complete general picture of what was happening. His alternative proposal was that Nelson allow the second, third and fourth ships of his line to precede the *Victory*. Nelson, however, would not even consider leaving his flagship, though he finally relented so far as to permit the second ship,

Téméraire, to precede him. Even so, only minutes before the first shots were fired, a mischievous Nelson ordered Captain Hardy to put on more sail in order to prevent Captain Harvey of the *Téméraire* from ever carrying out his orders.

Beneath a cloudy sky and with a slight west-north-westerly breeze behind them, the British fleet – each ship with two Union flags (in case one was shot down), one at the main topmast stay, another at the fore topgallant stay, and the white St George's ensign streaming – were closing the gap of the last few thousand yards between them and the Franco-Spanish battle line. At 11.25 am a long and fairly complex message began to be hoisted from the three masts and rigging of the *Victory*, a signal never before seen in the annals of the Royal Navy: 'England expects that every man will do his duty'. It was followed by a gradually increasing roar as thousands of sailors cheered their chief. Then came signals sixty-three and eight for the British fleet to anchor at the conclusion of the battle. This may have seemed odd to some midshipmen and younger officers approaching their first sea fight on this the 21st October, but, once the battle began, masts and yards would be shot away, ships would be dispersed over several square miles and thus this was the last occasion such a message could be relayed to all the ships of the fleet. In fact, by now, though the westerly wind was still weak, a low-pressure area was moving in and the ground swell growing at an alarming rate, warning an alert Nelson that gale-force winds far to the west were pushing these seas and would be upon them later that day at a time when many disabled ships would be unable to sail and in danger of being blown out of control upon the shoals and rocky shore round San Pedro and Cape Trafalgar. Ships at anchor would stand a better chance of avoiding this.

Nelson's last telegraphic message, for which there was no number, came at 11.40 am: 'I intend to push or go through the end of the enemy's line to prevent them from getting into Cadiz'. It was sent to only one ship, Collingwood's *Royal Sovereign*, just as she was coming under enemy fire.

By now Nelson definitely knew he was not going to be able to adhere to his original much vaunted battle plan that he had presented in his famous Memorandum, for he still did not know where the French Commander-in-Chief's ship was located and that information was essential. Ordinarily it would have been easy enough to find, even without a flag, as it would have been one of the largest three-deckers in the centre of their battle line, but, in fact, Villeneuve's flagship was the smallest three-decker available, an 80-gun ship, scarcely distinguishable from the 74s. Furthermore, Nelson was stymied by the higgledy-piggledy Franco-Spanish battle line, with bunches of ships, rather than the expected order of single ones, which would be impossible to pierce completely and attack in his planned spear-like fashion. Inadvertently, the hapless Villeneuve had established the one formation that did not fit the British plan. What is more, Lord Nelson really thought the French commander – having refused to hoist his flag and thereby revealing his position – might be having cold feet once again and preparing to break away to Cadiz. The fleet appeared to be in cruising – not battle – order, steering straight for Cadiz, which was only about twenty miles distant, and even if they did not make a break for it now at the outset of hostilities, they might attempt to seek refuge there later on. This led to Nelson's change of mind at 11.40 am when he decided to push through for the head of the Combined Fleet rather than for its centre. This signal took everyone by surprise, even Collingwood, one admiral who did not appreciate the naval virtuosity involved in such last-minute changes. What was happening?

In fact, for another five minutes, Nelson was still planning to strike at the van (Dumanoir's division), when, suddenly, at 11.45 am, the Combined Fleet (all except the *Bucentaure*) hoisted their colours, opening fire as they did so, the *Fougueux* letting out her topsail, foresail and topgallantsail in a feverish attempt to block the passage of the *Royal Sovereign* as she neared her.

Then at the last possible moment prior to making the final manoeuvre and entering the enemy line, everything was changed. Nelson spotted Villeneuve's hesitant flag being hoisted from the mast of the *Bucentaure* and, in a flash, he dropped his plans for attacking the head of the fleet and reverted to the former ones for sealing off the centre and attacking his opposite number. Only the alertness of his captain, Thomas Hardy, meant this could be translated into reality. Hardy hoped to pass under the stern of Villeneuve's flagship, but Captain Magendie of the *Bucentaure* did his best to discourage this. 'I gave orders to fire several well-directed volleys and a fusillade at her [*Victory*], but they failed to destroy all her rigging', Magendie noted. At the same time another French ship, the *Redoutable*, closed upon the *Bucentaure* so that *Victory* could not squeeze through, Hardy then bringing her astern of this interloper instead. Captain Hardy was as determined as Nelson to cross the enemy line and no one would stop him, cost what it may.

At 11.50 am, just as the first enemy shot fell close to his ship, Admiral Lord Nelson was standing on the poop with Captain Hardy, and Captain Blackwood was taking his leave to return to his ship. Nelson called him

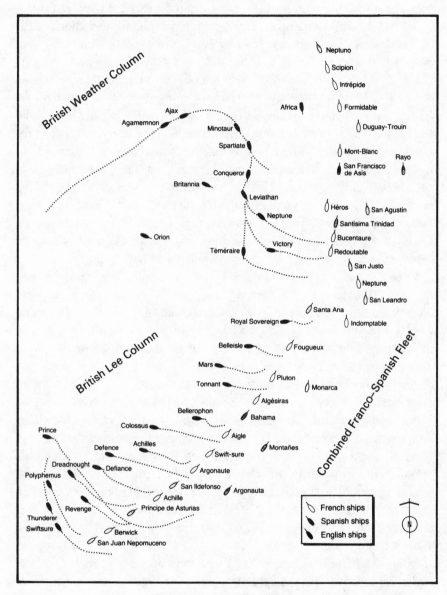

Commencement of hostilities.

back to inform him of his change of plans, that he would go for the centre of the enemy line at the thirteenth or fourteenth ship after all, and not for the van. Blackwood rushed off with orders to inform the ships directly astern of *Victory*, as shots from *Santísima Trinidad* and *Redoutable* peppered the sea, and Nelson's last general order rose quickly up the masts of *Victory*: 'Engage the enemy more closely.' Far off his port beam and to the north, the lone *Africa* could be seen running the gauntlet, under fire from Dumanoir's van and trying desperately to get back to her Commander-in-Chief's column, but in vain, for she was too far away and too late.

As hundreds of French and Spanish 32-, 24-, 18- and 12-pounders roared at him, an excited Nelson shouted, 'I'll give them such a dressing as they never had before!' though in no position yet even to return their fire. Collingwood signalled a final frantic message, that Villeneuve was on board the frigate *Rhin*, but he was mistaken and in any event *Victory* was already committed as, at 12.04 pm, she was about to crash through the enemy line, clouds of virgin black smoke belching forth from her foremost port guns. Meanwhile, a thousand yards off his starboard quarter, Nelson could see Collingwood's column, in practically no formation whatsoever, disappearing behind a curtain of wood, canvas and flashing guns.

If Nelson had been uncertain about how or where he would first attack the opposing line, the French were left just as uncertain about their onrushing opponent, and then taken by surprise, as Major-General Théodore Contamine, commanding the fleet's French marines and on deck with Villeneuve, relates. Nelson led his column, which followed 'in some disorder heading for our line ... Four of our ships, *Héros*, *Santísima Trinidad*, *Bucentaure* and *Redoutable*, presented him with a very brisk and solid wall of fire as he approached. All four of them were drawn up in a tight line and it did not seem possible for him to be able to cut through it at this place. *Victory* first wanted to pass astern of the *Santísima Trinidad*, the ship before us [*Bucentaure*]. We even thought she was going to board her; but just as she was about to do that, she suddenly fell off to her starboard, passing behind us. Now within musket range, she received several broadsides from our ships, including a terrible fusillade [by the marines] which caused her considerable damage; but it was not enough to prevent her from cutting through our line.'

At 12.15 pm the *Victory* received the first effective salvos fired into her port quarter from the French flagship, which was still steering in a northerly direction under the colourless grey Trafalgar sky, as clouds of black smoke settled gradually across French and Spanish gunports and decks, concealing the feverish activity of thousands of men. It now became apparent that the *Bucentaure* and *Redoutable* were indeed 'making an incredible effort to lock her [*Victory*] out', as Captain Prigny later confirmed, forcing Nelson at the last minute to abandon his intention of passing under the stern of the French flagship and dropping behind *Redoutable* instead, followed by *Téméraire*, while *Neptune* more success-fully cut in behind *Bucentaure*, followed in turn by *Leviathan*. Regardless of the difficulties they were encountering, Nelson was still intent upon slicing the enemy fleet cleanly in two, if it was at all possible, and had maintained his column for that precise purpose. On the other hand, Admiral Collingwood was failing to pierce his section of the rear-guard very effectively. Instead, six of his fifteen vessels concentrated on the last three ships of the Combined Fleet, the *San Juan Nepomuceno*, the French *Berwick*, and Gravina's flagship, *Príncipe de Asturias*.

Moments later Lord Nelson's secretary, John Scott, standing next to Captain Hardy on the quarterdeck, was truncated by a round shot. Meanwhile the enormous swell carried the *Victory* lurching forwards, as the French Captain Lucas's *Redoutable* maintained an almost ceaseless fire from her thirty-seven port-side guns, whilst *Victory*, coming at her bow first, remained almost helpless to retaliate, having so few guns in that forward direction. Behind *Victory*, *Téméraire* and *Neptune* were now breaking through the line. It was a 'hazardous . . . even desperate move' by Nelson, naval historian Julian Corbett admitted, as the weak British attack fizzled out into a near standstill, leaving Nelson's fairly isolated ship stranded in a lethal cross-fire. However, in spite of the French and Spanish ships' efforts to bunch up and keep out more of the British men of war, a large gap of nearly three-quarters of a mile opened between the first fourteen ships of the Combined Fleet's van, of which *Redoutable* was the last, and the first of the remaining nineteen ships, the *Santa Ana*. The enemy's fleet was severed as Nelson had hoped, but not by *his* ships.

Five hundred yards away *Bucentaure*'s guns now opened a barrage of fire, tearing right through *Victory*'s mizen topmast, bringing it down while she was still in a relatively defenceless position. The ship's masts – the mainmast, the largest one in the centre, the foremast ahead of it, and the mizenmast abaft (in the rear) – quickly became pockmarked with shot. Other shelling, mainly from the French *Redoutable*, smashed the enor-mous double-wheel not far behind Nelson, requiring the ship to be steered thereafter by the master and a lieutenant from the gunroom, far below deck. More double-headed shot rained over them, killing and wounding some dozen Royal Marines near Nelson and forcing him to order their commanding officer to remove them to safer quarters. Far above them, other shot carried away her fore topmast and yardarm, destroying the ship's two launches (stored on the booms), smashing part of the quarterdeck and whistling all round and between Nelson and

Hardy, a splinter shredding the buckle of one of Hardy's shoes in the process. 'This is too warm work, Hardy, to last long,' Nelson smiled, but neither of them moved to shelter. The *Victory* was taking a severe beating.

It was only now, however, as two French 74s, the *Neptune* (not to be confused with the nearby British ship of the same name) and *Redoutable* closed menacingly on *Victory*'s lee (starboard) quarter that Thomas Hardy realised they simply could not 'push ahead' as planned, so intense was the unexpected resistance they were meeting. It was obvious, Hardy pointed out, that he could never get to *Bucentaure* without colliding with one of the other ships blocking the way, and Nelson quipped: 'Take your choice!' By now *Victory* had already suffered some fifty casualties, had her studsail booms on the foremast destroyed, 100 square yards of her immense foresail were left hanging in shreds, and she still was not yet in a position to let off her first full broadside!

All British ships carried, in addition to their rated (official) firepower, other weapons, including between eight and fourteen deadly 32-pound short-range ship-smashing carronades. Unlike the other ships, however, *Victory* mounted instead two mighty 68-pound carronades on her forecastle (the raised deck at the bow), weapons ideal for use at very close quarters with an enemy and rigging, but which could not be reloaded quickly.

At one o'clock Captain Hardy gave the order to fire the 68-pounder (filled with one cannon ball and a keg of 500 musket balls) located on the port side of the forecastle into *Bucentaure*'s stern cabin windows, as *Victory*'s fifty double- and treble-shotted port-side guns raked the vessel at long last. The *Victory* now passed so closely that her yard-arms brushed against her opponent's as the 186-foot ship rolled in the ground swell. But while she still could not get in the right position to tackle Villeneuve's ship, her guns killed or wounded many dozens of men and dismounted twenty French guns. After firing at the *Victory* with impunity for nearly half an hour, it was finally *Bucentaure*'s turn to take a beating, Captain Magendie acknowledging that they received 'several devastating salvos' from her. A stunned Villeneuve now seemed incapable of giving the orders necessary to extricate himself or to disentangle the knot of ships round him, and 'no other vessel' came to his aid, Magendie complained. The noise of the powerful port guns was more deafening than the worst thunder storm; the British gun crews and their officers were caught in the sweltering and suffocating clouds of thick gunsmoke in the cramped gundecks where a man could scarcely stand upright, their eardrums bursting as the recoil threw them backwards, streams of sweat or blood

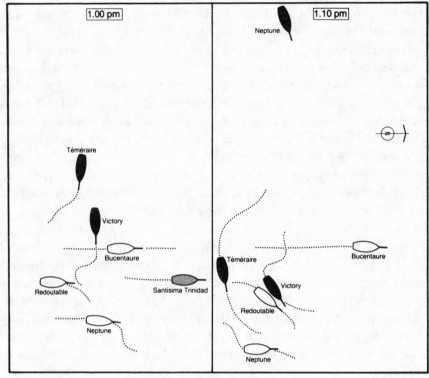

Victory engaging *Bucentaure*.

tracing across blackened bodies stripped to the waist. To the smoke on
the quarter deck was added a pall of fine wood dust drifting over them
from Villeneuve's pulverised ship.

An hour after crossing the enemy line, the *Victory* was continuing to
come under very heavy fire from the French, especially from the
Bucentaure and Commodore Maistral's powerful 80-gun *Neptune*, firing
primarily at *Victory*'s bow, while *Redoutable*'s effective broadsides raked
Victory's starboard side. As unrelenting as the cannonading were the
accompanying cries of agony of hundreds of unseen human beings from a
dozen nations, men and boys whose bodies were rent asunder by this
folly, only to be drowned out by the big guns.

By now French guns had shattered *Victory*'s flying jib-boom, bowsprit
and topsail yards, had severely damaged the thick timbers composing the
catheads (from which anchors were hoisted and lowered), had landed
several shot in her hull 'between wind and water' (the area between the
water level and deck), had destroyed two of her anchors and badly
damaged her foremast.

Having passed *Bucentaure*, Captain Hardy suddenly put *Victory*'s helm hard a-port in order to get at the *Redoutable* which had been causing such havoc as the murderous enfilade in which *Victory* had been caught up continued. Relief was in sight, however, as Captain Harvey's 98-gun *Téméraire* now pulled out of *Victory*'s wake passing to starboard of *Redoutable* and the French *Neptune*, firing into them both and drawing more and more French gunfire to herself, though *Victory*'s port side still lay completely exposed. Captain Hardy, however, timed and executed his move perfectly at 1.10 pm as he brought *Victory*'s starboard side crashing into *Redoutable*'s port side, their anchors striking and the sails of the *Victory* and *Redoutable* catching each other, locking the two warships together in a lethal embrace at the very moment *Téméraire* was passing off *Redoutable*'s starboard beam. The French ship had managed to roll her port-side guns in and close most of the lower-deck ports (where the larger guns were mounted) just before the collision, but this did not prevent *Victory*'s middle- and lower-deck starboard guns from blasting the hull from point-blank range while her upper guns swept the French decks. If some of *Redoutable*'s upper-deck 12-pounders were out of action, many of her main-deck guns continued to fire into the *Victory*, aided by the effective use of hand-grenades and musketry by sharpshooters up in her tops and through those few gun ports which remained open.

Because of the extreme danger of fire to sails and yards, Nelson had forbidden the deployment of sharpshooters aloft, unlike the French for whom the benefits of such a practice seemed to outweigh the risks. The French and British also varied in their gunnery objectives, the French generally aiming their big guns at masts and yards to disable their foe, while the British preferred to concentrate many of their heavy guns on the hulls of their opponents, though not excluding higher targets. Both sides fought with an unimaginable ferocity and bravery, neither side giving an inch as Hardy and the valiant, if greatly outgunned Lucas continued, their warships slowly drifting eastward. Despite the dearth of gun crews, several of the *Victory*'s port guns were also manned, their deadly volleys reaching the damaged *Bucentaure* and *Santísima Trinidad*.

Nelson and Hardy were walking abreast of one another and studying the situation before them, pacing the twenty-one foot stretch of quarter deck between the shattered wheel and the cabin ladder when, at 1.25 pm, in the din of battle, the dapper one-armed Admiral silently fell to his knees, supporting his slight body with his remaining arm, then collapsing on the very spot where his secretary had been killed shortly before. A ball from a French sharpshooter's musket in the mizen topmast of the

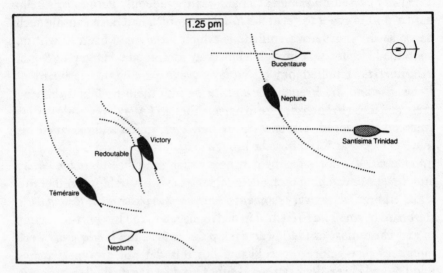

Redoutable engaging *Victory*.

Redoutable had pierced his left shoulder, tearing through the thick gold epaulette and his lung, finally lodging in his spine. Captain Hardy quickly ordered three men nearby to carry him to the surgeon's cockpit below the gun deck while the fighting continued to rage, gunfire spraying the upper deck of *Victory* bringing down some forty marines in a matter of minutes and sending everyone else scurrying for safety. The battle which had begun just before noon was now at its very height and would not begin to tail off for another hour and a half.

By this time most of the *Victory*'s upper-deck 12-pounders had been put out of action as a result of *Redoutable*'s intense and unrelenting fire, though some of her 24- and 32-pounders on the middle and lower decks continued as *Neptune* and other British ships in her wake came under the stern of *Bucentaure*, bombarding her port guns and those of the *Santísima Trinidad* close by while training their starboard guns on *Redoutable* and taking a very heavy toll on French crews and their guns. If *Victory* was receiving severe treatment from the French, Lucas' powerful *Redoutable* was suffering even more awesome damage and casualties from the double- and even treble-shotted cannonades along her port side at point-blank range from *Victory*'s guns which were literally scraping against the French ship's hull. *Téméraire* came astern and then between *Redoutable* and *Neptune*, and fired broadsides into *Redoutable*'s other, starboard beam, but still the French would not surrender. Carried by the ground swell, *Victory* and *Redoutable* now drifted slowly to the south-east, bringing them closer to Captain Eliab Harvey's *Téméraire*, herself under heavy fire from *Neptune*'s port guns which were in the process of shooting away *Téméraire*'s main topmast and badly damaging her fore yard.

A quarter of an hour after Nelson fell, the battered *Redoutable* crashed helplessly into the *Téméraire*, the French bowsprit passing over Harvey's quarter deck, which his crew quickly lashed to his ship, while *Redoutable*'s side also remained joined to the *Victory*. The French ship could not budge. Harvey now turned every available gun, including most of his fourteen 32-pound carronades, on the unfortunate *Redoutable*, remorselessly raking her hull and deck and inflicting appalling casualties on the most valiant French crew, which, of course, had just done the same to *Victory*, completely clearing her decks.

Despite her by now utterly dilapidated state, the French not only refused to surrender their ship, but even brazenly gathered a party of men to board the much disabled *Victory*! Nelson had wanted his pell-mell battle . . . Suddenly a group of British officers and marines appeared on deck (having come up unseen from the middle and lower decks) forcing the astonished French to remain on board and run for cover. Though the British suffered another few dozen casualties just in this single repulse, those of the French were continuing to mount even higher, much higher, as *Téméraire*'s carronades did their deadly work from the other side. Yet even now, with their ship a floating wreck, the French would not give in and continued with musketry fire from the tops and yard-arms, accompanied by 'hand-grenades' hurled down below. Some of these, falling short, landed in *Redoutable* and set fire to her starboard rigging, which was also entangled in *Téméraire*'s foresail, spreading the flames to both ships. The crews – French and British alike – then dropped their weapons in order to man the pumps to quench what could easily have proven to be a calamitous inferno, while on board the *Victory*, crews were rushed up from below to put out another fire spreading among some rigging and canvas on the booms.

Exhausted, in a state of shock and barely conscious now, Captain Lucas at last struck his colours, surrendering in order to prevent any further slaughter of his men. Two midshipmen from the *Victory*, accompanied by a mere ten marines, descended to their one remaining boat in tow at the stern and rowed the short distance over to *Redoutable* where they accepted the swords of the one or two remaining French officers still standing.

Even as Captain Harvey was beginning to catch his breath on board

Téméraire, the French 74-gun *Fougueux*, under the command of Captain
Louis Beaudouin, who had just left a skirmish with the British *Belleisle*,
to leeward of the *Royal Sovereign* and *Santa Ana*, sailed up, crossing the
gap of many hundreds of yards of open sea and now ranged close
alongside *Téméraire*, giving that immobile ship a terrific broadside. In
fact, by this stage *Téméraire* looked almost as battered as the *Redoutable*.
As both her Union flags had been shot away, Beaudouin thought that
she had in fact struck her colours, and prepared to board the mighty
three-decker. Like most of the British ships at Trafalgar, Captain
Harvey's 98-gun ship, which should have had a crew of close to 1,000
men, had been sent to war with only 660 (about the same complement as
a French 74!), which casualties had by now reduced to about 550, and
Beaudouin no doubt thought that the bleak-looking ship's crew had
been decimated.

Nevertheless Captain Beaudouin had seriously misjudged the situation, for Harvey was not even considering surrendering. Below decks,
Lieutenant Thomas Kennedy shifted crews from the port to the
starboard to man those fresh guns, keeping his men out of sight until
Fougueux got within a mere 100 yards of her. Without any warning,
Kennedy then gave the order for a most unexpected and terrible
broadside of forty-nine guns, followed several moments later by yet
another. At two o'clock a mortally wounded Captain Beaudouin was no
doubt stunned to find that his superb ship was now a veritable wreck, with
masts, spars and timbers raining down from every direction, and out of
control, crashing into the *Téméraire*! Captain Harvey immediately had the
French ship's fore rigging lashed to his spare anchor as the ubiquitous
Lieutenant Kennedy appeared, bounding on deck gathering the only
twenty-two men they could spare, and boarded Beaudouin's smouldering
ship. Ten minutes later the last of the French surrendered and the Union
flag rose over the *Fougueux* as well. Her captain, Louis Beaudouin, was
found on his quarter deck lying in a pool of blood, his sword near his hand
where it had fallen.

Five minutes later the *Victory* was finally able to disentangle herself
from the *Redoutable*. Dozens of men using the fire booms managed to
extricate her, *Victory*'s shattered bowsprit swinging free to the north.
Harvey, aboard the *Téméraire*, was now in charge of both French prizes –
Fougueux and *Redoutable* – and drifted in a southerly direction, just as the
main- and mizen masts of *Redoutable* crashed down, bringing with them
her remaining sails and even a few sharpshooters who had been holding
out in the tops. Her mainmast, falling right across the deck of the British

ship, severed the stump of *Téméraire*'s mizen topmast, smashing part of the poop deck, and crushing several bodies beneath the enormous pile of wreckage. Meanwhile the French *Neptune* continued to lay down a cannonade against *Téméraire*. The British ship tried to protect herself with her few remaining free guns, while many French shells also landed on the French prizes. With the sight of *Leviathan* coming to the rescue, however, *Neptune* ceased firing and bore away.

For the *Victory*, *Téméraire* and their two captured vessels, the battle was over by half past two. The *Victory*, the largest British first-rate, had had her mizen topmast shot away, while the mizenmast itself was left tottering, her fore- and mainmasts and their yards, bowsprit, jib-boom, and rigging all very badly shot up. Her enormous hull had proved to be a superb target for French cannoneers who had shattered it in many places above the waterline, while much of the outer woodwork along the gun ports was also badly shot through, and the starboard cathead had been blown right away. Her casualties were remarkably light considering the sustained intensity of the fighting, 57 dead and 102 wounded, among them Nelson.

The cockpit to which Nelson had been taken by marine Sergeant Secker and two sailors was a shallow deck immediately beneath the lowest gun deck, where the full brunt of the recoiling 32-pounder above them deafened eardrums and caused mighty oak timbers to shudder. It was a terrible place to bring the wounded and dying, but a British battleship was intended for one purpose only, to spew out death, not to allay it. The head of the cockpit was enclosed by a series of small rooms or lockers, barely wide enough for a man to stand in, one of which was designated as the ship's dispensary. As for 'hospital quarters', there were none, casualties being placed on the red-painted deck wherever a large enough space could be found, and today every inch was taken by the steady stream of wounded. As for the dead, they were simply thrown overboard. The thirty-seven-year-old Chaplain, Alexander Scott, was so sickened by what he saw there that day, that in the ensuing years he only referred to it once, with a succinct, 'it was like a butcher's shambles!'

Nelson was squeezed in about half-way along the deck in a recess on the port side. The ship's surgeon, Dr William Beatty, had the Admiral's clothes removed and replaced by a sheet as he examined and cleaned the wound, but he quickly realised there was nothing to be done. All round him lay officers, marines and seamen with a variety of wounds. Nelson could not long survive his own, the musket ball having gone completely through his lung. 'He felt "a gush of blood"', the chaplain said, who remained by his side. 'I felt it [the musket ball] break my back', Nelson told him weakly. The ball was indeed lodged in his spine and he lost all feeling below the waist, the internal haemorrhaging making any speech very difficult. Constantly thirsty, he was given lemonade and then water and wine. He was most anxious about Emma and Horatia. Naturally he was also concerned about what was happening in the battle and called for Captain Hardy – the good-natured Dorsetman who had served under him at both the battles of the Nile and Copenhagen. At nearly half past three, Hardy came down to see Nelson for the last time, informing him that they had already captured about fifteen enemy ships. 'I wish I had not left the deck, for I shall soon be gone', Nelson whispered, reminding Hardy that he must signal the fleet to anchor after the battle. It was then that Nelson asked him to give him the now famous parting embrace. The burly, but gentle Hardy kneeled awkwardly, kissed Nelson's forehead and then left quickly with tears in his eyes. Dr Beatty could no longer detect a pulse in his cold wrist. After receiving a final report that victory was theirs, Horatio Lord Nelson died at 4.30 pm. Meanwhile, however, the battle continued to rage and more men died.

Like the *Victory*, Captain Harvey's *Téméraire* had also suffered substantial damage. Her main topmast, the head of her mizenmast, her fore- and topsail yards shot away, while her remaining fore- and mainmasts were left in what the Royal Navy termed a 'tottering state', that is, so shot up as to be unfit to carry any sail. They would have to be replaced, as would her bowsprit, which provided support for the foremast. Her starboard cathead and bumpkin (the colourful name for the boom used to extend the foresail off the bow) were also shot away, as was part of her rudder, and 'Her rigging of every sort was cut to pieces', said William James. On the starboard side, eight feet of the lower deck next to the mainmast had caved in and the galleries there had been cut right off. She suffered a total of 123 casualties.

Captain Lucas' ship, the *Redoutable*, was left devastated, and that anyone survived the ordeal it had been through unscathed was little short of a miracle. Her main- and mizenmasts had been shot away, along with her fore topmast and bowsprit. Her rudder was shattered, her hull shot up everywhere, above and below water. Twenty-two of her guns had been dismounted or destroyed. Of her original crew of 643, 487 were killed and 81 wounded, leaving only 75 to man the ship. 88 per cent of her crew were put out of commission, a total of 568 men; among the survivors, a severely wounded and most valiant Captain Lucas. Later, writing on a wintry January day in 1806 from a prisoner-of-war camp in Berkshire, a convalescing Lucas praised the efforts of his superb men and those who had died in this 'bloody business off Cape Trafalgar', claiming for them a 'distinguished place in the annals of the French Navy'.

Beaudouin's ship the *Fougueux* suffered far less, at this stage, and had perhaps a little more than forty casualties, which included Captain Beaudouin himself who was to die of his wounds. In the storm that followed the battle, however, all her damaged masts collapsed and she foundered on the Spanish coast, resulting in a total of 532 casualties (most drowning) of her crew of 650.

Nevertheless, none of these figures in any way begin to tell of the woeful pain suffered by the dying or wounded who survived, some suffering from untreatable burns, others with arms and legs blown off or left dangling by bits of muscle and ligament, the remaining bone often crushed, or with eyes, head and body pierced by musket balls and metal and wooden splinters of all kinds.

Meanwhile, the British *Neptune*, having followed in Nelson's column, finally found herself close under the stern of Villeneuve's flagship at 1.45 pm, firing a broadside as she passed and levelling both *Bucentaure*'s main- and mizenmast right down to the deck. It was either incredible luck, or superb gunnery. Meanwhile *Leviathan*, following in *Neptune*'s wake, also poured a mighty volley into the *Bucentaure*'s already shattered stern from a distance of just thirty yards. She then passed, ceding her place to *Conqueror*, which would not be denied her turn, firing further broadsides into what remained of *Bucentaure*'s stern, cabins, lee quarter and beam, blasting her foremast into the sea and leaving her completely dismasted. 'Having anticipated our possible dismasting', Villeneuve wrote after the battle, 'I had had a boat lowered with the intention of transferring my flag to another vessel', but now he found it had been sunk. 'I had the *Santísima Trinidad* hailed, she being just ahead of us, asking her to send a boat for me and a tow for the ship. I received no reply.'

By 4.15 pm *Bucentaure*'s position was quite hopeless. Every officer on the upper deck had been killed or wounded, though some remained below decks. Captain Magendie had been shot in the face, and Captain Prigny had shrapnel in his right leg, even midshipman Donadieu (who had earlier helped parade the Imperial eagle) was wounded, but the French Commander-in-Chief survived unscathed. 'Admiral Villeneuve complained most bitterly', Captain Prigny noted in his battle report, 'having been spared in the midst of that hail of bullets and bursting shells.' It was all over, said Magendie. 'All rigging gone, entirely dismasted, having lost all the men on the upper decks, the battery of 24-pounders left totally 'dismounted and unmanned by the dead and wounded, the starboard guns covered by the fallen rigging, spars and timber, with close to 450 casualties and no longer even being in a state to defend ourselves . . . surrounded by 5 enemy ships, with no help in sight . . . Admiral Villeneuve had no choice but to put an end to this, to prevent the further useless killing of any more brave people, which he then did after three and a quarter hours of fighting, after first throwing the débris of the Imperial eagle into the sea along with the ship's signals.'

'I had to yield to my fate,' Villeneuve acknowledged, and thus surrendered to Captain Israel Pellew of *Conqueror* who sent *one officer and five marines* to claim the flagship of the Combined Fleet! Upon reaching the quarterdeck the marine captain found an unharmed Admiral Villeneuve, the ship's captain, Magendie (with his hideous face wound), Major-General Contamine, and a couple of other officers who were escorted from the ship, *only two Royal Marines* left as a boarding party to hold the *Bucentaure*. It did not seem quite fitting. Through a mix-up of orders, however, the French officers were rowed over – not to *Conqueror* but to the nearby *Mars*.

Meanwhile, after discharging her broadside against the *Bucentaure*, Captain Thomas Fremantle's powerful 98-gun *Neptune* (carrying an additional fourteen 32-pound carronades) continued in the same direction to approach the stern of the imposing four-deck 136-gun *Santísima Trinidad*, ranging alongside her and firing across her decks. Captain Henry Bayntun on board the 74-gun *Leviathan*, following in the wake of *Neptune*, was about to give the order to open fire on the Spanish vessel when they heard a terrible crash and tearing noise, as both the main- and mizenmast of the mighty *Trinidad* came thundering down. *Neptune*'s superb gunnery was evident as she now luffed along the Spanish ship's lee side while the *Conqueror* gave Admiral Cisneros' flagship a broadside with her starboard guns. A few minutes later, at 2.30 pm, the captain of Cisneros' *Trinidad*, Commodore Francisco de Uriarte, saw her last remaining mast, the foremast, shrivelled to a stump, leaving Uriarte, in the words of William James, with 'an unmanageable wreck.'

Meanwhile, the 64-gun *Africa*, which had found herself far to the north of Nelson's column at the commencement of hostilities just before noon, had at long last reached the heart of the fighting, and brought her guns to bear on the limping monster, the *Trinidad*, just at the moment the British

Neptune was distracted briefly by Rear-Admiral Dumanoir's van squadron making its way to the south-west. Apparently unimpressed by her size as she literally towered like a giant over his own vessel, the smallest ship of the line in that battle, and seeing no colours flying from that Spanish four-decker, now motionless in the water, Captain Henry Digby sent a party from *Africa* to take possession of her. Once on board he approached a Spanish officer to accept his sword, only to be informed that the Spanish ship had *not* surrendered. Such was the etiquette of the age that the boarding party was permitted to withdraw and disembark unmolested!

For the next few hours the *Santísima Trinidad*, though no longer firing a shot and just drifting in the heaving swell, remained without a prize crew, when finally Captain Richard Grindall, of the 98-gun *Prince*, no doubt not believing his eyes, manned it and took Admiral Cisneros and Commodore Uriarte prisoner, both of whom had been badly wounded and numbered amongst the warship's 300 casualties.

Captain Pellew's *Conqueror* had already lost her mizen topmast and main topgallantmasts, with her fore- and mainmasts 'badly wounded', her rigging left hanging in shreds, and her hull greatly shot up, but for all that somehow had suffered only twelve casualties. As for *Neptune*, she found herself with damaged masts but still capable of supporting her sails, the nine shot in her hull no hindrance to navigation, and her casualties were limited to forty-four.

Earlier, after leaving *Neptune* to cope with the *Trinidad*, *Leviathan* had continued on her way heading straight for the 80-gun French *Neptune*. The latter was already under fire from some of the *Téméraire*'s forward guns, but her commander, Esprit Tranquille Maistral, apparently not liking the looks of the advancing *Leviathan*, now wore his ship and fled to windward. But *Leviathan*'s youthful captain, Henry Bayntun, was not to be completely disappointed as he now spotted the van squadron under Rear-Admiral Dumanoir beyond the *Santísima Trinidad*, just as they were altering their course from a northerly direction to a southerly one that brought them back towards the pursuing British vessels.

Still without a prize to his name, Bayntun now headed his lone ship directly towards them. At 3 o'clock he was finally closing on Captain Felipe Jado Cajigal in the fresh Spanish 74, *San Agustín*, one of only three ships in Dumanoir's division of ten men of war willing to enter the fray. The *San Agustín*, when within 100 yards of *Leviathan*, slammed her helm hard a-starboard to bring her guns in position to rake Bayntun's ship. The British captain had other ideas about such a move, however, countering it in this naval ballet by immediately putting *Leviathan*'s helm hard a-port and swinging her guns round to bear faster than those of Cajigal. The *San Agustín* instead received the full brunt of the *Leviathan*'s treble-shotted port guns as they ruthlessly raked the length of her starboard side, bringing down the *Agustín*'s mizenmast. Nevertheless the Spanish ship, in her first serious fighting of the day, had the use of her other sails and could manoeuvre freely, unlike the *Leviathan* whose yards and rigging had been much damaged in the previous encounter. Fearing the Spaniards would attempt to escape just as the French *Neptune* had done earlier, a desperate Captain Bayntun made the one move which would definitely stop his opponent: he swung *Leviathan*'s helm hard a-starboard and ran aboard the *San Agustín*, fouling her bow and jib-boom in *Leviathan*'s standing rigging. The *Leviathan*'s 32-pound carronades now strafed the Spanish first-rate's upper deck, attended by heavy musket fire from the Royal Marines. Without losing a moment Bayntun sent his third lieutenant aboard Captain Cajigal's ship with a boarding party, and the Spaniards surrendered without further ado as the British

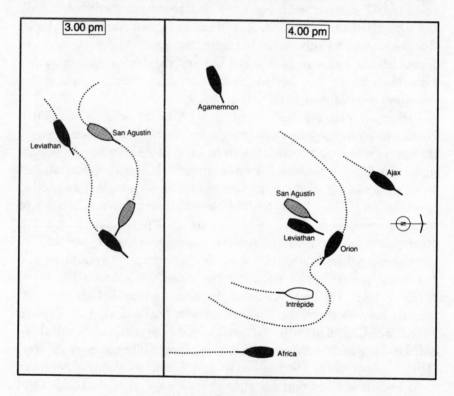

Leviathan engaging *San Agustín*.

crew lashed a stream-cable to the *Leviathan*. A triumphant Henry Bayntun finally had his prize after all.

The *Leviathan* had had her mizen topsail yard completely shot away and all three enormous masts shot through many times, as well as her bowsprit, lower and topsail yards, and much of her rigging was now almost useless, but for all that she had suffered only twenty-six casualties, while incredibly the *Agustín* had incurred 380, well over half her crew, including Commodore Cajigal amongst the wounded.

No sooner had the *San Agustín* been secured at 3.20 pm, however, than *Leviathan* found herself under attack by another ship from Dumanoir's van division, the 74-gun *Intrépide*, which first raked the *Leviathan* ahead and then came along her starboard side to enter upon a full exchange of destructive broadsides. At the sight of the fast approaching *Africa* under Captain Henry Digby (who was more than ready for a good scrap), Captain Louis Infernet of the *Intrépide* left off the attack on the *Leviathan* and for the next three quarters of an hour pounded the smaller *Africa* in a merciless duel that left the British guns silenced, though Digby staunchly refused to surrender. Captain Edward Codrington of the 74-gun *Orion* (being one of the last of Nelson's ships to enter the battle), seeing *Africa*'s plight, came after the *Intrépide*, crossing the bows of the *Leviathan* and *Agustín* and then closed quickly on the French ship's stern, with *Africa* lying off her port side. Coming between the *Intrépide* and the mauled *Africa* (which was immediately shielded from any further damage), *Orion* brought an intense and incessant cannonading (including the full force of her ten 32-pound carronades) to bear against the *Intrépide*. Within a quarter of an hour she had brought both the French ship's main and mizen masts crashing down over her decks and into the sea. At 5 o'clock with *Conqueror* now in view and *Agamemnon* and *Ajax* just on the other side of the *Leviathan* and the defeated *San Agustín*, Captain Infernet lowered his colours.

In addition to losing two masts, most of the *Intrépide*'s rigging was rendered useless, and her hull was peppered with shot from every direction. *Africa* had had her lower masts so badly damaged that they later collapsed, but none the less her casualty figure of sixty-two was surprisingly low, compared with the *Intrépide*'s 320, approximately half of her complement. Though the *Orion* lost her maintopsail yard and main topgallantmast with a 'wounded' foremast, she had only twenty-four casualties. As for the rest of Dumanoir's elusive and still pristine division, they continued to the south with apparent unconcern over those who had stayed to fight, and in many cases, to die.

MEANWHILE, WELL TO the south-east of the *Victory*, Admiral Collingwood's 100-gun *Royal Sovereign* was leading his column and was the first warship to reach the Franco-Spanish battle line. Just minutes before noon she came under a heavy and continuing concentration of fire, especially from the *Santa Ana*, *Indomptable* and *Fougueux*. Three more British vessels – the 74s *Belleisle* and *Mars*, and the 80-gun *Tonnant* – lagged some three-quarters of a mile behind her. Pulling astern of Admiral Álava's impressive flagship, the twenty-one-year-old 112-gun *Santa Ana*, at 12.10 pm, *Royal Sovereign* fired a full broadside of her fifty-six double-shotted port guns into her opponent, inflicting extremely high casualties on the crowded Spanish gundecks and disabling a dozen of her guns. Since British ships had enough gun crews for one side of the ship only, those of the *Sovereign* crossed over to the fresh starboard guns, to discharge them at the more distant *Fougueux* but with less effect, *Fougueux* returning this with a surprisingly heavy rain of French shot that raked Collingwood's ship.

Having reached the enemy line several minutes before *Victory* did to windward, the usually phlegmatic Collingwood shouted through the din to his captain, 'Rotheram, what would Nelson give to be here!' as they ranged along the *Santa Ana*'s starboard side, the muzzles of the two ships literally touching. To the rear Captain Beaudouin's *Fougueux* drew closer, raking the *Sovereign* from the stern as the 64-gun *San Leandro*, 400 yards to the east of the *Santa Ana*, came about to fire at the *Sovereign*'s bow. Collingwood immediately found himself in the unenviable situation of being caught up in a heavy enfilade from three directions! Two other ships of the Combined Fleet, a few hundred yards off the *Sovereign*'s starboard side, also joined in the battle, leaving the British ship under the decimating fire of five opposing warships from every direction! The ferocity of the ships' barrage was such that their shot collided in mid-air!

Captain William Hargood's *Belleisle* was finally approaching fast, determined to come to his admiral's relief, followed by *Mars* and *Tonnant*. Gradually the other four French and Spanish ships pulled out of range, leaving the *Santa Ana* to fight it out alone with the *Royal Sovereign* for the next fifteen minutes, the Spanish ship proving no match for British gunnery. The *Belleisle* gave the *Santa Ana*'s starboard quarter a passing broadside before continuing to the north-east after the French *Indomp-table*, leaving the rest of Collingwood's lee column under very concentrated gunfire from the rear, the last dozen vessels of both sides enveloped by a mantle of thickening sulphuric blackness above a nearly airless sea.

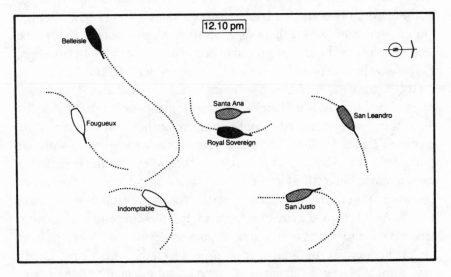

Royal Sovereign engaging *Santa Ana*.

Within three-quarters of an hour Rotheram's *Sovereign* had inflicted severe damage on Álava's flagship, having literally blasted away all three masts leaving a tangled mass of splinters and shredded canvas. Finally at 2.15 pm, after some two hours of unrelenting fighting, the crippled *Santa Ana* surrendered to the *Royal Sovereign* with some 340 casualties, including among the wounded the gallant ship's captain, José Gardoquí and Vice-Admiral Ignacio María de Álava y Navarrete. Having come under such heavy fire, it was hardly surprising that the *Sovereign* found herself nearly completely dismasted, her mizenmast gone, her mainmast going by the board an hour later, only her tottering foremast remaining, while down below in Collingwood's cabin every piece of furniture had been shattered. British casualties were surprisingly low, however, considering the murderous assault she had endured: 141 killed and wounded.

Meanwhile the *Belleisle*, after exchanging a few shots with the *Indomptable*, became continuously engaged with the Spanish *San Juan Nepomuceno*, some distance off her starboard side. The latter shot off the

Belleisle's main topmast at 12.45 pm with French reinforcements approaching quickly from astern. A quarter of an hour later the *Fougueux* appeared out of a hovering cloud of smoke and ranged up along the *Belleisle*'s starboard side, striking her quarter as she did so. But the French vessel had not reckoned on the *Belleisle* reducing her mizenmast to a splintered stump within a matter of minutes, the enormous wreckage of the mast and its rigging hanging over *Fougueux*'s port bow. George Duff's *Mars* now joined them and the three ships engaged in a fierce battle for the next hour; this proved to be too much for the none-too-fiery *Fougueux*, which dropped astern and hauled away to the north.

At 1.30 pm a more adventurous French man of war, the 74-gun *Achille*, commanded by Captain Gabriel Denieport, manoeuvred past the *Belleisle*'s stern and maintained a continuous fire on her port quarter, while another French 74, the *Aigle*, had replaced the *Nepomuceno* in a distant cannonade. It was beginning to look more threatening for the British ship as two more Spanish ships, the *San Leandro* and the 74 *San Justo* appeared off her bows and began a concentrated fire from that direction as well. As if Hargood's situation were not troublesome enough, Admiral Gravina's *Príncipe de Asturias* now let go a powerful salvo while passing under the stern of the surrounded *Belleisle*! Despite his extraordinary predicament Hargood remained calm and his superb men held their own, refusing to strike their colours, regardless of the beating they were taking. At 2.10 pm, with his rigging and sails already cut to pieces, his mainmast fell to add to the débris enmeshed with the remains of the mizenmast covering her port guns. The *Belleisle*'s situation became critical as the *Achille* continued to pour broadside after broadside into the British ship's port side, and it was beginning to look as if *Belleisle* might shortly become the first British man of war to surrender. At 2.30 pm her plight became even more acute as the French *Neptune* (which had earlier been driven away from *Victory* by *Téméraire* and *Leviathan*) ranged right across *Belleisle*'s starboard bow and within a quarter of an hour had shot away the British ship's bowsprit and one remaining mast, the foremast. It was now, however, that the long years of the most rigorous training and experience at sea and in battle paid dividends once again for the British, as Captain Hargood heroically stood his ground, firing his remaining starboard guns and carronades from the littered wreckage of the totally dismasted vessel. Surely someone would come to his aid, he must hold on. Somehow or other that vessel managed to maintain a nominal resistance for another *forty-five minutes*, *Belleisle*'s log recording what then transpired.

3.15 one of our Ships passed our bow and took the fire off one of the Enemy's Ships laying there. At 3.20 the Enemy's Ship, on our starboard side, was engaged by one of our Ships. At 3.25 the Swiftsure passed our stern, cheered us, and commenced firing on the Enemy's Ship on our larboard [port] quarter.

At 3.15 pm a most welcome Captain Robert Redmill had brought up his 64-gun *Polyphemus*, slipping between the *Belleisle* and the French *Neptune*, thereby absorbing some of the punishment herself. Five minutes later more help arrived as a determined Captain Philip Durham's 74, the *Defiance*, entered the fierce battle, returning the *Aigle*'s salvos and giving the *Belleisle*, still in desperate straits, a much needed breather. This was followed a few moments later by the arrival of another British warship, *Swiftsure* (not to be confused with the French ship of the same name, spelt *Swift-sure*), her men loudly cheering Captain Hargood and his magnificent crew as they cleared *Belleisle*'s stern, pouring lethal broadsides into *Achille* as she did so. Help had come with not a moment to spare, as Hargood recorded succinctly in the *Belleisle*'s log: 'Ceased firing, and turned the hands to clear the wreck.'

By 3.30 pm the tide of battle had turned for the battered *Belleisle*, now lying completely defenceless, her guns silent, not even the stump of a mast upon which to hoist her colours, though a proud seaman waved a ragged Union flag tied to a pike! It was valour above and beyond any

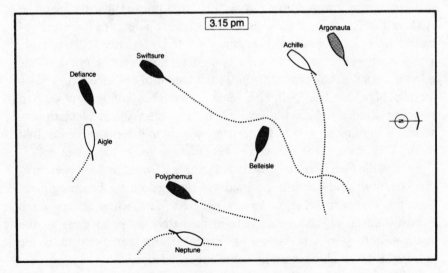

Belleisle under attack from all sides.

definition of the call of duty. Yet that was not the end of the tale, for Captain Hargood saw from the ruins of his quarter deck the 80-gun Spanish *Argonauta* striking her flag not too far away, and immediately rallied a token boarding party, sending them in his only remaining pinnace to seize her!

With the fighting having stopped for her, *Belleisle* was safe, but in the words of naval historian William James, her 'hull was knocked almost to pieces. . . . Ports, port-timbers, channels, chain-plates' all literally ground to bits and even her anchors destroyed. That she incurred only 126 casualties was simply astonishing, as the *Naiad* came up to attach a stream-cable to tow her and her prize.

The *Mars* too suffered grievously in her position downwind and astern of the *Belleisle* where she had fallen under the raking fire of two Spanish 74s, the *Nepomuceno* and *Monarca*, as well as that of two French ships, *Pluton* and *Algésiras*. Like the *Belleisle*, upon entering the enemy line (just ahead of Commodore Julien-Marie Cosmao-Kerjulien's *Pluton*) she had found herself tangling with that 74-gun ship. Although the *Mars* was able to avoid the brunt of that attack by hauling up suddenly, the French ship followed her, her gunfire cutting up the *Mars'* sails and rigging. Coming up sharply again to avoid running on board the *Santa Ana*, the *Mars* exposed her stern to the accurate fire of the Spanish *Monarca* and Rear-Admiral Charles Magon's flagship, the 74-gun *Algésiras*. At that very moment the British *Tonnant* broke through between *Pluton* and *Monarca*, alleviating *Mars*'s precarious situation somewhat, only to find her stern and quarter deck now coming under fire from the starboard guns of yet another French ship, the *Fougueux* (whose port-side guns were canno-nading *Belleisle*). *Mars*'s jovial captain, George Duff, had got himself into a very nasty predicament by 1.15 pm. As he stood at the break of the quarter deck assessing the situation, a cannon-shot fired from the *Pluton* literally blew his head off, the same round shot killing two seamen standing directly behind him as well. Lieutenant William Hennah now assumed command as Duff's teenage son, a midshipman in his first battle, helped carry the remains of his father below to his cabin.

By now the *Fougueux* had flitted off again, northward in the direction of the *Téméraire*, and Captain Cosmao was just ordering a boarding party from the *Pluton* to seize the much mangled *Mars*, when he saw fresh British ships coming forward. He immediately dropped away to the south-east to join Gravina's *Príncipe de Asturias* far away from the fighting. English ships were having many a close call.

In less than an hour, however, the damage had been done, the *Mars* having had her main topmast and spankerboom shot right off, all three masts, as well as her fore and main yards and fore topmast badly shot up and soon to topple overboard. Her rudder, stern and quarter deck were left 'much cut', several of her guns dismounted, and dozens of large round shot had been received in her hull 'between wind and water'. Her casualties came to just under 100 men and boys. But Captain Duff had also inflicted heavy casualties on the *Pluton* in exchange for his own life: some 280 men, and that ship taking in water quickly.

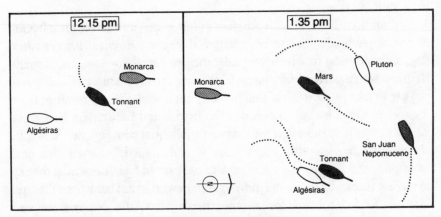

Tonnant engaging *Algésiras*.

When *Tonnant* had entered the contest on behalf of *Mars*, she had made straight for the port bow of the *Algésiras*, pouring in at least one good broadside before hauling up alongside and engaging the *Monarca* which briefly surrendered to the British ship at 1.10 pm.

On board the *Algésiras*, Admiral Magon ordered Captain Gabriel Brouard to fill her main and mizen topsails and cross the stern of *Tonnant* (by now in a bad state, with her foretopmast and main yard shot away). Anticipating just such a move, it seems, at 1.30 pm Captain Charles Tyler brought *Tonnant* hard a-port, deliberately running aboard the startled *Algésiras* entangling the bowsprit and anchors in *Tonnant*'s standing rigging. British sailors were most unpredictable! This new and unlikely position proved to be in *Tonnant*'s favour, providing her with a good field of fire, though in the mêlée no one seemed to notice well abaft of the English ship the *Monarca* rehoisting her colours.

With *Tonnant*'s starboard guns now pouring their shot into the *Algésiras*, Captain Tyler elevated his port guns to the maximum, firing over *Mars* at *Pluton*, while training his foremost port guns ahead on the

San Juan Nepomuceno. The French had rightly feared virtuoso English gunnery.

The intense exchange of fire between the *Tonnant* and the *Algésiras* was taking its toll and by 1.40 pm Captain Tyler had been wounded seriously and replaced on the quarter deck by his first lieutenant, John Bedford, who maintained the ship's salvos to good effect, shattering the *Algésiras's* foremast, but losing his own main and mizen topmasts. Bedford then had to fend off a French boarding party. If the British had been expecting an easy victory over the French and Spanish, they had found themselves in for a rude awakening.

Half an hour later, at 2.30 pm, just as her main- and mizenmast began to crash overboard, the terribly battered French *Algésiras* lowered her flag, surrendering to a nearly equally incapacitated *Tonnant*. Lieutenant Bedford sent a party of fifty men clambering through a maze of collapsed rigging to take possession of that brave French ship. Fifteen minutes later the *Nepomuceno* also surrendered to the British and Lieutenant Benjamin Clement was dispatched in the *Tonnant's* jollyboat with just two hands to claim her. *En route* the small boat was damaged by shell fire and swamped, and Lieutenant Clement was only saved from drowning thanks to a West Indian by the name of Macnamara who swam back for a lifeline. Having no more boats for another prize party, the *Nepomuceno* was abandoned, ultimately claimed an hour and a half later by the British *Defiance*.

Both ships, British and French, were badly damaged. In addition to losing her main and mizen topmasts the *Tonnant's* hull, rudder, starboard quarter deck, rails and gallery were badly shot up, and she had incurred 76 casualties, including her severely wounded captain, Charles Tyler. As for the French *Algésiras*, she was by now entirely dismasted with a casualty list of 219, including amongst the dead Admiral Magon (who though mortally wounded had refused to leave the deck), while a valiant Lieutenant Le Tourneur lay nearby, dying shortly thereafter. Indeed during the first hour of this battle, fighting had been so intense that it had not been at all clear who would emerge the winner.

The British *Bellerophon*, which had followed in *Tonnant's* wake as she crossed the battle line, passed astern of the *Monarca* just as the Spanish ship was rehoisting her colours. By 12.50 pm *Bellerophon* had worked her way to the lee side of *Monarca* when she ran foul of the French *Aigle*, engaging with her in a sharp duel. Within minutes Captain John Cooke found the 74-gun *Bellerophon* in a most disagreeable position. Nelson's earlier words: 'Nothing is sure in a sea fight beyond all others' now rang very true indeed, as two Spanish ships, the *Monarca* and *Montañes*, moved in closer to Cooke's port side, with a third Spanish man of war, Captain Dionisio Galiano's 74-gun *Bahama*, laying down a heavy fire across *Bellerophon*'s stern, and a fresh barrage off her starboard by the French *Swift-sure*! One after another British ships were paying an extremely heavy price for breaking through the enemy's battle line individually, where they were quickly surrounded, contrary to Nelson's plan of breaking through *en masse* and surrounding the enemy. Things were going badly wrong for the Royal Navy as *Bellerophon* now found herself in a similar dilemma to the *Victory*, *Royal Sovereign*, *Belleisle* and *Mars*.

By one o'clock the *Bellerophon*'s main and mizen topmasts had been blown off and her main topsail and topgallantsail had burst into flames. Five minutes later the ship's master was killed in the murderous crossfire, and at 1.11 pm her captain, John Cooke, fell as well, the senior lieutenant, William Pryce Cumby, assuming command. Fortunately for Cumby the *Montañes* soon dropped far astern and out of the skirmish while Galiano's *Bahama* (which had by now received a few devastating broadsides) and Captain Villemadrin's 74-gun *Swift-sure* began to concentrate on *Colossus*, fast approaching from astern – just in time. In fact, although the *Bellerophon*'s guns had badly damaged the French *Aigle*, musketry from the tops of the latter had continued to prove as deadly as that of the *Redoutable* had earlier for the *Victory*, leaving the *Bellerophon*'s deck strewn with dead and wounded. At least one French boarding party

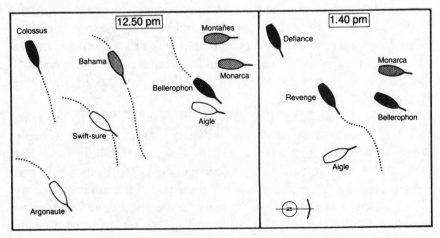

Bellerophon engaging *Aigle*, *Monarca* and *Montañes*.

from the *Aigle* had had to be repulsed already. Nelson's words were probably coming back to many a ship's captain.

At 1.45 pm Pierre-Paul Gourrège's *Aigle* dropped astern, catching a raking from *Bellerophon*'s starboard guns as well as from the foremost guns of another British 74, the *Revenge*, which was now coming straight for her. It was nearly too late for the crippled *Bellerophon*, which now lay an unmanoeuvrable wreck, though still capable of directing some shot from her port guns into the *Monarca*, which, ironically enough, struck her colours to the *Bellerophon*, whose topmasts were long gone and whose three lower masts were wavering and on the verge of collapse. The *Bellerophon*'s remaining canvas and standing and running rigging were left hanging or in shredded heaps, her lower deck badly mauled and lifeless, while her hull bore the marks of a complicated pattern of shot fired by the five different vessels.

Notwithstanding this near calamitous state and the high loss of life – 150 killed and wounded – the British crew kept up their spirits and Lieutenant Cumby sent a boat over with a nominal boarding party to take his first prize. The British found 241 dead and wounded throughout the blistered *Monarca*, including her brave captain, Argumosa, among the wounded, the ship itself a dismasted shambles.

Captain James Morris's *Colossus* had been most active in this part of the fighting and after raking the *Swift-sure*'s starboard side at about one o'clock emerged suddenly from a cloud of intense smoke close alongside the French 74-gun *Argonaute*, the yard-arms of the two vessels fouling as she did so. A fierce exchange of cannon shot between them continued for some ten minutes, after which most of the French guns abruptly ceased, but not before one final shot had nearly completely severed Captain Morris's leg above the knee at the very moment when the two ships were being driven apart by the concussion of their gun blasts. Captain Jacques Epron of the *Argonaute* then quickly hauled off to seek a quieter corner of the battle and, following a later skirmish with *Revenge*, was last sighted at 3.15 pm steering for Cadiz.

The *Colossus* remained, of course, her port guns exchanging fire again with both the French *Swift-sure* and the Spanish *Bahama*. Coming between the by now battered *Bahama* and *Colossus* at 3 pm the *Swift-sure* took such a beating from *Colossus*' port guns that the French ship was forced to fall astern, and leave *Bahama* to her fate. A few minutes later the mainmast crashed into the sea as the unmanoeuvrable and apparently deserted ship lowered her flag, a Union flag rising in its place over the stern.

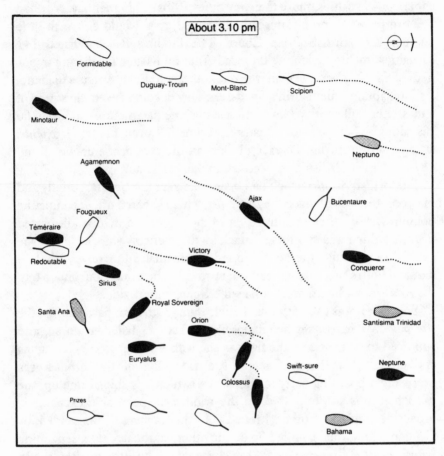

About 3.10 pm

Battle scene around the *Victory* at 3.10 pm.

The loyal Captain Villemadrin, not one to give up that easily, tried to rescue his Spanish ally, bringing *Swift-sure* under the stern of *Colossus* and preparing a broadside for her, when the British ship came about most unexpectedly, catching the French ship off guard, and raking her with a deadly starboard broadside that brought her mizenmast thundering down. When another British 74, the *Orion*, delivered the *Swift-sure* a 37-gun salvo at 3.30 pm it blasted off her already tottering mainmast. That was quite enough for *Swift-sure*, which joined *Bahama* in striking to the triumphant *Colossus*.

The *Colossus* hardly looked the victor, however, with her foremast badly shot through, her mizenmast floating in the sea, and a tottering mainmast about to join it. In human terms it was worse; she had suffered some 200 casualties, more than any other British ship that day. Nor had her two prizes come out unscathed, indeed, they would be worth little enough in a British Prize Court. The limping *Bahama* listed 141 casualties, including among the dead Admiral Magon's debating opponent of 8th October, the man who did not want to fight, Antonio Galiano. As for Captain Villemadrin's *Swift-sure*, now devoid of even the stump of a mast, her hull shot up badly and leaking, she had incurred at least 260 casualties. The none-too-illustrious Captain Epron of the *Argonaute*, later criticised for his disgraceful flight in the face of the enemy, listed 187 casualties. British guns were still taking their toll.

The British *Achilles* which had been following the *Colossus*, briefly and unsuccessfully challenged the *Montañes*, which sheered off, declining the honour; *Achilles* then continued on to the aid of the by now dismasted *Belleisle* (which was still under attack by three enemy ships). Before she could do so, though, the *Achilles* found the Spanish 74, *Argonauta*, before her, and both ships commenced what proved to be a one-hour shoot-out, the *Achilles*' starboard guns versus the Spanish port side.

The ordeal was causing considerable damage to both parties when the *Argonauta*, trying to set her mainsail and escape, failed to do so, and appeared to be giving up the fight as she withdrew her lower-deck guns and closed their ports. Captain Richard King of the *Achilles* was preparing a boarding party for her when two enemy ships came up: the French *Achille* slowly passed on the windward (port) side exchanging broadsides, while another French 74, the *Berwick* (commanded by Captain Jean Camas), pulled up on the other, starboard, side, separating King's *Achilles* from her prize, the *Argonauta*. The French *Achille* then continued in the direction of the already well outnumbered *Belleisle*, as the *Argonauta* dropped to leeward, leaving *Achilles* and *Berwick* to fight it out alone.

It was gruelling, demanding the greatest endurance on the part of King's by now thoroughly exhausted crew. None the less their perseverance paid off and at the end of yet another full hour's fight, the French *Berwick* struck her colours and was duly seized by *Achilles*, while nearby *Belleisle* was taking the drifting *Argonauta* (which she was forced to release at 4 o'clock due to the severity of her own damage).

As might be expected after more than two hours of non-stop fighting, *Achilles* was in a dreadful state, her bowsprit and all three masts barely standing, her hull reduced to a sieve, though astonishingly Captain King recorded only 74 casualties!

The French *Berwick* was left a floating shambles while casualties reached the 250 figure, including her gallant captain, Jean Camas, who died on deck with his men. In the case of the unfortunate *Argonauta* – not to be confused with the French *Argonaute* which had fled – it was even more tragic, for though she was still capable of sailing (in spite of considerable damage sustained), her casualty list exceeded 300 men, including her wounded captain, Antonio Pareja. The French and Spaniards were fighting with a ferocity and tenacity not seen in many a year, astounding their respectful British opponents.

A few thousand yards to the north, the Combined Fleet's van, comprising ten pristine ships under Rear-Admiral Dumanoir who commanded from the 80-gun *Formidable*, was maintaining the original north-easterly course, irrespective of the heavy fighting to the rear. At one o'clock Admiral Villeneuve had hoisted signal number five, which was repeated by the four frigates cruising between them and the coast along the length of the Combined Fleet's battle line, and then repeated again: 'All vessels which, in their present position are not fighting, are ordered to take one that will bring them under fire as quickly as possible'. The signal's meaning was 'perfectly clear' and 'easily seen', commented the official War Office historian, Edouard Desbrière, yet Dumanoir and his leading division 'continued north and away from the battle quite unperturbed'. The Rear-Admiral simply could not justify this open disobedience of orders. That Admiral Villeneuve and the rest of their fleet were heavily engaged, indeed, already fighting for their very existence, could hardly be ignored as thousands of cannon reverberated across the seas and clouds of gun smoke hovered over most of the area behind them.

At 1.45 pm, Villeneuve hoisted a final, desperate signal that included the *Formidable*'s own ship number and this was duly repeated by the two most forward frigates: '*Virer lof pour lof*'. They were to turn back immediately and come to the aid of the rest of the fleet, and this signal was seen and logged by at least three ships of Dumanoir's division, the *Duguay-Trouin*, *Intrépide* and *Scipion*, not to mention his own flagship, the *Formidable*. The question remains, however, why would any responsible naval commander even *need* to be reminded officially by signal to give the help that was so obviously necessary? Having foreseen just such a problem, Villeneuve had stated perfectly clearly in his pre-battle final instructions that 'any captain who is not under fire is not at his post'. Dumanoir could perhaps have changed the results of the battle had he followed Villeneuve's orders and intervened with his ten ships at the beginning.

Finally, *about 2.30 pm* Admiral Dumanoir slowly began to come about, altering his northerly course. To their credit, as has already been seen, two of his ships – *San Agustín* and *Intrépide* – had earlier abandoned his division to challenge the British, though three more ships – *Rayo*, *San Francisco de Asís* and *Héros* – continued on a separate northerly course away from the battle, ignoring both Villeneuve's and Dumanoir's signals. At 3 o'clock Admiral Dumanoir was finally nearing the battle area – if far to the windward or west of it – *three hours after the fighting had begun!*, his division by now reduced to five fresh 74-gun men of war: the *Formidable*, *Duguay-Trouin*, *Scipion*, *Mont-Blanc*, and *Neptuno*. Meanwhile, aboard the *Intrépide*, an excitable Captain Louis Infernet in his strong Provençal patois had ordered a course directly for the fighting much earlier, wishing to get as close as possible to Villeneuve's beleaguered flagship *Bucentaure*, though in his haste to separate from Dumanoir's division (and contrary to Dumanoir's orders) he had collided with the *Mont-Blanc* (which had refused to make way for him), and lost the foresail in the mishap, but this did not prevent the fiery young man from continuing. As already seen he exchanged cannon shot with the *Leviathan* at 2 o'clock (the English ship then fighting the *San Agustín*), then assaulted the *Africa* which was only saved later by the opportune arrival of *Orion*, Captain Edward Codrington proving himself a match for the young French captain. After a fierce two-hour-long duel with the *Orion*, the *Intrépide* was left completely dismasted, and with the approach of two more fresh Royal Navy vessels, *Ajax* and *Agamemnon*, that placed themselves between the *Intrépide* and the rest of Dumanoir's division (which was well to the west and, in any event, declining to come to her aid), while the nearby 98-gun *Britannia* was shelling the distant and fast departing Spanish *San Francisco de Asís* and *Rayo*, the heroic but by now less enthusiastic Captain Infernet finally gave up as yet two more British vessels, the *Spartiate* and *Minotaur*, arrived. He had seen more than half his men fall, the casualty list surpassing 320. His situation was hopeless. The equally valiant, but more skilful, Captain Codrington recorded a mere twenty-four casualties for the *Orion*, however.

After leaving the *Orion* in possession of the *Intrépide*, at about four o'clock the *Minotaur* and *Spartiate* caught up with the last ship of Dumanoir's elusive division, the 80-gun *Neptuno*, commanded by Commodore Cayetano Valdés, and ranged along either side of the hapless vessel. Remorselessly blasting her from both sides for the next hour with mighty salvos, they brought down her mizenmast and fore and main topmasts in succession. The outflanked *Neptuno* surrendered to them at 5.10 pm but then drifted out of control and collided with a startled *Téméraire*, (which had her hands full with the two prize ships already lashed to her sides). The *Neptuno*'s wounded Commodore Valdés was found among the seventy-three casualties; the British incurred a combined total of only forty-eight.

Passing the beaten *Intrépide* at three o'clock and with the besieged *Neptuno* astern of him – abandoning both with remarkable aplomb – the 'imperturbable' Dumanoir continued his southerly course, declining further challenges from the *Ajax* and *Agamemnon* even when they were within 'pistol shot range', though several of their broadsides hit his ship. Steering with true Villeneuvian panache and undaunted determination, he successfully bypassed the entire raging fight in the rear. Now refusing to bring his remaining four untouched ships to the aid of the valiant *Santa Ana*, Dumanoir sailed to the south-west, well out of harm's way, before ultimately turning to the north once again. Several days later, on 4th November, the rest of his division – the *Formidable*, *Duguay-Trouin*, *Mont-Blanc* and *Scipion* – was captured in good condition by Sir Richard Strachan's squadron off the Spanish coast.[3]

Most of the remaining heavy fighting was concentrated towards the rear of the Combined Fleet where Collingwood's slowest ships had been the last into battle. Among them was his former flagship, the *Dreadnought*, under the command of Captain John Conn, who, having swung round the tail end of the enemy's battle line at 2 o'clock, came into action with the 74-gun *San Juan Nepomuceno*, which had previously been badly mauled by the *Bellerophon*, *Defiance* and latterly by *Tonnant*. The *Tonnant* having been unable to board her at the time she surrendered, the *Nepomuceno* had since drifted and it was then that the *Dreadnought*, with her 98 guns and fourteen 32-pound carronades, had come upon her. Disregarding the proximity and cannonading of other enemy ships, including the *Príncipe de Asturias*, *San Justo* and *Indomptable*, the British warship deliberately rammed the nearly defenceless *Nepomuceno*, whose captain, Cosmé Churruca, had already been killed. She surrendered, this time, in just a quarter of an hour.

No sooner was Captain Conn preparing a prize party to board her, however, than he spotted Gravina's ship, *Príncipe de Asturias*, leaving the battlefield and, dropping his plans to board the stricken Spanish warship, set off in pursuit of the Spanish Admiral – the bewildered *Nepomuceno* now having surrendered twice, only to be abandoned. Conn exchanged a few broadsides with the 112-gun *Príncipe de Asturias* – one round of which nearly severing Gravina's left arm – from which wound he was to die many days later. But she was too fast for him, gradually leaving the plodding *Dreadnought* far behind as the Spaniards steered for home, effectively ending the battle for both of them.

Although the *Dreadnought* had received some shot in her masts and rigging, her casualties were light – thirty-three in all. When the *Nepomuceno* was finally seized later by the *Defiance*, she was found to be in a ruinous state and her Commander numbered among the 254 casualties. Although the *Príncipe de Asturias* did make good her escape, she carried 163 casualties back to Cadiz, including – in addition to Gravina – a wounded Rear-Admiral, Antonio de Escaño. Another British ship, the *Revenge*, which had entered the battle line astern of the *Dreadnought* and *Polyphemus*, after exchanging a few broadsides with the *Aigle*, *Príncipe de Asturias*, *Indomptable* and *San Justo*, incurred seventy-nine casualties.

Captain George Hope's 74-gun *Defence* – which had challenged the French *Berwick* for some thirty minutes before the French vessel broke off the action at 3 pm and disappeared – not despairing, soon found another sparring partner: the 74-gun *San Ildefonso*. The two ships then lambasted one another with mighty broadsides for an hour before the *San Ildefonso*'s wounded Captain Vargas, seeing the British *Polyphemus* approach, struck the red and white flag of the Spanish monarchy. The Spaniards had borne the brunt of the battle against Vice-Admiral Calder on 22nd July, and on 8th October had stated unequivocally to Admiral Villeneuve that they had no intention of repeating that performance. This hour-long battle had sustained their honour, attested to by the 165 casualties they suffered. Captain Hope's dead and wounded came to a total of only thirty-six.

Captain Philip Durham's 74-gun *Defiance* had followed the *Defence* across the Franco-Spanish battle line between the *San Ildefonso* and the French *Achille*, and shortly afterwards had received a good baptism of fire from the guns of the towering *Príncipe de Asturias*, which cut up her sails and rigging so badly that she could not pursue Gravina's flagship as she bore away. Nevertheless Captain Durham could still fight and, at three o'clock, his ship came alongside the *Aigle* (which had been so battered previously by the *Bellerophon* and *Revenge*) and, meeting no resistance, had her lashed to the *Defiance*. Upon boarding her, he hauled down the French flag, hoisting the Union flag in its place. Then, suddenly, the British marines found themselves under such a weltering fire of musketry from the forecastle, waist and even the yards above, that they were forced to run back to the *Defiance* and cut her loose. Drawing back no more than fifty yards, Captain Durham held his position beside Captain Pierre Courrège's *Aigle*, bent on giving her a good lesson. He poured in one merciless salvo after another, which were matched at first by retaliating French guns, but the battered *Aigle* could only sustain this effort for about twenty-five minutes, when she surrendered to the *Defiance*. Shortly after manning the *Aigle*, Captain Durham dispatched a second prize party to seize, successfully this time, the nearby silent, drifting *San Juan Nepomuceno*.

When the fighting had stopped, Durham found *Defiance* to be 'much wounded', with her masts, rigging, sails and hull terribly shot up and seventy casualties. As for the unfortunate *Aigle*, which had continued fighting long after she had been dismasted, she was quite simply a floating hulk and had lost upwards of *two-thirds of her crew and officers*, that is, well over 400 dead and wounded, her captain being among the dying. It was carnage.

It was not until nearly half past three that the British *Swiftsure*, which had earlier followed the *Colossus* into battle, began exchanging ferocious salvos with the French *Achille*, which until then had been raking the *Belleisle*. Pursuing her to the south-east and catching up with her, Captain William Rutherford's *Swiftsure* had passed under the stern of the French *Achille*, then, coming up along her port side, began engaging her closely, while the *Polyphemus*, which had been fighting with the French *Neptune*, in turn came alongside *Achille*'s other, starboard side in a brief artillery duel.

By now eleven out of the nineteen ships composing the second half of the Combined Fleet's battle line had been captured, seven more having fled the scene. The French *Achille*, battered and isolated, having survived previous harsh encounters with *Achilles* and *Belleisle*, during which her courageous captain, Gabriel Denieport had been killed, now stopped all serious resistance. Her mizenmast and fore yard had been shot away and her topsails and rigging were ablaze, the flames spreading out of control. Then at 4.30 pm the *Prince*'s guns brought down the flaming upper half of *Achille*'s mainmast, fanning the flames across the men, boats, guns and deck below.

As the smoke cleared following another couple of broadsides, Captain Richard Grindall of the *Prince*, now seeing what had happened, ordered his guns to cease fire and pulled back a distance, for what he beheld before him was horrifying. The *Achille* was a blazing inferno. Grindall immediately ordered all his boats away to come to the aid of the stricken ships. The captains of *Swiftsure*, the British cutter *Entreprenante* and schooner *Pickle* also joined in the rescue operation, all converging on the French ship in a desperate effort to save the trapped French crew they had been trying to kill just moments before. Flames now engulfed the lower deck, bursting through the gun ports, and British boats got as close as they could to the wall of intense heat which was now detonating loaded French guns in all directions, rendering an already dangerous rescue operation all the more hazardous. Still the British persisted, launching every boat available, as the screams of agony from those trapped below and burning alive pierced the gathering dusk. Flames reached voraciously down to the water-line and many a sombre British face, reflected in that terrible light, watched from rescue boats and high atop the decks of men of war at 5.45 pm as the magazines of the 74-gun French Imperial ship exploded into a burgeoning ball of fire hundreds of feet high against the darkening sky, flaming timbers, human limbs and torsos raining down upon them. These men, who had come out here excitedly to kill the foe and destroy their ships, stared blankly at the awesome product of their day's work. Over 100 French survivors were taken safely to the British ships ringing the litter-strewn patch of sea where the *Achille* had stood only a short time before. The entire French officer corps had been killed along with much of the crew, the death toll reaching 499 (excluding those who were to die of their wounds later).

The British casualties were light: a total of a couple of dozen for the *Swiftsure* and *Polyphemus*, while the *Prince* reported none, the only British warship to be that fortunate.

The explosion of the *Achille* marked the factual and symbolic end to the battle of Cape Trafalgar, the victory that Nelson and another 448 British sailors and officers were never to see. Another 1,241 men lay wounded, bringing the total dead and wounded to 1,690 British casualties.* Despite their strongly stated misgivings about entering this battle, the Spanish had joined their French allies and paid a heavy price. Fourteen of their commanding officers and admirals had been either killed or wounded, 1,038 men had been killed outright and another 1,385 men had been wounded – a total of 2,423 casualties. As for the French, they too had paid dearly. Six of their captains had been either killed or wounded, one admiral (Admiral Magon) had been killed, the overall number of men dead or drowned coming to 3,370, with another 1,160 wounded, bringing the total number of French casualties to 4,530. Altogether the Combined

*See appendix 3

Franco-Spanish Fleet casualty list bore 6,953 names. Such was the annihilation Nelson had longed for. Such too was the price Napoleon had demanded France and Spain to pay in order to satisfy his lust for war, wealth and power.

Vice-Admiral Collingwood had taken an initial total of nineteen French and Spanish prizes,* but the Royal Navy had given their enemy none.

The storm Nelson had anticipated that morning now broke over the battered British fleet and their equally battered 'prizes' as the exhausted winners slowly cleared away the débris and gathered their dispersed ships, now located some eight miles west-south-west of Trafalgar. Nelson had ordered the fleet to anchor immediately after the battle, knowing full well that many vessels would be incapable of sailing or manoeuvring, but Collingwood arrogantly rescinded that order, this, as it turned out, to the detriment of the fleet. There was no longer a Nelson to tell him what to do. Because of the gale-force winds, churning up those blood-stained waters later that night and the next few days, because the fleet did not anchor that first night after the battle and because some prize ships escaped, Collingwood ultimately ended up with a mere four of the original nineteen ships, only the *San Juan Nepomuceno*, *Swift-sure*, *San Ildefonso* and *Bahama* being safely escorted back to Gibraltar. 'I was afraid the people of England might have attributed our misfortunes to a want of skilful management', an anxious Collingwood confessed to a friend. 'I can only say that in my life I never saw such exertions as were made to save those ships'. Fortunately, Captain Sir Richard Strachan added another four to that list on 4th November when his four ships captured Dumanoir's four sail – *Formidable*, *Scipion*, *Mont-Blanc* and *Duguay-Trouin* – off Cape Viñano.

Of the initial nineteen prizes – excluding the four taken to Gibraltar - four were scuttled by Collingwood between 28th and 30th October (the *Santísima Trinidad*, *Argonauta*, *San Agustín* and *Intrépide*), two escaped from them to Cadiz (the *Algésiras* and *Santa Ana*) and the rest of the prizes either sank in the storm or were dashed upon the rocks, resulting in extremely high casualties, Villeneuve's flagship, the *Bucentaure*, among them. A mortally wounded and gallant Admiral Gravina on board the *Príncipe de Asturias*, now under tow by a French frigate, led another ten ships back to Cadiz, five French – the *Pluton*, *Héros*, *Neptune*, *Argonaute* and *Indomptable* – and five Spanish – the *San Francisco de Asís*, *Montañes*,

*See appendix 3

Rayo, *San Leandro* and the *San Justo* – the *Algésiras* and *Santa Ana* joining them later to make a total of thirteen. Three of these, however (the *Indomptable*, *San Francisco de Asís* and *Rayo*) broke up on the rocks within the next few days, reducing the remnant of the Combined Fleet to ten ships, of which only five had suffered little damage and fewer than fifty casualties, and were thus capable of putting to sea. The Royal Navy and nature together had reduced the enemy's fleet by a staggering *twenty-three* ships.

Vice-Admiral Collingwood re-established the blockade of Cadiz and personally introduced one at Cartagena. With the exception of one or two unsuccessful attempts to leave Cadiz, the ten surviving ships of the Combined Fleet remained locked in the port. Upon the invasion of Spain by Napoleon in 1808, the Spanish navy seized all five French ships (the *Pluton*, *Héros*, *Neptune*, *Argonaute* and *Algésiras*) and none of the ships at Cadiz was again used to wage war against the British during the final years of Napoleon's reign.[4]

Admiral Lord Nelson had had his 'pell-mell battle' – as, ironically, both he and Villeneuve had referred to it quite independently – and indeed his war of annihilation, resulting in the greatest British naval victory in history. The French and Spanish, though fighting with undaunted bravery and tenacity, suffered a shattering defeat, destroying French naval morale for decades to come. 'So much courage and devotion', Villeneuve afterwards lamented, 'deserved a better fate.'

13

A State Funeral

The Admiral [Cornwallis] grieves much over the death of Lord Nelson. Never a word or thought of envy for his glorious victory, only a deep regret that they did not meet and speak in August last when they might have.

Captain J. Whitby to his wife, 31st October 1805

All the men in our ship [the Victory] who have seen him [Nelson] are such soft toads they have done nothing but blast their eyes and cry ever since he was killed.

Seaman aboard the Victory

The skill and intrepidity of my officers and seamen were never more conspicuous than on this important occasion. The loss of the distinguished Commander under whom this great victory has been achieved, I most sincerely and deeply lament; his transcendant and heroic services will, I am persuaded, exist for ever in the recollection of my people . . .

King George III, 22nd November 1805

Nelson died in the fullest glory and the honours accorded his memory were hardly excessive when one considers that no victory ever had more decisive, nor especially more long-lasting, results. His country still enjoys [ie, 100 years later] the indisputable naval superiority that it acquired at the battle of Trafalgar.

Edouard Desbrière, 1907

'GIVEN THE TYPE of attack the enemy made against us, it was inevitable that a series of pell-mell battles would ensue, which, as it turned out, were executed with the greatest audacity by the English', prisoner-of-war Vice-Admiral Villeneuve wrote to Naval Minister Decrès from the cabin assigned to him by Captain Blackwood as the *Euryalus* approached the Breton coast on 15th November. But he continued, 'As for me, Monseigneur, deeply aware of the full extent of my misfortunes and of the full responsibility that I must bear for such a great disaster, my only wish is to come soon to prostrate myself before His Majesty, either to explain my actions or to serve as the sacrificial victim, not for the sake of the honour of our flag – which, I need hardly say, has remained intact –

but to appease the spirits of those who may have perished through my possible imprudence and thoughtlessness or as a result of the neglect of one of my duties'. As for the French navy, '. . . the officers and crews of His Majesty's ships could not have shown greater courage and devotion to the country and to the Emperor . . . but the time has not yet come when France can celebrate her naval victories together with those of the army on the Continent'.

During his three weeks of captivity, Pierre Villeneuve had apparently come to terms with himself and his situation, or at least in part, although still not fully acknowledging the dire consequences stemming from his own acts and personal inadequacies as a leader. Fourteen French and Spanish warships had abandoned their brethren in the midst of the battle, largely due to his own failure to lead and inspire. Now, however, he was longing to see his wife and willing to accept whatever lay in store for him in Paris. To be sure scarcely one of his fleet captains and staff members – not even the 'loyal Prigny' – mentioned his name in their battle reports and only one had dared praise him – the severely wounded Rear-Admiral Escaño, who described him as 'a most dignified and courageous man'.

Nevertheless, like Villeneuve, several high French and Spanish officers were, in fact, full of praise for what they witnessed during the battle, including Major-General Contamine, who in his official report to Admiral Decrès stated, 'I believe I can truthfully say that the battle of Cape Trafalgar must be considered as having . . . reflected the highest honour on the French and Spanish navies and shows what our navy will one day be capable of doing'. However, in his final report on Trafalgar to the French Emperor, Decrès laid the full blame for the loss of that battle on the desertion of so many ships, failing to heed Villeneuve's orders, and, in particular, Rear-Admiral Dumanoir's division. 'It is perfectly clear that . . . the commander of this avant-garde did not carry out his instructions . . . It is [also] to this cause that the flag captain of the *Bucentaure* [Captain Magendie] attributes the fleet's disaster and Captains Villemadrin, Lucas and Infernet have expressed a like opinion to me . . . As for Admiral Villeneuve, he has not complained about anyone in his report; indeed, he has praised the entire fleet under his command.'

In fact, Villeneuve impressed his British captors, especially the pernickety Francophobe Admiral Collingwood. 'Admiral Villeneuve is a well-bred man', he related to Admiral Lord Radstock, 'and I believe a very good Officer: he has nothing in his manners of the offensive vapouring and boasting which we, perhaps too often, attribute to Frenchmen'.

After being rowed ashore at Morlaix, Villeneuve, now bereft of both fleet and command, took the coach to the Hôtel de la Patrie at Rennes where on 17th November his body was discovered with an alleged note to his wife and six deep knife wounds in and around the heart, the blade of the dagger jammed brutally up to the hilt between his ribs and directly in the heart. Fouché and the Imperial Police closed the case immediately, however, without attempting a proper investigation, declaring it to be a 'suicide', a procedure and verdict unquestioned at the time, and indeed, for some curious reason never seriously queried by French historians since.

A weary but exhilarated crew aboard the schooner *Pickle* dropped anchor at Portsmouth late on 5th November even as the last embers of the bonfires were dying, the first vessel to reach England directly from the battlefield of Trafalgar. A team of six horses was quickly harnessed for a special post-chaise to carry the young frigate captain, Lieutenant John Richards Lapenotière, to London and the Admiralty where, at one o'clock in the morning, a crotchety eighty-year-old Admiral Lord Barham was aroused and brought from his chamber to hear the tidings. To Prime Minister William Pitt, who was woken up at 3 am, it was a much needed balm. Indeed, just four days earlier at a dinner party here at Downing Street with Lord Malmesbury present, the Prime Minister had been informed of another battle, a calamitous one in Swabia at Ulm, where, on the eve of Trafalgar, Britain's allies, the Austrians, had surrendered nearly 30,000 men to the French. A much weakened Pitt had greeted the news with an almost unique flash of anger, snapping at Malmesbury, 'Don't believe a word of it; it is all a fiction!'

By the crack of dawn on 6th November, the first copies of the 'Extraordinary' edition of the *London Gazette*'s initial report of the great victory at Trafalgar were being read in the British capital. Meanwhile, by seven o'clock that morning, further up the Thames, at Windsor Castle, King George III was being awakened with the glad tidings, even as cannon thundered from Hyde Park and the Tower of London to spread the news of the great event, indeed the first really splendid news received in many a month.

The cautious London Stock Exchange was not quite so ebullient, however. Government securities wavered, then sank, investors still wary as to what to expect next from a French Emperor last reported heading a powerful army towards the Habsburg capital at Vienna. Sir John Perring, the Lord Mayor of London, on the other hand, had no such qualms and at his annual banquet three days later hailed the Prime Minister as 'the Saviour of Europe'. With a partially defeated Austria and an untried Russia (and hopefully Prussia) on his mind, Pitt himself remained cautiously sanguine. 'England has saved herself by her exertions', he replied, 'and will, as I trust, save Europe by her example.'

The results of the great British naval victory of Trafalgar reassured John Bull's Britain in many respects. The ships of the Combined Fleet at Cadiz would never again pose a serious threat to British shipping or the Royal Navy, that much was clear, while along the Channel there were neither sufficient warships nor flotilla vessels to allow the French Emperor to indulge in any more invasion plans or ever again to threaten Britain. The British Isles were finally safe, thanks to Pitt's and Melville's rigorous policies, supported by a superbly trained and robust Royal Navy. British army and naval units protecting her shores could be reduced and there would be no more coastal inhabitants fleeing inland in alarm about French landings. Chatham, Sheerness and the London dockyards would not be burned. Although many French officers and seamen had fought with magnificent courage, the French Navy still lacked well-experienced crews and enough good officers and, further, Trafalgar had broken their spirit for decades to come.

Admiral Sir William Cornwallis' most skilful and determined job of restraining the French Imperial Navy all along the Channel for the past two years, despite the worst storms in living memory and insufficient numbers of ships at his command, capped by his timely creation and dispatch of a large fleet to cope with the menace of the Combined Fleet, had rendered the subsequent victory and the security of Britain a reality. Indeed, had Cornwallis not acted in this manner and so expeditiously, there would, most probably, have been no celebrations in London now. However, on the Continent Napoleon was making great strides towards conquering and dominating Central and Western Europe and not even the greatest naval victory in British history halted this. Years of hard work and sacrifice remained to achieve that.

The British were at once saddened and exhilarated by the news brought by the *Pickle*, however. 'I never saw so little public joy', Lord Malmesbury acknowledged, not because of the news of French victories on the Continent, but because the Battle of Trafalgar had cost the life of Nelson. The news of the naval victory had spread like wildfire through the streets, lanes, mews and markets of London, but there was little brash or noisy rejoicing. Instead, small mourning lamps were lit in windows, and above the Drury Lane Theatre, an immense anchor and the initials 'LN' were illuminated, while inside, patriotic sketches of the hero were read and performed. Regardless of the obvious delight businessmen dealing in colonial trade took in the victory as they gathered at Lloyd's Coffee House early that morning of 6th November, it was rarely mentioned without a reference to the loss of Nelson. The reactions of the *Annual Register* were typical. There was 'not an individual in the Country', it commented, 'even him before the most desponding of its fate, who did not feel that it [the victory] was purchased at too dear a rate, nor was there an individual in it who would not have given up the Victory to have saved the Victim!' These sentiments were echoed by the phlegmatic Earl of Malmesbury: 'No one individual who felt joy at this victory, so well-timed and so complete but first had an instinctive feeling of sorrow, not selfish sorrow . . . but the sorrow of affection and gratitude for what he had done for us . . . He was a true patriot, which is nearly as rare a character as to be the hero he was'. Some felt a real sense of personal grief at the loss of Nelson, including Captain Henry Blackwood, as he wrote in the aftermath of the battle, 'My heart . . . is sad, and penetrated with the deepest anguish. A victory, such a one as has never been achieved . . . took place in the course of five hours; but at such an expense, in the loss of the most gallant of men, and best of friends, as renders it to me a Victory I never wished to have witnessed – at least, on such terms . . . Such an Admiral has the Country lost, and every officer and man so kind, so good, so obliging a friend as never was'. 'Never did any man's death cause so universal a sorrow as Lord Nelson's', Vice-Admiral Collingwood echoed to Hugh Elliot, Minister at Naples.

On 7th November, King George III, who had personally been left deeply moved by the news of Nelson's death along with the welcome news of the attendant victory, issued a Royal Proclamation from the Queen's Palace calling for a day of thanksgiving:

We, taking into our most serious consideration the indispensable duty which we owe to Almighty God for the recent and signal interposition of his good Providence, in addition to the manifold and inestimable benefits which these Kingdoms have from time to time received at his hands, manifested by the blessing bestowed on our arms in the late signal and important Victory obtained by our Fleet under the command of the late Vice-Admiral Lord Viscount Nelson, over the Combined Fleets of France and Spain, have thought . . . to issue this our Royal Proclamation, hereby appointing and commanding that a General Thanksgiving to Almighty God for these his mercies to be observed throughout those parts of our

United Kingdom called England and Ireland, on Thursday the fifth day of
December next.

French reaction to the greatest naval disaster in their history was at first
one of stunned, then self-imposed, silence, followed later by their own
version of events. Rarely has there been such a total news blackout as took
place following the events of 21st October. Napoleon was found in the
white and gold Baroque splendour of the Schönbrunn Palace in Vienna
on 16th November (which his troops had just occupied three days
before), when a special courier arrived from Paris with the first news of
Trafalgar. So thoroughly were members of his general staff silenced by
him that not a word of what transpired there that day ever reached the
public. The French Emperor, however, hardly known for his admirable
temper, no doubt let fly the words 'treason' and 'cowardice', as he had in
August at Boulogne, before breaking camp there. So efficiently was the
most stringent silence imposed on the French press, that not even a hint
of the disaster reached the streets of Paris – the capital already suffering
from a critical financial situation – until 7th December 1805, five days
after his own magnificent victory at Austerlitz, where he destroyed the
combined Austro-Russian armies which Prime Minister Pitt had worked
so long and hard to field and subsidise, at once bringing down the third
anti-French coalition and any hopes for a European peace for many years
to come.

Napoleon was, without a doubt, one of the greatest military geniuses of
all time, but he was also one of the greatest liars, exceeded only by Stalin
and Hitler. On the morning of 7th December, the semi-official government newspaper, *Journal de Paris*, informed the French people that a
great naval battle had taken place off Trafalgar on 19th (not 21st)
October, a stupendous battle in which thirty-three British ships, it said,
faced the Combined Fleet, including fifteen British ships which were not
in fact present that day* and another three which did not even exist. The
Franco-Spanish Fleet, it continued, had won a spectacular victory
resulting in nineteen British ships either having been sunk, burned,
wrecked on the rocks or so mauled by gunfire as to be rendered useless.
The Combined Fleet's losses had been nominal in ships and men, while
the British had suffered 10,471 casualties! 'This report attests brilliantly
to the worth of the French Fleet,' the Parisian paper concluded, though
failing to explain why twenty-three battleships of the Combined Fleet

*See appendix 3

had suddenly disappeared, and why the French Government refused to celebrate such a splendid victory.

Thinking about the forthcoming battle, one of the last things Admiral Lord Nelson had attended to was requesting the Committee of the Patriotic Fund to provide for the wounded and the families of the deceased. Two days before the national day of thanksgiving set aside by the King, this Committee duly met on the first floor of Lloyd's Coffee House and, among other things:

> Resolved, That the sum of forty pounds be presented to every Seaman or Marine, whose wounds may be attended with disability or loss of limb; the sum of twenty pounds to each Seaman or Marine severely wounded; and the sum of ten pounds to each Seaman or Marine slightly wounded.
>
> Resolved, That relief be afforded to the widows, orphans, parents, and relatives, depending for support on the Captains, Officers, Petty Officers, Seamen, and Marines, who fell in these glorious engagements . . .
>
> Resolved, That the sums contributed on the Day of Thanksgiving [£100,000], be exclusively appropriated to the relief of the Seamen, Soldiers, Marines, and Volunteers, wounded; and to the widows, orphans, and relatives of those killed in His Majesty's Service . . .

Meanwhile in London, following the day of public thanksgiving, a rapidly declining William Pitt had his ministers arrange for a curious combination of both a celebration of the battle of Trafalgar and obsequies in the guise of a state funeral for Lord Nelson, who had personally requested that he be buried in St Paul's Cathedral.

> The remains [of Nelson's body] were wrapped in cotton vestments, and rolled from head to foot with bandages of the same material, in the ancient mode of embalming. The body was then put into a leaden coffin filled with brandy holding in solution of camphor and myrrh. This coffin was inclosed in a wooden one, and placed in the after-part of his Lordship's cabin: where it remained till the 21st of December when an order was received from the Admiralty for the removal of the body.
>
> *Dr William Beatty*

A MUCH BATTERED *Victory* reached England, approaching Portsmouth on 4th December 1805. Then, after proceeding to the Thames estuary on 22nd December, Nelson's body was transferred to Commissioner

Grey's yacht, the *Chatham*, subdued guns firing from the forts at Gravesend and Tilbury as it continued on its way to Greenwich Hospital where it was received on the 23rd by Nelson's former commanding officer, Admiral Lord Hood. Following a complete autopsy, Nelson's body was placed in the coffin made from the mainmast of *L'Orient* and lay in state in the Painted Hall of the naval hospital between 5th and 7th January 1806.

Fierce south-westerly winds on Wednesday 8th January challenged the floodtide rushing up the Thames. The river had been cleared in advance for the state barges taking part in the procession bearing the body of Admiral Viscount Nelson, accompanied by Lord Hood and the Lord Mayor of London, from Greenwich Hospital. All ships' flags were at half-mast along the wharves and guns boomed mournfully from the Tower of London, as dozens of tough oarsmen pulled against the waters whipped up by gale-force winds. But even biting winds could not prevent all of Britain from paying their respects to the greatest hero in British history as his barge reached Whitehall stairs.

Nor was it any different on Thursday, as vast throngs made their way from every direction to the heart of the British capital. 'Thousands of people were in motion' by 3 am on that 9th January, *The Times* reported, from St James's Park and the Admiralty – where hundreds of troops were assembled – all along the intended route of the funeral procession, up the Strand, Fleet Street and Ludgate Hill to St Paul's Cathedral. Dim street lamps along the winding cobblestoned roads cast a faint light over the clusters of dark figures huddling to keep warm against the pervading January damp and cold.

Then, one hour before daylight on 9th January, drums beat throughout every quarter of the city, summoning their respective volunteer corps to arms, as they converged from both sides of the river to take their places, lining every step of the way from the gates of the Admiralty to the heights of St Paul's. By daybreak the Life Guards were mounted at their posts in Hyde Park and St James's Park, where all the infantry and cavalry regiments quartered within a hundred miles of the capital (including the troops who had served in 'the glorious campaigns in Egypt' following Nelson's victory of the Nile) were assembled in their colourful uniforms and smart formations, as twelve field pieces and the ammunition tumbrils of a detachment of flying artillery were being made ready to be brought to Moorfields near the cathedral.

At eight o'clock, eight mourning coaches, each drawn by four horses, brought the Heralds and Pursuivants of Arms from their College to the

Admiralty, but the Prince of Wales and his six younger brothers, including the Duke of York, Commander-in-Chief of the army, had arrived even earlier, the splendour of their carriages set off from the dozens of others now gathering by their golden escutcheons on the doors.

All street traffic had been stopped along the route, except for foreign ambassadors, and access could only be gained to Hyde Park through Cumberland and Grosvenor Gates by special, numbered tickets, signed personally by Sir Isaac Heard and issued by the College of Arms, the same passes also being required at the gate to St James's Park at the top of Constitution Hill and at the Horse Guards.

By 8.30 am all the troops under the command of General Sir David Dundas, KB, had been assembled on parade in St James's Park. Before the Horse Guards, the eighty-five-year-old Admiral of the Fleet, Sir Peter Parker, the Chief Mourner, and his two 'Supporters', Admiral William Lord Radstock and Admiral Samuel Viscount Hood, took their places in the procession (their mourning carriages, like the rest, draped in black), surrounded by senior officers in navy blue dress uniforms, and officials in ancient gowns or habits, mostly in black, and wrapped in long black 'mourning cloaks'.

Finally, at noon, all was ready and the procession set off from the Admiralty, General Dundas and Lieutenant-General Harry Burrard leading the way at the head of the light dragoons and infantry, two Highland regiments, four Grenadier companies – seven files abreast – six cavalry squadrons – four by four – and the horse-drawn Royal artillery – two abreast.

The Marshal's men cleared the way for the procession, which now included hundreds of persons: representatives of the College of Arms bearing the Rouge Croix, Blue Mantle, Rouge Dragon and Portcullis, forty-eight pensioners from Greenwich Naval Hospital (in black mourning cloaks adorned with badges and black staves in their hands), forty-eight sailors and twelve marines from the *Victory*, in ordinary dress with black neckerchiefs, black stockings and black crape in their hats, watermen, drums and fifes setting the funereal pace, followed by resplendent trumpeters, the standard, borne in front of one black mourning coach in which sat Captain Laforey of the *Spartiate* and two naval lieutenants, the servants of the deceased, officers of His Majesty's wardrobe, 'Gentlemen and Esquires', deputations from the great commercial companies of London, the physicians and divines, chaplains and secretary of the deceased, the banner of the deceased (as a Knight of the Bath) preceding a mourning coach carrying Captain Durham of the

Defiance and two lieutenants, Attendants of the Body, Knights Bachelor, Sergeants at Law, Knights of the Bath, the Comptroller, Treasurer and Steward of the Household of the Deceased, all bearing white staves, a Gentleman Usher, the younger and eldest sons of the nobility, four Privy Counsellors, Lord Holland, Lord Mulgrave, Lord Hawkesbury, the Lord Bishop of Exeter, Viscount Castlereagh, Viscount Sidmouth, fourteen earls, several marquises, the Duke of Montrose, the Duke of Devonshire, the Duke of St Albans, the Duke of Norfolk, Earl Camden, as Lord President of the Council, and the Archbishop of Canterbury. These were followed by the Prince of Wales and Their Royal Highnesses the Dukes of Cambridge, Sussex, Cumberland, Kent, Clarence and York. Next came Richmond Herald, the Great Banner, preceding the mourning coach of Captain Robert Moorsom, of the *Revenge*, another four mourning coaches bearing the knightly accoutrements of the deceased – gauntlet and spurs, helm and crest, target and sword, and surcoat – followed by the coach bearing Nelson's coronet on a black cushion borne by Norroy King of Arms and attended by two Gentlemen Ushers, followed by six naval lieutenants bearing the two bannerols in two more coaches, then two mourning coaches conveying the six admirals who were to bear the canopy over the coffin in St Paul's, and another coach with the four admirals who were to support the pall, directly over the coffin.

Finally the body itself was placed on an open hearse designed by the Rev Mr M'Quin, and drawn by six led horses, the hearse in the shape of a ship with 'VICTORY' in raised letters over the poop. Each side of the hearse was decorated with escutcheons of Nelson's arms, three on each side, and, between them, four scrolls, ringed by branches of wreaths of palm and laurel, with the names of the four principal French and Spanish warships Nelson had been responsible for capturing at major battles – *San Joseph*, *L'Orient*, *Trinidad*, and *Bucentaure*. Three platforms, like decks, stood above the hearse. On the highest one the coffin was placed, head towards the stern where a Union Jack was hanging at half-mast. A large, black canopy hung over the coffin, supported by four pillars, black ostrich feathers adorning the four corners, the sides festooned with richly fringed black velvet. On the front of the canopy the word 'NILE' was inscribed in gold, on one side the motto: 'HOSTE DEVICTO, REQUIEVIT', on the opposite side: 'PALMAM QUI MERUIT FERAT', and in the back, above the Union Jack, the word 'TRAFAL-GAR'. This canopy was shortly removed, however, to permit the public to get a better view of the coffin, which, in fact, was concealed beneath the folds of a great black pall. The carriage was drawn by six horses 'in elegant furniture'. Nothing like it had ever been seen in London, although the hearse almost did not make it in time for the ceremony, having been twice modified at the last minute to permit it to squeeze through the gates at the Admiralty and then to pass beneath the arch at Temple Bar.

After stopping for some moments at Charing Cross opposite the statue of King Charles, the hearse passed on, the horses being led at a solemn pace. 'Every hat was off, every sound was hushed, and the most awful silence prevailed,' as many tens of thousands looked on. The hearse was followed by Garter Principal King of Arms, Sir Isaac Heard, 'in his official habit, with his Sceptre,' his coach being followed in turn by that of the Chief Mourner and his two Supporters in long black cloaks. They were followed by two more coaches with six assistant mourners, then by Windsor Herald with the Banner of Emblems, in front of a mourning coach bearing Captains Hardy and Bayntun, of the *Leviathan*. They were followed by the male relatives of the deceased in coaches, including Horatio Nelson Esq (as William Earl Nelson, the Admiral's sole surviving brother now called himself, to the anguish of Emma Hamilton: 'A man must have great courage to *accept* the honour of calling himself by *that* name!'). Also present were Nelson's three nephews, Viscount Merton, George Matcham and Thomas Bolton, then their fathers, the two brothers-in-law, George Matcham and Thomas Bolton, and four cousins.

The Grenadiers now entered the railings round St Paul's, lining the space from the western gate of the churchyard to the cathedral door, while the rest of the column proceeded round the church down Cheapside, along Old Jewry and Coleman Street, to Moorfields, where the troops, cavalry and artillery were posted.

Meanwhile, inside, the seats allotted to the public had been filled since 7 am even though the first members of the procession only reached the church at one o'clock, when the great western door was thrown open and a resplendent General Sir David Dundas marched in at the head of the Grenadier companies and the Highland regiments – 300 men altogether. They formed single files and gradually lined the north and south aisles of the nave and the transept, and from the gold and white dome along the black and white marble floor to the gate of the choir where they rested on their arms reversed. The Dean, the white-mitred Bishop of Lincoln, escorted His Royal Highness, the Prince of Wales, to the choir beneath immense Byzantine ceilings; next came Earl Camden (replacing the

Prime Minister this day), followed by the six Royal dukes, then by the Lord Mayor in a large black silk gown fringed with gold lace on the sleeves and collar. Behind them in the audience the Royal Navy was well represented by thirty-one admirals and ninety-three captains all wearing mourning swords and black crape arm bands. However, it was 'the brave Seamen of the *Victory*', bearing two tattered Union flags and the St George's Ensign that had been torn and singed while atop the *Victory*'s masts, who captured everyone's attention. The organ began to play, its rich, resonant sounds accompanied by 100 choristers singing, 'I am the resurrection and the life, saith the Lord,' followed by evening prayers and further anthems – 'Dixi Custodium', 'Domine, Refugium', and the 'Magnificat'.

By now a wintry dusk was settling quickly over the capital as the murky grey light from the windows at the base of the dome faded and large torches were lit in the choir and the galleries of Christopher Wren's seventeenth-century cathedral, even as the vast space beneath the immense dome was lighted by 130 'patent lamps' hoisted in a large multi-tiered black octagonal lanthorn far above. From the choir where the service was conducted, great long shadows were cast in all directions and a large bier, covered with black velvet, ornamented with gold fringe and tassels, bore the coffin. Over it lay another black velvet pall, adorned like the hearse with six golden escutcheons representing Lord Nelson's arms, and above it the heavy velvet canopy, supported by six rear-admirals, while the two supporters of the pall, Vice-Admiral James Hawkins Whitshed and Nelson's old foe, Vice-Admiral Sir John Orde, Bt, stood at the head of the bier, Rear-Admiral (as he now was) Eliab Harvey (of the *Téméraire*) and Vice-Admiral Thomas Taylor standing at its foot. Further ahead of the bier in the choir stood two naval lieutenants, Richmond Herald and Captain Robert Moorsom (of the *Revenge*) holding the Great Banner, while the Heralds of York, Somerset, Lancaster and Chester held Nelson's gauntlet and spurs, helm and crest, target and sword, and surcoat, two Gentlemen Ushers and Norroy King of Arms bearing the black velvet cushion with the Admiral's coronet as Viscount. Outside, on either side of the supporters of the canopy, three bannerols containing the family lineage were borne by two naval officers and behind each of them stood another officer, all of them serving on the *Victory*.

To the rear of the bier stood two more Gentlemen Ushers, Garter Principal King of Arms with his sceptre, Sir Isaac Heard, the Chief Mourner, Sir Peter Parker, Bt, Admiral of the Fleet, with two Supporters, Admiral Lord Radstock and Admiral Lord Hood, attended by six assistant mourners (all admirals), two more Gentlemen Ushers, Windsor Herald and, behind him, the Banner of Emblems borne by Captain Hardy and Captain Bayntun, aided by two naval lieutenants and, finally, behind them all, ten relatives of the deceased, William Earl Nelson, Viscount Merton, George Matcham and his son of the same name, Thomas Bolton and son of the same name and four cousins. In the nearby 'Royal Box', stood the Royal dukes and the Prince of Wales, each in a resplendent uniform, bedecked with medals and orders.

The canopy and pall were finally removed at five o'clock as the admirals carried the coffin from the bier and choir to the centre of the dome, where the stones of the floor had been removed earlier to permit the coffin to be lowered directly into the crypt below. The Gentleman Usher now carried the carpet and cushion along with the 'trophies' to a table near the grave behind the Chief Mourner, while the coronet, still on the velvet cushion, was placed by Clarenceux King of Arms on the body. As the Chief Mourner, his Supporters and assistants and the relatives of the deceased took their places around the coffin, the organ played a solemn dirge and the Bishop of Lincoln, his arms outstretched from his white chasuble, uttered the timeless funeral rites: 'Earth to earth, ashes to ashes, dust to dust'.

As the coffin was lowered into the torch-lit crypt below at 5.33 pm the artillery in nearby Moorfields boomed, attended by three volleys by the infantry, while, inside, Garter King at Arms, Sir Isaac Heard, now proclaimed in his powerful voice:

> Thus it hath pleased Almighty God to take out of this transitory life, unto his divine mercy, the Most Noble Lord Horatio Nelson, Viscount and Baron Nelson of the Nile and of Burnham Thorpe, in the County of Norfolk, Baron Nelson of the Nile, and of Hilborough, in the same County; Knight of the most Honourable Order of the Bath, Vice-Admiral of the White Squadron of the Fleet, and Commander-in-Chief of His Majesty's Ships and Vessels in the Mediterranean; also Duke of Brontë in Sicily; Knight Grand Cross of the Sicilian Order of St Ferdinand and of Merit; Member of the Ottoman Order of the Crescent; Knight Grand Commander of the Order of St Joachim, and Hero who, in the moment of Victory, fell covered with immortal glory! Let us humbly trust, that he is now raised to bliss ineffable, and to a glorious immortality.

With these closing words the Comptroller, Treasurer and Steward of Nelson's household now broke their white staves and gave the pieces to Garter, who threw them into the grave, while placing the two furled Union Jacks and St George's ensign on the coffin. Horatio Nelson had found peace at long last.

*

No women were invited to attend this state ceremony, and Emma Hamilton spent the afternoon at her little house in Clarges Street, while far to the north, in Scotland, Lord Melville passed the day in seclusion. At the same time, in the spa resort of Bath, William Pitt was being carried by his doctor and servants to a waiting coach to take him to Bowling Green House, at Putney Heath, where he died on 23rd January. On the same 9th January, aboard his new flagship *Queen*, Vice-Admiral Collingwood was on guard duty off the south-eastern Spanish port of Cartagena. Admiral Cornwallis, whose mastery had resulted in Britain holding and controlling the Channel for the past two years and keeping all French fleets – with the exception of the Rochefort squadron – successfully blockaded, rendering them incapable either of launching an invasion or joining Villeneuve's fleet, and who created and dispatched to the Spanish coast the fleet that Nelson commanded, was sheltering from a harsh gale with his fleet off the South Devon coast at Torbay. His presence had neither been required at St Paul's this day, nor his absence remarked upon. Nor, indeed, was he ever thanked for these most remarkable achievements.

'I can assure your lordship', a restrained William Cornwallis wrote to Lord Barham following receipt of the news from Trafalgar and hints from London that he might be reassigned to another command, 'that I never had any particular partiality for this employment [commanding the prestigious Channel Fleet]. The manner in which I was twice called to it by a great sea officer [St Vincent] was all that was flattering to me . . .' Three months after Nelson's obsequies, Admiral Cornwallis was summarily ordered ashore by Lord Grenville's new Government, never to sail again and subsequently forgotten by British historians, even as Admiral Lord St Vincent (the 'great sea officer' who had declined the honour of attending the recent state funeral of an even greater one) took his place, hoisting his own ensign over the *Ville de Paris* as Commander-in-Chief of the Channel Fleet.

Chronology of Events

1796–1802

19th August 1796	Secret Treaty of Ildefonso, Spain and France.
May 1798–June 1800	Second Coalition formed against France.
17th October 1798	Treaty of Campo Formio.
9th–10th November 1799	Napoleon's *coup d'état*.
10th April 1800	Robert Fulton launches first submarine at Rouen.
16th December 1800	Russia, Sweden, Denmark form Armed Neutrality of the North.
9th February 1801	Treaty of Lunéville.
2nd April 1801	Battle of Copenhagen.
15th July 1801	French Concordat with Vatican.
September 1801	French army in Egypt capitulates to English.
1st October 1801	Decrès named Minister of the Navy and Colonies.
8th October 1801	Franco-Russian Treaty.
December 1801	Napoleon named President of the Italian Republic.
24th March 1802	Treaty of Amiens signed.
26th December 1802	Treaty of Paris, Austria, France, Russia.

1803

19th February 1803	Act of Mediation drawn up, creating Helvetic Confederation.
April 1803	French high-tariff law vs Great Britain goes into effect.
27th April 1803	Imperial Recess of Ratisbon.
May 1803	Bonaparte appeals to nation for patriotic contributions. Blockade of Brest resumes.
1st May 1803	Work begins on new port and fortifications of Boulogne.
16th May 1803	Admiral Nelson named Commander-in-Chief of the Mediterranean Fleet.
23rd May 1803	Daru informs Tribunate to expect French invasion of England. War Minister Berthier announces first tentative plans for invasion camps along the Channel.

24th May 1803	Pierre Forfait named Inspector General of the National Flotilla. First Consul Bonaparte awards the first major contracts for flotilla vessels.
25th May 1803	Cornwallis assumes command of Channel Fleet, issuing orders to seize and destroy all French shipping.
28th May 1803	Bonaparte creates first coastal artillery units.
29th May 1803	Bonaparte obtains 20,000,000 franc bank loan for the flotilla.
June 1803	Bonaparte calls for creation of boatyards nationwide, and conscripts carpenters and labourers.
4th June 1803	War Minister Berthier assigns 60,000 troops to man coastal defences.
25th June 1803	Batavian Republic and France sign military convention, Holland joins French war effort against England.
Summer 1803	Robert Fulton tests submarine *Nautilus* for French navy.
5th July 1803	Bonaparte substantially increases boat orders for National Flotilla.
21st July 1803	Admiral de Bruix named Commander-in-Chief of the National Flotilla. Bonaparte prepares first general plan for all Channel embarkation ports and their development.
August 1803	Soult named as Commander-in-Chief of invasion forces.
10th September 1803	Bonaparte prepares project for initial invasion force of 114,000 men and 7,000 horses.
October 1803	24,000,000 francs' worth of patriotic contributions made by citizens of France for the flotilla.
19th October 1803	Secret Franco-Spanish military alliance.
21st October 1803	Wimereux now named for development as a port.
November 1803	Bonaparte names Admiral Verhuell to head Dutch navy and their flotilla contributions.

1804

January 1804	70,000 French troops encamped near Boulogne.
March 1804	Cochrane replaces Pellew off Cape Finisterre.

21st March 1804	Duke d'Enghien murdered by Bonaparte.
16th May 1804	Melville named First Lord of Admiralty, Sir Sidney Smith clashes with Dutch flotilla.
18th May 1804	Senate proclaims Napoleon Emperor of the French, Consulate ends. Prime Minister Pitt assumes office.
19th May 1804	Napoleon names first nine Imperial Marshals.
24th May 1804	Russo-Prussian Defence Pact signed.
June 1804	Admiral Ganteaume replaces Admiral Truguet at Brest.
July 1804	Major army/navy military review at Boulogne.
2nd July 1804	**Napoleon's first invasion plan:** Admiral Latouche-Tréville, named commander of Mediterranean Fleet, to sail from Toulon to Rochefort and Cherbourg, thence to Boulogne.
Summer 1804	Boulogne's defences nearly completed.
19th August 1804	Latouche-Tréville dies at Toulon, first invasion plan (of 2nd July) cancelled.
3rd September 1804	Villeneuve is named to replace Latouche-Tréville at Toulon.
22nd September 1804	Admiral Cornwallis orders Captain Moore to seize Spanish treasure ships.
29th September 1804	**Napoleon's second invasion plan:** Villeneuve to sail from Toulon to South America and Surinam. Smaller expedition to go to St Helena and west coast of Africa. Admiral Missiessy's Rochefort fleet to join Villeneuve at Martinique. Total fleet under Villeneuve to return to El Ferrol, then to Boulogne. Ganteaume's Brest fleet to go to northern Ireland to land troops and then join others at Boulogne. (English intercept this plan.)
5th October 1804	Captain Moore seizes Spanish treasure ships.
8th October 1804	Napoleon cancels second invasion plan (of 29th September).
26th October and 23rd December 1804	**Napoleon's third invasion plan:** Missiessy to sail to Martinique. Villeneuve to sail from Toulon to South America and Surinam to attack British ports and to return to Channel ports. No invasion actually mentioned.
27th October 1804	Lord Melville orders Sir John Orde to form squadron off Cadiz.

6th November 1804	Russo-Austrian Treaty signed and begins Third Coalition (ratified 17th June 1805).
2nd December 1804	Napoleon's Imperial Coronation, Paris.
3rd December 1804	King Gustavus IV of Sweden signs secret military convention with England.
12th December 1804	Spain declares war on England.
19th December 1804	Villeneuve assumes command at Toulon.
22nd December 1804	Spain closes El Ferrol/La Coruña to British ships.

1805

2nd January 1805	Napoleon writes to George III, proposing peace.
4th January 1805	New Franco-Spanish naval pact signed.
11th January 1805	Missiessy sails for Caribbean.
16th January 1805	**Napoleon's fourth invasion plan:** French squadrons at Brest, Rochefort, El Ferrol (including Spanish) to sail to West Indies. Villeneuve's Toulon fleet to meet there, ravage British ports, then return to Europe. Cancelled because Villeneuve returns to Toulon.
18th January 1805	Villeneuve's abortive attempt to leave Toulon.
24th January 1805	Great Britain declares war on Spain.
22nd February 1805	Missiessy reaches Martinique.
27th February–2nd March 1805	**Napoleon's fifth invasion plan:** rescinds orders of 16th January. Ganteaume to sail to El Ferrol to lead Gourdon's and Spanish squadron to Martinique. Missiessy to remain at Martinique. Villeneuve to sail from Toulon to Martinique. Ganteaume to take command of entire force at Martinique and lead it back to Boulogne for invasion (to arrive between 10th June and 10th July 1805).
2nd March 1805	Admiral Calder assumes command at El Ferrol, replacing Admiral Cochrane.
18th March 1805	Admiral de Bruix dies, replaced as Flotilla Commander-in-Chief by Admiral Lacrosse.
22nd March 1805	Napoleon rescinds orders of 27th February–2nd March.
28th March 1805	Missiessy sails from Martinique for France.
30th March 1805	Villeneuve sails from Toulon for Martinique.

30th March 1805	**Napoleon's sixth invasion plan**: Villeneuve to sail directly to Ireland (and not the West Indies) then down to Boulogne, but Napoleon rescinded this plan on 13th April and it was never sent.
3rd April 1805	Lord Gardner replaces Cornwallis at Ushant, who goes on leave.
4th April 1805	Nelson learns of Villeneuve's escape from Toulon.
8th April 1805	Parliament censures Melville, who resigns. He is replaced by Lord Barham later same month.
10th April 1805	Villeneuve, with Gravina's squadron, sails from Cadiz for Martinique.
11th April 1805	Anglo-Russian Treaty signed (ratified 28th July 1805), for Third Coalition.
13th April 1805	**Napoleon's seventh invasion plan**: Villeneuve to sail directly to West Indies (not Ireland), to be joined by Gravina's squadron (from Cadiz). Ganteaume (at Brest) to sail to Martinique. In Caribbean, French to attack and seize British colonies. At Martinique Villeneuve to assume full command and return to El Ferrol with Combined Fleet, thence to Boulogne.
12th May 1805	Nelson leaves Portugal for West Indies following Combined Fleet.
16th May 1805	Villeneuve's Combined Fleet reaches Fort de France, Martinique.
20th May 1805	Missiessy returns to Rochefort.
26th May 1805	Napoleon seizes crown of Italy.
30th May 1805	Villeneuve receives new orders of seventh invasion plan (13th April) to proceed to Brest and then Boulogne.
2nd June 1805	Villeneuve captures HMS *Diamond*.
4th June 1805	Nelson arrives at Carlisle Bay, Barbados. Napoleon seizes Ligurian Republic.
5th June 1805	Villeneuve sails north from Martinique.
June 1805	Lord Gardner (at Ushant) dispatches Collingwood to the south and ultimately Cadiz.
7th June 1805	Villeneuve captures convoy of fifteen British merchantmen and learns of Nelson's arrival.
11th June 1805	Villeneuve sails for Europe.
16th June 1805	Nelson learns of Villeneuve's departure for Europe.
25th June 1805	Captain Allemand replaces Missiessy at Rochefort.

7th July 1805	Cornwallis resumes command at Ushant.
17th July 1805	Allemand's squadron escapes from Rochefort.
18th July 1805	Nelson reaches southern Spain.
22nd July 1805	Calder's fleet clashes with Combined Fleet off El Ferrol.
25th July 1805	Nelson learns Villeneuve's fleet is somewhere to north.
26th July 1805	**Napoleon's eighth invasion plan** (or set of orders): Villeneuve to return to Europe stopping for ships at Cadiz, then El Ferrol and Brest, finally advancing to Boulogne. Allemand is ordered to join him.
27th July 1805	Villeneuve puts into Vigo Bay.
29th July 1805	Calder return to El Ferrol, before rejoining Cornwallis on 14th August.
31st July 1805	Villeneuve leaves Vigo for El Ferrol/La Coruña.
August 1805	French treasury is bankrupt.
2nd August 1805	Villeneuve reaches El Ferrol/La Coruña.
3rd August 1805	Napoleon reaches Boulogne for last time, to review troops and await Villeneuve.
8th August 1805	Napoleon learns of battle of 22nd July.
9th August 1805	Austria signs defence pact with England (Third Coalition complete).
11th August 1805	Combined Fleet sails south, for Cadiz.
14th August 1805	Calder's fleet rejoins Cornwallis at Ushant.
15th August 1805	Nelson stops at Ushant and gives Cornwallis his fleet.
16th August 1805	Cornwallis creates new fleet, under command of Calder, to pursue Villeneuve to El Ferrol and Cadiz.
18th August 1805	Nelson reaches Portsmouth.
19th August 1805	Cornwallis learns Villeneuve has left El Ferrol.
21st August 1805	Combined Fleet reaches Cadiz.
25th August 1805	Napoleon signs defence pact with Bavaria.
26th August 1805	Grande Armée at Boulogne breaks camp, marches to the Rhine.
August–September 1805	Major Russian and Austrian troop movements towards western frontiers. Nelson meets with Pitt and Barham several times.

5th September 1805	Napoleon signs defence pact with Württemberg. Cornwallis receives signal from Collingwood that Combined Fleet has reached Cadiz.
11th September 1805	Francis II (Austria) invades Bavaria.
15th September 1805	Nelson sails from Portsmouth.
16th September 1805	**Napoleon's ninth plan**: orders Combined Fleet to Mediterranean and Genoa.
17th September 1805	Napoleon names Admiral Rosily to replace Villeneuve at Cadiz.
28th September 1805	Nelson assumes command of new Mediterranean Fleet off Cadiz, replacing Calder who is ordered home.
8th October 1805	Conseil de Guerre. Captains of Combined Fleet revolt.
10th October 1805	Admiral Rosily reaches Madrid.
14th October 1805	Rosily leaves Madrid for Cadiz.
18th October 1805	Villeneuve orders Combined Fleet to sail.
19th October 1805	*Euryalus* signals appearance of first French ships leaving Cadiz. Nelson orders 'General Chase'.
20th October 1805	Remainder of Combined Fleet clears Cadiz at 3 pm, sailing for Gibraltar.
21st October 1805	Villeneuve wears fleet to north at 8 am, to face Nelson. Battle of Trafalgar, Nelson killed, Villeneuve captured.
4th November 1805	Strachan captures Dumanoir's division of four ships off Cape Ortegal.
6th November 1805	London learns of the victory at Trafalgar.
15th November 1805	Villeneuve repatriated by the English.
16th November 1805	Napoleon (in Vienna) learns of his defeat at Trafalgar.
2nd December 1805	Battle of Austerlitz.
4th December 1805	*Victory* returns to England with Nelson's body.
5th December 1805	National day of thanksgiving throughout British Isles.
1806	
9th January 1806	Nelson's state funeral at St Paul's Cathedral.
23rd January 1806	William Pitt dies, replaced by Lord Grenville.
March 1806	Admiral St Vincent replaces Cornwallis as Commander-in-Chief of the Channel Fleet.

Biographical Sketches

ADDINGTON, HENRY, 1ST VISCOUNT SIDMOUTH, 1757–1844. Prime Minister 1801–1804. In 1805 he served briefly under Pitt as Lord President of the Council.

ÁLAVA Y NAVARRETE, IGNACIO MARÍA DE, 1750–1817. Spanish admiral commanding the second division of the Combined Fleet who later died of wounds received at Trafalgar.

ALEXANDER I, 1777–1825. Tsar of Russia. Married Elizabeth of Baden, 1793, and succeeded his father, Tsar Paul, in 1801. In 1805 he finally agreed to join the coalition against Napoleon.

ALLEMAND, ZACHARIE-JACQUES-THÉODORE, 1762–1826. Like Captain Missiessy whom he succeeded in the summer of 1805 as commander of the squadron at Rochefort, he escaped the British blockade and managed to inflict heavy casualties on their merchant shipping in the English Channel. Failing to receive orders to join Admiral Villeneuve's Combined Fleet and following the defeat of the latter, he safely returned to port.

ARGUMOSA, TEODORO DE. Captain of the *Monarca*, wounded at Trafalgar.

AUGEREAU, PIERRE-FRANÇOIS-CHARLES, 1757–1816. Named Marshal of the Empire 0 in 1804, he commanded the army at Bayonne, 1803–1804, then at Morlaix and Brest for the invasion preparations, before being named Governor of Hanover.

BALL, SIR ALEXANDER JOHN, 1757–1809. Rear-admiral who had served under Nelson in the Mediterranean, and participated in the Battle of the Nile. Subsequently he was named the first British Governor of Malta. He remained a close friend of Nelson.

BARBÉ-MARBOIS, FRANÇOIS, 1745–1837. France's Treasury Minister until the end of 1805.

BARHAM, LORD, SIR CHARLES MIDDLETON, 1726–1813. Appointed by Pitt in April 1805 to replace Lord Melville as First Lord of the Admiralty, a post he held at the time of Trafalgar.

BAYNTUN, HENRY WILLIAM, 1766–1840. Captain of the *Leviathan* at Trafalgar.

BEAUDOUIN, LOUIS-ALEXIS, d.1805. Captain of the *Fougueux*, killed at Trafalgar.

BEDFORD, JOHN, 1773?–1814. Assumed command of the *Tonnant* when Captain Tyler was seriously wounded.

BEDOUT, JACQUES, 1751–1818. Rear-admiral who commanded the squadron returning from San Domingo in 1803 that sought refuge at El Ferrol and La Coruña where they were trapped by Pellew's squadron. While there the ailing Bedout was replaced by Admiral Gourdon.

BÉRENGER, CHARLES, b.1757. Captain of the *Scipion* at Trafalgar.

BERRY, SIR EDWARD, 1768–1831. Commanded the *Agamemnon* at Trafalgar.

BERTHIER, LOUIS-ALEXANDRE, 1753–1815. French War Minister, appointed Major General of the Grande Armée in 1805. One of the first nine Marshals of the Empire to be created by Napoleon. He was responsible for co-ordinating and preparing all aspects of the invasion army, 1803–1805.

BEURNONVILLE, PIERRE DE RUEL, 1752–1821. Army general under Napoleon who also distinguished himself in various diplomatic appointments; as ambassador to Berlin and then Madrid. He refused to inform Villeneuve that he had been superseded by Admiral Rosily, permitting him to sail instead of returning to Paris.

BLACKWOOD, SIR HENRY, 1770–1832. Ultimately achieving the rank of vice-admiral, Captain Blackwood commanded the inshore squadron at Cadiz in October 1805 from the *Euryalus*, which signalled Lord Nelson that the Combined Fleet had sailed prior to the battle of Trafalgar.

BOLTON, WILLIAM, 1777–1830. Captain of the *Eurydice* at Trafalgar.

BONAPARTE, JOSEPH, 1768–1844. Napoleon's elder brother who negotiated the Treaty of Amiens with Lord Cornwallis, 1801–1802, and later became King of Naples and then of Spain.

BONAPARTE, NAPOLEON, 1769–1821. Seized control of the French government on 18 Brumaire An VIII (9th–10th November 1799) and established the Consulate, imposed the peace Treaty of Lunéville on Austria in 1801, named Consul for life in 1802. In March 1802 he concluded the Treaty of Amiens with Great Britain, resuming a state of war on 18th May 1803 and becoming Emperor of the French on 18th May 1804.

BRERETON, ROBERT. Brigadier General commanding British forces on St Lucia, he relayed false information on purported sighting of the French fleet, resulting in Nelson's failure to meet them in the West Indies in June 1805.

BROUARD, GABRIEL–AUGUSTE, 1769–1841. Captain of Admiral Magon's flagship, the *Algésiras*.

BRUIX, EUSTACE DE, 1795–1805. Career officer who fought against the British during the American War of Independence, and in the West Indies. Promoted to rank of captain in 1793, then arrested by the revolutionary government, reinstated in 1794, and as 'major-général' headed expedition against Ireland (which failed). Promoted rear-admiral in 1797, then named Naval Minister in 1798 and 1799, and vice-admiral (1799), commanding the fleet at Rochefort. In 1803 was named Commander-in-Chief of the Invasion Flotilla. Upon his death in March 1805 he was replaced by his Second-in-Command, Admiral Lacrosse.

BULLEN, CHARLES, 1769–1821. Captain of the *Britannia* at Trafalgar.

CAFFARELLI, LOUIS-MARIE-JOSEPH, 1760–1845. Maritime Prefect of Brest, 1800–1805.

CAJIGAL, FELIPE JADO. Captain of the *San Agustín*, wounded at Trafalgar.

CALDER, SIR ROBERT, 1745–1818. On 2nd March 1805 assumed command of the squadron off El Ferrol and La Coruña, then was given command of an enlarged squadron with orders to prevent Admiral Villeneuve's Combined Fleet (*en route* from the West Indies) from reaching Europe, resulting in a clash between the two forces off Finisterre on 22nd July 1805. Technically a British victory, Calder was later criticised for his failure to act decisively in this battle and pursue the enemy, resulting in his court-martial and a severe reprimand. Following that battle, in summer/autumn 1805 Calder was given command of another fleet with orders to pursue the Combined Fleet; he followed them to Cadiz where, upon Nelson's assumption of command, he returned to England, thereby ending his career.

CAMDEN, JOHN JEFFREYS PRATT, 2ND EARL AND 1ST MARQUIS, 1759–1840. Secretary for War and Colonies under Pitt's second administration, then replacing Viscount Sidmouth (Addington) as Lord President of the Council June–July 1805 with Castlereagh replacing him in turn at the War Office.

CANNING, GEORGE, 1770–1827. Under-Secretary of State in 1796, pursuing strong policy against the French. Served as Treasurer of the Navy, 1804–1806, afterwards as Foreign Secretary under Lord Portland's administration.

CAPEL, THE HON. THOMAS BLADEN, 1776–1853. Captain of the frigate *Phoebe* at Trafalgar.

CASTLEREAGH, ROBERT STEWARD, VISCOUNT, 1769–1822. Beginning political life as a Whig, he turned Tory in 1795. Keeper of the Privy Seal, 1796, Irish Chief-Secretary from 1797, served as War Minister from July 1805 to 1806, later distinguishing himself as Foreign Secretary at the congresses of Châtillon and Vienna (1814–15) and in preparation of the Treaty of Paris (1815).

CHARLOTTE, QUEEN, 1744–1818. Charlotte Sophia, daughter of the Duke of Mecklenburg-Strelitz, and wife of George III.

CHURRUCA, COSMÉ DAMIÁN, 1761–1805. Commanded the *San Juan Nepomuceno* and was killed at Trafalgar.

CISNEROS, BÁLTASAR HIDALGO DE, b.1770. Spanish admiral commanding a division of seven ships (including *Bucentaure*) at Trafalgar where he was wounded.

CLARENCE, DUKE OF, 1765–1837. Third son of George III, served as midshipman in the Royal Navy when Nelson was a captain. Succeeded to the throne as William IV in 1830.

COCHRANE, SIR ALEXANDER, 1758–1832. Rear-admiral in charge of the squadron off El Ferrol–La Coruña, where in March 1804 he replaced Commodore Pellew. He was later dispatched with a squadron to Jamaica.

CODRINGTON, EDWARD, 1770–1851. Captain of the *Orion* at Trafalgar.

COLLINGWOOD, CUTHBERT, 1748–1810. British admiral under Cornwallis's command, dispatched in the late summer of 1805 to blockade Spanish ships at Cadiz. Was later placed under the command of Sir Robert Calder at that port, and finally under Nelson (September–October). Succeeded as Commander-in-Chief of the Mediterranean Fleet after Nelson's death on 21st October 1805.

CONN, JOHN, 1764–1810. Captain of the *Dreadnought* at Trafalgar.

CONTAMINE, THÉODORE, 1773–1845. Commander of the French expeditionary force, succeeding General Lauriston in this post with the Combined Fleet at Cadiz in September 1805.

COOKE, JOHN, 1763–1805. Captain of the *Bellerophon*, killed at Trafalgar.

CORNWALLIS, CHARLES, 1ST MARQUIS, 1738–1805. Elder brother of Admiral Sir William Cornwallis, Commander-in-Chief of the British Army against the American colonists, surrendering to General Washington at Yorktown, Virginia, 1781. Served as

Lord-Lieutenant of Ireland and twice as Governor General of India (1786–1793, and 1804–1805) and negotiated the peace of Amiens for Britain, 1801–1802.

CORNWALLIS, SIR WILLIAM, 1744–1819. Fourth son of Charles, fifth Lord, and first Earl Cornwallis, to which titles his elder brother Charles later succeeded. Born 20th February 1743 or 1744, entered the navy in 1755, appointed lieutenant in 1761 and captain in 1766. Served in the Channel, the Mediterranean, Atlantic and Caribbean, and off the African coast, and was in numerous actions against the French. Met Captain Horatio Nelson in the West Indies by 1780. Served under Admiral Sir Samuel Hood in the West Indies, fighting with distinction against Admiral de Grasse at St Kitts on 26th January 1782. Nominated Commodore in 1788 and named Commander-in-Chief of the East Indies station, returning to England in 1794, having been promoted to rear-admiral (1st February 1793), once again serving in the Channel. 4th February 1794 he was promoted to vice-admiral. February 1796 he was appointed Commander-in-Chief in the West Indies, but, due to ill health and damage sustained by his flagship, he delayed assuming that post and was court-martialled and censured, then striking his flag. 14th February 1799 he was made admiral and in 1801 succeeded Lord St Vincent on board the *Ville de Paris* in command of the Channel Fleet until March 1802, resuming that post in May 1803 until March 1806 when he was ordered ashore. Throughout 1803–1806 he maintained his post off Ushant, and in the summer of 1805 unilaterally created and dispatched the fleet to Cadiz in pursuit of Admiral Villeneuve, of which Nelson assumed command in September 1805 just prior to the battle of Trafalgar, 21st October 1805.

COSMAO-KERJULIEN, JULIEN-MARIE, 1761–1825. Commodore of the *Pluton* at Trafalgar.

COTTON, SIR CHARLES, 1753–1812. Served as Cornwallis's Second-in-Command during the blockade of Brest. *San Josef* served as his flagship.

CUMBY, WILLIAM PRYCE, 1771–1837. Assumed command of the *Bellerophon* when Captain Cook was killed at Trafalgar.

CUMMING, WILLIAM, 1757?–1824. Commanded Sir Robert Calder's flagship, the *Prince of Wales*.

DAVOUT, LOUIS-NICOLAS, 1770–1823. Created Marshal of the Empire, and commanded the army corps at Bruges, 1804–1805, during the invasion preparations.

DECRÈS, DENIS, 1761–1820. Joined navy 1779, promoted to lieutenant 1786 and captain in 1793, taking part in the Irish expedition of 1797. Promoted rear-admiral in 1798, named Minister of the Navy and Colonies 1801–1814, in charge of invasion operations against Great Britain, 1803–1805. Named Grand Aigle de la Légion d'Honneur and Grand Officier de l'Empire, and raised to the peerage as duke. His name is to be found on the Arc de Triomphe.

DENIEPORT, GABRIEL, 1765–1805. Commanded the *Achille* at Trafalgar where he was killed.

DIGBY, HENRY, 1770–1842. Captain of the *Africa* at Trafalgar.

DUFF, GEORGE, 1764–1805. Captain of the *Mars*, killed at Trafalgar.

DUMANOIR LE PELLEY, PIERRE-ETIENNE-RENÉ-MARIE, 1770–1829. Served as Villeneuve's Second-in-Command of the French Mediterranean fleet. He was against fighting the British and removed most of his division of ten ships from the battle at Trafalgar on 21st October 1805, thereby disobeying orders and abandoning Villeneuve. He was captured by Sir Richard Strachan shortly thereafter off Cape Viñano. Although finally cleared of all charges subsequently brought against his irregular conduct, he was not entrusted with another command until 1811.

DUMAS, MATHIEU, 1753–1837. General inspecting troops in Belgium and Holland during the invasion period and preparing coastal defences and army camps.

DUMOURIEZ, CHARLES FRANÇOIS DUPÉRIER, 1739–1823. Former army commander and foreign minister under the French revolutionary government, then military adviser to the Duke of York, 1803–1806.

DUNDAS, SIR DAVID, 1735–1820. General commanding the military district comprising Kent, Surrey and Sussex during the threat of French invasion, 1804–1806.

DUNDAS, HENRY, 1ST VISCOUNT MELVILLE AND BARON DUNIRA, 1742–1811. Early in his parliamentary career became a staunch Pitt supporter and in 1791 served as Secretary of State for the Home Department, later resigning with Pitt in 1801. In May 1804 he was named First Lord of the Admiralty, a post he held till April 1805. He was then impeached for "gross malversation and breach of duty" for his earlier conduct when Treasurer of the Navy, of which charges he was acquitted in 1806.

DUNDAS, WILLIAM, 1762–1845. Served as War Minister under Pitt.

DURHAM, PHILIP CHARLES, 1763–1845. Captain of the *Defiance*, wounded at Trafalgar.

ELPHINSTONE, GEORGE KEITH, 1ST VISCOUNT KEITH, 1746–1823. British admiral in command at the Downs station, 1803–1806, then commanding the Channel Fleet 1812–1815 and responsible for transporting Napoleon from Rochefort to Plymouth in 1815.

EPRON, JACQUES, 1766–1837. Captain of the *Argonaute* at Trafalgar.

ESCAÑO, ANTONIO DE, 1752–1814. Rear-admiral serving under Gravina, wounded at Trafalgar.

FILHOL-CAMAS, JEAN GILLES, 1760–1805. Commanded the *Berwick*, killed at Trafalgar.

FLORES, LUIS DE. Captain of the *San Francisco de Asís* at Trafalgar.

FORFAIT, PIERRE-ALEXANDRE-LAURENT, 1752–1807. Fired as Naval Minister in 1801 to be replaced by Admiral Decrès, during 1803–1805 was named Inspector General of the National Flotilla, was responsible for designing the new flat-bottomed vessels to partake in the crossing to England.

FOUCHÉ, JOSEPH, 1763–1820. Teacher of physics at the Oratoire college of Nantes, subsequently headmaster, then revolutionary, voting for the execution of Louis XVI in 1792. Later responsible for mass executions at Lyons. Police Minister under the Directory in 1799, then under the Consulate and the Empire until 1810, and briefly once more under Napoleon in 1815.

FOX, CHARLES JAMES, 1749–1806. Liberal statesman and third son of the first Lord Holland, entering Parliament at age of nineteen, and staunch Pitt opponent. A celebrated debater carrying out strenuous attacks opposing the continuation of the war against France.

FRANCIS II OF THE HOLY ROMAN EMPIRE, AND FRANCIS I OF AUSTRIA, 1768–1835. Succeeded his father, Leopold II, to the throne in 1792. His first war with revolutionary France ended in 1797 with the Treaty of Campo Formio, thereby losing Netherlands and Lombardy. Joined England and Russia in the Third Coalition against France in 1805.

FREDERICK AUGUSTUS, DUKE OF YORK AND ALBANY, 1763–1827. Second son of George III, named Commander-in-Chief of British forces in 1798 and in charge of defending England during the threat of French invasion, 1803–1805.

FREDERICK WILLIAM III, KING OF PRUSSIA, 1770–1840. Assumed throne of Prussia in 1797 and tried to maintain a neutral international policy *vis-à-vis* France and England, only finally declaring war on the French in 1806.

FREMANTLE, THOMAS FRANCIS, 1765–1819. Captain of the *Neptune* at Trafalgar.

FRERE, JOHN HOOKHAM, 1769–1841. Diplomat, wit, translator. Former Under Secretary of State for Foreign Affairs, and British Minister to Madrid from 1802.

FULTON, ROBERT, 1765–1815. American inventor who successfully launched the first submarine (the *Nautilus*) on the Seine on 10th April 1800, which Napoleon and Decrès declined to employ. He invented the first steamship (also in France) in 1803.

GALIANO, DIONISIO ALCALÁ, d.1805. Commander of the *Bahama*, killed at Trafalgar.

GAMBIER, JAMES. British consul-general, Lisbon.

GANTEAUME, HONORÉ-JOSEPH-ANTOINE, 1755–1818. Succeeded Admiral Truguet as Fleet Commander at Brest, 1804–1805.

GARDNER, ALAN, LORD, 1742–1809. Briefly commanded the Channel Fleet off Brest in the summer of 1805 during Admiral Cornwallis's absence. *Hibernia* served as his flagship.

GARDOQUÍ, JOSÉ, d.1816. Captain of Álava's flagship, the *Santa Ana*, he was wounded at Trafalgar.

GASTÓN, MIGUEL. Captain of the *San Justo* at Trafalgar.

GEORGE III, 1738–1820. Succeeded his grandfather, George II, as King of England and Elector of Hanover in 1760. Generally disliked Prime Minister William Pitt and several of his basic reforms.

GEORGE, PRINCE OF WALES, 1762–1830. Eldest son of George III and bitter enemy of Pitt. Became Prince Regent in 1810 and King, as George IV, in 1820.

GODOY, MANUEL DE, 'PRINCE OF PEACE', DUKE OF ALCUDIA, 1767–1851. Became Spanish prime minister in 1792 under Carlos IV, co-operating with Napoleon and the French against Britain, ending his life in exile in Rome and Paris.

GOURDON, ADRIEN-LOUIS, 1765–1833. Admiral Bedout's chief-of-staff, replacing him as squadron commander at El Ferrol in 1804.

GOURRÈGE, PIERRE-PAUL, 1762–1805. Captain of the *Aigle*, killed at Trafalgar.

GRANDALLANA, DOMINGO. Commanded the Spanish squadron at El Ferrol prior to the arrival of the Combined Fleet. He had hoped to replace Admiral Gravina as Commander-in-Chief of the Spanish Fleet.

GRAVES, SIR THOMAS, 1747–1814. Commanded squadron off the coast of Brittany, 1804–1805, under Admiral Cornwallis. It was he who on 17th January 1805 reported the escape of Missiessy's squadron from Rochefort.

GRAVINA, FEDERICO CARLOS, 1758–1806. Served as Second-in-Command of the Combined Fleet under Admiral Villeneuve during the technical defeat at the hands of Admiral Calder off the Spanish coast on 22nd July 1805. He held the same position at the battle of Trafalgar, 21st October, when he was mortally wounded.

HAMILTON, LADY EMMA LYON, 1768–1815. Nelson's common-law wife by whom he had a daughter, Horatia.

HARDY, THOMAS MASTERMAN, 1769–1839. Old friend of Nelson's, serving as captain of the *Victory* at Trafalgar.

HARGOOD, WILLIAM, 1762–1839. Captain of the *Belleisle* at Trafalgar.

HARRINGTON, EARL OF, CHARLES STANHOPE, 1753–1829. General commanding the military district of London during the period 1803–1806 at the time of a threatened French invasion.

HARROWBY, EARL OF, RICHARD RYDER, 1766–1832. Secretary of State for the Foreign Department under Pitt's second administration.

HARVEY, ELIAB, 1758–1830. Captain of the *Téméraire* at Trafalgar.

HAWKESBURY, LORD, ROBERT JENKINSON, 1770–1828. Son of Charles Jenkinson, Earl of Liverpool. Served as Foreign Secretary under Addington's government and as Secretary of State for the Home Department under Pitt's second administration.

HENNAH, WILLIAM, 1765?–1833. Assumed command of *Mars* following the death of Duff.

HOBART, ROBERT, EARL OF BUCKINGHAMSHIRE, 1760–1816. Secretary of War under Addington, 1801–1804.

HOPE, GEORGE, 1767–1818. Captain of the *Defence* at Trafalgar.

HORE, RAFAEL DE, 1770–1808. Captain of Gravina's flagship, the *Príncipe de Asturias*.

HOSTE, WILLIAM, 1780–1828. Captain of the *Amphion* (having replaced Captain Sutton) at Trafalgar.

HUBERT, JEAN-JOSEPH, 1765–1805. Commodore of the *Indomptable* at Trafalgar.

INFERNET, LOUIS-ANTOINE-CYPRIEN, 1756–1815. Captain of the *Intrépide* at Trafalgar.

KING, RICHARD, 1774–1834. Captain of the *Achilles* at Trafalgar.

LACROSSE, JEAN-BAPTISTE-RAYMOND, 1765–1829. Admiral replacing Bruix as Commander-in-Chief of the Invasion Flotilla at Boulogne in March 1805.

LAFOREY, SIR FRANCIS, 1767–1835. Captain of the *Spartiate* at Trafalgar.

LAGRANGE, JOSEPH, 1761–1836. General in command of the troops on board Missiessy's Rochefort squadron which sailed to the West Indies in January 1805.

LAPENOTIÈRE, JOHN RICHARDS, 1770–1834. Captain of the schooner *Pickle* which brought back the news of the victory at Trafalgar and Nelson's death to England in November 1805.

LATOUCHE-TRÉVILLE, LOUIS-RENÉ LEVASSOR DE, 1745–1804. In 1803 upon his return from the ill-fated San Domingo expedition, Vice-Admiral Latouche was named Commander-in-Chief of the Toulon fleet, where he died on board the *Bucentaure*, 14th August 1804, to be replaced by Villeneuve.

LAURISTON, JACQUES-ALEXANDRE-BERNARD LAW, 1768–1828. General commanding the troops aboard Villeneuve's Combined Fleet, 1804–1805, and deeply critical of Villeneuve's actions. He was called to Paris from Cadiz just prior to the battle of Trafalgar.

LAVILLEGRIS, GUILLAUME-JEAN-NOËL, d.1807. Captain of the *Mont-Blanc* at Trafalgar.

LE ROY. Commissaire Général des Relations Commerciales at Cadiz in 1805.

LETELLIER, JEAN-MARIE, 1767–1830. Captain of Dumanoir's flagship, the *Formidable*.

LE TOURNEUR, d.1805. Lieutenant on the *Algésiras*, killed at Trafalgar.

L'HOSPITALIER-VILLEMADRIN, CHARLES-EUSÈBE, b.1756. Commanded the *Swift-sure* at Trafalgar.

LOUIS, THOMAS, 1759–1807. Rear-admiral dispatched by Nelson to Gibraltar and Morocco for revictualling, hence not present at the battle of Trafalgar.

LUCAS, JEAN-JACQUES-ETIENNE, 1764–1819. Captain of the *Redoutable*, wounded at Trafalgar.

MACDONNELL, ENRIQUE. Commodore in the Spanish Navy commanding the *Rayo* at Trafalgar.

MAGENDIE, JEAN-JACQUES, 1766–1835. Captain of Villeneuve's flagship, *Bucentaure*, at Trafalgar where he was wounded.

MAGON DE MÉDCINE, CHARLES-RENÉ, 1763–1805. Briefly commanded the right wing of the Invasion Flotilla at Boulogne; the fiery Admiral Magon later bitterly opposed Villeneuve's failure to seek out the enemy. He was killed aboard the *Algésiras* at the battle of Trafalgar.

MAISTRAL, ESPRIT-TRANQUILLE, 1763–1815. Captain of the *Neptune* at Trafalgar.

MALMESBURY, EARL OF, JAMES HARRIS, 1746–1820. Career diplomat who served at Madrid, Berlin, St Petersburg and The Hague. A close friend of Pitt.

MANSFIELD, CHARLES JOHN MOORE, d.1813. Captain of the *Minotaur* at Trafalgar.

MARSDEN, WILLIAM, 1754–1836. First, or Permanent Secretary of the Admiralty throughout 1804–1805, having replaced Sir Evan Nepean.

MEYERS, SIR WILLIAM. Lieutenant-general and Commander-in-Chief of British forces at Barbados and the Leeward Islands in 1805, with whom Nelson conferred before pursuing Villeneuve.

MINTO, EARL OF, SIR GILBERT ELLIOT-MURRAY-KYNYNMOUND, 1751–1814. Old friend and confidant of Nelson's ever since Minto's days as Viceroy of Corsica. He later served as Governor-General of India.

MISSIESSY, EDOUARD-THOMAS DE BURGUES, 1756–1837. Commanded the French squadron at Rochefort, 1803–1805, which escaped the British blockade reaching the West Indies (1805), then returning safely to France. He was replaced by Captain Zacharie Allemand.

MOORE, GRAHAM, 1764–1843. Captain of the *Indefatigable*, ordered by Cornwallis on 22nd September 1804 to intercept and seize the Spanish treasure ships returning from America to Cadiz, which Moore duly executed on 5th October 1804, resulting in Spain's declaration of war against England on 12th December. He was the brother of General Sir John Moore who later commanded an expeditionary force against the French in Spain.

MOORSOM, ROBERT, d.1835. Captain of the *Revenge*, wounded at Trafalgar.

MORRIS, JAMES NICOLL, 1763–1830. Captain of the *Colossus*, wounded at Trafalgar.

NELSON, HORATIO, VISCOUNT, 1758–1805. Having served at all the major naval stations, in the Far East, Mediterranean, Channel and western Atlantic, he was responsible for the great victories of the Nile (1798) and Copenhagen (1801) (the latter under the nominal command of Sir Hyde Parker). He was killed off Cape Trafalgar on 21st October 1805 after effecting the greatest naval victory in the history of the Royal Navy.

NEY, MICHEL, 1769–1815. Later made Marshal of the Empire, commanded the army corps at Montreuil during the invasion preparations (1804–1805).

NORTHESK, EARL OF, WILLIAM CARNEGIE, 1758–1831. Rear-admiral and Third-in-Command at Trafalgar where his flagship, the *Britannia*, avoided almost all the fighting.

ORDE, SIR JOHN, 1751–1824. Vice-admiral and St Vincent's Third-in-Command off Cadiz in 1798, who protested so vehemently when St Vincent gave Nelson command of the Mediterranean Fleet that he was ordered to strike his flag. He was only given a new command six years later (1805) and was watching Cadiz once again when Admiral Villeneuve arrived

from the Mediterranean. He failed to notify Nelson of this important event or follow Villeneuve, thereby significantly delaying the action to be taken against the Combined Fleet. In 1805 Orde was again ordered to strike his flag, this time permanently.

OUVRARD, GABRIEL-JULIEN, 1770–1846. Financier and contractor for the French army and navy and responsible in part for victualling Villeneuve's ships at Cadiz prior to Trafalgar.

OWEN, RICHARD, 1771–1849. Captain of the *Immortalité*, serving under Lord Keith in the Channel and North Sea.

PAREJA, ANTONIO, d.1813. Captain of the *Argonauta*, wounded at Trafalgar.

PELLEW, SIR EDWARD, 1757–1833. Commodore and future Admiral Viscount Exmouth, in command of the squadron Cornwallis assigned to Cape Finisterre, Spain, summer 1803–March 1804, when he was replaced by Rear-Admiral Cochrane.

PELLEW, ISRAEL, 1758–1832. Captain of the *Conqueror* at Trafalgar.

PILFORD, JOHN, 1776–1834. Acting captain of the *Ajax* at Trafalgar.

PITT, WILLIAM, 1759–1806. Second son of the Earl of Chatham. Entered House of Commons in 1781, Prime Minister 1783–1801. Responsible for directing the British war effort against the revolutionary government of France, resuming office as Prime Minister 1804–1806.

PIUS VII, GREGORIO LUIGI BARNABA CHIARAMONTI, 1742–1823. Pope, 1800–1823; signed the Concordat with France, 15th July 1801 and performed the religious ceremonies at the imperial coronation of Napoleon on 2nd December 1804. He later excommunicated the French emperor, and was in turn arrested by him.

POULAIN, JEAN-BAPTISTE-JOSEPH-RENÉ, 1767–1805. Captain of the *Héros*, died at Trafalgar.

PRIGNY, JEAN-BAPTISTE-NICOLAS-GUILLAUME, b.1778. Villeneuve's chief of staff, wounded at Trafalgar.

PROWSE, WILLIAM, 1760?–1826. Captain of the frigate *Sirius* at Trafalgar.

QUEVEDO Y CHEZA, JOSÉ. Captain of the *San Leandro* at Trafalgar.

REDMILL, ROBERT, d.1819. Captain of the *Polyphemus* at Trafalgar.

REILLE, HONORÉ-CHARLES-MICHEL-JOSEPH, 1775–1860. General, Second-in-Command of expeditionary force under General Lauriston aboard the fleet with Villeneuve.

ROSE, HON. GEORGE, 1744–1818. English statesman, supporter and confidant of William Pitt. He served as Vice-President of the Board of Trade, Paymaster General, and Treasurer of the Navy.

ROSILY-MESROS, FRANÇOIS-ETIENNE, 1748–1832. Named by Napoleon to succeed Admiral Villeneuve as Commander of the Combined Fleet at Cadiz, September 1805. Only arriving after the battle of Trafalgar, he remained blockaded at Cadiz with the remnants of the fleet where he was captured by the Spanish in 1808. His name is to be found on the Arc de Triomphe.

ROTHERAM, EDWARD, 1753–1830. Captain of the *Royal Sovereign* at Trafalgar.

RUMBOLD, SIR GEORGE BERRIMAN, 1764–1807. The British diplomatic envoy to Cuxhaven

(Germany) who was kidnapped on 25th October 1804 on orders of Police Minister Fouché, resulting in a major international incident, only resolved just before Napoleon's imperial coronation that December.

RUTHERFORD, WILLIAM GEORGE, 1764–1818. Captain of the *Swiftsure* at Trafalgar.

ST VINCENT, EARL, JOHN JERVIS, 1735–1823. Created Earl St Vincent following his defeat of the enemy off Cape St Vincent in 1797. Named Admiral of the Fleet and served as First Lord of the Admiralty under Prime Minister Addington, relinquishing that post to Lord Melville in May 1804.

SCHIMMELPENNINCK, RUTGER JAN, 1761–1825. Dutch lawyer, statesman and Grand Pensionary.

SMITH, SIR WILLIAM SYDNEY, 1764–1840. Between 1803 and 1806 Commodore Smith served in various capacities in the Channel and off the Dutch coast under Admiral Lord Keith.

SOULT, NICOLAS JEAN DE DIEU, 1769–1851. Marshal of the Empire and Colonel General of the Imperial Guard, commanded the army corps at St Omer during the invasion preparations, 1803–1805, with overall command of the entire invasion army.

STANHOPE, LADY HESTER, 1776–1839. Eldest daughter of Charles, third Earl Stanhope, and William Pitt's sister, ran Pitt's establishment 1803–1806. In 1810 left England to live in the Levant.

STIRLING, CHARLES, 1760–1833. As a rear-admiral served as squadron commander under Cornwallis in the Channel.

STOCKHAM, JOHN, d.1814. Acting captain of the *Thunderer* at Trafalgar.

STRACHAN, SIR RICHARD, 1760–1828. On 4th November 1805 Captain (later Admiral) Strachan's squadron captured Admiral Dumanoir's remaining four ships off Cape Viñano as they were fleeing northward from Trafalgar.

SUTTON, SIR JOHN, b.1757? Second-in-Command at Plymouth, the admiral served as president of the court-martial board in the summer of 1804 trying three seamen – James Dunn, Patrick Gorman and Edward Plunkett – of the *Montagu*, for inciting mutiny off the coast of Brest. All three were convicted and executed in July 1805.

TALLEYRAND-PÉRIGORD, CHARLES MAURICE DE, PRINCE OF BENEVENTO, 1754–1838. Son of the Comte Talleyrand de Périgord, began career in the Church, serving as abbot of St Denis, 1775, and *agent-général* to the French clergy in 1780. Nominated as Bishop of Autun in 1788, in 1789 was elected for the clergy to the States General where he helped draft the Declaration of Rights of Man and Citizen. In 1790 he was elected president of the Assembly and also consecrated two new bishops, but was then excommunicated by Pope Pius VI. Spent 1793 as exile in London, and in 1794 went to America. In 1797 served as Foreign Minister to the Directory. Under the Consulate named Foreign Minister again, then was Emperor Napoleon's Foreign Minister. In 1814 he deserted Napoleon.

TOUFFET, CLAUDE, b.1767. Captain of the *Duguay-Trouin* at Trafalgar.

TRUGUET, LAURENT-JEAN-FRANÇOIS, 1752–1839. Former Naval Minister, the vice-admiral commanding the fleet at Brest until summer 1804 when he was replaced by Vice-Admiral Ganteaume.

TYLER, CHARLES, 1760–1835. Captain of the *Tonnant*, wounded at Trafalgar.

URIARTE Y BORJA, FRANCISCO DE, 1753–1842. Captain of Cisneros's flagship, the *Santísima Trinidad*, and wounded at Trafalgar.

VALDÉS, CAYETANO, b.1770. Commodore and captain of the *Neptuno*, wounded at Trafalgar.

VARGAS, JOSÉ DE, b.1769. Captain of the *San Ildefonso*, wounded at Trafalgar.

VERHUELL, CHARLES-HENRI, 1764–1845. Began his career as infantry officer, then took a naval commission and served in the north Atlantic, off the African coast, the West Indies, the Baltic and Mediterranean, becoming a captain in 1791, but retiring for political reasons shortly thereafter. Active duty again in 1803 with rank of rear-admiral with the French navy in the Channel, promoted vice-admiral in 1804. Very pro-French, almost anti-Dutch, commanding the right wing of the invasion armada, 1803–1805. He later became the Dutch Naval Minister, and field marshal, then serving as the Dutch Ambassador to Paris where he later retired and became a French citizen. His name is inscribed on the Arc de Triomphe.

VILLARET-DE-JOYEUSE, LOUIS-THOMAS, 1748–1812. In 1800 commanded the ill-fated expedition against San Domingo. Then named Captain-General of Martinique, a position he held throughout the period 1803–1805 when squadrons and fleets of the intended invasion force rendezvoused in the West Indies. This testy vice-admiral, who denounced every naval commander sent to his station throughout this period, was captured by the English in 1809. He concluded his career as Governor-General of Venice.

VILLENEUVE, PIERRE-CHARLES-JEAN-BAPTISTE-SILVESTRE DE, 1763–1806. Succeeded Latouche-Tréville as Commander of the Toulon fleet in 1804, then appointed to head the Combined Fleet of the French and Spanish navies which was ultimately defeated by Nelson off Cape Trafalgar on 21st October 1805.

WHITBY, JOHN, d.1806. Good friend of Admiral Cornwallis, who with his wife lived permanently at Cornwallis' estate of Newlands. Served for some time as captain of the *Ville de Paris*.

WHITWORTH, CHARLES, EARL, 1752–1825. Served as British ambassador to Paris following the signing of the Peace of Amiens, 1802–1803.

YOUNG, ROBERT BENJAMIN, 1773–1846. Captain of the cutter *Entreprenante* at Trafalgar.

APPENDIX 3

Fleets

Admiral Ganteaume's Brest Fleet:

SHIPS OF THE LINE

Impérial (118-gun)	*Jean-Bart* (74-gun)	*Batave* (74-gun)
Invincible (118-gun)	*Jupiter* (74-gun)	*Brave* (74-gun)
Républicain (110-gun,	*Patriote* (74-gun)	*Cassard* (74-gun)
formerly *Révolutionnaire)*	*Tourville* (74-gun)	*Conquérant* (74-gun)
Alexandre (80-gun)	*Ulysse* (74-gun)	*Diomède* (74-gun)
Foudroyant (80-gun)	*Vétéran* (74-gun)	*Eole* (74-gun)
Aquilon (74-gun)	*Wattignie* (74-gun)	*Impétueux* (74-gun)

FRIGATES

Comète (40-gun)	*Valeureuse* (40-gun)
Félicité (40-gun)	*Volontaire* (40-gun)
Indienne (40-gun)	

Ships detached by Admiral Cornwallis from the Channel Fleet, 16th August 1805, under the command of Sir Robert Calder to El Ferrol:

SHIPS OF THE LINE

Britannia (Northesk's flagship, 100-gun)	*Swiftsure** (74-gun)
Prince (98-gun)	*Conqueror** (74-gun)
Téméraire (98-gun)	*Leviathan** (74-gun)
Neptune (98-gun)	*Defence* (74-gun)
Prince of Wales (Calder's flagship, 90-gun)	*Goliath* (74-gun)
	Dragon (74-gun)
*Canopus** (Louis' flagship, 80-gun)	*Orion* (74-gun)
Revenge (74-gun)	
Zealous (74-gun)	FRIGATE
Spencer (74-gun)	*Sirius*
*Spartiate** (74-gun)	
*Donegal** (74-gun)	GUNBOAT
*Tigre** (74-gun)	*Attack*

The ships marked with an asterisk had formed part of Nelson's fleet that he left with Cornwallis on his way home to England after his voyage to the West Indies.

Villeneuve's Combined Franco-Spanish Fleet that left El Ferrol for Cadiz August 1805:

SHIPS OF THE LINE

(French)

Bucentaure (80-gun)
Formidable (80-gun)
Neptune (80-gun)
Indomptable (80-gun)
Pluton (74-gun)

Scipion (74-gun)
Swift-sure (74-gun)
Mont-Blanc (74-gun)
Fougueux (74-gun)
Redoutable (74-gun)

Argonaute (74-gun)
Duguay-Trouin (74-gun)
Héros (74-gun)

(Spanish)

Príncipe de Asturias
   (112-gun)
Neptuno (80-gun)
San Juan Nepomuceno
   (74-gun)

San Francisco de Asís
   (74-gun)
Monarca (74-gun)
San Agustín (74-gun)

San Ildefonso (74-gun)
Montañes (74-gun)
San Fulgencio (64-gun)

FRIGATES

(French)

Rhin (40-gun)
Hermione (40-gun)
Cornélie (40-gun)

Hortense (40-gun)
Thémis (32-gun)

(Spanish)
Flora (34-gun)

CORVETTES

(French)
Argus
Observateur

(Spanish)
Mercurio
Indagora

GOËLETTE

(French)
Téméraire

San Rafael and *Firma* of the Spanish fleet were captured 22nd July 1805. *España* and *America* (Spanish) and *Atlas* (French) were put into dry dock in Vigo as a result of that battle and three French boats, *Revanche*, *Guerrière* and *Syrène* (frigate) were put into dry dock at El Ferrol.

The Combined Franco-Spanish fleet at the battle of Trafalgar in order of sailing, with their nationality, name of ship's captain and number of guns:

1. *Neptuno* (Spanish, 80-gun, Commodore Cayetano Valdés)
2. *Scipion* (French, 74-gun, Captain Charles Bérenger)
3. *Intrépide* (French, 74-gun, Captain Louis-Antoine-Cyprien Infernet)
4. *Formidable* (French, 80-gun, Rear-Admiral Pierre-Etienne-René-Marie Dumanoir Le Pelley, Captain Jean-Marie Letellier)
5. *Duguay-Trouin* (French, 74-gun, Captain Claude Touffet)
6. *Mont-Blanc* (French, 74-gun, Commodore Guillaume-Jean-Noël Lavillegris)
7. *Rayo* (Spanish, 100-gun, Commodore Enrique MacDonnell)
8. *San Francisco de Asís* (Spanish, 74-gun, Captain Luis de Flores)

9. *Héros* (French, 74-gun, Captain Jean-Baptiste-Joseph-René Poulain)
10. *San Agustín* (Spanish, 74-gun, Captain Felipe Jado Cajigal)
11. *Santísima Trinidad* (Spanish, 136-gun, Rear-Admiral Báltasar Hidalgo de Cisneros, Commodore Francisco de Uriarte y Borja)
12. *Bucentaure* (French, 80-gun, Vice-Admiral Pierre-Charles-Jean-Baptiste-Silvestre de Villeneuve, Captain Jean-Jacques Magendie)
13. *Redoutable* (French, 74-gun, Captain Jean-Jacques-Etienne Lucas)
14. *San Justo* (Spanish, 74-gun, Captain Miguel Gastón)
15. *Neptune* (French, 80-gun, Commodore Esprit-Tranquille Maistral)
16. *San Leandro* (Spanish, 64-gun, Captain José Quevedo y Cheza)
17. *Santa Ana* (Spanish, 112-gun, Vice-Admiral Ignacio María de Álava y Navarrete, Captain José Gardoquí)
18. *Indomptable* (French, 80-gun, Commodore Jean-Joseph Hubert)
19. *Fougueux* (French, 74-gun, Captain Louis-Alexis Beaudouin)
20. *Pluton* (French, 74-gun, Commodore Julien-Marie Cosmao-Kerjulien)
21. *Monarca* (Spanish, 74-gun, Captain Teodoro de Argumosa)
22. *Algésiras* (French, 74-gun, Rear-Admiral Charles-René Magon, Captain Gabriel-Auguste Brouard)
23. *Bahama* (Spanish, 74-gun, Commodore Dionisio Alcalá Galiano)
24. *Aigle* (French, 74-gun, Captain Pierre-Paul Gourrège)
25. *Montañes* (Spanish, 74-gun, Captain Francisco Alcedo)
26. *Swift-sure* (French, 74-gun, Captain C. E. L'Hospitalier-Villemadrin)
27. *Argonaute* (French, 74-gun, Captain Jacques Epron)
28. *Argonauta* (Spanish, 80-gun, Captain Antonio Pareja)
29. *San Ildefonso* (Spanish, 74-gun, Captain José de Vargas)
30. *Achille* (French, 74-gun, Captain Gabriel Denieport)
31. *Príncipe de Asturias* (Spanish, 112-gun, Admiral Federico Carlos Gravina, Rear-Admiral Antonio de Escaño, Captain Rafael de Hore)
32. *Berwick* (French, 74-gun, Captain Jean-Gilles Filhol-Camas)
33. *San Juan Nepomuceno* (Spanish, 74-gun, Captain Cosmé Damián Churruca)

There were five frigates attached to the Combined Fleet: *Cornélie, Hermione, Hortense, Rhin* (all 40-gun) and *Thémis* (32-gun); and two brigs, *Argus* and *Furet*.

The British Fleet at the battle of Trafalgar was divided into two columns as follows, with the number of guns and name of the commander for each ship:

WEATHER COLUMN
1. *Victory* (100-gun, Vice-Admiral Lord Nelson, Captain Thomas Masterman Hardy)
2. *Téméraire* (98-gun, Captain Eliab Harvey)
3. *Neptune* (98-gun, Captain Thomas Francis Fremantle)
4. *Leviathan* (74-gun, Captain Henry William Bayntun)
5. *Conqueror* (74-gun, Captain Israel Pellew)
6. *Britannia* (100-gun, Rear-Admiral the Earl of Northesk, Captain Charles Bullen)

7. *Spartiate* (74-gun, Captain Sir Francis Laforey)
8. *Minotaur* (74-gun, Captain Charles John Moore Mansfield)
9. *Ajax* (74-gun, Lieutenant John Pilford, acting captain)
10. *Agamemnon* (64-gun, Captain Sir Edward Berry)
11. *Orion* (74-gun, Captain Edward Codrington, out of formation)
12. *Africa* (64-gun, Captain Henry Digby, out of formation)

LEE COLUMN
1. *Royal Sovereign* (100-gun, Vice-Admiral Cuthbert Collingwood, Captain Edward Rotheram)
2. *Belleisle* (74-gun, Captain William Hargood)
3. *Mars* (74-gun, Captain George Duff)
4. *Tonnant* (80-gun, Captain Charles Tyler)
5. *Bellerophon* (74-gun, Captain John Cooke)
6. *Colossus* (74-gun, Captain James Nicoll Morris)
7. *Achilles* (74-gun, Captain Richard King)
8. *Defence* (74-gun, Captain George Hope)
9. *Defiance* (74-gun, Captain Philip Charles Durham)
10. *Prince* (98-gun, Captain Richard Grindall)
11. *Dreadnought* (98-gun, Captain John Conn)
12. *Revenge* (74-gun, Captain Robert Moorsom)
13. *Swiftsure* (74-gun, Captain William George Rutherford)
14. *Thunderer* (74-gun, Lieutenant John Stockham, acting captain)
15. *Polyphemus* (64-gun, Captain Robert Redmill)

The British frigates included *Euryalus,* Captain the Hon. Henry Blackwood; *Naiad,* Captain Thomas Dundas; *Phoebe,* Captain the Hon. Thomas Bladen Capel; *Sirius,* Captain William Prowse and *Juno* (which was not present at the battle). Lieutenant John Lapenotière commanded the schooner *Pickle* and Lieutenant Robert Benjamin Young the cutter *Entreprenante.*

Six English captains were killed or wounded in addition to Lord Nelson: Duff of the *Mars* and Cooke of the *Bellerophon* were killed; Tyler of the *Tonnant,* Morris of the *Colossus,* Moorsom of the *Revenge* and Durham of the *Defiance* were wounded.

The nineteen prizes captured by the Royal Navy at the Battle of Trafalgar were:

(Spanish)

Santísima Trinidad	*San Agustín*	*Santa Ana*
San Ildefonso	*Argonauta*	*Monarca*
Bahama	*Neptuno*	*Argonauta*
	San Juan Nepomuceno	

(French)

Bucentaure	*Redoutable*	*Fougueux*
Algésiras	*Aigle*	*Intrépide*
Berwick	*Swift-sure*	*Achille*

NOTES AND SOURCES

PREFACE

1. Nelson was honoured with burial in the crypt of St Paul's Cathedral as were some of his fellow officers present at Trafalgar (e.g. Collingwood and Codrington) yet there is not even a small plaque to the memory of Sir William Cornwallis.
2. Although Sir William's brother the Marquis (a commanding general in the American Revolutionary War, Lieutenant-General of Ireland and twice Governor-General of India) is given substantial coverage in *Chambers Biographical Dictionary*, the Admiral is not even mentioned.

Sources

CORBETT, SIR JULIAN, *The Campaign of Trafalgar*, London, Longmans, Green, 1910

LEYLAND, JOHN (ed.), *Dispatches and Letters Relating to the Blockade of Brest, 1803–1805*, 2 vols, London, Navy Records Society, 1899, 1902

CHAPTER 1

1. Treaties of the Second Coalition: Austrian Treaty with Naples, 19th May 1798; Britain's Treaty with Naples, 29th November 1798; Russo-Neapolitan Treaty, 1st December 1798; Anglo-Russian Treaty, 29th December 1798; Russian Treaty with the Ottoman Empire, 23rd December 1798; Britain's Treaty with the Ottoman Empire, 29th December 1798; Anglo-Austrian Treaty, 20th June 1800 (valid until 28th February 1801).
2. Great Britain only insisted on France evacuating Holland and Switzerland, allowing her to remain in both Piedmont and the Italian Republic.
3. The asking price was 80,000,000 francs, but certain 'expenses' were deducted, including indemnities to the government in Washington D.C.
4. Rose, who had held numerous government posts including the Vice-Presidency of the Board of Trade, Paymaster General and Treasurer of the Navy, was a close and long-time confidant of Pitt.

Sources

The Annual Register, or a View of the History, Politics, and Literature for the Year 1804

AYLING, STANLEY, *George The Third*, London, Collins, 1972

BERTHAUT, JULES, *Manuel du Chef: Maximes Napoléoniennes*, Paris, Payot, 1919

BINGHAM, D. A., *A Selection from the Letters of the First Napoleon*, vol. 2, London, Chapman, Hall, 1884

BRUCE, H. A. (ed.), *Life of General Sir William Napier*, London, John Murray, 1864

CASTELOT, ANDRÉ, *Napoleon*, London, Harper & Row, 1971

CLARKE, JAMES STANIER, and MACARTHUR, JOHN, *The Life of Admiral Lord Nelson, from His Lordship's Manuscripts*, London, Cadwell & Davies, 1809

CLEVELAND, DUCHESS OF, *The Life and Letters of Lady Hester Stanhope*, London, John Murray, 1914

CONSTANT, LOUIS, *Mémoires de Constant, premier valet de chambre de l'Empereur sur la vie privée de Napoléon, sa famille et sa cour*, vol. 2, Paris, Lavocat, 1830

CORNWALLIS, MARQUIS, *The Correspondence of Charles First Marquis Cornwallis*, vols 2 and 3, London, John Murray, 1859

Dictionary of National Biography, Oxford, Oxford University Press

FAUVELET DE BOURRIENNE, *Mémoires*, vol. 1, London translation, Hutchinson, 1885

Foreign Relations, *see* Foreign Office correspondence in the Public Record Office, London: France FO 27; Miscellaneous FO 148; Portugal FO 63; Spain FO 72, 185, 186

GAGNON, *France since 1789*, New York, Harper & Row, 1972

Gentleman's Magazine, 1804

HARCOURT, LEVENSON VERNON (ed.), *The Diaries and Correspondence of the Right Hon. George Rose, containing original letters of the most distinguished statesman of his day*, London, Bentley, 1860

LAUGHTON, JOHN KNOX, *Letters and Despatches of Horatio, Viscount Nelson*, London, Longmans, Green, 1886

MAHAN, ALFRED T., *The Life of Nelson, the Embodiment of the Sea Power of Great Britain*, 2 vols, London, Sampson, Low, Marston, 1897

MALMESBURY, EARL OF, *Diaries and Correspondence of James Harris, First Earl of Malmesbury*, London, Bentley, 1844

MARKHAM, CLEMENTS (ed.), *Selections from the Correspondence of Admiral John Markham*, London, Navy Records Society, 1904

MARKHAM, JOHN, *see* Markham, Clements

MATHESON, CYRIL, *The Life of Henry Dundas, First Viscount Melville 1742–1811*, London, Constable, 1933

MOWAT, R.B., *The Diplomacy of Napoleon*, London, Arnold, 1924

PITT, WILLIAM, *see* 'Prime Ministers' Papers' in the Public Record Office, London, PRO 36/8, bundles 101–363

REILLY, ROBIN, *William Pitt the Younger*, New York, Putnam, 1979

RÉMUSAT, MME DE, *Mémoires de Madame de Rémusat, 1802–1808*, vol. 2, Paris, Hachette, 1959

ROSE, GEORGE, *see* Harcourt, Levenson (ed.)

STANHOPE, LADY HESTER, *Memoirs of the Lady Hester Stanhope, As Related by Herself in Conversations with her Physician*, vol. 2, London, Colburn, 1845

The Times, May–December 1804

WARDROPPER, JOHN, *Kings, Lords and Wicked Libellers, Satire and Protest 1760–1837*, London, John Murray, 1973

WHEELER, H.F.B., and BROADLEY, A.M., *Napoleon and the Invasion of England, the Story of the Great Terror*, vol. 2, London, John Lane, 1908

CHAPTER 2

1. Curiously enough, the most precise figures on the British army's regimental strength comes from Desbrière's *Projets*. See also *Hansard* and the *Annual Register* for 1804, the latter claiming the army was now up to 120,000 men, volunteers in England reaching the figure of 380,000 and 84,000 more in Scotland, for a total of 464,000 volunteers.

2. Lord Castlereagh in summer 1805 stated there were 84,000 militia in the UK; 25,000 sea-fencibles, 96,000 regular troops, 340,000 volunteers. 'In truth, there are 120,000 men in Great Britain who still do not have rifles.'

Sources

CRUIKSHANK, GEORGE, *A Pop Gun fired off by George Cruikshank, in defence of the British Volunteers of 1803*, London, W. Kent & Co., 1860

DESBRIÈRE, EDOUARD, *Projets et Tentatives de Débarquement aux Iles Britanniques*, vol. 3, Paris, Chapelot, 1902

HARCOURT, LEVENSON VERNON, *op. cit.*

JAMES, WILLIAM, *The Naval History of Great Britain, from the Declaration of War by France in 1793, to the Accession of George IV*, vols 3 and 4, London, Bentley, 1837

The John Johnson Collection ('Military II, Irregulars'), Bodleian Library, Oxford

Liverpool Chronicle, 28th August 1805

MARKHAM, JOHN, *op. cit.*

MONTAGU, JOHN LORD, *Buckler's Hard and Its Ships, Some Historical Reflections*, London, private printing, 1909

Morning Post, October 1803

ROSE, J. HOLLAND, and BROADLEY, A.M., *Dumouriez and the Defence of England against Napoleon*, vol. 2, London, John Lane, 1904

The Times, September–December 1803, May 1804

WATSON, J. STEVEN, *The Reign of George III, 1760–1815*, Oxford, Clarendon Press, 1985

WHEELER, H.F.B., and BROADLEY, A.M., *op. cit.*

CHAPTER 3

1. All this work was directed by the local district commission, each of which was headed by a naval captain and comprised three other naval officers.
2. Sixteen *prames* were on order costing an average of 70,000 francs each, 318 *chaloupes* were placed on tender at a cost of between 32,000 and 42,000 francs each, and were built as far away as Strasbourg and Colmar. The total cost was approximately 11,766,000 francs but, as shall be seen, Napoleon found other means of financing these boats for the most part. The cost of the 289 *bateaux canonniers* (there were already 165 older ones in existence); averaging 18,000 to 23,000 francs each came to 6,358,000 francs, while the typical cost of a *péniche* ran at about 8,500 francs, or 3,833,500 francs for all 452 of them. Thus the total cost of the new flotilla came to 23,077,500 francs exclusive of its armament, which must be estimated at at least another 5,000,000 francs, and the bill for an additional 709 transport vessels (mostly fishing boats or small coastal freighters) bought up and down the entire coast from as far south as Bayonne, and as far north as Anvers and Ostend, which came to 6,840,430 francs, without the costs of modifying them.

3. Admiral Bruix found only 241 *chaloupes* (instead of the 342 Napoleon said they had, 392 *bateaux canonniers* (not 432) and only 393 *péniches*, and in fact these included all vessels built or on order.

4. As will be seen later, the contradictions and incredible complexity created by these movements of ships, ship orders, and estimates of supplies was to prove equally troublesome in the creation of the Army as well, when units of men were transferred – companies, half-brigades, brigades and regiments from all over France and Europe broken up, often for years at a time, lent to various other armies and services – all so utterly scrambled as to create a logistical nightmare which even War Minister Alexandre Berthier could scarcely begin to cope with.

5. By the end of 1803 the Dutch had the following results for Napoleon: 89 flat-bottomed boats completely rigged and armed, but lacking both crews and food supplies; 10 more flat-bottom boats shortly to be ready at Rotterdam; 10 more such boats under construction at Flushing (all these were armed with two small guns – 4- or 6-pounders – and with a 16-inch howitzer); 23 *chaloupes canonnières*, completely rigged and

fitted out both with crews and armament (three cannon – 12-, 18- or 24-pound guns); 108 stable-ships to be ready shortly (the Dutch version being only 50 feet long and 20 feet wide, hence smaller than the French model).

6. This figure conflicts, of course, with the Dutch figure.

7. By the end of May, however, the three divisions of *chaloupes* and four divisions of *bateaux canonniers* at Ostend came to a total of 54 *chaloupes* and 144 *bateaux canonniers*. The Dutch-designed *chaloupes* and *bateaux* were smaller but more seaworthy. A Dutch *chaloupe* could carry 30 to 40 sailors and 21 soldiers, as compared to a maximum of 152 for the French equivalent; Dutch *bateaux canonniers* also carried a much smaller crew, 3 or 4 sailors and 22 men, compared to the French design allowing for 112 men.

Sources

Archives des affaires étrangères: 607, Hollande, 1803 (An XI and XII); 608, Hollande, 1804 (An XII and XIII), Paris

Archives Nationales, Paris: AF⁴, Archives du pouvoir executif et relations extérieures, 1789–1815 (Napoléon), 1190, 1191, 1202, 1203; BB¹ Décisions (including correspondence between Napoleon and Decrès), 26; BB² Correspondance du Départ, 1790–1869, 91; BB⁴ Campagnes (including Boulogne and Flottille Nationale et Impériale), 167

BERTHAUT, JULES, *op. cit.*

BONAPARTE, NAPOLEON, *Correspondance de Napoléon Premier, publiée par ordre de L'Empereur Napoléon III*, Paris, Imprimerie Impériale, 1858–1869: 1803, Letters 6870, 6967, 7030, 7066, 7100, 7105, 7375

DESBRIÈRE, EDOUARD, *Projets, op. cit.*, vol. 3

Le Moniteur, May–September 1803

THOMAZI, AUGUSTE, *Les Marins de Napoléon*, Paris, Tallandier, 1978

TOLSTOY, LEO, *War and Peace*, London, Heinemann, 1904

WHEELER, H.F.B., and BROADLEY, A.M., *op. cit.*

CHAPTER 4

1. In July 1803 he complained to Berthier, 'Ostend is not properly armed; they need eight 12-inch Gomer mortars and twelve 36-pounders . . . I have ordered naval engineers to build two batteries at the end of the jetty and another on the dyke, one, two hundred yards from the sea, the other 500 yards, which will effectively shelter this port from any bombardment'. And when passing *en route* to St Valéry he noted, 'The batteries at St Quentin have not even been armed.'

2. Among other things this Treaty called for French recognition of Spanish neutrality in exchange for a monthly subsidy to France of 6,000,000 *livres*, and for Spanish aid to French warships in Spanish ports. Spain, on the other hand, was to receive 1,000,000 *livres* per month from Portugal.

Sources

Archives de la Guerre: Section Historique, Registres, 1803

Archives Nationales: AF⁴, 1190, 1191, 1203; BB⁴, 167, 173

BONAPARTE, NAPOLEON, *Correspondance de Napoléon Iᵉʳ, op. cit.*, 1803, Letters 6870, 6967, 7030, 7066, 7105, 7186, 7375

CONSTANT, LOUIS, *op. cit.*, vol. 2

DESBRIÈRE, EDOUARD, *Projets, op. cit.*, vol. 2

LEJEUNE, GENERAL BARON, *Mémoires*, vol. 2, Paris, F. Didot, 1895

Le Moniteur, 14th August 1803

REICHARDT, J.F., *Un Hiver à Paris*, Paris, Plon, Nourrit, 1896

STAËL, MME DE, *Mémoires de Madame de Staël, Dix Ans d'Exil*, Paris, Charpentier, 1866

VIGÉE-LEBRUN, MME, *Souvenirs*, 3 vols, Paris, Fournier, 1835–1837

ZIESENISS, JÉROME, *Berthier, Frère d'armes de Napoléon*, Paris, Belfond, 1985

CHAPTER 5

1. Pitt's budget for 1805 was raised to £15,035,630.
2. These figures from St Vincent's *Memoirs* were probably taken just before St Vincent left office in May 1804, and will appear to differ statistically somewhat with those provided in James's *Naval History*.
3. From 473 ships in commission in January 1805 the number rose to 551 by January 1806, an increase of sixty-four per cent since January 1804.
4. James writes this in 1837.

Sources

Dictionary of National Biography, *op. cit.*

CORNWALLIS-WEST, GEORGE, *The Life and Letters of Admiral Cornwallis*, London, Holden, 1927

JAMES, WILLIAM, *op. cit.*, vol. 3

LEYLAND, JOHN (ed.), *op. cit.*, vol. 1 *Naval Chronicle*, January–June 1805

RODGER, N.A.M., *The Wooden World, An Anatomy of the Georgian Navy*, London, Collins, 1986

ST VINCENT, EARL OF, *Memoirs of the Administration of the Board of Admiralty under the Presidency of the Earl of St Vincent*, vol. 2, appendix XI, London, 1805

CHAPTER 6

1. Craig's expedition sailed for the Mediterranean on 19th April 1805.

2. For example, one of the reasons the British navy was superior throughout the period 1803–1805, was that 'English ships were in better condition' (Lefebvre, *Napoleon*, vol. 1, p. 190); and that the reason Villeneuve was able to escape from Toulon in 1805 was because Nelson 'tarried in the Neapolitan waters, lured by the proximity of Lady Hamilton' (*ibid.*), though of course she was then living at Merton, in England. He also claimed England had a navy of '115 ships of the line' (*ibid.*), which was out by nearly thirty battleships. In short, almost everything he has to say regarding the naval side of Napoleon's regime should be considered with the utmost caution.

Sources

BERTHAUT, JULES, *op. cit.*

CASTELOT, ANDRÉ, *op. cit.*

CORBETT, J.S., *The Trafalgar Campaign*, London, Longmans, Green, 1910

DESBRIÈRE, EDOUARD, *Projets*, *op. cit.*

Historical Manuscripts Commission, London, Dropmore mss (1892–1927), vol. 8

LEFEBVRE, GEORGES, *Napoleon, from 18 Brumaire to Tilsit, 1799–1807*, vol. 1, London, Routledge & Kegan Paul, 1969

MALMESBURY, EARL OF, *op. cit.*, vol. 4

MAXWELL, HERBERT (ed.), *The Creevey Papers*, vol. 2, London, John Murray, 1904

MINTO, NORA, *Life and Letters of Sir Gilbert Elliot, First Earl of Minto, from 1751–1806*, vol. 3, London, Longmans, 1874

MIOT DE MELITO, ANDRÉ FRANÇOIS, *Mémoires du comte Miot de Melito*, vol. 2, Paris, Michel Lévy, 1858

PRICE, C. (ed.), *The Letters of Richard Brinsley Sheridan*, vol. 2, Oxford, Oxford University Press, 1966

REILLY, ROBIN, *op. cit.*

ROSE, J. HOLLAND, *William Pitt and the Great War*, London, Bell, 1911

STANHOPE, EARL, *Life of the Right Honourable William Pitt*, vol. 4, London, John Murray, 1862

CHAPTER 7

1. Following Spain's declaration of war later against Britain on 12th December 1804 another secret pact linking Napoleon I and the Spanish monarchy was signed in Paris on 4th January 1805, by which Spain pledged the contribution of twenty-nine ships of the line and four frigates in the war against Great Britain.
2. Nevertheless, the unscheduled presence of Bedout's fleet was to be taken advantage of by Napoleon in the preparation of new expeditions in the Channel. Pellew was to remain there watching the French refit until March 1804 when he was recalled to London to testify in Parliament on behalf of Lord St Vincent (against Pitt's attack calling for a British flotilla to match the one Bonaparte was assembling).
3. His haul comprised: 3,166,850 silver dollars, 1,119,658 gold dollars, 150,011 'ingots of gold reduced into dollars', 1,735 pigs of copper, 4,723 bars of tin, 25,925 seal skins, 10 pipes of seal oil, 75 sacks of Vidona wool, 60 chests or sacks of Cascarilla, 2 chests of Ratina, 28 planks of rare wood.

Sources
Archives Nationales: AF⁴, 1195; BB³, Lettres Reçues 1790–1869, 210, 213, 244; BB⁴, 168
CORNWALLIS-WEST, GEORGE, *op. cit.*
BONAPARTE, NAPOLEON, *Correspondance de Napoléon I⁰ʳ, op. cit.*, 1804, Letters 7994, 7996, 8048, 8060, 8061, 8063
— *Correspondance de Napoléon avec le Ministre de la Marine, depuis 1804 jusqu'en avril 1815*, vol. 1, Paris, Delloye & Lecou, 1837

DESBRIÈRE, EDOUARD, *Projets, op. cit.*, vol. 4
DUMAS, MATHIEU, *Précis des Evénements*, vol. 2, Paris, Treuttel & Wurtz, 1817–26
JAMES, WILLIAM, *op. cit.*, vol. 3
LEYLAND, JOHN (ed.), *op. cit.*, vol. 1
ST VINCENT, EARL OF, *op. cit.*, vol. 2 (republished in *Letters of Admiral of the Fleet, The Earl of St Vincent whilst First Lord of the Admiralty, 1801–1804*, vol. 2, London, Navy Records Society, 1927)

CHAPTER 8

1. In addition to the 6,000,000 francs a month Spain was required to pay France, on 19th December 1803 Portugal agreed to pay 16,000,000 francs.
2. Napoleon had been giving open support to several thousand young Irish émigrés in France, enrolling them when possible in special units of the invasion army.
3. Privately Napoleon demanded 4,700 troops.
4. Edouard Desbrière gives a figure of 48 battleships if all forces met there.
5. There was a standing feud between Nelson and Orde, Nelson claiming rightly that Cádiz was always part of the Mediterranean command (but which Melville had given to Orde who was under the Channel Fleet command). Nelson complained bitterly to Commissioner Otway on 4th May 1805 that Orde had not dispatched a vessel to Gibraltar to apprise him of the situation.
6. Interestingly, Nelson had anticipated the French thinking this, see his letter to Melville, 5th April 1805 in Nicolas, *The Dispatches and Letters of Vice-Admiral Lord Viscount Nelson*, vol. 4.

Sources
Archives Nationales: AF⁴, 1190, 1192,

1204; BB⁴, 207, 216, 227, 230, 233;
BB⁷ Marines étrangères (includes
Flottille Nationale), 245, 247
BONAPARTE, NAPOLEON, *Correspondance
de Napoléon Ier*, *op. cit.*, 1804, 1805,
Letters 8231, 8261, 8279, 8309,
8350, 8360, 8369, 8379, 8381,
8382, 8436, 8467, 8480, 8518,
8542, 8570, 8582, 8615, 8618,
8654, 8670, 8938
— *Correspondance avec le Ministre de la
Marine*, *op. cit.*, vol. 1
CLARKE, J.S., and M'ARTHUR, J., *The
Life of Admiral Lord Nelson, KB*, vol.
2, London, 1809
DESBRIÈRE, EDOUARD, *Projets*, *op. cit.*,
vol. 4
— *Trafalgar, la campagne maritime de
1805*, Paris, Chapelot, 1907
JAMES, WILLIAM, *op. cit.*, vol. 3
LEYLAND, JOHN (ed.), *op. cit.*, vol. 2
MIOT DE MELITO, *op. cit.*, vol. 2
MORRISON, ALFRED (ed.), *The Hamilton
and Nelson Letters*, vol. 2, London,
privately printed, 1893–1894
NICOLAS, SIR NICHOLAS HARRIS, *The
Dispatches and Letters of Vice-Admiral
Lord Viscount Nelson*, vol. 6, London,
Colburn, 1846
REILLE, GENERAL, *Journal* (Archives
Nationales BB⁴, 233)

CHAPTER 9

1. Allemand had five ships: *Majestueux, Jemmapes, Magnanime, Suffren* and *Lion*; three frigates: *Armide, Gloire* and *Thétis*; and two brigs: *Sylphe* and *Palmyre*
2. As late as 22nd August 1805 Napoleon clearly stated, in a letter to Admiral Ganteaume, his intention of seeing Villeneuve *at Boulogne*.

Sources

Archives Nationales: BB⁴, 224, 230,
233, 234, 235
BONAPARTE, NAPOLEON, *Correspondance
de Napoléon Ier*, *op. cit.*, 1805, Letters

8583, 8618, 9020, 9022, 9026,
9043, 9057, 9059, 9060, 9065,
9066, 9072, 9073, 9076, 9114
CLARKE, J.S., and M'ARTHUR, J., *op. cit.*,
vol. 2
DESBRIÈRE, EDOUARD, *Projets*, *op. cit.*,
vol. 1
JAMES, WILLIAM, *op. cit.*, vols 3 and 4
LEYLAND, JOHN (ed.), *op. cit.*, vol. 2
NICOLAS, SIR NICHOLAS HARRIS, *op. cit.*,
vol. 6

CHAPTER 10

1. *The Times* reported 101 ships of the line in service, (which William James does not agree with), 19 50-gun ships and 140 frigates, exclusive of 18 older battleships now relegated to hospital, prison and guard service.
2. Not all *The Times*' pronouncements were so portentous:

'T'invade, or not t'invade – that is
  the question –
Whether 'tis nobler in my soul, to
  suffer
Those haughty Islands to check my
  power,
Or to send forth my troops upon
  their coast,
And by attacking, crush them. –
  T'invade – to fight –
No more; – and by a fight, to say I
  end
The glory, and the thousand natural
  blessings
That England's heir to; – 'tis a
  consummation
Devoutly to be wish'd. – To invade
  – to fight –
To fight – perchance to fail: – Aye,
  there's the rub,
For in that failure, what dire fate
  may come,
When they have shuffled all from
  Gallia's shore,
Must give me pause. – There's the
  respect,

That makes me thus procrastinate
  the deed:
For would I bear the scoff and
  scorn of foes,
The oppressive thought of English
  liberty,
The pangs of despis'd threats,
  th'attempt's delay,
The insolence of Britain, and the
  spurns,
That I impatient and unwilling take,
When I myself might head the
  plund'ring horde,
And grasp at conquest? Would I
  tamely bear
To groan and sweat under a long
  suspense,
But that the dread of something
  after battle,
That undecided trial, from whose
  hazard
I never may return, – puzzles my
  will,
And makes me rather bear unsated
  vengeance,
Than fly from Boulogne at the risk
  of all.
Thus the contemplation stays my
  deep designs,
And thus my native passion of
  ambition
Is clouded o'er with sad, presaging
  thought;
And this momentous, tow'ring
  enterprise,
With this regard, is yearly turn'd
  aside,
And waits the name of action.'

'Buonaparte's soliloquy on the cliff
  at Boulogne', *The Times*, 11th
  September 1805
3. The flotilla comprised: 14 divisions
  of *chaloupes*, of 252 boats; 18
  divisions of *bateaux canonniers*, of
  324 boats; 16 divisions of *péniches*,
  of 228 boats.
4. It was Ouvrard who had presented
  Josephine with the cash required
  (but which Napoleon had been able
  to provide) for the purchase of
  Malmaison, one of the many acts

which Bonaparte could never
forgive. On 18th December 1804
Ouvrard received drafts from the
Spanish government for 52,500,000
piastres, also making him a partner
with King Carlos. On 6th May
1805 Labouchère agreed to
undertake the transfer of the
Mexican treasure (with the help of
Ouvrard's brother in Philadelphia),
Baring in turn consenting to partake
in the venture (for a stiff
commission) by obtaining from
William Pitt approval of the
transaction as well as the use of *four
British frigates with which to transport
the treasure in the name of the Bank of
England*, the latter then paying
Labouchère, who would pay
Ouvrard. Ultimately this would have
brought Hope and Labouchère
£900,000 or 225,000,000 French
francs and a commission of
24,000,000 francs to Ouvrard, who
was literally partners now with
Napoleon, Carlos IV and the Bank
of England! This extraordinary
operation finally fell through for
several reasons. See Lefebvre,
Napoleon, I, pp. 234–235, and for
greater detail, Otto Wolfe's
biography of Ouvrard.
5. The Confederation of the Rhine
  was formed on 12th July 1806.

Sources
Archives Nationales: BB^1, 31; BB^2, 10
BONAPARTE, NAPOLEON, *Correspondance
  de Napoléon Ier, op. cit.*, 1805; Letters
  8551, 8835, 9037
DESBRIÈRE, EDOUARD, *Projets, op. cit.*,
  vol. 4
FRASER, FLORA, *Beloved Emma, The Life
  of Emma Lady Hamilton*, London,
  Weidenfeld & Nicolson, 1986
LEFEBVRE, GEORGES, *op. cit.*, vol. 1
KENNEDY, LUDOVIC, *Nelson's Band of
  Brothers*, London, Odhams Press,
  1952
Le Moniteur, 16th August 1805
London Gazette, 6th September 1805

MAHAN, A.T., *op. cit.*, vol. 2

MINTO, EARL OF, *op. cit.*, vol. 3

MORRISON, ALFRED, *op. cit.*

NAISH, GEORGE P.B., *Nelson's Letters to His Wife, and Other Documents, 1785–1831*, London, Routledge & Kegan Paul, 1958

NICOLAS, SIR NICHOLAS HARRIS, *op. cit.*, vol. 7

OMAN, CAROLA, *Nelson*, London, Hodder & Stoughton, 1967

ROSE, GEORGE, *op. cit.*, vol 2

ROSE, J. HOLLAND, *op. cit.*

SICHEL, WALTER, *Emma Lady Hamilton*, London, Archibald Constable, 1905

The Times, August–September 1805

TULARD, JEAN, *Napoleon, the Myth of the Saviour*, London, Methuen, 1985

WATSON, J. STEVEN, *op. cit.*

WHEELER, H.F.B., and BROADLEY, A.M., *op. cit.*, vol. 1

CHAPTER 11

1. Among other orders issued on 10th October 1805 were the following:

   '. . . [for] the Captains and Commanders of His Majesty's Ships and Vessels under my command, who may purchase bullocks, fresh beef, lemons, onions, or any other species of provisions or refreshments . . . whether it is made by my order or other, [it is directed] that a Voucher [be] transmitted to me, immediately. . . .'
   '. . . the Captains and Commanders of His Majesty's Ships and Vessels under my command respectively, [are to] have their Muster-Books in readiness when the Naval Officers at Gibraltar and Malta go on board to muster their Ships' Companies . . . .'
   'It is my directions that whenever any men are sent to the Hospitals, a statement of their case is sent with them, that the Medical Gentlemen belonging to the Hospital may know what has been done [previously] in order to remove the diseases.'
   'It is expected in fine weather that the Ships in Order of Sailing do not keep more than two cables' length from each other.'
   'When in presence of an Enemy, all the Ships under my command are to bear white Colours, and a Union Jack is to be suspended from the fore top-gallant stay.'

   For a complete list see Nicolas, *op. cit.*, vol. 6.

2. For the most recent statistics to appear regarding the strength of the Spanish squadron, see John D. Harbron, *Trafalgar and the Spanish Navy*. There were five French frigates present at the battle, despite varying earlier reports: four 40-gun frigates – *Cornélie, Rhin, Hortense, Hermione* – and the 32-gun *Thémis*. See Desbrière, *Trafalgar, op. cit*, pp. 222–224.

3. Le munitionnaire général des vivres de la marine.

4. The list of vessels not in shape to put to sea included two 80-gun vessels, the *Formidable* and *Indomptable*, and six 74s, the *Algésiras, Mont-Blanc, Fougueux, Swift-sure, Héros* and *Intrépide*.

5. 'Procès-verbal du Conseil de Guerre tenu le 8 octobre 1805 à bord du *Bucentaure*', Archives Nationales (BB^4, 230) signed by Prigny, Galiano, Hore, Lavillegris, Maistral, Cosmao, Macdonnell, Magon, Cisneros, Escaño, Dumanoir Le Pelley, Álava, Gravina and Villeneuve. Gravina's report on the proceedings of 8th October has been removed from the Spanish archives. It is thanks to the diligence of Edouard Desbrière that the first hint of a mutiny came to light, though he never used the word 'mutiny'. See Desbrière, *Trafalgar, op. cit.*, and Villeneuve to

Decrès, 8th October 1805 (Archives Nationales, BB⁴, 230) in which he discusses these proceedings. The only English author to acknowledge this rebellion was Julian S. Corbett in *The Campaign of Trafalgar* having been in communication with Colonel Desbrière who pointed it out to him.

6. These figures include guns of ships of the line only (excluding frigates). James gives the Combined Fleet 2,626 guns, or an additional 478 guns. But there were even more guns aboard many ships – of both fleets – than their official ratings would indicate. Thus for instance *Victory* actually mounted 102 guns (and not 100) while the 98-gun *Téméraire* had 102. The 80-gun *Tonnant* carried an additional ten, giving her 90 all told, while the 74-gun *Belleisle* really boasted 90 guns. Many of the British 74s carried up to 82 guns each. The same principle applied to the Combined Fleet, thus maintaining a relative balance in their extra guns. The *San Ildefonso* mounted 74 guns in theory, but in reality had 78. The *Bucentaure* and other French 80s carried 86 guns each, and most of the French 74s carried between 82 and 84 guns.

7. The next news Rosily received was that *his* fleet had been destroyed and defeated by Nelson. The remnants that survived were not able to put to sea again for another two years, and then briefly, only to find themselves captured in the very port of Cadiz by Spanish revolutionary forces on 14th June 1808. Rosily and his general staff were finally repatriated to France where Napoleon allegedly offered him the Naval Ministry, though he never held that post, preferring the less political and controversial Direction Générale du Dépôt de la Marine, which he held until 1826.

Sources
Archives des affaires étrangères: 668, Espagne, Correspondance politique
Archives Nationales: AF⁴, 1196, 1597; BB⁴, 228, 230, 233, 234, 237
BONAPARTE, NAPOLEON, *Correspondance de Napoléon Iᵉʳ, op. cit.*, 1805, Letters 9179, 9190, 9220
CORBETT, J.S., *op. cit.*
DESBRIÈRE, EDOUARD, *Projets, op. cit.*, vol. 4
— *Trafalgar, op. cit.*
HARBRON, JOHN D., *Trafalgar and the Spanish Navy*, London, Conway Maritime Press, 1988
JAMES, WILLIAM, *op. cit.*, vol. 4
KEEGAN, JOHN, *The Price of Admiralty, War at Sea from Man of War to Submarine*, London, Hutchinson, 1988
LEYLAND, JOHN (ed.), *op. cit.*, vol. 2
NICOLAS, SIR NICHOLAS HARRIS, *op. cit.*, vol. 2

CHAPTER 12

1. John Keegan gives Nelson's fleet 2,232 guns in *The Price of Admiralty* (*op. cit.*).
2. Admiral Sir Cyprian Bridge puts Nelson's fleet at 17,256 men in *Nelson; The Centenary of Trafalgar*, a speech delivered before the Navy Records Society in July 1905, quoted in A.T. Mahan's *Life of Nelson* (*op. cit.*).
3. Dumanoir's implausible behaviour at Trafalgar and subsequent capture resulted in a series of hearings and commissions established to investigate this, lasting until 1810. He was exonerated.
4. Upon seizing the French ships in the spring of 1808, the Spanish renamed three of them, *Pluton* becoming *Montañes*, *Neptune* becoming *Neptuno*, and *Argonaute* the new *Argonauta*.

Sources
Archives Nationales: BB⁴, 237

BEATTY, DR WILLIAM, *The Authentic Narrative of the Death of Lord Nelson*, London, T. Cadell, 1807

CORBETT, J.S., *op. cit.*; *Fighting Instructions, 1530–1816*, London, Navy Records Society, 1905; *Signals and Instructions, 1776–1794*, London, Navy Records Society, 1909

CRESWELL, JOHN, *British Admirals of the Eighteenth Century: Tactics in Battle*, London, George Allen & Unwin, 1972

DESBRIÈRE, EDOUARD, *Trafalgar, op. cit.*

GOODWIN, PETER, *The Constructions and Fitting of English Ships of War, 1600–1815*, London, Conway Maritime Press, 1987

HARBRON, JOHN D., *op. cit.*

JAMES, WILLIAM, *op. cit.*, vol. 4

KEEGAN, JOHN, *op. cit.*

LAVERY, B., *The Ship of the Line*, London, Conway Maritime Press, Vol. 1 'The Development of the Battle Fleet, 1650–1850', 1983; Vol. 2 'Design, Constructions and Fittings', 1984

MAHAN, A.T., *op. cit.*, vol. 2

McKAY, JOHN, *Anatomy of the Ship: The 100-gun Ship Victory*, London, Conway Maritime Press, 1987

NICOLAS, SIR NICHOLAS HARRIS, *op. cit.*, vol. 7

ROBERTSON, F.L., *The Evolution of Naval Armament*, London, Constable, 1921

CHAPTER 13

Sources

Annual Register, 1805

Archives Nationales: BB[4], 230, 237

CORNWALLIS-WEST, GEORGE, *op. cit.*

DESBRIÈRE, EDOUARD, *Trafalgar, op. cit.*

FRASER, FLORA, *op. cit.*

Journal de Paris, 7th December 1805

London Gazette, 18th December 1805

MALMESBURY, EARL OF, *op. cit.*

Naval Chronicle, 1805

NICOLAS, SIR NICHOLAS HARRIS, *op. cit.*, vol. 7

ROSE, J. HOLLAND, *op. cit.*

The Times, December 1805–January 1806

INDEX

Abbott, Speaker Charles, 150, 151
Aboukir Bay *see* Nile, Battle of the
Act of Mediation (1803), 12
Acton, Sir John, 156, 219
Adams, Henry, shipwright, 43
Addington, Dr Anthony, 26
Addington, Henry, 1st Viscount
    Sidmouth, 8, 11, 12, 26–7, 30, 38,
    39, 45, 52, 128, 129, 136, 148, 149,
    152, 265, 366, 378
Additional Forces Act (1804), 46, 47
Additional Forces Act (1805), 265
Admiralty, 44, 47, 49, 129, 131, 132,
    140, 152, 167, 170, 175, 179, 251,
    256, 262, 359, 364
Admiralty Board, 40, 70, 129, 144, 145–
    6, 153, 160, 168, 200, 205, 214,
    234, 248, 255, 281, 282, 283, 289,
    290
Álava y Navarrete, Vice-Admiral Ignacio
    María de, 312, 313, 338, 339, 378,
    402n
Alexander I, Tsar of Russia, 15, 155–7,
    378
Allemand, Captain Zacharie, 216, 218,
    235, 237, 241, 276, 278, 280, 378,
    400n
Ambleteuse, 36, 101, 102, 106–7, 109,
    113, 124, 125, 193, 266
American War of Independence, 245,
    246
Amiens, Treaty of (1802), 11–12, 13, 26,
    71, 101, 157, 216
Anson, Admiral Lord, 144
Antigua, 129, 184, 209, 220, 222, 225,
    226, 227, 228
Argumosa, Captain Teodoro de, 346,
    378
Arman, Midshipman, 311
Armed Neutrality of the North (1800), 9
Armiston, Lady, 29
Armiston, Robert Dundas, Lord of, 28
Ascott, Lieutenant, 177
Auersperg, Prince, 269

Augereau, Marshal Pierre-François-
    Charles, 18, 123, 174, 186, 378
Austerlitz, Battle of (1805), 122, 272,
    362
Austria, Austrians, 9, 15, 46, 122, 154,
    265, 269, 270; Treaty of Lunéville,
    10, 154; Treaty of Paris, 10;
    Russian Treaty, 157; Bavaria
    invaded by, 157; French War
    against, 272–3; Battle of Ulm, 359;
    Battle of Austerlitz, 362

Badini, spy, 59
Ball, Sir Alexander, John, 213, 281, 294,
    378
balloon, montgolfière hot air, 84
Banks, Sir Joseph, 261
Banque de France, 8, 271
Barbados, 217, 220, 225, 226, 227;
    Nelson arrives at Carlisle Bay, 213,
    219, 226
Barbé-Marbois, François, 238, 270, 271,
    378
Barham, Lord, First Lord of the
    Admiralty, 152, 153, 256, 257, 262–
    3, 275, 282, 283, 285, 359, 370, 378
Barker, Admiral Sir Peter, 365
Batavian-French Convention (1803), 91
Batavian Republic *see* Holland
bateaux canonniers, French, 72, 74, 75,
    78–9, 91, 92, 93, 95, 96, 98, 100,
    105, 106, 266, 396n, 397n, 401n
Bayntun, Captain Henry, 334, 335–6,
    367, 368, 378
Bayonne army camp, 122, 123
beacons, signal, 54
Beatty, Dr William, 331, 332, 363
Beaudouin, Captain Louis-Alexis, 330,
    333, 338, 378
Beauharnais, Colonel-General Eugène,
    21
Bedford, Lieutenant John, 344, 378
Bedout, Rear-Admiral Jacques, 162, 173,
    378, 399n

Belgium, 10, 108, 140, 156
Bernadotte, Marshal, 21, 272
Berry, Captain Sir Edward, 288, 307, 378
Berthier, Marshal Louis-Alexandre, War Minister, 5, 21, 67, 69, 98, 107, 110, 111, 112, 113, 115–25, 206, 239, 266, 267, 272, 379, 396n, 397n; ball held by, 115–16, 117–19; Napoleon's relations with, 119–22; created Marshal, 121, 124; organisation of invasion troops by, 122–5
Bessborough, Lady, 149
Bessières, Marshal Jean Baptiste, 18
Betanzos Bay, 162, 179, 180
Beurnonville, General Pierre de Ruel, 12, 188, 190, 191–2, 207, 275, 299, 300, 301, 305, 306, 379
Bickerton, Sir Richard, 215, 217
Blackwood, Captain Sir Henry, 43, 44, 254, 262, 264, 275, 284, 285, 286, 288, 295, 306, 308, 309, 311, 357, 361, 379; at Battle of Trafalgar, 312, 316, 319, 321
Bolton, Mrs (Nelson's sister), 251
Bolton, Thomas, Jr, 367, 369
Bolton Thomas, Sr, 367, 369
Bolton, Sir William, 288, 379
Bonaparte, Elisa (Napoleon's sister), 18
Bonaparte, Princess Hortense (née de Beauharnais), 18
Bonaparte, Prince Joseph, King of Naples and Spain, 18, 37–9
Bonaparte, Princess Julia Marie (née Clary), 18
Bonaparte, Louis, King of Holland, 18
Bonaparte, Lucien, 18
Bonaparte, Pauline, 18
Bonnefoux, Naval Prefect, 197–8
Boulogne, 74, 80, 90, 110, 113, 131, 140, 169, 171, 174, 190, 196, 205, 206, 237, 239, 242, 257; invasion preparations, 19, 35–7, 40, 71, 81, 93, 100, 101–5, 107, 109, 110, 111, 112, 114, 124–5, 193, 237–8, 266, 272; storm tragedy, 97–9; Napoleon at, 97–9, 111, 266, 267, 271, 272, 276, 362; Fort Rouge (floating fort), 102–3, 104, 105, 193; Fort de l'Heurt, 102–3, 104, 105, 115, 124, 125; Fort de la Crèche, 102–3, 104, 105, 125; British attacks on, 103–4, 105, 115; Camp César, 105;

Imperial Guard barracks, 125; invasion forces leave for Germany from, 272
Bourrienne, Louis Antoine Fauvelet de, 12
Boyles, Captain Charles, 232
Brereton, Brigadier-General Robert, 219, 220, 222, 229, 379
Brest, 35, 63, 73, 81, 86, 99, 110, 113, 114, 138, 139, 141, 160, 163, 168, 169, 170, 171–2, 178, 179, 180, 190, 206, 209, 216, 237; British blockade of, 1, 2, 81, 169, 171, 172, 179, 196, 202, 206, 212, 216, 242; army camp, 122, 123
Brest Squadron, 81, 161, 163, 169, 171–2, 174, 183, 193, 195–6, 202–4, 205, 209, 215, 218, 224, 225, 241, 258, 260, 262, 266, 276, 277, 278–9, 296
Briche, Engineer de, 100
Bridge, Admiral Sir Cyprian, 403n
British Army, 49, 155, 268; volunteers, 41, 42, 45, 47, 50–1, 52, 59, 155, 265, 268–9; Blackheath review (1804), 41, 50; strength, 45, 47, 58; bounties offered to recruits, 45, 47, 51; militia, 45, 47, 49, 59, 155, 265; regulars, 47, 155, 268; Hyde Park review (1804), 50; Dumouriez's advice on defence by, 55–6; new exploding shells tested, 268; deserters from, 47, 269
British Army units, 50; Royal Surrey Militia, 49; St James's Loyal Volunteers, 51; 2nd Regiment of Liverpool Volunteers, 52; Chertsey Volunteers, 52; City Horse Volunteers, 57; St James's Dragoons, 59; Cinque Port Volunteers, 128; South Gloucester Militia, 269
Brome, Viscount, 11
Brouard, Captain Gabriel-Auguste, 343, 379
Brueys, Admiral François-Paul de, 65, 203
Bruges army camp, 37, 73, 123, 124, 125–6, 266, 272
Bruix, Admiral Eustace de, C-in-C National Flotilla, 39, 72, 79, 81, 84–5, 96, 98, 102, 103–4, 105, 106, 109, 113, 171, 173, 379, 396n
Brune, General, 12

Buckingham House, 24
Buckler's Hard, launching of *Euryalus* at, 42–4
Burney, Fanny, 26
Burrard, Lieutenant-General Harry, 365
Bustamente, Rear-Admiral Don José, 177
Byng, Admiral George, 106

Cadiz, 81, 139, 162, 173, 176, 178, 189, 191, 196, 204, 207, 216, 217, 226, 229, 236, 237, 246, 280, 399n; Collingwood arrives at, 214, 216–17; Villeneuve sails for, 242, 275, 276; Nelson assumes command of new Mediterranean Fleet off, 280–4, 298, 302; Franco-Spanish Fleet sails out of (October 1805), 295, 304–6, 311–12; Battle of Trafalgar, 307–56; British re-establish blockade of, 356
Cadiz Fleet (Franco-Spanish), 191, 192, 193, 197–8, 205, 208–9, 210, 211, 212, 213, 218, 237, 262, 279–80, 281, 284, 298–306; Rosily replaces Villeneuve as Commander of, 296, 301, 303–4
Caffarelli, General Louis, 86, 161, 171, 172–3, 379
Cajigal, Captain Felipe Jado, 335–6, 379
Calais, 41, 74, 89, 90, 100, 107–8, 112, 113, 190, 197, 198
Calder, Admiral Sir Robert, 136, 163, 200, 201, 202, 210, 224, 243, 248, 255, 259–60, 276, 277, 280, 379–80; Commander of El Ferrol Squadron, 200–1, 204, 209, 214, 215, 216, 217, 218, 229, 230, 259, 276; clash off El Ferrol between Franco-Spanish Fleet and (July 1805), 230–6, 238, 239, 255, 275, 312, 352; public criticism in Britain of, 259, 282; given command of new Mediterranean Fleet, 277–8; board of inquiry into conduct of, 282–3; replaced by Nelson and returns home, 283–4, 288, 294
Camas, *see* Filhol-Camas
Cambacérès, Jean-Jacques, 41, 69, 73, 105, 238
Camden, John Jeffreys Pratt, 2nd Earl and 1st Marquis, 38, 41, 152, 366, 367, 380
Campbell, Rear-Admiral Donald, 213

Campbell, Rear-Admiral George, 135
Campo Formio, Treaty of (1798), 9, 10, 12
Canaries, 196, 229, 247
Canning, George, 38, 148, 150, 256, 264, 380
Cape Finisterre, 162, 163, 169, 173, 179, 200, 201, 210, 214, 236, 275
Cape of Good Hope, 11, 169, 260
Cape St Vincent, Battle of (1797), 130, 140, 200, 216, 247, 248–9
Cape Spartel, 223, 285, 287
Caprara, Cardinal, 18
Carlos III, King of Spain, 189
Carlos IV, King of Spain, 121, 189, 190, 191, 401n
Carrier, Jean-Baptiste, 7
Cartagena, 191, 192, 207, 217, 260, 285, 302, 356, 370
Castlereagh, Robert Steward, Viscount, 150, 152, 256, 261, 268, 284, 290, 366, 380, 395n
chaloupes canonnières, French, 72, 74, 75, 77, 78, 82, 83, 88, 91, 92, 94, 95, 96, 98, 100, 105, 266, 396n, 297n, 401n
Channel Fleet, British (Western Squadron), 2, 101, 109, 129, 137, 153, 160–1, 163–6, 170–3, 174–5, 182–3, 200–1, 213, 214, 215, 218, 249, 276, 277, 370; Cornwallis appointed C-in-C, 136, 138–9; St Vincent replaces Cornwallis (1806), 370; *see also* Royal Navy; ships, British
Channel ports, French: Royal Navy's blockade of, 1, 2, 81, 169, 170–3, 174, 175–6, 178–9, 181, 182–3, 200, 206, 211, 216, 217, 218; invasion preparations, 35–7, 55–9, 71–83, 88–115; coastal redoubts and batteries, 55–6, 61, 112, 161, 397n; British attacks on, 103–4, 105, 109, 114; defence of, 109–15; gathering of invasion troops at, 122–7, 266–7; *see also* Combined Fleet; France; National Flotilla
Charles X, King of France, 50
Charles, Archduke of Austria, 269
Charlotte Sophia, Queen, 23–4, 25, 380
Chatham, Baroness (*née* Hester Grenville), 26, 148
Chatham, William Pitt (the Elder), 1st Earl of, 24, 26, 27

Chatham, 49, 54, 57, 152, 258, 297, 360

Cherbourg, 67, 73, 110, 169

Churruca, Captain Cosmé Damián, 351, 380

Cisalpine or Italian Republic, 10, 12–13, 154

Cisneros, Admiral Báltasar Hidalgo de, 312, 334, 335, 380, 402n

Clarence, William Henry, Duke of (later William IV), 51, 60, 245, 366, 380

Clement, Lieutenant Benjamin, 344

Cochrane, Rear-Admiral Sir Alexander, 144, 163, 168, 169, 174, 175–6, 179, 180, 183, 187, 200, 201, 219, 225, 380

Codrington, Captain Edward, 336, 350, 380, 394

Collingwood, Vice-Admiral Cuthbert, 136, 180, 181, 182, 223, 245, 262, 263, 275, 279, 280, 358, 370, 380, 394n; assumes command of new squadron, 201, 204, 210–11; arrives at Cadiz, 214, 216–17; as Nelson's Second-in-Command, 283, 289, 290, 292, 293, 294–5, 299; transferred from *Dreadnought* to *Royal Sovereign*, 293, 294; Battle of Trafalgar, 308, 317–19, 320, 321, 323, 324, 338–9, 351, 355, 356; re-establishes blockade of Cadiz, 356; mourns death of Nelson, 361

Combined Franco-Spanish Fleet, 2, 192–3, 196–7, 200, 204–18, 230–42, 243, 266; Villeneuve appointed C-in-C of, 205–6; sails to West Indies, 206–10, 211, 217, 220, 222–3, 224–8; Nelson's pursuit of, 212–13, 214, 220, 222–4; 15 British merchantmen captured by, 227; returns to El Ferrol, 228–30; clash off El Ferrol with British Fleet, 230–6, 238–40, 255, 275, 276, 312; at Cadiz, 262, 275, 276, 279–80, 281, 282, 284, 285–6, 298–306; lack of supplies and manpower, 290, 298–302; strength, 295, 298, 301–2, 304, 315, 403n; ordered to sail to Naples, 296, 298, 301, 302, 303; Rosily replaces Villeneuve as Fleet Commander, 296, 301, 359; *Conseil de Guerre* against leaving Cadiz, 302–4; sails out of Cadiz (19 October 1805), 295, 304–6, 311–12; Battle of Trafalgar, 307–56, 358,

360, 362; Observation Squadron, 312, 313, 314; First, Second and Third Squadrons, 312; casualties at Trafalgar, 354–5, 362; British blockade of Cadiz re-established, 356; *see also* French Navy; National Flotilla; Spanish Navy

Commissioners for Sick and Wounded Seamen, 147

Commissioners of the Dockyards, British, 146

Committee of the Patriotic Fund, 363

Compiègne army camp, 122, 123

Concordat (French-Vatican: 1801), 5, 6

Confederation of the Rhine (1806), 10, 272

Congreve, Colonel, 261, 284

Conn, Captain John, 351–2, 380

Connor, Sarah, 256

Constant, Benjamin, 8–9

Constant, Louis (Napoleon's valet), 14, 97–8

Contamine, Major-General Theodore, 311, 323, 334, 358, 380

Cooke, Captain John, 344–5, 380

Copenhagen, Battle of (1801), 9, 130, 140, 248, 249, 250, 253, 259, 332

Corbett, Sir Julian, 1, 2, 324, 402n

Cornwallis, Charles, 1st Earl (father), 136, 381

Cornwallis, Charles, General, 1st Marquis (William's brother), 11, 12, 136, 137, 381, 394

Cornwallis, Admiral Sir William ('Blue Billy'), 43, 104, 109–10, 134, 135, 136–9, 140, 141, 144, 145, 146, 167, 175, 214, 223, 224, 275; C-in-C Channel Fleet, 1, 2–3, 136–9, 160, 161–3, 168, 169, 170, 174, 175, 176–81, 183, 184, 195, 196, 200, 201–2, 211, 215, 218, 229, 236, 276–72, 279–80, 360, 370; distinctive role of, 2–3; Nelson's friendship with, 138, 244–5, 248; authorised attacks on Spanish treasure ships, 176–8, 187; creates new fleet (1805), 277–8; replaced by St Vincent as C-in-C Channel Fleet (1806), 202, 370

Cosmao-Kerjulien, Commodore Julien-Marie, 341, 342, 380, 402n

Cotton, Sir Charles, 138, 170, 203, 380–1

Courrège, Captain Pierre, 353

Craig, General Sir James, 156, 285
Cravan, Lord, 48
Creevey, Thomas, 148, 149, 153
Cribb, Thomas, gardener, 262
Cruikshank, George, 52
Cumby, Lieutenant William Pryce, 345, 346, 381
Cumming, Captain William, 230, 381

Dacre, Rear-Admiral, 219
Daru, Pierre-Antoine, 72
David, Admiral, 80
Davison, Alexander, 222, 245, 246, 253, 262, 263, 284
Davout, Marshal Louis-Nicolas, 18, 114, 118, 123, 126, 381
Decrès, Rear-Admiral Denis, 63–70, 71, 117, 119, 131, 144, 172, 175, 178, 185, 186, 189, 190, 191, 192, 193, 208, 209, 216, 237, 239, 286, 296, 381; naval career, 64, 65–7; Maritime Prefect at Lorient, 64, 66–7; Napoleon's relations with, 64–5, 66, 67, 68–9, 70, 173; Naval Minister (1801–14), 64–5, 67, 68–9, 70, awarded sword of honour (1801), 66; and National Flotilla, 72, 74, 77, 78, 80, 82, 88–9, 90, 94–5, 266; and Channel ports and batteries, 102–3, 108–9, 110, 112–13; and Villeneuve, 173, 194–5, 198–9, 206–7, 219, 224, 225, 226, 228–9, 234, 238, 240, 241–2, 260, 276, 295, 296, 298, 299, 301, 302, 303, 304, 306, 314, 357–8; 'Secret Project' rejected by Napoleon, 296–7; and shortage of supplies at Cadiz, 299–301; Battle of Trafalgar, 311, 315, 358
Defence Act (1803), 47
Denieport, Captain Gabriel, 309, 340, 353, 381
Derval, Dupon, 57–8
Desbrière, Colonel Edouard, 1, 157, 315, 349, 357, 395n, 399n, 402–3n
deserters and shirkers, 47, 53, 269
Diamond Rock, Martinique (HMS Diamond), captured by Villeneuve, 225, 226, 228
Dieppe, 74, 90, 99, 101, 109, 110
Digby, Captain Henry, 335, 336, 381
Disbrowe, Colonel, 23
dockyards, British Royal, 129–30, 131, 132, 133, 146

Dode, Deputy Director of Fortifications, 104
Dominica, 184, 185, 205, 225, 227
Donadieu, Midshipman, 311, 333
Duckworth, Sir John, 140
Duff, Captain George, 281, 284, 286, 288, 293, 295, 318, 340, 342, 343, 381
Dumanoir Le Pelley, Admiral Pierre, 312, 314, 315, 321, 323, 334, 335, 336, 337, 349–51, 355, 358, 381–2, 402n, 403n
Dumas, General Mathieu, 122, 125–6, 382
Dumouriez, General Charles François Dupérier, 42, 46, 48, 54, 55–6, 62, 263
Dunbar, Captain James, 289
Dundas, Captain, 278
Dundas, General Sir David, 46, 54, 365, 367, 382
Dundas, Henry see Melville, 1st Viscount
Dundas, Robert see Arniston
Dundas, William, 38, 382
Dunkirk, 37, 63, 74, 89, 90, 96, 99, 100, 110, 113, 140, 190, 205, 266, 297
Dunn, Seaman James, 167, 168
Durham, Captain Philip, 341, 352–3, 365, 382

Edward, Duke of Kent, 263, 366
Egypt, 9, 11, 155, 163, 208, 212, 260
El Ferrol, 139, 141, 161, 162, 163, 168, 169, 170, 174, 175, 176, 179, 183, 193, 196, 204, 206, 210, 218, 223, 225, 226, 236, 237, 241, 275, 287; French and Spanish Squadrons, 183–4, 191, 192, 193, 195, 196, 197, 200, 205, 208–9, 210–11, 212, 215, 216, 217, 218, 225, 236, 240, 242, 259; British Squadron off, 187, 196, 200, 204, 206, 209, 214, 215, 229, 230–6, 276; Villeneuve returns from West Indies to, 228–9, 278; clash between Combined Fleet and British (July 1805), 230–6, 238–9, 275
Elliot, Hugh, British Minister at Naples, 34, 361
Elphinstone, Captain, 163
Elphinstone, George see Keith, Admiral Lord
Emeriaux, Rear-Admiral, 199
Enghien, Louis Antoine de Bourbon,

Duke d', kidnapping of, 14, 17, 121, 156
Epron, Captain Jacques, 346, 348, 382
Escaño, Rear-Admiral Antonio de, 303, 304, 352, 358, 382, 402n
Etaples, 90, 101, 106, 107, 109, 113, 140, 266
Exmouth, Admiral Viscount *see* Pellew, Commodore

Farquhar, Walter, physician, 148
Fernandez, British Vice-Consul, 179
Fesch, Cardinal, 18, 21
Filhol-Camas, Captain Jean Gilles, 348, 349, 382
First Lord of the Admiralty, 144–5; *see also* Barham; Melville; St Vincent
Fitsharris, Lord, 151
Fitzgerald, W. T., 61
Flushing, 35, 37, 67, 100, 108–9, 110, 140, 165, 297, 396n
Forfait, Pierre-Alexandre, 65, 67, 71–2, 74, 79–80, 81, 85, 102–3; Inspector-General of National Flotilla (1803), 72–3, 79, 80, 88, 89–90; Minister of the Navy (1799–1801), 80, 86–7; Maritime Prefect of Genoa (1805), 80
Fort de France, Martinique, 185, 196, 224, 225–6
Fouché, Joseph, 7, 15, 19, 67–8, 69, 238, 359, 382
Fox, Charles James, 24, 30, 38, 52, 119, 148, 150, 152, 382–3
France, French: Napoleon's invasion of Britain plans, 1, 2, 3, 35–7, 39, 40–1, 44–62, 71–83, 88–115, 122–7, 168–70, 173–5, 178, 184, 186, 193, 195–7, 205–6, 215–16, 217–18, 224–5, 237–8, 239, 240–2, 296–7; Concordat (1801), 5, 6; Imperial Coronation (1804), 5–6, 13–14, 15, 16, 18–22, 34, 121; Napoleon's reorganisation of, 7–9; Civil Code, 8; foreign policy/conquests, 9–13, 14–18, 154–5; Treaty of Lunéville (1801), 10, 12, 17, 154, 157; Russian relations with, 10, 18, 155–6; Treaty of Amiens (1802), 11–12, 13, 26, 71, 101, 157, 216; war resumed against Britain (1803), 13, 16, 18, 26, 44, 155, 162, 265; Battle of the Nile (1798), 66, 140, 194, 203, 250, 259, 332; Dutch relations with, 90–6, 155, 396–7n; Battle of Austerlitz (1805), 122, 272, 362; Spanish relations with, 155, 161–2, 186–93, 399n; Continental War, 269–70, 272–3, 359–60; financial problems, 270–1, 362; Battle of Trafalgar, 307–56, 362–3; invasion of Spain by (1808), 356; Battle of Ulm (1805), 359; *see also* Channel ports; Combined Navy; French Navy; National Flotilla
Francis II, Holy Roman Emperor, 154, 157, 270, 383
Franco-American Convention (1800), 9–10
Franco-Portuguese Pact (June 1801), 10
Franco-Russian Treaty (1801), 10
Franco-Spanish Pact (1805), 190–1, 399n
Franco-Spanish Treaty (1803), 123, 155, 161, 186, 187, 190
Frederick Augustus, Duke of York and Albany, 26, 41, 42, 48, 50–1, 55, 366; C-in-C British Forces (1803), 26, 46
Frederick Louis, Prince of Wales, 23
Frederick William III, King of Prussia, 15, 154, 156, 157, 383
Fremantle, Captain Thomas, 243, 251, 334, 383
French Army (*Grande Armée*), 2, 9, 19, 69, 197, 272; coastal batteries and redoubts, 55–6, Corps de Garde, 83; 'patriotic contribution' from units of, 83; 43rd Regiment, 107; mobile artillery batteries, 110; coastal defence by, 109–15; coastguard companies, 110–11; Continental War (1805), 269–70, 272–3, 296; *see also* Channel ports; France; National Flotilla
French Imperial Navy, 44, 48, 64, 65, 66, 69–70, 84, 136, 139, 161, 162, 163, 167, 168–79, 182; shortage of manpower and supplies, 95, 173, 290, 298–302; Missiessy's expedition to West Indies, 183, 184–6, 209; Franco-Spanish Naval Pact (1805), 190–1, 399n; Villeneuve fails to escape from Toulon, 193–5, 198, 206; Battle of Trafalgar, 307–56; *see also* Brest Squadron; Cadiz Fleet; Channel ports; Combined Fleet; National Flotilla; Rochefort

Squadron
French Revolution, 7, 17, 240
Frere, John Hookham, 163, 383
Fulton, Robert, inventor, 84–8, 261, 383

Galiano, Captain Dionisio Alcalá, 303–4,
    345, 348, 383 402n
Gambier, James, 279, 289, 383
Ganteaume, Vice-Admiral Honoré-
    Joseph-Antoine, 41, 72, 81, 171,
    173, 175, 194, 199, 205, 206, 223,
    228, 383, 400n; Fleet Commander,
    Brest, 171–2, 174, 195–7, 202–3,
    204–5, 209, 210, 211, 215–16, 218,
    224, 225, 241, 258, 260, 276, 277,
    278–9, 296
Gardner, Alan, Admiral Lord, 140, 201,
    203–4, 209–10, 211, 212, 213–14,
    215, 216, 217, 248, 383
Gardoquí, Captain José, 339, 383
Genoa, 80, 81, 157, 260, 293, 298
George II, King of England, 23, 24
George III, King of England, 15, 23–6,
    27, 31, 32, 38, 42, 48, 49, 50–1, 52,
    55, 148, 152–3, 250, 273–4, 383;
    illness of, 24–5; King's Speech
    (1804), 46; Napoleon's peace letter
    to (1805), 157–9; and Battle of
    Trafalgar, 357, 359, 361–2
George, Prince of Wales (Prince Regent:
    George IV), 25, 26, 31, 48, 51, 251,
    252, 268, 364, 366, 367, 369, 383
Gibraltar, 129, 223, 229, 269, 281, 285,
    288, 289, 305, 306, 308, 318, 355,
    402n
Gillray, James, 40
Godoy, Manuel de, Duke of Alcudia
    ('Prince of Peace'), 155, 188–9, 191,
    192–3, 234, 239, 271, 300, 383
Gordon, Sir William, 29
Gorman, Seaman Patrick, 167
Gourdon, Admiral Adrien-Louis, 162,
    168, 195, 196, 236, 383
Gourrège, Captain Pierre-Paul, 345, 383
Grandallana, Rear-Admiral Domingo,
    236, 383
Grasse, Admiral de, 291
Gravelines, 100, 108, 113
Graves, Rear-Admiral Sir Thomas, 183,
    215, 216, 218, 384
Gravina, Admiral Federico Carlos, 16,
    187, 188, 189, 190, 191, 192, 204,
    205, 219, 222, 226, 228, 229, 230,
    259, 275, 282, 287, 298, 300, 309;

C-in-C Spanish Fleet (1805), 191;
    sails to Martinique, 207–8; battle off
    El Ferrol, 230–6, 238, 240; Battle of
    Trafalgar, 312, 313, 314, 315, 324,
    340, 342, 351, 384, 402n; mortally
    wounded, 352, 355
Great Britain: 'the Great Terror' and
    defence of, 1, 2, 3, 35–7, 39, 40–1,
    44–62, 71–83, 88, 267–9; Peace of
    Amiens (1802), 11–12, 13, 26, 71,
    101, 157, 216; French high-tariff
    law against, 13; resumption of war
    with France (1803), 13, 16, 18, 26,
    44, 155, 162, 265; economy, 45,
    155; 16 military districts, 46–7;
    Melville Affair, 133–4, 149–51, 152,
    153, 216, 270; Third Coalition
    against Napoleon (1805), 148, 154,
    156–7; Russian Treaty with (1805),
    156–7; Swedish secret convention
    with (1804), 156; Napoleon's peace
    offer to George III, 158–9; Spain
    declares war against (1804), 179,
    181, 188, 190, 399n; Battle of
    Trafalgar, 307–56, 359–62, 363;
    and Nelson's state funeral (January
    1806), 363–9; see also British Army;
    Royal Navy; ships, British
'the Great Terror' (1803–5), 1, 2, 3, 35–
    7, 39, 40–1, 44–62, 71–83, 88, 267–
    9
Greenwich Naval Hospital, 49, 363–4,
    365
Grenada, 209, 225; St George's Bay,
    220–1
Grenville, William Wyndham, 1st Baron,
    30, 148, 149, 152, 370
Grindall, Captain Richard, 335, 353
Guadeloupe, 205, 224, 225, 226, 227,
    228, 240
Guion, Captain, 180
Gustavus IV, King of Sweden, 156

Hallowell, Captain Ben, 250, 264
Hamilton, Lady Emma Lyon, 52, 224,
    244, 247, 250–4, 255, 261–2, 264,
    291, 332, 367, 369–70, 384, 398n
Hamilton, Horatia (Nelson's daughter),
    224, 252–3, 262, 332
Hamilton, Sir William, 251, 253, 264
Hancock, Captain John, 164–5
Hardenberg, Karl von, 15
Hardy, Captain Thomas Masterman,
    136, 264, 319, 321, 324, 325,

327–8, 332, 367, 368, 384
Hargood, Captain William, 318, 338,
    340–1, 384
Harrington, Charles Stanhope, Earl of,
    46, 384
Harrowby, Richard Ryder, Earl of, 38,
    154, 384
Harvey, Captain Eliab (later Rear-
    Admiral), 319, 327, 329–30, 332,
    368, 384
Hawkesbury, Lord, Robert Jenkinson,
    11, 12, 38, 366, 384
Heard, Sir Isaac, Garter King of Arms,
    365, 367, 368, 369
Hennah, Lieutenant William, 342, 384
Hobart, Robert, Earl of
    Buckinghamshire, 152, 384
Holland, 1st Lord, 24
Holland, Lord and Lady, 119
Holland, Henry Richard, 3rd Baron, 366
Holland/Dutch (Batavian Republic), 9,
    10, 11, 12, 16, 26, 108–9, 122, 124,
    154, 156, 164–6, 190, 266; invasion
    preparations, 35; war contribution,
    91–6, 396–7n; French Convention
    with (1803), 155; battle off Ostend
    (1804), 164–6; see also ships, Dutch
Holy Roman Empire, dissolution of, 10,
    272
Hood, Samuel, Admiral Lord, 138, 140,
    245, 246, 248, 277, 363, 364, 365,
    368
Hope, Captain George, 352, 384
Hoste, Captain William, 288, 384
Hotham, Admiral Sir William, 248

Imperial Recess (1803), 10
income tax, British, 45, 155
Infernet, Captain Louis-Antoine, 336,
    337, 350, 358, 384
'The Invasion' (popular song), 61
Ireland, Irish, 35, 57, 58, 81, 123, 157,
    160, 162, 163, 172, 174, 175, 212,
    214, 217, 218, 237, 266, 399n
Italy, 9, 10, 17, 120, 121, 154, 157

Jamaica, 129, 139, 219, 220, 245
James, William, 1, 143, 231, 234, 236,
    332, 334, 341, 398n, 400n, 403n
Jeffrey, Lord, 30
Jervis, Sir John see St Vincent, Lord
Jervis, Mr Justice, 129
John, Archduke of Austria, 269
Jordan, Mrs Dorothea, 60, 274

Josephine, Empress, 18, 19, 20, 21–2,
    116, 401n
Junot, Colonel-General Andoche, 118,
    192–3, 197

Keats, Captain, 258, 259
Keith, George Elphinstone, Admiral
    Lord, 35, 36, 37, 40, 48, 52, 110,
    114, 128, 139, 140, 141, 145, 163,
    175, 248, 249, 251, 382
Kellermann, Marshal François Etienne,
    Duke of Valmy, 21
Kennedy, Lieutenant Thomas, 330
King, Captain Richard, 348, 384
Knight, Rear-Admiral Alexander, 280,
    282
Kutusow, General, 270

La Coruña, 139, 141, 161, 162, 179,
    184, 210, 217, 223, 237, 240, 242,
    259, 275
Labouchère, Peter, 271, 401n
Lacrosse, Admiral Jean-Baptiste, 384
Lafond, CGS National Flotilla, 266
Laforey, Captain Sir Francis, 365, 384
Lagrange, General Joseph, 174, 184, 384
Laharpe, writer, 119
Lamb, Charles, 25
Lannes, Marshal Jean, Duc de
    Montebello, 18, 118
Lapenotière, Lieutenant John Richards,
    359, 384–5
Latouche-Tréville, Admiral Louis-René
    Levassor de, 81, 84, 106, 168–9,
    171, 173, 385
Lauriston, General Jacques-Alexandre-
    Bernard Law, 193, 196, 199, 205,
    219, 226, 228, 242, 302, 385
Le Havre, 37, 86, 110, 112, 114, 140,
    190, 197
Le Roy, Commissioner-General at
    Cadiz, 299–300, 301, 305, 385
Le Tourneur, Lieutenant, 344, 385
Le Tréport, 90, 110
Lebrun, Charles-François, 73
Lefebvre, Marshal François Joseph,
    Duke of Danzig, 18, 21, 157
Lefebvre, Georges, historian, 270, 398n
Lejeune, General Baron, 120
Lescallier, 297
Lesueur, M., Imperial Chapel Master, 19
Leyland, John, 1, 2–3
Liddell, Robert, 167
Limeux, M. de, 301

Lincoln, Bishop of, 367, 369
Lloyds Coffee House, 361, 363
London: threat of French invasion and defence of, 48, 49, 50, 52, 57–8, 59; theatres and amusements, 59–61; Nelson's state funeral, 364–9
London Stock Exchange, 359
Lorient, 64, 66, 111, 139, 160, 163, 170, 179, 211
Louis XVI, King of France, 63, 79, 115
Louis XVIII, King of France, 17, 50
Louis de Narbonne, 119
Louis, Rear-Admiral Thomas, 140, 278, 288–9, 294, 305, 306, 308, 317, 318, 385
Louise, Queen of Prussia, 154
Louisiana, 37, 121
Louis-Philippe, King of France, 17
Lucas, Captain Jean-Jacques, 309, 324, 327, 328, 329, 332–3, 358, 385
Lucchesini, Ambassador Marchese di, 270
Lunéville, Treaty of (1801), 10, 12, 17, 154, 157
lycée system of education, French, 7–8

MacDonnell, Commodore Enrique, 304, 309, 385, 402n
Mack, Field-Marshal Lieutenant Baron, 270
Magendie, Captain Jean-Jacques, 311, 314, 321, 325, 333, 334, 358, 385
Magon, Rear-Admiral Charles-René, 98, 226, 303–4, 308, 309, 312, 342, 343, 344, 348, 354, 385, 402n
Maistral, Commodore Esprit-Tranquille, 326, 335, 385, 402n
Malmesbury, James Harris, Earl of, 359, 360, 361, 385
Malmesbury, Lady, 259–60
Malta, 9, 11, 13, 65, 66, 155–6, 257, 260, 285, 402n
Marengo, Battle of (1800), 118, 120
Maria Carolina, Queen of Naples, 156
Maria Luisa, Queen of Spain, 121
Markham, Admiral John, 35, 36, 48
Marmont, Marshal Auguste Frédéric de, 118, 175
Mars, Mlle (Anne Boulet), 118
Marsden, William, First Secretary to Admiralty, 145, 180, 200, 222, 223, 279, 288, 385
Martello Towers, 54–5, 149, 267
Martinique, 184, 185, 193, 196, 199,
202, 205, 206, 208, 214, 228, 240; Villeneuve sails to, 206–10, 211, 212, 213, 224–6; and departs from, 226–7, 228
Mason, Captain Francis, 164, 165
Masséna, Marshal André, Duke of Rivoli, 18
Matcham, George, Jr, 367, 369
Matcham, George, Sr, 367, 369
Matcham, Mrs (Nelson's sister), 251
Mediterranean Fleet, British, 140, 153, 160–1, 173, 175, 194, 207, 208, 211–13, 220–4, 227, 229, 255, 263, 276, 278, 280–356; Nelson assumes command of new (September 1805), 263, 280–4; strength, 287–8, 304, 315, 316, 403n; supplies for, 288–90, 293, 294; Battle of Trafalgar, 307–56; blockade of Cadiz re-established by, 356; casualties, 354–5, 362; see also Royal Navy; ships, British
Melito, Miot de, 159
Melville, Elizabeth Rannie, Lady, 28–9
Melville, Henry Dundas, 1st Viscount, First Lord of the Admiralty, 28–9, 30, 31, 32, 40, 48, 70, 129, 136, 143, 144–5, 148, 149–51, 152, 155, 160, 166, 169–70, 175, 178–9, 181, 201, 202, 204, 210, 212, 261, 360, 370, 382; impeachment of, 133–4, 149–51, 202, 216, 270
Menou, General, 5
Merton, Viscount, 367, 369
Merton Place (Nelson's and Lady Hamilton's home), 251, 254, 256, 258, 261–2, 264, 398n
Meyers, Lieutenant-General Sir William, 219, 220, 385
Middleton, Sir Charls see Barham, Lord
Militia Act (1802), 45
Minto, Earl of, Sir Gilbert Elliot, 149, 247, 251, 254, 257, 258, 259, 260, 272, 385
Minto, Lady, 259, 272
Missiessy, Admiral Edouard-Thomas de Burgues, 1, 173, 174, 183, 193, 199, 211, 216, 385; West Indian expedition of, 184–6, 193, 196, 197, 209, 214
Moncey, Marshal, 18, 21
Montmorency, Adrien de, 119
Montreuil army camp, 37, 123, 124, 266, 272

Montrose, Duke of, 366
Moore, Captain Graham, 176–7, 188,
    385–6
Moore, General Sir John, 176
Moorsom, Captain Robert, 366, 368, 386
Morris, Captain Charles, 31
Morris, Captain James Nicoll, 346, 386
Mulgrave, Lord, 154, 256, 261, 366
Murat, Prince, 240

Napier, General Sir William, 31, 33–4
Naples, 9, 11, 156, 247, 251, 296, 298,
    301, 314
Napoleon I Bonaparte, Emperor, 30, 34–
    7, 39, 46, 56, 141, 152, 154, 157–9,
    225, 243, 266, 295–8; Coronation of
    (1804), 5–6, 13–14, 15, 16, 18–22,
    34, 41, 121, 189, 190; social and
    economic reorganisation of France,
    7–9; foreign policy, 9–13, 157–9;
    Continental System, 16; coup d'état
    (1799), 17, 81, 121; invasion of
    Russia (1812), 18; invasion of
    Britain plans, 35–7, 39, 40–1, 56–9,
    62, 71–83, 88–115, 122–7, 157,
    168–9, 170, 171, 173–5, 178, 184,
    186, 193, 195–7, 205–11, 215–16,
    217–18, 224–5, 237–8, 239, 240–2,
    266–7, 269, 272, 295–6; Decrès's
    relations with, 64–5, 66, 67, 68–9;
    National Flotilla, 71–9, 81, 82–3,
    88–90, 91–6, 97–9, 100; and
    'patriotic contributions', 82–3;
    Fulton's submarine, 86–8; Dutch
    relations with, 90–6, 109; Boulogne
    storm tragedy, 97–9; preparation of
    Channel ports, 99–115; Berthier's
    relations with, 119–232; and
    gathering of invasion troops, 122–7;
    letter to George III (1805), 158–9;
    Spanish relations with, 186, 187,
    188, 189, 190–1, 192, 193, 195,
    399n; and Villeneuve, 193, 195,
    196, 198–9, 205–6, 207, 209, 236–
    7, 240–2, 276, 295, 296, 298, 308,
    314, 357; and Ganteaume, 195–7,
    202–3, 204–5, 209, 210, 215–16;
    battle off El Ferrol, 238–40; at
    Boulogne (August 1805), 266, 267,
    271, 272, 276, 362; Continental
    War, 269–70, 272–3, 296, 359, 360;
    financial difficulties, 270–1; 36th
    birthday celebrations, 271; invasion
    of Spain by (1808), 356; Battle of

Trafalgar, 362; and Battle of
    Austerlitz, 362
National/Imperial Flotilla, French, 71–9,
    80, 81–3, 88–90, 91–6, 97–9, 100,
    122, 136, 140, 190, 193, 197–8,
    206, 266–7, 296–7; 4 main classes
    of vessels, 74–7, 396n; cost, 77,
    396n; patriotic contributions to, 82–
    3; strength, 90, 266, 396–7n, 401n;
    Dutch contribution to, 91–6, 396n;
    shortage of crews, 95; Channel ports
    for, 99–115; see also Combined
    Fleet; French Navy
Nautilus (Fulton's submarine), 85–8
Naval Chronicle, 66, 136, 137, 139, 163
Navy Board, 132–3, 144, 146, 147, 153
Nelson, Horatio, Admiral Lord, 2, 3, 34,
    39, 41, 42, 43, 52, 55, 63, 74, 130,
    136, 139, 141, 145, 153, 163, 169,
    182, 211–13, 217, 219, 275, 277,
    280–4, 299, 304, 344, 345, 398n;
    Battle of Copenhagen, 130, 248,
    249, 250, 259; and Battle of Cape
    St Vincent, 130, 200, 247, 248–9;
    Cornwallis's friendship with, 138,
    244–5, 248; C-in-C Mediterranean
    Fleet, 140, 153, 173, 194–5, 207,
    208, 211–13, 255, 276; Orde's feud
    with, 211, 248, 399n; gives chase to
    Villeneuve's Fleet, 212–13, 214,
    220–4, 229, 236, 254–5; in West
    Indies, 219–23, 226, 227, 228, 240,
    244–5, 248; character, 243–4, 246,
    248–9; life and career, 244–54;
    malaria suffered by, 244, 245;
    marriage to Fanny Nisbet, 245; love
    affair with Lady Hamilton, 247,
    250–4; injuries sustained by, 247,
    327–8, 331–2; St Vincent's relations
    with, 248–50, 251; promotion and
    honours, 249–50, 251; legal
    separation from Fanny, 250; money
    troubles, 253–4; home leave, 255–
    64, 269; assumes command of new
    Mediterranean Fleet, 263, 280–4,
    298; sails from Portsmouth, 264–5;
    joins Fleet off Cadiz, 280–2, 302;
    and Calder's return home, 282–4;
    and Trafalgar Memorandum, 291–
    3; orders issued to captains (10th
    October 1805), 294, 402n; gives
    chase to Franco-Spanish Fleet, 295,
    311; Battle of Trafalgar, 307–32,
    354, 355, 356, 363; death of, 327–8;

331–2, 357, 360–1; and state
funeral (9th January 1806), 363–9
Nelson, Lady (*née* Fanny Nisbet), 245–6,
250, 253
Nelson, William Earl (brother), 367
'the Nelson touch' (battle plan of attack),
258, 291, 320
Nepean, Sir Evan, 128, 145
Ney, Marshal Michel, 18, 118, 123, 267,
386
Nieuport, 67, 100, 108, 113, 114
Nile (Aboukir Bay), Battle of the (1798),
66, 140, 194, 203, 250, 259, 332
Nisbet, Captain Josiah (stepson of
Nelson), 245–6, 247
North, Lord, 28
Northesk, William Carnegie, Rear-
Admiral the Earl of, 278, 319, 386
Novosiltzoff, Ambassador Nikolai, 156

Orde, Vice-Admiral Sir John, 178, 208,
211, 214, 226, 248, 368, 386, 399n
Ordnance Board, British Naval, 144, 147
Ostend, 74, 82, 96, 100, 101, 108, 113,
114, 126, 165, 166, 190, 266, 397n;
Anglo-Dutch naval clash off (1804),
164–6
Otto, Louis Guillaume, 57
Ottoman Empire, 9, 155
Otway, Captain, 167, 399n
Oudinot, General, 271
Ouvrard, Gabriel Julien, 271, 300, 301,
386, 401n
Owen, Captain Richard, 35–6, 114, 386

Paget, Lord, 268
Pareja, Captain Antonio, 349, 386
Paris, Napoleon's Coronation in Notre-
Dame Cathedral (1804), 5, 6, 14,
16, 18–22, 121, 190
Paris, Treaty of (1802), 10
Parker, Admiral Sir Hyde, 130, 138, 248,
250, 277
Parker, Admiral Sir Peter, 368
Parker, Captain, 280
Paul, Tsar of Russia, 9, 15
Pellew, Commodore Sir Edward (later
Admiral Viscount Exmouth), 36,
161–2, 163, 168, 200, 201, 386,
399n
Pellew, Captain Israel, 334, 335, 386
péniches, French, 74, 75, 78–9, 82, 88,
98, 126, 266, 396n, 401n
Perceval, Spencer, Attorney-General,
150
Perignon, Marshal, 21
Perring, Sir John, Lord Mayor of
London, 359–60
Petty, Lord Henry, 150
Pitt, William, the Elder *see* Chatham
Pitt, William, the Younger, 8, 11, 12, 15,
24, 29, 30–4, 45, 56, 62, 268, 271,
274; biography and character, 26–8,
31, 32–4; and Lady Hester
Stanhope, 31–3; Prime Minister
(1804–6), 32–3, 38–40, 46, 47–8,
49, 50, 61, 70, 109, 114, 134, 141,
143, 148–59, 164, 187, 265; conflict
between St Vincent and, 128–9,
130–4; ill-health, 148–9, 152; and
Melville Affair, 148, 149–51, 152,
153; Third Coalition, 148, 154,
156–7; appoints Barham 1st Lord of
Admiralty, 152, 153; foreign policy,
154–5, 156–7, 159; and Nelson,
254, 256, 257, 259, 260, 262, 263,
287; authorises submarine and
torpedo tests, 261; Battle of
Trafalgar, 359, 363; and Nelson's
state funeral, 369; death (1806), 370
Pius VI, Pope, 5, 6, 121
Pius VII, Pope, 386–7; and Napoleon's
Coronation, 5–7, 13–14, 17, 21–2
Pléville, Naval Minister, 84
Plunkett, Seaman Edward, 167, 168
Plymouth, 49, 53, 57, 130, 138, 141,
146, 152, 167, 180, 181, 183, 211,
236, 258, 264
Ponsonby, George, 150
Popham, Admiral Sir Home, 261, 285
Portsmouth, 44, 49, 53, 54, 57, 152, 255,
264, 359, 363
Portugal, 155, 160, 289, 399n
prames, French, 74, 75, 77, 79, 82, 164,
165, 166, 266, 396n
press gangs, 39
Prigny, Captain Jean Baptiste, 302, 303,
309, 314, 323, 333, 358, 387, 402n
Prince of Peace *see* Godoy
profiteers, war, 88–9
Prussia, 9, 15, 16, 46, 154, 156

Radstock, Admiral William Lord, 358,
365, 368
Rannie, Elizabeth *see* Melville, Lady
Redmill, Captain Robert, 341, 387
Regnault de Saint-Jean d'Angély, Mme,
116

Reille, General Honoré-Charles, 228, 240, 387

Rémusat, Claire, Comtesse de, 20

Rennie, Sir Charles, 261

Robespierre, Maximilien de, 7

Rochefort, 1, 73, 99, 109, 123, 139, 141, 160, 163, 169, 170, 174, 179, 180, 183, 184, 185, 186, 190, 199, 214, 236

Rochefort Squadron, 173, 174, 182, 183, 184–6, 193, 196, 205, 211, 214, 215, 216, 217, 218, 229, 237, 276

Rodney, George, 1st Baron, 291

Rodger, N. A. M., 145

Rose, Hon. George, 38, 48, 256, 257, 259, 260, 263, 264, 281, 387, 394n

Rose, Holland, 152

Rose, M., Imperial Chapel Master, 19

Rosily-Mesros, Admiral François-Etienne, 80, 85, 173, 387, 403n; replaces Villeneuve as Fleet Commander at Cadiz, 296, 301, 304–5, 306, 308

Rotely, Second-Lieutenant, 307

Rotheram, Captain Edward, 338, 339, 387

Royal Military College, 45

Royal Navy, British, 1, 39, 40, 47, 50, 70, 91, 128–47; blockade of French/Spanish ports, 1, 2, 81, 169, 170–3, 174, 175–6, 178–9, 181, 182–3, 200, 206, 211, 216, 217, 218; stength, 47–8, 131, 139, 140, 141–3, 403n; budget, 48, 132, 133; sea-fencibles, 48, 49; triple line of barricade, 49; attacks on channel ports by, 103–4, 105, 109, 114, 115; administration, 132–3, 144–7, 149; disposition of, 139–41; loss of ships, 142, 143; manpower, 132, 143–4; mutiny, 129, 166–7; North American command, 140; officers, 143–4; St Vincent's inquiry into administration, 132–3, 149; Dutch skirmish off Ostend with (1804), 164–6; alleged superiority at sea of, 170, 181; Spanish treasure ships attacked by, 176–8, 187, 188; storm damage to ships, 179–81, 183; Nelson gives chase to Villeneuve's Fleet, 212–13, 214, 219–24, 229; HMS *Diamond* captured by Villeneuve, 225; and 15 merchantmen captured, 227, 228;

clash off El Ferrol with Franco-Spanish Fleet (July, 1805), 230–6, 238–9, 275; Nelson takes over command of new Mediterranean Fleet, 263, 280–4; new flag signalling system, 285–6; Trafalgar Memorandum, 291–3; Battle of Trafalgar, 307–56; state funeral of Nelson, 363–9; *see also* Channel Fleet; dockyards; Mediterranean Fleet; ships, British

Rumbold, Sir George Berriman, kidnapping of, 15, 387

Russell, Vice-Admiral, 53

Russia, 9, 14–15, 16, 46, 122, 154, 155–7, 265, 269, 270; French Treaty with (1801), 10; Treaty of Paris (1802), 10; Prussian Defence Pact (1804), 16, 156; Napoleon's invasion of (1812), 18; British Treaty (1805), 156–7; Swedish Treaty (1805), 156; Austrian Treaty (1805), 157; Battle of Austerlitz (1805), 362

Rutherford, Captain William, 353, 387

Ryan, Seaman John, 167

St Cyr, General Gouvion, 12

St Helena, 174

St Lucia, 184, 205, 219, 220, 222, 225

St Omer army camp, 37, 89, 90, 110, 122, 124, 266, 272

St Paul's Cathedral, Nelson's burial in, 363, 367–9, 370, 394

Saint-Valéry, 74, 90, 110

Saint-Valéry-sur-Somme, 90, 110, 112

St Vincent, John Jervis, Earl, 39, 40, 45, 49, 53, 128–34, 136, 137, 138, 139, 141, 143, 146, 147, 149, 152, 160, 163, 181, 199, 202, 248, 249, 370, 387; conflict between Pitt and, 128–34; inquiry into naval administration by, 132–3, 149, 199; and Melville Affair, 133–4, 150; *Memoirs*, 134, 398n; replaces Cornwallis as C-in-C Channel Fleet (1806), 202, 370; Nelson's relations with, 248–50, 251; against Fulton's submarine, 261

San Domingo, 67, 156, 168, 185, 189, 196, 205

Sardinia, 206, 208, 211, 212, 226, 257, 293

Saumaurez, Sir James, 140

Saxton, Sir Richard, 264

Scherer, General, 120
Schimmelpenninck, Rutger Jan, 91–3,
    94, 95, 387
Scott, Chaplain Alexander, 331
Scott, John, 324
Scott, Sir Walter, 54
sea-fencibles, 48, 49
Seaforth, Lord, 219, 220
Sebastiani, Colonel, 12
Second Coalition, 9, 12, 394n
Serurier, French Ambassador at
    Amsterdam, 239
Sganzin, engineer, 101–2, 106–7
Sheerness, 57, 59, 297, 360
Shelbourne, Lord, 31, 150
Sheridan, Richard Brinsley, 31, 61, 149
Ships, British, 390, 392–3
    Acasta, 288
    Achilles, 348
    Aetna, 281, 288
    Africa, 288, 319, 323, 334–5, 336, 337,
        350
    Agamemnon, 43, 44, 208, 230, 233,
        246, 264, 288, 307, 312, 318, 337,
        350, 351
    Aimable, 164, 165, 166, 288
    Ajax, 204, 209, 230, 232, 233, 264,
        318, 337, 350, 351
    Amazon, 280
    Amphion, 176, 177, 288
    Antelope, 164, 165, 166
    Argo, 66
    Barfleur, 215, 230
    Belleisle, 288, 318, 330, 338–41, 342,
        345, 348, 353, 403n
    Bellerophon, 344–6, 351, 352
    Boadicea, 180
    Britannia, 319, 350
    Calcutta, 278
    Canopus, 288
    Colossus, 286, 318, 345, 346–8, 353
    Colpoys, 218
    Conqueror, 333, 334, 335, 337
    Cruiser, 164, 165, 166
    Curieux, 223
    Defence, 208, 286, 288, 318, 352
    Defiance, 200, 215, 230, 264, 288, 341,
        344, 351, 352–3, 365
    Donegal, 288
    Dorothea, 261
    Dragon, 215, 230, 232, 233
    Dreadnought, 180, 181, 201, 204, 210,
        244, 288, 293, 351–2
    Egyptienne, 215

    Endymion, 287, 288
    Entreprenante, 353
    Euryalus, 43–4, 262, 264, 286, 295,
        306, 311, 312, 319, 357
    Eurydice, 288
    Felix, 183
    Foudroyant, 66, 180, 183, 215
    Glory, 208, 230
    Hero, 200, 215, 230, 231, 232
    Hibernia, 204
    Hydra, 288
    Illustrious, 180, 201
    Immortalité, 35
    Impetueux, 180, 200
    Indefatigable, 176, 177, 200, 215
    Juno, 288
    Leviathan, 288, 324, 331, 333, 334,
        335–6, 337, 340, 350, 367
    Lion, 66, 244
    Lively, 176, 177
    Louis, 180
    Magnificent, 181
    Malabar, 289
    Malta, 200, 204, 209, 215, 230, 233,
        236
    Mars, 138, 201, 281, 286, 295, 318,
        334, 338, 340, 341–3, 345
    Medusa, 176
    Mercury, 226
    Minotaur, 201, 350–1
    Montagu, 167, 200
    Naiad, 278, 286, 287, 311, 341
    Neptune, 324, 328, 333, 335
    Niger, 288
    Nimble, 218
    Northumberland, 168, 179
    Orion, 319, 336–7, 347, 350
    Penelope, 66, 164, 165, 166
    Phoebe, 211, 286, 287, 311, 316
    Phoenix, 237
    Pickle, 166, 288, 311, 354, 359, 360
    Plantagenet, 180
    Polyphemus, 208, 341, 352, 353, 354
    Prince, 180, 335, 353, 354
    Prince George, 180
    Prince of Wales, 200, 215, 229, 230,
        231, 233, 283, 288
    Queen, 215, 288, 370
    Raisonnable, 215, 230, 244
    Ranger, 278
    Rattler, 164, 165, 166
    Renommée, 288
    Renown, 208
    Repulse, 200, 215, 230

418　　　　　　　　　　　　INDEX

Revenge, 345, 346, 352, 366, 368
Royal Sovereign, 213, 215, 264, 288,
　293, 294, 318, 319, 320, 321, 330,
　338, 339, 345
Ruby, 208
Salvador del Mundo, 167
San Joseph, 180
Sirius, 231, 288, 311, 312
Spartiate, 180, 350–1, 365
Spencer, 288
Stag, 164
Sterling, 181
Swiftsure, 43, 44, 341, 353, 354
Swinger, 210
Téméraire, 319, 324, 327, 328–31, 332,
　335, 340, 342, 351, 368, 403n
Terrible, 200, 204, 209, 215
Thunderer, 230, 264
Tigre, 288
Tonnant, 162, 201, 338, 342, 343–4,
　351, 403n
Triumph, 215, 230
Venerable, 180
Victory, 41, 153, 211, 212, 219, 223,
　262, 263, 264, 274, 275, 277, 280,
　284, 286, 294, 295, 307, 316, 318,
　319, 320, 357, 363, 403n; Battle of
　Trafalgar, 319, 320, 321–32, 338,
　340, 345; and Nelson's state funeral,
　363–9
Ville de Paris, 160, 179, 180, 201, 202,
　277, 370
Warrior, 215, 230
Weazle, 286, 287, 311
Windsor Castle, 215, 230, 232, 233,
　234, 236
Zealous, 287, 288
Ships, Dutch, 48, 91–6, 163
　Chatam, 95
　Fortitude, 94
　Grondeur, 94
　Hertzeller, 95
　Triton, 94
　Victor-Polus, 95
　Ville d'Aix, 164
　Ville-d'Anvers, 164, 165, 166
　Wreker, 95
　Zoontmorn, 95
Ships, French, 390, 391–2
　Achille, 226, 231, 309, 312, 313, 340,
　　341, 348, 353, 353–4
　Aigle, 231, 313, 340, 341, 344, 345,
　　352, 353
　Algésiras, 226, 231, 312, 313, 341, 342,

343–4, 355, 356, 402n
Argonaute, 312, 346, 348, 349, 355,
　356
Armide, 400n
Atlas, 207, 231, 232, 233
Berwick, 207, 231, 313, 324, 348–9,
　352
Bucentaure, 169, 194, 195, 206, 207,
　231, 233, 302, 306, 311, 312, 313,
　321, 323, 324, 325–6, 327, 328,
　333–4, 350, 355, 358, 366, 402n,
　403n
Cornélie, 207, 402n
Didon, 211, 224–5, 237
Duguay-Trouin, 312, 313, 349, 350,
　351, 355
Formidable, 65, 207, 231, 313, 349,
　350, 351, 355, 402n
Fougueux, 313, 321, 330, 333, 338,
　340, 342, 402n
Furieuse, 95
Gloire, 400
Glorieux, 65
Guillaume Tell, 66, 67, 194
Hermione, 207, 311, 402n
Héros, 312, 313, 323, 350, 355, 356,
　402n
Hortense, 207, 402n
Indomptable, 207, 231, 313, 338, 339,
　351, 352, 355, 356, 402n
Intrépide, 207, 231, 313, 336–7, 349,
　350, 351, 355, 402n
Jemmapes, 184, 185
Lion, 185, 400n
Magnanime, 185, 400n
Majestueux, 184, 185, 400n
Mont-Blanc, 207, 231, 232, 233, 313,
　350, 351, 355, 402n
Muiron, 121
Neptune, 207, 231, 312, 313, 325, 326,
　327, 331, 334, 335, 336, 340, 341,
　353, 355, 356
Normandie, 79
Orient, 250, 364, 366
Palmyre, 400n
Pluton, 207, 231, 232, 233, 313, 341–
　2, 343, 355, 356
Redoutable, 309, 313, 321, 323–4, 325,
　326, 327, 328–9, 330, 332, 345
Rhin, 207, 312, 323, 402n
Scipion, 207, 231, 313, 349, 350, 351,
　355
Sirène, 207
Suffren, 185, 400n

Swift-sure, 207, 231, 313, 341, 345, 346, 347, 348, 355, 402n
Sylphe, 400n
Thémis, 207, 311, 402n
Thétis, 400n
Ships, Spanish, 391–2
America, 231
Argonauta, 192, 229, 230, 231, 232, 313, 341, 348, 349, 355
Bahama, 312, 313, 345, 346, 347, 348, 355
Clara, 177
España, 231, 232
Fama, 177
Firma, 231, 232, 234
Medea, 177
Medusa, 177
Mercedes, 177
Monarca, 313, 341, 342, 343, 344, 345–6
Montañes, 313, 345, 348, 355
Neptuno, 313, 350–1
Príncipe de Asturias, 179, 313, 324, 340, 342, 351–2, 355
Rayo, 302, 309, 312, 313, 350, 356
San Agustín, 313, 335–6, 337, 350, 355
San Francisco de Asís, 313, 350, 355, 356
San Ildefonso, 313, 352, 355, 403n
San Joseph, 366
San Juan Nepomuceno, 179, 313, 324, 339–40, 341, 344, 351, 352, 353, 355
San Justo, 302, 313, 340, 351, 352, 356
San Leandro, 313, 338, 340, 356
San Rafael, 231, 232, 234
Santa Ana, 302, 313, 324, 330, 338, 339, 342, 351, 355, 356
Santísima Trinidad, 313, 321, 323, 327, 328, 333, 334, 335, 355, 366
Terrible, 231
Ships, US
Demologus, (steam-driven), 261
Sicily, 156, 206, 208, 211, 212
Siddons, Mrs, 273
Sidmouth, Viscount *see* Addington, Henry
Smith, Commodore Sir William Sydney, 140, 163, 164, 165–6, 175, 268, 387
Soult, Marshal Nicolas Jean de Dieu, 18, 58, 107, 111, 114, 118, 123, 124, 193, 267, 272, 387
Spain, Spanish, 163, 168, 169, 170, 176–8, 223, 229, 269; secret French Treaty with (1803), 123, 155, 161, 186, 187, 190; and French relations, 155, 161–2, 186–93, 399n; declares war on Britain (1804), 179, 181, 188, 190, 399n; new French Pact with (1805), 190–1, 399n; financial problems, 271; Napoleon's invasion of (1808), 356
Spanish Royal Navy, 162, 175–6, 179, 183–4, 189, 190–3, 196, 197, 402n; British attack on treasure ships of, 176–8, 187, 188, 190; French ships seized in Cadiz by (1808), 356, 403n; *see also* Combined Franco-Spanish Fleet; ships, Spanish
Spencer, George John Spencer, 2nd Earl of, 30
Spithead Fleet, 40
Staël, Mme de, 8, 116
Stanhope, Charles, 33, 34
Stanhope, Lady Harriet, 31
Stanhope, Lady Hester, 31–3, 34, 387
Stanhope, James, 34
Steward, Brigadier General William, 281
Stirling, Rear-Admiral Charles, 218, 229, 236, 280, 387
Strachan, Captain Sir Richard John, 280, 351, 355, 388
submarines and torpedoes, Fulton's, 84–8, 261
Suckling, Captain Maurice, 244
Sutton, Captain, 288
Sutton, Rear-Admiral Sir John, 167, 388
Sweden, 9, 16, 156
Switzerland, 9, 10, 12, 154

Talleyrand-Périgord, Charles Maurice de, Prince of Benevento (French Foreign Minister), 11, 12, 14, 16, 17–18, 20, 21, 34, 57, 58, 68, 69, 72, 73, 91, 93, 94, 95, 118, 154, 186, 187, 188, 191, 237, 295, 300, 388
Tallien, Mme, 116
Talma, Francis Joseph, actor, 118
Taylor, Simon, 219
Taylor, Vice-Admiral Thomas, 368
Texada, Captain-General, 175–6
Texel (Dutch island), 35, 140, 175, 190, 241, 272
theatres, London, 59–60, 274
Thilorier, Jean-Charles, 84
Third Coalition (1805), 46, 148, 154,

156–7, 362
Thornborough, Admiral, 140
Tierney, George, 39
Tilbury, 49, 57, 59
The Times, 34, 35, 38, 40, 46, 49, 53, 61,
    243, 254, 255, 256, 258, 260, 265,
    268, 273, 274, 364, 400–1n
Tobago, 220, 225
Tooke, John Horne, 30
Torbay, 170, 183, 201, 370
Toulon, 63, 73, 99, 110, 123, 139, 140,
    168, 169, 185, 189, 190, 194, 195,
    293, 298
Toulon Fleet, 168, 173, 174, 184, 193,
    194–5, 196, 197, 198–9, 204, 205,
    206–8, 211, 212, 213, 216, 229,
    240, 260, 284, 314
Trafalgar, Battle of (21st October 1805),
    1–2, 258, 275, 287, 307–56, 359–
    69; casualties, 354–5, 362;
    Thanksgiving Day, 361–2; provision
    for wounded and families of dead,
    363; Nelson's state funeral, 363–9
Trafalgar Memorandum, Nelson's, 291–
    3, 320
Treasurer of the Navy, 146, 150
Trinidad, 11, 220, 225
Trotter, Paymaster Alexander, 149, 150
Troubridge, Thomas, 251
Truguet, Admiral Laurent-Jean, 72, 163,
    171, 388
Twining, Thomas, 54
Tyler, Captain Charles, 343–4, 388

Ulm, Battle of (1805), 272, 359
Uriarte y Borja, Commodore Francisco
    de, 334, 335, 388
Ushant, 141, 160, 168, 176, 178, 179,
    202, 204, 209, 210, 217, 218, 223,
    224, 237, 276, 277, 278, 279

Valdés, Commodore Cayetano, 350, 351,
    388
Vargas, Captain José de, 352, 388
Vatican, 10; Concordat (1801), 5, 6
Verhuell, Rear-Admiral Charles-Henri,
    91, 94, 95, 96, 163, 164–5, 166,
    192, 388
Victualling Board, British Naval, 144,
    147
Vigée-LeBrun, Mme, 52, 116
Villaret-de-Joyeuse, Admiral Louis-
    Thomas, 86, 138, 168, 185, 186,
    224, 228–9, 388

Villemadrin, Captain Charles-Eusèbe,
    345, 347, 348, 358, 384
Villeneuve, Vice-Admiral Pierre-Charles
    Silvestre de, 2, 81, 184, 185, 189,
    193–5, 202, 205, 218, 219, 236–7,
    238–42, 259, 260, 266, 271, 275,
    282, 285, 286–7, 298–306, 389,
    398n, 402n; Fleet Commander,
    Toulon, 173, 174, 193–5, 196, 199;
    Gravina's relations with, 189;
    abortive attempt to escape from
    Toulon, 193–5, 198, 206; letter of
    resignation to Decrès, 198–9; C-in-
    C Combined Fleet, 205–6; escapes
    from Toulon (to Martinique), 206–
    10, 211, 212, 213, 220, 224–6;
    Nelson's pursuit of, 212–13, 214,
    220, 222–4, 254–5; captures HMS
    Diamond, 225, 226, 228; leaves
    Martinique, 226–7; captures 15
    British merchantmen, 227, 228;
    returns to El Ferrol, 228–9, 240–1,
    278; clash off El Ferrol with
    Calder's Fleet (July 1805), 230–6,
    238–40; sails for Cadiz (August
    1805), 242, 275, 276; ordered by
    Napoleon to sail to Naples, 206,
    298, 301, 302, 303; replaced by
    Rosily as Fleet Commander, Cadiz,
    296, 304–5, 306, 308; and shortage
    of supplies and manpower, 298–302;
    Conseil de Guerre countermands
    Napoleon's orders, 302–4; sails out
    of Cadiz (18th October 1805), 304–
    6, 311–12; Battle of Trafalgar, 307–
    11, 312–16, 317, 321, 325, 333–4,
    341, 350, 352, 356; as PoW, 357–8;
    suicide of (November 1805), 359
Visconti, Marchioness Giuseppa, 116–18
Vorontzoff, Count Simon, 157

Wagram, Battle of (1809), 122
Walmer Castle, Kent, 31, 32, 33, 48, 49,
    148, 261
Walpole, Horace, 23, 27
Ward, John, 148
Watson, Steven, 45
West Indies (Caribbean), 137, 139, 140,
    169, 174, 182, 189, 190, 191, 193,
    205, 210, 212, 214, 217, 240, 244–
    5, 248, 255, 314; Missiessy's
    expedition to, 183, 184–6, 209;
    Villeneuve sails to, 206–10, 211,
    212, 213, 217, 224–8; and Nelson's

pursuit of Villeneuve to, 219–23
Weymouth, 273, 274
Whitbread, Samuel, 150, 151
Whitby, Captain John, 357, 389
Whitshed, Vice-Admiral James Hawkins, 368
Whitworth, Charles, Earl, 13, 72, 101, 389
Wilberforce, William, 30, 150

William, Prince, Duke of Gloucester, 273
Wimereux, 36, 102, 107, 109, 124, 125, 193, 266, 271
Windham, William, 46
Wissant, 100, 101, 105–6, 113, 114

York, Duke of see Frederick Augustus
Young, Admiral, 167